An Invitation to Read the Book of Mormon

HAVE YOU EVER wondered about the source of the prehistoric ruins now being discovered on the American continents? Have you ever been curious to know who some of the prehistoric forefathers of the American Indian were? In the Book of Mormon you'll find answers to these questions, and many others.

But—you'll find more than factual answers. You'll also discover a philosophy of life! You'll be able to live with a people and witness their moral and spiritual growth—and their downfall. This book takes you back through time and space to an age 3000-2000 B.C. and allows you to travel forward to the fourth century after Christ.

Not only will you discover a prehistoric people, but you will have a marvelous experience with Jesus Christ—the same Savior recorded in the New Testament! Into the midst of a people who had nearly forgotten God, Christ appears. He teaches them; he heals them. He establishes his church on this continent, and instructs them in the ways of peace and prosperity. You will be there and will live through the wondering moment when he leaves them, promising to return again to his "other sheep."

The Book of Mormon is primarily the religious history of two Hebrew colonies who left Jerusalem nearly six hundred years before Christ—just prior to the capture of Jerusalem by the warriors of Babylon. By divine guidance, they are both led to America. Unknown to each other they develop civilizations. Centuries later, they meet and unite. They also find the remains of an earlier civilization—people who had come to America following the confusion of languages at the tower of Babel. This intriguing history unfolds the political, scientific, and religious experiences of a people specifically preserved to become witnesses to the power of God in the lives of men.

How to Read the Book of Mormon

There are three ways to read the Book of Mormon. One way—perhaps the best—is to start at page one and read through to the end. But if the thought of wading through 374 pages frightens you, there are two alternatives. Either of these introduces you to the book and stimulates you to desire a more intimate contact with the record.

First, you may want the highlights of the story sequence. If you do, the following suggested list of readings will carry you through the major thread of the history. The accent here is on action—the major events of their experiences. It includes 34 narrative excerpts.

Warned of God, Lehi and party leave Jerusalem: page 1 to page 9, verse 41.

Journey into the wilderness: p. 22:7 to p. 25:102; p. 26:153 to p. 27:174.

The ocean voyage: p. 27:175 to p. 28:217.

Battle of Cumorah; extinction of Nephite nation: p. 336:1 to p. 339:16.

An Alternative Study Plan

The second alternative is to study the distinctive teachings and prophetic writings of the book. The list below contains some of the finest passages in the Book of Mormon. Here the accent is on its philosophy, its moral and religious flavor. Even a hasty skimming of these portions would reveal the primary objective of the book: to testify to the divinity of Jesus Christ and his message to the world.

Adam's fall; that man might be: p. 38:81 to p. 39:128.

Baptism essential to salvation: p. 75:7 to p. 76:32; p. 122:35 to p. 123:48; p. 154:24-28; p. 303:18 to p. 304:46.

Book of Mormon relation to Bible: p. 17:190 to p. 18:200; p. 72:35 to p. 73:72.

Brother of Jared sees preexistent Christ: p. 346:68 to p. 347:85.

Calling and ordination of "Twelve Disciples"; p. 303:18 to page 304:46; p. 313:1 to p. 314:15; p. 365: chapter 2:1-3.

Christ speaks during great darkness: p. 300:26 to p. 302:73.

Christ's first appearance in America: p. 302:1 to p. 313:75.

Christ's second appearance in America: p. 314:16 to p. 322:13.

Christ's last recorded appearance in America: p. 322:14 to p. 325:24.

A GUIDE TO UNDERSTANDING

One of the authors of the Book of Mormon presents a challenge we'd like you to accept. He invites each reader of this book to "ask God, the eternal Father, in the name of Christ, if these things are not true." His firm belief is that if you pray "sincerely, with real intent, having faith in Christ, he will manifest the truth of it unto you, by the power of the Holy Ghost."

We're sure you'll enjoy reading the Book of Mormon. Your life will be benefited by its message.

THE
BOOK OF MORMON

TRANSLATED BY

JOSEPH SMITH, JR.

COMPARED WITH THE ORIGINAL MANUSCRIPT AND THE
KIRTLAND EDITION OF 1837, WHICH WAS CARE-
FULLY RE-EXAMINED AND COMPARED WITH
THE ORIGINAL MANUSCRIPT BY JOSEPH
SMITH AND OLIVER COWDERY

Published by the Board of Publication of the Reorganized
Church of Jesus Christ of Latter Day Saints

INDEPENDENCE, MISSOURI

THE BOOK OF MORMON

Wherefore, it is an abridgment of the record of the people of Nephi, and also of the Lamanites; written to the Lamanites, who are a remnant of the house of Israel; and also to Jew and Gentile; written by way of commandment, and also by the spirit of prophecy and of revelation. Written, and sealed up, and hid unto the Lord, that they might not be destroyed; to come forth by the gift and power of God unto the interpretation thereof; sealed by the hand of Moroni, and hid up unto the Lord, to come forth in due time by the way of Gentile; the interpretation thereof by the gift of God.

An abridgment taken from the Book of Ether; also, which is a record of the people of Jared; who were scattered at the time the Lord confounded the language of the people, when they were building a tower to get to heaven: which is to shew unto the remnant of the house of Israel what great things the Lord hath done for their fathers; and that they may know the covenants of the Lord, that they are not cast off for ever; and also to the convincing of the Jew and Gentile that Jesus is the Christ, the Eternal God, manifesting himself unto all nations. And now if there are faults, they are the mistakes of men; wherefore, condemn not the things of God, that ye may be found spotless at the judgment seat of Christ.

THE TESTIMONY OF THREE WITNESSES

Be it known unto all nations, kindreds, tongues, and people, unto whom this work shall come, that we, through the grace of God the Father, and our Lord Jesus Christ, have seen the plates which contain this record, which is a record of the people of Nephi, and also of the Lamanites, their brethren, and also of the people of Jared, who came from the tower of which hath been spoken; and we also know that they have been translated by the gift and power of God, for his voice hath declared it unto us; wherefore we know of a surety, that the work is true. And we also testify that we have seen the engravings which are upon the plates; and they have been shewn unto us by the power of God, and not of man. And we declare with words of soberness, that an angel of God came down from heaven, and he brought and laid before our eyes, that we beheld and saw the plates, and the engravings thereon; and we know that it is by the grace of God the Father, and our Lord Jesus Christ, that we beheld and bear record that these things are true; and it is marvelous in our eyes, nevertheless, the voice of the Lord commanded us that we should bear record of it; wherefore, to be obedient unto the commandments of God, we bear testimony of these things. And we know that if we are faithful in Christ, we shall rid our garments of the blood of all men, and be found spotless before the judgment seat of Christ, and shall dwell with him eternally in the heavens. And the honor be to the Father, and to the Son, and to the Holy Ghost, which is one God. Amen.

OLIVER COWDERY

DAVID WHITMER

MARTIN HARRIS

AND ALSO THE TESTIMONY OF EIGHT WITNESSES

Be it known unto all nations, kindreds, tongues, and people, unto whom this work shall come, that Joseph Smith, Jr., the translator of this work, has shewn unto us the plates of which hath been spoken, which have the appearance of gold; and as many of the leaves as the said Smith has translated, we did handle with our hands: and we also saw the engravings thereon, all of which has the appearance of ancient work, and of curious workmanship. And this we bear record with words of soberness, that the said Smith has shewn unto us, for we have seen and hefted, and know of a surety that the said Smith has got the plates of which we have spoken. And we give our names unto the world, to witness unto the world that which we have seen; and we lie not, God bearing witness of it.

CHRISTIAN WHITMER

JACOB WHITMER

PETER WHITMER, JR.

JOHN WHITMER

HIRAM PAGE

JOSEPH SMITH, SEN.

HYRUM SMITH

SAMUEL H. SMITH

FOREWORD
TO THE 1966 EDITION

This edition of the Book of Mormon has been prepared in response to the need for treating grammatical and language problems. No conscious attempt has been made to modernize the language of the text.

The corrections made are in the grammatical area of punctuation, ambiguous construction, substitution of synonyms for obsolete and archaic words, revision of out-of-date spellings, and other grammatical changes as needed. Many of the adjustments were in punctuation to solve problems which have persisted from the first edition. Others relate to the translation into English from another language, and still others were made because of the constant changes in a living language during the past 130 years.

The versification numbering has been kept the same as in the 1908 Authorized Edition, although the paragraphing has been altered to some extent. Unless the preceding verse ends with a period, question mark, or exclamation point, the next numbered verse is made a part of the preceding paragraph, with the verse number retained in reduced size, as in the Revised Standard Version of the Bible.

The original record was written by twenty-four authors, and their work was finally condensed, or abridged, by Mormon. When Moroni hid the plates in the earth, he wrote that the record

> "is of great worth, and whoever shall bring it to light, him will the Lord bless. . . . It shall be brought out of the earth, and it shall shine forth out of darkness, and come unto the knowledge of the people, and it shall be done by the power of God, and if there be faults, they be the faults of man."

John H. Gilbert who set the type for the 1830 edition of the Book of Mormon, in a memorandum dated September 8, 1892, said:

> "The manuscript was supposed to be in the handwriting of Cowdery. Every chapter, if I remember correctly, was one solid paragraph without a punctuation mark from beginning to end. . . . I punctuated it to make it read as I supposed the author intended."

Without affirming the accuracy of this claim, we may conclude that the punctuating and paragraphing were not specifically indicated by inspiration.

The greatest number of changes in this edition relate to punctuation. Much care has been given to see that each mark helps to express the exact meaning of the author.

All the direct, or first-person, quotations have been indicated by quotation marks. The use of the familiar forms (now traditionally associated with the English Scriptures) of the pronouns and verbs, such as *thou art*, have been restricted to quotations ascribed to Deity (either the Father or the Son), angels, the Holy Spirit as in prophecy, or when the speaker is praying to God or talking to royalty. In all ordinary conversation the terms of daily use have been substituted. Archaic spellings in words such as *shew*, *wo*, and *spake* have been modernized.

The work of this edition is largely that of Elder Chris B. Hartshorn, formerly editorial assistant to the First Presidency. In this very difficult task he has had the technical assistance of Mrs. Audrey Stubbart, proofreader and copy editor of twenty years experience, and of Dr. Ronald W. McReynolds, English professor at Central Missouri State College. The final editorial review was made by the Herald House managing editor, Elder Paul Wellington. The arduous hours of help they have given to this work are hereby acknowledged. While no claim can be made for perfection, this edition is offered in the conviction that the readers of the Book of Mormon will find that the changes facilitate its reading and clarify its meaning, without altering its message.

THE FIRST PRESIDENCY

PREFACE

(Appearing in all Editions since 1908)

At a General Conference of the Reorganized Church of Jesus Christ of Latter Day Saints, in April, 1906, the following preamble and resolution were adopted:

"Whereas, There are several editions of the Book of Mormon extant, differing in divisions of chapters and paragraphs, thereby rendering it impossible to prepare concordance and works of reference, therefore,

"Resolved, That we recommend. . . the appointment of a committee . . . to investigate and prepare a uniform plan for the divisions of chapters and verses, and, if thought advisable, to prepare or adopt a system of references."

Frederick M. Smith, Heman C. Smith, Richard S. Salyards, Francis M. Sheehy, Columbus Scott, Edmund L. Kelley, and Frederick B. Blair were appointed.

The committee appointed Frederick M. Smith, Heman C. Smith, and Richard S. Salyards as a sub-committee to do the work of reversification, etc., with instructions to use the large type, Lamoni edition as a basis; to leave the chapters as in the original Palmyra edition.

The sub-committee completed the work of reversification, and in so doing made "all verses from the Book of Isaiah to correspond in their divisions" to the versification of the Inspired Translation of the Holy Scriptures, and indicated such matter by reference notes.

The general committee indorsed the work of the sub-committee. It concluded to broaden the scope of its work by making provision for comparison of the Lamoni edition with the Original Manuscript and the Kirtland edition. It adopted the following as instruction to the sub-committee for the completion of the work:

"Resolved, That it be the sense of this committee that in the publication of the new work we follow the corrections of the Book of Mormon so as to make the new work in accordance with the Original Manuscript and the Kirtland edition of the Book of Mormon, published by Pratt & Goodson, of 1837, that the work may be completed as corrected by Joseph Smith and Oliver Cowdery."

The sub-committee were authorized to "examine proofs and corrections" according to the foregoing resolution; to proofread the matter as published;

and to prepare a suitable index. They were also instructed to indicate by paragraph signs the divisions into paragraphs according to the Palmyra edition, and to hand over the work for publication.

The sub-committee carefully compared the Original Manuscript with the Kirtland and the large-type editions. One member of the committee read from the Manuscript, one followed the Kirtland edition, the other recorded all corrections in the large-type edition. The Manuscript is legible; there was little difficulty in reading it. They also referred to the Palmyra edition in the examination of the text. There is very little difference in the paragraphs in the Palmyra and the Kirtland editions.

The Preface to the Kirtland edition contains the following paragraph:

"Individuals acquainted with book printing, are aware of the numerous typographical errors which always occur in manuscript editions. It is only necessary to say, that the whole has been carefully re-examined and compared with the original manuscripts, by Elder Joseph Smith, Jr., the translator of the Book of Mormon, assisted by the present printer, Brother O. Cowdery, who formerly wrote the greatest portion of the same, as dictated by Brother Smith."

The committee found errors, including omissions, in the Lamoni edition; also some matter in the Original Manuscript omitted in the Palmyra or the Kirtland edition, or in both those editions; such omissions evidently being overlooked in proofreading.

Where differences occurred between the Manuscript and the Kirtland edition, the committee were governed by the subject-matter of the context. There were no material differences in the sense of the text of the Manuscript and of the Kirtland edition.

Numerous minor changes were made, many of which have improved the subject-matter. Among the more important corrections we note the following:

Concerning the prohibition of polygamy; Book of Jacob, chapter 2: 6,7: "I *must* testify unto you concerning the wickedness of your hearts"; *must*, instead of *might*. 2: 45: "Behold ye have done greater *iniquity* than the Lamanites, our brethren." *Iniquity*, singular form, specific; instead of *iniquities* in other editions. Ether 1: 16: The Palmyra and Kirtland editions both read, "thy families," referring to the Brother of Jared and the commandment to migrate. The manuscript reads, "thy family"; the singular instead of the plural form of the word. The text was made to read according to the Manuscript.

Samples of matter omitted in one or all early editions, included in this correct edition:

Book of Alma 4: 8: "there having been a city built which was called the city of Gideon." 12: 5: "even as with the power and authority." 15: 55: "yea, decreeth unto them decrees which are unalterable." 16: 157: "And now behold, will not this strengthen your faith? Yea, it will strengthen your faith, for ye will say, I know that this is a good seed, for behold, it sprouteth and beginneth to grow." 25: 59: "yea, they would not partake of wine."

Book of Nephi 2: 32. "and the land which was between the land of Zara-hemla."

Samples of corrections:

I Nephi 3: 219: The Palmyra and Kirtland editions read "whose foundation is the devil"; the Manuscript reads, "founder"; the text was made to conform to the Manuscript.

II Nephi 12: 84: "*White* and a delightsome," instead of "*pure* and a delight-some."

Mosiah 11: 190: *wading*, instead of *wandering*.

Alma 3: 89: *inherit*, instead of "*enter* the kingdom." 15: 27: "*where* they had pitched their tents," instead of *whence*. 21: 108: "armies" should march, instead of *servants*.

IV Nephi 1: 9: "*build* cities," instead of "*fill* cities."

Names corrected:

Ammoron, for *Ammaron*, wherever given. (This does not refer to *Amaron*, Book of Omni.) *Jeneum*, instead of *Joneam*, Mormon 3: 15. *Cumenihah*, instead of *Camenihah*, wherever given.

Mosiah 9: 170: The Manuscript reads, "King Benjamin had a gift from God"; the Kirtland edition reads, "King Mosiah." The text was made to read, "King Mosiah."

The name *Mosiah* was inserted in brackets after the words *King Benjamin* in Book of Ether 1: 95, in harmony with the reading of the Book of Mosiah 9: 170.

The committee concluded that instead of providing marginal references, a concordance to the Book of Mormon should be provided.

FREDERICK M. SMITH, *Chairman*

RICHARD S. SALYARDS, *Secretary*

LAMONI, IOWA, July 17, 1908

FOREWORD

This is a book of scripture. It is holy because it was presented to the world by the gift of the Holy Spirit through Joseph Smith, Jr., and because it has been an inspiration to generations of readers.

It describes from the human perspective how God interacts with individuals and cultures. We encounter many similar problems and opportunities today. Therefore, this book is valuable and deserves careful study, as do our other sacred scriptures, the Bible and the Doctrine and Covenants.

The Reorganized Church of Jesus Christ of Latter Day Saints, through its publishing division, Herald House, Independence, Missouri, makes this book available in several bindings and formats. This 1966 version uses modestly updated sentence structure and punctuation. Herald House also publishes the 1908 authorized edition which follows closely the original text of 1830.

We urge all people seeking to know the message of Jesus Christ to read this scripture and consider its testimony. It represents an additional witness to the divinity of Christ and his timeless message of God the creator who calls us to love each other and to live with him in eternity.

THE FIRST PRESIDENCY

Wallace B. Smith
Howard S. Sheehy, Jr.
Alan D. Tyree

INDEPENDENCE, MISSOURI
MAY 1986

CONTENTS

THE BOOK OF MORMON

THE FIRST BOOK OF NEPHI

HIS REIGN AND MINISTRY

CHAPTER 1

An account of Lehi and his wife Sariah, and his four sons, being called (beginning at the eldest) Laman, Lemuel, Sam, and Nephi. The Lord warned Lehi to depart out of the land of Jerusalem, because he prophesied to the people concerning their iniquity; and they sought to destroy his life. He took three days' journey into the wilderness with his family. Nephi took his brothers and returned to the land of Jerusalem after the record of the Jews. The account of their sufferings. They took the daughters of Ishmael to wife. They took their families and departed into the wilderness. Their sufferings and afflictions in the wilderness. The course of their travels. They came to the large waters. Nephi's brothers rebelled against him. He confounded them, and built a ship. They called the place Bountiful. They crossed the large waters into the promised land. This is according to the account of Nephi; or in other words, I, Nephi wrote this record.

I, Nephi, having been born of goodly parents, therefore I was taught somewhat in all the learning of my father; and having seen many afflictions in the course of my days—nevertheless, having been highly favored of the Lord in all my days—and having had a great knowledge of the goodness and the mysteries of God, therefore I make a record of my proceedings in my days; and I make a record in the language of my father, which consists of the learning of the Jews and the language of the Egyptians.

2 I know that the record which I make is true; and I make it with my own hand; and I make it according to my knowledge.

3 For it came to pass, in the commencement of the first year of the reign of Zedekiah, king of Judah (my father Lehi having dwelt at Jerusalem all his days), there came many prophets prophesying to the people that they must repent or the great city Jerusalem must be destroyed.

4 Wherefore my father Lehi, as he went forth, prayed to the Lord, even with all his heart, in behalf of his people.

5 As he prayed to the Lord, there came a pillar of fire and dwelt upon a rock before him; and he saw and heard much; and because of the things which he saw and heard, he quaked and trembled exceedingly.

6 He returned to his own house at Jerusalem; and he cast himself upon his bed, being overcome with the Spirit and the things which he had seen.

7 Being thus overcome with the Spirit, he was carried away in a vision, even that he saw the heavens open, and he thought he saw God sitting upon his throne, surrounded with numberless concourses of angels in the attitude of singing and praising their God.

8 And he saw one descending out

1

600 B. C.

of the midst of heaven, and he beheld that his luster was above that of the sun at noonday.

9 He also saw twelve others following him, and their brightness exceeded that of the stars in the firmament; and they came down and went forth upon the face of the earth; 10and the first came and stood before my father, and gave him a book, and bade him that he should read.

11 As he read, he was filled with the Spirit of the Lord, and he read, saying, "Woe, woe to Jerusalem, for I have seen thine abominations!"

12 And many things did my father read concerning Jerusalem—that it should be destroyed, and of the inhabitants thereof many should perish by the sword and many should be carried away captive into Babylon.

13 When my father had read and seen many great and marvelous things, he exclaimed many things to the Lord, such as "Great and marvelous are thy works, O Lord God Almighty! Thy throne is high in the heavens, and thy power, and goodness, and mercy are over all the inhabitants of the earth; and because thou art merciful, thou wilt not suffer those who come to thee that they shall perish!"

14 And after this manner was the language of my father in the praising of his God; for his soul rejoiced, and his whole heart was filled, because of the things which he had seen, which the Lord had shown him.

15 Now I, Nephi, do not make a full account of the things which my father has written, for he has written many things which he saw in visions and in dreams.

16 He also has written many things which he prophesied and spoke to his children, of which I shall not make a full account; but I shall make an account of my proceedings in my days.

17 Behold, I make an abridgment of the record of my father, upon plates which I have made with my own hands; wherefore after I have abridged the record of my father, then will I make an account of my own life.

18 Therefore, I would that you should know that after the Lord had shown so many marvelous things to

my father Lehi concerning the destruction of Jerusalem, behold, he went forth among the people, and began to prophesy and to declare to them concerning the things which he had both seen and heard.

19 And it came to pass that the Jews mocked him because of the things which he testified of them; for he truly testified of their wickedness and their abominations.

20 He testified that the things which he saw and heard, and also the things which he read in the book, manifested plainly of the coming of a Messiah, and also the redemption of the world.

21 And when the Jews heard these things, they were angry with him, even as with the prophets of old, whom they had cast out, and stoned, and slain ; 22and they also sought his life, that they might take it away.

23 But, behold, I, Nephi, will show you that the tender mercies of the Lord are over all those whom he has chosen, because of their faith, to make them mighty even to the power of deliverance.

24 Behold, it came to pass that the Lord spoke to my father in a dream, and said to him, "Blessed art thou, Lehi, because of the things which thou hast done.

25 "Because thou hast been faithful and declared to this people the things which I commanded thee, behold, they seek to take away thy life."

26 And the Lord commanded my father, in a dream, that he should take his family and depart into the wilderness.

27 And he was obedient to the word of the Lord, wherefore he did as the Lord commanded him, 28and he departed into the wilderness.

29 He left his house, and the land of his inheritance, and his gold, and his silver, and his precious things, and took nothing with him, save his family, and provisions, and tents, and he departed into the wilderness; 30and he came down by the borders near the shore of the Red Sea.

31 And he traveled in the wilderness in the borders which were nearer the Red Sea ; 32and he traveled in the wilderness with his family which consisted of my mother Sariah, and my

elder brothers, who were Laman, Lemuel, and Sam.

33 When he had traveled three days in the wilderness, he pitched his tent in a valley by the side of a river of water.

34 And he built an altar of stones, and he made an offering to the Lord and gave thanks to the Lord our God.

35 He called the name of the river Laman, and it emptied into the Red Sea; and the valley was in the borders near the mouth thereof.

36 When my father saw that the waters of the river emptied into the fountain of the Red Sea, he spoke to Laman, saying, "O that you might be like this river, continually running into the fountain of all righteousness."

37 He also spoke to Lemuel: "O that you might be like this valley, firm and steadfast, and immovable in keeping the commandments of the Lord."

38 Now this he spoke because of the stiff-neckedness of Laman and Lemuel; for, behold, they murmured many things against their father because he was a visionary man and had led them out of the land of Jerusalem, to leave the land of their inheritance, and their gold, and their silver, and their precious things, to perish in the wilderness.

39 This they said he had done because of the foolish imaginations of his heart.

40 And thus Laman and Lemuel, being the eldest, murmured against their father.

41 They murmured because they knew not the dealings of that God who had created them.

42 Neither did they believe that Jerusalem, that great city, could be destroyed according to the words of the prophets.

43 They were like the Jews, who were at Jerusalem, who sought to take away the life of my father.

44 And my father spoke to them in the valley of Lemuel with power, being filled with the Spirit, until their frames shook before him.

45 He confounded them, that they dared not utter against him; wherefore they did as he commanded them.

46 And my father dwelt in a tent.

47 And it came to pass that I, Nephi, being exceedingly young, nevertheless being large in stature, had great desires to know of the mysteries of God.

48 Wherefore I cried to the Lord; and, behold, he visited me, and softened my heart that I believed all the words which had been spoken by my father; wherefore I did not rebel against him like my brothers.

49 I spoke to Sam, making known to him the things which the Lord had manifested to me by his Holy Spirit, 50and he believed in my words.

51 But, behold, Laman and Lemuel would not hearken to my words; 52and being grieved because of the hardness of their hearts, I cried to the Lord for them.

53 And the Lord spoke to me, saying, "Blessed art thou, Nephi, because of thy faith, for thou hast sought me diligently, with lowliness of heart.

54 "Inasmuch as ye shall keep my commandments, ye shall prosper, and shall be led to a land of promise, even a land which I have prepared for you, a land which is choice above all other lands.

55 "And inasmuch as thy brethren shall rebel against thee, they shall be cut off from the presence of the Lord.

56 "And inasmuch as thou shalt keep my commandments, thou shalt be made a ruler and a teacher over thy brethren.

57 "For, behold, in that day that they shall rebel against me, I will curse them even with a sore curse, and they shall have no power over thy seed, except they shall rebel against me also.

58 "If it so be that they rebel against me, they shall be a scourge to thy seed, to stir them up in the ways of remembrance."

59 And I, Nephi, returned from speaking with the Lord, to the tent of my father.

60 And he spoke to me, saying: "Behold, I have dreamed a dream, in which the Lord has commanded me that you and your brethren should return to Jerusalem.

61 "For, behold, Laban has the record of the Jews, and also a genealogy of our forefathers, and they are engraved upon plates of brass.

62 "Wherefore the Lord has commanded me that you and your brothers should go to the house of Laban,

600–592 B. C.

and seek the records, and bring them down here into the wilderness.

63 "Now, behold, your brothers murmur, saying it is a hard thing which I have required of them; but, behold, I have not required it of them, but it is a commandment of the Lord.

64 "Therefore go, my son, and you shall be favored of the Lord, because you have not murmured."

65 And I, Nephi, said to my father, "I will go and do the things which the Lord has commanded, for I know that the Lord gives no commandments to the children of men save he shall prepare a way for them that they may accomplish the thing which he commands them."

66 When my father had heard these words, he was exceedingly glad, for he knew that I had been blessed of the Lord.

67 And I, Nephi, and my brethren took our journey in the wilderness with our tents, to go up to the land of Jerusalem.

68 When we had come up to the land of Jerusalem, I and my brethren consulted one with another; and we cast lots who of us should go in to the house of Laban.

69 The lot fell upon Laman; and Laman went in to the house of Laban, and he talked with him as he sat in his house.

70 He desired of Laban the records which were engraved upon the plates of brass, which contained the genealogy of my father.

71 And, behold, Laban was angry, and thrust him out from his presence; and he would not that he should have the records.

72 Wherefore, he said to him, "Behold, you are a robber, and I will slay you."

73 But Laman fled out of his presence, and told us the things which Laban had done.

74 We began to be exceedingly sorrowful, and my brethren were about to return to my father in the wilderness.

75 But, behold, I said to them, "As the Lord lives, and as we live, we will not go down to our father in the wilderness until we have accomplished the thing which the Lord has commanded us.

76 "Wherefore let us be faithful in keeping the commandments of the Lord; 77therefore let us go down to the land of our father's inheritance, for, behold, he left gold and silver, and all manner of riches.

78 "All this he has done because of the commandments of the Lord; for he knew that Jerusalem must be destroyed because of the wickedness of the people.

79 "For, behold, they have rejected the words of the prophets.

80 "Wherefore if my father should dwell in the land, after he has been commanded to flee out of the land, behold, he would also perish.

81 "Wherefore it must needs be that he flee out of the land.

82 "Behold, it is wisdom in God that we should obtain these records, that we may preserve to our children the language of our fathers; 83and also that we may preserve to them the words which have been spoken by the mouth of all the holy prophets, which have been delivered to them by the spirit and power of God, since the world began, even down to this present time."

84 After this manner of language I persuaded my brethren, that they might be faithful in keeping the commandments of God.

85 And it came to pass that we went down to the land of our inheritance and gathered together our gold and our silver and our precious things; 86and after we had gathered these things together, we went up again to the house of Laban.

87 We went to Laban, and desired of him that he would give us the records which were engraved upon the plates of brass, for which we would give him our gold, and our silver, and all our precious things.

88 When Laban saw our property, that it was exceedingly great, he lusted after it, insomuch that he thrust us out, and sent his servants to slay us that he might obtain our property.

89 We fled before the servants of Laban, and we were obliged to leave behind our property, and it fell into the hands of Laban.

90 And we fled into the wilderness, and the servants of Laban did not

overtake us, and we hid ourselves in the cavity of a rock.

91 Laman was angry with me, and also with my father, as also was Lemuel; for he hearkened to the words of Laman.

92 Wherefore Laman and Lemuel spoke many hard words to us, their younger brothers, and they smote us even with a rod.

93 As they smote us with a rod, behold, an angel of the Lord came and stood before them, and he spoke to them saying, "Why do ye smite your younger brother with a rod?

94 "Know ye not that the Lord hath chosen him to be a ruler over you, and this because of your iniquities?

95 "Behold, ye shall go up to Jerusalem again, and the Lord will deliver Laban into your hands."

96 And after the angel had spoken to us, he departed.

97 After the angel had departed, Laman and Lemuel again began to murmur, saying "How is it possible that the Lord will deliver Laban into our hands?

98 "Behold, he is a mighty man, and he can command fifty, even he can slay fifty; then why not us?"

99 But I spoke to my brethren, saying, "Let us go up again to Jerusalem, and let us be faithful in keeping the commandments of the Lord; for, behold, he is mightier than all the earth, then why not mightier than Laban and his fifty, or even than his tens of thousands?

100 "Therefore let us go up; let us be strong like Moses; for he truly spoke to the waters of the Red Sea, and they divided here and there, and our fathers came through out of captivity on dry ground, and the armies of Pharaoh followed and were drowned in the waters of the Red Sea.

101 "Now, behold, you know that this is true; and you also know that an angel has spoken to you, wherefore can you doubt?

102 "Let us go up; the Lord is able to deliver us, even as our fathers, and to destroy Laban even as the Egyptians."

103 Now when I had spoken these words, they were yet angry, and still continued to murmur; nevertheless they followed me until we came without the walls of Jerusalem.

104 It was night; and I caused that they should hide themselves without the walls.

105 After they had hid themselves, I, Nephi, crept into the city, and went forth toward the house of Laban.

106 I was led by the Spirit, not knowing beforehand the things which I should do.

107 Nevertheless I went forth, and as I came near the house of Laban, I beheld a man, and he had fallen to the earth before me, for he was drunken with wine.

108 When I came to him I found that it was Laban.

109 I beheld his sword, and I drew it forth from the sheath thereof, and the hilt thereof was of pure gold, and the workmanship thereof was exceedingly fine; and I saw that the blade thereof was of the most precious steel.

110 And it came to pass that I was constrained by the Spirit that I should kill Laban.

111 But I said in my heart, "Never at any time have I shed the blood of man." And I shrank and would that I might not slay him.

112 And the Spirit said to me again, "Behold, the Lord hath delivered him into thy hands"; and I also knew that he had sought to take away my own life; and he would not hearken to the commandments of the Lord, and he also had taken away our property.

113 The Spirit again said to me, "Slay him, for the Lord hath delivered him into thy hands.

114 "Behold, the Lord slayeth the wicked to bring forth his righteous purposes.

115 "It is better that one man should perish, than that a nation should dwindle and perish in unbelief."

116 When I, Nephi, had heard these words, I remembered the words of the Lord which he spoke to me in the wilderness, saying, "Inasmuch as thy seed shall keep my commandments, they shall prosper in the land of promise."

117 I also thought that they could not keep the commandments of the

Lord according to the law of Moses, save they should have the law.

118 And I also knew that the law was engraved upon the plates of brass.

119 Again, I knew that the Lord had delivered Laban into my hands for this cause, that I might obtain the records according to his commandments.

120 Therefore I obeyed the voice of the Spirit, and took Laban by the hair of the head, and I smote off his head with his own sword.

121 After I had smitten off his head with his own sword, I took the garments of Laban and put them on my own body, even every whit; and I girded on his armor about my loins.

122 And after I had done this, I went to the treasury of Laban.

123 As I went toward the treasury of Laban, behold, I saw the servant of Laban, who had the keys of the treasury.

124 And I commanded him in the voice of Laban that he should go with me into the treasury; and he supposed me to be his master Laban, for he beheld the garments and also the sword girded about my loins.

125 He spoke to me concerning the elders of the Jews, he knowing that his master Laban had been out by night among them.

126 And I spoke to him as if I had been Laban.

127 I also spoke to him that I should carry the engravings which were upon the plates of brass to my elder brethren who were without the walls.

128 And I also bade him that he should follow me.

129 He supposed that I spoke of the brethren of the church, and that I was truly that Laban whom I had slain, wherefore he followed me.

130 And he spoke to me many times concerning the elders of the Jews, as I went forth to my brethren who were without the walls.

131 When Laman saw me, he was exceedingly frightened, and also Lemuel and Sam.

132 And they fled from my presence; for they supposed it was Laban, and that he had slain me, and sought to take away their lives also.

133 I called after them, and they heard me; wherefore they ceased to flee from my presence.

134 When the servant of Laban beheld my brethren, he began to tremble, and was about to flee from me and return to the city of Jerusalem.

135 Now I, Nephi, being a man large in stature, and also having received much strength of the Lord, seized upon the servant of Laban and held him that he should not flee.

136 And I spoke with him, that if he would hearken to my words, as the Lord lives, and as I live, even so that if he would hearken to our words, we would spare his life.

137 I spoke to him, even with an oath, that he need not fear; that he should be a free man like us, if he would go down in the wilderness with us.

138 I also spoke to him, saying, "Surely the Lord has commanded us to do this thing, and shall we not be diligent in keeping the commandments of the Lord?

139 "Therefore, if you will go down into the wilderness to my father, you shall have place with us."

140 Zoram took courage at the words which I spoke.

141 Now Zoram was the name of the servant; and he promised that he would go down into the wilderness to our father.

142 And he also made an oath to us, that he would tarry with us from that time forth.

143 Now we were desirous that he should tarry with us for this cause, that the Jews might not know concerning our flight into the wilderness lest they should pursue us and destroy us.

144 But when Zoram had made an oath to us, our fears ceased concerning him.

145 And it came to pass that we took the plates of brass and the servant of Laban, and departed into the wilderness, and journeyed to the tent of our father.

146 After we had come down into the wilderness to our father, behold, he was filled with joy, and also my mother Sariah was exceedingly glad, for she truly had mourned because of us; for she had supposed that we had perished in the wilderness.

147 She also had complained against my father, telling him that he was a visionary man, saying, "Behold, you have led us forth from the land of our inheritance, and my sons are no more, and we shall perish in the wilderness."

148 After this manner of language had my mother complained against my father.

149 And my father spoke to her, saying, "I know that I am a visionary man; for if I had not seen the things of God in a vision, I should not have known the goodness of God, but would have tarried at Jerusalem and perished with my brethren.

150 "But, behold, I have obtained a land of promise, in which things I rejoice.

151 "And I know that the Lord will deliver my sons out of the hands of Laban, and bring them down again to us in the wilderness."

152 After this manner of language my father Lehi comforted my mother Sariah concerning us, while we journeyed in the wilderness up to the land of Jerusalem to obtain the record of the Jews.

153 And when we had returned to the tent of my father, behold, their joy was full, and my mother was comforted.

154 She spoke, saying, "Now I know of a surety that the Lord has commanded my husband to flee into the wilderness.

155 "I also know of a surety that the Lord has protected my sons, and delivered them out of the hands of Laban, and has given them power whereby they could accomplish the thing which the Lord had commanded them."

156 After this manner of language she spoke.

157 And they rejoiced exceedingly, and offered sacrifice and burnt offerings to the Lord; and they gave thanks to the God of Israel.

158 After they had given thanks to the God of Israel, my father Lehi took the records which were engraved upon the plates of brass, and he searched them from the beginning.

159 He beheld that they contained the five books of Moses, which gave an account of the creation of the world, 160and also of Adam and Eve who were our first parents; 161and also a record of the Jews from the beginning even down to the commencement of the reign of Zedekiah, king of Judah; 162and also the prophecies of the holy prophets, from the beginning even down to the commencement of the reign of Zedekiah; 163and also many prophecies which have been spoken by the mouth of Jeremiah.

164 And it came to pass that my father Lehi also found upon the plates of brass a genealogy of his fathers.

165 Wherefore he knew that he was a descendant of Joseph; even that Joseph who was the son of Jacob, who was sold into Egypt, and who was preserved by the hand of the Lord, that he might preserve his father Jacob and all his household from perishing with famine.

166 And they were also led out of captivity and out of the land of Egypt, by that same God who had preserved them.

167 Thus my father Lehi discovered the genealogy of his fathers.

168 Laban also was a descendant of Joseph, wherefore he and his fathers had kept the records.

169 Now when my father saw all these things he was filled with the Spirit, and began to prophesy concerning his seed, that these plates of brass should go forth to all nations, kindreds, tongues and people, who were of his seed.

170 Wherefore he said that these plates of brass should never perish, neither should they be dimmed any more by time.

171 And he prophesied many things concerning his seed.

172 Thus far I and my father had kept the commandments wherewith the Lord had commanded us.

173 And we had obtained the records which the Lord had commanded us, and searched them and found that they were desirable, even of great worth to us, insomuch that we could preserve the commandments of the Lord to our children.

174 Wherefore it was wisdom in the Lord that we should carry them

with us as we journeyed in the wilderness toward the land of promise.

CHAPTER 2

NOW I, Nephi, do not give the genealogy of my fathers in this part of my record; neither at any time shall I give it hereafter upon these plates which I am writing; for it is given in the record which has been kept by my father; wherefore I do not write it in this work.

2 For it suffices me to say that we are descendants of Joseph.

3 And it matters not to me that I am particular to give a full account of all the things of my father, for they cannot be written upon these plates, for I desire the room that I may write of the things of God.

4 For the fullness of my intent is that I may persuade men to come to the God of Abraham, and the God of Isaac, and the God of Jacob, and be saved.

5 Wherefore the things which are pleasing to the world I do not write, but the things which are pleasing to God and to those who are not of the world.

6 Wherefore I shall give commandment to my seed, that they shall not occupy these plates with things which are not of worth to the children of men.

7 Now I would that you might know that after my father Lehi had made an end of prophesying concerning his seed, it came to pass that the Lord spoke to him again, saying that it was not meet for him, Lehi, that he should take his family into the wilderness alone; but that his sons should take daughters to wife that they might raise up seed to the Lord in the land of promise.

8 And the Lord commanded him that I, Nephi, and my brethren should again return to the land of Jerusalem, and bring down Ishmael and his family into the wilderness.

9 I, Nephi, with my brethren, went forth again into the wilderness to go up to Jerusalem.

10 We went to the house of Ishmael, and we gained favor in the sight of Ishmael, insomuch that we spoke to him the words of the Lord.

11 The Lord softened the heart of Ishmael and also his household, insomuch that they took their journey with us down into the wilderness to the tent of our father.

12 As we journeyed in the wilderness, behold, Laman and Lemuel, and two of the daughters of Ishmael, and the two sons of Ishmael, and their families, rebelled against us—even against me, Nephi, and Sam, and their father Ishmael, and his wife, and his three other daughters—13 and were desirous to return to the land of Jerusalem.

14 Now I, Nephi, being grieved for the hardness of their hearts, therefore I spoke to Laman and Lemuel saying, "Behold, you are my elder brethren; and how is it that you are so hard in your hearts, and so blind in your minds, that you have need that I, your younger brother, should speak to you and set an example for you?

15 "How is it that you have not hearkened to the word of the Lord?

16 "How is it that you have forgotten that you have seen an angel of the Lord?

17 "And how is it that you have forgotten what great things the Lord has done for us in delivering us out of the hands of Laban, and also that we should obtain the record?

18 "And how is it that you have forgotten that the Lord is able to do all things, according to his will, for the children of men, if it so be that they exercise faith in him; wherefore let us be faithful to him.

19 "If it so be that we are faithful to him, we shall obtain the land of promise; and you shall know at some future period that the word of the Lord shall be fulfilled concerning the destruction of Jerusalem; 20 for all things which the Lord has spoken concerning the destruction of Jerusalem must be fulfilled.

21 "For, behold, the Spirit of the Lord ceases soon to strive with them; 22 for, behold, they have rejected the prophets and they have cast Jeremiah into prison.

23 "And they have sought to take away the life of my father, insomuch that they have driven him out of the land.

24 "Now, behold, I say to you that if you will return to Jerusalem you shall also perish with them.

25 "And now, if you have choice, go up to the land, and remember the words which I speak to you, that if you go you will also perish; for thus the Spirit of the Lord constrains me that I should speak."

26 When I, Nephi, had spoken these words to my brethren they were angry with me.

27 They laid their hands upon me —for, behold, they were exceedingly angry—and they bound me with cords, for they sought to take away my life, that they might leave me in the wilderness to be devoured by wild beasts.

28 But I prayed to the Lord, saying, "O Lord, according to my faith which is in thee, wilt thou deliver me from the hands of my brethren; ²⁹and even give me strength that I may burst these bands with which I am bound."

30 When I had said these words, behold, the bands were loosed from my hands and feet, and I stood before my brethren, and I spoke to them again.

31 And they were angry with me again, and sought to lay hands upon me; ³²but, behold, one of the daughters of Ishmael, and also her mother, and one of the sons of Ishmael pleaded with my brethren, insomuch that they softened their hearts; and they ceased striving to take away my life.

33 They were sorrowful because of their wickedness, insomuch that they bowed down before me, and pleaded with me that I would forgive them of the thing that they had done against me.

34 I frankly forgave them all that they had done, and I exhorted them that they would pray to the Lord their God for forgiveness, ³⁵and they did so.

36 After they had prayed to the Lord we again traveled on our journey toward the tent of our father.

37 And it came to pass that we came down to the tent of our father.

38 After I and my brethren and all the house of Ishmael had come down to the tent of my father, we gave thanks to the Lord our God; ³⁹and we offered sacrifice and burnt offerings to him, ⁴⁰for we had gathered all manner of seeds of every kind, both of grain of every kind and also of the seeds of fruits of every kind.

41 And while my father tarried in the wilderness he spoke to us, saying, "Behold, I have dreamed a dream; or in other words, I have seen a vision.

42 "And, behold, because of the thing which I have seen, I have reason to rejoice in the Lord because of Nephi, and also of Sam; for I have reason to suppose that they, and also many of their seed, will be saved.

43 "But, behold, Laman and Lemuel, I fear exceedingly because of you; for, behold, I thought I saw in my dream a dark and dreary wilderness.

44 "And I saw a man, and he was dressed in a white robe; and he came and stood before me.

45 "He spoke to me, and bade me follow him.

46 "As I followed him I beheld myself that I was in a dark and dreary waste.

47 "After I had traveled for the space of many hours in darkness I began to pray to the Lord that he would have mercy on me according to the multitude of his tender mercies.

48 "And after I had prayed to the Lord, I beheld a large and spacious field.

49 "And I beheld a tree, whose fruit was desirable to make one happy.

50 "I went forth and partook of the fruit thereof; and I beheld that it was most sweet above all that I ever before tasted.

51 "And I beheld that the fruit thereof was white, to exeed all the whiteness that I had ever seen.

52 "As I partook of the fruit thereof, it filled my soul with exceedingly great joy; ⁵³wherefore I began to be desirous that my family should partake of it also; for I knew that it was desirable above all other fruit.

54 "As I looked about, that perhaps I might discover my family also, I beheld a river of water; and it ran along, and it was near the tree of which I was partaking the fruit.

55 "And I looked to behold whence

9

it came; and I saw the head thereof a little way off.

56 "At the head thereof I beheld your mother Sariah, and Sam, and Nephi; and they stood as if they knew not where they should go.

57 "I beckoned to them; and I also said to them with a loud voice that they should come to me and partake of the fruit, which was desirable above all other fruit.

58 "And they came to me, and partook of the fruit also.

59 "I was desirous that Laman and Lemuel should come and partake of the fruit also; 60wherefore, I cast my eyes toward the head of the river that perhaps I might see them.

61 "I saw them, but they would not come to me and partake of the fruit.

62 "And I beheld a rod of iron; and it extended along the bank of the river, and led to the tree by which I stood.

63 "I also beheld a straight and narrow path, which came along by the rod of iron, even to the tree by which I stood; 64and it also led by the head of the fountain to a large and spacious field, as if it had been a world.

65 "And I saw numberless concourses of people, many of whom were pressing forward that they might obtain the path which led to the tree by which I stood.

66 "They came forth and commenced in the path which led to the tree.

67 "But there arose a mist of darkness, even an exceedingly great mist of darkness, insomuch that they who had commenced in the path lost their way, that they wandered off and were lost.

68 "And it came to pass that I beheld others pressing forward, and they came forth and caught hold of the end of the rod of iron; 69and they pressed forward through the mist of darkness, clinging to the rod of iron, even until they came forth and partook of the fruit of the tree.

70 "After they had partaken of the fruit of the tree they cast their eyes about as if they were ashamed.

71 "I also cast my eyes round about, and beheld on the other side

of the river of water a great and spacious building; 72and it stood as if it were in the air, high above the earth.

73 "It was filled with people, both old and young, both male and female; 74and their manner of dress was exceedingly fine; 75and they were in the attitude of mocking and pointing their fingers toward those who had come, and were partaking of the fruit.

76 "After they had tasted of the fruit they were ashamed, because of those that were scoffing at them; and they fell away into forbidden paths and were lost."

77 Now I, Nephi, do not speak all the words of my father.

78 But, to be short in writing, behold, he saw other multitudes pressing forward; and they came and caught hold of the end of the rod of iron; and they pressed their way forward, continually holding fast to the rod of iron, until they came forth and fell down and partook of the fruit of the tree.

79 He also saw other multitudes feeling their way toward that great and spacious building.

80 Many were drowned in the depths of the fountain; 81and many were lost from his view, wandering in strange roads.

82 And great was the multitude that entered into that strange building.

83 After they entered into that building they pointed the finger of scorn at me, and those that were partaking of the fruit also; but we heeded them not.

84 These are the words of my father: "For as many as heeded them had fallen away.

85 "And Laman and Lemuel partook not of the fruit," said my father.

86 After my father had spoken all the words of his dream or vision, which were many, he said to us that because of these things which he saw in a vision he exceedingly feared for Laman and Lemuel; 87and he feared lest they should be cast off from the presence of the Lord.

88 He exhorted them then with all the feeling of a tender parent, that they would hearken to his words, that perhaps the Lord would be mer-

ciful to them and not cast them off; [89]and my father preached to them.

90 After he had preached to them, and also prophesied to them of many things, he bade them to keep the commandments of the Lord; [91]and he ceased speaking to them.

92 All these things my father saw and heard and spoke as he dwelt in a tent in the valley of Lemuel, and also a great many more things, which cannot be written upon these plates.

93 Now as I have spoken concerning these plates, behold, they are not the plates upon which I make a full account of the history of my people; [94]for the plates upon which I make a full account of my people, I have given the name of Nephi; [95]wherefore, they are called the plates of Nephi after my own name; and these plates also are called the plates of Nephi.

96 Nevertheless, I have received a commandment of the Lord that I should make these plates for the special purpose that there should be an account engraved of the ministry of my people.

97 Upon the other plates should be engraved an account of the reign of the kings, and the wars and contentions of my people.

98 Wherefore, these plates are for the greater part of the ministry; and the other plates are for the greater part of the reign of the kings, and the wars and contentions of my people.

99 Wherefore, the Lord has commanded me to make these plates for a wise purpose in him; which purpose I know not.

100 But the Lord knows all things from the beginning; [101]wherefore, he prepares a way to accomplish all his works among the children of men; for, behold, he has all power to the fulfilling of all his words.

102 Thus it is. Amen.

CHAPTER 3

NOW I, Nephi, proceed to give an account upon these plates of my proceedings, and of my reign and ministry; wherefore, to proceed with my account, I must speak somewhat of the things of my father, and also of my brethren.

2 For, behold, after my father had made an end of speaking the words of his dream, and also of exhorting them to all diligence, he spoke to them concerning the Jews, that after they should be destroyed, even that great city Jerusalem, and many be carried away captive into Babylon, according to the own due time of the Lord they should return again, and even be brought back out of captivity.

3 And after they should be brought back out of captivity they should possess again the land of their inheritance.

4 And even six hundred years from the time that my father left Jerusalem, a prophet would the Lord God raise up among the Jews, even a Messiah; or, in other words, a Savior of the world.

5 He also spoke concerning the prophets, how great a number had testified of these things, concerning this Messiah of whom he had spoken, or this Redeemer of the world.

6 Wherefore, all mankind were in a lost and in a fallen state, and ever would be, save they should rely on this Redeemer.

7 And he spoke also concerning a prophet who should come before the Messiah, to prepare the way of the Lord.

8 He should go forth and cry in the wilderness, "Prepare ye the way of the Lord and make his paths straight; [9]for there standeth one among you whom ye know not; and he is mightier than I, whose shoe's latchet I am not worthy to unloose."

10 And much spoke my father concerning this thing.

11 My father also said he should baptize in Bethabara, beyond Jordan, and that he should baptize with water; even that he should baptize the Messiah with water.

12 And after he had baptized the Messiah with water, he should behold and bear record that he had baptized the Lamb of God, who should take away the sins of the world.

13 After my father had spoken these words, he spoke to my brethren concerning the gospel which should be preached among the Jews, [14]and also concerning the dwindling of the Jews in unbelief.

15 After they had slain the Messiah who should come, he should rise from the dead, and should make himself manifest by the Holy Ghost to the Gentiles.

16 And my father spoke much concerning the Gentiles, and also concerning the house of Israel, that they should be compared to an olive tree whose branches should be broken off and should be scattered upon all the face of the earth.

17 Wherefore he said that we should be led with one accord into the land of promise, to the fulfilling of the word of the Lord that we should be scattered upon all the face of the earth.

18 And after the house of Israel should be scattered, they should be gathered together again; 19or, in fine, after the Gentiles had received the fullness of the gospel, the natural branches of the olive tree, or the remnants of the house of Israel, should be grafted in, or come to the knowledge of the true Messiah, their Lord and their Redeemer.

20 After this manner of language my father prophesied and spoke to my brethren; 21and also many more things, which I do not write in this book; for I have written as many of them as were expedient for me in my other book.

22 All these things of which I have spoken were done as my father dwelt in a tent in the valley of Lemuel.

23 And it came to pass after I, Nephi, had heard all the words of my father concerning the things which he saw in a vision, 24and also the things which he spoke by the power of the Holy Ghost, which power he received by faith on the Son of God—25and the Son of God was the Messiah who should come—26I, Nephi, was desirous also that I might see, and hear, and know of these things, by the power of the Holy Ghost, which is the gift of God to all those who diligently seek him, as well in times of old as in the time that he should manifest himself to the children of men; 27for he is the same yesterday, today, and forever.

28 And the way is prepared from the foundation of the world, if it so be that they repent and come to him.

29 For he that diligently seeks shall find; 30and the mysteries of God shall be unfolded to him by the power of the Holy Ghost, as well in this time as in times of old; 31and as well in times of old as in times to come.

32 Wherefore, the course of the Lord is one eternal round.

33 Therefore remember, O man, for all your doings you shall be brought into judgment.

34 Wherefore, if you have sought to do wickedly in the days of your probation, then you are found unclean before the judgment seat of God; 35and no unclean thing can dwell with God; wherefore you must be cast off forever.

36 And the Holy Ghost gives authority that I should speak these things and deny them not.

37 After I had desired to know the things that my father had seen, and believing that the Lord was able to make them known to me, 38as I sat pondering in my heart I was caught away in the Spirit of the Lord into an exceedingly high mountain which I never had before seen, and upon which I never had set my foot.

39 And the Spirit said to me, "Behold, what desirest thou?"

40 I said, "I desire to behold the things which my father saw."

41 And the Spirit said to me, "Believest thou that thy father saw the tree of which he hath spoken?"

42 I said, "Thou knowest that I believe all the words of my father."

43 When I had spoken these words, the Spirit cried with a loud voice, saying, "Hosanna to the Lord, the most high God; for he is God over all the earth, even above all.

44 "Blessed art thou, Nephi, because thou believest in the son of the most high God; wherefore, thou shalt behold the things which thou hast desired.

45 "Behold, this thing shall be given thee for a sign, that after thou hast beheld the tree which bore the fruit which thy father tasted, thou shalt also behold a man descending out of heaven; and him shall ye witness; and after ye have witnessed him, ye shall bear record that it is the Son of God."

46 And it came to pass that the

Spirit said to me, "Look!" And I looked and beheld a tree; and it was like the tree which my father had seen; and the beauty thereof was far beyond, even exceeding all beauty; and the whiteness thereof exceeded the whiteness of the driven snow.

47 After I had seen the tree, I said to the Spirit, "I behold thou hast shown me the tree which is precious above all."

48 And he said to me, "What desirest thou?"

49 I said to him, "To know the interpretation thereof."

50 For I spoke to him as a man speaks; for I beheld that he was in the form of a man; yet, nevertheless, I knew that it was the Spirit of the Lord; and he spoke to me as a man speaks with another.

51 And he said to me, "Look!" And I looked as if to look upon him, and I saw him not; for he had gone from my presence.

52 And I looked and beheld the great city of Jerusalem, and also other cities.

53 And I beheld the city of Nazareth; and in the city of Nazareth I beheld a virgin, and she was exceedingly fair and white.

54 And I saw the heavens open; and an angel came down and stood before me; and he said to me, "Nephi, what beholdest thou?"

55 I said to him, "A virgin, most beautiful and fair above all other virgins."

56 And he said to me, "Knowest thou the condescension of God?"

57 I said to him, "I know that he loveth his children; nevertheless I do not know the meaning of all things."

58 And he said to me, "Behold, the virgin whom thou seest is the mother of the Son of God, after the manner of the flesh."

59 And I beheld that she was carried away in the Spirit; 60and after she had been carried away in the Spirit for the space of a time, the angel spoke to me, saying, "Look!"

61 I looked and beheld the virgin again, bearing a child in her arms.

62 And the angel said to me, "Behold the Lamb of God, even the Son of the Eternal Father!

63 "Knowest thou the meaning of the tree which thy father saw?"

64 I answered him, saying, "It is the love of God, which sheddeth itself abroad in the hearts of the children of men; wherefore it is the most desirable above all things."

65 And he spoke to me, saying, "And the most joyous to the soul."

66 After he had said these words, he said to me, "Look!" And I looked, and I beheld the Son of God going forth among the children of men; 67and I saw many fall down at his feet and worship him.

68 And I beheld that the rod of iron, which my father had seen, was the word of God, which led to the fountain of living waters, or to the tree of life, which waters are a representation of the love of God; 69and I also beheld that the tree of life was a representation of the love of God.

70 The angel again said to me, "Look and behold the condescension of God!"

71 I looked and beheld the Redeemer of the world, of whom my father had spoken; 72and I also beheld the prophet who should prepare the way before him.

73 And the Lamb of God went forth and was baptized of him; 74and after he was baptized, I beheld the heavens open and the Holy Ghost came down out of heaven and abode on him in the form of a dove.

75 I beheld that he went forth ministering to the people in power and great glory; 76and the multitudes were gathered together to hear him; 77and I beheld that they cast him out from among them.

78 I also beheld twelve others following him.

79 And they were carried away in the Spirit from before my face, and I saw them not.

80 And it came to pass that the angel spoke to me again, saying, "Look!" And I looked, and I beheld the heavens open again, 81and I saw angels descending upon the children of men; and they ministered to them.

82 And he spoke to me again, saying, "Look!" And I looked, and I beheld the Lamb of God going forth among the children of men.

83 I beheld multitudes of people

who were sick, and who were afflicted with all manner of diseases, and with devils, and unclean spirits; 84and the angel spoke and showed all these things to me.

85 They were healed by the power of the Lamb of God, and the devils and the unclean spirits were cast out.

86 And the angel spoke to me again, saying, "Look!" And I looked and beheld the Lamb of God, that he was taken by the people; even the Son of the everlasting God was judged of the world; and I saw and bear record.

87 I, Nephi, saw that he was lifted upon the cross and slain for the sins of the world.

88 And after he was slain, I saw the multitudes of the earth, that they were gathered together to fight against the apostles of the Lamb; for thus were the twelve called by the angel of the Lord.

89 And the multitude of the earth was gathered together; 90and I beheld that they were in a large and spacious building, like the building which my father saw.

91 And the angel of the Lord spoke to me again, saying, "Behold the world and the wisdom thereof; 92behold, the house of Israel hath gathered together to fight against the twelve apostles of the Lamb."

93 I saw and bear record that the great and spacious building was the pride of the world; 94and it fell; and the fall thereof was exceedingly great.

95 The angel of the Lord spoke to me again, saying, "Thus shall be the destruction of all nations, kindreds, tongues and people that shall fight against the twelve apostles of the Lamb."

96 And the angel said to me, "Look and behold thy seed, and also the seed of thy brethren!"

97 I looked and beheld the land of promise; 98and I beheld multitudes of people, even as it were in number as many as the sand of the sea.

99 And I beheld multitudes gathered together to battle, one against the other; and I beheld wars, and rumors of wars, and great slaughters with the sword among my people.

100 And I beheld many generations pass away, after the manner of wars and contentions in the land;

101and I beheld many cities, even that I did not number them.

102 And I saw a mist of darkness on the face of the land of promise; 103and I saw lightnings, and I heard thunderings, and earthquakes, and all manner of tumultuous noises.

104 And I saw the earth and the rocks that they rent; 105and I saw mountains tumbling into pieces; 106and I saw the plains of the earth that they were broken up.

107 And I saw many cities that they were sunk; 108and I saw many that they were burned with fire; 109and I saw many that tumbled to the earth because of the quaking thereof.

110 After I saw these things, I saw the vapor of darkness that it passed from off the face of the earth; 111and, behold, I saw multitudes who had fallen because of the great and terrible judgments of the Lord.

112 And I saw the heavens open, and the Lamb of God descending out of heaven; and he came down and showed himself to them.

113 I also saw and I bear record that the Holy Ghost fell upon twelve others, and they were ordained of God, and chosen.

114 Again the angel spoke to me, saying, "Behold the twelve disciples of the Lamb, who are chosen to minister to thy seed."

115 And he said to me, "Thou remembereth the twelve apostles of the Lamb? Behold, they are they who shall judge the twelve tribes of Israel.

116 Wherefore, the twelve ministers of thy seed shall be judged of them; for ye are of the house of Israel; and these twelve ministers whom thou beholdest shall judge thy seed.

117 "Behold, they are righteous forever; for because of their faith in the Lamb of God, their garments are made white in his blood."

118 And the angel said to me, "Look!" And I looked and beheld three generations pass away in righteousness, and their garments were white, even like the Lamb of God.

119 And the angel said to me, "These are made white in the blood of the Lamb, because of their faith in him."

120 I, Nephi, also saw many of the fourth generation, who passed away in righteousness.

121 And it came to pass that I saw the multitudes of the earth gathered together.

122 Then the angel said to me, "Behold thy seed, and also the seed of thy brethren."

123 I looked and beheld the people of my seed gathered in multitudes against the seed of my brethren; and they were gathered together to battle.

124 And the angel spoke to me, saying, "Behold the fountain of filthy water which thy father saw, even the river of which he spoke; and the depths thereof are the depths of hell; 125and the mists of darkness are the temptations of the devil, which blindeth the eyes, and hardeneth the hearts of the children of men, and leadeth them away into broad roads, that they may perish, and are lost; 126and the large and spacious building which thy father saw is vain imaginations and the pride of the children of men.

127 "A great and a terrible gulf divideth them, even the word of the justice of the eternal God, and the Messiah who is the Lamb of God, of whom the Holy Ghost beareth record, from the beginning of the world until this time, and from this time henceforth and forever."

128 While the angel spoke these words, I beheld and saw that the seed of my brethren contended against my seed, according to the word of the angel; 129and because of the pride of my seed, and the temptations of the devil, I beheld that the seed of my brethren overpowered the people of my seed.

130 And I beheld and saw the people of the seed of my brethren, that they had overcome my seed; and they went forth in multitudes upon the face of the land.

131 I saw them gathered together in multitudes; 132and I saw wars and rumors of wars among them; and in wars, and rumors of wars, I saw many generations pass away.

133 And the angel said to me, "Behold, these shall dwindle in unbelief."

134 And I beheld after they had dwindled in unbelief, they became a dark and loathsome, and a filthy people, full of idleness and all manner of abominations.

135 Then the angel spoke to me, saying, "Look!" And I looked and beheld many nations and kingdoms.

136 And the angel said to me, "What beholdest thou?"

137 I said, "I behold many nations and kingdoms."

138 And he said to me, "These are the nations and kingdoms of the Gentiles."

139 And I saw among the nations of the Gentiles the foundation of a great church.

140 And the angel said to me, "Behold the foundation of a church, which is most abominable above all other churches, which slayeth the saints of God, and tortureth them and bindeth them down, and yoketh them with a yoke of iron, and bringeth them down into captivity."

141 I beheld this great and abominable church; and I saw the devil that he was the foundation of it.

142 I also saw gold and silver, and silks, and scarlets, and fine twined linen, and all manner of precious clothing; and I saw many harlots.

143 And the angel spoke to me, saying, "Behold the gold, and the silver, and the silks, and the scarlets, and the fine twined linen, and the precious clothing, and the harlots are the desires of this great and abominable church.

144 "Also for the praise of the world do they destroy the saints of God, and bring them down into captivity."

145 And it came to pass that I looked and beheld many waters; and they divided the Gentiles from the seed of my brethren.

146 And the angel said to me, "Behold, the wrath of God is upon the seed of thy brethren!"

147 I looked and beheld a man among the Gentiles, who was separated from the seed of my brethren by the many waters; and I beheld the Spirit of God, that it came down and wrought upon the man; and he went forth upon the many waters, even to the seed of my brethren, who were in the promised land.

148 And I beheld the Spirit of

600–592 B. C.

God, that it wrought upon other Gentiles; and they went forth out of captivity upon the many waters.

149 And I beheld many multitudes of the Gentiles upon the land of promise.

150 I beheld the wrath of God that it was upon the seed of my brethren; and they were scattered before the Gentiles and were smitten.

151 And I beheld the Spirit of the Lord, that it was upon the Gentiles, that they prospered and obtained the land for their inheritance; and I beheld that they were white, and exceedingly fair and beautiful, like my people before they were slain.

152 Then I, Nephi, beheld that the Gentiles who had gone forth out of captivity humbled themselves before the Lord, and the power of the Lord was with them.

153 I also beheld that their mother Gentiles were gathered together upon the waters, and upon the land also, to battle against them.

154 But I beheld that the power of God was with them; and also that the wrath of God was upon all those that were gathered together against them to battle.

155 And I, Nephi, beheld that the Gentiles that had gone out of captivity were delivered by the power of God out of the hands of all other nations; 156and I, Nephi, beheld that they prospered in the land.

157 I also beheld a book, and it was carried forth among them.

158 And the angel said unto me, "Knowest thou the meaning of the book?"

159 I said to him, "I know not."

160 And he said, "Behold, it proceedeth out of the mouth of a Jew"; and I, Nephi, beheld it.

161 Then he said to me, "The book that thou beholdest is a record of the Jews, which containeth the covenants of the Lord which he hath made to the house of Israel.

162 "It also containeth many of the prophecies of the holy prophets; 163and it is a record like the engravings which are upon the plates of brass, save there are not so many; nevertheless, they containeth the covenants of the Lord which he hath made to the house of Israel; 164where-

fore, they are of great worth to the Gentiles."

165 And the angel of the Lord said to me, "Thou hast beheld that the book proceeded forth from the mouth of a Jew; and when it proceeded forth from the mouth of a Jew it contained the plainness of the gospel of the Lord, of whom the twelve apostles bear record; and they bear record according to the truth which is in the Lamb of God.

166 "Wherefore, these things go forth from the Jews in purity to the Gentiles, according to the truth which is in God.

167 "After they go forth by the hand of the twelve apostles of the Lamb, from the Jews to the Gentiles, thou seest the foundation of a great and abominable church, which is most abominable above all other churches.

168 "For, behold, they have taken away from the gospel of the Lamb many parts which are plain and most precious; 169and also many covenants of the Lord have they taken away.

170 "All this have they done that they might pervert the right ways of the Lord, that they might blind the eyes and harden the hearts of the children of men.

171 "Wherefore, thou seest that after the book hath gone forth through the hands of the great and abominable church that there are many plain and precious things taken away from the book, which is the book of the Lamb of God.

172 "And after these plain and precious things were taken away, it goeth forth to all the nations of the Gentiles.

173 "And after it goeth forth to all the nations of the Gentiles, even across the many waters which thou hast seen, with the Gentiles which have gone forth out of captivity; 174thou seest because of the many plain and precious things which have been taken out of the book, which were plain to the understanding of the children of men, according to the plainness which is in the Lamb of God; 175because of these things which are taken away out of the gospel of the Lamb, an exceedingly great many

do stumble, insomuch that Satan hath great power over them.

176 "Nevertheless thou beholdest that the Gentiles who have gone forth out of captivity, and have been lifted up by the power of God above all other nations upon the face of the land—which is choice above all other lands, 177which is the land that the Lord God hath covenanted with thy father that his seed should have for the land of their inheritance—will not utterly destroy the mixture of thy seed, which are among thy brethren.

178 "Neither will He suffer that the Gentiles shall destroy the seed of thy brethren.

179 "Neither will the Lord God suffer that the Gentiles shall forever remain in that awful state of blindness, which thou beholdest they are in because of the plain and most precious parts of the gospel of the Lamb which have been kept back by that abominable church, whose formation thou hast seen.

180 "'Wherefore,' says the Lamb of God, 'I will be merciful to the Gentiles, to the visiting of the remnant of the house of Israel in great judgment.'"

181 Again the angel of the Lord spoke to me, saying, "'Behold,' says the Lamb of God, 'after I have visited the remnant of the house of Israel, and this remnant of whom I speak is the seed of thy father; 182wherefore, after I have visited them in judgment, and smitten them by the hand of the Gentiles; 183and after the Gentiles stumble exceedingly because of the most plain and precious parts of the gospel of the Lamb which have been kept back by that abominable church, which is the mother of harlots,' says the Lamb, 'I will be merciful to the Gentiles in that day, insomuch that I will bring forth to them in my own power much of my gospel, which shall be plain and precious,' says the Lamb.

184 "'For, behold,' says the Lamb, 'I will manifest myself to thy seed, that they shall write many things which I shall minister to them, which shall be plain and precious.

185 "'And after thy seed shall be destroyed and dwindle in unbelief, and also the seed of thy brethren, be-

hold, these things shall be hidden, to come forth to the Gentiles by the gift and power of the Lamb.

186 "'In them shall be written my gospel,' says the Lamb, 'and my rock and my salvation.

187 "'Blessed are they who shall seek to bring forth my Zion at that day, for they shall have the gift and the power of the Holy Ghost; 188and if they endure to the end, they shall be lifted up at the last day, and shall be saved in the everlasting kingdom of the Lamb.

189 "'And whoso shall publish peace, even tidings of great joy, how beautiful upon the mountains shall they be.'"

190 And it came to pass that I beheld the remnant of the seed of my brethren, and also the book of the Lamb of God which had proceeded forth from the mouth of the Jew, that it came forth from the Gentiles to the remnant of the seed of my brethren.

191 After it had come forth to them, I beheld other books which came forth by the power of the Lamb from the Gentiles to them, to the convincing of the Gentiles, and the remnant of the seed of my brethren, and also the Jews, who were scattered upon all the face of the earth, that records of the prophets and of the twelve apostles of the Lamb are true.

192 And the angel spoke to me, saying, "These last records which thou hast seen among the Gentiles shall establish the truth of the first, which are of the twelve apostles of the Lamb, and shall make known the plain and precious things which have been taken away from them.

193 "They shall make known to all kindreds, tongues and people that the Lamb of God is the son of the Eternal Father and the Savior of the world; and that all men must come to him or they cannot be saved; 194and they must come according to the words which shall be established by the mouth of the Lamb.

195 "And the words of the Lamb shall be made known in the records of thy seed, as well as in the records of the twelve apostles of the Lamb; 196wherefore, they both shall be established in one; 197for there is one God

17

and one Shepherd over all the earth.

198 "The time cometh that he shall manifest himself to all nations, to the Jews, and also to the Gentiles.

199 "And after he hath manifested himself to the Jews and also to the Gentiles, then he shall manifest himself to the Gentiles, and also to the Jews, 200and the last shall be first, and the first shall be last.

201 "And if the Gentiles shall hearken to the Lamb of God in that day that he shall manifest himself to them in word, and also in power, in very deed, to the taking away of their stumbling blocks, and harden not their hearts against the Lamb of God, they shall be numbered among the seed of thy father.

202 "They shall be numbered among the house of Israel; 203and they shall be a blessed people upon the promised land forever.

204 "They shall be no more brought down into captivity; 205and the house of Israel shall no more be confounded.

206 "And that great pit which hath been digged for them by that great and abominable church, which was founded by the devil and his children that he might lead away the souls of men down to hell—207even that great pit which hath been digged for the destruction of men—shall be filled by those who digged it, to their utter destruction, says the Lamb of God; 208but not to the destruction of their soul, save it be the casting of it into that hell which hath no end.

209 "For, behold, this is according to the captivity of the devil, and also according to the justice of God upon all those who will work wickedness and abomination before him."

210 And the angel spoke to me, Nephi, saying, "Thou hast beheld that if the Gentiles repent, it shall be well with them.

211 "Thou also knowest concerning the covenants of the Lord to the house of Israel; 212and thou also hast heard that whoso repenteth not, must perish.

213 "Therefore, woe be to the Gentiles if it so be that they harden their hearts against the Lamb of God.

214 "'For the time cometh,' says the Lamb of God, 'that I will work a great and a marvelous work among the children of men—215a work which shall be everlasting, either on the one hand or on the other; 216either to the convincing of them to peace and life eternal, or to the deliverance of them to the hardness of their hearts and the blindness of their minds, to their being brought down into captivity and also to destruction, both temporally and spiritually, according to the captivity of the devil, of which I have spoken.'"

217 When the angel had spoken these words, he said to me, "Remember thou the covenants of the Father to the house of Israel?"

218 I said to him, "Yes."

219 Then he said to me, "Look and behold that great and abominable church, which is the mother of abominations, whose founder is the devil."

220 And he said to me, "Behold, there are save two churches only: 221the one is the church of the Lamb of God, and the other is the church of the devil.

222 "Wherefore, whoso belongeth not to the church of the Lamb of God belongeth to that great church, which is the mother of abominations; 223and she is the whore of all the earth."

224 I looked and beheld the whore of all the earth, and she sat upon many waters; 225and she had dominion over all the earth, among all nations, kindreds, tongues, and people.

226 And I beheld the church of the Lamb of God, and its numbers were few, because of the wickedness and abominations of the whore who sat upon many waters.

227 Nevertheless, I beheld that the church of the Lamb, who were the saints of God, were also upon all the face of the earth; 228and their dominions upon the face of the earth were small, because of the wickedness of the great whore whom I saw.

229 I also beheld that the great mother of abominations gathered in multitudes upon the face of all the earth, among all the nations of the Gentiles, to fight against the Lamb of God.

230 And I, Nephi, beheld the power of the Lamb of God, that it descended upon the saints of the church of the

Lamb, and upon the covenant people of the Lord, who were scattered upon all the face of the earth; 231and they were armed with righteousness and with the power of God in great glory.

232 And I beheld that the wrath of God was poured out upon the great and abominable church, insomuch that there were wars and rumors of wars among all the nations and kindreds of the earth.

233 As there began to be wars and rumors of wars among all the nations which belonged to the mother of abominations, the angel spoke to me, saying, 234"Behold, the wrath of God is upon the mother of harlots; 235and, behold, thou seest all these things.

236 "When the day cometh that the wrath of God is poured out upon the mother of harlots, which is the great and abominable church of all the earth, whose foundation is the devil, 237then at that day, the work of the Father shall commence, in preparing the way for the fulfilling of his covenants which he has made to his people, who are of the house of Israel."

238 And it came to pass that the angel spoke to me, saying, "Look!" And I looked and beheld a man, and he was dressed in a white robe.

239 And the angel said to me, "Behold one of the twelve apostles of the Lamb!

240 "Behold, he shall see and write the remainder of these things; 241and also many things which have been.

242 "He shall also write concerning the end of the world.

243 "Wherefore, the things which he shall write are just and true.

244 "Behold, they are written in the book which thou beheld proceeding out of the mouth of the Jew.

245 "And at the time they proceeded out of the mouth of the Jew, or at the time the book proceeded out of the mouth of the Jew, the things which were written were plain and pure, and most precious and easy to the understanding of all men.

246 "Behold, the things which this apostle of the Lamb shall write are many things which thou hast seen; 247and, behold, the remainder shalt thou see.

248 "But the things which thou shalt see hereafter thou shalt not write; for the Lord God hath ordained the apostle of the Lamb of God that he should write them.

249 "And also others who have been, to them hath he shown all things, and they have written them; 250and they are sealed up to come forth in their purity according to the truth which is in the Lamb, in the own due time of the Lord, to the house of Israel."

251 I, Nephi, heard and bear record that the name of the apostle of the Lamb was John, according to the word of the angel.

252 And, behold, I, Nephi, am forbidden that I should write the remainder of the things which I saw and heard; wherefore, the things which I have written suffice me; 253and I have written but a small part of the things which I saw.

254 I bear record that I saw the things which my father saw, and the angel of the Lord made them known to me.

255 Now I make an end of speaking concerning the things which I saw while I was carried away in the Spirit.

256 And if all the things which I saw are not written, the things which I have written are true. And thus it is. Amen.

CHAPTER 4

AFTER I, Nephi, had been carried away in the Spirit, and had seen all these things, I returned to the tent of my father.

2 And I beheld my brethren, and they were disputing one with another concerning the things which my father had spoken to them.

3 For he truly spoke many great things to them, which were hard to be understood save a man should inquire of the Lord; 4and they being hard in their hearts, therefore they did not look to the Lord as they ought.

5 Now I, Nephi, was grieved because of the hardness of their hearts, and also because of the things which I had seen, and knew they must unavoidably come to pass because of the great wickedness of the children of men.

6 I was overcome because of my afflictions, for I considered that my

afflictions were great above all, because of the destruction of my people; for I had beheld their fall.

7 But after I had received strength, I spoke to my brethren, desiring to know of them the cause of their disputations.

8 And they said, "Behold, we cannot understand the words which our father has spoken concerning the natural branches of the olive tree, and also concerning the Gentiles."

9 And I said to them, "Have you inquired of the Lord?"

10 They said, "We have not; for the Lord makes no such thing known to us."

11 Behold, I said to them, "How is it that you do not keep the commandments of the Lord?

12 "How is it that you will perish because of the hardness of your hearts?

13 "Do you not remember the things which the Lord has said, 'If you will not harden your hearts, and will ask me in faith, believing that you shall receive, with diligence in keeping my commandments, surely these things shall be made known to you'?

14 "Behold, I say to you that the house of Israel was compared to an olive tree by the Spirit of the Lord which was in our fathers; 15and, behold, are we not broken off from the house of Israel; and are we not a branch of the house of Israel?

16 "Now the thing which our father means concerning the grafting in of the natural branches through the fullness of the Gentiles is, that in the latter days, when our seed shall have dwindled in unbelief, even for the space of many years and many generations after the Messiah shall be manifested in body to the children of men, then shall the fullness of the gospel of the Messiah come to the Gentiles, and from the Gentiles to the remnant of our seed.

17 "At that day shall the remnant of our seed know that they are of the house of Israel, and that they are the covenant people of the Lord.

18 "Then shall they know and come to the knowledge of their forefathers, and also to the knowledge of the gospel of their Redeemer, which was ministered to their fathers by him.

19 "Wherefore, they shall come to the knowledge of their Redeemer, and the very points of his doctrine, that they may know how to come to him and be saved.

20 "Then at that day, will they not rejoice and give praise to their everlasting God, their rock and their salvation?

21 "And at that day, will they not receive the strength and nourishment from the true vine?

22 "Will they not come to the true fold of God?

23 "Behold, I say to you, Yes: they shall be remembered again among the house of Israel; 24they shall be grafted in, being a natural branch of the olive tree, into the true olive tree.

25 "This is what our father means.

26 "He means that it will not come to pass until after they are scattered by the Gentiles.

27 "And he means that it shall come by way of the Gentiles, that the Lord may show his power to the Gentiles, for the very cause that he shall be rejected by the Jews or by the house of Israel.

28 "Wherefore, our father has not spoken of our seed alone, but also of all the house of Israel, pointing to the covenant which should be fulfilled in the latter days; 29which covenant the Lord made to our father Abraham, saying, 'In thy seed shall all the kindreds of the earth be blessed.'"

30 I, Nephi, spoke much to them concerning these things; 31and I spoke to them concerning the restoration of the Jews in the latter days.

32 I rehearsed to them the words of Isaiah, who spoke concerning the restoration of the Jews, or of the house of Israel; 33that after they were restored, they should no more be confounded, neither should they be scattered again.

34 And I spoke many words to my brethren, that they were pacified and humbled themselves before the Lord.

35 And it came to pass that they spoke to me again, saying, "What means this thing which our father saw in a dream?

36 "What means the tree which he saw?"

37 And I said to them, "It was a representation of the tree of life."

38 Then they said to me, "What means the rod of iron which our father saw that led to the tree?"

39 And I said to them that it was the word of God; and whoever would hearken to the word of God and would hold fast to it would never perish; 40neither could the temptations nor the fiery darts of the adversary overpower them to blindness, to lead them away to destruction.

41 Wherefore, I, Nephi, exhorted them to give heed to the word of the Lord.

42 And I exhorted them with all the energies of my soul, and with all the faculty which I possessed, that they would give heed to the word of God and remember to keep his commandments always in all things.

43 Then they said to me, "What means the river of water which our father saw?"

44 And I said to them that the water which my father saw was filthiness; 45and so much was his mind swallowed up in other things that he beheld not the filthiness of the water.

46 I also said to them that it was an awful gulf which separates the wicked from the tree of life, and also from the saints of God, 47and that it was a representation of that awful hell, which the angel said to me was prepared for the wicked.

48 Then I said to them that our father also saw that the justice of God also divided the wicked from the righteous; 49and the brightness thereof was like the brightness of a flaming fire, which ascends up to God for ever and ever, and has no end.

50 And they said to me, "Does this thing mean the torment of the body in the days of probation, or does it mean the final state of the soul after the death of the temporal body, or does it speak of the things which are temporal?"

51 I said to them that it was a representation of things both temporal and spiritual; 52for the day should come that they must be judged of their works, even the works which were done by the temporal body in their days of probation.

53 Wherefore, if they should die in their wickedness, they must be cast off also as to the things which are spiritual, which are pertaining to righteousness.

54 Wherefore, they must be brought to stand before God to be judged of their works: 55and if their works have been filthiness, they must be filthy.

56 And if they be filthy, they cannot dwell in the kingdom of God; 57if so, the kingdom of God must be filthy also.

58 "But, behold, I say to you, the kingdom of God is not filthy, and there cannot any unclean thing enter into the kingdom of God; 59wherefore, there must be a place of filthiness prepared for that which is filthy.

60 "There is a place prepared, even that awful hell of which I have spoken, and the devil is the foundation of it.

61 "Wherefore, the final state of the souls of men is to dwell in the kingdom of God, or to be cast out because of that justice of which I have spoken.

62 "Wherefore, the wicked are rejected from the righteous and also from that tree of life, whose fruit is most precious and most desirable above all other fruits; 63and it is the greatest of all the gifts of God."

64 Thus I spoke to my brethren. Amen.

CHAPTER 5

AFTER I, Nephi, had made an end of speaking to my brethren, behold, they said to me, "You have declared to us hard things, more than we are able to bear."

2 I said to them that I knew I had spoken hard things against the wicked, according to the truth; and the righteous have I justified, and testified that they should be lifted up at the last day; wherefore, the guilty take the truth to be hard, for it cuts them to the very center.

3 "Now, my brethren, if you were righteous, and were willing to hearken to the truth, and give heed to it, that you might walk uprightly before God, then you would not murmur because of the truth, and say, 'You speak hard things against us.'"

21

4 And I, Nephi, exhorted my brethren with all diligence to keep the commandments of the Lord; ⁵and they humbled themselves before the Lord, insomuch that I had joy and great hopes of them that they would walk in the paths of righteousness.

6 Now all these things were said and done as my father dwelt in a tent in the valley which he called Lemuel.

7 And it came to pass that I, Nephi, took one of the daughters of Ishmael to wife; and also my brethren took of the daughters of Ishmael to wife; and also Zoram took the eldest daughter of Ishmael to wife.

8 Thus my father had fulfilled all the commandments of the Lord which had been given him.

9 Also I, Nephi, had been blessed of the Lord exceedingly.

10 And it came to pass that the voice of the Lord spoke to my father by night and commanded him that on the morrow he should take his journey into the wilderness.

11 As my father arose in the morning and went forth to the tent door, to his great astonishment, he beheld upon the ground a round ball of curious workmanship; and it was of fine brass.

12 Within the ball were two spindles; and the one pointed the way which we should go into the wilderness.

13 And it came to pass that we gathered together what things we should carry into the wilderness, and all the remainder of our provisions which the Lord had given to us.

14 We took seed of every kind, that we might carry into the wilderness; ¹⁵and we took our tents and departed into the wilderness, across the river Laman.

16 We traveled for the space of four days, nearly a south southeast direction, and we pitched our tents again; and we called the name of the place Shazer.

17 And we took our bows and our arrows, and went forth into the wilderness to slay food for our families; and after we had slain food for our families, we returned again to our families in the wilderness, to the place of Shazer.

18 Then we went forth again in the wilderness, following the same direction, keeping in the most fertile parts of the wilderness, which were in the borders near the Red Sea.

19 We traveled for the space of many days, slaying food by the way, with our bows and our arrows, and our stones and our slings.

20 And we followed the directions of the ball, which led us in the more fertile parts of the wilderness.

21 After we had traveled for the space of many days, we pitched our tents for the space of a time that we might again rest ourselves and obtain food for our families.

22 As I, Nephi, went forth to slay food, behold, I broke my bow, which was made of fine steel; and after I broke my bow, behold, my brethren were angry with me, because of the loss of my bow, for we could obtain no food.

23 And we returned without food to our families.

24 Being much fatigued because of their journeying, they suffered much for the want of food.

25 Then Laman and Lemuel and the sons of Ishmael began to murmur exceedingly because of their sufferings and afflictions in the wilderness; and also my father began to murmur against the Lord his God; and they were all exceedingly sorrowful, even that they murmured against the Lord.

26 Now I, Nephi, had been afflicted with my brethren because of the loss of my bow, and their bows had lost their spring; therefore it began to be exceedingly difficult, insomuch that we could obtain no food.

27 And I, Nephi, spoke much to my brethren because they had hardened their hearts again, even to complaining against the Lord their God.

28 And it came to pass that I, Nephi, made out of wood a bow, and out of a straight stick an arrow; wherefore, I armed myself with a bow and an arrow, with a sling, and with stones.

29 Then I said to my father, "Where shall I go to obtain food?"

30 And he inquired of the Lord, for they had humbled themselves because of my word; for I said many things to them in the energy of my soul.

31 And the voice of the Lord came to my father; and he was truly chastened because of his murmuring against the Lord, insomuch that he was brought down into the depths of sorrow.

32 The voice of the Lord said to him, "Look upon the ball, and behold the things which are written!"

33 And when my father beheld the things which were written upon the ball, he feared and trembled exceedingly; and also my brethren, and the sons of Ishmael, and our wives.

34 I, Nephi, beheld the pointers which were in the ball, that they worked according to the faith and diligence and heed which we gave to them.

35 And there was also written upon them a new writing, which was plain to be read, which gave us understanding concerning the ways of the Lord; and it was written and changed from time to time, according to the faith and diligence which we gave to it.

36 Thus we see that by small means the Lord can bring about great things.

37 And it came to pass that I, Nephi, went forth up to the top of the mountain, according to the directions which were given upon the ball; ³⁸and I slew wild beasts, insomuch that I obtained food for our families.

39 Then I returned to our tents, bearing the beasts which I had slain.

40 Now when they beheld that I had obtained food, how great was their joy.

41 And they humbled themselves before the Lord, and gave thanks to him.

42 And it came to pass that we again took our journey, traveling nearly the same course as in the beginning.

43 After we had traveled for the space of many days, we pitched our tents again that we might tarry for the space of a time.

44 And it came to pass that Ishmael died, and was buried in the place which was called Nahom.

45 The daughters of Ishmael mourned exceedingly because of the loss of their father, and because of their afflictions in the wilderness.

46 And they murmured against my father because he had brought them out of the land of Jerusalem, saying, "Our father is dead; and we have wandered much in the wilderness, and we have suffered much affliction, hunger, thirst, and fatigue; and after all these sufferings, we must perish in the wilderness with hunger."

47 Thus they murmured against my father, and also against me; and they were desirous to return again to Jerusalem.

48 And Laman said to Lemuel, and also to the sons of Ishmael, "Behold, let us slay our father, and also our brother Nephi, who has taken it upon himself to be our ruler and our teacher, who are his elder brethren.

49 "Now he says that the Lord has talked with him, and also that angels have ministered to him!

50 "But, behold, we know that he lies to us; and he tells us these things, and he works many things by his cunning arts, that he may deceive our eyes, thinking, perhaps, that he may lead us away into some strange wilderness.

51 "And after he has led us away, he has thought to make himself a king and a ruler over us, that he may do with us according to his will and pleasure."

52 After this manner my brother Laman stirred up their hearts to anger.

53 But the Lord was with us; even the voice of the Lord came and spoke many words to them, and chastened them exceedingly.

54 And after they were chastened by the voice of the Lord, they turned away their anger, and repented of their sins, insomuch that the Lord blessed us again with food, that we did not perish.

55 And it came to pass that we again took our journey in the wilderness; and we traveled nearly eastward from that time forth.

56 We traveled and waded through much affliction in the wilderness; and our women bore children in the wilderness.

57 But so great were the blessings of the Lord upon us that while we lived on raw meat in the wilderness, our women gave plenty of suck for their children, and were strong, even like the men; and they began to bear

their journeyings without murmurings.

58 Thus we see that the commandments of God must be fulfilled.

59 And if it so be that the children of men keep the commandments of God, he will nourish and strengthen them and provide means whereby they can accomplish the thing which he has commanded them.

60 Wherefore, he provided means for us while we sojourned in the wilderness.

61 And we sojourned for the space of many years, even eight years in the wilderness.

62 Then we came to the land which we called Bountiful, because of its much fruit, and also wild honey.

63 And all these things were prepared of the Lord that we might not perish.

64 And we beheld the sea, which we called Irreantum, which being interpreted is "many waters."

65 We pitched our tents by the seashore; 66and notwithstanding we had suffered many afflictions, and much difficulty, even so much that we cannot write them all, we exceedingly rejoiced when we came to the seashore.

67 And we called the place Bountiful, because of its much fruit.

68 After I, Nephi, had been in the land of Bountiful for the space of many days, the voice of the Lord came to me, saying, "Arise, and get thee into the mountain."

69 I arose and went up into the mountain, and cried to the Lord.

70 And the Lord spoke to me, saying, "Thou shalt construct a ship, after the manner which I shall show thee, that I may carry thy people across these waters."

71 And I said, "Lord, where shall I go that I may find ore to smelt that I may make tools to construct the ship after the manner which thou hast shown me?"

72 Then the Lord told me where I should go to find ore that I might make tools.

73 And I, Nephi, made bellows wherewith to blow the fire, of the skins of beasts.

74 After I had made bellows that I might have wherewith to blow the

fire, I smote two stones together that I might make fire.

75 For the Lord had not hitherto suffered that we should make much fire as we journeyed in the wilderness.

76 For he said, "I will make thy food become sweet that ye cook it not; 77and I will also be your light in the wilderness; 78and I will prepare the way before you, if it so be that ye shall keep my commandments.

79 "Wherefore, inasmuch as ye shall keep my commandments, ye shall be led toward the promised land; and ye shall know that it is by me that ye are led."

80 And the Lord said also, "After ye have arrived at the promised land, ye shall know that I, the Lord, am God; 81and that I, the Lord, delivered you from destruction; 82that I brought you out of the land of Jerusalem."

83 Wherefore, I, Nephi, strove to keep the commandments of the Lord, and I exhorted my brethren to faithfulness and diligence.

84 And it came to pass that I made tools of the ore which I smelted out of the rock.

85 When my brethren saw that I was about to build a ship, they began to murmur against me, saying, 86"Our brother is a fool, for he thinks that he can build a ship; 87and he also thinks that he can cross these great waters."

88 Thus my brethren complained against me, and were desirous that they might not labor, for they did not believe that I could build a ship; 89neither would they believe that I was instructed of the Lord.

90 Now I, Nephi, was exceedingly sorrowful, because of the hardness of their hearts.

91 When they saw that I began to be sorrowful, they were glad in their hearts, insomuch that they rejoiced over me, saying, 92"We knew that you could not construct a ship, for we knew that you were lacking in judgment; wherefore, you cannot accomplish so great a work.

93 "You are like our father, led away by the foolish imaginations of your heart.

94 "He has led us out of the land of Jerusalem; and we have wandered in the wilderness for these many years; 95and our women have toiled,

being big with child; and they have borne children in the wilderness and suffered all things, save it were death.

96 "It would have been better that they had died before they came out of Jerusalem than to have suffered these afflictions.

97 "Behold, these many years we have suffered in the wilderness, which time we might have enjoyed our possessions and the land of our inheritance; and we might have been happy.

98 "We know that the people who were in the land of Jerusalem were a righteous people.

99 "For they kept the statutes and the judgments of the Lord, and all his commandments according to the law of Moses; wherefore, we know that they are a righteous people.

100 "But our father has judged them, and has led us away because we hearkened to his word; 101and our brother is like him."

102 After this manner of language my brethren murmured and complained against us.

103 And I, Nephi, spoke to them, saying, "Do you believe that our fathers, who were the children of Israel, would have been led away out of the hands of the Egyptians, if they had not hearkened to the words of the Lord?

104 "Do you suppose that they would have been led out of bondage if the Lord had not commanded Moses that he should lead them out of bondage?

105 "Now you know that the children of Israel were in bondage; and you know that they were laden with tasks which were grievous to be borne; 106wherefore, you know that it must be a good thing for them that they should be brought out of bondage.

107 "Now you know that Moses was commanded of the Lord to do that great work; 108and you know that by his word the waters of the Red Sea were divided, and they passed through on dry ground.

109 "But you know that the Egyptians were drowned in the Red Sea, who were the armies of Pharaoh.

110 "You also know that our fathers were fed with manna in the wilderness.

111 "And you also know that Moses, by his word, according to the power of God which was in him, smote the rock, and there came forth water that the children of Israel might quench their thirst.

112 "Notwithstanding their being led, the Lord their God, their Redeemer, going before them, leading them by day and giving light to them by night, and doing all things for them which were expedient for man to receive, they hardened their hearts, and blinded their minds, and reviled against Moses and against the true and living God.

113 "And it came to pass that according to his word, he destroyed them.

114 "And according to his word, he led them; 115and according to his word, he did all things for them; 116and there was not anything done except by his word.

117 "After they had crossed the river Jordan, he made them mighty, to the driving out the children of the land, to the scattering of them to destruction.

118 "Now do you suppose that the children of this land, who were in the land of promise, who were driven out by our fathers, do you suppose that they were righteous? Behold, I say to you, No.

119 "Do you suppose that our fathers would have been more choice than they, if they had been righteous? 120 "I say to you, No.

121 "Behold, the Lord esteems all flesh in one.

122 "He that is righteous is favored of God.

123 "But, behold, this people had rejected every word of God, and they were ripe in iniquity; and the fullness of the wrath of God was upon them.

124 "And the Lord cursed the land against them, and blessed it to our fathers; he cursed it against them to their destruction; 125and he blessed it to our fathers, to their obtaining power over it.

126 "Behold, the Lord has created the earth that it should be inhabited; 127and he has created his children that they should possess it.

128 "He raises up a righteous na-

591 B. C.

tion, and destroys the nations of the wicked.

129 "And he leads away the righteous into precious lands, and the wicked he destroys, and curses the land to them for their sakes.

130 "He rules high in the heavens, for it is his throne, and this earth is his footstool.

131 "And he loves those who will have him to be their God.

132 "Behold, he loved our fathers; and he covenanted with them, even Abraham, Isaac, and Jacob; and he remembered the covenants which he had made.

133 "Wherefore, he brought them out of the land of Egypt, and he straightened them in the wilderness with his rod, for they hardened their hearts, even as you have; and the Lord straightened them because of their iniquity.

134 "He sent fiery-flying serpents among them; and after they were bitten, he prepared a way that they might be healed; 135and the labor which they had to perform was to look! And because of the simpleness of the way, or the easiness of it, there were many who perished.

136 "And they hardened their hearts from time to time, and they reviled against Moses, and also against God; 137nevertheless you know that they were led forth by his matchless power into the land of promise.

138 "Now after all these things, the time has come that they have become wicked, nearly to ripeness.

139 "I know not but they are at this day about to be destroyed; 140for I know that the day must surely come that they must be destroyed, save a few only who shall be led away into captivity.

141 "Wherefore, the Lord commanded my father that he should depart into the wilderness.

142 "And the Jews also sought to take away his life; and you also have sought to take away his life; 143wherefore, you are murderers in your hearts, and you are like them.

144 "You are swift to do iniquity, but slow to remember the Lord your God.

145 "You have seen an angel, and he spoke to you; you have heard his voice from time to time; 146and he has spoken to you in a still, small voice, but you were past feeling, that you could not feel his words.

147 "Wherefore, he has spoken to you like the voice of thunder, which caused the earth to shake as if it were to divide asunder.

148 "And you also know that by the power of his almighty word he can cause the earth that it shall pass away; 149and you know that by his word he can cause the rough places to be made smooth, and smooth places to be broken up.

150 "O then, why is it that you can be so hard in your hearts?

151 "Behold, my soul is rent with anguish because of you, and my heart is pained; I fear lest you shall be cast off forever.

152 "Behold, I am full of the Spirit of God, insomuch that my frame has no strength."

153 When I had spoken these words, they were angry with me and were desirous to throw me into the depths of the sea.

154 As they came forth to lay their hands upon me, I spoke to them, saying, "In the name of the Almighty God, I command you that you touch me not, for I am filled with the power of God, even to the consuming of my flesh.

155 "Whoever shall lay his hands upon me shall wither even as a dried reed; and he shall be as nought before the power of God, for God shall smite him."

156 And I, Nephi, said to them that they should murmur no more against their father, neither should they withhold their labor from me, for God had commanded me that I should build a ship.

157 And I said to them, "If God had commanded me to do all things, I could do them.

158 "If he should command me that I should say to this water, 'Be thou earth,' it should be earth; and if I should say it, it would be done.

159 "Now, if the Lord has such great power, and has wrought so many miracles among the children of men, how is it that he cannot instruct me that I should build a ship?"

160 And I, Nephi, said many things to my brethren, insomuch that they were confounded, and could not contend against me; 161neither dared they lay their hands upon me, nor touch me with their fingers, even for the space of many days.

162 Now they dared not do this, lest they should wither before me, so powerful was the Spirit of God; and thus it had wrought upon them.

163 And it came to pass that the Lord said to me, "Stretch forth thine hand again to thy brethren, and they shall not wither before thee, but I will shake them," said the Lord; "and this will I do that they may know that I am the Lord their God."

164 And I stretched forth my hand to my brethren, and they did not wither before me; but the Lord shook them, even according to the word which he had spoken.

165 Now they said, "We know of a surety that the Lord is with you, for we know that it is the power of the Lord that has shaken us."

166 They fell down before me, and were about to worship me, but I would not suffer them, saying, "I am your brother, even your younger brother.

167 "Wherefore worship the Lord your God, and honor your father and your mother, that your days may be long in the land which the Lord your God shall give you."

168 And they worshiped the Lord, and went forth with me; and we worked timbers of curious workmanship.

169 And the Lord showed me from time to time after what manner I should work the timbers of the ship.

170 Now I, Nephi, did not work the timbers after the manner which was learned by men, neither did I build the ship after the manner of men; 171but I built it after the manner which the Lord had shown me; wherefore, it was not after the manner of men.

172 And I, Nephi, went into the mount often, and I prayed often to the Lord; wherefore, the Lord showed me great things.

173 After I had finished the ship according to the word of the Lord, my brethren beheld that it was good, and that the workmanship thereof was exceedingly fine; 174wherefore, they humbled themselves again before the Lord.

175 And it came to pass that the voice of the Lord came to my father that we should arise and go down into the ship.

176 And on the morrow, after we had prepared all things, much fruits and meat from the wilderness, and honey in abundance, and provisions according to that which the Lord had commanded us, 177we went down into the ship with all our loading and our seeds, and whatever thing we had brought with us, every one according to his age.

178 Wherefore, we all went down into the ship, with our wives and our children.

179 Now my father had begotten two sons in the wilderness; the elder was called Jacob, and the younger, Joseph.

180 And after we had all gone down into the ship, and had taken with us our provisions and things which had been commanded us, 181we put forth into the sea, and were driven forth before the wind toward the promised land.

182 After we had been driven forth before the wind for the space of many days, behold, my brethren, and the sons of Ishmael, and also their wives, began to make themselves merry, insomuch that they began to dance, and to sing, and to speak with much rudeness, 183even that they forgot by what power they had been brought there; and 184they were lifted up to exceeding rudeness.

185 And I, Nephi, began to fear exceedingly lest the Lord should be angry with us, and smite us because of our iniquity, that we should be swallowed up in the depths of the sea.

186 Wherefore, I, Nephi, began to speak to them with much soberness.

187 But, behold, they were angry with me, saying, "We will not that our younger brother shall be a ruler over us."

188 And Laman and Lemuel took me and bound me with cords, and they treated me with much harshness; 189nevertheless, the Lord suffered it that he might show forth his power

to the fulfilling of his word which he had spoken concerning the wicked.

190 After they had bound me insomuch that I could not move, the compass, which had been prepared of the Lord, ceased to work.

191 Wherefore, they knew not where they should steer the ship, insomuch that there arose a great storm, even a great and terrible tempest, 192and we were driven back upon the waters for the space of three days.

193 They began to be frightened exceedingly lest they should be drowned in the sea; 194nevertheless, they did not loosen me.

195 And on the fourth day which we had been driven back, the tempest began to be exceedingly sore.

196 We were about to be swallowed up in the depths of the sea.

197 And after we had been driven back upon the waters for the space of four days, my brethren began to see that the judgments of God were upon them, and that they must perish, save that they should repent of their iniquities.

198 Wherefore, they came to me and loosed the bands which were upon my wrists, and, behold, they had swollen exceedingly; and also my ankles were much swollen, and great was the soreness thereof.

199 Nevertheless, I looked to my God, and I praised him all the day long; and I did not murmur against the Lord because of my afflictions.

200 Now my father, Lehi, had said many things to them, and also to the sons of Ishmael; but, behold, they breathed out many threatenings against anyone that should speak for me.

201 And my parents, being stricken in years and having suffered much grief because of their children, were brought down, even upon their sick beds.

202 Because of their grief, and much sorrow, and the iniquity of my brethren, they were brought near even to be carried out of this time to meet their God; 203their gray hairs were about to be brought down to lie low in the dust; 204even they were near to be cast, with sorrow, into a watery grave.

205 Jacob and Joseph also, being young and having need of much nourishment, were grieved because of the afflictions of their mother.

206 Also my wife, with her tears and prayers, and also my children did not soften the hearts of my brethren, that they would loosen me.

207 There was nothing, save it were the power of God which threatened them with destruction, could soften their hearts.

208 Wherefore, when they saw that they were about to be swallowed up in the depths of the sea, they repented of the thing which they had done, insomuch that they loosened me.

209 And after they had loosened me, behold, I took the compass, and it worked whenever I desired it.

210 I prayed to the Lord; and after I had prayed, the winds ceased, and the storm ceased, and there was a great calm.

211 And I, Nephi, guided the ship, that we sailed again toward the promised land.

212 And it came to pass that after we had sailed for the space of many days, we arrived at the promised land.

213 We went forth upon the land, and pitched our tents; and we called it the promised land.

214 Then we began to till the earth, and we began to plant seeds, and we put all our seeds into the earth, which we had brought from the land of Jerusalem.

215 And they grew exceedingly; wherefore, we were blessed in abundance.

216 And it came to pass that we found upon the land of promise, as we journeyed in the wilderness, that there were beasts in the forests of every kind, both the cow, and the ox, and the ass, and the horse, and the goat, and the wild goat, and all manner of wild animals, which were for the use of men.

217 And we found all manner of ore, both of gold and of silver, and of copper.

218 And the Lord commanded me, wherefore I made plates of ore that I might engrave upon them the record of my people.

219 Upon the plates which I made,

I engraved the record of my father, and also our journeyings in the wilderness, and the prophecies of my father; and also many of my own prophecies have I engraved upon them.

220 I knew not at the time when I made them that I should be commanded of the Lord to make these plates; 221wherefore, the record of my father, and the genealogy of his forefathers, and the greater part of all our proceedings in the wilderness are engraved upon those plates of which I have spoken; 222wherefore, the things which transpired before I made these plates are, of a truth, more particularly made mention upon the first plates.

223 After I had made these plates by way of commandment, I, Nephi, received a commandment that the ministry, and the prophecies, the more plain and precious parts of them should be written upon these plates; 224and that the things which were written should be kept for the instruction of my people who should possess the land, and also for other wise purposes, which purposes are known to the Lord.

225 Wherefore I, Nephi, made a record upon the other plates, which gives an account, or which gives a greater account of the wars and contentions and destructions of my people.

226 This have I done, and commanded my people what they should do after I am gone, and that these plates should be handed down from one generation to another, or from one prophet to another, until further commandments of the Lord.

227 An account of my making these plates shall be given hereafter; 228and then, behold, I proceed according to that which I have spoken; and this I do that the more sacred things may be kept for the knowledge of my people.

229 Nevertheless, I do not write anything upon plates, save it be that I think it is sacred.

230 Now if I err, even did they err of old.

231 Not that I would excuse myself because of other men, but because of the weakness which is in me, according to the flesh, I would excuse myself.

232 For the things which some men esteem to be of great worth, both to the body and soul, others set at nought and trample under their feet.

233 Even the very God of Israel do men trample under their feet.

234 I say trample under their feet; but I would speak in other words: 235They set him at nought, and hearken not to the voice of his counsels.

236 Behold, he will come, according to the words of the angel, in six hundred years from the time my father left Jerusalem.

237 And the world, because of their iniquity, shall judge him to be a thing of nought; wherefore, they will scourge him, and he will suffer it; and they will smite him, and he will suffer it.

238 They will spit upon him, and he will suffer it, because of his loving-kindness and his long-suffering toward the children of men.

239 And the God of our fathers who were led out of Egypt, out of bondage, and also were preserved in the wilderness by him—240the God of Abraham, and of Isaac, and the God of Jacob—yields himself, according to the words of the angel, as a man into the hands of wicked men, to be lifted up according to the words of Zenock, 241to be crucified, according to the words of Neum, 242to be buried in a sepulcher, according to the words of Zenos, which he spoke concerning the three days of darkness, 243which should be a sign given of his death to those who should inhabit the isles of the sea, 244 more especially given to those who are of the house of Israel.

245 For thus spoke the prophet, "The Lord God surely shall visit all the house of Israel at that day; 246some with his voice, because of their righteousness, to their great joy and salvation; 247and others with the thunderings and the lightnings of his power, by tempest, by fire, and by smoke, and vapor of darkness, and by the opening of the earth, and by mountains which shall be carried up.

248 "All these things must surely come," said the prophet Zenos.

249 "The rocks of the earth must rend; ²⁵⁰and because of the groanings of the earth, many of the kings of the isles of the sea shall be wrought upon by the Spirit of God, to exclaim, 'The God of nature suffers.'

251 "As for those who are at Jerusalem," said the prophet, "they shall be scourged by all people, because they crucify the God of Israel, and turn their hearts aside, rejecting signs and wonders and power and glory of the God of Israel.

252 "And because they turn their hearts aside," said the prophet, "and have despised the Holy One of Israel, they shall wander in the flesh, and perish, and become a hiss and a by-word, and be hated among all nations.

253 "Nevertheless, when that day comes," said the prophet, "that they no more turn aside their hearts against the Holy One of Israel, then will he remember the covenants which he made to their fathers; ²⁵⁴then will he remember the isles of the sea.

255 "'And all the people who are of the house of Israel will I gather in,' said the Lord, according to the words of the prophet Zenos, 'from the four quarters of the earth.'

256 "And all the earth shall see the salvation of the Lord," said the prophet; ²⁵⁷"every nation, kindred, tongue and people shall be blessed."

258 I, Nephi, have written these things to my people that perhaps I might persuade them that they would remember the Lord their Redeemer.

259 Wherefore, I speak to all the house of Israel, if it so be that they should obtain these things.

260 For, behold, I have workings in the spirit, which weary me, even that all my joints are weak, for those who are at Jerusalem.

261 For had not the Lord been merciful to show me concerning them, even as he had prophets of old, I should have perished also.

262 And he surely showed the prophets of old all things concerning them; ²⁶³and also he showed many concerning us.

264 Wherefore, we know concerning them, for they are written upon the plates of brass.

CHAPTER 6

NOW it came to pass that I, Nephi, taught my brethren these things.

2 And I read many things to them, which were engraved upon the plates of brass, that they might know concerning the doings of the Lord in other lands among people of old.

3 I read many things to them which were written in the book of Moses.

4 But that I might more fully persuade them to believe in the Lord their Redeemer, I read to them that which was written by the prophet Isaiah; ⁵for I likened all scriptures to us that it might be for our profit and learning.

6 Wherefore, I spoke to them, saying, "Hear the words of the prophet, you who are a remnant of the house of Israel, a branch who have been broken off; hear the words of the prophet which were written to all the house of Israel, and liken them to yourselves, that you may have hope as well as your brethren, from whom you have been broken off.

7 "For after this manner has the prophet written:

8 *Hearken and hear this, O house of Jacob, who are called by the name of Israel, and are come forth out of the waters of Judah, who swear by the name of the Lord, and make mention of the God of Israel; yet they swear not in truth, nor in righteousness.

9 Nevertheless, they call themselves of the holy city, but they do not stay themselves upon the God of Israel, who is the Lord of hosts; the Lord of hosts is his name.

10 "Behold, I have declared the former things from the beginning; and they went forth out of my mouth, and I showed them; I showed them suddenly.

11 "And I did it because I knew that thou art obstinate, and thy neck was an iron sinew, and thy brow brass.

12 "And I have, even from the beginning, declared them to thee; before they came to pass I showed them to thee; and I showed them

_____
*Isaiah 48

30

for fear lest thou shouldst say, 'My idol hath done them, and my graven image, and my molten image hath commanded them.'

13 "Thou hast seen and heard all this; and will ye not declare them? And that I have showed thee new things from this time, even hidden things, and thou didst not know them.

14 "They are created now, and not from the beginning; even before the day when thou heardest them not, they were declared to thee, lest thou shouldst say, 'Behold, I knew them.'

15 "And thou heardest not; thou knewest not; from that time thine ear was not opened; for I knew that thou wouldst deal very treacherously, and wast called a transgressor from the womb.

16 "Nevertheless, for my name's sake will I defer my anger, and for my praise will I refrain from thee, that I cut thee not off.

17 "For, behold, I have refined thee; I have chosen thee in the furnace of affliction.

18 "For my own sake, for my own sake, will I do this; for I will not suffer my name to be polluted, and I will not give my glory to another.

19 "Hearken to me, O Jacob, and Israel, my called; for I am he; I am the first, and I am also the last.

20 "My hand hath also laid the foundation of the earth, and my right hand hath spanned the heavens; I call to them, and they stand up together.

21 "All ye, assemble yourselves, and hear; who among them hath declared these things to them? The Lord hath loved him; and he will fulfill his word which he hath declared by them; and he will do his pleasure on Babylon, and his arm shall come upon the Chaldeans."

22 Also, says the Lord: "I, the Lord, I have spoken; I have called him, to declare, I have brought him, and he shall make his way prosperous.

23 "Come ye near to me: I have not spoken in secret from the beginning; from the time that it was declared have I spoken"; and the

Lord God, and his Spirit, hath sent me.

24 And thus says the Lord, your Redeemer, the Holy One of Israel: "I have sent him, the Lord thy God who teacheth thee to profit, who leadeth thee by the way thou shouldst go, has done it.

25 "O that thou hadst hearkened to my commandment, then had thy peace been as a river, and thy righteousness as the waves of the sea.

26 "Thy seed also had been as the sand; the offspring of thy bowels like the gravel thereof; his name should not have been cut off nor destroyed from before me."

27 Go ye forth of Babylon, flee ye from the Chaldeans, with a voice of singing declare ye, tell this, utter to the end of the earth; say ye, "The Lord hath redeemed his servant Jacob."

28 And they thirsted not when he led them through the deserts; he caused the waters to flow out of the rock for them; he cleft the rock also, and the waters gushed out.

29 And notwithstanding he hath done all this, and greater also, "There is no peace," says the Lord, "to the wicked."

30 Again: Hearken, O ye house of Israel, all ye that are broken off and are driven out, because of the wickedness of the pastors of my people; all ye that are broken off, that are scattered abroad, who are of my people, O house of Israel.

31 *Listen, O isles, to me; and hearken, ye people, from far; the Lord hath called me from the womb; from the bowels of my mother hath he made mention of my name.

32 And he hath made my mouth like a sharp sword; in the shadow of his hand hath he hid me, and made me a polished shaft; in his quiver hath he hid me,

33 And said to me, "Thou art my servant, O Israel, in whom I will be glorified."

34 Then I said, "I have labored

*Isaiah 49

31   588–570 B. C.

in vain, I have spent my strength for nought, and in vain; surely my judgment is with the Lord, and my work with my God."

35 And now, says the Lord that formed me from the womb that I should be his servant, to bring Jacob again to him, though Israel be not gathered, yet shall I be glorious in the eyes of the Lord, and my God shall be my strength.

36 And he said, "It is a light thing that thou shouldst be my servant to raise up the tribes of Jacob, and to restore the preserved of Israel. I will also give thee for a light to the Gentiles, that thou mayest be my salvation to the ends of the earth."

37 Thus says the Lord, the Redeemer of Israel, his Holy One, to him whom man despiseth, to him whom the nations abhorreth, to a servant of rulers, "Kings shall see and arise, princes also shall worship, because of the Lord that is faithful."

38 Thus says the Lord, "In an acceptable time have I heard thee, O isles of the sea, and in a day of salvation have I helped thee; and I will preserve thee, and give thee my servant for a covenant of the people, to establish the earth, to cause to inherit the desolate heritages; 39that thou mayest say to the prisoners, 'Go forth'; to them that sit in darkness, 'Show yourselves.' They shall feed in the ways, and their pastures shall be in all high places.

40 "They shall not hunger nor thirst, neither shall the heat nor the sun smite them; for he that hath mercy on them shall lead them, even by the springs of water shall he guide them.

41 "And I will make all my mountains a way, and my highways shall be exalted.

42 "And then, O house of Israel, behold, these shall come from far; and, lo, these from the north and from the west; and these from the land of Sinim."

43 Sing, O heavens; and be joyful, O earth; for the feet of those who are in the east shall be established; and break forth into sing-

ing, O mountains; for they shall be smitten no more; for the Lord hath comforted his people, and will have mercy upon his afflicted.

44 But, behold, Zion hath said, "The Lord hath forsaken me, and my Lord hath forgotten me"; but he will show that he hath not.

45 "For can a woman forget her sucking child, that she should not have compassion on the son of her womb?" Yea, they may forget, yet will I not forget thee, O house of Israel.

46 Behold, I have graven thee upon the palms of my hands; thy walls are continually before me.

47 Thy children shall make haste against thy destroyers; and they that made thee waste shall go forth of thee.

48 Lift up thine eyes round about, and behold; all these gather themselves together, and they shall come to thee. And as I live, says the Lord, thou shalt surely clothe thee with them all, as with an ornament, and bind them on even as a bride.

49 "For thy waste and thy desolate places, and the land of thy destruction, shall even now be too narrow by reason of the inhabitants; and they that swallowed thee up shall be far away.

50 "The children whom thou shalt have, after thou hast lost the first, shall again in thine ears say, 'The place is too strait for me; give place to me that I may dwell.'

51 "Then shalt thou say in thine heart, 'Who hath begotten me these, seeing I have lost my children, and am desolate, a captive, and removing to and fro, and who hath brought up these? Behold, I was left alone; these, where have they been?'"

52 Thus says the Lord God, "Behold, I will lift up my hand to the Gentiles, and set up my standard to the people; and they shall bring thy sons in their arms, and thy daughters shall be carried upon their shoulders.

53 "And kings shall be thy nursing fathers, and their queens thy nursing mothers; they shall bow down to thee with their face toward

the earth, and lick up the dust of thy feet; and thou shalt know that I am the Lord; for they shall not be ashamed that wait for me."

54 For shall the prey be taken from the mighty, or the lawful captives delivered?

55 But thus says the Lord, "Even the captives of the mighty shall be taken away, and the prey of the terrible shall be delivered; for I will contend with him that contendeth with thee, and I will save thy children.

56 "And I will feed them that oppress thee with their own flesh: they shall be drunken with their own blood, as with sweet wine; and all flesh shall know that I the Lord am thy Savior and thy Redeemer, the mighty one of Jacob."

CHAPTER 7

AFTER I, Nephi, had read these things which were engraved upon the plates of brass, my brethren came to me and said to me, "What do these things mean which you have read?

2 "Behold, are they to be understood according to the things which are spiritual, which shall come to pass according to the spirit and not the flesh?"

3 And I, Nephi, said to them, "Behold, they were made manifest to the prophet, by the voice of the Spirit; 4for by the Spirit are all things made known to the prophets, which shall come upon the children of men according to the flesh.

5 "Wherefore, the things of which I have read are things pertaining to things both temporal and spiritual.

6 "For it appears that the house of Israel, sooner or later, will be scattered upon all the face of the earth, and also among all nations, 7and, behold, there are many who are already lost from the knowledge of those who are at Jerusalem.

8 "The greater part of all the tribes have been led away; 9and they are scattered to and fro upon the isles of the sea; 10and where they are, none of us know, save that we know that they have been led away.

11 "Since they have been led away,

these things have been prophesied concerning them, and also concerning all those who shall hereafter be scattered and be confounded, because of the Holy One of Israel; for against him will they harden their hearts; 12wherefore, they shall be scattered among all nations, and shall be hated of all men.

13 "Nevertheless, after they have been nursed by the Gentiles, and the Lord has lifted up his hand upon the Gentiles and set them up for a standard, and their children have been carried in their arms, and their daughters have been carried upon their shoulders, behold, these things of which are spoken are temporal; for thus are the covenants of the Lord with our fathers; 14and it means us in the days to come, and also all our brethren who are of the house of Israel.

15 "And it means that the time will come that after all the house of Israel has been scattered and confounded, the Lord God will raise up a mighty nation among the Gentiles, even upon the face of this land; 16and by them shall our seed be scattered.

17 "And after our seed are scattered, the Lord God will proceed to do a marvelous work among the Gentiles, which shall be of great worth to our seed; 18wherefore, it is likened to their being nourished by the Gentiles, and being carried in their arms, and upon their shoulders.

19 "And it shall also be of worth to the Gentiles; 20and not only to the Gentiles, but also to all the house of Israel, to the making known of the covenants of the Father of heaven to Abraham, saying, 'In thy seed shall all the kindreds of the earth be blessed.'

21 "I would, my brethren, that you should know that all the kindreds of the earth cannot be blessed unless he shall make bare his arm in the eyes of the nations.

22 "Wherefore, the Lord God will proceed to make bare his arm in the eyes of all the nations, in bringing about his covenants and his gospel to those who are of the house of Israel.

23 "Wherefore, he will bring them again out of captivity, and they shall be gathered together to the lands of their inheritance.

24 "And they shall be brought out of obscurity, and out of darkness; 25and they shall know that the Lord is their Savior and their Redeemer, the mighty one of Israel.

26 "And the blood of that great and abominable church, which is the whore of all the earth, shall turn upon their own heads; 27for they shall war among themselves, and the sword of their own hands shall fall upon their own heads, and they shall be drunken with their own blood.

28 "And every nation which shall war against you, O house of Israel, shall be turned one against another, 29and they shall fall into the pit which they digged to ensnare the people of the Lord.

30 "All that fight against Zion shall be destroyed.

31 "And the great whore, who has perverted the right ways of the Lord even that great and abominable church, shall tumble to the dust, and great shall be the fall of it.

32 " 'For, behold,' said the prophet, 'the time will come speedily that Satan shall have no more power over the hearts of the children of men; 33for the day soon will come that all the proud and they who do wickedly shall be as stubble; and the day will come that they must be burned.

34 " 'For the time soon will come that the fullness of the wrath of God shall be poured out upon all the children of men; 35for he will not suffer that the wicked shall destroy the righteous.

36 " 'Wherefore, he will preserve the righteous by his power, even if it be so that the fullness of his wrath must come, and the righteous be preserved, even to the destruction of their enemies by fire.

37 " 'Wherefore, the righteous need not fear'; for thus says the prophet, 'They shall be saved, even if it so be as by fire.'

38 "Behold, my brethren, I say to you that these things must shortly come; even blood, and fire, and vapor of smoke must come; 39and it must be upon the face of this earth.

40 "And it will come to men according to the flesh, if it so be that they will harden their hearts against the Holy One of Israel.

41 "For, behold, the righteous shall not perish; 42for the time surely must come that all they who fight against Zion shall be cut off.

43 "The Lord will surely prepare a way for his people, to the fulfilling of the words of Moses, which he spoke, saying:

44 " 'A prophet shall the Lord your God raise up to you, like me; him shall ye hear in all things whatsoever he shall say to you.'

45 "And all those who will not hear that prophet shall be cut off from among the people.

46 "Now I, Nephi, declare to you that this prophet of whom Moses spoke was the Holy One of Israel.

47 "Wherefore, he shall execute judgment in righteousness; 48and the righteous need not fear, for they are those who shall not be confounded.

49 "But it is the kingdom of the devil which shall be built up among the children of men, which kingdom is established among them which are in the flesh.

50 "For the time speedily shall come that all churches which are built up to get gain, and all those which are built up to get power over the flesh, and those which are built up to become popular in the eyes of the world, and those which seek the lusts of the flesh and the things of the world, and to do all manner of iniquity—51all those which belong to the kingdom of the devil—are those which need to fear, and tremble, and quake.

52 "They are those which must be brought low in the dust; 53they are those which must be consumed as stubble; 54and this is according to the words of the prophet.

55 "The time comes speedily that the righteous must be led up as calves of the stall, and the Holy One of Israel must reign in dominion, and might, and power, and great glory.

56 "He will gather his children from the four quarters of the earth; 57and he will number his sheep, and they will know him; 58and there shall be one fold and one shepherd.

59 "He shall feed his sheep, and in him they shall find pasture.

60 "And because of the righteousness of his people, Satan will have no

power; [61]wherefore, he cannot be loosed for the space of many years; [62]for he will have no power over the hearts of the people, for they dwell in righteousness, and the Holy One of Israel will reign.

63 "Now, behold, I, Nephi, say to you that all these things must come according to the flesh.

64 "But, behold, all nations, kindreds, tongues, and people shall dwell safely in the Holy One of Israel, if it so be that they will repent.

65 "Now I, Nephi, make an end; for I dare not speak further as yet, concerning these things.

66 "Wherefore, my brethren, I would that you should consider that the things which have been written upon the plates of brass are true; [67]and they testify that a man must be obedient to the commandments of God.

68 "Wherefore, you need not suppose that I and my father are the only ones that have testified, and also taught them.

69 "Wherefore, if you will be obedient to the commandments, and endure to the end, you shall be saved at the last day.

70 "Thus it is. Amen."

THE SECOND BOOK OF NEPHI

CHAPTER 1

An account of the death of Lehi. Nephi's brothers rebel against him. The Lord warns Nephi to depart into the wilderness. His journeyings in the wilderness.

NOW it came to pass after I, Nephi, had made an end of teaching my brethren, our father, Lehi, also spoke many things to them, of what great things the Lord had done for them in bringing them out of the land of Jerusalem.

2 He spoke to them concerning their rebellions upon the waters, and the mercies of God in sparing their lives that they were not swallowed up in the sea.

3 And he also spoke to them concerning the land of promise which they had obtained, how merciful the Lord had been in warning us that we should flee out of the land of Jerusalem.

4 "For, behold," he said, "I have seen a vision, in which I know that Jerusalem is destroyed; [5]and had we remained in Jerusalem, we should also have perished.

6 "But," he said, "notwithstanding our afflictions, we have obtained a land of promise, a land which is choice above all other lands, [7]a land which the Lord God has covenanted with me should be a land for the inheritance of my seed.

8 "The Lord has covenanted this land to me and to my children forever; [9]and also to all those who should be led out of other countries by the hand of the Lord.

10 "Wherefore, I, Lehi, prophesy, according to the workings of the Spirit which is in me, that there shall none come into this land save they shall be brought by the hand of the Lord.

11 "Wherefore, this land is consecrated to him whom he shall bring.

12 "And if they shall serve him according to the commandments which he has given, it shall be a land of liberty to them.

13 "Wherefore, they shall never be brought down into captivity; if so, it shall be because of iniquity.

14 "For if iniquity shall abound, cursed shall be the land for their sakes; [15]but to the righteous, it shall be blessed forever.

16 "Behold, it is wisdom that this land should be kept as yet from the knowledge of other nations; [17]for, behold, many nations would overrun the land, that there would be no place for an inheritance.

18 "Wherefore, I, Lehi, have obtained a promise that inasmuch as those whom the Lord God shall bring out of the land of Jerusalem shall keep his commandments, they shall prosper upon the face of this land; ¹⁹and they shall be kept from all other nations, that they may possess this land to themselves.

20 "And if it so be that they shall keep his commandments, they shall be blessed upon the face of this land; ²¹and there shall be none to molest them, nor to take away the land of their inheritance; and they shall dwell safely forever.

22 "But, behold, when the time comes that they shall dwindle in unbelief, after they have received so great blessings from the hand of the Lord, having a knowledge of the creation of the earth and all men, knowing the great and marvelous works of the Lord from the creation of the world, having power given them to do all things by faith, having all the commandments from the beginning, and having been brought by his infinite goodness into this precious land of promise; ²³behold, I say, if the day shall come that they will reject the Holy One of Israel, the true Messiah, their Redeemer and their God, behold, the judgments of him that is just shall rest upon them.

24 "He will bring other nations to them, and he will give to them power, and he will take away from them the lands of their possessions, and he will cause them to be scattered and smitten.

25 "As one generation passes to another, there shall be bloodsheds and great visitations among them; ²⁶therefore, my sons, I would that you would remember; I would that you would hearken to my words.

27 "O that you would awake; awake from a deep sleep, even from the sleep of hell, and shake off the awful chains by which you are bound, which are the chains which bind the children of men, that they are carried away captive down to the eternal gulf of misery and woe!

28 "Awake, and rise from the dust, and hear the words of a trembling parent, whose limbs you must soon lay down in the cold and silent grave,

whence no traveler can return; a few more days, and I go the way of all the earth.

29 "But, behold, the Lord has redeemed my soul from hell; I have beheld his glory, and I am encircled eternally in the arms of his love.

30 "And I desire that you should remember to observe the statutes and the judgments of the Lord; behold, this has been the anxiety of my soul, from the beginning.

31 "My heart has been weighed down with sorrow from time to time; for I have feared lest for the hardness of your hearts the Lord your God should come out in the fullness of his wrath upon you, that you be cut off and destroyed forever; ³²or that a cursing should come upon you for the space of many generations; and you are visited by sword, and by famine, and are hated, and are led according to the will and captivity of the devil.

33 "O my sons, that these things might not come upon you, but that you might be a choice and a favored people of the Lord!

34 "But, behold, his will be done, for his ways are righteousness forever; and he has said that, 'Inasmuch as ye shall keep my commandments ye shall prosper in the land; but inasmuch as ye will not keep my commandments ye shall be cut off from my presence.'

35 "Now that my soul might have joy in you, and that my heart might leave this world with gladness because of you, that I might not be brought down with grief and sorrow to the grave, ³⁶arise from the dust, my sons, and be men, and be determined in one mind, and in one heart united in all things, that you may not come down into captivity; that you may not be cursed with a sore cursing; ³⁷and also, that you may not incur the displeasure of a just God upon you, to the eternal destruction of both soul and body.

38 "Awake, my sons; put on the armor of righteousness.

39 "Shake off the chains with which you are bound, and come forth out of obscurity, and arise from the dust.

40 "Rebel no more against your brother, whose views have been

glorious, and who has kept the commandments from the time that we left Jerusalem, and who has been an instrument in the hands of God in bringing us forth into the land of promise.

41 "For were it not for him we must have perished with hunger in the wilderness.

42 "Nevertheless, you sought to take away his life; and he has suffered much sorrow because of you.

43 "I exceedingly fear and tremble because of you lest he shall suffer again; 44for, behold, you have accused him that he sought power and authority over you.

45 "But I know that he has not sought for power nor authority over you; but he has sought the glory of God and your own eternal welfare.

46 "You have murmured because he has been plain to you.

47 "You say that he has used sharpness; you say that he has been angry with you.

48 "But, behold, his sharpness was the sharpness of the power of the word of God, which was in him; 49and that which you call anger was the truth, according to that which is in God, which he could not restrain, manifesting boldly concerning your iniquities.

50 "And it must be that the power of God must be with him, even to his commanding you that you must obey.

51 "But, behold, it was not he, but it was the Spirit of the Lord which was in him which opened his mouth to utterance that he could not shut it.

52 "Now my son, Laman, and also Lemuel and Sam, and also my sons who are the sons of Ishmael, behold, if you will hearken to the voice of Nephi, you shall not perish.

53 "And if you will hearken to him, I leave you a blessing, even my first blessing.

54 "But if you will not hearken to him, I will take away my first blessing, even my blessing, and it shall rest upon him.

55 "Now, Zoram, I speak to you: Behold, you are the servant of Laban; nevertheless, you have been brought out of the land of Jerusalem, and I

know that you are a true friend to my son Nephi, forever.

56 "Wherefore, because you have been faithful, your seed shall be blessed with his seed, that they dwell in prosperity long upon the face of this land; 57and nothing, save it shall be iniquity among them, shall harm or disturb their prosperity upon the face of this land forever.

58 "Wherefore, if you shall keep the commandments of the Lord, the Lord has consecrated this land for the security of your seed with the seed of my son.

59 "Now, Jacob, I speak to you: You are my first born in the days of my tribulation in the wilderness.

60 "Behold, in your childhood you have suffered afflictions and much sorrow because of the rudeness of your brethren.

61 "Nevertheless, Jacob, my first born in the wilderness, you know the greatness of God; and he shall consecrate your afflictions for your gain.

62 "Wherefore your soul shall be blessed, and you shall dwell safely with your brother Nephi; and your days shall be spent in the service of your God.

63 "Wherefore, I know that you are redeemed, because of the righteousness of your Redeemer; for you have beheld that in the fullness of time he will come to bring salvation to men.

64 "And you have beheld in your youth his glory; wherefore you are blessed even as they to whom he shall minister in the flesh.

65 "For the Spirit is the same, yesterday, today, and forever.

66 "The way is prepared from the fall of man, and salvation is free.

67 "And men are instructed sufficiently that they know good from evil.

68 "And the law is given to men.

69 "By the law, no flesh is justified, or, by the law, men are cut off.

70 "By the temporal law, they were cut off; and also by the spiritual law they perish from that which is good, and become miserable forever.

71 "Wherefore, redemption comes in and through the holy Messiah, for he is full of grace and truth.

72 "Behold, he offers himself a

sacrifice for sin, to answer the ends of the law to all those who have a broken heart and a contrite spirit; and to none else can the ends of the law be answered.

73 "Wherefore, how great the importance to make these things known to the inhabitants of the earth, that they may know that there is no flesh that can dwell in the presence of God, save it be through the merits, and mercy, and grace of the holy Messiah, [74]who will lay down his life according to the flesh, and take it again by the power of the Spirit, [75]that he may bring to pass the resurrection of the dead, being the first that should rise.

76 "Wherefore, he is the first fruits unto God, inasmuch as he shall make intercession for all the children of men.

77 "And they that believe in him shall be saved.

78 "Because of the intercession for all, all men come to God; [79]wherefore, they stand in the presence of him, to be judged of him according to the truth and holiness which is in him.

80 "Wherefore, the ends of the law which the Holy One has given, to the inflicting of the punishment which is affixed, which punishment that is affixed is in opposition to that of the happiness which is affixed, to answer the ends of the atonement; [81]for there must be an opposition in all things.

82 "If not so, my first born in the wilderness, righteousness could not be brought to pass; neither wickedness; neither holiness nor misery; neither good nor bad.

83 "Wherefore, all things must be a compound in one.

84 "Wherefore, if it should be one body, it must remain as dead, having no life, neither death nor corruption, nor incorruption, happiness nor misery, neither sense nor insensibility.

85 "Wherefore, it must have been created for a thing of nought; [86]wherefore, there would have been no purpose in the end of its creation.

87 "Wherefore, this thing must needs destroy the wisdom of God and his eternal purposes, and also the power, and the mercy, and the justice of God.

88 "And if you shall say there is no law, you shall also say there is no sin.

89 "And if you shall say there is no sin, you shall also say there is no righteousness.

90 "And if there be no righteousness, there be no happiness.

91 "And if there be no righteousness nor happiness, there be no punishment nor misery.

92 "And if these things are not, there is no God.

93 "And if there is no God, we are not, neither the earth, for there could have been no creation of things, neither to act nor to be acted upon; wherefore, all things must have vanished away.

94 "Now, my son, I speak to you these things, for your profit and learning.

95 "For there is a God, and he has created all things, both the heavens and the earth, and all things that are in them; [96]both things to act, and things to be acted upon.

97 "And to bring about his eternal purposes in the end of man, after he had created our first parents, and the beasts of the field and the fowls of the air, and in fine, all things which are created, there must be an opposition; [98]even the forbidden fruit in opposition to the tree of life; the one being sweet and the other bitter.

99 "Wherefore, the Lord God gave to man that he should act for himself.

100 "Wherefore, man could not act for himself save it should be that he was enticed by the one or the other.

101 "And I, Lehi, according to the things which I have read, must suppose that an angel of God, according to that which is written, had fallen from heaven; [102]wherefore he became a devil, having sought that which was evil before God.

103 "Because he had fallen from heaven and had become miserable forever, he sought also the misery of all mankind.

104 "Wherefore, that old serpent, who is the devil, who is the father of all lies, said to Eve, 'Partake of the forbidden fruit, and ye shall not die, but ye shall be as God, knowing good and evil.'

105 "And after Adam and Eve had partaken of the forbidden fruit,

they were driven out of the garden of Eden, to till the earth.

106 "And they have brought forth children, even the family of all the earth.

107 "And the days of the children of men were prolonged, according to the will of God, that they might repent while in the flesh.

108 "Wherefore, their state became a state of probation, and their time was lengthened, according to the commandments which the Lord God gave to the children of men.

109 "For he gave commandment that all men must repent; [110]for he showed to all men that they were lost, because of the transgression of their parents.

111 "Now, behold, if Adam had not transgressed, he would not have fallen; but he would have remained in the garden of Eden.

112 "And all things which were created must have remained in the same state which they were, after they were created; and they must have remained forever, and had no end.

113 "They would have had no children; wherefore, they would have remained in a state of innocence, having no joy, for they knew no misery; doing no good, for they knew no sin.

114 "But, behold, all things have been done in the wisdom of him who knows all things.

115 "Adam fell, that men might be; and men are, that they might have joy.

116 "And the Messiah will come in the fullness of time, that he may redeem the children of men from the fall.

117 "And because they are redeemed from the fall, they have become free forever, knowing good from evil—[118]to act for themselves, and not to be acted upon, save it be by the punishment of the Lord, at the great and last day, according to the commandments which God has given.

119 "Wherefore, men are free according to the flesh; and all things are given them which are expedient to man.

120 "And they are free to choose liberty and eternal life, through the great mediation of all men, or to choose captivity and death, according to the captivity and power of the devil; [121]for he seeks that all men might be miserable like himself.

122 "Now, my sons, I would that you should look to the great Mediator, and hearken to his great commandments, [123]and be faithful to his words, and choose eternal life, according to the will of his Holy Spirit, [124]and not choose eternal death, according to the will of the flesh and the evil which is therein, [125]which gives the spirit of the devil power to captivate, to bring you down to hell, that he may reign over you in his own kingdom.

126 "I have spoken these few words to you all, my sons, in the last days of my probation; [127]and I have chosen the good part, according to the words of the prophet.

128 "I have no other object, save it be the everlasting welfare of your souls. Amen."

CHAPTER 2

NOW I speak to you, Joseph, my last born.

2 "You were born in the wilderness of my afflictions; in the days of my greatest sorrow your mother bore you.

3 "May the Lord consecrate also to you this land, which is a most precious land, for your inheritance and the inheritance of your seed with your brethren, for your security forever, if it so be that you shall keep the commandments of the Holy One of Israel.

4 "Now, Joseph, my last born, whom I have brought out of the wilderness of my afflictions, may the Lord bless you forever, for your seed shall not utterly be destroyed.

5 "For, behold, you are the fruit of my loins; and I am a descendant of Joseph, who was carried captive into Egypt.

6 "And great were the covenants of the Lord which he made to Joseph; wherefore, Joseph truly saw our day.

7 "And he obtained a promise of the Lord, that out of the fruit of his loins the Lord God would raise up a righteous branch to the house of Israel; [8]not the Messiah, but a branch

which was to be broken off, nevertheless to be remembered in the covenants of the Lord, [9]that the Messiah should be made manifest to them in the latter days, in the spirit of power, to the bringing of them out of darkness into light, out of hidden darkness and out of captivity into freedom.

10 "For Joseph truly testified, saying: 'A seer shall the Lord my God raise up, who shall be a choice seer to the fruit of my loins.'

11 "Joseph truly said, 'Thus said the Lord to me: "A choice seer will I raise up out of the fruit of thy loins; and he shall be esteemed highly among the fruit of thy loins.

12 """"To him will I give commandment that he shall do a work for the fruit of thy loins, his brethren, which shall be of great worth to them, even to the bringing of them to the knowledge of the covenants which I have made with thy fathers.

13 """"And I will give to him a commandment that he shall do no other work, save the work which I shall command him.

14 """"I will make him great in my eyes; for he shall do my work.

15 """"And he shall be great like Moses, whom I have said I would raise up to you, to deliver my people, O house of Israel.

16 """"And Moses will I raise up, to deliver thy people out of the land of Egypt.

17 """"But a seer will I raise up out of the fruit of thy loins; and to him will I give power to bring forth my word to the seed of thy loins; [18]and not to the bringing forth of my word only," saith the Lord, "but to the convincing them of my word, which shall have already gone forth among them.

19 """"Wherefore, the fruit of thy loins shall write; and the fruit of the loins of Judah shall write.

20 """"And that which shall be written by the fruit of thy loins, and also that which shall be written by the fruit of the loins of Judah shall grow together, [21]to the confounding of false doctrines, and laying down of contentions, and establishing peace among the fruit of thy loins, [22]and bringing them to the knowledge of their fathers in the latter days; [23]and

also to the knowledge of my covenants," saith the Lord.

24 """"Out of weakness he shall be made strong, in that day when my work shall commence among all my people, to the restoring thee, O house of Israel," saith the Lord.'

25 "Thus prophesied Joseph, saying: 'Behold, that seer will the Lord bless; [26]and they that seek to destroy him shall be confounded; [27]for this promise, which I have obtained of the Lord, of the fruit of thy loins, shall be fulfilled.

28 "'Behold, I am sure of the fulfilling of this promise.

29 "'His name shall be called after me; and it shall be after the name of his father.

30 "'He shall be like me; for the thing which the Lord shall bring forth by his hand, by the power of the Lord shall bring my people to salvation.'

31 "Thus prophesied Joseph, 'I am sure of this thing, even as I am sure of the promise of Moses; for the Lord has said to me, "I will preserve thy seed forever."

32 "'And the Lord has said, "I will raise up a Moses; and I will give power to him in a rod; [33]and I will give judgment to him in writing.

34 """"Yet I will not loose his tongue that he shall speak much; for I will not make him mighty in speaking.

35 """"But I will write to him my law, by the finger of my own hand; and I will make a spokesman for him."

36 "'Also the Lord, said to me, "I will raise up to the fruit of thy loins; and I will make for him a spokesman.

37 """"Behold, I will give to him, that he shall write the writing of the fruit of thy loins, to the fruit of thy loins; and the spokesman of thy loins shall declare it.

38 """"And the words which he shall write shall be the words which are expedient in my wisdom should go forth to the fruit of thy loins.

39 """"It shall be as if the fruit of thy loins had cried to them from the dust; for I know their faith.

40 """"They shall cry from the dust, even repentance to their brethren, even after many generations have gone by them.

41 """"And their cry shall go even according to the simpleness of their words.

42 """"Because of their faith, their words shall proceed forth out of my mouth to their brethren, who are the fruit of thy loins; 43and the weakness of their words will I make strong in their faith, to the remembering of my covenant which I made to thy fathers.""'

44 "Now, behold, my son, Joseph, after this manner did my father of old prophesy.

45 "Wherefore, because of this covenant you are blessed; for your seed shall not be destroyed, for they shall hearken to the words of the book.

46 "And there shall arise one mighty among them, who shall do much good, both in word and in deed, being an instrument in the hands of God, with exceeding faith, 47to work mighty wonders, and do that thing which is great in the sight of God to the bringing to pass much restoration to the house of Israel, and to the seed of your brethren.

48 "Now, blessed are you, Joseph.

49 "Behold, you are little; wherefore, hearken to the words of your brother Nephi, and it shall be done to you even according to the words which I have spoken.

50 "Remember the words of your dying father. Amen."

CHAPTER 3

NOW I, Nephi, speak concerning the prophecies of which my father has spoken concerning Joseph, who was carried into Egypt.

2 For, behold, he truly prophesied concerning all his seed.

3 And of the prophecies which he wrote, there are not many greater.

4 He prophesied concerning us, and our future generations; 5and they are written upon the plates of brass.

6 Wherefore, after my father had made an end of speaking concerning the prophecies of Joseph, he called the children of Laman, his sons, and his daughters, and said to them:

7 "Behold, my sons and my daughters, who are the sons and the daughters of my first born, I would that you should give ear to my words.

8 "For the Lord God has said, 'Inasmuch as ye shall keep my commandments, ye shall prosper in the land; 9and inasmuch as ye will not keep my commandments, ye shall be cut off from my presence.'

10 "But, behold, my sons and my daughters, I cannot go down to my grave save I should leave a blessing upon you; 11for, behold, I know that if you are brought up in the way you should go, you will not depart from it.

12 "Wherefore, if you are cursed, behold, I leave my blessing upon you that the cursing may be taken from you and be answered upon the heads of your parents.

13 "Wherefore, because of my blessing, the Lord God will not suffer that you shall perish; wherefore, he will be merciful to you, and to your seed forever."

14 And it came to pass that after my father had made an end of speaking to the sons and daughters of Laman, he caused the sons and daughters of Lemuel to be brought before him.

15 And he spoke to them, saying: "Behold, my sons and my daughters, who are the sons and the daughters of my second son; 16I leave to you the same blessing which I left to the sons and daughters of Laman; wherefore, you shall not utterly be destroyed; but in the end your seed shall be blessed."

17 When my father had made an end of speaking to them, behold, he spoke to the sons of Ishmael, and even all his household.

18 And after he had made an end of speaking to them, he spoke to Sam, saying:

19 "Blessed are you and your seed; for you shall inherit the land, like your brother Nephi.

20 "Your seed shall be numbered with his seed; 21and you shall be even like your brother, and your seed like his seed; and you shall be blessed in all your days."

22 After my father Lehi had spoken to all his household, according to the feelings of his heart and the Spirit of the Lord which was in him, he waxed old.

23 And it came to pass that he died, and was buried.

24 Not many days after his death, Laman and Lemuel, and the sons of Ishmael were angry with me because of the admonitions of the Lord; 25for I, Nephi, was constrained to speak to them, according to his word.

26 For I had spoken many things to them, as also had my father before his death, 27many of which sayings are written upon my other plates; for the more historical part is written upon my other plates.

28 And upon these, I write the things of my soul, and many of the scriptures which are engraved upon the plates of brass.

29 For my soul delights in the scriptures, and my heart ponders them, and writes them for the learning and the profit of my children.

30 Behold, my soul delights in the things of the Lord; and my heart ponders continually upon the things which I have seen and heard.

31 Nevertheless for the great goodness of the Lord in showing me his great and marvelous works, my heart exclaims, O wretched man that I am; my heart sorrows because of my flesh.

32 My soul grieves because of my iniquities.

33 I am encompassed about because of the temptations and the sins which so easily beset me.

34 When I desire to rejoice my heart groans because of my sins; nevertheless, I know in whom I have trusted.

35 My God has been my support; he has led me through my afflictions in the wilderness; and he has preserved me upon the waters of the great deep.

36 He has filled me with his love, even to the consuming of my flesh.

37 He has confounded my enemies, to the causing of them to quake before me.

38 Behold, he has heard my cry by day, and he has given me knowledge by visions in the nighttime.

39 By day have I waxed bold in mighty prayer before him; my voice have I sent up on high; and angels came down and ministered to me.

40 Upon the wings of his Spirit has my body been carried away upon exceedingly high mountains.

41 And my eyes have beheld great things, even too great for man; therefore I was bidden that I should not write them.

42 Oh, then, if I have seen so great things—if the Lord in his condescension to the children of men, has visited me in so much mercy—why should my heart weep, and my soul linger in the valley of sorrow, and my flesh waste away, and my strength slacken because of my afflictions?

43 Why should I yield to sin because of my flesh?

44 Why should I give way to temptations, that the evil one has place in my heart to destroy my peace and afflict my soul?

45 Why am I angry because of my enemy?

46 Awake, my soul! No longer droop in sin.

47 Rejoice, O my heart, and give place no more for the enemy of my soul.

48 Do not anger again because of my enemies.

49 Do not slacken my strength because of my afflictions.

50 Rejoice, O my heart, and cry to the Lord, and say, "O Lord, I will praise thee forever; my soul will rejoice in thee, my God, and the rock of my salvation.

51 "O Lord, wilt thou redeem my soul.

52 "Wilt thou deliver me out of the hands of mine enemies.

53 "Wilt thou make me that I may shake at the appearance of sin.

54 "May the gates of hell be shut continually before me, because my heart is broken and my spirit is contrite.

55 "O Lord, wilt thou not shut the gates of thy righteousness before me, that I may walk in the path of the low valley, that I may be strict in the plain road.

56 "O Lord, wilt thou encircle me around in the robe of thy righteousness.

57 "O Lord, wilt thou make a way for my escape before my enemies.

58 "Wilt thou make my path straight before me.

59 "Wilt thou not place a stum-

bling block in my way, 60but clear my way before me, and hedge not up my way, but the ways of my enemy.

61 "O Lord, I have trusted in thee, and I will trust in thee forever.

62 "I will not put my trust in the arm of flesh; for I know that cursed is he that puts his trust in the arm of flesh.

63 "Cursed is he that puts his trust in man, or makes flesh his arm.

64 "I know that God will give liberally to him that asks.

65 "And my God will give me, if I ask not amiss; therefore I will lift up my voice to thee; I will cry to thee, my God, the rock of my righteousness.

66 "Behold, my voice shall forever ascend to thee, my rock and my everlasting God. Amen."

CHAPTER 4

BEHOLD, I, Nephi, cried much to the Lord my God, because of the anger of my brethren.

2 But, behold, their anger increased against me, insomuch that they sought to take away my life.

3 They murmured against me, saying: "Our younger brother thinks to rule over us; and we have had much trial because of him; wherefore, now let us slay him that we may not be afflicted more because of his words.

4 "For, behold, we will not have him to be our ruler; for it belongs to us, who are the elder brethren, to rule over this people."

5 Now I do not write upon these plates all the words which they murmured against me.

6 But it suffices me to say that they sought to take away my life.

7 And it came to pass that the Lord warned me that I, Nephi, should depart from them and flee into the wilderness with all those who would go with me.

8 Wherefore, I, Nephi, took my family; and also Zoram and his family; and Sam, my elder brother, and his family; and Jacob and Joseph, my younger brethren; and also my sisters, and all those who would go with me.

9 And all those who would go with me were those who believed in the warnings and the revelations of God; wherefore, they hearkened to my words.

10 And we took our tents and whatever things were possible for us, and journeyed in the wilderness for the space of many days.

11 After we had journeyed for the space of many days, we pitched our tents.

12 My people would that we should call the name of the place Nephi; wherefore, we called it Nephi.

13 And all those who were with me took upon them to call themselves the people of Nephi.

14 We observed to keep the judgments, and the statutes, and the commandments of the Lord in all things, according to the law of Moses.

15 And the Lord was with us; and we prospered exceedingly; for we sowed seed, and we reaped again in abundance.

16 We began to raise flocks, and herds, and animals of every kind.

17 And I, Nephi, had also brought the records which were engraved upon the plates of brass; and also the ball, or compass, which was prepared for my father by the hand of the Lord, according to that which is written.

18 And we began to prosper exceedingly, and to multiply in the land.

19 I, Nephi, took the sword of Laban, and after the manner of it made many swords, lest by any means the people who were now called Lamanites should come upon us and destroy us; 20for I knew their hatred toward me and my children, and those who were called my people.

21 And I taught my people to build buildings, and to work in all manner of wood, and of iron, and of copper, and of brass, and of steel, and of gold, and of silver, and of precious ores, which were in great abundance.

22 And I, Nephi, built a temple; and I constructed it after the manner of the temple of Solomon, save it was not built of so many precious things; 23for they were not to be found upon the land; 24wherefore, it could not be built like Solomon's temple.

25 But the manner of the construction was like the temple of Solomon; and the workmanship thereof was exceedingly fine.

43   588–570 B. C.

26 And it came to pass that I, Nephi, caused my people to be industrious, and to labor with their hands.

27 And it came to pass that they would that I should be their king.

28 But I, Nephi, was desirous that they should have no king; nevertheless, I did for them according to that which was in my power.

29 And, behold, the words of the Lord had been fulfilled to my brethren, which he spoke concerning them, that I should be their ruler and their teacher; ³⁰wherefore, I had been their ruler and their teacher, according to the commandment of the Lord, until the time they sought to take away my life.

31 Wherefore, the word of the Lord was fulfilled which he spoke to me, saying: "Inasmuch as they will not hearken to thy words, they shall be cut off from the presence of the Lord."

32 And, behold, they were cut off from his presence.

33 And he had caused the cursing to come upon them, even a sore cursing, because of their iniquity.

34 For, behold, they had hardened their hearts against him, that they had become like flint.

35 Wherefore, as they were white, and exceedingly fair and delightsome, the Lord God caused a skin of blackness to come upon them that they might not be enticing to my people.

36 Thus said the Lord God, "I will cause that they shall be loathsome to thy people, save they shall repent of their iniquities.

37 "And cursed shall be the seed of him that mixes with their seed; for they shall be cursed even with the same cursing."

38 And the Lord spoke it, and it was done.

39 Because of their cursing which was upon them, they became an idle people, full of mischief and subtlety, and sought in the wilderness for beasts of prey.

40 And the Lord God said to me, "They shall be a scourge to thy seed, to stir them up in remembrance of me; ⁴¹and inasmuch as they will not remember me, and hearken to my words, they shall scourge them even to destruction."

42 And it came to pass that I, Nephi, consecrated Jacob and Joseph that they should be priests and teachers over the land of my people.

43 And we lived after the manner of happiness.

44 And thirty years had passed away from the time we left Jerusalem.

45 And I, Nephi, had kept the records upon my plates, which I had made of my people, thus far.

46 And it came to pass that the Lord God said to me, "Make other plates; and thou shalt engrave many things upon them which are good in my sight, for the profit of thy people."

47 Wherefore, I, Nephi, to be obedient to the commandments of the Lord, went and made these plates upon which I have engraved these things.

48 And I engraved that which is pleasing to God.

49 If my people are pleased with the things of God, they will be pleased with my engravings which are upon these plates.

50 And if my people desire to know the more particular part of the history of my people, they must search my other plates.

51 It suffices me to say that forty years had passed away, and we had already had wars and contentions with our brethren.

CHAPTER 5

THE word of Jacob, the brother of Nephi, which he spoke to the people of Nephi:

2 "Behold, my beloved brethren, I, Jacob, have been called of God, and ordained after the manner of his holy order, ³and have been consecrated by my brother, Nephi, to whom you look as a king or a protector, and on whom you depend for safety.

4 "Behold, you know that I have spoken to you exceedingly many things; ⁵nevertheless, I speak to you again; for I am desirous for the welfare of your souls.

6 "My anxiety is great for you; and you yourselves know that it ever has been.

7 "For I have exhorted you with all diligence; and I have taught you the words of my father; 8and I have spoken to you concerning all things which are written from the creation of the world.

9 "Now, behold, I would speak to you concerning things which are, and which are to come; 10wherefore, I will read you the words of Isaiah.

11 "And they are the words which my brother has desired that I should speak to you.

12 "I speak them to you for your sakes, that you may learn and glorify the name of your God.

13 "Now the words which I shall read are those which Isaiah spoke concerning all the house of Israel.

14 "Wherefore, they may be likened to you; for you are of the house of Israel.

15 "And there are many things which have been spoken by Isaiah, which may be likened to you, because you are of the house of Israel.

16 "Now, these are the words:

17* Thus says the Lord God, "Behold, I will lift up my hand to the Gentiles, and set up my standard to the people; 18and they shall bring thy sons in their arms, and thy daughters shall be carried upon their shoulders.

19 "And kings shall be thy nursing fathers, and their queens thy nursing mothers.

20 "They shall bow down to thee with their faces toward the earth, and lick up the dust of thy feet; 21and thou shalt know that I am the Lord; for they shall not be ashamed that wait for me."

22 "Now I, Jacob, would speak somewhat concerning these words; for, behold, the Lord has shown me that those who were at Jerusalem, from which we came, have been slain and carried away captive; 23nevertheless, the Lord has shown me that they should return again.

24 "He also has shown me that the Lord God, the Holy One of Israel, should manifest himself to them in the flesh.

25 "And after he should manifest
───────────
*Isaiah 49:22, 23

himself, they should scourge him and crucify him, according to the words of the angel who spoke it to me.

26 "And after they have hardened their hearts and stiffened their necks against the Holy One of Israel, behold, the judgments of the Holy One of Israel shall come upon them.

27 "The day will come that they shall be smitten and afflicted.

28 "Wherefore, after they are driven to and fro (for thus said the angel), many shall be afflicted in the flesh and shall not be suffered to perish because of the prayers of the faithful; they shall be scattered, and smitten, and hated.

29 "Nevertheless, the Lord will be merciful to them, that when they shall come to the knowledge of their Redeemer, they shall be gathered again to the lands of their inheritance.

30 "Blessed are the Gentiles, they of whom the prophet has written; 31for, behold, if it so be that they shall repent and fight not against Zion, and do not unite themselves to that great and abominable church, they shall be saved.

32 "For the Lord God will fulfill his covenants which he has made to his children; and for this cause the prophet has written these things.

33 "Wherefore, they that fight against Zion and the covenant people of the Lord shall lick up the dust of their feet; 34and the people of the Lord shall not be ashamed.

35 "For the people of the Lord are they who wait for him; for they still wait for the coming of the Messiah.

36 "And, behold, according to the words of the prophet, the Messiah will set himself again the second time to recover them.

37 "Wherefore, he will manifest himself to them in power and great glory, to the destruction of their enemies, when that day comes when they shall believe in him; 38and none will he destroy that believe in him.

39 "And they that believe not in him shall be destroyed, both by fire, and by tempest, and by earthquakes, and by bloodsheds, and by pestilence, and by famine.

40 "They shall know that the Lord is God, the Holy One of Israel.

41* For shall the prey be taken from the mighty, or the lawful captive delivered?

42 But thus says the Lord: "Even the captives of the mighty shall be taken away, and the prey of the terrible shall be delivered; for the mighty God shall deliver his covenant people."

43 For thus says the Lord: "I will contend with them that contend with thee, and I will feed them that oppress thee with their own flesh; 44and they shall be drunken with their own blood, as with sweet wine; 45and all flesh shall know that I the Lord am thy Savior and thy Redeemer, the mighty One of Jacob."

46** Yea, for thus says the Lord: "Have I put thee away, or have I cast thee off forever?"

47 For thus says the Lord: "Where is the bill of your mother's divorcement? 48To whom have I put thee away, or to which of my creditors have I sold you? 49Yea, to whom have I sold you?

50 "Behold, for your iniquities have ye sold yourselves, and for your transgressions is your mother put away.

51 "Wherefore, when I came, there was no man; when I called, there was none to answer.

52 "O house of Israel, is my hand shortened at all that it cannot redeem, or have I no power to deliver?

53 "Behold, at my rebuke, I dry up the sea, I make the rivers a wilderness and their fish to stink because the waters are dried up, and they die because of thirst.

54 "I clothe the heavens with blackness, and I make sackcloth their coverings."

55 The Lord God hath given me the tongue of the learned, that I should know how to speak a word in season to thee, O house of Israel.

56 When ye are weary, he waketh morning by morning.

57 He waketh my ear to hear as the learned.

58 The Lord God hath opened

my ear, and I was not rebellious, neither turned away back.

59 I gave my back to the smiter, and my cheeks to them that plucked off the hair.

60 I hid not my face from shame and spitting, for the Lord God will help me; therefore shall I not be confounded.

61 Therefore have I set my face like a flint, and I know that I shall not be ashamed; and the Lord is near, and he justifieth me.

62 Who will contend with me?

63 Let us stand together.

64 Who is my adversary?

65 Let him come near me, and I will smite him with the strength of my mouth; for the Lord God will help me.

66 And all they who shall condemn me, behold, all they shall wax old as a garment, and the moth shall eat them up.

67 Who is among you that feareth the Lord, that obeyeth the voice of his servant, that walketh in darkness, and hath no light?

68 Behold, all ye that kindle a fire, that compass yourselves about with sparks, walk in the light of your fire, and in the sparks which ye have kindled.

69 This shall ye have of my hand: Ye shall lie down in sorrow.

70* "Hearken to me, ye that follow after righteousness; look to the rock from whence ye are hewn, and to the hole of the pit from whence ye are digged.

71 "Look to Abraham your father, and to Sarah, she that bare you; for I called him alone, and blessed him.

72 "For the Lord shall comfort Zion; he will comfort all her waste places; 73and he will make her wilderness like Eden, and her desert like the garden of the Lord.

74 "Joy and gladness shall be found therein, thanksgiving and the voice of melody.

75 "Hearken to me, my people; and give ear to me, O my nation; 76for a law shall proceed from me, and I will make my judgment to rest for a light for the people.

77 "My righteousness is near;

*Isaiah 49:24–26
**Isaiah 50

*Isaiah 51

my salvation is gone forth, and my arm shall judge the people.

78 "The isles shall wait upon me, and on my arm shall they trust.

79 "Lift up your eyes to the heavens, and look upon the earth beneath; 80for the heavens shall vanish away like smoke, and the earth shall wax old like a garment; and they that dwell therein shall die in like manner.

81 "But my salvation shall be forever; and my righteousness shall not be abolished.

82 "Hearken to me, ye that know righteousness, the people in whose heart I have written my law.

83 "Fear ye not the reproach of men; neither be ye afraid of their revilings.

84 "For the moth shall eat them up like a garment, and the worm shall eat them like wool.

85 "But my righteousness shall be forever; and my salvation from generation to generation."

86 Awake, awake! Put on strength, O arm of the Lord; awake as in the ancient days.

87 Art thou not it that hath cut Rahab and wounded the dragon?

88 Art thou not it which hath dried the sea, the waters of the great deep; 89that hath made the depths of the sea a way for the ransomed to pass over?

90 Therefore, the redeemed of the Lord shall return, and come with singing to Zion; and everlasting joy and holiness shall be upon their heads; 91and they shall obtain gladness and joy; sorrow and mourning shall flee away.

92 "I am he, I am he that comforteth you.

93 "Behold, who art thou, that thou shouldst be afraid of man, who shall die, and of the son of man, who shall be made like unto grass; 94and forgettest the Lord thy maker, that hath stretched forth the heavens, and laid the foundations of the earth; 95and hast feared continually every day, because of the fury of the oppressor, as if he were ready to destroy?

96 "And where is the fury of the oppressor?

97 "The captive exile hasteneth,

that he may be loosed, and that he should not die in the pit, nor that his bread should fail.

98 "But I am the Lord thy God, that divided the sea, whose waves roared; the Lord of hosts is my name.

99 "And I have put my words in thy mouth, and have covered thee in the shadow of my hand, that I may plant the heavens and lay the foundations of the earth, and say unto Zion, 'Behold, thou art my people.'"

100 Awake, awake, stand up, O Jerusalem, which hast drunk at the hand of the Lord the cup of his fury.

101 Thou hast drunken the dregs of the cup of trembling wrung out; 102and none to guide her among all the sons she hath brought forth; 103neither that taketh her by the hand, of all the sons she hath brought up.

104 These two sons are come to thee—who shall be sorry for thee—thy desolation and destruction, and the famine and the sword.

105 And by whom shall I comfort thee?

106 Thy sons have fainted, save these two; they lie at the head of all the streets, as a wild bull in a net; they are full of the fury of the Lord, the rebuke of thy God.

107 Therefore, hear now this, thou afflicted, and drunken, and not with wine:

108 Thus says thy Lord, "The Lord and thy God pleadeth the cause of his people: 109Behold, I have taken out of thine hand the cup of trembling, the dregs of the cup of my fury; thou shalt no more drink it again.

110 "But I will put it into the hand of them that afflict thee; who have said to thy soul, 'Bow down, that we may go over'; 111and thou hast laid thy body as the ground, and as the street to them that went over."

112* Awake, awake, put on thy strength, O Zion; put on thy beautiful garments, O Jerusalem, the holy city; 113for henceforth there shall no more come into thee

_____
*Isaiah 52:1, 2

the uncircumcised and the unclean.

114 Shake thyself from the dust; arise, sit down, O Jerusalem; loose thyself from the bands of thy neck, O captive daughter of Zion.

CHAPTER 6

NOW, my beloved brethren, I have read these things that you might know concerning the covenants of the Lord, that he has covenanted with all the house of Israel, 2that he has spoken to the Jews, by the mouth of his holy prophets, even from the beginning down, from generation to generation, until the time comes that they shall be restored to the true church and fold of God, 3when they shall be gathered home to the lands of their inheritance, and shall be established in all their lands of promise.

4 "Behold, my beloved brethren, I speak to you these things that you may rejoice and lift up your heads forever because of the blessings which the Lord God shall bestow upon your children.

5 "For I know that you have searched much, many of you, to know of things to come.

6 "Wherefore I know that you know that our flesh must waste away and die; 7nevertheless, in our bodies we shall see God.

8 "I know that you know that in the body he shall show himself to those at Jerusalem, whence we came; 9for it is expedient that he should be among them.

10 "For it behooves the great Creator that he suffer himself to become subject to man in the flesh, and die for all men, that all men might become subject to him.

11 "For as death has passed upon all men, to fulfill the merciful plan of the great Creator there must be a power of resurrection.

12 "And the resurrection must come to man by reason of the fall; 13and the fall came by reason of transgression.

14 "And because man became fallen, he was cut off from the presence of the Lord; 15wherefore, there must be an infinite atonement.

16 "Save it should be an infinite atonement, this corruption could not put on incorruption.

17 "Wherefore, the first judgment which came upon man must have remained to an endless duration.

18 "If so, this flesh must have lain down to rot and to crumble to its mother earth, to rise no more.

19 "Oh, the wisdom of God, his mercy and grace!

20 "For, behold, if the flesh should rise no more, our spirits must become subject to that angel who fell from before the presence of the eternal God, and became the devil, to rise no more.

21 "And our spirits must have become like him, and we become devils, angels to a devil, to be shut out from the presence of our God, and to remain with the father of lies, in misery like himself; 22even to that being who beguiled our first parents; 23who transforms himself nigh to an angel of light, and stirs up the children of men to secret combinations of murder and all manner of secret works of darkness.

24 "Oh, how great the goodness of our God, who prepares a way for our escape from the grasp of this awful monster, 25even that monster, death and hell, which I call the death of the body, and also the death of the spirit.

26 "Because of the way of deliverance of our God the Holy One of Israel, this death of which I have spoken, which is the temporal, shall deliver up its dead, which death is the grave.

27 "And this death of which I have spoken, which is the spiritual death, shall deliver up its dead; which spiritual death is hell.

28 "Wherefore, death and hell must deliver up their dead, and hell must deliver up its captive spirits; 29and the grave must deliver up its captive bodies; and the bodies and the spirits of men will be restored, one to the other; 30and it is by the power of the resurrection of the Holy One of Israel.

31 "Oh, how great the plan of our God! For on the other hand, the paradise of God must deliver up the spirits of the righteous, and the grave deliver up the body of the righteous.

32 "And the spirit and the body is restored to itself again, and all men become incorruptible, and immortal, and they are living souls, having a perfect knowledge like us, in the flesh, [33]save it be that our knowledge shall be perfect.

34 "Wherefore, we shall have a perfect knowledge of all our guilt, and our uncleanness, and our nakedness.

35 "And the righteous shall have a perfect knowledge of their enjoyment, and their righteousness, being clothed with purity, even with the robe of righteousness.

36 "And it shall come to pass that when all men shall have passed from this first death to life, insomuch as they have become immortal, they must appear before the judgment seat of the Holy One of Israel.

37 "Then comes the judgment; and then must they be judged according to the holy judgment of God.

38 "Assuredly, as the Lord lives, for the Lord God has spoken it, and it is his eternal word, which cannot pass away, they who are righteous shall be righteous still, and they who are filthy shall be filthy still.

39 "Wherefore, they who are filthy are the devil and his angels; [40]and they shall go away into everlasting fire, prepared for them; and their torment is as a lake of fire and brimstone, whose flames ascend for ever and ever, and has no end.

41 "Oh, the greatness and the justice of our God! For he executes all his words, and they have gone forth out of his mouth, and his law must be fulfilled.

42 "But, behold, the righteous, the saints of the Holy One of Israel, they who have believed in the Holy One of Israel; they who have endured the crosses of the world, and despised the shame of it; they shall inherit the kingdom of God, which was prepared for them from the foundation of the world; and their joy shall be full forever.

43 "Oh, the greatness of the mercy of our God, the Holy One of Israel! For he delivers his saints from that awful monster the devil, and death, and hell, and that lake of fire and brimstone, which is endless torment.

44 "Oh, how great the holiness of our God! For he knows all things, and there is not anything save he knows it.

45 "He will come into the world that he may save all men, if they will hearken to his voice; [46]for, behold, he will suffer the pains of all men, the pains of every living creature (men, women and children) who belongs to the family of Adam.

47 "And he will suffer this that the resurrection might pass upon all men, that all might stand before him at the great and judgment day.

48 "And he commands all men that they must repent, and be baptized in his name, having perfect faith in the Holy One of Israel, or they cannot be saved in the kingdom of God.

49 "And if they will not repent and believe in his name, and be baptized in his name, and endure to the end, they must be damned; [50]for the Lord God, the Holy One of Israel, has spoken it.

51 "Wherefore he has given a law; and where there is no law given there is no punishment; [52]and where there is no punishment, there is no condemnation; [53]and where there is no condemnation, the mercies of the Holy One of Israel have claim upon them, because of the atonement.

54 "They are delivered by the power of him; for the atonement satisfies the demands of his justice upon all those who have not the law given to them, that they are delivered from that awful monster, death and hell, and the devil, and the lake of fire and brimstone, which is endless torment.

55 "And they are restored to that God who gave them breath, which is the Holy One of Israel.

56 "But woe to him that has the law given, that has all the commandments of God, like us, and that transgresses them, and that wastes the days of his probation; for awful is his state!

57 "Oh, that cunning plan of the evil one!

58 "Oh, the vainness, and the frailties, and the foolishness of men!

59 "When they are learned, they think they are wise, and they hearken not to the counsel of God, for they

49

set it aside, supposing they know of themselves; [60]wherefore, their wisdom is foolishness, and it profits them not. And they shall perish.

61 "But to be learned is good, if they hearken to the counsels of God.

62 "But woe to the rich, who are rich as to the things of the world.

63 "For because they are rich, they despise the poor, and they persecute the meek, and their hearts are upon their treasures; wherefore their treasure is their god.

64 "And, behold, their treasure shall perish with them also.

65 "Woe to the deaf that will not hear; for they shall perish.

66 "Woe to the blind that will not see; for they shall perish also.

67 "Woe to the uncircumcised of heart; for a knowledge of their iniquities shall smite them at the last day.

68 "Woe to the liar; for he shall be thrust down to hell.

69 "Woe to the murderer, who deliberately kills; for he shall die.

70 "Woe to them who commit whoredoms; for they shall be thrust down to hell.

71 "Woe to those who worship idols; for the devil of all devils delights in them.

72 "In fine, woe to all those who die in their sins; for they shall return to God, and behold his face, and remain in their sins.

73 "O my beloved brethren, remember the awfulness in transgressing against that Holy God, and also the awfulness of yielding to the enticings of that cunning one.

74 "Remember, to be carnally minded is death, and to be spiritually minded is life eternal.

75 "O my beloved brethren, give ear to my words.

76 "Remember the greatness of the Holy One of Israel.

77 "Do not say that I have spoken hard things against you; for if you do, you will revile against the truth; for I have spoken the words of your Maker.

78 "I know that the words of truth are hard against all uncleanness; but the righteous fear them not, for they love the truth, and are not shaken.

79 "Oh, then, my beloved brethren, come to the Lord, the Holy One.

80 "Remember that his paths are righteousness.

81 "Behold, the way for man is narrow, but it lies in a straight course before him, and the keeper of the gate is the Holy One of Israel; and he employs no servant there.

82 "And there is no other way, save it be by the gate, for he cannot be deceived; for the Lord God is his name.

83 "And whoever knocks, to him will he open; and the wise, and the learned, and they that are rich, who are puffed up because of their learning, and their wisdom, and their riches, they are they whom he despises.

84 "And save they shall cast these things away, and consider themselves fools before God, and come down in the depths of humility, he will not open to them.

85 "But the things of the wise and the prudent shall be hid from them forever, even that happiness which is prepared for the saints.

86 "O my beloved brethren, remember my words: Behold, I take off my garments and I shake them before you.

87 "I pray the God of my salvation that he view me with his all-searching eye; [88]wherefore, you shall know at the last day, when all men shall be judged of their works, that the God of Israel witnessed that I shook your iniquities from my soul, and that I stand with brightness before him, and am rid of your blood.

89 "O my beloved brethren, turn away from your sins; shake off the chains of him that would bind you fast; [90]come to that God who is the rock of your salvation.

91 "Prepare your souls for that glorious day when justice shall be administered to the righteous, even the day of judgment, that you may not shrink with awful fear, [92]that you may not remember your awful guilt in perfectness, and be constrained to exclaim, 'Holy, holy are thy judgments, O Lord God Almighty.

93 "'But I know my guilt; I transgressed thy law, and my transgressions are mine; and the devil has obtained me, that I am a prey to his awful misery.'

94 "But, behold, my brethren, is it expedient that I should awake you to an awful reality of these things?

95 "Would I harrow up your souls if your minds were pure?

96 "Would I be plain to you according to the plainness of the truth, if you were freed from sin?

97 "Behold, if you were holy, I would speak to you of holiness; but as you are not holy, and you look upon me as a teacher, it is expedient that I teach you the consequences of sin.

98 "Behold, my soul abhors sin, and my heart delights in righteousness; and I will praise the holy name of my God.

99 "Come, my brethren, every one that thirsts, come to the waters; and he that has no money, come buy and eat; come buy wine and milk without money and without price.

100 "Wherefore, do not spend money for that which is of no worth, nor your labor for that which cannot satisfy.

101 "Hearken diligently to me, and remember the words which I have spoken; come to the Holy One of Israel, 102and feast upon that which perishes not, neither can be corrupted, and let your soul delight in fatness.

103 "Behold, my beloved brethren, remember the words of your God; pray to him continually by day and give thanks to his holy name by night.

104 "Let your hearts rejoice, and behold how great the covenants of the Lord, and how great his condescensions to the children of men.

105 "Because of his greatness, and his grace and mercy, he has promised us that our seed shall not utterly be destroyed, according to the flesh, but that he would preserve them; and in future generations they shall become a righteous branch to the house of Israel.

106 "And now, my brethren, I would speak to you more; but on the morrow I will declare to you the remainder of my words. Amen."

CHAPTER 7

NOW I, Jacob, speak to you again, my beloved brethren, concerning this righteous branch of which I have spoken.

2 "For, behold, the promises which we have obtained are promises to us according to the flesh.

3 Wherefore, it has been shown me that many of our children shall perish in the flesh because of unbelief, nevertheless God will be merciful to many; 4and our children shall be restored that they may come to that which will give them the true knowledge of their Redeemer.

5 "Wherefore, as I said to you, it is expedient that Christ (for in the last night the angel spoke to me that this should be his name) should come among the Jews, among those who are the more wicked part of the world; 6and they shall crucify him; for thus it behooves our God; 7and there is no other nation on earth that would crucify their God.

8 "For should the mighty miracles be wrought among other nations, they would repent and know that he is their God.

9 "But because of priestcrafts and iniquities, they at Jerusalem will stiffen their necks against him, that he will be crucified.

10 "Wherefore, because of their iniquities, destructions, famines, pestilence and bloodsheds shall come upon them; 11and they who shall not be destroyed shall be scattered among all nations.

12 "But, behold, thus says the Lord God: 'When the day cometh that they shall believe in me, that I am Christ, then have I covenanted with their fathers that they shall be restored in the flesh, upon the earth, to the lands of their inheritance.

13 "'And it shall come to pass that they shall be gathered in from their long dispersion from the isles of the sea and from the four parts of the earth.

14 "'And the nations of the Gentiles shall be great in my eyes,' says God, 'in carrying them forth to the lands of their inheritance.

15 "'The kings of the Gentiles shall be nursing fathers to them, and their queens shall become nursing mothers; 16wherefore the promises of the Lord are great to the Gentiles, for he has spoken it, and who can dispute?

17 "'But, behold, this land,' says

God, 'shall be a land of thine inheritance; and the Gentiles shall be blessed upon the land.

18 "'And this land shall be a land of liberty to the Gentiles; and there shall be no kings upon the land who shall rise up to the Gentiles.

19 "'I will fortify this land against all other nations.

20 "'And he that fights against Zion shall perish,' says God; 'for he that raiseth up a king against me shall perish.

21 " 'For I, the Lord, the King of heaven, will be their king; and I will be a light to them forever, that hear my words.

22 "'Wherefore, for this cause, that my covenants may be fulfilled which I have made to the children of men that I will do to them while they are in the flesh, I must destroy the secret works of darkness, and of murders, and of abominations.

23 "'Wherefore, he that fights against Zion, both Jew and Gentile, both bond and free, both male and female, shall perish.

24 " 'For they are they who are the whore of all the earth; 25for they who are not for me, are against me,' says our God.

26 "'For I will fulfill my promises which I have made to the children of men, that I will do unto them while they are in the flesh.

27 " 'Wherefore, my beloved brethren,' thus says our God, 'I will afflict thy seed by the hand of the Gentiles; 28nevertheless, I will soften the hearts of the Gentiles, that they shall be like a father to them; 29wherefore, the Gentiles shall be blessed and numbered among the house of Israel.

30 "'Wherefore, I will consecrate this land to thy seed, and they who shall be numbered among thy seed, forever, for the land of their inheritance; 31for it is a choice land,' says God, 'to me, above all other lands; 32wherefore, I will have all men that dwell thereon, that they shall worship me.'

33 "Now, my beloved brethren, seeing that our merciful God has given us so great knowledge concerning these things, let us remember him, and lay aside our sins, and not hang down our heads, for we are not cast off.

34 "Nevertheless, we have been driven out of the land of our inheritance; but we have been led to a better land; 35for the Lord has made the sea our path, and we are upon an isle of the sea.

36 "But great are the promises of the Lord to those who are upon the isles of the sea; 37wherefore, as it says isles, there must be more than this; and they are inhabited also by our brethren.

38 "For, behold, the Lord God has led away from time to time from the house of Israel, according to his will and pleasure.

39 "Now, behold, the Lord remembers all those who have been broken off; wherefore, he remembers us also.

40 "Therefore cheer up your hearts, and remember that you are free to act for yourselves, to choose the way of everlasting death or the way of eternal life.

41 "Wherefore, my beloved brethren, reconcile yourselves to the will of God, and not to the will of the devil and the flesh.

42 "And remember after you are reconciled to God that it is only in and through the grace of God that you are saved.

43 "Wherefore, may God raise you from death by the power of the resurrection, and also from everlasting death by the power of the atonement, 44that you may be received into the eternal kingdom of God, that you may praise him through grace divine. Amen."

CHAPTER 8

JACOB spoke many more things to my people at that time; nevertheless, only these things have I caused to be written, for the things which I have written suffice me.

2 Now I, Nephi, write more of the words of Isaiah; for my soul delights in his words.

3 For I will liken his words to my people; and I will send them forth to all my children; for he verily saw my Redeemer, even as I have seen him.

4 And my brother Jacob also has seen him as I have seen him; wherefore, I will send their words forth to my children to prove to them that my words are true.

5 "Wherefore, by the words of three," God has said, "I will establish my word."

6 Nevertheless, God sends more witnesses; and he proves all his words.

7 Behold, my soul delights in proving to my people the truth of the coming of Christ; [8]for, for this end has the law of Moses been given; [9]and all things which have been given of God from the beginning of the world, to man, are the typifying of him.

10 Also, my soul delights in the covenants of the Lord which he has made to our fathers; [11]my soul delights in his grace, and his justice, and power, and mercy, in the great and eternal plan of deliverance from death.

12 And my soul delights in proving to my people that, save Christ should come, all men must perish.

13 For if there be no Christ, there be no God; and if there be no God, we are not, for there could have been no creation.

14 But there is a God, and he is Christ; and he comes in the fullness of his own time.

15 Now I write some of the words of Isaiah, that whoever of my people shall see these words may lift up their hearts and rejoice for all men.

16 These are the words; and you may liken them to you, and to all men.

17* The word that Isaiah, the son of Amoz, saw, concerning Judah and Jerusalem:

18 And it shall come to pass in the last days that the mountain of the Lord's house shall be established in the top of the mountains, and shall be exalted above the hills, and all nations shall flow to it.

19 And many people shall go and say, "Come ye, and let us go up to the mountain of the Lord, to the house of the God of Jacob; and he will teach us of his ways, and we will walk in his paths." For out of Zion shall go forth the law, and the

word of the Lord from Jerusalem.

20 And he shall judge among the nations, and shall rebuke many people; and they shall beat their swords into plow shares, and their spears into pruning hooks; nation shall not lift up sword against nation, neither shall they learn war any more.

21 O house of Jacob, come ye and let us walk in the light of the Lord; come, for ye have all gone astray, every one to his wicked ways.

22 Therefore, O Lord, thou hast forsaken thy people, the house of Jacob, because they be replenished from the east, and hearken to soothsayers like the Philistines, and they please themselves in the children of strangers.

23 Their land also is full of silver and gold, neither is there any end of their treasures; their land is also full of horses, neither is there any end of their chariots.

24 Their land also is full of idols; they worship the work of their own hands, that which their own fingers have made.

25 And the mean man bows not down, and the great man humbles himself not; therefore forgive him not.

26 O ye wicked ones, enter into the rock, and hide thee in the dust, for the fear of the Lord and the glory of his majesty shall smite thee.

27 And it shall come to pass that the lofty looks of man shall be humbled, and the haughtiness of men shall be bowed down, and the Lord alone shall be exalted in that day.

28 For the day of the Lord of hosts will soon come upon all nations, upon every one; upon the proud and lofty, and upon every one who is lifted up; and he shall be brought low.

29 And the day of the Lord shall come upon all the cedars of Lebanon, for they are high and lifted up, and upon all the oaks of Bashan; [30]and upon all the high mountains, and upon all the hills, and upon all the nations which are lifted up;

*Isaiah 2

31and upon every people, and upon every high tower, and upon every fenced wall; 32and upon all the ships of the sea, and upon all the ships of Tarshish, and upon all pleasant pictures.

33 And the loftiness of man shall be bowed down, and the haughtiness of men shall be made low; and the Lord alone shall be exalted in that day.

34 And the idols he shall utterly abolish.

35 And they shall go into the holes of the rocks and into the caves of the earth, for the fear of the Lord shall come upon them; and the glory of his majesty shall smite them, when he ariseth to shake terribly the earth.

36 In that day a man shall cast his idols of silver and his idols of gold, which he has made for himself to worship, to the moles and to the bats, 37to go into the clefts of the rocks and into the tops of the ragged rocks, for the fear of the Lord shall come upon him and the majesty of his glory shall smite him when He arises to shake terribly the earth.

38 Cease ye from man, whose breath is in his nostrils; for wherein is he to be accounted of?

39* For, behold, the Lord, the Lord of hosts, is taking away from Jerusalem and from Judah the stay and the staff, the whole staff of bread, and the whole stay of water, 40the mighty man, and the man of war, the judge, and the prophet, and the prudent, and the ancient, 41the captain of fifty, and the honorable man, and the counselor, and the cunning artificer, and the eloquent orator.

42 And I will give children to them to be their princes, and babes shall rule over them.

43 And the people shall be oppressed, every one by another, and every one by his neighbor; the child shall behave himself proudly against the ancient, and the base against the honorable.

44 When a man shall take hold of his brother of the house of his father, and shall say, "Thou hast

clothing, be thou our ruler, and let not this ruin come under thy hand";

45 In that day shall he swear, saying: "I will not be a healer; for in my house there is neither bread nor clothing: make me not a ruler of the people."

46 For Jerusalem is ruined, and Judah is falllen; because their tongues and their doings have been against the Lord, to provoke the eyes of his glory.

47 The show of their countenance witnesses against them, and declares their sin to be even as Sodom, and they cannot hide it. Woe to their souls, for they have rewarded evil to themselves.

48 Say to the righteous that it is well with them; for they shall eat the fruit of their doings.

49 Woe to the wicked, for they shall perish; for the reward of their hands shall be upon them.

50 And my people, children are their oppressors, and women rule over them. O my people, they who lead thee cause thee to err, and destroy the way of thy paths.

51 The Lord stands up to plead, and stands to judge the people.

52 The Lord will enter into judgment with the ancients of his people, and the princes thereof: "For ye have eaten up the vineyard, and the spoil of the poor in your houses.

53 "What mean ye? Ye beat my people to pieces, and grind the faces of the poor," says the Lord God of hosts.

54 Moreover the Lord says because the daughters of Zion are haughty, and walk with stretched forth necks and wanton eyes, walking and mincing as they go, and making a tinkling with their feet; 55therefore the Lord will smite with a scab the crown of the head of the daughters of Zion, and the Lord will discover their secret parts.

56 In that day the Lord will take away the bravery of their tinkling ornaments, and cauls, and round tires like the moon, 57the chains and the bracelets, and the mufflers, 58the bonnets, and the ornaments of the legs, and the head-bands, and the tablets, and the ear-rings,

*Isaiah 3

59the rings, and nose-jewels, 60the changeable suits of apparel, and the mantles, and the wimples, and the crisping-pins, 61the glasses, and the fine linen, and hoods and the veils.

62 And it shall come to pass, instead of sweet smell, there shall be stink; and instead of a girdle, a rent; and instead of well-set hair, baldness; and instead of a stomacher, a girding of sackcloth; burning instead of beauty.

63 Thy men shall fall by the sword, and thy mighty in the war.

64 And her gates shall lament and mourn; and she shall be desolate, and shall sit upon the ground.

65* And in that day, seven women shall take hold of one man, saying, "We will eat our own bread, and wear our own apparel; only let us be called by thy name, to take away our reproach."

66 In that day shall the branch of the Lord be beautiful and glorious; the fruit of the earth excellent and comely to them that are escaped of Israel.

67 And it shall come to pass, those that are left in Zion, and remain in Jerusalem, shall be called holy, everyone that is written among the living in Jerusalem, 68when the Lord shall have washed away the filth of the daughters of Zion, and shall have purged the blood of Jerusalem from the midst thereof by the spirit of judgment, and by the spirit of burning.

69 And the Lord will create upon every dwelling place of mount Zion, and upon her assemblies, a cloud and smoke by day, and the shining of a flaming fire by night; for upon all the glory of Zion shall be a defense.

70 And there shall be a tabernacle for a shadow in the daytime from the heat, and for a place of refuge, and a covert from storm and from rain.

71** And then will I sing to my well beloved a song of my beloved touching his vineyard. My well beloved had a vineyard in a very fruitful hill.

72 And he fenced it, and gathered out the stones thereof, and planted it with the choicest vine, and built a tower in the midst of it, and also made a wine press therein; and he looked that it should bring forth grapes, and it brought forth wild grapes.

73 And now, O inhabitants of Jerusalem, and men of Judah, judge, I pray you, between me and my vineyard.

74 What could have been done more to my vineyard that I have not done in it? Wherefore, when I looked that it should bring forth grapes, it brought forth wild grapes.

75 And now go to; I will tell you what I will do to my vineyard: I will take away the hedge thereof, and it shall be eaten up; and I will break down the wall thereof, and it shall be trodden down.

76 And I will lay it waste; it shall not be pruned nor digged; but there shall come up briers and thorns. I will also command the clouds that they rain no rain upon it.

77 For the vineyard of the Lord of hosts is the house of Israel, and the men of Judah his pleasant plant; and he looked for judgment, and, behold, oppression; for righteousness, but, behold, a cry.

78 Woe to them that join house to house, till there can be no place, that they may be placed alone in the midst of the earth!

79 In my ears, says the Lord of hosts, "Of a truth many houses shall be desolate, and great and fair cities without inhabitant.

80 "Ten acres of vineyard shall yield one bath, and the seed of a homer shall yield an ephah."

81 Woe to them that rise up early in the morning, that they may follow strong drink; that continue until night, till wine inflame them!

82 And the harp, and the viol, the tabret and pipe, and wine are in their feasts; but they regard not the works of the Lord, neither consider the operation of his hands.

83 Therefore, my people are gone into captivity, because they have no knowledge; and their hon-

*Isaiah 4
**Isaiah 5

orable men are famished, and their multitude dried up with thirst.

84 Therefore, hell has enlarged herself, and opened her mouth without measure; and their glory, and their multitude, and their pomp, and he that rejoices shall descend into it.

85 And the mean man shall be brought down, and the mighty man shall be humbled, and the eyes of the lofty shall be humbled.

86 But the Lord of hosts shall be exalted in judgment, and God that is holy shall be sanctified in righteousness.

87 Then shall the lambs feed after their manner, and the waste places of the fat ones shall strangers eat.

88 Woe to them that draw iniquity with cords of vanity, and sin as it were with a cart rope; 89that say, "Let him make speed, hasten his work that we may see it; and let the counsel of the Holy One of Israel draw nigh and come, that we may know it."

90 Woe to them that call evil good, and good evil; that put darkness for light, and light for darkness; that put bitter for sweet, and sweet for bitter!

91 Woe to the wise in their own eyes, and prudent in their own sight!

92 Woe to the mighty to drink wine, and men of strength to mingle strong drink; 93who justify the wicked for reward, and take away the righteousness of the righteous from him!

94 Therefore, as the fire devours the stubble, and the flame consumes the chaff, their root shall be rottenness, and their blossoms shall go up as dust; because they have cast away the law of the Lord of hosts, and despised the word of the Holy One of Israel.

95 Therefore is the anger of the Lord kindled against his people, and he has stretched forth his hand against them, and has smitten them; and the hills trembled and their carcasses were torn in the midst of the streets. For all this his anger is not turned away, but his hand is stretched out still.

96 And he will lift up an ensign to the nations from far, and will hiss to them from the end of the earth; and, behold, they shall come with speed swiftly.

97 None shall be weary nor stumble among them; none shall slumber nor sleep; neither shall the girdle of their loins be loosed, nor the latchet of their shoes be broken; 98whose arrows shall be sharp, and all their bows bent, and their horses' hoofs shall be counted like flint, and their wheels like a whirlwind, their roaring like a lion.

99 They shall roar like young lions; they shall roar, and lay hold of the prey, and shall carry it away safe, and none shall deliver.

100 And in that day they shall roar against them like the roaring of the sea; and if they look to the land, behold, darkness and sorrow, and the light is darkened in the heavens thereof.

CHAPTER 9

*IN the year that king Uzziah died, I saw also the Lord sitting upon a throne, high and lifted up, and his train filled the temple.

2 Above it stood the seraphims; each one had six wings; with twain he covered his face, and with twain he covered his feet, and with twain he flew.

3 And one cried to another, and said, "Holy, holy, holy is the Lord of hosts; the whole earth is full of his glory."

4 And the posts of the door moved at the voice of him that cried, and the house was filled with smoke.

5 Then said I, "Woe is me, for I am undone; because I am a man of unclean lips, and I dwell in the midst of a people of unclean lips; for my eyes have seen the King, the Lord of hosts."

6 Then flew one of the seraphims to me, having a live coal in his hand, which he had taken with the tongs from off the altar.

7 And he laid it upon my mouth, and said, "Lo, this has touched your lips; and your in-

*Isaiah 6

iquity is taken away, and your sin purged."

8 Also I heard the voice of the Lord, saying, "Whom shall I send, and who will go for us?" Then I said, "Here am I; send me."

9 And he said, "Go, and tell this people, 'Hear ye indeed but understand not,' and 'See ye indeed but perceive not.'

10 "Make the heart of this people fat, and make their ears heavy, and shut their eyes; lest they see with their eyes, and hear with their ears, and understand with their heart, and be converted, and be healed."

11 Then said I, "Lord, how long?" And he said, "Until the cities be wasted without inhabitant, and the houses without man, and the land be utterly desolate; 12and the Lord has removed men far away, for there shall be a great forsaking in the midst of the land.

13 "But yet in it there shall be a tenth, and they shall return, and shall be eaten; as a teil tree, and as an oak whose substance is in them when they cast their leaves, so the holy seed shall be the substance thereof."

14* And it came to pass in the days of Ahaz the son of Jotham, the son of Uzziah, king of Judah, that Rezin, king of Syria, and Pekah, the son of Remaliah, king of Israel, went up toward Jerusalem to war against it, but could not prevail against it.

15 And it was told the house of David saying, "Syria is confederate with Ephraim." And his heart was moved, and the heart of his people, as the trees of the wood are moved with the wind.

16 Then said the Lord to Isaiah, "Go forth now to meet Ahaz, thou, and Shear-jashub thy son, at the end of the çonduit of the upper pool in the highway of the fuller's field;

17 "And say to him, 'Take heed, and be quiet; fear not, neither be fainthearted for the two tails of these smoking firebrands, for the fierce anger of Rezin with Syria, and the son of Remaliah.

18 "'Because Syria, Ephraim, and the son of Remaliah have taken evil counsel against thee, saying, 19"Let us go up against Judah, and vex it, and let us make a breach therein for us, and set a king in the midst of it, even the son of Tabeal.'"

20 Thus says the Lord God, "It shall not stand, neither shall it come to pass.

21 "For the head of Syria is Damascus; and the head of Damascus, Rezin; and within threescore and five years shall Ephraim be broken, that it be not a people.

22 "And the head of Ephraim is Samaria, and the head of Samaria is Remaliah's son. If ye will not believe, surely ye shall not be established."

23 Moreover, the Lord spoke again to Ahaz, saying,

24 "Ask thee a sign of the Lord thy God; ask it either in the depths, or in the heights above."

25 But Ahaz said, "I will not ask, neither will I tempt the Lord."

26 And he said: "Hear ye now, O house of David; is it a small thing for you to weary men, but will ye weary my God also?

27 "Therefore the Lord himself shall give you a sign: Behold, a virgin shall conceive, and shall bear a son, and shall call his name Immanuel.

28 "Butter and honey shall he eat, that he may know to refuse the evil, and to choose the good.

29 "For before the child shall know to refuse the evil and choose the good, the land that thou abhorrest shall be forsaken of both her kings.

30 "The Lord shall bring upon thee, and upon thy people and upon thy father's house, days that have not come, from the day that Ephraim departed from Judah, the king of Assyria."

31 And it shall come to pass in that day that the Lord shall hiss for the fly that is in the uttermost part of Egypt, and for the bee that is in the land of Assyria.

32 And they shall come, and shall rest all of them in the desolate valleys, and in the holes of the

*Isaiah 7

rocks, and upon all thorns, and upon all bushes.

33 In the same day shall the Lord shave with a razor that is hired, by them beyond the river, by the king of Assyria, the head, and the hair of the feet, and it shall also consume the beard.

34 And it shall come to pass in that day, a man shall nourish a young cow and two sheep; 35and it shall come to pass, for the abundance of milk they shall give, he shall eat butter; for butter and honey shall everyone eat that is left in the land.

36 And it shall come to pass in that day, every place shall be, where there were a thousand vines at a thousand silverlings, which shall be for briers and thorns.

37 With arrows and with bows shall men come thither; because all the land shall become briers and thorns.

38 And all hills that shall be digged with the mattock, there shall not come thither the fear of briers and thorns; but it shall be for the sending forth of oxen, and the treading of lesser cattle.

39* Moreover, the word of the Lord said to me, "Take thee a great roll, and write in it with a man's pen concerning Maher-shalal-hash-baz."

40 And I took faithful witnesses to record, Uriah the priest, and Zechariah the son of Jeberechiah.

41 And I went to the prophetess; and she conceived and bare a son. Then said the Lord to me, "Call his name Maher-shalal-hash-baz.

42 "For, behold, the child shall not have knowledge to cry, 'My father,' and 'My mother,' before the riches of Damascus and the spoil of Samaria shall be taken away before the king of Assyria."

43 The Lord spoke also to me again, saying,

44 "Forasmuch as this people refuseth the waters of Shiloah that go softly and rejoice in Rezin and Remaliah's son; 45now therefore, behold, the Lord bringeth up upon them the waters of the river, strong and many, even the king of Assyria,

*Isaiah 8

and all his glory; and he shall come up over all his channels, and go over all his banks.

46 "And he shall pass through Judah; he shall overflow and go over; and he shall reach even to the neck; and the stretching out of his wings shall fill the breadth of thy land, O Immanuel."

47 Associate yourselves, O ye people, and ye shall be broken in pieces; and give ear all ye of far countries: gird yourselves, and ye shall be broken in pieces; gird yourselves, and ye shall be broken in pieces.

48 Take counsel together, and it shall come to nought; speak the word, and it shall not stand; for God is with us.

49 For the Lord spoke thus to me with a strong hand, and instructed me that I should not walk in the way of this people, saying,

50 "Say ye not, 'A confederacy,' to all to whom this people shall say, 'A confederacy'; neither fear ye their fear, nor be afraid.

51 "Sanctify the Lord of hosts himself, and let him be your fear, and let him be your dread.

52 "And he shall be for a sanctuary; but for a stone of stumbling and for a rock of offense to both the houses of Israel, for a gin and a snare to the inhabitants of Jerusalem.

53 "And many among them shall stumble, and fall, and be broken, and be snared, and be taken."

54 Bind up the testimony, seal the law among my disciples.

55 And I will wait upon the Lord that hideth his face from the house of Jacob, and I will look for him.

56 Behold, I and the children whom the Lord hath given me are for signs and for wonders in Israel from the Lord of hosts, which dwelleth in mount Zion.

57 And when they shall say to you, "Seek to them that have familiar spirits, and to wizards that peep, and mutter": should not a people seek to their God? for the living to hear from the dead?

58 To the law and to the testi-

mony; and if they speak not according to this word, it is because there is no light in them.

59 And they shall pass through it hardly bestead and hungry; and it shall come to pass that when they shall be hungry they shall fret themselves, and curse their king and their God, and look upward.

60 And they shall look to the earth; and behold trouble, and darkness, dimness of anguish, and shall be driven to darkness.

61* Nevertheless the dimness shall not be such as was in her vexation, when at the first he lightly afflicted the land of Zebulun, and the land of Naphtali, and afterward did more grievously afflict by the way of the Red Sea beyond Jordan, in Galilee of the nations.

62 The people that walked in darkness have seen a great light: they that dwell in the land of the shadow of death, upon them hath the light shined.

63 Thou hast multiplied the nation, and increased the joy; they joy before thee according to the joy in harvest, and as men rejoice when they divide the spoil.

64 For thou hast broken the yoke of his burden, and the staff of his shoulder, the rod of his oppressor.

65 For every battle of the warrior is with confused noise, and garments rolled in blood; but this shall be with burning and fuel of fire.

66 For to us a child is born, to us a son is given, and the government shall be upon his shoulder; and his name shall be called "Wonderful, Counselor, The mighty God, The everlasting Father, The Prince of Peace."

67 Of the increase of government and peace there is no end, upon the throne of David, and upon his kingdom, to order it, and to establish it with judgment and with justice from henceforth even forever. The zeal of the Lord of hosts will perform this.

68 The Lord sent his word to Jacob and it hath lighted upon Israel.

69 And all the people shall know, even Ephraim and the inhabitants of Samaria, that say in the pride and stoutness of heart:

70 "The bricks are fallen down, but we will build with hewn stones; the sycamores are cut down, but we will change them into cedars."

71 Therefore the Lord shall set up the adversaries of Rezin against him, and join his enemies together; 72the Syrians before, and the Philistines behind; and they shall devour Israel with open mouth. For all this his anger is not turned away, but his hand is stretched out still.

73 For the people turneth not to him that smiteth them, neither do they seek the Lord of hosts.

74 Therefore, will the Lord cut off from Israel head and tail, branch and rush in one day.

75 The ancient, he is the head; and the prophet that teacheth lies, he is the tail.

76 For the leaders of this people cause them to err; and they that are led of them are destroyed.

77 Therefore the Lord shall have no joy in their young men, neither shall have mercy on their fatherless and widows; for every one of them is a hypocrite and an evildoer, and every mouth speaketh folly. For all this his anger is not turned away, but his hand is stretched out still.

78 For wickedness burneth as the fire; it shall devour the briers and thorns, and shall kindle in the thickets of the forests, and they shall mount up like the lifting up of smoke.

79 Through the wrath of the Lord of hosts is the land darkened, and the people shall be as the fuel of the fire; no man shall spare his brother.

80 And he shall snatch on the right hand, and be hungry; and he shall eat on the left hand, and they shall not be satisfied; they shall eat every man the flesh of his own arm:

81 Manasseh, Ephraim; and Ephraim, Mannasseh; they together shall be against Judah. For all this his anger is not turned away, but his hand is stretched out still.

*Isaiah 9

82* Woe to them that decree unrighteous decrees, and that write grievousness which they have prescribed; [83]to turn aside the needy from judgment, and to take away the right from the poor of my people, that widows may be their prey, and that they may rob the fatherless.

84 And what will ye do in the days of visitation, and in the desolation which shall come from far? To whom will ye flee for help, and where will ye leave your glory?

85 Without me they shall bow down under the prisoners, and they shall fall under the slain. For all this his anger is not turned away, but his hand is stretched out still.

86 O Assyrian, the rod of my anger, and the staff in their hand is their indignation.

87 I will send him against a hypocritical nation, and against the people of my wrath will I give him a charge, to take the spoil, and to take the prey, and to tread them down like the mire of the streets.

88 Howbeit he means not so, neither does his heart think so; but in his heart it is to destroy and cut off nations not a few.

89 For he says, "Are not my princes altogether kings?

90 "Is not Calno as Carchemish? Is not Hamath as Arpad? Is not Samaria as Damascus?

91 "As my hand hath founded the kingdoms of the idols, and whose graven images did excel them of Jerusalem and of Samaria; [92]shall I not, as I have done to Samaria and her idols, so do to Jerusalem and to her idols?"

93 Wherefore it shall come to pass that when the Lord has performed his whole work upon mount Zion and upon Jerusalem, I will punish the fruit of the stout heart of the king of Assyria, and the glory of his high looks.

94 For he says, "By the strength of my hand and by my wisdom I have done these things; for I am prudent; and I have moved the borders of the people, and have robbed their treasures, and I have put down the inhabitants like a valiant man.

95 "And my hand hath found as a nest the riches of the people; and as one gathered eggs that are left, have I gathered all the earth; and there was none that moved the wing, or opened the mouth, or peeped."

96 Shall the axe boast itself against him that hews therewith? Shall the saw magnify itself against him that shakes it? As if the rod should shake itself against them that lift it up, or as if the staff should lift up itself as if it were no wood!

97 Therefore shall the Lord, the Lord of hosts, send among his fat ones, leanness; and under his glory he shall kindle a burning like the burning of a fire.

98 And the light of Israel shall be for a fire, and his Holy One for a flame, and it shall burn and shall devour his thorns and his briers in one day; [99]and shall consume the glory of his forest, and of his fruitful field, both soul and body; and they shall be as when a standard-bearer fainteth.

100 And the rest of the trees of his forest shall be few, that a child may write them.

101 And it shall come to pass in that day that the remnant of Israel, and such as are escaped of the house of Jacob, shall no more again stay upon him that smote them, but shall stay upon the Lord, the Holy One of Israel, in truth.

102 The remnant shall return, even the remnant of Jacob, to the mighty God.

103 For though thy people Israel be as the sand of the sea, yet a remnant of them shall return; the consumption decreed shall overflow with righteousness.

104 For the Lord God of hosts shall make a consumption, even determined, in all the land.

105 Therefore, thus says the Lord God of hosts, "O my people that dwellest in Zion, be not afraid of the Assyrian; he shall smite thee with a rod, and shall lift up his staff against thee, after the manner of Egypt.

*Isaiah 10

106 "For yet a very little while and the indignation shall cease, and my anger in their destruction.

107 "And the Lord of hosts shall stir up a scourge for him according to the slaughter of Midian at the rock of Oreb; and as his rod was upon the sea, so shall he lift it up after the manner of Egypt.

108 "And it shall come to pass in that day that his burden shall be taken away from off thy shoulder, and his yoke from off thy neck, and the yoke shall be destroyed because of the anointing."

109 He is come to Aiath, he is passed to Migron; at Michmash he has laid up his carriages;

110 They are gone over the passage; they have taken up their lodging at Geba; Ramath is afraid; Gibeah of Saul is fled.

111 Lift up the voice, O daughter of Gallim; cause it to be heard to Laish, O poor Anathoth.

112 Madmenah is removed; the inhabitants of Gebim gather themselves to flee.

113 As yet shall he remain at Nob that day; he shall shake his hand against the mount of the daughter of Zion, the hill of Jerusalem.

114 Behold, the Lord, the Lord of hosts shall lop the bough with terror; and the high ones of stature shall be hewn down, and the haughty shall be humbled.

115 And he shall cut down the thickets of the forest with iron, and Lebanon shall fall by a mighty one.

116* And there shall come forth a rod out of the stem of Jesse, and a branch shall grow out of his roots.

117 And the Spirit of the Lord shall rest upon him, the spirit of wisdom and understanding, the spirit of counsel and might, the spirit of knowledge and of the fear of the Lord; 118and shall make him of quick understanding in the fear of the Lord; and he shall not judge after the sight of his eyes, neither reprove after the hearing of his ears; 119but with righteousness shall he judge the poor, and reprove with equity for the meek of the earth; and he shall smite the earth

with the rod of his mouth, and with the breath of his lips shall he slay the wicked.

120 And righteousness shall be the girdle of his loins, and faithfulness the girdle of his reins.

121 The wolf also shall dwell with the lamb, and the leopard shall lie down with the kid, and the calf and the young lion and the fatling together; and a little child shall lead them.

122 And the cow and the bear shall feed; their young ones shall lie down together; and the lion shall eat straw like the ox.

123 And the sucking child shall play on the hole of the asp, and the weaned child shall put his hand on the cockatrice's den.

124 They shall not hurt nor destroy in all my holy mountain; for the earth shall be full of the knowledge of the Lord as the waters cover the sea.

125 And in that day there shall be a root of Jesse, which shall stand for an ensign of the people; to it shall the Gentiles seek, and his rest shall be glorious.

126 And it shall come to pass in that day that the Lord shall set his hand again the second time to recover the remnant of his people, which shall be left from Assyria, and from Egypt, and from Pathros, and from Cush, and from Elam, and from Shinar, and from Hamath, and from the islands of the sea.

127 And he shall set up an ensign for the nations, and shall assemble the outcasts of Israel, and gather together the dispersed of Judah from the four corners of the earth.

128 The envy of Ephraim also shall depart, and the adversaries of Judah shall be cut off; Ephraim shall not envy Judah, and Judah shall not vex Ephraim.

129 But they shall fly upon the shoulders of the Philistines toward the west; they shall spoil them of the east together; they shall lay their hand upon Edom and Moab; and the children of Ammon shall obey them.

130 And the Lord shall utterly

destroy the tongue of the Egyptian sea; and with his mighty wind he shall shake his hand over the river, and shall smite it in the seven streams, and make men go over dry shod.

131 And there shall be a highway for the remnant of his people, which shall be left, from Assyria, like as it was to Israel in the day that he came up out of the land of Egypt.

132* And in that day you shall say, "O Lord, I will praise thee; though thou wast angry with me, thine anger is turned away, and thou comfortedst me.

133 "Behold, God is my salvation; I will trust, and not be afraid; for the Lord Jehovah is my strength and my song; he also is become my salvation."

134 Therefore, with joy shall you draw water out of the wells of salvation.

135 And in that day shall you say, "Praise the Lord, call upon his name, declare his doings among the people, make mention that his name is exalted.

136 "Sing to the Lord; for he hath done excellent things: this is known in all the earth.

137 "Cry out and shout, thou inhabitant of Zion; for great is the Holy One of Israel in the midst of thee."

CHAPTER 10

**THE burden of Babylon, which Isaiah the son of Amoz did see.

2 Lift ye up a banner upon the high mountain, exalt the voice to them, shake the hand, that they may go into the gates of the nobles.

3 I have commanded my sanctified ones, I have also called my mighty ones, for my anger is not upon them that rejoice in my highness.

4 The noise of the multitude in the mountains like as of a great people; a tumultuous noise of the kingdoms of nations gathered to-

*Isaiah 12
**Isaiah 13

gether: the Lord of hosts mustereth the hosts of the battle.

5 They come from a far country, from the end of heaven, the Lord and the weapons of his indignation, to destroy the whole land.

6 Howl ye; for the day of the Lord is at hand; it shall come as a destruction from the Almighty.

7 Therefore shall all hands be faint; every man's heart shall melt; 8and they shall be afraid; pangs and sorrows shall take hold of them; they shall be amazed one at another; their faces shall be as flames.

9 Behold, the day of the Lord cometh, cruel both with wrath and fierce anger, to lay the land desolate; and he shall destroy the sinners thereof out of it.

10 For the stars of heaven and the constellations thereof shall not give their light; the sun shall be darkened in his going forth, and the moon shall not cause her light to shine.

11 And I will punish the world for evil, and the wicked for their iniquity; I will cause the arrogancy of the proud to cease, and will lay down the haughtiness of the terrible.

12 I will make a man more precious than fine gold; even a man than the golden wedge of Ophir.

13 Therefore I will shake the heavens, and the earth shall remove out of her place, in the wrath of the Lord of hosts, and in the day of his fierce anger.

14 And it shall be as the chased roe, and as a sheep that no man takes up; they shall every man turn to his own people, and flee every one into his own land.

15 Every one that is proud shall be thrust through; and every one that is joined to the wicked shall fall by the sword.

16 Their children also shall be dashed to pieces before their eyes; their houses shall be spoiled and their wives ravished.

17 Behold, I will stir up the Medes against them, which shall not regard silver and gold, nor they shall not delight in them.

18 Their bows shall also dash

the young men to pieces; and they shall have no pity on the fruit of the womb; their eyes shall not spare children.

19 And Babylon, the glory of kingdoms, the beauty of the Chaldee's excellency, shall be as when God overthrew Sodom and Gomorrah.

20 It shall never be inhabited, neither shall it be dwelt in from generation to generation; neither shall the Arabian pitch tent there; neither shall the shepherds make their fold there:

21 But wild beasts of the desert shall lie there; and their houses shall be full of doleful creatures; and owls shall dwell there, and satyrs shall dance there.

22 And the wild beasts of the islands shall cry in their desolate houses, and dragons in their pleasant palaces; and her time is near to come, and her day shall not be prolonged. For I will destroy her speedily; for I will be merciful to my people; but the wicked shall perish.

23* For the Lord will have mercy on Jacob, and will yet choose Israel, and set them in their own land; and the strangers shall be joined with them, and they shall cleave to the house of Jacob.

24 And the people shall take them and bring them to their place, from far to the ends of the earth; and they shall return to their lands of promise. And the house of Israel shall possess them, and the land of the Lord shall be for servants and handmaids; and they shall take them captives, to whom they were captives; and they shall rule over their oppressors.

25 And it shall come to pass in that day that the Lord shall give you rest from your sorrow, and from your fear, and from the hard bondage wherein you were made to serve.

26 And it shall come to pass in that day that you shall take up this proverb against the king of Babylon, and say, "How hath the oppressor ceased, the golden city ceased!

27 "The Lord hath broken the staff of the wicked, the scepters of the rulers.

28 "He who smote the people in wrath with a continual stroke, he that ruled the nations in anger, is persecuted, and none hindereth.

29 "The whole earth is at rest and is quiet; they break forth into singing.

30 "The fir trees rejoice at thee, and also the cedars of Lebanon, saying, 'Since thou art laid down, no feller is come up against us.'

31 "Hell from beneath is moved for thee to meet thee at thy coming; it stirreth up the dead for thee, even all the chief ones of the earth; it hath raised up from their thrones all the kings of the nations.

32 "All they shall speak and say to thee, 'Art thou also become weak as we? Art thou become like us?'

33 "Thy pomp is brought down to the grave; the noise of thy viols is not heard; the worm is spread under thee, and the worms cover thee.

34 "How art thou fallen from heaven, O Lucifer, son of the morning! How art thou cut down to the ground, which did weaken the nations!

35 "For thou hast said in thy heart, 'I will ascend into heaven; I will exalt my throne above the stars of God. I will sit also upon the mount of the congregation, in the sides of the north.

36 "'I will ascend above the heights of the clouds; I will be like the Most High.'

37 "Yet thou shalt be brought down to hell, to the sides of the pit.

38 "They that see thee shall narrowly look upon thee, and shall consider thee, and shall say, 'Is this the man that made the earth to tremble, that shook kingdoms, 39and made the world as a wilderness, and destroyed the cities thereof, and opened not the house of his prisoners?'

40 "All the kings of the nations, even all of them, lie in glory, every one of them in his own house.

41 "But thou art cast out of thy grave like an abominable branch, and the remnant of those that are

63

slain, thrust through with a sword, that go down to the stones of the pit, as a carcass trodden under feet.

42 "Thou shalt not be joined with them in burial, because thou hast destroyed thy land, and slain thy people; the seed of evildoers shall never be renowned.

43 "Prepare slaughter for his children for the iniquities of their fathers, that they do not rise, nor possess the land, nor fill the face of the world with cities."

44 "For I will rise up against them," says the Lord of hosts, "and cut off from Babylon the name, and remnant, and son, and nephew," says the Lord.

45 "I will also make it a possession for the bittern, and pools of water; and I will sweep it with the besom of destruction," says the Lord of hosts.

46 The Lord of hosts has sworn, saying "Surely as I have thought, so shall it come to pass; and as I have purposed, so shall it stand:

47 "That I will break the Assyrian in my land, and upon my mountains tread him under foot; then shall his yoke depart from off them, and his burden depart from off their shoulders."

48 This is the purpose that is purposed upon the whole earth; and this is the hand that is stretched out upon all nations.

49 For the Lord of Hosts has purposed, and who shall disannul? And his hand is stretched out, and who shall turn it back?

50 In the year that King Ahaz died was this burden:

51 "Rejoice not thou, whole Palestina, because the rod of him that smote thee is broken; for out of the serpent's root shall come forth a cockatrice, and his fruit shall be a fiery flying serpent.

52 "And the first born of the poor shall feed, and the needy shall lie down in safety; and I will kill thy root with famine, and he shall slay thy remnant.

53 "Howl, O gate; cry, O city; thou, whole Palestina, art dissolved; for there shall come from the north a smoke, and none shall be alone in his appointed times."

54 What shall one then answer the messengers of the nations? "That the Lord hath founded Zion, and the poor of his people shall trust in it."

CHAPTER 11

NOW I, Nephi, speak somewhat concerning the words which I have written, which have been spoken by the mouth of Isaiah.

2 For, behold, Isaiah spoke many things which were hard for many of my people to understand; for they know not concerning the manner of prophesying among the Jews.

3 For I, Nephi, have not taught them many things concerning the manner of the Jews; for their works were works of darkness, and their doings were doings of abomination.

4 Wherefore, I write to my people, to all those that shall receive hereafter these things which I write, that they may know the judgments of God, that they come upon all nations, according to the word which he has spoken.

5 Wherefore hearken, O my people, which are of the house of Israel, and give ear to my words; for though the words of Isaiah are not plain to you, nevertheless they are plain to all those that are filled with the spirit of prophecy.

6 But I give you a prophecy, according to the spirit which is in me; wherefore I shall prophesy according to the plainness which has been with me from the time that I came out from Jerusalem with my father:

7 For, behold, my soul delights in plainness unto my people, that they may learn; 8and my soul delights in the words of Isaiah, for I came out from Jerusalem, and my eyes have beheld the things of the Jews, and I know that the Jews understand the things of the prophets, and there are no other people that understand the things which were spoken to the Jews, save it be that they are taught after the manner of the things of the Jews.

9 But, behold, I, Nephi, have not taught my children after the manner

of the Jews; but, behold, I myself have dwelt at Jerusalem, wherefore I know concerning the regions round about.

10 I have made mention to my children concerning the judgments of God, which have come to pass among the Jews, according to all that which Isaiah has spoken, and I do not write them.

11 But, behold, I proceed with my own prophecy according to my plainness, in which I know that no man can err.

12 Nevertheless, in the days that the prophecies of Isaiah shall be fulfilled, men shall know of a surety at the times when they shall come to pass.

13 Wherefore, they are of worth to the children of men, and he that supposes that they are not, to him will I speak particularly, and confine the words to my own people.

14 For I know that they shall be of great worth to them in the latter days; for in that day shall they understand them; wherefore, for their good have I written them.

15 As one generation has been destroyed among the Jews because of iniquity, even so have they been destroyed from generation to generation, according to their iniquities; 16and never has any of them been destroyed, save it were foretold them by the prophets of the Lord.

17 Wherefore, it has been told them concerning the destruction which should come upon them immediately after my father left Jerusalem.

18 Nevertheless, they hardened their hearts; and according to my prophecy, they have been destroyed, save it be those which are carried away captive into Babylon.

19 Now this I speak because of the spirit which is in me.

20 Notwithstanding they have been carried away, they shall return again and possess the land of Jerusalem; wherefore they shall be restored again to the lands of their inheritance.

21 But, behold, they shall have wars and rumors of wars; and when the day comes that the Only Begotten of the Father, even the Father of heaven and of earth, shall mani-

fest himself to them in the flesh, behold, they will reject him, because of their iniquities, and the hardness of their hearts, and the stiffness of their necks.

22 Behold, they will crucify him, and after he is laid in a sepulcher for the space of three days, he shall rise from the dead, with healing in his wings, and all those who shall believe on his name shall be saved in the kingdom of God.

23 Wherefore, my soul delights to prophesy concerning him, for I have seen his day, and my heart magnifies his holy name.

24 Behold, it shall come to pass that after the Messiah has risen from the dead, and has manifested himself to his people, to as many as will believe on his name, behold, Jerusalem shall be destroyed again; for woe to them that fight against God and the people of his church.

25 Wherefore, the Jews shall be scattered among all nations; and also Babylon shall be destroyed; wherefore, the Jews shall be scattered by other nations.

26 After they have been scattered, and the Lord God has scourged them by other nations for the space of many generations, even down from generation to generation, until they shall be persuaded to believe in Christ, the Son of God, and the atonement, which is infinite for all mankind; 27and when that day shall come that they shall believe in Christ, and worship the Father in his name, with pure hearts, and clean hands, and look not forward any more for another Messiah, then, at that time, the day will come that it must be expedient that they should believe these things.

28 And the Lord will set his hand again the second time to restore his people from their lost and fallen state.

29 Wherefore, he will proceed to do a marvelous work and a wonder among the children of men.

30 Wherefore, he shall bring forth his words to them, which words shall judge them at the last day.

31 For they shall be given them for the purpose of convincing them of the true Messiah, who was rejected by them; 32and to the convincing of

them that they need not look forward any more for a Messiah to come.

33 For there should not any come, save it should be a false Messiah which should deceive the people; 34for there is but one Messiah spoken of by the prophets, and that Messiah is he who should be rejected of the Jews.

35 For according to the words of the prophets, the Messiah will come in six hundred years from the time that my father left Jerusalem.

36 And according to the words of the prophets, and also the word of the angel of God, his name shall be Jesus Christ, the Son of God.

37 Now my brethren, I have spoken plainly, that you cannot err.

38 As the Lord God lives that brought Israel up out of the land of Egypt, and gave Moses power that he should heal the nations after they had been bitten by the poisonous serpents, if they would cast their eyes to the serpent which he raised up before them, and also gave him power that he should smite the rock and the water should come forth; 39behold, I say to you, that as these things are true, and as the Lord God lives, there is no other name given under heaven, save it be this Jesus Christ of which I have spoken, whereby man can be saved.

40 Wherefore, for this cause has the Lord God promised me that these things which I write shall be kept and preserved, and handed down to my seed, from generation to generation, that the promise may be fulfilled to Joseph that his seed should never perish as long as the earth should stand.

41 Wherefore, these things shall go from generation to generation as long as the earth shall stand; and they shall go according to the will and pleasure of God.

42 And the nations which shall possess them shall be judged of them according to the words which are written.

43 For we labor diligently to write, to persuade our children, and also our brethren, to believe in Christ, and to be reconciled to God; 44for we know that it is by grace that we are saved, after all we can do.

45 Notwithstanding we believe in Christ, we keep the law of Moses, and look forward with steadfastness to Christ, until the law shall be fulfilled; for, for this end was the law given.

46 Wherefore, the law has become dead to us, and we are made alive in Christ, because of our faith; 47yet we keep the law because of the commandments.

48 And we talk of Christ, we rejoice in Christ, we preach of Christ, we prophesy of Christ, and we write according to our prophecies, that our children may know to what source they may look for a remission of their sins.

49 Wherefore, we speak concerning the law, that our children may know the deadness of the law.

50 And they, by knowing the deadness of the law, may look forward to that life which is in Christ, and know for what end the law was given.

51 And after the law is fulfilled in Christ, that they need not harden their hearts against him, the law ought to be done away.

52 Now, behold, my people, you are a stiff-necked people; wherefore, I have spoken plainly to you, that you cannot misunderstand.

53 The words which I have spoken shall stand as a testimony against you; for they are sufficient to teach any man the right way.

54 For the right way is to believe in Christ and deny him not; for by denying him, you also deny the prophets and the law.

55 Now, behold, I say to you that the right way is to believe in Christ, and deny him not; and Christ is the Holy One of Israel.

56 Wherefore you must bow down before him and worship him with all your might, mind, and strength, and your whole soul, and if you do this, you shall in no wise be cast out.

57 Inasmuch as it shall be expedient, you must keep the performances and ordinances of God until the law shall be fulfilled which was given to Moses.

58 And after Christ shall have risen from the dead, he shall show himself to you, my children, and my beloved brethren; 59and the words

which he shall speak to you shall be the law which you shall do.

60 For, behold, I say to you that I have beheld that many generations shall pass away, and there shall be great wars and contentions among my people.

61 And after the Messiah shall come, there shall be signs given to my people of his birth, and also of his death and resurrection.

62 Great and terrible shall that day be to the wicked; for they shall perish; 63and they perish because they cast out the prophets and the saints, and stone them, and slay them; 64wherefore the cry of the blood of the saints shall ascend up to God from the ground against them.

65 "Wherefore all those who are proud, and that do wickedly, the day that comes shall burn them up," says the Lord of hosts, "for they shall be as stubble.

66 "And they that kill the prophets, and the saints, the depths of the earth shall swallow them up," says the Lord of hosts; 67"and mountains shall cover them, and whirlwinds shall carry them away, and buildings shall fall upon them, and crush them to pieces and grind them to powder.

68 "And they shall be visited with thunderings, and lightnings, and earthquakes, and all manner of destructions; 69for the fire of the anger of the Lord shall be kindled against them, and they shall be as stubble, and the day that cometh shall consume them," says the Lord of hosts.

70 Oh, the pain, and the anguish of my soul for the loss of the slain of my people!

71 For I, Nephi, have seen it, and it well nigh consumes me before the presence of the Lord; but I must cry to my God, "Thy ways are just."

72 But, behold, the righteous that hearken to the words of the prophets, and destroy them not, but look forward to Christ with steadfastness for the signs which are given, notwithstanding all persecutions; behold, they are they which shall not perish.

73 But the Son of Righteousness shall appear to them; and he shall heal them, and they shall have peace with him, until three generations shall have passed away, and many of the fourth generation shall have passed away in righteousness.

74 When these things shall have passed away, a speedy destruction will come to my people; for, notwithstanding the pains of my soul, I have seen it; wherefore, I know that it shall come to pass.

75 They sell themselves for nought; for, for the reward of their pride, and their foolishness, they shall reap destruction.

76 For because they yield to the devil, and choose works of darkness rather than light, therefore they must go down to hell; for the Spirit of the Lord will not always strive with man.

77 When the Spirit ceases to strive with man, then comes speedy destruction; and this grieves my soul.

78 As I spoke concerning the convincing of the Jews that Jesus is the very Christ, it is necessary that the Gentiles be convinced also that Jesus is the Christ, the Eternal God; and that he manifests himself to all those who believe in him, by the power of the Holy Ghost; 79to every nation, kindred, tongue, and people, working mighty miracles, signs and wonders among the children of men, according to their faith.

80 But, behold, I prophesy to you concerning the last days; concerning the days when the Lord God shall bring these things forth to the children of men.

81 After my seed and the seed of my brethren shall have dwindled in unbelief, and shall have been smitten by the Gentiles; 82after the Lord God shall have camped against them round about, and shall have laid siege against them with a mount, and raised forts against them; 83and after they shall have been brought down low in the dust, even that they are not, yet the words of the righteous shall be written, and the prayers of the faithful shall be heard, and all those who have dwindled in unbelief shall not be forgotten.

84 For those who shall be destroyed shall speak to them out of the ground, and their speech shall be low out of the dust, and their voice shall be as one that has a familiar spirit; 85for the Lord God will give him power that he may whisper concern-

ing them, even as it were out of the ground; and their speech shall whisper out of the dust.

86 For thus says the Lord God: "They shall write the things which shall be done among them, and they shall be written and sealed up in a book, and those who have dwindled in unbelief shall not have them, for they seek to destroy the things of God.

87 "Wherefore, those who have been destroyed, have been destroyed speedily; and the multitude of their terrible ones shall be as chaff that passes away."

88 Thus says the Lord God: "It shall be at an instant, suddenly."

89 And it shall come to pass that those who have dwindled in unbelief shall be smitten by the hand of the Gentiles.

90 And the Gentiles are lifted up in the pride of their eyes, and have stumbled because of the greatness of their stumbling block, that they have built up many churches.

91 Nevertheless they put down the power and the miracles of God, and preach to themselves their own wisdom, and their own learning, that they may get gain and grind upon the face of the poor.

92 And there are many churches built up which cause envyings, and strifes, and malice.

93 There are also secret combinations, even as in times of old, according to the combinations of the devil, for he is the foundation of all these things; the foundation of murder and works of darkness.

94 And he leads them by the neck with a flaxen cord, until he binds them with his strong cords forever.

95 For, behold, my beloved brethren, I say to you that the Lord God works not in darkness.

96 He does not anything except it be for the benefit of the world; for he loves the world, even that he lays down his own life that he may draw all men to him.

97 Wherefore, he commands none that they shall not partake of his salvation.

98 Behold, does he cry to any, saying, "Depart from me"?

99 Behold, I say to you, No; but he says, "Come to me all ye ends of the earth; buy milk and honey, without money and without price."

100 Behold, has he commanded any that they should depart out of the synagogues, or out of the houses of worship?

101 Behold, I say to you, No.

102 Has he commanded any that they should not partake of his salvation?

103 Behold, I say to you, No; but he has given it free for all men; and he has commanded his people that they should persuade all men to repentance.

104 Behold, has the Lord commanded any that they should not partake of his goodness?

105 Behold, I say to you, No; but all men are privileged the one like the other, and none are forbidden.

106 He commands that there shall be no priestcrafts; for, behold, priestcrafts are that men preach and set themselves up for a light to the world that they may get gain and praise of the world; but they seek not the welfare of Zion.

107 Behold, the Lord has forbidden this thing; wherefore, the Lord God has given a commandment that all men should have charity, which charity is love.

108 And except they should have charity, they were nothing; wherefore, if they should have charity, they would not suffer the laborer in Zion to perish.

109 But the laborers in Zion shall labor for Zion; for if they labor for money, they shall perish.

110 And again, the Lord God has commanded that men should not murder, that they should not lie, that they should not steal, that they should not take the name of the Lord their God in vain, that they should not envy, that they should not have malice, that they should not contend one with another, that they should not commit whoredoms, and that they should do none of these things.

111 For whoever does them shall perish. For none of these iniquities come of the Lord; for he does that which is good among the children of men; 112and he does nothing save it be plain to the children of men.

113 And he invites them all to come to him and partake of his goodness; [114]and he denies none that come to him, black and white, bond and free, male and female; [115]and he remembers the heathen, and all are alike to God, both Jew and Gentile.

116 But, behold, in the last days, or in the days of the Gentiles, all the nations of the Gentiles, and also the Jews, both those who shall come upon this land and those who shall be upon other lands, even upon all the lands of the earth; behold, they will be drunken with iniquity and all manner of abominations.

117* And when that day shall come, they shall be visited of the Lord of hosts with thunder, and with earthquake, and with a great noise, and with storm, and with tempest, and with the flame of devouring fire.

118 And all the nations that fight against Zion, and that distress her, shall be as a dream of a night vision.

119 It shall be to them even as to a hungry man, who dreams and, behold, he eats, but he awakes and his soul is empty; [120]or like a thirsty man who dreams, and, behold he drinks, but he awakes and, behold, he is faint and his soul has appetite.

121 Even so shall the multitude of all the nations be that fight against mount Zion.

122 For, behold, all you that do iniquity, stay yourselves and wonder; for you shall cry out, and cry; you shall be drunken, but not with wine; you shall stagger, but not with strong drink; [123]for, behold, the Lord has poured out upon you the spirit of deep sleep.

124 For, behold, you have closed your eyes, and you have rejected the prophets and your rulers, and the seers has he covered because of your iniquity.

125 And it shall come to pass that the Lord God shall bring forth to you the words of a book, and they shall be the words of them which have slumbered.

126 And, behold, the book shall be sealed; and in the book shall be

a revelation from God, from the beginning of the world to the ending thereof.

127 Wherefore, because of the things which are sealed up, the things which are sealed shall not be delivered in the day of the wickedness and abominations of the people.

128 Wherefore the book shall be kept from them.

129 But the book shall be delivered to a man, and he shall deliver the words of the book, which are the words of those who have slumbered in the dust; and he shall deliver these words to another; but the words which are sealed he shall not deliver, neither shall he deliver the book.

130 For the book shall be sealed by the power of God, and the revelation which was sealed shall be kept in the book until the own due time of the Lord, that they may come forth; for, behold, they reveal all things from the foundation of the world to the end thereof.

131 And the day will come that the words of the book which were sealed shall be read upon the housetops; and they shall be read by the power of Christ.

132 And all things shall be revealed to the children of men which ever have been among the children of men, and which ever will be, even to the end of the earth.

133 Wherefore, at that day when the book shall be delivered to the man of whom I have spoken, the book shall be hidden from the eyes of the world, that the eyes of none shall behold it, save it be that three witnesses shall behold it by the power of God, besides him to whom the book shall be delivered; and they shall testify to the truth of the book and the things therein.

134 And there is no other which shall view it, save it be a few, according to the will of God, to bear testimony of his word to the children of men; for the Lord God has said that the words of the faithful should speak as if it were from the dead.

135 Wherefore, the Lord God will proceed to bring forth the

*Isaiah 29:6–32

words of the book; and in the mouth of as many witnesses as seem to him good will he establish his word; and woe be to him that rejects the word of God.

136 But, behold, it shall come to pass that the Lord God shall say to him to whom he shall deliver the book, "Take these words which are not sealed, and deliver them to another, that he may show them to the learned, saying, 'Read this, I pray thee.'"

137 And the learned shall say, "Bring the book, and I will read it."

138 And now because of the glory of the world and to get gain will they say this, and not for the glory of God.

139 And the man shall say, "I cannot bring the book, for it is sealed."

140 Then shall the learned say, "I cannot read it."

141 Wherefore it shall come to pass that the Lord God will deliver again the book and the words thereof to him that is not learned; and the man that is not learned shall say, "I am not learned."

142 Then shall the Lord God say to him, "The learned shall not read them, for they have rejected them, and I am able to do my own work; wherefore, thou shalt read the words which I shall give thee.

143 "Touch not the things which are sealed, for I will bring them forth in my own due time; for I will show the children of men that I am able to do my own work.

144 "Wherefore, when thou hast read the words which I have commanded thee, and obtained the witnesses which I have promised thee, then shalt thou seal up the book again, and hide it up to me that I may preserve the words which thou hast not read until I shall see fit in my own wisdom to reveal all things to the children of men.

145 "For, behold, I am God; and I am a God of miracles; and I will show the world that I am the same yesterday, today, and forever; and I work not among the children of men save it be according to their faith."

146 And again it shall come to pass that the Lord shall say to him that shall read the words that shall be delivered him, "Forasmuch as this people draw near me with their mouth, and with their lips do honor me, but have removed their hearts far from me, and their fear toward me is taught by the precepts of men, therefore I will proceed to do a marvelous work among this people; [147]even a marvelous work, and a wonder, for the wisdom of their wise and learned shall perish, and the understanding of their prudent shall be hid.

148 "And woe to them that seek deep to hide their counsel from the Lord.

149 "And their works are in the dark; and they say, 'Who sees us; and who knows us?'

150 "And they also say, 'Surely, your turning of things upside down shall be esteemed as the potter's clay.'

151 "But, behold, I will show them," says the Lord of hosts, "that I know all their works.

152 "For shall the work say of him that made it, 'He made me not'?

153 "Or shall the thing framed say of him that framed it, 'He had no understanding'?

154 "But, behold," says the Lord of hosts, "I will show the children of men that it is yet a very little while and Lebanon shall be turned into a fruitful field; and the fruitful field shall be esteemed as a forest.

155 "And in that day shall the deaf hear the words of the book, and the eyes of the blind shall see out of obscurity and out of darkness.

156 "And the meek also shall increase, and their joy shall be in the Lord; and the poor among men shall rejoice in the Holy One of Israel.

157 "For assuredly as the Lord liveth, they shall see that the terrible one is brought to nought, and the scorner is consumed, and all that watch for iniquity are cut off, and they that make a man an offender for a word, and lay a snare

for him that reproveth in the gate, and turn aside the just for a thing of nought.

158 "Therefore," thus says the Lord who redeemed Abraham, concerning the house of Jacob, "Jacob shall not now be ashamed, neither shall his face now wax pale.

159 "But when he sees his children, the work of my hands, in the midst of him, they shall sanctify my name, and sanctify the Holy One of Jacob, and shall fear the God of Israel.

160 "They also that erred in spirit shall come to understanding, and they that murmured shall learn doctrine."

CHAPTER 12

NOW, behold, my brethren, I have spoken to you according as the Spirit has constrained me; wherefore, I know that they must surely come to pass.

2 And the things which shall be written out of the book shall be of great worth to the children of men, and especially to our seed which is a remnant of the house of Israel.

3 For it shall come to pass in that day that the churches, which are built up and not to the Lord, shall say one to another, "Behold, I, I am the Lord's," and the other shall say, "I, I am the Lord's."

4 Thus shall everyone say that has built up churches, and not to the Lord.

5 They shall contend one with another; and their priests shall contend one with another; and they shall teach with their learning, and deny the Holy Ghost which gives utterance.

6 And they deny the power of God, the Holy One of Israel; and they say to the people, "Hearken to us, and hear our precept; 7for, behold, there is no God today, for the Lord, the Redeemer, has done his work, and he has given his power to men.

8 "Behold, hearken to my precept; if any shall say there is a miracle wrought by the hand of the Lord, believe it not; for this day he is not a God of miracles; he has done his work."

9 And there shall be many who shall say, "Eat, drink, and be merry, for tomorrow we die; and it shall be well with us."

10 And there shall also be many who shall say, "Eat, drink, and be merry; nevertheless, fear God, he will justify in committing a little sin; lie a little, take the advantage of one because of his words, dig a pit for your neighbor; there is no harm in this.

11 "And do all these things, for tomorrow we die; and if it so be that we are guilty, God will beat us with a few stripes, and at last we shall be saved in the kingdom of God."

12 And there shall be many who shall teach after this manner false, and vain, and foolish doctrines, and shall be puffed up in their hearts, and shall seek deep to hide their counsels from the Lord; and their works shall be in the dark; and the blood of the saints shall cry from the ground against them.

13 They have all gone out of the way; they have become corrupted.

14 Because of pride, and because of false teachers and false doctrine, their churches have become corrupted, and their churches are lifted up; because of pride they are puffed up.

15 They rob the poor because of their fine sanctuaries; they rob the poor because of their fine clothing; and they persecute the meek and the poor in heart, because in their pride they are puffed up.

16 They wear stiff necks and high heads; and because of pride, and wickedness, and abominations, and whoredoms, they have all gone astray, save it be a few who are the humble followers of Christ.

17 Nevertheless, they are led that in many instances they err, because they are taught by the precepts of men.

18 O the wise, and the learned, and the rich, that are puffed up in the pride of their hearts, and all those who preach false doctrines, and all those who commit whoredoms, and pervert the right way of the Lord; "Woe, woe, woe be to them," says the Lord God Almighty, "for they shall be thrust down to hell."

19 Woe to them that turn aside

the just for a thing of nought, and revile against that which is good, and say that it is of no worth; ²⁰for the day shall come that the Lord God will speedily visit the inhabitants of the earth; and in that day that they are fully ripe in iniquity, they shall perish.

21 "But, behold, if the inhabitants of the earth shall repent of their wickedness and abominations, they shall not be destroyed," says the Lord of hosts.

22 But, behold, that great and abominable church, the whore of all the earth, must tumble to the earth; and great must be the fall thereof.

23 For the kingdom of the devil must shake, and they which belong to it must be stirred up to repentance, or the devil will grasp them with his everlasting chains, and they will be stirred up to anger and perish.

24 For, behold, at that day shall he rage in the hearts of the children of men, and stir them up to anger against that which is good; ²⁵and others will he pacify, and lull them away into carnal security, that they will say, "All is well in Zion; Zion prospers, all is well."

26 Thus the devil cheats their souls, and leads them away carefully down to hell.

27 Behold, others he flatters away, and tells them there is no hell; and he says to them, "I am no devil, for there is none."

28 Thus he whispers in their ears, until he grasps them with his awful chains, from which there is no deliverance.

29 They are grasped with death and hell; and death, and hell, and the devil, and all that have been seized therewith must stand before the throne of God and be judged according to their works, whence they must go into the place prepared for them, even a lake of fire and brimstone, which is endless torment.

30 Therefore, woe be to him that is at ease in Zion.

31 Woe be to him that cries, "All is well"; woe be to him that hearkens to the precepts of men, and denies the power of God and the gift of the Holy Ghost.

32 Woe be to him that says, "We have received, and we need no more."

33 In fine, woe to all those who tremble and are angry because of the truth of God.

34 For, behold, he that is built upon the rock receives it with gladness; and he that is built upon a sandy foundation trembles lest he shall fall.

35 Woe be to him that shall say, "We have received the word of God, and we need no more of the word of God, for we have enough."

36 For, behold, thus says the Lord God: "I will give to the children of men line upon line, precept upon precept, here a little and there a little; ³⁷and blessed are those who hearken to my precepts and lend an ear to my counsel, for they shall learn wisdom.

38 "For to him that receives, I will give more; and from them that shall say, 'We have enough,' shall be taken away even that which they have.

39 "Cursed is he that puts his trust in man, or makes flesh his arm, or shall hearken to the precepts of men, save their precepts shall be given by the power of the Holy Ghost.

40 "Woe be to the Gentiles," says the Lord God of hosts; "for notwithstanding I shall lengthen out my arm to them from day to day, they will deny me.

41 "Nevertheless, I will be merciful to them," says the Lord God, "if they will repent and come to me; for my arm is lengthened out all the day long," says the Lord God of hosts.

42 "But, behold, there shall be many at that day when I shall proceed to do a marvelous work among them that I may remember my covenants which I have made to the children of men, that I may set my hand again the second time to recover my people which are of the house of Israel, ⁴³and also that I may remember the promises which I have made to you, Nephi, and also to your father, that I would remember your seed, and that the words of your seed should proceed forth out of my mouth to your seed.

44 "My words shall hiss forth to the ends of the earth for a standard to my people who are of the house of Israel.

45 "And because my words shall hiss forth, many of the Gentiles shall say, 'A bible, a bible, we have got a

bible, and there cannot be any more bible.'"

46 But thus says the Lord God: "O fools, they shall have a bible; and it shall proceed forth from the Jews, my ancient covenant people.

47 "And what thank they the Jews for the bible which they received from them?

48 "What do the Gentiles mean?

49 "Do they remember the travels, and the labors, and the pains of the Jews, and their diligence to me, in bringing forth salvation to the Gentiles?

50 "O ye Gentiles, have ye remembered the Jews, my ancient covenant people?

51 "No; but ye have cursed them, and have hated them, and have not sought to recover them.

52 "But, behold, I will return all these things upon your own heads; for I, the Lord, have not forgotten my people.

53 "Thou fool, that shall say, 'A bible, we have got a bible, and we need no more bible.'

54 "Have ye obtained a bible, save it were by the Jews?

55 "Know ye not that there are more nations than one?

56 "Know ye not that I, the Lord your God, have created all men, and that I remember those who are upon the isles of the sea; and that I rule in the heavens above, and in the earth beneath; 57and I bring forth my word to the children of men, even upon all the nations of the earth?

58 "Wherefore murmur ye, because that ye shall receive more of my word?

59 "Know ye not that the testimony of two nations is a witness to you that I am God, that I remember one nation like another?

60 "Wherefore, I speak the same words to one nation as to another.

61 "And when the two nations shall run together, the testimony of the two nations shall run together also.

62 "I do this that I may prove to many that I am the same yesterday, today, and forever; and that I speak forth my words according to my own pleasure.

63 "And because I have spoken one word, ye need not suppose that I cannot speak another; for my work is not yet finished; neither shall it be until the end of man; neither from that time henceforth and forever.

64 "Wherefore, because ye have a bible, ye need not suppose that it contains all my words; neither need ye suppose that I have not caused more to be written.

65 "For I command all men, both in the east, and in the west, and in the north, and in the south, and in the islands of the sea, that they shall write the words which I speak to them.

66 "For out of the books which shall be written, I will judge the world, every man according to his works, according to that which is written.

67 "For, behold, I shall speak to the Jews, and they shall write it; 68and I shall also speak to the Nephites, and they shall write it.

69 "I shall also speak to the other tribes of the house of Israel, which I have led away, and they shall write it; 70and I shall also speak to all nations of the earth, and they shall write it.

71 "And it shall come to pass that the Jews shall have the words of the Nephites, and the Nephites shall have the words of the Jews.

72 "And the Nephites and the Jews shall have the words of the lost tribes of Israel; and the lost tribes of Israel shall have the words of the Nephites and the Jews.

73 "And it shall come to pass that my people which are of the house of Israel shall be gathered home to the lands of their possessions; and my word also shall be gathered in one.

74 "And I will show those who fight against my word and against my people, who are of the house of Israel, that I am God, and that I covenanted with Abraham that I would remember his seed forever."

75 Now, behold, my beloved brethren, I would speak to you: for I, Nephi, would not suffer that you should suppose that you are more righteous than the Gentiles shall be.

76 For, behold, except you shall keep the commandments of God you shall all likewise perish; and because of the words which have been spoken,

you need not suppose that the Gentiles are utterly destroyed.

77 For, behold, I say to you that as many of the Gentiles as will repent are the covenant people of the Lord; and as many of the Jews as will not repent shall be cast off.

78 For the Lord covenants with none, save it be with them that repent and believe in his Son, who is the Holy One of Israel.

79 Now I would prophesy somewhat more concerning the Jews and the Gentiles.

80 For after the book of which I have spoken shall come forth, and be written to the Gentiles, and sealed up again to the Lord, there shall be many which shall believe the words which are written; and they shall carry them forth to the remnant of our seed.

81 Then shall the remnant of our seed know concerning us, how that we came out from Jerusalem, and that they are descendants of the Jews.

82 And the gospel of Jesus Christ shall be declared among them; wherefore, they shall be restored to the knowledge of their fathers, and also to the knowledge of Jesus Christ, which was had among their fathers.

83 Then shall they rejoice; for they shall know that it is a blessing to them from the hand of God.

84 And their scales of darkness shall begin to fall from their eyes; and many generations shall not pass away among them, save they shall be a white and a delightsome people.

85 And it shall come to pass that the Jews which are scattered also shall begin to believe in Christ, and they shall begin to gather in upon the face of the land; 86and as many as shall believe in Christ shall also become a delightsome people.

87 And it shall come to pass that the Lord God shall commence his work among all nations, kindreds, tongues, and people, to bring about the restoration of his people upon the earth.

88 With righteousness shall the Lord God judge the poor, and reprove with equity for the meek of the earth.

89 He shall smite the earth with the rod of his mouth; and with the breath of his lips shall he slay the wicked; 90for the time will speedily come that the Lord God shall cause a great division among the people; and the wicked will he destroy; and he will spare his people, even if it so be that he must destroy the wicked by fire.

91 And righteousness shall be the girdle of his loins, and faithfulness the girdle of his reins.

92 Then shall the wolf dwell with the lamb, and the leopard shall lie down with the kid, and the calf and the young lion and the fatling together; and a little child shall lead them.

93 And the cow and the bear shall feed; their young ones shall lie down together; and the lion shall eat straw like the ox.

94 The sucking child shall play on the hole of the asp, and the weaned child shall put his hand on the cockatrice's den.

95 They shall not hurt nor destroy in all my holy mountain; for the earth shall be full of the knowledge of the Lord, as the waters cover the sea.

96 Wherefore, the things of all nations shall be made known; even all things shall be made known to the children of men.

97 There is nothing which is secret save it shall be revealed; there is no work of darkness save it shall be made manifest in the light; and there is nothing which is sealed upon the earth save it shall be loosed.

98 Wherefore, all things which have been revealed to the children of men shall at that day be revealed; 99and Satan shall have power over the hearts of the children of men no more, for a long time.

100 Now, my beloved brethren, I must make an end of my sayings.

CHAPTER 13

NOW I, Nephi, make an end of my prophesying to you, my beloved brethren.

2 I can write but a few things which I know must surely come to pass; and I can write but a few of the words of my brother Jacob.

3 Wherefore, the things which I have written suffice me, save it be a

few words which I must speak concerning the doctrine of Christ; wherefore I shall speak to you plainly, according to the plainness of my prophesying.

4 For my soul delights in plainness; for after this manner does the Lord God work among the children of men.

5 For the Lord God gives light to the understanding; for he speaks to men according to their language, to their understanding.

6 Wherefore, I would that you should remember that I have spoken to you concerning that prophet which the Lord showed me that should baptize the Lamb of God which should take away the sin of the world.

7 Now if the Lamb of God, he being holy, should have need to be baptized by water to fulfill all righteousness, oh, then, how much more need have we, being unholy, to be baptized, even by water.

8 And now I would ask of you, my beloved brethren, wherein the Lamb of God fulfilled all righteousness in being baptized by water? Know you not that he was holy?

9 But notwithstanding being holy, he shows the children of men that according to the flesh he humbled himself before the Father, and witnessed to the Father that he would be obedient to him in keeping his commandments.

10 Wherefore, after he was baptized with water, the Holy Ghost descended upon him in the form of a dove.

11 And again: He showed to the children of men the straitness of the path, and the narrowness of the gate by which they should enter, he having set the example before them.

12 And he said to the children of men, "Follow thou me."

13 Wherefore, my beloved brethren, can we follow Jesus, save we shall be willing to keep the commandments of the Father?

14 The Father said, "Repent ye, repent ye, and be baptized in the name of my beloved Son."

15 Also, the voice of the Son came to me, saying, "He that is baptized in my name, to him will the Father give the Holy Ghost, like to me; where-

fore, follow me and do the things which ye have seen me do."

16 Wherefore, my beloved brethren, I know that if you shall follow the Son with full purpose of heart, acting no hypocrisy and no deception before God, but with real intent, repenting of your sins, witnessing to the Father that you are willing to take upon you the name of Christ by baptism, by following your Lord and your Savior down into the water, according to his word, behold, then shall you receive the Holy Ghost.

17 Then comes the baptism of fire and of the Holy Ghost; and then can you speak with the tongue of angels and shout praises to the Holy One of Israel.

18 But, behold, my beloved brethren, thus came the voice of the Son to me, saying, "After ye have repented of your sins, and witnessed to the Father that ye are willing to keep my commandments, by the baptism of water, and have received the baptism of fire and of the Holy Ghost, and can speak with a new tongue, even with the tongue of angels, and after this, should deny me, it would have been better for you that ye had not known me."

19 And I heard a voice from the Father, saying, "The words of my beloved are true and faithful.

20 "He that endureth to the end, the same shall be saved."

21 Now, my beloved brethren, I know by this that unless a man shall endure to the end in following the example of the Son of the living God, he cannot be saved.

22 Wherefore, do the things which I have told you I have seen that your Lord and your Redeemer should do; 23for, for this cause have they been shown to me, that you might know the gate by which you should enter.

24 For the gate by which you should enter is repentance and baptism by water; and then comes a remission of your sins by fire and by the Holy Ghost.

25 Then are you in this strait and narrow path which leads to eternal life; you have entered in by the gate; you have done according to the commandments of the Father and the Son; 26and you have received the Holy

Ghost which witnesses of the Father and the Son, to the fulfilling of the promise which he has made that if you enter in by the way, you shall receive.

27 Now, my beloved brethren, after you have gotten into this strait and narrow path, I would ask if all is done?

28 Behold, I say to you, No; for you have not come thus far save it were by the word of Christ, with unshaken faith in him, relying wholly upon the merits of him who is mighty to save.

29 Wherefore, you must press forward with a steadfastness in Christ, having a perfect brightness of hope, and a love of God and of all men.

30 Wherefore, if you shall press forward, feasting upon the word of Christ, and endure to the end, behold, thus says the Father: "Ye shall have eternal life."

31 Now, behold, my beloved brethren, this is the way; and there is no other way nor name given under heaven whereby man can be saved in the kingdom of God.

32 Behold, this is the doctrine of Christ, and the only and true doctrine of the Father, and of the Son, and of the Holy Ghost, which is one God, without end. Amen.

CHAPTER 14

NOW, behold, my beloved brethren, I suppose that you ponder somewhat in your hearts concerning what you should do after you have entered in by the way.

2 But, behold, why do you ponder these things in your hearts? Do you not remember that I said to you that after you had received the Holy Ghost you could speak with the tongue of angels?

3 Now, how could you speak with the tongue of angels save it were by the Holy Ghost? Angels speak by the power of the Holy Ghost; wherefore, they speak the words of Christ.

4 Wherefore, I said to you, "Feast upon the words of Christ; for, behold, the words of Christ will tell you all things that you should do."

5 Wherefore, now after I have spoken these words, if you cannot

understand them, it will be because you ask not, neither do you knock; wherefore, you are not brought into the light, but must perish in the dark.

6 For, behold, again I say to you that if you will enter in by the way and receive the Holy Ghost, it will show you all things that you should do.

7 Behold, this is the doctrine of Christ; and there will be no more doctrine given until after he shall manifest himself to you in the flesh.

8 And when he shall manifest himself to you in the flesh, the things which he shall say to you shall you observe to do.

9 Now I, Nephi, cannot say more; the Spirit stops my utterance, and I am left to mourn because of the unbelief, and the wickedness, and the ignorance, and the stiffneckedness of men; for they will not search knowledge, nor understand great knowledge when it is given to them in plainness, even as plain as word can be.

10 My beloved brethren, I perceive that you ponder still in your hearts; and it grieves me that I must speak concerning this thing.

11 For if you would hearken to the Spirit which teaches a man to pray, you would know that you must pray; for the evil spirit teaches not a man to pray, but teaches him that he must not pray.

12 But, behold, I say to you that you must pray always, and not faint; that you must not perform anything to the Lord, save in the first place you shall pray to the Father in the name of Christ that he will consecrate your performance to you, that your performance may be for the welfare of your soul.

CHAPTER 15

NOW I, Nephi, cannot write all the things which were taught among my people; neither am I mighty in writing, as in speaking; for when a man speaks by the power of the Holy Ghost, the power of the Holy Ghost carries it to the hearts of the children of men.

2 But, behold, there are many that harden their hearts against the Holy Spirit, that it has no place in them;

wherefore, they cast many things away which are written, and esteem them as things of nought.

3 But I, Nephi, have written what I have written; and I esteem it as of great worth, and especially to my people.

4 For I pray continually for them by day, and my eyes water my pillow by night because of them; I cry to my God in faith, and I know that he will hear my cry;, and I know that the Lord God will consecrate my prayers for the gain of my people.

5 The words which I have written in weakness will he make strong to them; for it persuades them to do good; it makes known to them of their fathers; and it speaks of Jesus, and persuades them to believe in him, and to endure to the end, which is life eternal.

6 And it speaks harsh against sin according to the plainness of the truth; wherefore, no man will be angry at the words which I have written, save he shall be of the spirit of the devil.

7 I glory in plainness; I glory in truth; I glory in my Jesus, for he has redeemed my soul from hell.

8 I have charity for my people, and great faith in Christ that I shall meet many souls spotless at his judgment seat.

9 I have charity for the Jew: I say Jew, because I mean them whence I came. I also have charity for the Gentiles.

10 But, behold, for none of these can I hope, except they shall be reconciled to Christ, and enter into the narrow gate, and walk in the strait path which leads to life, and continue in the path until the end of the day of probation.

11 Now, my beloved brethren, and also Jew, and all you ends of the earth, hearken to these words, and believe in Christ; and if you believe not in these words, believe in Christ.

12 If you shall believe in Christ, you will believe in these words; for they are the words of Christ, and he has given them to me; and they teach all men that they should do good.

13 And if they are not the words of Christ, judge you; for Christ will show you, with power and great glory, that they are his words, at the last day.

14 You and I shall stand face to face before his bar; and you shall know that I have been commanded of him to write these things, notwithstanding my weakness.

15 I pray the Father in the name of Christ that many of us, if not all, may be saved in his kingdom at that great and last day.

16 Now, my beloved brethren, all those who are of the house of Israel, and all you ends of the earth, I speak to you, as the voice of one crying from the dust: Farewell until that great day shall come.

17 And you that will not partake of the goodness of God, and respect the words of the Jews, and also my words, and the words which shall proceed forth out of the mouth of the Lamb of God, behold, I bid you an everlasting farewell, for these words shall condemn you at the last day.

18 For what I seal on earth shall be brought against you at the judgment bar; for thus has the Lord commanded me, and I must obey. Amen.

THE BOOK OF JACOB

THE BROTHER OF NEPHI

CHAPTER 1

The words of his preaching to his brethren. He confounds a man who seeks to overthrow the doctrine of Christ. A few words concerning the history of the people of Nephi.

FOR, behold, it came to pass that fifty-five years had passed away from the time that Lehi left Jerusalem; wherefore, Nephi gave me, Jacob, a commandment concerning these small plates upon which these things are engraved.

2 And he gave me, Jacob, a commandment that I should write upon these plates a few of the things which I considered to be most precious; that I should not touch, save it were lightly, concerning the history of this people which are called the people of Nephi.

3 For he said that the history of his people should be engraved upon his other plates, and that I should preserve these plates and hand them down to my seed, from generation to generation; 4and if there were preaching which was sacred, or revelation which was great, or prophesying, I should engrave the heads of them upon these plates, and touch upon them as much as it were possible, for Christ's sake, and for the sake of our people.

5 For because of faith and great anxiety, it truly had been made manifest to us concerning our people, what things should happen to them.

6 We also had many revelations, and the spirit of much prophecy; wherefore, we knew of Christ and his kingdom which should come.

7 Wherefore, we labored diligently among our people, that we might persuade them to come to Christ and partake of the goodness of God, that they might enter into his rest, lest by any means he should swear in his wrath they should not enter in, as in the provocation in the days of temp-

tation while the children of Israel were in the wilderness.

8 Wherefore, we would to God that we could persuade all men not to rebel against God, to provoke him to anger, but that all men would believe in Christ, and view his death, and suffer his cross, and bear the shame of the world; wherefore, I, Jacob, take it upon me to fulfill the commandment of my brother Nephi.

9 Now Nephi began to be old, and he saw that he must soon die; wherefore, he anointed a man to be a king and a ruler over his people now, according to the reigns of the kings.

10 The people having loved Nephi exceedingly, he having been a great protector for them, having wielded the sword of Laban in their defense, and having labored in all his days for their welfare; wherefore, the people were desirous to retain in remembrance his name.

11 And those who should reign in his stead were called by the people, second Nephi, third Nephi, and so forth, according to the reigns of the kings; and thus they were called by the people, let them be of whatever name they would.

12 And it came to pass that Nephi died.

13 Now the people which were not Lamanites were Nephites; nevertheless, they were called Nephites, Jacobites, Josephites, Zoramites, Lamanites, Lemuelites, and Ishmaelites.

14 But I, Jacob, shall not hereafter distinguish them by these names, but I shall call them Lamanites that seek to destroy the people of Nephi; and those who are friendly to Nephi I

shall call Nephites, or the people of Nephi, according to the reigns of the kings.

15 Now it came to pass that the people of Nephi, under the reign of the second king, began to grow hard in their hearts, and indulge themselves somewhat in wicked practices, such as like David of old, and also Solomon, his son, desiring many wives and concubines.

16 And they also began to search for much gold and silver, and began to be lifted up somewhat in pride.

17 Wherefore, I, Jacob, gave them these words as I taught them in the temple, having first obtained my errand from the Lord.

18 For I, Jacob, and my brother Joseph had been consecrated priests and teachers of this people by the hand of Nephi.

19 We magnified our office to the Lord, taking upon us the responsibility, answering the sins of the people upon our own heads, if we did not teach them the word of God with all diligence; 20wherefore, by laboring with our mights, their blood might not come upon our garments; otherwise, their blood would come upon our garments, and we would not be found spotless at the last day.

CHAPTER 2

THE words which Jacob, the brother of Nephi, spoke to the people of Nephi, after the death of Nephi:

2 "Now, my beloved brethren, I, Jacob, according to the responsibility which I am under to God to magnify my office with soberness, and that I might rid my garments of your sins, I come up into the temple this day that I might declare to you the word of God.

3 "You yourselves know that I have hitherto been diligent in the office of my calling; but I this day am weighed down with much more desire and anxiety for the welfare of your souls than I have hitherto been.

4 "For, behold, as yet, you have been obedient to the word of the Lord, which I have given to you.

5 "But, behold, hearken to me, and know that by the help of the all-powerful Creator of heaven and earth, I can tell you concerning your thoughts, how that you are beginning to labor in sin, which sin appears very abominable to me, and abominable to God.

6 "It grieves my soul and causes me to shrink with shame before the presence of my Maker that I must testify to you concerning the wickedness of your hearts.

7 "Also, it grieves me that I must use so much boldness of speech concerning you before your wives and your children, many of whose feelings are exceedingly tender and chaste and delicate before God, which thing is pleasing to God.

8 "I suppose that they have come up here to hear the pleasing word of God, even the word which heals the wounded soul.

9 "Wherefore, it burdens my soul that I should be constrained because of the strict commandment which I have received from God, to admonish you, according to your crimes, to enlarge the wounds of those which are already wounded, instead of consoling and healing their wounds; 10and those which have not been wounded, instead of feasting upon the pleasing word of God, have daggers placed to pierce their souls and wound their delicate minds.

11 "But, notwithstanding the greatness of the task, I must do according to the strict commands of God, and tell you concerning your wickedness and abominations, in the presence of the pure in heart, and the broken heart, and under the glance of the piercing eye of the Almighty God.

12 "Wherefore, I must tell you the truth, according to the plainness of the word of God.

13 "For, behold, as I inquired of the Lord, thus came the word to me, saying, 'Jacob, get thou up into the temple on the morrow, and declare the word which I shall give thee, to this people.'

14 "Now, behold, my brethren, this is the word which I declare to you: that many of you have begun to search for gold, and for silver, and all manner of precious ores, in which this land, which is a land of promise

to you and to your seed, abounds most plentifully.

15 "The hand of providence has smiled upon you most pleasingly, that you have obtained many riches.

16 "And because some of you have obtained more abundantly than your brethren, you are lifted up in the pride of your hearts, and wear stiff necks, and high heads, because of the costliness of your apparel, and persecute your brethren, because you suppose that you are better than they.

17 "Now, my brethren, do you suppose that God justifies you in this thing? Behold, I say to you, No.

18 "But he condemns you, and if you persist in these things, his judgments must speedily come to you.

19 "Oh, that he would show you that he can pierce you, and with one glance of his eye he can smite you to the dust.

20 "Oh, that he would rid you from this iniquity and abomination.

21 "And, oh, that you would listen to the word of his commands, and let not this pride of your hearts destroy your souls.

22 "Think of your brethren as being like yourselves, and be familiar with all, and free with your substance, that they may be rich like you.

23 "But before you seek for riches, seek for the kingdom of God.

24 "And after you have obtained a hope in Christ, you shall obtain riches, if you seek them; and you will seek them, for the intent to do good, to clothe the naked, and to feed the hungry, and to liberate the captive, and administer relief to the sick and the afflicted.

25 "Now, my brethren, I have spoken to you concerning pride; and those of you which have afflicted your neighbor, and persecuted him because you were proud in your hearts of the things which God has given you, what say you of it?

26 "Do you not suppose that such things are abominable to him, who created all flesh?

27 "One being is as precious in his sight as the other.

28 "And all flesh is of the dust; and for the selfsame end has he created them, that they should keep his commandments, and glorify him forever.

29 "Now I make an end of speaking to you concerning this pride.

30 "And were it not that I must speak to you concerning a grosser crime, my heart would rejoice exceedingly because of you.

31 "But the word of God burdens me because of your grosser crimes.

32 "For, behold, thus says the Lord, 'This people begin to wax in iniquity; they understand not any man the scriptures; for they seek to excuse themselves in committing whoredoms because of the things which were written concerning David and Solomon his son.

33 "'Behold, David and Solomon truly had many wives and concubines, which thing was abominable before me,' says the Lord.

34 "'Wherefore,' thus says the Lord, 'I have led this people forth out of the land of Jerusalem by the power of my arm, that I might raise up to me a righteous branch from the fruit of the loins of Joseph.

35 "'Wherefore, I, the Lord God, will not suffer that this people shall do like them of old.'

36 "Wherefore, my brethren, hear me, and hearken to the word of the Lord: 'For there shall not any man among you have, save it be one wife; and concubines he shall have none; for I, the Lord God, delighteth in the chastity of women.

37 "'Whoredoms are an abomination before me,' thus says the Lord of hosts.

38 "'Wherefore, this people shall keep my commandments,' says the Lord of hosts, 'or cursed be the land for their sakes.

39 "'For if I will,' says the Lord of hosts, 'raise up seed to me, I will command my people; otherwise, they shall hearken to these things.

40 "'For, behold, I, the Lord, have seen the sorrow, and heard the mourning of the daughters of my people in the land of Jerusalem, and in all the lands of my people, because of the wickedness and abominations of their husbands.

41 "'And I will not suffer,' says the Lord of hosts, 'that the cries of the fair daughters of this people, which I have led out of the land of Jerusalem, shall come up to me

against the men of my people,' says the Lord of hosts.

42 "'For they shall not lead away captive the daughters of my people, because of their tenderness, save I shall visit them with a sore curse, even to destruction.

43 "'For they shall not commit whoredoms like to them of old,' says the Lord of hosts.

44 "Behold, my brethren, you know that these commandments were given to our father Lehi; wherefore you have known them before; and you have come to great condemnation; for you have done these things which you ought not to have done.

45 "Behold, you have done greater iniquity than the Lamanites, our brethren.

46 "You have broken the hearts of your tender wives and lost the confidence of your children because of your bad examples before them, and the sobbings of their hearts ascend up to God against you.

47 "And because of the strictness of the word of God, which comes down against you, many hearts died, pierced with deep wounds.

48 "But, behold, I, Jacob, would speak to you that are pure in heart.

49 "Look to God with firmness of mind, and pray to him with exceeding faith, and he will console you in your afflictions, and he will plead your cause, and send down justice upon those who seek your destruction.

50 "Oh, all you that are pure in heart, lift up your heads and receive the pleasing word of God, and feast upon his love; for you may, if your minds are firm forever.

51 "But woe, woe to you that are not pure in heart, that are filthy this day before God; for except you repent, the land is cursed for your sakes.

52 "And the Lamanites which are not filthy like you (nevertheless, they are cursed with a sore cursing) shall scourge you even to destruction.

53 "And the time will speedily come that, except you repent, they shall possess the land of your inheritance, and the Lord God will lead away the righteous out from among you.

54 "Behold, the Lamanites, your brethren, whom you hate because of their filthiness and the cursings which have come upon their skins, are more righteous than you.

55 "For they have not forgotten the commandments of the Lord, which were given our fathers, that they should have save it were one wife, and concubines they should have none, and there should not be whoredoms committed among them.

56 "This commandment they observe to keep; wherefore because of this observance in keeping this commandment, the Lord God will not destroy them, but will be merciful to them; and one day they shall become a blessed people.

57 "Behold, their husbands love their wives, and their wives love their husbands, and their husbands and their wives love their children.

58 "And their unbelief and their hatred toward you is because of the iniquity of their fathers; wherefore, how much better are you than they in the sight of your great Creator?

59 "O my brethren, I fear that, unless you shall repent of your sins, their skins will be whiter than yours when you shall be brought with them before the throne of God.

60 "Wherefore, a commandment I give you, which is the word of God, that you revile no more against them because of the darkness of their skins; neither shall you revile against them because of their filthiness.

61 "But you shall remember your own filthiness, and remember that their filthiness came because of their fathers.

62 "Wherefore, you shall remember your children, how that you have grieved their hearts because of the example that you have set before them.

63 "Also, remember that you may, because of your filthiness, bring your children to destruction, and their sins be heaped upon your heads at the last day.

64 "O my brethren, hearken to my word; arouse the faculties of your soul; shake yourselves that you may awake from the slumber of death.

65 "And loose yourselves from the pains of hell that you may not become

angels to the devil, to be cast into that lake of fire and brimstone, which is the second death."

66 Now I, Jacob, spoke many more things to the people of Nephi, warning them against fornication, and lasciviousness, and every kind of sin, telling them the awful consequences of them.

67 And a hundredth part of the proceedings of this people, which now began to be numerous, cannot be written upon these plates.

68 But many of their proceedings are written upon the larger plates, and their wars, and their contentions, and the reigns of their kings.

69 These plates are called the plates of Jacob; and they were made by the hand of Nephi.

70 And I make an end of speaking these words.

CHAPTER 3

NOW, behold, I, Jacob, have ministered much to my people in word. And I can write but little of my words because of the difficulty of engraving our words upon plates, and we know that the things which we write upon plates must remain.

2 But whatever things we write upon anything, save it be upon plates, must perish and vanish away; but we can write a few words upon plates which will give our children, and also our beloved brethren, a small degree of knowledge concerning us, or concerning their fathers.

3 Now in this thing we rejoice; and we labor diligently to engrave these words upon plates, hoping that our beloved brethren and our children will receive them with thankful hearts, and look upon them that they may learn with joy, and not with sorrow, neither with contempt concerning their first parents.

4 For, for this intent have we written these things, that they may know that we knew of Christ, and we had a hope of his glory many hundred years before his coming, and not only we ourselves had a hope of his glory, but also all the holy prophets which were before us.

5 Behold, they believed in Christ and worshiped the Father in his name; and also, we worship the Father in his name.

6 For this intent we keep the law of Moses, it pointing our souls to him; and for this cause it is sanctified to us for righteousness, even as it was accounted to Abraham in the wilderness to be obedient to the commands of God in offering up his son Isaac, which is a similitude of God and his only begotten Son.

7 Wherefore, we search the prophets; and we have many revelations and the spirit of prophecy, and having all these witnesses, we obtain a hope, and our faith becomes unshaken, insomuch that we truly can command in the name of Jesus, and the very trees obey us, or the mountains, or the waves of the sea.

8 Nevertheless, the Lord God shows us our weakness, that we may know that it is by his grace, and his great condescensions to the children of men, that we have power to do these things.

9 Behold, great and marvelous are the works of the Lord.

10 How unsearchable are the depths of the mysteries of him; and it is impossible that man should find out all his ways.

11 No man knows of his ways save it be revealed to him; wherefore, brethren, despise not the revelations of God.

12 For, behold, by the power of his word man came upon the face of the earth, which earth was created by the power of his word.

13 Wherefore, if God, being able to speak and the world was, and to speak and man was created, oh, then, why is he not able to command the earth, or the workmanship of his hands upon the face of it, according to his will and pleasure?

14 Wherefore, brethren, seek not to counsel the Lord, but to take counsel from his hand.

15 For, behold, you yourselves know that he counsels in wisdom, and in justice, and in great mercy over all his works.

16 Wherefore, beloved brethren, be reconciled to him, through the atonement of Christ, his only begotten Son, 17that you may obtain a

resurrection, according to the power of the resurrection which is in Christ, and be presented as the first fruits of Christ unto God, having faith, and obtaining a good hope of glory in him, before he manifests himself in the flesh.

18 Now, beloved, marvel not that I tell you these things; for why not speak of the atonement of Christ, and attain to a perfect knowledge of him, as to attain to the knowledge of a resurrection and the world to come?

19 Behold, my brethren, he that prophesies, let him prophesy to the understanding of men; for the Spirit speaks the truth, and lies not.

20 Wherefore, it speaks of things as they really are, and of things as they really will be; wherefore, these things are manifested to us plainly for the salvation of our souls.

21 But, behold, we are not witnesses alone in these things; for God also spoke them to prophets of old.

22 But, behold, the Jews were a stiff-necked people; and they despised the words of plainness, and killed the prophets, and sought for things that they could not understand.

23 Wherefore, because of their blindness, which blindness came by looking beyond the mark, they must fall.

24 For God has taken away his plainness from them, and delivered to them many things which they cannot understand, because they desired it.

25 And because they desired it, God has done it that they may stumble.

26 Now I, Jacob, am led on by the Spirit to prophesying; for I perceive by the workings of the Spirit which is in me that by the stumbling of the Jews they will reject the stone upon which they might build and have a safe foundation.

27 But, behold, according to the scriptures, this stone shall become the great, and the last, and the only sure foundation upon which the Jews can build.

28 Now, my beloved, how is it possible that these, after having rejected the sure foundation, can ever build upon it, that it may become the head of their corner?

29 Behold, my beloved brethren, I will unfold this mystery to you, if I do not by any means get shaken from my firmness in the Spirit and stumble because of my overanxiety for you.

30 Behold, my brethren, do you not remember having read the words of the prophet Zenos, who spoke to the house of Israel, saying: "Hearken, O ye house of Israel, and hear the words of me, a prophet of the Lord.

31 "For, behold," thus says the Lord, "I will liken thee, O house of Israel, to a tame olive tree, which a man took and nourished in his vineyard; and it grew, and waxed old, and began to decay.

32 "And the master of the vineyard went forth and saw that his olive tree began to decay; and he said, 'I will prune it, and dig about it, and nourish it, that perhaps it may shoot forth young and tender branches, and not perish.'

33 "And he pruned it, and dug about it, and nourished it, according to his word.

34 "After many days, it began to put forth somewhat a little, young and tender branches; but, behold, the main top thereof began to perish.

35 "The master of the vineyard saw it and said to his servant, 'It grieves me that I should lose this tree.

36 "'Wherefore, go and pluck the branches from a wild olive tree, and bring them to me; and we will pluck off those main branches which are beginning to wither away, and we will cast them into the fire that they may be burned.

37 "'And, behold,' said the lord of the vineyard, 'I will take away many of these young and tender branches, and I will graft them wherever I will.

38 "'It matters not that if it so be that the root of this tree will perish, I may preserve the fruit thereof to myself; 39wherefore, I will take these young and tender branches, and I will graft them wherever I will.

40 "'Take the branches of the wild olive tree, and graft them in, in the stead thereof; 41and these

which I have plucked off, I will cast into the fire, and burn them, that they may not cumber the ground of my vineyard.'

42 "And it came to pass that the servant of the lord of the vineyard did according to the word of the lord of the vineyard, and grafted in the branches of the wild olive tree.

43 "And the lord of the vineyard caused that it should be dug about, and pruned, and nourished, saying to his servant, 'It grieves me that I should lose this tree; ⁴⁴wherefore, that perhaps I might preserve the roots thereof that they perish not, that I might preserve them to myself, I have done this thing.

45 " 'Wherefore, go your way; watch the tree, and nourish it, according to my words.

46 " 'These will I place in the nethermost part of my vineyard, wherever I will, it matters not to you.

47 " 'And I do it that I may preserve to myself the natural branches of the tree; and also that I may lay up fruit thereof, against the season, to myself; for it grieves me that I should lose this tree and the fruit thereof.'

48 "The Lord of the vineyard went his way, and hid the natural branches of the tame olive tree in the nethermost parts of the vineyard; some in one, and some in another, according to his will and pleasure.

49 "And a long time passed away, and the lord of the vineyard said to his servant, 'Come, let us go down into the vineyard, that we may labor in the vineyard.'

50 "The lord of the vineyard, and also the servant, went down into the vineyard to labor.

51 "And the servant said to his master, 'Behold, look here; behold the tree.'

52 "The lord of the vineyard looked and beheld the tree in which the wild olive branches had been grafted; and it had sprung forth and begun to bear fruit.

53 "And he beheld that it was good, and the fruit thereof was like the natural fruit.

54 "And he said to the servant,

'Behold, the branches of the wild tree have taken hold of the moisture of the root thereof, that the root thereof has brought forth much strength; ⁵⁵and because of the much strength of the root thereof, the wild branches have brought forth tame fruit.

56 " 'Now if we had not grafted in these branches, the tree would have perished.

57 " 'Behold, I shall lay up much fruit which the tree thereof has brought forth; and the fruit thereof I shall lay up, against the season, to myself.'

58 "And the lord of the vineyard said to the servant, 'Come, let us go to the nethermost parts of the vineyard, and behold if the natural branches of the tree have not brought forth much fruit also, that I may lay up of the fruit thereof, against the season, to myself.'

59 "And they went forth where the master of the vineyard had hid the natural branches of the tree, and he said to the servant, 'Behold these.'

60 "He beheld the first, that it had brought forth much fruit; and he beheld also that it was good.

61 "And he said to the servant, 'Take of the fruit thereof, and lay it up, against the season, that I may preserve it to myself.

62 " 'For, behold,' said he, 'this long time have I nourished it, and it has brought forth much fruit.'

63 "And the servant said to his master, 'How did you come to plant this tree, or this branch of the tree, here? For, behold, it was the poorest spot in all the land of your vineyard.'

64 "And the lord of the vineyard said to him, 'Counsel me not. I knew that it was a poor spot of ground; wherefore, I said to you, I have nourished it this long time; and you behold that it has brought forth much fruit.'

65 "And the lord of the vineyard said to his servant, 'Look here; behold, I have planted another branch of the tree also; and you know that this spot of ground was poorer than the first.

66 " 'But, behold the tree; I have

nourished it this long time, and it has brought forth much fruit; therefore, gather it and lay it up, against the season, that I may preserve it to myself.'

67 "The lord of the vineyard said again to his servant, 'Look here, and behold another branch also which I have planted; behold that I have nourished it also, and it has brought forth fruit.'

68 "And he said to the servant, 'Look here, and behold the last; behold, this have I planted in a good spot of ground; and I have nourished it this long time, and only a part of the tree has brought forth tame fruit; and the other part of the tree has brought forth wild fruit; behold, I have nourished this tree like the others.'

69 "And the lord of the vineyard said to the servant, 'Pluck off the branches that have not brought forth good fruit, and cast them into the fire.'

70 "But the servant said to him, 'Let us prune it, and dig about it, and nourish it a little longer that perhaps it may bring forth good fruit that you can lay it up against the season.'

71 "And the lord of the vineyard and the servant of the lord of the vineyard nourished all the fruit of the vineyard.

72 "After a long time had passed away, the lord of the vineyard said to his servant, 'Come, let us go down into the vineyard, that we may labor again in the vineyard.

73 "'For, behold, the time draws near, and the end soon will come; wherefore, I must lay up fruit, against the season, to myself.'

74 "And the lord of the vineyard and the servant went down into the vineyard; and they came to the tree whose natural branches had been broken off and the wild branches had been grafted in; and, behold, all sorts of fruit cumbered the tree.

75 "And the lord of the vineyard tasted of the fruit, every sort according to its number.

76 "And the lord of the vineyard said, 'Behold, this long time have we nourished this tree, and I have laid up to myself against the season, much fruit.

77 "'But, behold, this time it has brought forth much fruit, and there is none of it which is good.

78 "'There are all kinds of bad fruit; and it profits me nothing, notwithstanding all our labor; and now, it grieves me that I should lose this tree.'

79 "And the lord of the vineyard said to the servant, 'What shall we do to the tree, that I may preserve again good fruit thereof to myself?'

80 "The servant said to his master, 'Behold, because you grafted in the branches of the wild olive tree, they have nourished the roots that they are alive, and they have not perished; wherefore, you behold that they are yet good.'

81 "And the lord of the vineyard said to his servant, 'The tree profits me nothing; and the roots thereof profit me nothing, as long as it shall bring forth evil fruit.

82 "'Nevertheless, I know that the roots are good; and for my own purpose I have preserved them; and because of their much strength they have hitherto brought forth from the wild branches good fruit.

83 "'But, behold, the wild branches have grown and have overrun the roots thereof; and because the wild branches have overcome the roots thereof, it has brought forth much evil fruit.

84 "'And because it has brought forth so much evil fruit, you behold that it begins to perish; and it will soon become ripened that it may be cast into the fire except we should do something for it to preserve it.'

85 "Then the lord of the vineyard said to his servant, 'Let us go down into the nethermost parts of the vineyard and behold if the natural branches have also brought forth evil fruit.'

86 "And they went down into the nethermost parts of the vineyard.

87 "And they beheld that the fruit of the natural branches had become corrupt also, even the first, and the second, and also the last; and they had all become corrupt.

88 "The wild fruit of the last had

overcome that part of the tree which brought forth good fruit, even that the branch had withered away and died.

89 "The lord of the vineyard wept, and said to the servant, 'What could I have done more for my vineyard?

90 "'Behold, I knew that all the fruit of the vineyard, save it were these, had become corrupted.

91 "'Now these which have once brought forth good fruit have also become corrupted.

92 "'All the trees of my vineyard are good for nothing save it be to be hewn down and cast into the fire.

93 "'Behold, this last, whose branch has withered away, I planted in a good spot of ground, even that which was choice to me above all other parts of the land of my vineyard.

94 "'And you beheld that I also cut down that which cumbered this spot of ground that I might plant this tree in the stead thereof.

95 "'And you beheld that a part thereof brought forth good fruit, and a part thereof brought forth wild fruit.

96 "'Because I plucked not the branches thereof and cast them into the fire, behold, they have overcome the good branch that it has withered away.

97 "'Now, behold, notwithstanding all the care which we have taken of my vineyard, the trees thereof have become corrupted that they bring forth no good fruit.

98 "'And these I had hoped to preserve, to have laid up fruit thereof, against the season, to myself.

99 "'But, behold, they have become like the wild olive tree; and they are of no worth but to be hewn down and cast into the fire; and it grieves me that I should lose them.

100 "'But what could I have done more in my vineyard?

101 "'Have I slackened my hand that I have not nourished it?

102 "'No; I have nourished it, and I have dug about it, and I have pruned it, and I have dunged it;

and I have stretched forth my hand almost all the day long; and the end draws nigh.

103 "'It grieves me that I should hew down all the trees of my vineyard and cast them into the fire that they should be burned.

104 "'Who is it that has corrupted my vineyard?'

105 "And the servant said to his master, 'Is it not the loftiness of your vineyard?

106 "'Have not the branches thereof overcome the roots, which are good?

107 "'And because the branches have overcome the roots thereof, behold, they grew faster than the strength of the roots, taking strength to themselves.

108 "'Behold, I say, Is not this the cause that the trees of your vineyard have become corrupted?'

109 "Then the lord of the vineyard said to the servant, 'Let us go to, and hew down the trees of the vineyard, and cast them into the fire, that they shall not cumber the ground of my vineyard; for I have done all; what could I have done more for my vineyard?'

110 "But, behold, the servant said to the lord of the vineyard, 'Spare it a little longer.'

111 "And the lord said, 'I will spare it a little longer; for it grieves me that I should lose the trees of my vineyard.

112 "'Wherefore let us take of the branches of these which I have planted in the nethermost parts of my vineyard, and let us graft them into the tree from which they came.

113 "'And let us pluck from the tree those branches whose fruit is most bitter, and graft in the natural branches of the tree in the stead thereof.

114 "'This will I do that the tree may not perish, that perhaps I may preserve to myself the roots thereof for my own purpose.

115 "'Behold, the roots of the natural branches of the tree, which I planted wherever I would, are yet alive; 116wherefore, that I may preserve them also, for my purpose, I will take of the branches of this

tree, and I will graft them into them.

117 "'I will graft in them the branches of their mother tree, that I may preserve the roots also to myself, that when they shall be sufficiently strong perhaps they may bring forth good fruit to me, and I may yet have glory in the fruit of my vineyard.'

118 "And they took from the natural tree which had become wild, and grafted into the natural trees which also had become wild.

119 "They also took of the natural trees which had become wild, and grafted into their mother tree.

120 "And the lord of the vineyard said to the servant, 'Pluck not the wild branches from the trees, save it be those which are most bitter; and in them you shall graft, according to that which I have said.

121 "'We will nourish again the trees of the vineyard, and we will trim up the branches thereof; and we will pluck from the trees those branches which are ripened that must perish, and cast them into the fire.

122 "'This I do that perhaps the roots thereof may take strength, because of their goodness; and because of the change of the branches, that the good may overcome the evil; [123]and because I have preserved the natural branches, and the roots thereof; and have grafted in the natural branches again into their mother tree; and have preserved the roots of their mother tree that perhaps the trees of my vineyard may bring forth again good fruit; [124]and that I may have joy again in the fruit of my vineyard, and perhaps that I may rejoice exceedingly that I have preserved the roots and the branches of the first fruit.

125 "'Wherefore, go and call servants that we may labor diligently with our mights in the vineyard, that we may prepare the way, that I may bring forth again the natural fruit, which natural fruit is good and the most precious above all other fruit.

126 "'Wherefore, let us go and labor with our mights this last time; for, behold, the end draws nigh, and this is the last time that I shall prune my vineyard.

127 "'Graft in the branches; begin at the last that they may be first and that the first may be last, and dig about the trees, both old and young, the first and the last, and the last and the first, that all may be nourished once again for the last time.

128 "'Wherefore, dig about them, and prune them, and dung them once more for the last time; for the end draws nigh.

129 "'And if it so be that these last grafts shall grow and bring forth the natural fruit, then shall you prepare the way for them that they may grow.

130 "'And as they begin to grow, you shall clear away the branches which bring forth bitter fruit, according to the strength of the good and the size thereof.

131 "'But you shall not clear away the bad thereof all at once lest the roots thereof should be too strong for the graft, and the graft thereof shall perish, and I lose the trees of my vineyard.

132 "'For it grieves me that I should lose the trees of my vineyard; wherefore, you shall clear away the bad, according as the good shall grow, that the root and the top may be equal in strength, until the good shall overcome the bad, and the bad be hewn down and cast into the fire, that they cumber not the ground of my vineyard; and thus will I sweep away the bad out of my vineyard.

133 "'And the branches of the natural tree will I graft again into the natural tree; and the branches of the natural tree will I graft into the natural branches of the tree; [134]and thus will I bring them together again that they shall bring forth the natural fruit; and they shall be one.

135 "'And the bad shall be cast away, even out of all the land of my vineyard; for, behold, only this once will I prune my vineyard.'

136 "The lord of the vineyard

sent his servant; and the servant did as the lord had commanded him, and brought other servants; and they were few.

137 "And the lord of the vineyard said to them, 'Go and labor in the vineyard with your mights.

138 "'For, behold, this is the last time that I shall nourish my vineyard; for the end is nigh at hand, and the season speedily comes.

139 "'If you labor with your mights with me, you shall have joy in the fruit which I shall lay up to myself, against the time which will soon come.'

140 "And the servants went, and labored with their mights, and the lord of the vineyard labored also with them; and they obeyed the commandments of the lord of the vineyard in all things.

141 "And there began to be the natural fruit again in the vineyard; and the natural branches began to grow and thrive exceedingly.

142 "And the wild branches began to be plucked off and to be cast away; and they kept the root and the top thereof equal, according to the strength thereof.

143 "Thus they labored with all diligence, according to the commandments of the lord of the vineyard, even until the bad had been cast away out of the vineyard, and the lord had preserved to himself that the trees had become again the natural fruit.

144 "And they became like one body; and the fruits were equal; and the lord of the vineyard had preserved to himself the natural fruit, which was most precious to him from the beginning.

145 "When the lord of the vineyard saw that his fruit was good, and that his vineyard was no more corrupt, he called up his servants and said to them, 'Behold, for this last time have we nourished my vineyard; and you behold that I have done according to my will.

146 "'I have preserved the natural fruit, that it is good even as it was in the beginning; and blessed are you.

147 "'For because you have been diligent in laboring with me in my vineyard, and have kept my commandments, and have brought to me again the natural fruit that my vineyard is no more corrupted, and the bad is cast away, behold, you shall have joy with me, because of the fruit of my vineyard.

148 "'For, behold, for a long time will I lay up of the fruit of my vineyard to myself, against the season which speedily comes.

149 "'For the last time have I nourished my vineyard, and pruned it, and dug about it, and dunged it; 150wherefore I will lay up to myself of the fruit for a long time, according to that which I have spoken.

151 "'And when the time comes that evil fruit shall again come into my vineyard, then will I cause the good and the bad to be gathered; 152and the good will I preserve to myself, and the bad will I cast away into its own place.

153 "'Then comes the season and the end; and my vineyard will I cause to be burned with fire.'"

CHAPTER 4

NOW, behold, my brethren, as I said to you that I would prophesy, behold, this is my prophecy:

2 "The things which this prophet Zenos spoke concerning the house of Israel, in which he likened them to a tame olive tree, must surely come to pass.

3 "In the day that he shall set his hand again the second time to recover his people is the day, even the last time that the servants of the Lord shall go forth in his power to nourish and prune his vineyard; and after that, the end will soon come.

4 "How blessed are they who have labored diligently in his vineyard; and how cursed are they who shall be cast out into their own place!

5 "And the world shall be burned with fire.

6 "And how merciful is our God to us; for he remembers the house of Israel, both roots and branches; and he stretches forth his hands to them all the day long.

7 "They are a stiff-necked and a

gainsaying people; but as many as will not harden their hearts shall be saved in the kingdom of God.

8 "Wherefore, my beloved brethren, I beseech of you in words of soberness that you would repent, and come with full purpose of heart, and cleave to God as he cleaves to you.

9 "And while his arm of mercy is extended toward you in the light of the day, harden not your hearts.

10 "Today, if you will hear his voice, harden not your hearts; for why will you die?

11 "For, behold, after you have been nourished by the good word of God all the day long, will you bring forth evil fruit that you must be hewn down and cast into the fire?

12 "Behold, will you reject these words?

13 "Will you reject the words of the prophets, and will you reject all the words which have been spoken concerning Christ, after so many have spoken concerning him, and deny the good word of Christ, and the power of God, and the gift of the Holy Ghost, and quench the Holy Spirit, and make a mock of the great plan of redemption which has been laid for you?

14 "Know you not that if you will do these things, the power of the redemption and the resurrection which is in Christ will bring you to stand with shame and awful guilt before the bar of God?

15 "According to the power of justice, for justice cannot be denied, you must go away into that lake of fire and brimstone whose flames are unquenchable and whose smoke ascends up for ever and ever, which lake of fire and brimstone is endless torment.

16 "Oh, then, my beloved brethren, repent, and enter in at the strait gate, and continue in the way which is narrow until you shall obtain eternal life.

17 "Oh, be wise; what can I say more?

18 "Finally, I bid you farewell until I shall meet you before the pleasing bar of God, which bar strikes the wicked with awful dread and fear. Amen."

CHAPTER 5

AFTER some years had passed away, there came a man among the people of Nephi, whose name was Sherem.

2 And he began to preach among the people, and to declare to them that there should be no Christ.

3 He preached many things which were flattering to the people; and this he did that he might overthrow the doctrine of Christ.

4 And he labored diligently that he might lead away the hearts of the people, insomuch that he led away many hearts.

5 Knowing that I, Jacob, had faith in Christ who should come, he sought much opportunity that he might come to me.

6 And he was learned, that he had a perfect knowledge of the language of the people; wherefore, he could use much flattery, and much power of speech, according to the power of the devil.

7 He had hope to shake me from the faith, notwithstanding the many revelations, and the many things which I had seen concerning these things; for I truly had seen angels, and they had ministered to me.

8 Also I had heard the voice of the Lord speaking to me in very word, from time to time; wherefore, I could not be shaken.

9 And it came to pass that he came to me; and on this wise he spoke to me, saying: "Brother Jacob, I have sought much opportunity that I might speak to you; for I have heard and also know that you go about much, preaching that which you call the gospel, or the doctrine of Christ.

10 "You have led away many of this people, that they pervert the right way of God, and keep not the law of Moses, which is the right way; and convert the law of Moses into the worship of a being, which you say shall come many hundred years hence.

11 "And now, behold, I, Sherem, declare to you that this is blasphemy; for no man knows of such things; for he cannot tell of things to come."

12 After this manner Sherem contended against me.

13 But, behold, the Lord God poured his Spirit into my soul, insomuch that I confounded him in all his words.

14 I said to him, "Do you deny the Christ which shall come?"

15 And he said, "If there should be a Christ, I would not deny him; but I know that there is no Christ, neither has been, nor ever will be."

16 Then I said to him, "Do you believe the scriptures?"

17 And he said, "Yes."

18 And I said to him, "Then you do not understand them; for they truly testify of Christ.

19 "Behold, I say to you that none of the prophets have written, nor prophesied, save they have spoken concerning this Christ.

20 "And this is not all: it has been made manifest to me, for I have heard and seen; and it also has been made manifest to me by the power of the Holy Ghost.

21 "Wherefore, I know if there should be no atonement made, all mankind must be lost."

22 And he said to me, "Show me a sign by this power of the Holy Ghost, in which you know so much."

23 And I said to him, "What am I, that I should tempt God to show you a sign, in the thing which you know to be true?

24 "Yet you will deny it, because you are of the devil.

25 "Nevertheless, not my will be done; but if God shall smite you, let that be a sign to you that he has power, both in heaven and in earth; and also, that Christ shall come.

26 "Thy will, O Lord, be done, and not mine."

27 And when I, Jacob, had spoken these words, the power of the Lord came upon him insomuch that he fell to the earth.

28 And he had to be nourished for the space of many days.

29 And it came to pass that he said to the people, "Gather together on the morrow, for I shall die; wherefore, I desire to speak to the people before I shall die."

30 On the morrow, the multitude were gathered together; and he spoke plainly to them, and denied the things which he had taught them; and confessed the Christ, and the power of the Holy Ghost, and the ministering of angels.

31 He spoke plainly to them, that he had been deceived by the power of the devil.

32 And he spoke of hell, and of eternity, and of eternal punishment.

33 And he said, "I fear lest I have committed the unpardonable sin, for I have lied to God; for I denied the Christ, and said that I believed the scriptures, and they truly testify of him.

34 "Because I have thus lied to God, I greatly fear lest my case shall be awful; but I confess to God."

35 And when he had said these words, he could say no more; and he gave up the ghost.

36 When the multitude had witnessed that he spoke these things as he was about to give up the ghost, they were astonished exceedingly; insomuch that the power of God came down upon them, and they were overcome, that they fell to the earth.

37 Now this thing was pleasing to me, Jacob; for I had requested it of my Father who was in heaven; for he had heard my cry and answered my prayer.

38 And it came to pass that peace and the love of God were restored again among the people; and they searched the scriptures and hearkened no more to the words of this wicked man.

39 Many means were devised to reclaim and restore the Lamanites to the knowledge of the truth; but it all was vain; for they delighted in wars and bloodshed; and they had an eternal hatred against us, their brethren, 40and they sought by the power of their arms to destroy us continually.

41 Wherefore, the people of Nephi fortified against them with their armies, and with all their might, trusting in the God and rock of their salvation; wherefore, they became, as yet, conquerors of their enemies.

42 And it came to pass that I, Jacob, began to be old; and the record of this people is kept on the other plates of Nephi, wherefore, I conclude this record, declaring that I

have written according to the best of
my knowledge, by saying ⁴³that the
time passed away with us, and also
our lives passed away, like as it were
to us a dream, we being a lonesome
and a solemn people, wanderers, cast
out from Jerusalem; ⁴⁴born in tribulation, in a wilderness, and hated of
our brethren, which caused wars and
contentions; wherefore, we mourned
out our days.

45 I, Jacob, saw that I must soon
go down to my grave; wherefore, I
said to my son Enos, "Take these
plates."

46 And I told him the things which
my brother Nephi had commanded
me; and he promised obedience to
the commands.

47 Now I make an end of my writing upon these plates, which writing
has been small.

48 And to the reader I bid farewell,
hoping that many of my brethren
may read my words. Brethren, farewell.

THE BOOK OF ENOS

CHAPTER 1

BEHOLD, it came to pass that I,
Enos, knew that my father was a
just man; for he taught me in his
language, and also in the nurture and
admonition of the Lord.

2 Blessed be the name of my God
for it.

3 Now I will tell you of the wrestle
which I had before God, before I
received a remission of my sins.

4 Behold, I went to hunt beasts in
the forest; and the words which I had
often heard my father speak, concerning eternal life, and the joy of the
saints had sunk deep into my heart.

5 My soul hungered; and I knelt
before my Maker, and I cried to him
in mighty prayer and supplication for
my soul.

6 All the day long I cried to him;
and when the night came, I still
raised my voice high, that it reached
the heavens.

7 And there came a voice to me,
saying, "Enos, thy sins are forgiven
thee, and thou shalt be blessed."

8 I, Enos, knew that God could
not lie; wherefore, my guilt was swept
away.

9 And I said, "Lord, how is it
done?"

10 He said to me, "Because of thy
faith in Christ, whom thou hast never
before heard nor seen.

11 "Many years will pass away
before he shall manifest himself in
the flesh; wherefore, go, thy faith
hath made thee whole."

12 Now, when I had heard these
words, I began to feel a desire for the
welfare of my brethren, the Nephites;
wherefore, I poured out my whole
soul to God for them.

13 While I was thus struggling in
the spirit, behold, the voice of the
Lord came into my mind again,
saying,

14 "I will visit thy brethren according to their diligence in keeping
my commandments.

15 "I have given them this land,
and it is a holy land; and I curse it not
save it be for the cause of iniquity;
¹⁶wherefore, I will visit thy brethren
according as I have said; and their
transgressions will I bring down with
sorrow upon their own heads."

17 After I, Enos, had heard these
words, my faith began to be unshaken
in the Lord; and I prayed to him with
many long strugglings for my brethren, the Lamanites.

18 And after I had prayed and
labored with all diligence, the Lord
said to me, "I will grant thee according to thy desires, because of thy
faith."

19 Now, behold, this was the desire which I desired of him: that if it
should so be that my people, the

Nephites, should fall into transgression and by any means be destroyed, and the Lamanites should not be destroyed, the Lord God would preserve a record of my people, the Nephites, [20]even if it so be, by the power of his holy arm, that it might be brought forth at some future day to the Lamanites, that perhaps they might be brought to salvation.

21 For at the present, our strugglings were vain in restoring them to the true faith.

22 They swore in their wrath that if it were possible they would destroy our records and us, and also all the traditions of our fathers.

23 Wherefore, knowing that the Lord God was able to preserve our records, I cried to him continually.

24 For he had said to me, "Whatsoever thing ye shall ask in faith, believing that ye shall receive in the name of Christ, ye shall receive it."

25 I had faith, and I cried to God that he would preserve the records.

26 And he covenanted with me that he would bring them forth to the Lamanites in his own due time.

27 And I, Enos, knew it would be according to the covenant which he had made; wherefore, my soul rested.

28 Then the Lord said to me, "Thy fathers have also required of me this thing; and it shall be done to them according to their faith, for their faith was like thine."

29 And I, Enos, went about among the people of Nephi, prophesying of things to come and testifying of the things which I had heard and seen.

30 I bear record that the people of Nephi sought diligently to restore the Lamanites to the true faith in God.

31 But our labors were in vain; their hatred was fixed, and they were led by their evil nature, so that they became wild and ferocious, and a bloodthirsty people, full of idolatry and filthiness, [32]feeding upon beasts of prey, dwelling in tents, and wandering about in the wilderness with a short skin girted about their loins, and their heads shaven; and their skill was in the bow, and the cimeter, and the ax.

33 Many of them ate nothing, save it was raw meat; and they were continually seeking to destroy us.

34 But the people of Nephi tilled the land, and raised all manner of grain and fruit, and flocks of herds, and flocks of all manner of cattle of every kind, and goats, and wild goats and also many horses.

35 And there were exceedingly many prophets among us.

36 And the people were a stiffnecked people, hard to understand.

37 There was nothing, save it was exceeding harshness, preaching and prophesying of wars, and contentions, and destructions, and continually reminding them of death, and the duration of eternity, and the judgments and the power of God, [38]and all these things stirring them up continually to keep them in the fear of the Lord.

39 I say there was nothing short of these things, and exceedingly great plainness of speech, would keep them from going down speedily to destruction.

40 And after this manner I write concerning them.

41 I saw wars between the Nephites and the Lamanites in the course of my days.

42 And it came to pass that I began to be old, and one hundred and seventy-nine years had passed away from the time that our father, Lehi, left Jerusalem.

43 I saw that I must soon go down to my grave, having been wrought upon by the power of God that I must preach and prophesy to this people, and declare the word according to the truth which is in Christ.

44 And I have declared it in all my days, and have rejoiced in it above all of the world.

45 I soon go to the place of my rest, which is with my Redeemer; for I know that in him I shall rest.

46 I rejoice in the day when my mortal shall put on immortality and shall stand before him; then shall I see his face with pleasure, and he will say to me, "Come to me, ye blessed, there is a place prepared for you in the mansions of my Father." Amen.

THE BOOK OF JAROM

CHAPTER 1

NOW, behold, I, Jarom, write a few words, according to the commandment of my father Enos, that our genealogy may be kept.

2 As these plates are small, and as these things are written for the intent of the benefit of our brethren, the Lamanites, wherefore, I must write a little; but I shall not write the things of my prophesying, nor of my revelations.

3 For what could I write more than my fathers have written?

4 For have not they revealed the plan of salvation?

5 I say to you, Yes; and this suffices me.

6 Behold, it is expedient that much should be done among this people because of the hardness of their hearts, and the deafness of their ears, and the blindness of their minds, and the stiffness of their necks.

7 Nevertheless, God is exceedingly merciful to them, and has not as yet swept them off from the face of the land.

8 There are many among us who have many revelations; for they are not all stiff-necked.

9 And as many as are not stiff-necked, and have faith, have communion with the Holy Spirit, which makes manifest to the children of men according to their faith.

10 Now, behold, two hundred years had passed away, and the people of Nephi had waxed strong in the land.

11 They observed to keep the law of Moses and the Sabbath day holy to the Lord.

12 And they profaned not; neither did they blaspheme.

13 And the laws of the land were exceedingly strict.

14 They were scattered upon much of the face of the land; and the Lamanites also.

15 And they were exceedingly more numerous than were the Nephites; and they loved murder and would drink the blood of beasts.

16 And they came many times against us, the Nephites, to battle.

17 But our kings and our leaders were mighty men in the faith of the Lord; and they taught the people the ways of the Lord; 18wherefore, we withstood the Lamanites, and swept them away out of our lands, and began to fortify our cities, or whatever place of our inheritance.

19 And we multiplied exceedingly, and spread upon the face of the land, and became exceedingly rich in gold, and in silver, and in precious things, and in fine workmanship of wood, in buildings, and in machinery, and also in iron, and copper, and brass, and steel, making all manner of tools of every kind to till the ground, and weapons of war 20—the sharp pointed arrow, and the quiver, and the dart, and the javelin, and all preparations for war.

21 And because we were prepared to meet the Lamanites, they did not prosper against us.

22 But the word of the Lord was verified which he spoke to our fathers, saying, "Inasmuch as ye will keep my commandments, ye shall prosper in the land."

23 And it came to pass that the prophets of the Lord threatened the people of Nephi, according to the word of God, that if they did not keep the commandments, but should fall into transgression, they should be destroyed from off the face of the land.

24 Wherefore, the prophets, and the priests, and the teachers, labored diligently, exhorting with all long-suffering the people to diligence; teaching the law of Moses and the intent for which it was given; 25persuading them to look forward unto the Messiah, and to believe in him yet to come, as though he already was.

26 After this manner they taught them.

27 By so doing they kept them from being destroyed upon the face of the land; 28for they pricked their hearts with the word, continually stirring them up to repentance.

29 And it came to pass that two hundred and thirty-eight years had passed away after the manner of wars, and contentions, and dissensions, for the space of much of the time.

30 And I, Jarom, do not write more, for the plates are small.

31 But, behold, my brethren, you can go to the other plates of Nephi; for, behold, upon them the record of our wars are engraved, according to the writings of the kings, or those which they caused to be written.

32 I deliver these plates into the hands of my son Omni, that they may be kept according to the commandments of my fathers.

THE BOOK OF OMNI

CHAPTER 1

BEHOLD, it came to pass that I, Omni, was commanded by my father Jarom, that I should write somewhat on these plates to preserve our genealogy.

2 Wherefore, in my days, I would that you should know that I fought much with the sword to preserve my people, the Nephites, from falling into the hands of their enemies, the Lamanites.

3 But, behold, I of myself am a wicked man, and I have not kept the statutes and the commandments of the Lord as I ought to have done.

4 And it came to pass that two hundred and seventy-six years had passed away, and we had many seasons of peace; and we had many seasons of serious war and bloodshed.

5 In fine, two hundred and eighty-two years had passed away, and I had kept these plates according to the commandments of my fathers; and I conferred them upon my son Amaron. And I make an end.

6 Now I, Amaron, write the things whatever I write, which are few, in the book of my father.

7 Behold, it came to pass that three hundred and twenty years had passed away, and the more wicked part of the Nephites were destroyed.

8 For the Lord would not suffer, after he had led them out of the land of Jerusalem and kept and preserved them from falling into the hands of their enemies, that the words should not be verified which he spoke to our fathers, saying, "Inasmuch as ye will not keep my commandments, ye shall not prosper in the land."

9 Wherefore, the Lord visited them in great judgment; nevertheless, he spared the righteous that they should not perish, but delivered them out of the hands of their enemies.

10 And it came to pass that I delivered the plates to my brother Chemish.

11 Now I, Chemish, write what few things I write in the same book with my brother; for, behold, I saw the last which he wrote, that he wrote it with his own hand; and he wrote it in the day that he delivered them to me.

12 And after this manner we keep the records, for it is according to the commandments of our fathers. And I make an end.

13 Behold, I, Abinadom, am the son of Chemish.

14 I have seen much war and contention between my people, the Nephites, and the Lamanites.

15 And I, with my own sword, have taken the lives of many of the Lamanites, in the defense of my brethren.

94

16 Behold, the record of this people is engraved upon plates which record is had by the kings, according to the generations.

17 And I know of no revelation, save that which has been written, nor prophecy; wherefore, that which is sufficient is written. And I make an end.

18 Behold, I am Amaleki, the son of Abinadom.

19 Behold, I will speak to you somewhat concerning Mosiah, who was made king over the land of Zarahemla; 20for, behold, he was warned of the Lord that he should flee out of the land of Nephi, and as many as would hearken to the voice of the Lord should also depart out of the land with him, into the wilderness.

21 And he did according as the Lord had commanded him.

22 And they departed out of the land into the wilderness, as many as would hearken to the voice of the Lord; and they were led by many preachings and prophesyings.

23 They were admonished continually by the word of God; and they were led by the power of his arm through the wilderness, until they came down into the land which is called the land of Zarahemla.

24 And they discovered a people, who were called the people of Zarahemla.

25 Now there was great rejoicing among the people of Zarahemla; and also Zarahemla rejoiced exceedingly because the Lord had sent the people of Mosiah with the plates of brass which contained the record of the Jews.

26 Behold, Mosiah discovered that the people of Zarahemla came out from Jerusalem at the time that Zedekiah, king of Judah, was carried away captive into Babylon.

27 And they journeyed in the wilderness, and were brought by the hand of the Lord across the great waters into the land where Mosiah discovered them; and they had dwelt there from that time forth.

28 At the time that Mosiah discovered them, they had become exceedingly numerous.

29 Nevertheless, they had had many wars and serious contentions, and had fallen by the sword from time to time.

30 And their language had become corrupted; and they had brought no records with them.

31 And they denied the being of their Creator; and neither Mosiah nor the people of Mosiah could understand them.

32 But it came to pass that Mosiah caused that they should be taught in his language.

33 And after they were taught in the language of Mosiah, Zarahemla gave a genealogy of his fathers, according to his memory; and it is written, but not in these plates.

34 And it came to pass that the people of Zarahemla and of Mosiah united, and Mosiah was appointed to be their king.

35 And in the days of Mosiah, there was a large stone brought to him, with engravings on it; and he interpreted the engravings by the gift and power of God.

36 They gave an account of one Coriantumr and the slain of his people.

37 Coriantumr was discovered by the people of Zarahemla; and he dwelt with them for the space of nine moons.

38 It also spoke a few words concerning his fathers.

39 His first parents came out from the tower at the time the Lord confounded the language of the people; and the severity of the Lord fell upon them, according to his judgments, which are just; and their bones lay scattered in the land northward.

40 Behold, I, Amaleki, was born in the days of Mosiah; and I have lived to see his death; and Benjamin, his son, reigns in his stead.

41 And, behold, I have seen in the days of King Benjamin a serious war, and much bloodshed between the Nephites and the Lamanites.

42 But, behold, the Nephites obtained much advantage over them, insomuch that King Benjamin drove them out of the land of Zarahemla.

43 And I began to be old; and having no seed, and knowing King Benjamin to be a just man before the Lord, wherefore I shall deliver up

these plates to him, exhorting all men to come to God, the Holy One of Israel, 44and believe in prophesying, and in revelations, and in the ministering of angels, and in the gift of speaking with tongues, and in the gift of interpreting languages, and in all things which are good.

45 For there is nothing which is good save it comes from the Lord; and that which is evil comes from the devil.

46 Now, my beloved brethren, I would that you should come to Christ, who is the Holy One of Israel, and partake of his salvation and the power of his redemption.

47 Come to him, and offer your whole souls as an offering to him, and continue in fasting and praying, and endure to the end; and as the Lord lives, you will be saved.

48 And now I would speak some-

what concerning a certain number who went up into the wilderness to return to the land of Nephi; 49for there was a large number who desired to possess the land of their inheritance; wherefore, they went up into the wilderness.

50 Their leader being a strong and a mighty man, and a stiff-necked man, wherefore he caused a contention among them; and they were all slain, save fifty, in the wilderness, and they returned again to the land of Zarahemla.

51 They also took others, to a considerable number, and took their journey again into the wilderness.

52 And I, Amaleki, had a brother, who also went with them; and I have not since known concerning them.

53 And I am about to lie down in my grave; and these plates are full.

54 I make an end of my speaking.

THE WORDS OF MORMON

CHAPTER 1

I, Mormon, am about to deliver up the record which I have been making into the hands of my son Moroni; behold, I have witnessed almost all the destruction of my people, the Nephites.

2 It is many hundred years after the coming of Christ that I deliver these records into the hands of my son; and I suppose that he will witness the entire destruction of my people.

3 But may God grant that he may survive them, that he may write somewhat concerning them, and somewhat concerning Christ, that perhaps someday it may profit them.

4 Now I speak somewhat concerning that which I have written; for after I had made an abridgment from the plates of Nephi, down to the reign of this King Benjamin, of whom Amaleki spoke, 5I searched among the records which had been delivered into my hands, and I found

these plates which contained this small account of the prophets, from Jacob down to the reign of this King Benjamin, and also many of the words of Nephi.

6 And the things which are upon these plates please me, because of the prophecies of the coming of Christ; and my fathers know that many of them have been fulfilled.

7 And I also know that as many things as have been prophesied concerning us down to this day have been fulfilled; and as many as go beyond this day must surely come to pass.

8 Wherefore, I chose these things to finish my record upon them, which remainder of my record I shall take from the plates of Nephi; and I cannot write the hundredth part of the things of my people.

9 But, behold, I shall take these plates, which contain these prophesyings and revelations, and put them

with the remainder of my record, for they are choice to me; and I know they will be choice to my brethren.

10 And I do this for a wise purpose; for thus it is whispered to me, according to the workings of the Spirit of the Lord which is in me.

11 Now I do not know all things; but the Lord knows all things which are to come; wherefore, he works in me to do according to his will.

12 And my prayer to God is concerning my brethren, that they may once again come to the knowledge of God, even the redemption of Christ, that they may once again be a delightsome people.

13 Now I, Mormon, proceed to finish out my record, which I take from the plates of Nephi; and I make it according to the knowledge and the understanding which God has given me.

14 Wherefore, it came to pass that after Amaleki had delivered up these plates into the hands of King Benjamin, he took them and put them with the other plates, which contained records which had been handed down by the kings, from generation to generation, until the days of King Benjamin.

15 And they were handed down from King Benjamin, from generation to generation, until they have fallen into my hands.

16 I, Mormon, pray to God that they may be preserved from this time henceforth.

17 And I know that they will be preserved; for there are great things written upon them, out of which my people and their brethren shall be judged at the great and last day, according to the word of God which is written.

18 Now concerning this King Benjamin: he had some contentions among his own people.

19 And it came to pass also that the armies of the Lamanites came down out of the land of Nephi to battle against his people.

20 But, behold, King Benjamin gathered together his armies, and he stood against them; and he fought with the strength of his own arm, with the sword of Laban.

21 In the strength of the Lord they contended against their enemies, until they had slain many thousands of the Lamanites.

22 And they contended against the Lamanites until they had driven them out of all the lands of their inheritance.

23 There had been false Christs, and their mouths had been shut, and they had been punished according to their crimes.

24 And there had been false prophets, and false preachers and teachers among the people, and all these had been punished according to their crimes.

25 After there had been much contention, and many dissensions away to the Lamanites, behold, it came to pass that King Benjamin, with the assistance of the holy prophets who were among his people (for, behold, King Benjamin was a holy man, and he reigned over his people in righteousness, 26and there were many holy men in the land) spoke the word of God with power and with authority; and they used much sharpness because of the stiff-neckedness of the people.

27 Wherefore, with the help of these, King Benjamin, by laboring with all the might of his body and the faculty of his whole soul, and also the prophets, once more established peace in the land.

THE BOOK OF MOSIAH

CHAPTER 1

NOW there was no more conten- tion in all the land of Zara- hemla, among all the people who belonged to King Benjamin, so that King Benjamin had continual peace all the remainder of his days.

2 And it came to pass that he had three sons; and he called their names Mosiah, and Helorum, and Helaman.

3 And he caused that they should be taught in all the language of his fathers, that thereby they might be- come men of understanding, and that they might know concerning the prophecies which had been spoken by the mouths of their fathers which were delivered them by the hand of the Lord.

4 He also taught them concerning the records which were engraved on the plates of brass, saying, "My sons, I would that you should remember that were it not for these plates which contain these records and these commandments, we must have suf- fered in ignorance, even at this pres- ent time, not knowing the mysteries of God.

5 "For it would not have been possible that our father Lehi could have remembered all these things, to have taught them to his children, except for the help of these plates.

6 "For he having been taught in the language of the Egyptians, there- fore he could read these engravings, and teach them to his children that thereby they could teach them to their children, and so fulfill the command- ments of God, even down to this present time.

7 "I say to you, my sons, that were it not for these things which have been kept and preserved by the hand of God that we might read and under- stand of his mysteries and have his commandments always before our eyes, even our fathers would have dwindled in unbelief 8and we should have been like our brethren, the La- manites, who know nothing concern- ing these things, or even do not believe them when they are taught them, because of the traditions of their fathers, which are not correct.

9 "O my sons, I would that you should remember that these sayings are true, and also that these records are true.

10 "And, behold, also the plates of Nephi which contain the records and the sayings of our fathers from the time they left Jerusalem until now, and they are true; and we can know of their surety because we have them before our eyes.

11 "Now, my sons, I would that you should remember to search them diligently, that you may profit thereby.

12 "And I would that you should keep the commandments of God, that you may prosper in the land, according to the promises which the Lord made to our fathers."

13 Many more things King Ben- jamin taught his sons, which are not written in this book.

14 And after King Benjamin had made an end of teaching his sons, he waxed old; and he saw that he must very soon go the way of all the earth; therefore, he thought it expedient that he should confer the kingdom upon one of his sons.

15 Therefore, he had Mosiah brought before him; and these are the words which he spoke to him, saying: "My son, I would that you should make a proclamation through- out all this land, among all this peo- ple, or the people of Zarahemla and the people of Mosiah who dwell in this land, that thereby they may be gathered together.

16 "For on the morrow I shall pro- claim to this my people out of my own mouth, that you are a king and a ruler over this people whom the Lord our God has given us.

17 "Moreover, I shall give this

98

people a name that thereby they may be distinguished above all the people which the Lord God has brought out of the land of Jerusalem; and this I do because they have been a diligent people in keeping the commandments of the Lord.

18 "And I give to them a name that never shall be blotted out, except it be through transgression.

19 "Moreover I say to you that if this highly favored people of the Lord should fall into transgression, and become a wicked and an adulterous people, the Lord will deliver them up, that thereby they become weak like their brethren.

20 "And he will no more preserve them by his matchless and marvelous power, as he has hitherto preserved our fathers.

21 "For I say to you that if he had not extended his arm in the preservation of our fathers, they would have fallen into the hands of the Lamanites and become victims to their hatred."

22 After King Benjamin had made an end of these sayings to his son, he gave him charge concerning all the affairs of the kingdom.

23 And moreover, he also gave him charge concerning the records which were engraved on the plates of brass, and also the plates of Nephi, 24and also the sword of Laban, and the ball or director which led our fathers through the wilderness, which was prepared by the hand of the Lord that thereby they might be led, every one, according to the heed and diligence which they gave him.

25 Therefore, as they were unfaithful, they did not prosper nor progress in their journey, but were driven back and incurred the displeasure of God upon them, 26and we re smitten with famine and sore afflictions to stir them up in remembrance of their duty.

27 Now it came to pass that Mosiah did as his father had commanded him, and proclaimed to all the people who were in the land of Zarahemla that they should gather together, to go up to the temple to hear the words which his father should speak to them.

28 And after Mosiah had done as his father had commanded him, and had made a proclamation throughout all the land, the people gathered together that they might go up to the temple to hear the words which King Benjamin should speak to them.

29 And there were a great number, even so many that they did not number them; for they had multiplied exceedingly and waxed great in the land.

30 And they also took of the firstlings of their flocks that they might offer sacrifice and burnt offerings according to the law of Moses; 31and also that they might give thanks to the Lord their God, who had brought them out of the land of Jerusalem, and who had delivered them out of the hands of their enemies, and had appointed just men to be their teachers, and also a just man to be their king, 32who had established peace in the land of Zarahemla, and who had taught them to keep the commandments of God, that thereby they might rejoice and be filled with love toward God and all men.

33 And when they came up to the temple, they pitched their tents round about, every man according to his family, consisting of his wife, and his sons, and his daughters, and their sons, and their daughters, from the eldest down to the youngest, every family being separate one from another.

34 And they pitched their tents round about the temple, every man having his tent with the door thereof toward the temple, that thereby they might remain in their tents and hear the words which King Benjamin should speak to them.

35 For the multitude was so great that King Benjamin could not teach them all within the walls of the temple, therefore he caused a tower to be erected that thereby his people might hear the words which he should speak to them.

36 And he began to speak to his people from the tower, and they could not hear all his words because of the greatness of the multitude.

37 Therefore, he caused that the words which he spoke should be written and sent forth among those that were not under the sound of his voice that they might also receive his words.

38 And these are the words which he spoke and caused to be written,

saying, "My brethren, all you that have assembled yourselves together, you that can hear my words which I shall speak to you this day:

39 "I have not commanded you to come up here to trifle with the words which I shall speak, but that you should hearken to me, and open your ears that you may hear, and your hearts that you may understand, and your minds that the mysteries of God may be unfolded to your view.

40 "I have not commanded you to come up here that you should fear me, or that you should think that I, of myself, am more than a mortal man.

41 "For I am like yourselves, subject to all manner of infirmities in body and mind.

42 "Yet I have been chosen by this people, and was consecrated by my father, and was suffered by the hand of the Lord that I should be a ruler and a king over this people, and have been kept and preserved by his matchless power to serve you with all the might, mind, and strength which the Lord has granted to me.

43 "I say to you that I have been suffered to spend my days in your service, even up to this time, and have not sought gold nor silver, nor any manner of riches of you.

44 "Neither have I suffered that you should be confined in dungeons, nor that you should make slaves one of another, nor that you should murder, or plunder, or steal, or commit adultery.

45 "Nor have I suffered that you should commit any manner of wickedness, but have taught you that you should keep the commandments of the Lord in all things which he has commanded you.

46 "And even I myself have labored with my own hands that I might serve you, and that you should not be laden with taxes, and that there should nothing come upon you which was grievous to be borne; and of all these things which I have spoken, you yourselves are witnesses this day.

47 "Yet, my brethren, I have not done these things that I might boast, neither do I tell these things that thereby I might accuse you; but I tell you these things that you may know

that I can answer with a clear conscience before God this day.

48 "Behold, because I said to you that I had spent my days in your service, I do not desire to boast, for I have only been in the service of God.

49 "And, behold, I tell you these things that you may learn wisdom, that you may learn that when you are in the service of your fellow beings you are only in the service of your God.

50 "Behold, you have called me your king; and if I, whom you call your king, labor to serve you, then ought you not labor to serve one another?

51 "And also, if I, whom you call your king, who have spent my days in your service and yet have been in the service of God, merit any thanks from you, oh, how much ought you to thank your heavenly King!

52 "I say to you, my brethren, that if you should render all the thanks and praise which your whole souls have power to possess to that God who has created you, and has kept and preserved you, and has caused that you should rejoice, and has granted that you should live in peace one with another; 53if you should serve him who has created you from the beginning, and is preserving you from day to day by lending you breath, that you may live and move and do according to your own will, and is even supporting you from one moment to another; 54if you should serve him with all your whole soul, yet ye would be unprofitable servants.

55 "And, behold, all that he requires of you is to keep his commandments; and he has promised you that if you would keep his commandments you should prosper in the land.

56 "He never varies from that which he has said; therefore, if you will keep his commandments, he will bless you, and prosper you.

57 "Now in the first place, he has created you and granted to you your lives, for which you are indebted to him.

58 "And second, he requires that you should do as he has commanded you, for which if you do, he immedi-

ately blesses you; and therefore he has paid you.

59 "And you are still indebted to him; and are, and will be, for ever and ever; therefore, of what have you to boast?

60 "Now I ask, 'Can you say aught of yourselves?' I answer you, 'No.'

61 "You cannot say that you are even as much as the dust of the earth; yet you were created of the dust of the earth; but, behold, it belongs to him who created you.

62 "And I, even I, whom you call your king, am no better than you yourselves are; for I am also of the dust.

63 "You behold that I am old and am about to yield up this mortal frame to its mother earth.

64 "Therefore, as I said to you that I had served you, walking with a clear conscience before God, even so I at this time have caused that you should assemble yourselves together that I might be found blameless, and that your blood should not come upon me when I shall stand to be judged of God of the things whereof he has commanded me concerning you.

65 "I say to you that I have caused that you should assemble yourselves together that I might rid my garments of your blood at this period of time when I am about to go down to my grave, 66that I might go down in peace, and my immortal spirit may join the choirs above in singing the praises of a just God.

67 "Moreover, I say to you that I have caused that you should assemble yourselves together that I might declare to you that I can no longer be your teacher, nor your king.

68 "For even at this time my whole frame trembles exceedingly while attempting to speak to you.

69 "But the Lord God supports me, and has suffered me that I should speak to you, and has commanded me that I should declare to you this day that my son, Mosiah, is a king and a ruler over you.

70 "Now, my brethren, I would that you should do as you have hitherto done.

71 "As you have kept my commandments, and also the commandments of my father, and have pros-

pered, and have been kept from falling into the hands of your enemies, 72even so if you shall keep the commandments of my son, or the commandments of God which shall be delivered to you by him, you shall prosper in the land, and your enemies shall have no power over you.

73 "But, O my people, beware lest there shall arise contentions among you, and you list to obey the evil spirit which was spoken of by my father Mosiah.

74 "For, behold, there is a woe pronounced upon him who lists to obey that spirit; for if he lists to obey him, and remains and dies in his sins, the same drinks damnation to his own soul.

75 "For he receives for his wages an everlasting punishment, having transgressed the law of God contrary to his own knowledge.

76 "I say to you that there are not any among you, except it be your little children that have not been taught concerning these things, but knows that you are eternally indebted to your heavenly Father 77to render to him all that you have, and are. You also have been taught concerning the records which contain the prophecies which have been spoken by the holy prophets, even down to the time our father Lehi left Jerusalem, and also all that has been spoken by our fathers until now.

78 "And, behold, also they spoke that which was commanded them of the Lord; therefore, they are just and true.

79 "And now I say to you, my brethren, that, after you have known and have been taught all these things, if you should transgress and go contrary to that which has been spoken, you withdraw yourselves from the Spirit of the Lord, that it may have no place in you to guide you in wisdom's path, that you may be blessed, prospered, and preserved.

80 "I say to you that the man that does this, the same comes out in open rebellion against God.

81 "Therefore he lists to obey the evil spirit and becomes an enemy to all righteousness; 82therefore, the Lord has no place in him, for he dwells not in unholy temples.

83 "Therefore, if that man repents not, and remains and dies an enemy to God, the demands of divine justice will awaken his immortal soul to a lively sense of his own guilt, ⁸⁴which will cause him to shrink from the presence of the Lord, and will fill his breast with guilt, and pain, and anguish, which is like an unquenchable fire whose flames ascend up for ever and ever.

85 "Now I say to you that mercy has no claim on that man; therefore, his final doom is to endure a never ending torment.

86 "O all you old men, and also you young men, and you little children who can understand my words (for I have spoken plainly to you, that you might understand), ⁸⁷I pray that you should awake to a remembrance of the awful situation of those that have fallen into transgression.

88 "Moreover, I would desire that you should consider the blessed and happy state of those that keep the commandments of God.

89 "For, behold, they are blessed in all things, both temporal and spiritual; ⁹⁰and if they hold out faithful to the end, they are received into heaven, that thereby they may dwell with God in a state of never ending happiness.

91 "Oh, remember, remember that these things are true; for the Lord God has spoken it.

92 "Again, my brethren, I would call your attention, for I have somewhat more to speak to you.

93 "For, behold, I have things to tell you concerning that which is to come; and the things which I shall tell you are made known to me by an angel from God.

94 "He said to me, 'Awake'; and I awoke, and, behold, he stood before me.

95 "And he said to me, 'Awake, and hear the words which I shall tell thee; for, behold, I am come to declare to thee glad tidings of great joy.

96 "'For the Lord hath heard thy prayers, and hath judged of thy righteousness, and hath sent me to declare to thee that thou mayest rejoice; and that thou mayest declare to thy people that they may also be filled with joy.

97 "'For, behold, the time cometh, and is not far distant, that with power, the Lord Omnipotent who reigneth, who was, and is from all eternity to all eternity, shall come down from heaven among the children of men and shall dwell in a tabernacle of clay, ⁹⁸and shall go forth amongst men, working mighty miracles, such as healing the sick, raising the dead, causing the lame to walk, the blind to receive their sight, and the deaf to hear, and curing all manner of diseases.

99 "'And he shall cast out devils, or the evil spirits which dwell in the hearts of the children of men.

100 "'And, lo, he shall suffer temptations, and pain of body, hunger, thirst, and fatigue, even more than man can suffer, except it be to death; ¹⁰¹for, behold, blood cometh from every pore, so great shall be his anguish for the wickedness and the abominations of his people.

102 "'And he shall be called Jesus Christ, the Son of God, the Father of heaven and earth, the Creator of all things, from the beginning; and his mother shall be called Mary.

103 "'And, lo, he cometh to his own that salvation might come to the children of men, even through faith on his name.

104 "'Even after all this, they shall consider him a man, and say that he hath a devil, and shall scourge him, and shall crucify him.

105 "'And he shall rise the third day from the dead; and, behold, he standeth to judge the world.

106 "'Behold, all these things are done that a righteous judgment might come upon the children of men.

107 "'For, behold, and also his blood atoneth for the sins of those who have fallen by the transgression of Adam, who have died not knowing the will of God concerning them, or who have ignorantly sinned.

108 "'But woe, woe to him who knoweth that he rebelleth against God; for salvation cometh to none such, except it be through repentance and faith on the Lord Jesus Christ.

109 "'And the Lord God hath sent his holy prophets among all the children of men to declare these things to every kindred, nation, and tongue,

that thereby whoever should believe that Christ should come, the same might receive remission of his sins, and rejoice with exceedingly great joy, even as though he had already come among them.

110 "'Yet the Lord God saw that his people were a stiff-necked people, and he appointed to them a law, even the law of Moses.

111 "'And many signs, and wonders, and types, and shadows he showed to them, concerning his coming.

112 "'Also holy prophets spoke to them concerning his coming.

113 "'Yet they hardened their hearts, and understood not that the law of Moses availeth nothing except it were through the atonement of his blood; 114and even if it were possible that little children could sin, they could not be saved; but I say to you, they are blessed;

115 "'For, behold, as in Adam, or by nature, they fall, even so the blood of Christ atoneth for their sins.

116 "'Moreover, I say to you that there shall be no other name given, nor any other way nor means whereby salvation can come to the children of men only in and through the name of Christ, the Lord Omnipotent.

117 "'For, behold, he judgeth, and his judgment is just, and the infant perisheth not that dieth in his infancy; 118but men drink damnation to their own souls except they humble themselves, and become as little children, and believe that salvation was, and is, and is to come, in and through the atoning blood of Christ, the Lord Omnipotent.

119 "'For the natural man is an enemy to God, and has been from the fall of Adam, and will be, for ever and ever; 120unless he yields to the enticings of the Holy Spirit, and puts off the natural man, and becomes a saint, through the atonement of Christ, the Lord, and becomes as a child, submissive, meek, humble, patient, full of love, willing to submit to all things which the Lord sees fit to inflict upon him, even as a child doth submit to his father.

121 "'Moreover, I say to you that the time shall come when the knowledge of a Savior shall spread through-out every nation, kindred, tongue, and people.

122 "'Behold, when that time cometh, none shall be found blameless before God, except it be little children, only through repentance and faith on the name of the Lord God Omnipotent.

123 "'And even at this time, when thou shalt have taught thy people the things which the Lord thy God hath commanded thee, even then are they found no more blameless in the sight of God, only according to the words which I have spoken to thee.'

124 "Now I have spoken the words which the Lord God has commanded me.

125 "And thus says the Lord: 'They shall stand as a bright testimony against this people, at the judgment day; 126whereof they shall be judged, every man according to his works, whether they be good, or whether they be evil.

127 "'If they be evil, they are consigned to an awful view of their own guilt and abominations, which doth cause them to shrink from the presence of the Lord into a state of misery and endless torment, whence they can no more return; therefore, they have drunk damnation to their own souls.

128 "'Therefore, they have drunk out of the cup of the wrath of God, which justice could no more deny to them than it could deny that Adam should fall, because of his partaking of the forbidden fruit; therefore, mercy could have claim on them no more forever.

129 "'And their torment is as a lake of fire and brimstone, whose flames are unquenchable, and whose smoke ascendeth up for ever and ever.'

130 "Thus has the Lord commanded me. Amen."

CHAPTER 2

WHEN King Benjamin had made an end of speaking the words which had been delivered to him by the angel of the Lord, he cast his eyes round about on the multitude, and, behold, they had fallen to the earth, for the fear of the Lord had come upon them; 2and they had viewed themselves in their own carnal state even less than the dust of the earth.

3 Then they all cried aloud with one voice, saying, "Oh, have mercy, and apply the atoning blood of Christ that we may receive forgiveness of our sins, and our hearts may be purified; ⁴for we believe in Jesus Christ, the Son of God, who created heaven and earth, and all things, who shall come down among the children of men."

5 And after they had spoken these words, the Spirit of the Lord came upon them, and they were filled with joy, ⁶having received a remission of their sins and having peace of conscience because of the exceeding faith which they had in Jesus Christ who should come, according to the words which King Benjamin had spoken to them.

7 King Benjamin again opened his mouth, and began to speak to them, saying, "My friends and my brethren, my kindred and my people, I would again call your attention that you may hear and understand the remainder of my words which I shall speak to you.

8 "For, behold, if the knowledge of the goodness of God at this time, has awakened you to a sense of your nothingness, and your worthless and fallen state; ⁹I say to you, if you have come to a knowledge of the goodness of God, and his matchless power, and his wisdom, and his patience, and his long-suffering toward the children of men, ¹⁰and also, the atonement which has been prepared from the foundation of the world that thereby salvation might come to him that should put his trust in the Lord, and should be diligent in keeping his commandments, and continue in the faith even to the end of his life—I mean the life of the mortal body—¹¹I say that this is the man who will receive salvation through the atonement which was prepared from the foundation of the world for all mankind, which ever were, ever since the fall of Adam, or who are or who ever shall be, even to the end of the world; and this is the means whereby salvation comes.

12 "And there is no other salvation, save this which has been spoken of; neither are there any conditions

whereby man can be saved except the conditions which I have told you.

13 "Believe in God; believe that he is, and that he created all things, both in heaven and in earth.

14 "Believe that he has all wisdom, and all power, both in heaven and in earth.

15 "Believe that man does not comprehend all things which the Lord can comprehend.

16 "And again: Believe that you must repent of your sins and forsake them, and humble yourselves before God; and ask in sincerity of heart that he would forgive you.

17 "Now if you believe all these things, see that you do them.

18 "Again I say to you, as I have said before, that as you have come to the knowledge of the glory of God, ¹⁹or if you have known of his goodness, and have tasted of his love, and have received a remission of your sins, which causes such exceedingly great joy in your souls, ²⁰even so I would that you should remember, and always retain in remembrance the greatness of God and your own nothingness, and his goodness and long suffering toward you unworthy creatures, ²¹and humble yourselves even in the depths of humility, calling on the name of the Lord daily, and standing steadfastly in the faith of that which is to come, which was spoken by the mouth of the angel.

22 "Behold, I say to you that if you do this, you shall always rejoice and be filled with the love of God, and always retain a remission of your sins; ²³and you shall grow in the knowledge of the glory of him that created you, or in the knowledge of that which is just and true.

24 "And you will not have a mind to injure one another, but to live peaceably, and to render to every man according to that which is his due.

25 "And you will not suffer your children that they go hungry, or naked; ²⁶neither will you suffer that they transgress the laws of God, and fight and quarrel one with another, and serve the devil, who is the master of sin, or who is the evil spirit which has been spoken of by our fathers, he being an enemy to all righteousness;

27but you will teach them to walk in the ways of truth and soberness; you will teach them to love one another and to serve one another.

28 "Also, you yourselves will succor those that stand in need of your succor; you will administer of your substance to him that stands in need; 29and you will not suffer that the beggar will put up his petition to you in vain, and turn him out to perish.

30 "Perhaps you will say, 'The man has brought upon himself his misery; therefore I will stay my hand, and will not give to him of my food, nor impart to him of my substance that he may not suffer, for his punishments are just.'

31 "But I say to you, O man, whoever does this, the same has great cause to repent; and except he repents of that which he has done, he will perish forever, and have no interest in the kingdom of God.

32 "For, behold, are we not all beggars? Do we not all depend upon the same being, even God, for all the substance which we have; for both food and raiment, and for gold, and for silver, and for all the riches which we have of every kind?

33 "Behold, even at this time, you have been calling on his name and begging for a remission of your sins.

34 "And has he suffered that you have begged in vain?

35 "No; he has poured out his Spirit upon you, and has caused that your hearts should be filled with joy, and has caused that your mouths should be stopped that you could not find utterance, so exceedingly great was your joy.

36 "Now, if God, who has created you, on whom you are dependent for your lives and for all that you have and are, grants to you whatever you ask that is right, in faith, believing that you shall receive, oh, then, how had you ought to impart of the substance that you have, one to another?

37 "And if you judge the man who puts up his petition to you for your substance that he perish not, and condemn him, how much more just will be your condemnation for withholding your substance, which does not belong to you but to God, to whom also your life belongs; 38and

yet you put up no petition, nor repent of the thing which you have done.

39 "I say to you, woe be to that man, for his substance shall perish with him; and now, I say these things to those who are rich as pertaining to the things of this world.

40 "Again, I say to the poor, you who have not and yet have sufficient that you remain from day to day—I mean all you who deny the beggar because you have not—I would that you say in your hearts 'I give not because I have not; but if I had, I would give.'

41 "Now, if you say this in your hearts, you remain guiltless, otherwise you are condemned, and your condemnation is just; for you covet that which you have not received.

42 "And now for the sake of these things which I have spoken to you— that is, for the sake of retaining a remission of your sins from day to day that you may walk guiltless before God—43I would that you should impart of your substance to the poor, every man according to that which he has, such as feeding the hungry, clothing the naked, visiting the sick, and administering to their relief, both spiritually and temporally, according to their wants.

44 "And see that all these things are done in wisdom and order; for it is not requisite that a man should run faster than he has strength.

45 "Again, it is expedient that he should be diligent, that thereby he might win the prize; therefore, all things must be done in order.

46 "And I would that you should remember that whoever among you borrows of his neighbor should return the thing that he borrows, according as he agreed, 47or else you will commit sin, and perhaps you will cause your neighbor to commit sin also.

48 "Finally, I cannot tell you all the things whereby you may commit sin; for there are divers ways and means, even so many that I cannot number them.

49 "But this much I can tell you, that if you do not watch yourselves, and your thoughts, and your words, and your deeds, and observe to keep the commandments of God, and continue in the faith of what you have

heard concerning the coming of our Lord, even to the end of your lives, you must perish.

50 "Now, O man, remember, and perish not."

CHAPTER 3

WHEN King Benjamin had thus spoken to his people, he sent among them, desiring to know of his people if they believed the words which he had spoken to them.

2 And they all cried with one voice, saying, "We believe all the words which you have spoken to us.

3 "Also we know of their surety and truth, because of the Spirit of the Lord Omnipotent, which has wrought a mighty change in us, or in our hearts, that we have no more disposition to do evil, but to do good continually.

4 "We ourselves also, through the infinite goodness of God and the manifestations of his Spirit, have great views of that which is to come; and were it expedient, we could prophesy of all things.

5 "And it is the faith which we have had on the things which our king has spoken to us and has brought us to this great knowledge, whereby we rejoice with such exceedingly great joy.

6 "And we are willing to enter into a covenant with our God to do his will, and to be obedient to his commandments in all things that he shall command us, all the remainder of our days, that we may not bring upon ourselves a never ending torment, as has been spoken by the angel, that we may not drink out of the cup of the wrath of God."

7 Now these are the words which King Benjamin desired of them; and therefore he said to them, "You have spoken the words that I desired; and the covenant which you have made is a righteous covenant.

8 "And because of the covenant which you have made you shall be called the children of Christ, his sons, and his daughters.

9 "For, behold, this day he has spiritually begotten you; for you say that your hearts are changed through faith on his name; therefore, you are born of him and have become his sons and his daughters.

10 "And under this head you are made free; and there is no other head whereby you can be made free.

11 "There is no other name given whereby salvation comes; therefore, I would that you should take upon you the name of Christ, all you that have entered into the covenant with God that you would be obedient to the end of your lives.

12 "And it shall come to pass that whoever will do this shall be found at the right hand of God, for he shall know the name by which he is called; for he shall be called by the name of Christ.

13 "And whoever will not take upon him the name of Christ must be called by some other name; therefore, he will find himself on the left hand of God.

14 "I would that you should remember also that this is the name that I said I should give to you, that never should be blotted out except it be through transgression; 15therefore, take heed that you do not transgress, so the name will not be blotted out of your hearts.

16 "I say to you, I would that you should remember to retain the name written always in your hearts, that you are not found on the left hand of God, but that you hear and know the voice by which you shall be called, and also the name by which he shall call you.

17 "For how does a man know the master whom he has not served, and who is a stranger to him, and is far from the thoughts and intents of his heart?

18 "Again: Does a man take an ass which belongs to his neighbor, and keep him?

19 "I say to you, No; he will not even suffer that he shall feed among his flocks, but will drive him away and cast him out.

20 "I say to you, that even so shall it be among you, if you know not the name by which you are called.

21 "Therefore, I would that you should be steadfast and immovable, always abounding in good works, that Christ, the Lord God Omnipotent, may seal you his, that you may

be brought to heaven, that you may have everlasting salvation and eternal life through the wisdom, and power, and justice, and mercy of him who created all things in heaven and in earth, who is God above all. Amen."

CHAPTER 4

NOW King Benjamin thought it was expedient, after having finished speaking to the people, that he should take the names of all those who had entered into a covenant with God to keep his commandments.

2 And there was not one soul, except it were little children, but what had entered into the covenant and had taken upon him the name of Christ.

3 And when King Benjamin had made an end of all these things, and had consecrated his son Mosiah, to be a ruler and a king over his people, and had given him all the charges concerning the kingdom, 4and also had appointed priests to teach the people that thereby they might hear and know the commandments of God, and to stir them up in remembrance of the oath which they had made, he dismissed the multitude, and they returned, every one according to his family, to their own houses.

5 And Mosiah began to reign in his father's stead.

6 He began to reign in the thirtieth year of his age, making in the whole four hundred and seventy-six years from the time that Lehi left Jerusalem.

7 And King Benjamin lived three years and he died.

8 And it came to pass that King Mosiah walked in the ways of the Lord, and observed his judgments, and his statutes, and kept his commandments in all things whatever he commanded him.

9 And King Mosiah caused his people that they should till the earth.

10 He himself also tilled the earth that thereby he might not become burdensome to his people, that he might do according to that which his father had done in all things.

11 And there was no contention among all his people for the space of three years.

CHAPTER 5

NOW after King Mosiah had had continual peace for the space of three years, he was desirous to know concerning the people who went up to dwell in the land of Lehi-Nephi, or in the city of Lehi-Nephi; 2for his people had heard nothing from them from the time they left the land of Zarahemla; therefore, they wearied him with their teasings.

3 King Mosiah granted that sixteen of their strong men might go up to the land of Lehi-Nephi, to inquire concerning their brethren.

4 And on the morrow they started to go up, having with them one Ammon, he being a strong and mighty man, and a descendant of Zarahemla; and he was also their leader.

5 Now they knew not the course they should travel in the wilderness to go up to the land of Lehi-Nephi; therefore, they wandered many days in the wilderness, even forty days they wandered.

6 And when they had wandered forty days, they came to a hill which is north of the land of Shilom, and there they pitched their tents.

7 Ammon took three of his brethren, and their names were Amaleki, Helem, and Hem, and they went down into the land of Nephi.

8 And, behold, they met the king of the people who were in the land of Nephi and in the land of Shilom; 9and they were surrounded by the king's guard, and were taken, and were bound, and were committed to prison.

10 When they had been in prison two days, they were again brought before the king, and their bands were loosed; 11and they stood before the king, and were permitted, or rather commanded, that they should answer the questions which he should ask them.

12 And he said to them, "Behold, I am Limhi, the son of Noah, who was the son of Zeniff who came up out of the land of Zarahemla to inherit this land which was the land of their fathers, who was made a king by the voice of the people.

13 "Now I desire to know the cause whereby you were so bold as

to come near the walls of the city when I myself was with my guards without the gate?

14 "For this cause have I suffered that you should be preserved that I might inquire of you, or else I should have caused that my guards should have put you to death. You are permitted to speak."

15 When Ammon saw that he was permitted to speak, he went forth and bowed himself before the king; and rising again he said, "O king, I am very thankful before God this day that I am yet alive and am permitted to speak.

16 "I will endeavor to speak with boldness; for I am assured that if you had known me, you would not have suffered that I should have worn these bands.

17 "For I am Ammon, a descendant of Zarahemla, and have come up out of the land of Zarahemla to inquire concerning our brethren whom Zeniff brought up out of that land."

18 After Limhi had heard the words of Ammon, he was exceedingly glad, and said, "Now I know of a surety that my brethren who were in the land of Zarahemla are yet alive.

19 "And now I will rejoice; and on the morrow I will cause that my people shall rejoice also.

20 "For, behold, we are in bondage to the Lamanites and are taxed with a tax which is grievous to be borne.

21 "Now, behold, our brethren will deliver us out of our bondage, or out of the hands of the Lamanites, and we will be their slaves; 22for it is better that we be slaves to the Nephites than to pay tribute to the king of the Lamanites."

23 Then King Limhi commanded his guards that they should no more bind Ammon or his brethren, but caused that they should go to the hill which was north of Shilom and bring their brethren into the city, that thereby they might eat, and drink, and rest themselves from the labors of their journey; 24for they had suffered many things; they had suffered hunger, thirst, and fatigue.

25 And on the morrow, King Limhi sent a proclamation among all his people that thereby they might gather themselves to the temple to hear the words which he should speak to them.

26 When they had gathered themselves together, he spoke to them in this wise, saying,

27 "O my people, lift up your heads and be comforted; for, behold, the time is at hand, or is not far distant, when we shall no longer be in subjection to our enemies, notwithstanding our many strugglings which have been in vain; yet I trust there remains an effectual struggle to be made.

28 "Therefore, lift up your heads and rejoice, and put your trust in God, in that God who was the God of Abraham, and Isaac, and Jacob, 29and also, that God who brought the children of Israel out of the land of Egypt, and caused that they should walk through the Red Sea on dry ground, and fed them with manna that they might not perish in the wilderness; and many more things he did for them.

30 "Again, that same God has brought our fathers out of the land of Jerusalem, and has kept and preserved his people, even until now.

31 "Behold, it is our iniquities and abominations that have brought us into bondage.

32 "And you all are witnesses this day that Zeniff, who was made king over this people, was overzealous to inherit the land of his fathers.

33 "Therefore he was deceived by the cunning and craftiness of King Laman, who entered into a treaty with King Zeniff and yielded up into his hands the possessions of a part of the land, even the city of Lehi-Nephi, and the city of Shilom, and the land round about.

34 "And all this he did for the sole purpose of bringing this people into subjection, or into bondage.

35 "Behold, we at this time pay tribute to the king of the Lamanites to the amount of one half of our corn and our barley and even all our grain of every kind, and one half of the increase of our flocks and our herds.

36 "Even one half of all we have or possess, the king of the Lamanites exacts of us, or our lives.

37 "Is not this grievous to be borne?

38 "And is not this our affliction great?

39 "Behold, how great reason have we to mourn!

40 "I say to you, great are the reasons which we have to mourn; for, behold, how many of our brethren have been slain, and their blood has been spilt in vain, and all because of iniquity.

41 "For if this people had not fallen into transgressions, the Lord would not have suffered that this great evil should come upon them.

42 "But, behold, they would not hearken to his words; but there arose contentions among them, even so much that they shed blood among themselves.

43 "And a prophet of the Lord have they slain, even a chosen man of God, who told them of their wickedness and abominations, and prophesied of many things which are to come, even the coming of Christ.

44 "He said to them that Christ was the God, the Father of all things, and that he should take upon him the image of man, and it should be the image after which man was created in the beginning; 45or in other words, he said that man was created after the image of God, and that God should come down among the children of men, and take upon him flesh and blood, and go forth upon the face of the earth.

46 "And because he said this, they put him to death; and many more things they did which brought down the wrath of God upon them.

47 "Therefore, who wonders that they are in bondage and that they are smitten with sore afflictions?

48 "For, behold, the Lord has said, 'I will not succor my people in the day of their transgression; but I will hedge up their ways that they prosper not; and their doings shall be as a stumbling block before them.'

49 "Again, he says, 'If my people shall sow filthiness, they shall reap the chaff thereof in the whirlwind; and the effect thereof is poison.'

50 And again, he says, 'If my people shall sow filthiness, they shall reap the east wind, which bringeth immediate destruction.'

51 "Now, behold, the promise of the Lord is fulfilled; and you are smitten and afflicted.

52 "But if you will turn to the Lord with full purpose of heart, and put your trust in him, and serve him with all diligence of mind, he will, according to his own will and pleasure, deliver you out of bondage."

53 After King Limhi had made an end of speaking to his people (for he spoke many things to them, and only a few of them have I written in this book), he told his people all the things concerning their brethren who were in the land of Zarahemla.

54 And he caused that Ammon should stand up before the multitude, and rehearse to them all that had happened to their brethren, from the time that Zeniff went up out of the land, even until the time that he himself came up out of the land.

55 He also rehearsed to them the last words which King Benjamin had taught them, and explained them to the people of King Limhi so that they might understand all the words which he spoke.

56 After he had done all this, King Limhi dismissed the multitude, and caused that they should return, every one to his own house.

57 Then he caused that the plates which contained the record of his people, from the time that they left the land of Zarahemla, should be brought before Ammon that he might read them.

58 As soon as Ammon had read the record, the king inquired of him to know if he could interpret languages.

59 Ammon told him that he could not.

60 Then the king said to him, "Being grieved for the afflictions of my people, I caused that forty-three of my people should take a journey into the wilderness, that thereby they might find the land of Zarahemla, that we might appeal to our brethren to deliver us out of bondage.

61 "And they were lost in the wilderness for the space of many days; yet they were diligent, and found not

the land of Zarahemla, but returned to this land, having traveled in a land among many waters, 62having discovered a land which was covered with bones of men, and of beasts, and was also covered with ruins of buildings of every kind—63a land which had been peopled with a people who were as numerous as the hosts of Israel.

64 "And for a testimony that the things that they have said are true, they have brought twenty-four plates which are filled with engravings; and they are of pure gold.

65 "Behold, also they have brought breastplates which are large; and they are of brass and of copper, and are perfectly sound.

66 "Again, they have brought swords, the hilts thereof have perished, and the blades thereof are cankered with rust.

67 "And there is no one in the land that is able to interpret the language or the engravings that are on the plates.

68 "Therefore, I said to you, Can you translate?

69 "And I say to you again, Do you know of any one who can translate? I am desirous that these records should be translated into our language.

70 "For perhaps they will give us a knowledge of a remnant of the people who have been destroyed, whence these records came; 71or, perhaps they will give us a knowledge of this very people who have been destroyed; and I am desirous to know the cause of their destruction."

72 Now Ammon said to him, "I can assuredly tell thee, O king, of a man that can translate the records; for he has wherewith he can look and translate all records that are of ancient date; and it is a gift from God.

73 "The things are called interpreters; and no man can look in them except he be commanded, lest he should look for that he ought not, and he should perish.

74 "And whoever is commanded to look in them, the same is called seer.

75 "Behold, the king of the people who is in the land of Zarahemla is the man who is commanded to do these things and has this high gift from God."

76 Then the king said, "A seer is greater than a prophet?"

77 And Ammon said, "A seer is a revelator, and a prophet also; and a gift which is greater can no man have except he should possess the power of God, which no man can; yet a man may have great power given him from God.

78 "But a seer can know of things which have past, and also of things which are to come.

79 "By them shall all things be revealed, or rather shall secret things be made manifest, and hidden things shall come to light, and things which are not known shall be made known by them.

80 "Also, things shall be made known by them which otherwise could not be known.

81 "Thus God has provided a means that man, through faith, might work mighty miracles; therefore, he becomes a great benefit to his fellow beings."

82 When Ammon had made an end of speaking these words, the king rejoiced exceedingly and gave thanks to God, saying,

83 "Doubtless a great mystery is contained within these plates; and these interpreters were doubtless prepared for the purpose of unfolding all such mysteries to the children of men.

84 "Oh, how marvelous are the works of the Lord, and how long does he suffer with his people; 85and how blind and impenetrable are the understandings of the children of men; for they will not seek wisdom, neither do they desire that she should rule over them.

86 "They are as a wild flock, which flees from the shepherd, and are scattered, and are driven, and are devoured by the beasts of the forest."

CHAPTER 6

THE RECORD OF ZENIFF—*An account of his people from the time they left the land of Zarahemla until the time that they were delivered out of the hands of the Lamanites.*

I, Zeniff, having been taught in all the language of the Nephites, and having had a knowledge of the land of Nephi, or of the land of our fathers' first inheritance, was sent as a spy among the Lamanites that I might spy out their forces, so our army might come upon them and destroy them.

2 But when I saw that which was good among them, I was desirous that they should not be destroyed; therefore, I contended with my brethren in the wilderness; for I would that our ruler should make a treaty with them.

3 But he being an austere and a bloodthirsty man, commanded that I should be slain; but I was rescued by the shedding of much blood; 4for father fought against father, and brother against brother, until the greater number of our army was destroyed in the wilderness.

5 And we returned, those of us that were spared, to the land of Zarahemla to relate that tale to their wives and their children.

6 Yet, I, being overzealous to inherit the land of our fathers, collected as many as were desirous to go up to possess the land, and started again on our journey into the wilderness to go up to the land; but we were smitten with famine and sore afflictions, for we were slow to remember the Lord our God.

7 Nevertheless, after many days' wandering in the wilderness, we pitched our tents in the place where our brethren were slain, which was near to the land of our fathers.

8 Then I went again with four of my men into the city to the king, that I might know of the disposition of the king; and that I might know if I might go in with my people and possess the land in peace.

9 And I went in to the king, and he covenanted with me that I might possess the land of Lehi-Nephi and the land of Shilom.

10 He also commanded that his people should depart out of that land; and I and my people went into the land that we might possess it.

11 We began to build buildings and to repair the walls of the city, even the walls of the city of Lehi-Nephi and the city of Shilom.

12 And we began to till the ground, even with all manner of seeds, with seeds of corn, and of wheat, and of barley, and with neas, and with sheum, and with seeds of all manner of fruits; and we began to multiply and prosper in the land.

13 Now it was the cunning and the craftiness of King Laman to bring my people into bondage, that he yielded up the land that we might possess it.

14 Therefore, after we had dwelt in the land for the space of twelve years, King Laman began to grow uneasy, lest by any means my people should wax strong in the land, and that they could not overpower us and bring us into bondage.

15 Now they were a lazy and an idolatrous people; therefore, they were desirous to bring us into bondage that they might glut themselves with the labors of our hands, and that they might feast themselves upon the flocks of our fields.

16 Therefore, it came to pass that King Laman began to stir up his people that they should contend with my people; therefore, there began to be wars and contentions in the land.

17 For in the thirteenth year of my reign in the land of Nephi, away on the south of the land of Shilom, when my people were watering and feeding their flocks, and tilling their lands, a numerous host of Lamanites came upon them and began to slay them, and to take of their flocks and the corn of their fields.

18 And my people fled, all that

were not overtaken, even into the city of Nephi, and called upon me for protection.

19 And it came to pass that I armed them with bows, and with arrows, with swords, and with cimeters, and with clubs, and with slings, and with all manner of weapons which we could invent, and I and my people went forth against the Lamanites to battle.

20 In the strength of the Lord we went forth to battle against the Lamanites; 21for I and my people cried mightily to the Lord that he would deliver us out of the hands of our enemies, for we were awakened to a remembrance of the deliverance of our fathers.

22 And God heard our cries and answered our prayers; and we went forth in his might.

23 We went forth against the Lamanites; and in one day and a night we slew three thousand and forty-three; we slew them even until we had driven them out of our land.

24 And I myself, with my own hands, helped bury their dead.

25 Behold, to our great sorrow and lamentation, two hundred and seventy-nine of our brethren were slain.

26 And it came to pass that we again began to establish the kingdom; and we again began to possess the land in peace.

27 And I caused that there should be made weapons of war of every kind, that thereby I might have weapons for my people against the time the Lamanites should come up again to war against my people.

28 And I set guards round about the land that the Lamanites might not come upon us again unawares and destroy us.

29 Thus I guarded my people, and my flocks, and kept them from falling into the hands of our enemies.

30 And it came to pass that we inherited the land of our fathers for many years, even for the space of twenty-two years.

31 And I caused that the men should till the ground, and raise all manner of grain and all manner of fruit of every kind.

32 And I caused that the women should spin, and toil, and work, and make all manner of fine linen and cloth of every kind that we might clothe our nakedness.

33 Thus we prospered in the land; thus we had continual peace in the land for the space of twenty-two years.

34 And it came to pass that King Laman died, and his son began to reign in his stead.

35 And he began to stir his people up in rebellion against my people; therefore, they began to prepare for war, and to come up to battle against my people.

36 But I had sent my spies out round about the land of Shemlon that I might discover their preparation, that I might guard against them, that they might not come upon my people and destroy them.

37 And it came to pass that they came up upon the north of the land of Shilom, with their numerous hosts, men armed with bows, and with arrows, and with swords, and with cimeters, and with stones, and with slings; 38and they had their heads shaved, that they were naked; and they were girded with a leathern girdle about their loins.

39 And it came to pass that I caused that the women and children of my people should be hid in the wilderness; 40and I also caused that all my old men that could bear arms, and also all my young men that were able to bear arms, should gather themselves together to go to battle against the Lamanites; and I placed them in their ranks, every man according to his age.

41 Then we went up to battle against the Lamanites.

42 And I, even I, in my old age, went up to battle against the Lamanites.

43 And we went up in the strength of the Lord, to battle.

44 Now the Lamanites knew nothing concerning the Lord, nor the strength of the Lord; therefore they depended upon their own strength.

45 Yet they were a strong people, as to the strength of men; they were a wild, and a ferocious, and a bloodthirsty people, believing in the tradition of their fathers, which is this: 46That they were driven out of the

land of Jerusalem because of the iniquities of their fathers, and that they were wronged in the wilderness by their brethren; and they were also wronged while crossing the sea.

47 And again: That they were wronged while in the land of their first inheritance, after they had crossed the sea.

48 But all this was because Nephi was more faithful in keeping the commandments of the Lord, therefore he was favored of the Lord, for the Lord heard his prayers and answered them, and he took the lead of their journey in the wilderness.

49 And his brethren were angry with him because they understood not the dealings of the Lord.

50 They were also angry with him upon the waters because they hardened their hearts against the Lord.

51 Again, they were angry with him when they had arrived in the promised land because they said that he had taken the ruling of the people out of their hands; and they sought to kill him.

52 And again, they were angry with him because he departed into the wilderness as the Lord had commanded him, and took the records which were engraved on the plates of brass; for they said that he robbed them.

53 And thus they have taught their children, that they should hate them, and that they should murder them, and that they should rob and plunder them, and do all they could to destroy them; therefore, they have an eternal hatred, toward the children of Nephi.

54 For this very cause has King Laman, by his cunning and lying craftiness and his fair promises, deceived me, that I have brought this, my people, up into this land that they may destroy them; and we have suffered this many years in the land.

55 Now I, Zeniff, after having told all these things to my people concerning the Lamanites, stimulated them to go to battle with their might, putting their trust in the Lord; therefore, we contended with them face to face.

56 And we again drove them out of our land; and we slew them with a great slaughter, even so many that we did not number them.

57 And it came to pass that we returned again to our own land, and my people again began to tend their flocks and to till their ground.

58 Now I, being old, conferred the kingdom upon one of my sons; therefore, I say no more. And may the Lord bless my people. Amen.

CHAPTER 7

NOW it came to pass that Zeniff conferred the kingdom upon Noah, one of his sons; therefore Noah began to reign in his stead; and he did not walk in the ways of his father.

2 For, behold, he did not keep the commandments of God, but he walked after the desires of his own heart.

3 He had many wives and concubines, 4and caused his people to commit sin and do that which was abominable in the sight of the Lord.

5 And they committed whoredoms and all manner of wickedness.

6 And he laid a tax of one fifth part of all they possessed—a fifth part of their gold and of their silver, and a fifth part of their ziff, and of their copper, and of their brass and their iron, and a fifth part of their fatlings, and also a fifth part of all their grain.

7 All this he took to support himself and his wives and his concubines, and also his priests and their wives and their concubines; thus he had changed the affairs of the kingdom.

8 For he put down all the priests that had been consecrated by his father and consecrated new ones in their stead, such as were lifted up in the pride of their hearts.

9 Thus they were supported in their laziness, and in their idolatry, and in their whoredoms by the taxes which King Noah had put upon his people; thus the people labored exceedingly to support iniquity.

10 And they also became idolatrous because they were deceived by the vain and flattering words of the king and priests; for they spoke flattering things to them.

11 And it came to pass that King Noah built many elegant and spacious buildings; and he ornamented them with fine work of wood, and of all

manner of precious things, of gold, and of silver, and of iron, and of brass, and of ziff, and of copper.

12 He also built him a spacious palace and a throne in the midst thereof, all of which was of fine wood and was ornamented with gold, and silver, and with precious things.

13 And he also caused that his workmen should work all manner of fine work within the walls of the temple, of fine wood, and of copper, and of brass.

14 And the seats which were set apart for the high priests, which were above all the other seats, he ornamented with pure gold; 15and he caused a breastwork to be built before them that they might rest their bodies and their arms upon while they should speak lying and vain words to his people.

16 And he built a tower near the temple, a very high tower, even so high that he could stand upon the top thereof and overlook the land of Shilom, and also the land of Shemlon which was possessed by the Lamanites; and he could even look over all the land round about.

17 He also caused many buildings to be built in the land Shilom.

18 And he caused a great tower to be built on the hill north of the land Shilom which had been a resort for the children of Nephi at the time they fled out of the land.

19 Thus he did with the riches which he obtained by the taxation of his people.

20 And he placed his heart upon his riches, and he spent his time in riotous living with his wives and his concubines; and so did also his priests spend their time with harlots.

21 And he planted vineyards round about in the land; and he built winepresses and made wine in abundance; and therefore he became a winebibber, and also his people.

22 And it came to pass that the Lamanites began to come in upon his people, upon small numbers, and to slay them in their fields and while they were tending their flocks.

23 King Noah sent guards round about the land to keep them off; but he did not send a sufficient number, and the Lamanites came upon them and killed them and drove many of their flocks out of the land.

24 Thus the Lamanites began to destroy them and to exercise their hatred upon them.

25 And it came to pass that King Noah sent his armies against them, and they were driven back, or they drove them back for a time; therefore, they returned rejoicing in their spoil.

26 Because of this great victory, they were lifted up in the pride of their hearts; they boasted in their own strength, saying that their fifty could stand against thousands of the Lamanites.

27 Thus they boasted, and delighted in blood and the shedding of the blood of their brethren, and this because of the wickedness of their king and priests.

28 But there was a man among them whose name was Abinadi; and he went forth among them and began to prophesy, saying,

29 "Behold, thus says the Lord, and thus has he commanded me, saying, 30'Go forth and say to this people, Thus saith the Lord: 31woe be to this people, for I have seen their abominations, and their wickedness, and their whoredoms; and except they repent, I will visit them in my anger.

32 "'And except they repent, and turn to the Lord their God, behold, I will deliver them into the hands of their enemies; 33and they shall be brought into bondage; and they shall be afflicted by the hand of their enemies.

34 "'And it shall come to pass that they shall know that I am the Lord their God, and am a jealous God, visiting the iniquities of my people.

35 "'And except this people repent, and turn unto the Lord their God, they shall be brought into bondage; and none shall deliver them except it be the Lord, the Almighty God.

36 "'And when they shall cry to me, I will be slow to hear their cries; and I will suffer them to be smitten by their enemies.

37 "'And except they repent in sackcloth and ashes, and cry mightily

to the Lord their God, I will not hear their prayers, neither will I deliver them out of their afflictions.'

38 "Thus says the Lord, and thus has he commanded me."

39 Now when Abinadi had spoken these words to them, they were angry with him and sought to take away his life; but the Lord delivered him out of their hands.

40 And when King Noah had heard of the words which Abinadi had spoken to the people, he was also angry.

41 He said, "Who is Abinadi, that I and my people should be judged of him? Or who is the Lord that shall bring upon my people such great affliction?

42 "I command you to bring Abinadi here that I may slay him; for he has said these things that he might stir up my people to anger, one with another, and to raise contentions among my people; therefore I will slay him."

43 Now the eyes of the people were blinded; therefore, they hardened their hearts against the words of Abinadi, and they sought from that time forward to take him.

44 And King Noah hardened his heart against the word of the Lord; and he did not repent of his evil doings.

45 After the space of two years, Abinadi came among them in disguise that they knew him not, and began again to prophesy among them, saying,

46 "Thus has the Lord commanded me, saying, 'Abinadi, go and prophesy to this my people, for they have hardened their hearts against my words; they have repented not of their evil doings; 47therefore, I will visit them in my anger, in my fierce anger will I visit them in their iniquities and abominations; woe be to this generation.'

48 "And the Lord said to me, 'Stretch forth thy hand, and prophesy, saying, Thus says the Lord: It shall come to pass that this generation, because of their iniquities, shall be brought into bondage and shall be smitten on the cheek, 49and shall be driven by men, and shall be slain; and the vultures of the air, and the dogs,

and the wild beasts shall devour their flesh.

50 "'And the life of King Noah shall be valued even as a garment in a hot furnace; for he shall know that I am the Lord.

51 "'And I will smite this my people with sore afflictions, even with famine and with pestilence; and I will cause that they shall howl all the day long.

52 "'And I will cause that they shall have burdens lashed upon their backs; and they shall be driven before, like a dumb ass.

53 "'I will send forth hail among them, and it shall smite them; and they shall also be smitten with the east wind; and insects shall pester their land also, and devour their grain.

54 "'And they shall be smitten with a great pestilence; and all this will I do because of their iniquities and abominations.

55 "'Except they repent, I will utterly destroy them from off the face of the earth.

56 "'Yet they shall leave a record behind them, and I will preserve it for other nations which shall possess the land; 57even this will I do that I may discover the abominations of this people to other nations.'"

58 Many things Abinadi prophesied against this people.

59 And it came to pass that they were angry with him; and they took him and carried him bound before the king, and said to the king,

60 "Behold, we have brought a man before thee who has prophesied evil concerning thy people and has said that God will destroy them; 61and he also prophesied evil concerning thy life, and said that thy life shall be as a garment in a furnace of fire.

62 "Again, he said that thou shalt be as a stalk, even as a dry stalk of the field, which is run over by the beasts and trodden under foot.

63 "And again, he said thou shalt be as the blossom of a thistle, which when it is fully ripe, if the wind bloweth, it is driven forth upon the face of the land; and he pretendeth the Lord hath spoken it.

64 "He said all this shall come up-

on thee except thou repent; and this because of thine iniquities.

65 "And now, O king, what great evil hast thou done, or what great sins have thy people committed that we should be condemned of God or judged of this man?

66 "O king, behold, we are guiltless, and thou, O king, hast not sinned; therefore, this man has lied concerning thee, and he has prophesied in vain.

67 "Behold, we are strong, we shall not come into bondage, or be taken captive by our enemies; and thou hast prospered in the land, and thou shalt also prosper.

68 "Behold, here is the man, we deliver him into thy hands; thou mayest do with him as seemeth thee good."

69 And King Noah caused that Abinadi should be cast into prison.

70 And he commanded that the priests should gather themselves together that he might hold a council with them as to what he should do with him.

71 They said to the king, "Bring him here that we may question him."

72 And the king commanded that he should be brought before them.

73 They began to question him that they might cross him, that thereby they might have wherewith to accuse him.

74 But he answered them boldly and withstood all their questions, to their astonishment; 75for he withstood them in all their questions, and confounded them in all their words.

76 And one of them said to him, "What mean the words which are written and which have been taught by our fathers?"

77 *How beautiful upon the mountains are the feet of him that bringeth good tidings; that publisheth peace; that bringeth good tidings of good; that publisheth salvation; that saith to Zion, Thy God reigneth.

78 Thy watchmen shall lift up the voice; with the voice together shall they sing, for they shall see eye to eye, when the Lord shall bring again Zion.

*Isaiah 52:7–10

79 Break forth into joy; sing together, ye waste places of Jerusalem; for the Lord hath comforted his people; he hath redeemed Jerusalem.

80 The Lord hath made bare his holy arm in the eyes of all the nations; and all the ends of the earth shall see the salvation of our God.

81 Abinadi said to them, "Are you priests, and pretend to teach this people and to understand the spirit of prophesying, and yet desire to know of me what these things mean?

82 "I say to you, Woe be to you for perverting the ways of the Lord. For if you understand these things, you have not taught them; therefore you have perverted the ways of the Lord.

83 "You have not applied your hearts to understanding; therefore, you have not been wise. Therefore, what teach you this people?"

84 And they said, "We teach the law of Moses."

85 Again he said to them, "If you teach the law of Moses, why do you not keep it?

86 "Why do you set your hearts upon riches?

87 "Why do you commit whoredoms, and spend your strength with harlots, and cause this people to commit sin, that the Lord has cause to send me to prophesy against this people, even a great evil against this people?

88 "Know you not that I speak the truth?

89 "You know that I speak the truth; and you ought to tremble before God.

90 "And it shall come to pass that you shall be smitten for your iniquities; for you have said that you teach the law of Moses.

91 "And what know you concerning the law of Moses?

92 "Does salvation come by the law of Moses? What say you?"

93 They answered and said that salvation did come by the law of Moses.

94 But now Abinadi said to them, "I know if you keep the commandments of God, you shall be saved; 95if you keep the commandments

which the Lord delivered to Moses in the mount of Sinai, saying: 'I am the Lord thy God, who has brought thee out of the land of Egypt, out of the house of bondage.

96 "'Thou shalt have no other God before me.

97 "'Thou shalt not make thee any graven image, or any likeness of anything in heaven above, or things which are in the earth beneath.'"

98 Now Abinadi said to them, "Have you done all this? I say to you, you have not.

99 "Have you taught this people that they should do all these things? I say to you, you have not."

100 When the king had heard these words, he said to his priests, "Away with this fellow and slay him; for what have we to do with him, for he is mad."

101 And they stood forth and attempted to lay their hands on him; but he withstood them and said to them, "Touch me not, for God shall smite you if you lay your hands upon me, for I have not delivered the message which the Lord sent me to deliver.

102 "Neither have I told you that which you requested that I should tell; therefore, God will not suffer that I shall be destroyed at this time.

103 "But I must fulfill the commandments wherewith God has commanded me, and because I have told you the truth, you are angry with me.

104 "Again, because I have spoken the word of God, you have judged me that I am mad."

105 After Abinadi had spoken these words, the people of King Noah dared not lay their hands on him; 106for the Spirit of the Lord was upon him; and his face shone with exceeding luster, even as Moses' did while in the mount of Sinai while speaking with the Lord.

107 He spoke with power and authority from God; and he continued his words, saying, "You see that you have not power to slay me, therefore I finish my message.

108 "I perceive that it cuts you to your hearts, because I tell you the truth concerning your iniquities; and my words fill you with wonder and amazement, and with anger.

109 "But I finish my message; and then it matters not where I go, if it so be that I am saved.

110 "But this much I tell you: What you do with me, after this, shall be as a type and a shadow of things which are to come.

111 "Now I read to you the remainder of the commandments of God, for I perceive that they are not written in your hearts.

112 "I perceive that you have studied and taught iniquity the most part of your lives.

113 "Now, remember that I said to you, 'Thou shalt not make to thee any graven image, or any likeness of things which are in heaven above, or which are in the earth beneath, or which are in the water under the earth.'

114 "Again: 'Thou shalt not bow down thyself to them, nor serve them; for I the Lord thy God am a jealous God, visiting the iniquities of the fathers upon the children, to the third and fourth generations of them that hate me, and showing mercy to thousands of them that love me, and keep my commandments.

115 "'Thou shalt not take the name of the Lord thy God in vain; for the Lord will not hold him guiltless that taketh his name in vain.

116 "'Remember the Sabbath day, to keep it holy.

117 "'Six days shalt thou labor and do all thy work; but the seventh day, the Sabbath of the Lord thy God, thou shalt not do any work, thou, nor thy son, nor thy daughter, thy man servant, nor thy maid servant, nor thy cattle, nor thy stranger that is within thy gates.

118 "'For in six days the Lord made heaven and earth, and the sea and all that in them is; wherefore the Lord blessed the Sabbath day and hallowed it.

119 "'Honor thy father and thy mother, that thy days may be long upon the land which the Lord thy God giveth thee.

120 "'Thou shalt not kill.

121 "'Thou shalt not commit adultery.

122 "'Thou shalt not steal.

123 "'Thou shalt not bear false witness against thy neighbor.

124 "'Thou shalt not covet thy neighbor's house, thou shalt not covet thy neighbor's wife, nor his man servant, nor his maid servant, nor his ox, nor his ass, nor anything that is thy neighbor's.'"

CHAPTER 8

AFTER Abinadi had made an end of these sayings, he said to them, "Have you taught this people that they should observe to do all these things and to keep these commandments?

2 "I say to you, No; for if you had, the Lord would not have caused me to come forth and to prophesy evil concerning this people.

3 "You have said that salvation comes by the law of Moses.

4 "I say to you that it is expedient that you should keep the law of Moses as yet; but I say to you that the time shall come when it shall no more be expedient to keep the law of Moses.

5 "Moreover, I say to you that salvation does not come by the law alone; and were it not for the atonement which God himself shall make for the sins and iniquities of his people, they must unavoidably perish, notwithstanding the law of Moses.

6 "Now I say to you that it was expedient that there should be a law given to the children of Israel, even a very strict law; for they were a stiff-necked people, quick to do iniquity and slow to remember the Lord their God.

7 "Therefore there was a law given them, a law of performances and of ordinances, a law which they were to observe strictly from day to day, to keep them in remembrance of God and their duty toward him.

8 "But, behold, I say to you that all these things were types of things to come.

9 "And now, did they understand the law?

10 "I say to you, No, they did not all understand the law; and this because of the hardness of their hearts; for they understood not that there could not any man be saved except it were through the redemption of God.

11 "For, behold, did not Moses prophesy to them concerning the coming of the Messiah, and that God should redeem his people, and even all the prophets who have prophesied ever since the world began?

12 "Have they not spoken more or less concerning these things?

13 "Have they not said that God himself should come down among the children of men, and take upon him the form of man, and go forth in mighty power upon the face of the earth?

14 "And have they not said also that he should bring to pass the resurrection of the dead, and that he himself should be oppressed and afflicted?

15 "Even does not Isaiah say:

16 *Who hath believed our report, and to whom is the arm of the Lord revealed?

17 For he shall grow up before him as a tender plant, and as a root out of dry ground; he hath no form nor comeliness; and when we shall see him, there is no beauty that we should desire him.

18 He is despised and rejected of men, a man of sorrows, and acquainted with grief; and we hid as it were our face from him; he was despised, and we esteemed him not.

19 Surely he has borne our griefs and carried our sorrows; yet we did esteem him stricken, smitten of God, and afflicted.

20 But he was wounded for our transgressions, he was bruised for our iniquities; the chastisement of our peace was upon him; and with his stripes we are healed.

21 All we, like sheep, have gone astray; we have turned every one to his own way; and the Lord hath laid on him the iniquities of us all.

22 He was oppressed, and he was afflicted, yet he opened not his mouth; he is brought as a lamb to the slaughter, and as a sheep before her shearers is dumb, so he opened not his mouth.

23 He was taken from prison and from judgment; and who shall declare his generation? For he was cut off out of the land of the living;

*Isaiah 53

118

for the transgressions of my people was he stricken.

24 And he made his grave with the wicked, and with the rich in his death; because he had done no evil, neither was any deceit in his mouth.

25 Yet it pleased the Lord to bruise him; he hath put him to grief; when thou shalt make his soul an offering for sin, he shall see his seed, he shall prolong his days, and the pleasure of the Lord shall prosper in his hand.

26 He shall see of the travail of his soul and shall be satisfied; by his knowledge shall my righteous servant justify many; for he shall bear their iniquities.

27 Therefore will I divide him a portion with the great, and he shall divide the spoil with the strong; because he hath poured out his soul unto death; and he was numbered with the transgressors; and he bare the sins of many, and made intercession for the transgressors.

28 Now Abinadi said to them, "I would that you should understand that God himself shall come down among the children of men and shall redeem his people.

29 "And because he dwells in flesh, he shall be called the Son of God; 30and having subjected the flesh to the will of the Father, being the Father and the Son—the Father because he was conceived by the power of God, and the Son because of the flesh; thus becoming the Father and Son—31they are one God, the very eternal Father of heaven and of earth.

32 "Thus the flesh becoming subject to the Spirit, or the Son to the Father, being one God, suffers temptation, and yields not to the temptation, but suffers himself to be mocked, and scourged, and cast out, and disowned by his people.

33 "And after all this, and after working many mighty miracles among the children of men, he shall be led, even as Isaiah said, as a sheep before the shearer is dumb, so he opened not his mouth; 34even so he shall be led, crucified, and slain, the flesh becoming subject even to death, the will of the Son being swallowed up in the will of the Father.

35 "Thus God breaks the bands of death, having gained the victory over death, giving the Son power to make intercession for the children of men, 36having ascended into heaven, having the bowels of mercy, being filled with compassion toward the children of men, 37standing between them and justice, having broken the bands of death, having taken upon himself their iniquity and their transgressions, having redeemed them and satisfied the demands of justice.

38 "Now I say to you, Who shall declare his generation?

39 "Behold, I say to you that when his soul has been made an offering for sin, he shall see his seed.

40 "And now what say you? And who shall be his seed?

41 "Behold, I say to you that whoever has heard the words of the prophets, even all the holy prophets who have prophesied concerning the coming of the Lord; 42I say to you that all those who have hearkened to their words, and believed that the Lord would redeem his people, and have looked forward to that day for a remission of their sins; 43I say to you that these are his seed, or they are heirs of the kingdom of God.

44 "For these are they whose sins he has borne; these are they for whom he has died to redeem them from their transgressions.

45 "And now, are they not his seed?

46 "And are not the prophets every one that has opened his mouth to prophesy, that has not fallen into transgression; I mean all the holy prophets ever since the world began?

47 "I say to you that they are his seed; and these are they who have published peace, who have brought good tidings of good, who have published salvation, and said to Zion, Thy God reigneth!

48 "Oh, how beautiful upon the mountains were their feet!

49 "And again, how beautiful upon the mountains are the feet of those that are still publishing peace!

50 "And again, how beautiful upon the mountains are the feet of those who shall herafter publish peace,

from this time henceforth and forever!

51 "Behold, I say to you, This is not all: for, oh, how beautiful upon the mountains are the feet of him that brings good tidings, that is the founder of peace, 52even the Lord, who has redeemed his people, who has granted salvation to his people.

53 "For were it not for the redemption which he has made for his people, which was prepared from the foundation of the world—I say to you, were it not for this—all mankind must have perished.

54 "But, behold, the bands of death shall be broken, and the Son shall reign and have power over the dead; therefore, he will bring to pass the resurrection of the dead.

55 "And there will come a resurrection, even a first resurrection, even a resurrection of those that have been, and who are, and who shall be, even until the resurrection of Christ, for so shall he be called.

56 "Now the resurrection of all the prophets, and all those that have believed in their words, or all those that have kept the commandments of God, shall come forth in the first resurrection; therefore, they are the first resurrection.

57 "They are raised to dwell with God, who has redeemed them; thus they have eternal life through Christ, who has broken the bands of death.

58 "And these are those who have part in the first resurrection; and these are they that have died before Christ came, in their ignorance, not having salvation declared to them.

59 "Thus the Lord brings about the restoration of these; and they have a part in the first resurrection, or have eternal life, being redeemed by the Lord.

60 "And little children also have eternal life.

61 "But, behold, and fear, and tremble before God; for you ought to tremble; for the Lord redeems none such that rebel against him and die in their sins; 62even all those that have perished in their sins ever since the world began, that have willfully rebelled against God, that have known the commandments of God and would not keep them; these are they that have no part in the first resurrection.

63 "Therefore had you not ought to tremble?

64 "For salvation comes to none such; for the Lord has redeemed none such; 65neither can the Lord redeem such; for he cannot deny himself; for he cannot deny justice when it has its claim.

66 "Now I say to you that the time shall come that the salvation of the Lord shall be declared to every nation, kindred, tongue, and people."

67 *Lord, thy watchmen shall lift up the voice; with the voice together shall they sing; for they shall see eye to eye when the Lord shall bring again Zion.

68 Break forth into joy; sing together, ye waste places of Jerusalem; for the Lord hath comforted his people, he hath redeemed Jerusalem.

69 The Lord hath made bare his holy arm in the eyes of all the nations; and all the ends of the earth shall see the salvation of our God.

70 After Abinadi had spoken these words, he stretched forth his hand and said, "The time shall come when all shall see the salvation of the Lord; 71when every nation, kindred, tongue, and people shall see eye to eye, and shall confess before God that his judgments are just.

72 "Then shall the wicked be cast out, and they shall have cause to howl, and weep, and wail, and gnash their teeth; 73and this because they would not hearken to the voice of the Lord; therefore the Lord redeems them not, for they are carnal and devilish, and the devil has power over them; 74even that old serpent that beguiled our first parents, which was the cause of their fall; 75which was the cause of all mankind becoming carnal, sensual, devilish, knowing evil from good, subjecting themselves to the devil.

76 "Thus all mankind were lost; and, behold, they would have been endlessly lost were it not that God redeemed his people from their lost and fallen state.

*Isaiah 52:8–10

120

77 "But remember that he that persists in his own carnal nature, and goes on in the ways of sin and rebellion against God, remains in his fallen state, and the devil has all power over him.

78 "Therefore he is as though there was no redemption made, being an enemy to God; and also is the devil an enemy to God.

79 "Now if Christ had not come into the world, speaking of things to come as though they had already come, there could have been no redemption.

80 "And if Christ had not risen from the dead, or had not broken the bands of death that the grave should have no victory and that death should have no sting, there could have been no resurrection.

81 "But there is a resurrection, therefore the grave has no victory, and the sting of death is swallowed up in Christ.

82 "He is the light and the life of the world, a light that is endless, that can never be darkened; and also a life which is endless, that there can be no more death.

83 "Even this mortal shall put on immortality, and this corruption shall put on incorruption, and all shall be brought to stand before the bar of God to be judged of him according to their works, whether they be good or whether they be evil.

84 "If they be good, to the resurrection of endless life and happiness; and if they be evil, to the resurrection of endless damnation, 85being delivered up to the devil, who has subjected them, which is damnation; 86having gone according to their own carnal wills and desires; having never called upon the Lord while the arms of mercy were extended toward them.

87 "For the arms of mercy were extended toward them, and they would not; they being warned of their iniquities, and yet they would not depart from them.

88 "They were commanded to repent, yet they would not repent.

89 "Now had you not ought to tremble and repent of your sins, and remember only in and through Christ you can be saved?

90 "Therefore, if you teach the law of Moses, also teach that it is a shadow of those things which are to come.

91 "Teach them that redemption comes through Christ the Lord, who is the very eternal Father. Amen."

CHAPTER 9

WHEN Abinadi had finished these sayings, the king commanded that the priests should take him and cause that he should be put to death.

2 But there was one among them whose name was Alma; he also was a descendant of Nephi.

3 And he was a young man, and he believed the words which Abinadi had spoken, for he knew concerning the iniquity which Abinadi had testified against them; 4therefore he began to plead with the king that he would not be angry with Abinadi, but would suffer that he might depart in peace.

5 But the king was more angry, and caused that Alma should be cast out from among them, and sent his servants after him that they might slay him.

6 But he fled from before them and hid himself that they found him not.

7 And he, being concealed for many days, wrote all the words which Abinadi had spoken.

8 And it came to pass that the king caused that his guards should surround Abinadi and take him; and they bound him and cast him into prison.

9 After three days, having counseled with his priests, he caused that he should again be brought before him.

10 And he said to him, "Abinadi, we have found an accusation against you, and you are worthy of death.

11 "For you have said that God himself should come down among the children of men.

12 "For this cause you shall be put to death, unless you will recall all the evil words which you have spoken concerning me and my people."

13 Now Abinadi said to him: "I say to you, I will not recall the words which I have spoken to you concerning this people, for they are true; 14and that you may know of their surety, I have suffered myself that I have fallen into your hands.

15 "And I will suffer even until death, and I will not recall my words, and they shall stand as a testimony against you.

16 "If you slay me, you will shed innocent blood, and this shall also stand as a testimony against you at the last day."

17 Now King Noah was about to release him, for he feared his word; for he feared that the judgments of God would come upon him.

18 But the priests lifted up their voices against him, and began to accuse him, saying, "He has reviled the king."

19 Therefore the king was stirred up in anger against him, and he delivered him up that he might be slain.

20 And they took him, and bound him, and scourged his skin with fagots, even to death.

21 When the flames began to scorch him, he cried to them, saying, "Behold, even as you have done to me, so shall it come to pass that your seed shall cause that many shall suffer the pains that I suffer, even the pains of death by fire; and this because they believe in the salvation of the Lord their God.

22 "And it will come to pass that you shall be afflicted with all manner of diseases because of your iniquities.

23 "And you shall be smitten on every hand and shall be driven and scattered to and fro, even as a wild flock is driven by wild and ferocious beasts.

24 "And in that day you shall be hunted, and you shall be taken by the hand of your enemies, and then you shall suffer, as I suffer, the pains of death by fire.

25 "Thus God executes vengeance upon those that destroy his people.

26 "O God, receive my soul."

27 When Abinadi had said these words, he fell, having suffered death by fire, having been put to death because he would not deny the commandments of God, having sealed the truth of his words by his death.

28 Now it came to pass that Alma, who had fled from the servants of King Noah, repented of his sins and iniquities, and went about privately among the people, and began to teach the words of Abinadi ²⁹concerning that which was to come, and also concerning the resurrection of the dead, and the redemption of the people which was to be brought to pass through the power, and sufferings, and death of Christ and his resurrection and ascension into heaven.

30 And as many as would hear his word he taught.

31 And he taught them privately that it might not come to the knowledge of the king. And many believed his words.

32 As many as believed him went forth to a place which was called Mormon, having received its name from the king, being in the borders of the land having been infested at times or at seasons by wild beasts.

33 Now there was in Mormon a fountain of pure water where Alma resorted, there being near the water a thicket of small trees where he hid himself in the day time from the searches of the king.

34 And as many as believed him went there to hear his words.

35 After many days, there were a goodly number gathered together to the place of Mormon to hear the words of Alma.

36 All were gathered together that believed on his word to hear him.

37 And he taught them and preached to them repentance, and redemption, and faith on the Lord.

38 And he said to them, "Behold, here are the waters of Mormon"; for thus were they called.

39 "If you are desirous to come into the fold of God and to be called his people, and are willing to bear one another's burdens that they may be light, ⁴⁰and are willing to mourn with those that mourn, and comfort those that stand in need of comfort, and to stand as witnesses of God at all times, and in all things, and in all places that you may be in, even until death, that you may be redeemed of God, and be numbered with those of the first resurrection, that you may have eternal life; ⁴¹I say to you, If this be the desire of your hearts, what have you against being baptized in the name of the Lord, as a witness before him that you have entered into a covenant with him that you will serve him and keep his command-

ments, that he may pour out his Spirit more abundantly upon you?"

42 When the people heard these words, they clapped their hands for joy and exclaimed, "This is the desire of our hearts."

43 And Alma took Helam, he being one of the first, and went and stood forth in the water and cried, saying, "O Lord, pour out thy Spirit upon thy servant that he may do this work with holiness of heart."

44 When he had said these words, the Spirit of the Lord was upon him, and he said, "Helam, I baptize you, having authority from the Almighty God, as a testimony that you have entered into a covenant to serve him until you are dead as to the mortal body; and may the Spirit of the Lord be poured out upon you, and may he grant you eternal life through the redemption of Christ, whom he has prepared from the foundation of the world."

45 After Alma had said these words, both Alma and Helam were buried in the water; and they arose and came forth out of the water rejoicing, being filled with the Spirit.

46 And again, Alma took another, and went forth a second time into the water, and baptized him according to the first, only he did not bury himself again in the water.

47 After this manner he baptized every one that went forth to the place of Mormon; and they were in number two hundred and four souls.

48 And they were baptized in the waters of Mormon and were filled with the grace of God.

49 And they were called the church of God, or the church of Christ, from that time forward, [50]and whoever was baptized by the power and authority of God was added to his church.

51 And it came to pass that Alma, having authority from God, ordained priests; even one priest to every fifty of their number he ordained to preach to them, and to teach them concerning the things pertaining to the kingdom of God.

52 And he commanded them that they should teach nothing, save the things which he had taught and which had been spoken by the mouth of the holy prophets.

53 Even he commanded them that they should preach nothing, save repentance and faith on the Lord who had redeemed his people.

54 And he commanded them that there should be no contention one with another, but that they should look forward with one eye, having one faith and one baptism, having their hearts knit together in unity and in love, one toward another.

55 Thus he commanded them to preach. And thus they became the children of God.

56 And he commanded them that they should observe the Sabbath day and keep it holy, and also every day they should give thanks to the Lord their God.

57 He also commanded them that the priests whom he had ordained should labor with their own hands for their support.

58 And there was one day in every week that was set apart that they should gather themselves together to teach the people, and to worship the Lord their God, and also, as often as it was in their power, to assemble themselves together.

59 The priests were not to depend upon the people for their support; but for their labor they were to receive the grace of God that they might wax strong in the Spirit, having the knowledge of God, that they might teach with power and authority from God.

60 Again, Alma commanded that the people of the church should impart of their substance, every one according to that which he had.

61 If he had more abundantly, he should impart more abundantly; and of him that had but little, but little should be required; and to him that had not should be given.

62 Thus they should impart of their substance of their own free will and good desires toward God, and to those priests that stood in need, and to every needy, naked soul.

63 And this he said to them, having been commanded of God.

64 And they walked uprightly before God, imparting to one another, both temporally and spiritually, according to their needs and their wants.

65 Now it came to pass that all

this was done in Mormon, by the waters of Mormon, in the forest that was near the waters of Mormon.

66 The place of Mormon, the waters of Mormon, the forest of Mormon, how beautiful are they to the eyes of them who there came to the knowledge of their Redeemer.

67 And how blessed are they, for they shall sing to his praise forever.

68 And these things were done in the borders of the land that they might not come to the knowledge of the king.

69 But, behold, it came to pass that the king, having discovered a movement among the people, sent his servants to watch them.

70 Therefore on the day that they were assembling themselves together to hear the word of the Lord, they were discovered by the king's men.

71 Now the king said that Alma was stirring up the people to rebellion against him; therefore he sent his army to destroy them.

72 But Alma and the people of the Lord were apprised of the coming of the king's army; therefore they took their tents and their families, and departed into the wilderness.

73 And they were in number about four hundred and fifty souls.

74 And it came to pass that the army of the king returned, having searched in vain for the people of the Lord.

75 Now the forces of the king were small, having been reduced, and there began to be a division among the remainder of the people.

76 And the lesser part began to breathe out threatenings against the king, and there began to be a great contention among them.

77 Now there was a man among them whose name was Gideon, and he being a strong man and an enemy to the king, therefore he drew his sword and swore in his wrath that he would slay the king.

78 And he fought with the king; and when the king saw that he was about to overpower him, he fled and ran and got upon the tower, which was near the temple.

79 Gideon pursued him and was about to get upon the tower to slay the king, when the king cast his eyes round about toward the land of Shemlon, and, behold, the army of the Lamanites were within the borders of the land.

80 The king cried out in the anguish of his soul, saying, "Gideon, spare me, for the Lamanites are upon us, and they will destroy us; they will destroy my people."

81 Now the king was not so much concerned about his people as he was about his own life; nevertheless, Gideon spared his life.

82 And the king commanded the people that they should flee before the Lamanites, and he himself went before them, and they fled into the wilderness with their women and their children.

83 The Lamanites pursued them, and overtook them, and began to slay them.

84 And it came to pass that the king commanded them that all the men should leave their wives and their children and flee before the Lamanites.

85 Now there were many that would not leave them but had rather stay and perish with them.

86 And the rest left their wives and their children and fled.

87 Those who tarried with their wives and their children caused that their fair daughters should stand forth and plead with the Lamanites that they would not slay them.

88 And the Lamanites had compassion on them, for they were charmed with the beauty of their women.

89 Therefore the Lamanites spared their lives, and took them captives, and carried them back to the land of Nephi, and granted them that they might possess the land under the conditions that they would deliver up King Noah into the hands of the Lamanites, and deliver up their property, 90even one half of all they possessed—one half of their gold, and their silver, and all their precious things; and thus they should pay tribute to the king of the Lamanites from year to year.

91 Now there was one of the sons of the king among those that were taken captive whose name was Limhi.

92 Limhi was desirous that his fa-

ther should not be destroyed; nevertheless, Limhi was not ignorant of the iniquities of his father, he himself being a just man.

93 And it came to pass that Gideon sent men into the wilderness secretly to search for the king and those that were with him.

94 And they met the people in the wilderness, all save the king and his priests.

95 Now those who had fled with the king had sworn in their hearts that they would return to the land of Nephi, and if their wives and their children were slain, and also those that had tarried with them, they would seek revenge, and also perish with them.

96 But the king had commanded them that they should not return; and they were angry with the king and caused that he should suffer death by fire.

97 They were about to take the priests also to put them to death, but they fled before them.

98 And they were about to return to the land of Nephi when they met the men of Gideon.

99 The men of Gideon told them of all that had happened to their wives and their children; and that the Lamanites had granted them that they might possess the land by paying a tribute to the Lamanites of one half of all they possessed.

100 And the people told the men of Gideon that they had slain the king, and his priests had fled from them farther into the wilderness.

101 After they had ended the ceremony, they returned to the land of Nephi, rejoicing because their wives and their children were not slain; and they told Gideon what they had done to the king.

102 And it came to pass that the king of the Lamanites made an oath to them that his people would not slay them.

103 Also Limhi, being the son of the king, having the kingdom conferred upon him by the people, made oath to the king of the Lamanites that his people would pay tribute to him, even one half of all they possessed.

104 And Limhi began to establish the kingdom and to establish peace among his people.

105 The king of the Lamanites set guards round about the land that he might keep the people of Limhi in the land, that they might not depart into the wilderness; 106and he supported his guards out of the tribute which he received from the Nephites.

107 And King Limhi had continual peace in his kingdom for the space of two years, that the Lamanites did not molest them nor seek to destroy them.

108 Now there was a place in Shemlon where the daughters of the Lamanites gathered themselves together to sing, and to dance, and to make themselves merry.

109 One day a small number of them gathered there to sing and to dance.

110 The priests of King Noah, being ashamed to return to the city of Nephi, and also fearing that the people would slay them, dared not return to their wives and their children.

111 And having tarried in the wilderness, and having discovered the daughters of the Lamanites, they lay and watched them; and when there were but few of them gathered to dance, they came forth out of their secret places and took them and carried them into the wilderness; 112even twenty-four of the daughters of the Lamanites they carried into the wilderness.

113 When the Lamanites found that their daughters had been missing, they were angry with the people of Limhi; for they thought it was the people of Limhi.

114 Therefore they sent their armies forth; even the king himself went before his people. And they went up to the land of Nephi to destroy the people of Limhi.

115 Now Limhi had discovered them from the tower; even all their preparations for war he discovered; therefore he gathered his people together, and laid wait for them in the fields and in the forests.

116 When the Lamanites had come up, the people of Limhi began to fall upon them from their waiting places and began to slay them.

117 And the battle became exceed-

145–123 B. C.

ingly sore, for they fought like lions for their prey.

118 And the people of Limhi began to drive the Lamanites before them, yet they were not half so numerous as the Lamanites.

119 But they fought for their lives, and for their wives, and for their children; therefore they exerted themselves, and they fought like dragons.

120 And it came to pass that they found the king of the Lamanites among the number of their dead; yet he was not dead, having been wounded and left upon the ground, so speedy was the flight of his people.

121 They took him and bound up his wounds, and brought him before Limhi, and said, "Behold, here is the king of the Lamanites; he, having received a wound, has fallen among their dead, and they have left him; and, behold, we have brought him before you; and now let us slay him."

122 But Limhi said to them, "You shall not slay him, but bring him here that I may see him." And they brought him.

123 And Limhi said to him, "What cause have you to come up to war against my people?

124 "Behold, my people have not broken the oath that I made to you; therefore, why should you break the oath which you made to my people?"

125 And the king said, "I have broken the oath because your people carried away the daughters of my people; therefore in my anger I caused my people to come up to war against your people."

126 Now Limhi had heard nothing concerning this matter; therefore he said, "I will search among my people, and whoever has done this thing shall perish."

127 Therefore he caused a search to be made among his people.

128 Now when Gideon had heard these things, he being the king's captain, he went forth and said to the king, "I pray thee forbear, and do not search this people, and lay not this thing to their charge.

129 "For do you not remember the priests of your father, whom this people sought to destroy?

130 "Are they not in the wilderness? And are not they the ones who have stolen the daughters of the Lamanites?

131 "Behold, tell the king of these things, that he may tell his people, that they may be pacified toward us; for, behold, they are already preparing to come against us; and there are but few of us.

132 "They come with their numerous hosts; and except the king pacifies them toward us, we must perish.

133 "For are not the words of Abinadi fulfilled which he prophesied against us? And all this because we would not hearken to the word of the Lord and turn from our iniquities.

134 "Let us pacify the king, and fulfill the oath which we have made to him; for it is better that we should be in bondage than that we should lose our lives; therefore, let us put a stop to the shedding of so much blood."

135 Now Limhi told the king all the things concerning his father and the priests that had fled into the wilderness, and attributed the carrying away of their daughters to them.

136 And it came to pass that the king was pacified toward this people; and he said to them, "Let us go forth to meet my people without arms; and I swear to you with an oath that my people shall not slay your people."

137 They followed the king and went forth without arms to meet the Lamanites.

138 And they met the Lamanites; and the king of the Lamanites bowed himself down before them and pleaded in behalf of the people of Limhi.

139 When the Lamanites saw the people of Limhi, that they were without arms, they had compassion on them, and were pacified toward them, and returned with their king in peace to their own land.

140 And Limhi and his people returned to the city of Nephi and began to dwell in the land again in peace.

141 But after many days, the Lamanites began again to be stirred up in anger against the Nephites; and they began to come into the borders of the land round about.

142 Now they dared not slay them because of the oath which their king had made to Limhi; but they would

smite them on their cheeks and exercise authority over them, and they began to put heavy burdens upon their backs and to drive them as they would a dumb ass; and all this was done that the word of the Lord might be fulfilled.

143 The afflictions of the Nephites were great; and there was no way that they could deliver themselves out of their hands, for the Lamanites had surrounded them on every side.

144 And the people began to murmur with the king because of their afflictions; and they began to be desirous to go against them to battle.

145 They afflicted the king sorely with their complaints; therefore he granted them that they should do according to their desires.

146 And they gathered themselves together again, and put on their armor, and went forth against the Lamanites to drive them out of their land.

147 And it came to pass that the Lamanites beat them, and drove them back, and slew many of them.

148 There was a great mourning and lamentation among the people of Limhi: the widow mourning for her husband, the son and the daughter mourning for their father, and the brothers for their brethren.

149 Now there were a great many widows in the land; and they cried mightily from day to day, for a great fear of the Lamanites had come upon them.

150 And their continual cries stirred up the remainder of the people of Limhi to anger against the Lamanites.

151 And they went again to battle; but they were driven back again, suffering much loss.

152 They went again, even the third time, and suffered in like manner; and those that were not slain returned again to the city of Nephi.

153 Then they humbled themselves even to the dust, subjecting themselves to the yoke of bondage, submitting themselves to be smitten, and to be driven to and fro and burdened, according to the desires of their enemies.

154 And they humbled themselves even in the depths of humility; and

they cried mightily to God; even all the day long they cried to their God that he would deliver them out of their afflictions; 155but the Lord was slow to hear their cry, because of their iniquities.

156 Nevertheless the Lord heard their cries and began to soften the hearts of the Lamanites that they began to ease their burdens; yet the Lord did not see fit to deliver them out of bondage.

157 And they began to prosper by degrees in the land, and began to raise grain more abundantly, and flocks, and herds, that they did not suffer with hunger.

158 Now there were a great number of women more than there were of men; therefore King Limhi commanded that every man should impart to the support of the widows and their children that they might not perish with hunger; and this they did because of the greatness of their number that had been slain.

159 Now the people of Limhi kept together in a body as much as it was possible to do and still secure their grain and flocks; 160and the king himself did not trust his person without the walls of the city unless he took his guards with him, fearing that he might by some means fall into the hands of the Lamanites.

161 And he caused that his people should watch the land round about, that by some means they might take those priests that fled into the wilderness, who had stolen the daughters of the Lamanites and had caused such a great destruction to come upon them.

162 For they were desirous to take them that they might punish them; for they had come into the land of Nephi by night and carried off their grain and many of their precious things; therefore they laid wait for them.

163 And there was no more disturbance between the Lamanites and the people of Limhi, even until the time that Ammon and his brethren came into the land.

164 The king, having been without the gates of the city with his guard, discovered Ammon and his brethren; and supposing them to be priests of Noah, he caused that they should be

taken, and bound, and cast into prison.

165 Had they been the priests of Noah, he would have caused that they should be put to death; but when he found that they were not, but that they were his brethren and had come from the land of Zarahemla, he was filled with exceedingly great joy.

166 Now King Limhi had sent, previous to the coming of Ammon, a small number of men to search for the land of Zarahemla; but they could not find it, and they were lost in the wilderness.

167 Nevertheless they found a land which had been peopled; a land which was covered with dry bones; a land which had been peopled, and which had been destroyed.

168 And they, having supposed it to be the land of Zarahemla, returned to the land of Nephi, having arrived in the borders of the land not many days before the coming of Ammon.

169 And they brought a record with them, even a record of the people whose bones they had found, which record was engraved on plates of ore.

170 Now Limhi was again filled with joy on learning from the mouth of Ammon that King Mosiah had a gift from God whereby he could interpret such engravings; and Ammon also rejoiced.

171 Yet Ammon and his brethren were filled with sorrow because so many of their brethren had been slain, and also that King Noah and his priests had caused the people to commit so many sins and iniquities against God.

172 They also mourned for the death of Abinadi, and also for the departure of Alma, and the people that went with him, who had formed a church of God through the strength and power of God and faith on the words which had been spoken by Abinadi; 173they mourned for their departure, for they knew not where they had fled.

174 Now they would have gladly joined with them, for they themselves had entered into a covenant with God to serve him and keep his commandments.

175 Since the coming of Ammon,

King Limhi had also entered into a covenant with God, and also many of his people, to serve him and keep his commandments.

176 And King Limhi and many of his people were desirous to be baptized; but there were none in the land that had authority from God.

177 Ammon declined doing this thing, considering himself an unworthy servant; therefore they did not at that time form themselves into a church, waiting upon the Spirit of the Lord.

178 Now they were desirous to become even as Alma and his brethren who had fled into the wilderness.

179 They were desirous to be baptized as a witness and a testimony that they were willing to serve God with all their hearts; 180nevertheless they prolonged the time; and an account of their baptism shall be given hereafter.

181 Now all the study of Ammon and his people, and King Limhi and his people, was to deliver themselves out of the hands of the Lamanites and from bondage.

CHAPTER 10

AND it came to pass that Ammon and King Limhi began to consult with the people how they should deliver themselves out of bondage.

2 They even caused that all the people should gather themselves together; and this they did that they might have the voice of the people concerning the matter.

3 But they could find no way to deliver themselves out of bondage except to take their women and children, and their flocks and their herds, and their tents, and depart into the wilderness; 4for the Lamanites were so numerous it was impossible for the people of Limhi to contend with them, thinking to deliver themselves out of bondage by the sword.

5 Now Gideon went forth and stood before the king, and said to him, "Now, O king, thou hast hitherto hearkened to my words many times when we have been contending with our brethren, the Lamanites.

6 "And now, O king, if thou hast not found me to be an únprofitable

servant, or if thou hast hitherto listened to my words in any degree, and they have been of service to thee, even so I desire that thou wouldst listen to my words at this time, and I will be thy servant, and deliver this people out of bondage."

7 And the king granted him that he might speak.

8 Gideon said to him, "Behold the back pass through the back wall, on the back side of the city.

9 "The Lamanites, or the guards of the Lamanites, by night are drunken; therefore let us send a proclamation among all this people that they gather their flocks and herds that they may drive them into the wilderness by night.

10 "And I will go according to thy command and pay the last tribute of wine to the Lamanites, and they will be drunken; and we will pass through the secret pass on the left of their camp, when they are drunken and asleep.

11 "Thus we will depart with our women and our children, our flocks and our herds, into the wilderness; and we will travel around the land of Shilom."

12 And the king hearkened to the words of Gideon ¹³and caused that his people should gather their flocks;

and he sent the tribute of wine to the Lamanites; and he also sent more wine as a present to them; and they drank freely of the wine which King Limhi sent to them.

14 And it came to pass that the people of King Limhi departed by night into the wilderness with their flocks and their herds, and they went round about the land of Shilom in the wilderness and bent their course toward the land of Zarahemla, being led by Ammon and his brethren.

15 They took all their gold, and silver, and their precious things which they could carry, and also their provisions with them into the wilderness; and they pursued their journey.

16 After being many days in the wilderness, they arrived in the land of Zarahemla, and joined the people of Mosiah, and became his subjects.

17 And Mosiah received them with joy; and he also received their records, and also the records which had been found by the people of Limhi.

18 Now when the Lamanites found that the people of Limhi had departed out of the land by night, they sent an army into the wilderness to pursue them; ¹⁹but after they had pursued them two days, they could no longer follow their tracks; therefore they were lost in the wilderness.

CHAPTER 11

An account of Alma and the people of the Lord who were driven into the wilderness by the people of King Noah.

NOW Alma, having been warned of the Lord that the armies of King Noah would come upon them, made it known to his people, therefore they gathered together their flocks, and took of their grain, and departed into the wilderness before the armies of King Noah.

2 The Lord strengthened them that the people of King Noah could not overtake them to destroy them, ³and they fled eight days' journey into the wilderness, ⁴and came to a land, a very beautiful and pleasant land, a land of pure water.

5 They pitched their tents, and began to till the ground, and began to

build buildings, for they were industrious, and labored exceedingly.

6 And the people were desirous that Alma should be their king, for he was beloved by his people.

7 But he said to them, "Behold, it is not expedient that we should have a king; for thus says the Lord: 'Ye shall not esteem one flesh above another, or one man shall not think himself above another'; therefore I say to you, It is not expedient that you should have a king.

8 "Nevertheless, if it were possible that you could always have just men to be your kings, it would be well for you to have a king.

129   145–123 B. C.

9 "But remember the iniquity of King Noah and his priests; for I myself was caught in a snare, and did many things which were abominable in the sight of the Lord, which caused me sore repentance.

10 "Nevertheless, after much tribulation, the Lord heard my cries, and answered my prayers, and has made me an instrument in his hands in bringing so many of you to a knowledge of his truth.

11 "Nevertheless, in this I do not glory, for I am unworthy to glory of myself.

12 "Now I say to you, you have been oppressed by King Noah, and have been in bondage to him and his priests, and have been brought into iniquity by them; therefore you were bound with the bands of iniquity.

13 "Now as you have been delivered by the power of God, out of these bonds, ¹⁴even out of the hands of King Noah and his people, and also from the bonds of iniquity, even so I desire that you should stand fast in this liberty wherewith you have been made free, and that you trust no man to be a king over you.

15 "Also trust no one to be your teacher nor your minister except he be a man of God, walking in his ways and keeping his commandments."

16 Thus Alma taught his people, that every man should love his neighbor as himself, that there should be no contention among them.

17 Now Alma was their high priest, he being the founder of their church. ¹⁸and none received authority to preach or to teach except by him from God.

19 Therefore he consecrated all their priests and all their teachers, and none were consecrated except they were just men.

20 Therefore they watched over their people and nourished them with things pertaining to righteousness.

21 And they began to prosper exceedingly in the land; and they called the land Helam.

22 And it came to pass that they multiplied and prospered exceedingly in the land of Helam; and they built a city, which they called the city of Helam.

23 Nevertheless the Lord sees fit to chasten his people; he tries their patience and their faith.

24 Nevertheless, whoever puts his trust in him, the same shall be lifted up at the last day.

25 Thus it was with this people.

26 For, behold, I will show you that they were brought into bondage, and none could deliver them but the Lord their God, even the God of Abraham, and of Isaac, and of Jacob.

27 And it came to pass that he delivered them, and he showed forth his mighty power to them, and great were their rejoicings.

28 For, behold, while they were in the land of Helam, in the city of Helam, while tilling the land round about, behold, an army of the Lamanites were in the borders of the land.

29 Now the brethren of Alma fled from their fields, and gathered themselves together into the city of Helam; and they were much frightened because of the appearance of the Lamanites.

30 But Alma went forth and stood among them, and exhorted them that they should not be frightened, but that they should remember the Lord their God, and he would deliver them.

31 Therefore they hushed their fears and began to cry to the Lord that he would soften the hearts of the Lamanites, that they would spare them, and their wives, and their children.

32 And the Lord did soften the hearts of the Lamanites.

33 And Alma and his brethren went forth and delivered themselves up into their hands; and the Lamanites took possession of the land of Helam.

34 Now the armies of the Lamanites which had followed after the people of King Limhi had been lost in the wilderness for many days.

35 And, behold, they had found those priests of King Noah in a place which they called Amulon; and they had begun to possess the land of Amulon, and had begun to till the ground.

36 Now the name of the leader of those priests was Amulon.

37 And Amulon pleaded with the

Lamanites; and he also sent forth their wives, who were the daughters of the Lamanites, to plead with their brethren that they should not destroy their husbands.

38 And the Lamanites had compassion on Amulon and his brethren and did not destroy them, because of their wives.

39 Now Amulon and his brethren joined the Lamanites, and they were traveling in the wilderness in search of the land of Nephi when they discovered the land of Helam, which was possessed by Alma and his brethren.

40 The Lamanites promised Alma and his brethren that if they would show them the way which led to the land of Nephi, they would grant them their lives and their liberty.

41 But after Alma had showed them the way that led to the land of Nephi, the Lamanites would not keep their promise; but they set guards round about the land of Helam, over Alma and his brethren.

42 And the remainder of them went to the land of Nephi; and a part of them returned to the land of Helam, and also brought with them the wives and the children of the guards who had been left in the land.

43 The king of the Lamanites had granted Amulon that he should be a king and a ruler over his people who were in the land of Helam; nevertheless he should have no power to do anything contrary to the will of the king of the Lamanites.

44 But in time Amulon gained favor in the eyes of the king of the Lamanites; therefore the king of the Lamanites granted him and his brethren that they should be appointed teachers over his people; 45even over the people who were in the land of Shemlon, and in the land of Shilom, and in the land of Amulon; 46for the Lamanites had taken possession of all these lands; therefore the king of the Lamanites had appointed kings over all these lands.

47 Now the name of the king of the Lamanites was Laman, being called after the name of his father; and therefore he was called King Laman.

48 He was king over a numerous people; and he appointed teachers of the brethren of Amulon in every land which was possessed by his people.

49 Thus the language of Nephi began to be taught among all the people of the Lamanites.

50 And they were a people friendly one with another; nevertheless they knew not God; neither did the brethren of Amulon teach them anything concerning the Lord their God, neither the law of Moses.

51 Nor did they teach them the words of Abinadi; but they taught them that they should keep their record, and that they might write one to another.

52 Now the Lamanites began to increase in riches, and began to trade one with another and wax great, and began to be a cunning and a wise people as to the wisdom of the world, 53even a very cunning people, delighting in all manner of wickedness and plunder except among their own brethren.

54 And it came to pass that Amulon began to exercise authority over Alma and his brethren, and began to persecute him, and cause that his children should persecute their children.

55 For Amulon knew Alma, that he had been one of the king's priests, and that it was he that believed the words of Abinadi, and was driven out before the king; and therefore he was angry with him, for he was subject to King Laman; 56yet he exercised authority over them, and put tasks upon them, and put taskmasters over them.

57 So great were their afflictions that they began to cry mightily to God.

58 Amulon commanded them that they should stop their cries; and he put guards over them to watch them that whoever should be found calling upon God should be put to death.

59 And Alma and his people did not raise their voices to the Lord their God, but poured out their hearts to him; and he knew the thoughts of their hearts.

60 And the voice of the Lord came to them in their afflictions, saying, "Lift up your heads and be of good comfort, for I know of the covenant which ye have made to me; and I will

covenant with this my people and deliver them out of bondage.

61 "I will also ease the burdens which are put upon your shoulders, that even you cannot feel them upon your backs, even while you are in bondage; 62and this will I do that ye may stand as witnesses for me hereafter and that ye may know of a surety that I, the Lord God, do visit my people in their afflictions."

63 And it came to pass that the burdens which were laid upon Alma and his brethren were made light; 64the Lord strengthened them that they could bear their burdens with ease, and they submitted cheerfully and with patience to all the will of the Lord.

65 And so great was their faith and their patience that the voice of the Lord came to them again, saying, "Be of good comfort, for on the morrow I will deliver you out of bondage."

66 And he said to Alma, "Thou shalt go before this people, and I will go with thee and deliver this people out of bondage."

67 Now it came to pass that Alma and his people in the nighttime gathered their flocks, and also of their grain; even all the nighttime were they gathering their flocks together.

68 In the morning the Lord caused a deep sleep to come upon the Lamanites, and all their taskmasters were in a profound sleep.

69 And Alma and his people departed into the wilderness; and when they had traveled all day, they pitched their tents in a valley, and they called the valley Alma because he led their way in the wilderness.

70 And in the valley of Alma they poured out their thanks to God because he had been merciful to them, and eased their burdens, and had delivered them out of bondage; 71for they were in bondage, and none could deliver them, except the Lord their God.

72 They gave thanks to God; all their men, and all their women, and all their children that could speak, lifted their voices in the praises of their God.

73 Now the Lord said to Alma, "Haste thee and get thou and this people out of this land, for the Lamanites have awakened and do pursue thee.

74 "Therefore get thee out of this land, and I will stop the Lamanites in this valley, that they come no farther in pursuit of this people."

75 And they departed out of the valley, and took their journey into the wilderness.

76 After they had been in the wilderness twelve days, they arrived to the land of Zarahemla; and King Mosiah also received them with joy.

77 And King Mosiah caused that all the people should be gathered together.

78 Now there were not so many of the children of Nephi, or so many of those who were descendants of Nephi, as there were of the people of Zarahemla, who was a descendant of Mulek, and those who came with him into the wilderness.

79 And there were not so many of the people of Nephi and of the people of Zarahemla as there were of the Lamanites; they were not half so numerous.

80 Now all the people of Nephi were assembled together, and also all the people of Zarahemla, and they were gathered in two bodies.

81 And Mosiah read, and caused to be read, the records of Zeniff to his people from the time they left the land of Zarahemla until they returned again.

82 He also read the account of Alma and his brethren, and all their afflictions from the time they left the land of Zarahemla until the time they returned again.

83 When Mosiah had made an end of reading the records, his people who tarried in the land were struck with wonder and amazement, for they knew not what to think; 84for when they beheld those that had been delivered out of bondage, they were filled with exceedingly great joy.

85 Again, when they thought of their brethren who had been slain by the Lamanites, they were filled with sorrow, and even shed many tears of sorrow.

86 And when they thought of the immediate goodness of God and his power in delivering Alma and his

brethren out of the hands of the Lamanites, and of bondage, they raised their voices and gave thanks to God.

87 And again, when they thought upon the Lamanites, who were their brethren, of their sinful and polluted state, they were filled with pain and anguish for the welfare of their souls.

88 And it came to pass that those who were the children of Amulon and his brethren, who had taken to wife the daughters of the Lamanites, were displeased with the conduct of their fathers.

89 They would no longer be called by the names of their fathers, therefore they took upon themselves the name of Nephi, that they might be called the children of Nephi and be numbered among those who were called Nephites.

90 And all the people of Zarahemla were numbered with the Nephites, and this because the kingdom had been conferred upon none but those who were descendants of Nephi.

91 Now when Mosiah had made an end of speaking and reading to the people, he desired that Alma should also speak to the people.

92 And Alma spoke to them when they were assembled together in large bodies, and he went from one body to another preaching to the people repentance and faith on the Lord.

93 And he exhorted the people of Limhi and his brethren, all those that had been delivered out of bondage, that they should remember that it was the Lord that delivered them.

94 After Alma had taught the people many things, and had made an end of speaking to them, King Limhi was desirous that he might be baptized; and all his people were desirous that they might be baptized also.

95 Therefore Alma went forth into the water, and baptized them after the manner he did his brethren in the waters of Mormon.

96 And as many as he baptized belonged to the church of God, and this because of their belief on the words of Alma.

97 And it came to pass that King Mosiah granted Alma, that he might establish churches throughout all the land of Zarahemla and gave him power to ordain priests and teachers over every church.

98 Now this was done because there were so many people that they could not all be governed by one teacher; neither could they all hear the word of God in one assembly; therefore they assembled themselves together in different bodies, being called churches, 99every church having its priests and its teachers, and every priest preaching the word according as it was delivered to him by the mouth of Alma.

100 Thus, notwithstanding there were many churches they were all one church, even the church of God; 101for there was nothing preached in all the churches except repentance and faith in God.

102 And there were seven churches in the land of Zarahemla.

103 And it came to pass that those who were desirous to take upon them the name of Christ, or of God, joined the churches of God; and they were called the people of God.

104 And the Lord poured out his Spirit upon them, and they were blessed, and prospered in the land.

105 But there were many of the rising generation that could not understand the words of King Benjamin, being little children at the time he spoke to his people; and they did not believe the tradition of their fathers.

106 They did not believe what had been said concerning the resurrection of the dead; neither did they believe concerning the coming of Christ.

107 And because of their unbelief, they could not understand the word of God; and their hearts were hardened.

108 They would not be baptized; neither would they join the church.

109 And they were a separate people as to their faith, and remained so ever after, even in their carnal and sinful state; for they would not call upon the Lord their God.

110 In the reign of Mosiah, they were not half so numerous as the people of God; but because of the dissensions among the brethren, they became more numerous; 111for they deceived many with their flattering words who were in the church, and caused them to commit many sins.

112 Therefore it became expedient that those who committed sin who were in the church should be admonished by the church.

113 And they were brought before the priests, and delivered to the priests by the teachers; and the priests brought them before Alma, who was the high priest.

114 (King Mosiah had given Alma the authority over the church.)

115 Alma did not know concerning them, but there were many witnesses against them; the people stood and testified of their iniquity in abundance.

116 Now there had not any such thing happened before in the church; therefore Alma was troubled in his spirit, and he caused that they should be brought before the king.

117 And he said to the king, "Behold, here are many whom we have brought before thee who are accused of their brethren; and they have been taken in divers iniquities.

118 "And they do not repent of their iniquities; therefore we have brought them before thee that thou mayest judge them according to their crimes."

119 But King Mosiah said to Alma, "Behold, I judge them not; therefore I deliver them into your hands to be judged."

120 The spirit of Alma was again troubled; and he went and inquired of the Lord what he should do concerning this matter, for he feared that he should do wrong in the sight of God.

121 And after he had poured out his whole soul to God, the voice of the Lord came to him, saying, "Blessed art thou, Alma, and blessed are they who were baptized in the waters of Mormon.

122 "Thou art blessed because of thy exceeding faith in the words alone of my servant, Abinadi.

123 "And blessed are they because of their exceeding faith in the words alone which thou hast spoken to them.

124 "Blessed art thou because thou hast established a church among this people; and they shall be established, and they shall be my people.

125 "And blessed is this people who are willing to bear my name; for in my name shall they be called; and they are mine.

126 "And because thou hast inquired of me concerning the transgressor, thou art blessed.

127 "Thou art my servant; and I covenant with thee that thou shalt have eternal life; and thou shalt serve me, and go forth in my name, and shall gather my sheep.

128 "He that will hear my voice shall be my sheep; and him shall ye receive into the church; and him will I also receive.

129 "For, behold, this is my church: whoever is baptized, shall be baptized unto repentance.

130 "And he whom ye receive shall believe in my name; and him will I freely forgive.

131 "For it is I that taketh upon me the sins of the world; for it is I that hath created man; and it is I that granteth him that believeth in the end a place at my right hand.

132 "For, behold, in my name are they called; and if they know me, they shall come forth, and shall have a place eternally at my right hand.

133 "When the second trump shall sound, then shall they that never knew me come forth and shall stand before me; [134]and then shall they know that I am the Lord their God, that I am their Redeemer; but they would not be redeemed.

135 "Then will I confess to them that I never knew them; and they shall depart into everlasting fire prepared for the devil and his angels.

136 "Therefore I say to you that he that will not hear my voice, the same shall ye not receive into my church, for him I will not receive at the last day.

137 "Therefore I say to you, Go; and whoever transgresseth against me, him shall ye judge according to the sins which he has committed.

138 If he confess his sins before thee and me, and repenteth in the sincerity of his heart, him shall ye forgive, and I will forgive him also; [139]and as often as my people repent, will I forgive them their trespasses against me.

140 "And ye shall also forgive one another your trespasses; for verily I

say to you, He that forgiveth not his neighbor's trespasses when he says that he repents, the same hath brought himself under condemnation.

141 "Now I say to you, Go; and whoever will not repent of his sins, the same shall not be numbered among my people; and this shall be observed from this time forward."

142 When Alma had heard these words, he wrote them down that he might have them and that he might judge the people of that church according to the commandments of God.

143 And it came to pass that Alma went and judged those that had been taken in iniquity according to the word of the Lord.

144 Whoever repented of his sins and confessed them, he was numbered among the people of the church; 145and those that would not confess their sins and repent of their iniquity, the same were not numbered among the people of the church, and their names were blotted out.

146 Thus Alma regulated all the affairs of the church; 147and they began again to have peace and to prosper exceedingly in the affairs of the church, walking circumspectly before God, receiving many and baptizing many.

148 Now all these things Alma and his fellow laborers did who were over the church, walking in all diligence, teaching the word of God in all things, suffering all manner of afflictions, being persecuted by all those who did not belong to the church of God.

149 And they admonished their brethren; and they were also admonished by the word of God, every one according to his sins or to the sins which he had committed, being commanded of God to pray without ceasing and to give thanks in all things.

150 Now it came to pass that the persecutions which were inflicted on the church by the unbelievers became so great that the church began to murmur and complain to their leaders concerning the matter; and they complained to Alma.

151 Alma laid the case before their King Mosiah, and Mosiah consulted with his priests.

152 And it came to pass that King Mosiah sent a proclamation throughout the land round about that there should not any unbeliever persecute any of those who belonged to the church of God.

153 And there was a strict command throughout all the churches that there should be no persecutions among them, that there should be an equality among all men, that they should let no pride nor haughtiness disturb their peace, 154that every man should esteem his neighbor as himself, laboring with his own hands for his support, 155and that all their priests and teachers should labor with their own hands for their support, in all cases save it were in sickness or in much want; and doing these things they abounded in the grace of God.

156 There began to be much peace again in the land; and the people began to be very numerous and began to scatter abroad upon the face of the earth, 157on the north and on the south, on the east and on the west, building large cities and villages in all quarters of the land.

158 And the Lord visited them, and prospered them, and they became a large and a wealthy people.

159 Now the sons of Mosiah were numbered among the unbelievers; and also one of the sons of Alma was numbered among them, he being called Alma after his father; nevertheless he became a very wicked and an idolatrous man.

160 He was a man of many words, and spoke much flattery to the people; therefore he led many of the people to do after the manner of his iniquities.

161 And he became a great hindrance to the prosperity of the church of God, stealing away the hearts of the people, causing much dissension among the people, giving a chance for the enemy of God to exercise his power over them.

162 Now while he and the sons of Mosiah were going about to destroy the church of God—for he went about secretly with them, seeking to destroy the church and to lead astray the people of the Lord, contrary to the commandments of God or even the king—163and as

they were going about rebelling against God, behold, the angel of the Lord appeared to them; and he descended as it were in a cloud; and he spoke as it were with a voice of thunder, which caused the earth to shake upon which they stood.

164 So great was their astonishment that they fell to the earth and understood not the words which he spoke to them.

165 Nevertheless he cried again, saying, "Alma, arise, and stand forth, for why persecuteth thou the church of God?

166 "For the Lord has said, 'This is my church, and I will establish it; and nothing shall overthrow it save it is the transgression of my people.'"

167 Again, the angel said, "Behold, the Lord hath heard the prayers of his people and also the prayers of his servant Alma, who is thy father; 168for he has prayed with much faith concerning thee that thou mightest be brought to the knowledge of the truth.

169 "Therefore for this purpose have I come to convince thee of the power and authority of God, that the prayers of his servants might be answered according to their faith.

170 "Now, behold, can ye dispute the power of God?

171 "For, behold, doth not my voice shake the earth?

172 "And can ye not also behold me before you?

173 "I am sent from God.

174 "Now I say to thee, Go, and remember the captivity of thy fathers in the land of Helam and in the land of Nephi; and remember how great things he has done for them; for they were in bondage, and he has delivered them.

175 "And I say to thee, Alma, go thy way, and seek to destroy the church no more, that their prayers may be answered; and this even if thou wilt of thyself be cast off."

176 These were the last words which the angel spoke to Alma, and he departed.

177 Alma and those that were with him fell again to the earth, for great was their astonishment; for with their own eyes they had beheld an angel of the Lord; and his voice was as thunder which shook the earth.

178 And they knew that there was nothing, save the power of God, that could shake the earth and cause it to tremble as though it would part asunder.

179 The astonishment of Alma was so great that he became dumb that he could not open his mouth; and he became weak, even that he could not move his hands.

180 Therefore he was taken by those that were with him and carried helpless, even until he was laid before his father.

181 And they rehearsed to his father all that had happened to them; and his father rejoiced, for he knew that it was the power of God.

182 He caused that a multitude should be gathered together that they might witness what the Lord had done for his son, and also for those that were with him.

183 And he caused that the priests should assemble themselves together; and they began to fast and to pray to the Lord their God that he would open the mouth of Alma that he might speak; 184and also that his limbs might receive their strength that the eyes of the people might be opened to see and know of the goodness and glory of God.

185 After they had fasted and prayed for the space of two days and two nights, the limbs of Alma received their strength, and he stood up and began to speak to them, bidding them to be of good comfort.

186 "For," said he, "I have repented of my sins, and have been redeemed of the Lord; behold, I am born of the Spirit.

187 "And the Lord said to me, 'Marvel not that all mankind, men, and women, all nations, kindreds, tongues and people, must be born again—188born of God, changed from their carnal and fallen state to a state of righteousness, being redeemed of God, becoming his sons and daughters; and thus they become new creatures—and unless they do this, they can in no wise inherit the kingdom of God.'

189 "I say to you, Unless this be the case, they must be cast off; and

this I know because I was like to be cast off.

190 "Nevertheless, after wading through much tribulation, repenting nigh to death, the Lord in mercy has seen fit to snatch me out of an everlasting burning, and I am born of God.

191 "My soul has been redeemed from the gall of bitterness and bonds of iniquity.

192 "I was in the darkest abyss; but now I behold the marvelous light of God.

193 "My soul was racked with eternal torment; but I am snatched, and my soul is pained no more.

194 "I rejected my Redeemer and denied that which had been spoken of by our fathers.

195 "But now that they may foresee that he will come and that he remembers every creature of his creating, 196he will make himself manifest to all; every knee shall bow, and every tongue confess before him.

197 "Even at the last day, when all men shall stand to be judged of him, then shall they confess that he is God.

198 "Then shall they confess, who live without God in the world, that the judgment of an everlasting punishment is just upon them; 199and they shall quake, and tremble, and shrink beneath the glance of his all-searching eye."

200 And Alma began from this time forward to teach the people, and those who were with Alma at the time the angel appeared to them 201traveled round about through all the land, publishing to all the people the things which they had heard and seen, and preaching the word of God in much tribulation, being greatly persecuted by those who were unbelievers, being smitten by many of them.

202 But notwithstanding all this, they imparted much consolation to the church, confirming their faith, and exhorting them with long-suffering and much travail to keep the commandments of God.

203 Four of them were the sons of Mosiah; and their names were Ammon, and Aaron, and Omner, and Himni; these were the names of the sons of Mosiah.

204 And they traveled throughout all the land of Zarahemla and among all the people who were under the reign of King Mosiah, zealously striving to repair all the injuries which they had done to the church, 205confessing all their sins, and publishing all the things which they had seen, and explaining the prophecies and the scriptures to all who desired to hear them.

206 Thus they were instruments in the hands of God in bringing many to the knowledge of the truth, and to the knowledge of their Redeemer.

207 How blessed are they! For they published peace; they published good tidings of good; and they declared to the people that the Lord reigns.

CHAPTER 12

AFTER the sons of Mosiah had done all these things, they took a small number with them and returned to their father, the king, and desired of him that he would grant them that they might, with those whom they had selected, go up to the land of Nephi, 2that they might preach the things which they had heard, and that they might impart the word of God to their brethren, the Lamanites, that perhaps they might bring them to the knowledge of the Lord their God and convince them of the iniquity of their fathers.

3 They also desired that perhaps they might cure them of their hatred toward the Nephites, that they might also be brought to rejoice in the Lord their God, 4that they might become friendly to one another, and that there should be no more contentions in all the land which the Lord their God had given them.

5 Now they were desirous that salvation should be declared to every creature, for they could not bear that any human soul should perish.

6 Even the very thoughts that any soul should endure endless torment caused them to quake and tremble.

7 Thus did the Spirit of the Lord work upon them, for they had been the very vilest of sinners.

8 And the Lord saw fit in his infinite mercy to spare them; neverthe-

less they suffered much anguish of soul because of their iniquities, fearing that they should be cast off forever.

9 And it came to pass that they pleaded with their father many days that they might go up to the land of Nephi.

10 King Mosiah went and inquired of the Lord if he should let his sons go up among the Lamanites to preach the word.

11 And the Lord said to Mosiah, "Let them go, for many shall believe on their words, and they shall have eternal life; and I will deliver thy sons out of the hands of the Lamanites."

12 And Mosiah granted that they might go, and do according to their request.

13 And they took their journey into the wilderness, to go to preach the word among the Lamanites; and I shall give an account of their proceedings hereafter.

14 Now King Mosiah had no one to confer the kingdom upon, for there was not any of his sons who would accept of the kingdom.

15 Therefore he took the records which were engraved on the plates of brass, and also the plates of Nephi, and all the things which he had kept and preserved according to the commandments of God, 16after having translated and caused to be written the records which were on the plates of gold which had been found by the people of Limhi, which were delivered to him by the hand of Limhi.

17 This he did because of the great anxiety of his people, for they were desirous beyond measure to know concerning those people who had been destroyed.

18 And he translated them by the means of those two stones which were fastened into the two rims of a bow.

19 Now these things were prepared from the beginning, and were handed down from generation to generation, for the purpose of interpreting languages.

20 And they have been kept and preserved by the hand of the Lord, that he should discover to every creature who should possess the land the iniquities and abominations of his people; 21and whoever has these things is called seer, after the manner of old times.

22 Now after Mosiah had finished translating these records, behold, they gave an account of the people who were destroyed, from the time that they were destroyed, back to the building of the great tower at the time the Lord confounded the language of the people, 23and they were scattered abroad upon the face of all the earth, even from that time until the creation of Adam.

24 Now this account caused the people of Mosiah to mourn exceedingly; and they were filled with sorrow; 25nevertheless it gave them much knowledge in which they rejoiced.

26 And this account shall be written hereafter; for, behold, it is expedient that all people should know the things which are written in this account.

CHAPTER 13

NOW, as I said to you, after King Mosiah had done these things, he took the plates of brass, and all the things which he had kept and conferred them upon Alma, who was the son of Alma.

2 All the records and also the interpreters he conferred upon him and commanded him that he should keep and preserve them, and also keep a record of the people, handing them down from one generation to another, even as they had been handed down from the time that Lehi left Jerusalem.

3 Now when Mosiah had done this, he sent out through all the land, among all the people, desiring to know their will concerning who should be their king.

4 And the voice of the people came, saying, "We are desirous that Aaron, thy son, should be our king, and our ruler."

5 Now Aaron had gone up to the land of Nephi, therefore the king could not confer the kingdom upon him; neither would Aaron take upon him the kingdom.

6 Neither were any of the sons of Mosiah willing to take upon them the kingdom. Therefore King Mosiah sent again among the people, even a

written word sent he among the people.

7 These were the words that were written, saying: "Behold, O my people, or my brethren, for I esteem you as such; for I desire that you should consider the cause which you are called to consider; for you are desirous to have a king.

8 "Now I declare to you that he to whom the kingdom rightly belongs has declined and will not take upon him the kingdom.

9 "If there should be another appointed in his stead, behold, I fear there would rise contentions among you.

10 "And who knows but what my son, to whom the kingdom belongs, should turn to be angry and draw away a part of this people after him, which would cause wars and contentions among you, which would be the cause of shedding much blood and perverting the way of the Lord, and would destroy the souls of many people.

11 "Now I say to you, Let us be wise and consider these things, for we have no right to destroy my son, neither should we have any right to destroy another if he should be appointed in his stead.

12 "And if my son should turn again to his pride and vain things, he would recall the things which he had said, and claim his right to the kingdom, which would cause him and also this people to commit much sin.

13 "Let us be wise and look forward to these things, and do that which will make for the peace of this people.

14 "Therefore I will be your king the remainder of my days; 15nevertheless, let us appoint judges to judge this people according to our law, and we will newly arrange the affairs of this people, for we will appoint wise men to be judges that will judge this people according to the commandments of God.

16 "Now it is better that a man should be judged of God than of man, for the judgments of God are always just, but the judgments of man are not always just.

17 "Therefore, if it were possible that you could have just men to be your kings, who would establish the laws of God, and judge this people according to his commandments; if you could have men for your kings, who would do even as my father Benjamin did for this people, I say to you, if this could always be the case, then it would be expedient that you should always have kings to rule over you.

18 "Even I myself have labored with all the power and faculties which I have possessed to teach you the commandments of God and to establish peace throughout the land, 19that there should be no wars nor contentions, no stealing, nor plundering, nor murdering, nor any manner of iniquity.

20 "And whoever has committed iniquity, him have I punished according to the crime which he has committed, according to the law which has been given to us by our fathers.

21 "Now I say to you that, because all men are not just, it is not expedient that you should have a king or kings to rule over you.

22 "For, behold, how much iniquity one wicked king can cause to be committed, and what great destruction!

23 "Remember King Noah, his wickedness and his abominations; and also the wickedness and abominations of his people.

24 "Behold what great destruction came upon them; and also because of their iniquities they were brought into bondage.

25 "And were it not for the interposition of their all-wise Creator, and this because of their sincere repentance, they must unavoidably have remained in bondage until now.

26 "But, behold, he delivered them because they humbled themselves before him; and because they cried mightily to him, he delivered them out of bondage.

27 "Thus the Lord works with his power in all cases among the children of men, extending the arm of mercy toward them that put their trust in him.

28 "Behold, now I say to you, You cannot dethrone an iniquitous king save it be through much contention and the shedding of much blood.

29 "For, behold, he has his friends in iniquity, and he keeps his guards about him; and he tears up the laws of those who have reigned in righteousness before him; and he tramples under his feet the commandments of God.

30 "And he enacts laws and sends them forth among his people, laws after the manner of his own wickedness; and whoever does not obey his laws, he causes to be destroyed.

31 "And those who rebel against him, he will send his armies against them to war, and if he can, he will destroy them.

32 "Thus an unrighteous king perverts the ways of all righteousness.

33 "Now, behold, I say to you, It is not expedient that such abominations should come upon you.

34 "Therefore choose you, by the voice of this people, judges that you may be judged according to the laws which have been given you by our fathers, which are correct, and which were given them by the hand of the Lord.

35 "Now it is not common that the voice of the people desires anything contrary to that which is right; but it is common for the lesser part of the people to desire that which is not right; 36therefore this shall you observe and make it your law to do your business by the voice of the people.

37 "And if the time comes that the voice of the people chooses iniquity, then is the time that the judgments of God will come upon you; 38then is the time he will visit you with great destruction, even as he has hitherto visited this land.

39 "Now if you have judges, and they do not judge you according to the law which has been given, you can cause that they may be judged of a higher judge.

40 "If your higher judges do not judge righteous judgments, you shall cause that a small number of your lower judges shall be gathered together, and they shall judge your higher judges, according to the voice of the people.

41 "I command you to do these things in the fear of the Lord.

42 "And I command you to do these things, and that you have no king, that if these people commit sins and iniquities, they shall be answered upon their own heads.

43 "For, behold, I say to you, The sins of many people have been caused by the iniquities of their kings; therefore their iniquities are answered upon the heads of their kings.

44 "Now I desire that this inequality should be no more in this land, especially among this my people.

45 "But I desire that this land be a land of liberty, and that every man may enjoy his rights and privileges alike as long as the Lord sees fit that we may live and inherit the land, 46even as long as any of our posterity remains upon the face of the land."

47 Many more things King Mosiah wrote to them, unfolding to them all the trials and troubles of a righteous king, 48and all the travails of soul for their people, and also all the murmurings of the people to their king; and he explained it all to them.

49 And he told them that these things ought not to be; but that the burden should come upon all the people, that every man might bear his part.

50 He also unfolded to them all the disadvantages they labored under by having an unrighteous king to rule over them—51all his iniquities and abominations, and all the wars, and contentions, and bloodshed, and the stealing, and the plundering, and the committing of whoredoms, and all manner of iniquities, which cannot be enumerated.

52 He told them that these things ought not to be, that they were expressly repugnant to God.

53 After King Mosiah had sent these things forth among the people, they were convinced of the truth of his words; 54therefore they relinquished their desires for a king and became exceedingly anxious that every man should have an equal chance throughout all the land; 55and every man expressed a willingness to answer for his own sins.

56 Therefore it came to pass that they assembled themselves together in bodies throughout the land to cast in their voices concerning who should be their judges to judge them accord-

ing to the law which had been given them.

57 They rejoiced exceedingly because of the liberty which had been granted to them, ⁵⁸and they waxed strong in love toward Mosiah; they esteemed him more than any other man; ⁵⁹for they did not look upon him as a tyrant, who was seeking for gain, for that lucre which corrupts the soul.

60 He had not exacted riches of them, neither had he delighted in the shedding of blood; but he had established peace in the land, and he had granted his people that they should be delivered from all manner of bondage.

61 Therefore they esteemed him exceedingly, beyond measure.

62 And it came to pass that they appointed judges to rule over them or to judge them according to the law; and this they did throughout all the land.

63 Alma was appointed to be the chief judge, he being also the high priest, his father having conferred the office upon him and given him the charge concerning all the affairs of the church.

64 And Alma walked in the ways of the Lord, and he kept his commandments, and he judged righteous judgments; and there was continual peace through the land.

65 Thus commenced the reign of the judges throughout all the land of Zarahemla, among all the people who were called the Nephites; and Alma was the first and chief judge.

66 Now it came to pass that his father died, being eighty-two years old, having lived to fulfill the commandments of God.

67 And Mosiah died also, in the thirty-third year of his reign, being sixty-three years old, making in the whole, five hundred and nine years from the time Lehi left Jerusalem.

68 Thus ended the reign of the kings over the people of Nephi; and thus ended the days of Alma, who was the founder of their church.

THE BOOK OF ALMA

THE SON OF ALMA

CHAPTER 1

The account of Alma, who was the son of Alma, the first and chief judge over the people of Nephi, and also the high priest over the church. An account of the reign of the judges, and the wars and contentions among the people. Also an account of a war between the Nephites and the Lamanites, according to the record of Alma, the first and chief judge.

IN the first year of the reign of the judges over the people of Nephi, from this time forward—King Mosiah having gone the way of all the earth, having warred a good warfare, walking uprightly before God, leaving none to reign in his stead; ²nevertheless he established laws, and they were acknowledged by the people— they were obliged to abide by the laws which he had made.

3 And it came to pass that, in the first year of the reign of Alma in the judgment seat, there was a man brought before him to be judged, a man who was large and was noted for his much strength.

4 And he had gone about among the people, preaching to them that which he termed to be the word of God, bearing down against the church, ⁵declaring to the people that

every priest and teacher ought to become popular, and they ought not to labor with their own hands, but that they ought to be supported by the people.

6 He also testified to the people that all mankind should be saved at the last day, and that they need not fear nor tremble, but that they might lift up their heads and rejoice; 7for the Lord had created all men and had also redeemed all men; and in the end, all men should have eternal life.

8 And he taught these things so much that many believed in his words, even so many that they began to support him and give him money.

9 And he began to be lifted up in the pride of his heart, and to wear very costly apparel, and even began to establish a church after the manner of his preaching.

10 As he was going to preach to those who believed on his word, he met a man who belonged to the church of God, even one of their teachers.

11 And he began to contend with him sharply, that he might lead away the people of the church; but the man withstood him, admonishing him with the words of God.

12 The name of the man was Gideon; and it was he who was an instrument in the hands of God in delivering the people of Limhi out of bondage.

13 Now because Gideon withstood him with the words of God, he was angry with Gideon, and drew his sword and began to smite him.

14 Gideon, being stricken with many years, was not able to withstand his blows; therefore he was slain by the sword.

15 And the man who slew him was taken by the people of the church, and was brought before Alma to be judged according to the crime which he had committed.

16 And he stood before Alma and pleaded for himself with much boldness.

17 But Alma said to him, "Behold, this is the first time that priestcraft has been introduced among this people.

18 "And, behold, you are not only guilty of priestcraft, but you also have endeavored to enforce it by the sword; and were priestcraft to be enforced among this people, it would prove their entire destruction.

19 "You have shed the blood of a righteous man, a man who has done much good among this people; and were we to spare you, his blood would come upon us for vengeance.

20 "Therefore, you are condemned to die, according to the law which has been given us by Mosiah, our last king; 21and it has been acknowledged by this people; therefore this people must abide by the law."

22 They took him, and his name was Nehor, and they carried him upon the top of the hill Manti, 23and there he acknowledged, between the heavens and the earth, that what he had taught to the people was contrary to the word of God; and there he suffered an ignominious death.

24 Nevertheless, this did not put an end to the spreading of priestcraft through the land; for there were many who loved the vain things of the world, and they went forth preaching false doctrines, and this they did for the sake of riches and honor.

25 But they dared not lie, if it were known, for fear of the law, for liars were punished; therefore they pretended to preach according to their belief, 26since the law could have no power on any man for his belief.

27 And they dared not steal, for fear of the law, for such were punished; neither dared they rob, nor murder; for he that murdered was punished by death.

28 But it came to pass that whoever did not belong to the church of God began to persecute those that did belong to the church of God and had taken upon them the name of Christ.

29 They persecuted them, and afflicted them with all manner of words, and this because of their humility, 30because they were not proud in their own eyes, and because they imparted the word of God, one with another, without money and without price.

31 Now there was a strict law among the people of the church that there should not any man belonging to the church arise and persecute those that did not belong to the

church, and that there should be no persecution among themselves.

32 Nevertheless, there were many among them who began to be proud, and began to contend warmly with their adversaries, even to blows; and they would smite one another with their fists.

33 This was in the second year of the reign of Alma, and it was a cause of much affliction to the church; and it was the cause of much trial within the church.

34 For the hearts of many were hardened, and their names were blotted out that they were remembered no more among the people of God.

35 And also many withdrew themselves from among them.

36 Now this was a great trial to those that stood fast in the faith; nevertheless, they were steadfast and immovable in keeping the commandments of God, and they bore with patience the persecution which was heaped upon them.

37 When the priests left their labors to impart the word of God to the people, the people also left their labors to hear the word of God.

38 And when the priest had imparted to them the word of God, they all returned again diligently to their labors.

39 And the priest did not esteem himself above his hearers; for the preacher was no better than the hearer, neither was the teacher any better than the learner; and thus they were all equal, and they all labored, every man according to his strength.

40 They imparted of their substance, every man according to that which he had, to the poor, and the needy, and the sick, and the afflicted.

41 And they did not wear costly apparel, yet they were neat and comely.

42 Thus they established the affairs of the church; and thus they began to have continual peace again, notwithstanding all their persecutions.

43 Now because of the steadiness of the church, they began to be exceedingly rich, having abundance of all things whatever they stood in need —44an abundance of flocks, and herds, and fatlings of every kind, and

also abundance of grain, and of gold, and of silver, and of precious things, and abundance of silk and fine twined linen, and all manner of good homely cloth.

45 Thus in their prosperous circumstances they did not send away any who were naked, or that were hungry, or that were athirst, or that were sick, or that had not been nourished.

46 And they did not set their hearts upon riches; therefore they were liberal to all, both old and young, both bond and free, both male and female, whether out of the church or in the church, having no respect to persons as to those who stood in need.

47 Thus they prospered and became far more wealthy than those who did not belong to their church.

48 For those who did not belong to their church indulged themselves in sorceries, and in idolatry or idleness, and in babblings, and in envyings and strife, 49and wearing costly apparel, being lifted up in the pride of their own eyes, persecuting, lying, thieving, robbing, committing whoredoms, and murdering, and all manner of wickedness.

50 Nevertheless, the law was put in force upon all those who transgressed it, inasmuch as it were possible.

51 By thus exercising the law upon them, every man suffering according to that which he had done, they became more still, and dared not commit any wickedness, if it were known.

52 Therefore there was much peace among the people of Nephi, until the fifth year of the reign of the judges.

53 In the commencement of the fifth year of their reign, there began to be a contention among the people for a certain man called Amlici, he being a very cunning man, a wise man as to the wisdom of the world, he being after the order of the man that slew Gideon by the sword, who was executed according to the law.

54 Now this Amlici had, by his cunning, drawn away many people after him, even so many that they began to be very powerful; and they began to endeavor to establish Amlici to be a king over the people.

55 This was alarming to the people

of the church, and also to all those who had not been drawn away after the persuasions of Amlici; ⁵⁶for they knew that according to their law such things must be established by the voice of the people.

57 Therefore, if it were possible that Amlici should gain the voice of the people, he, being a wicked man, would deprive them of their rights and privileges of the church; for it was his intent to destroy the church of God.

58 And it came to pass that the people assembled themselves together throughout all the land, every man according to his mind, whether it were for or against Amlici, in separate bodies, having much dispute and wonderful contentions one with another.

59 Thus they assembled themselves together to cast in their voices concerning the matter; and they were laid before the judges.

60 And the voice of the people came against Amlici that he was not made king over the people.

61 This caused much joy in the hearts of those who were against him; but Amlici stirred up those who were in his favor to anger against those who were not in his favor.

62 And they gathered themselves together and consecrated Amlici to be their king.

63 Now when Amlici was made king over them, he commanded them that they should take up arms against their brethren; and this he did that he might subject them to him.

64 (The people of Amlici were distinguished by the name of Amlici, being called Amlicites; and the remainder were called Nephites, or the people of God.)

65 The people of the Nephites were aware of the intent of the Amlicites, therefore they prepared to meet them.

66 They armed themselves with swords, and with cimeters, and with bows, and with arrows, and with stones, and with slings, and with all manner of weapons of war of every kind; ⁶⁷and thus they were prepared to meet the Amlicites at the time of their coming.

68 And there were appointed captains, and higher captains, and chief captains, according to their numbers.

69 And Amlici armed his men with all manner of weapons of war of every kind; and he also appointed rulers and leaders over his people to lead them to war against their brethren.

70 And it came to pass that the Amlicites came upon the hill of Amnihu, which was east of the river Sidon which ran by the land of Zarahemla, and there they began to make war with the Nephites.

71 Now Alma, being the chief judge and the governor of the people of Nephi, went up with his people, with his captains and chief captains at the head of his armies, against the Amlicites to battle; and they began to slay the Amlicites upon the hill east of Sidon.

72 And the Amlicites contended with the Nephites with great strength, insomuch that many of the Nephites fell before the Amlicites.

73 Nevertheless the Lord strengthened the hand of the Nephites that they slew the Amlicites with a great slaughter, that they began to flee before them.

74 The Nephites pursued the Amlicites all that day, and slew them insomuch that there were slain of the Amlicites twelve thousand five hundred and thirty-two souls.

75 And there were slain of the Nephites six thousand five hundred and sixty-two souls.

76 When Alma could pursue the Amlicites no longer, he caused that his people should pitch their tents in the valley of Gideon, the valley being called after that Gideon who was slain by the hand of Nehor with the sword; and in this valley the Nephites pitched their tents for the night.

77 And Alma sent spies to follow the remnant of the Amlicites, that he might know of their plans and their plots, whereby he might guard himself against them, that he might preserve his people from being destroyed.

78 Now those whom he had sent out to watch the camp of the Amlicites were called Zeram, and Amnor, and Manti, and Limher; these were they who went out with their men to watch the camp of the Amlicites.

79 On the morrow they returned into the camp of the Nephites in great haste, being greatly astonished and struck with much fear, saying:

80 "Behold, we followed the camp of the Amlicites, and to our great astonishment, in the land of Minon, above the land of Zarahemla, in the course of the land of Nephi, we saw a numerous host of the Lamanites.

81 "And, behold, the Amlicites have joined them; and they are upon our brethren in that land; and they are fleeing before them with their flocks, and their wives, and their children, toward our city.

82 "Except we make haste, they will obtain possession of our city; and our fathers, and our wives, and our children will be slain."

83 And it came to pass that the people of Nephi took their tents and departed out of the valley of Gideon toward their city, which was the city of Zarahemla.

84 And, behold, as they were crossing the river Sidon, the Lamanites and the Amlicites, being as numerous almost, as it were, as the sands of the sea, came upon them to destroy them.

85 Nevertheless the Nephites were strengthened by the hand of the Lord, having prayed mightily to him that he would deliver them out of the hands of their enemies; [86]therefore the Lord heard their cries and strengthened them, and the Lamanites and Amlicites fell before them.

87 And Alma fought with Amlici with the sword, face to face; and they contended mightily, one with another.

88 And Alma, being a man of God, being exercised with much faith, cried, saying, "O Lord, have mercy and spare my life that I may be an instrument in thy hands to save and protect this people."

89 When Alma had said these words, he contended again with Amlici; and he was strengthened insomuch that he slew Amlici with the sword.

90 And he also contended with the king of the Lamanites; but the king of the Lamanites fled back from before Alma and sent his guards to contend with Alma.

91 But Alma, with his guards, contended with the guards of the king of the Lamanites until he slew and drove them back.

92 Thus he cleared the ground, or rather the bank, which was on the west of the river Sidon, throwing the bodies of the Lamanites who had been slain into the waters of Sidon, that thereby his people might have room to cross and contend with the Lamanites and the Amlicites on the west side of the river Sidon.

93 When they had all crossed the river Sidon, the Lamanites and the Amlicites began to flee before them, notwithstanding they were so numerous that they could not be numbered.

94 They fled before the Nephites toward the wilderness which was west and north, away beyond the borders of the land.

95 And the Nephites pursued them with their might and slew them; they were met on every hand, and slain and driven until they were scattered on the west and on the north, until they had reached the wilderness which was called Hermounts.

96 And it was that part of the wilderness which was infested by wild and ravenous beasts.

97 Many died in the wilderness of their wounds, and were devoured by those beasts, and also by the vultures of the air; and their bones have been found and have been heaped upon the earth.

98 The Nephites who were not slain by the weapons of war, after having buried those who had been slain (now the number of the slain were not numbered, because of the greatness of their number) all returned to their lands, and to their houses, and their wives and their children.

99 Now many women and children had been slain with the sword, and also many of their flocks and their herds; [100]and also many of their fields of grain were destroyed, for they were trodden down by the hosts of men.

101 Now many of the Lamanites and the Amlicites who had been slain upon the bank of the river Sidon were cast into the waters of Sidon; and, behold, their bones are in the depths of the sea, and they are many.

102 And the Amlicites were distinguished from the Nephites; for they had marked themselves with red in their foreheads after the manner of the Lamanites; nevertheless they had not shorn their heads like the Lamanites.

103 Now the heads of the Lamanites were shorn; and they were naked save it were skin which was girded about their loins, and also their armor which was girded about them, and their bows, and their arrows, and their stones, and their slings.

104 And the skins of the Lamanites were dark according to the mark which was set upon their fathers, which was a curse upon them because of their transgression and their rebellion against their brethren, who consisted of Nephi, Jacob, and Joseph, and Sam, who were just and holy men.

105 And their brethren sought to destroy them; therefore they were cursed; and the Lord God set a mark upon them, upon Laman and Lemuel, and also the sons of Ishmael, and the Ishmaelitish women.

106 This was done that their seed might be distinguished from the seed of their brethren, that thereby the Lord God might preserve his people, that they might not mix and believe in incorrect traditions which would prove their destruction.

107 And it came to pass that whoever mingled his seed with that of the Lamanites brought the same curse upon his seed.

108 Therefore whoever suffered himself to be led away by the Lamanites was called under that head, and there was a mark set upon him.

109 And those who would not believe in the tradition of the Lamanites, but believed those records which were brought out of the land of Jerusalem, and also in the tradition of their fathers, which were correct, who believed in the commandments of God and kept them, were called the Nephites, or the people of Nephi, from that time forth.

110 It is they who have kept the records which are true of their people, and also of the people of the Lamanites.

111 Now we will return again to the Amlicites, for they also had a mark set upon them; they set the mark upon themselves, even a mark of red upon their foreheads.

112 Thus the word of God is fulfilled, for these are the words which he said to Nephi:

113 "Behold, the Lamanites have I cursed; and I will set a mark upon them, that they and their seed may be separated from thee and thy seed from this time henceforth and forever, except they repent of their wickedness and turn to me, that I may have mercy upon them.

114 "And again: I will set a mark upon him that mingleth his seed with thy brethren, that they may be cursed also.

115 "Again: I will set a mark upon him that fighteth against thee and thy seed.

116 "And again I say, He that departeth from thee shall no more be called thy seed; and I will bless thee and whoever shall be called thy seed, henceforth and forever." These were the promises of the Lord to Nephi and to his seed.

117 Now the Amlicites knew not that they were fulfilling the words of God when they began to mark themselves in their foreheads.

118 Nevertheless they had come out in open rebellion against God; therefore it was expedient that the curse should fall upon them.

119 And I would that you should see that they brought upon themselves the curse; 120and even so does every man that is cursed bring upon himself his own condemnation.

121 Now it came to pass that not many days after the battle which was fought in the land of Zarahemla by the Lamanites and the Amlicites, another army of the Lamanites came in upon the people of Nephi in the same place where the first army met the Amlicites.

122 And there was an army sent to drive them out of their land.

123 Alma himself, being afflicted with a wound, did not go up to battle at this time against the Lamanites; but he sent up a numerous army against them.

124 And they went up and slew many of the Lamanites and drove the

remainder of them out of the borders of their land.

125 Then they returned again and began to establish peace in the land, being troubled no more for a time with their enemies.

126 Now all these things were done, all these wars and contentions were commenced and ended in the fifth year of the reign of the judges.

127 And in one year were thousands and tens of thousands of souls sent to the eternal world, 128that they might reap their rewards according to their works, whether they were good or whether they were bad, to reap eternal happiness or eternal misery according to the spirit which they listed to obey, whether it be a good spirit or a bad one.

129 For every man receives wages of him whom he lists to obey, and this according to the words of the spirit of prophecy; therefore let it be according to the truth.

130 Thus ended the fifth year of the reign of the judges.

CHAPTER 2

IN the sixth year of the reign of the judges over the people of Nephi, there were no contentions nor wars in the land of Zarahemla.

2 But the people were greatly afflicted for the loss of their brethren, and also for the loss of their flocks and herds, and also for the loss of their fields of grain which were trodden under foot and destroyed by the Lamanites.

3 So great were their afflictions that every soul had cause to mourn; and they believed that it was the judgments of God sent upon them because of their wickedness and their abominations; therefore they were awakened to a remembrance of their duty.

4 And they began to establish the church more fully; and many were baptized in the waters of Sidon and were joined to the church of God.

5 They were baptized by the hand of Alma, who had been consecrated the high priest over the people of the church by the hand of his father Alma.

6 In the seventh year of the reign of the judges, there were about three thousand five hundred souls that united themselves to the church of God and were baptized.

7 Thus ended the seventh year of the reign of the judges over the people of Nephi, and there was continual peace in all that time.

8 In the eighth year of the reign of the judges, the people of the church began to wax proud because of their exceeding riches, and their fine silks, and their fine twined linen, 9and because of their many flocks and herds, and their gold, and their silver, and all manner of precious things, which they had obtained by their industry.

10 And in all these things were they lifted up in the pride of their eyes, for they began to wear very costly apparel.

11 Now this was the cause of much affliction to Alma, and to many of the people whom Alma had consecrated to be teachers, and priests, and elders, over the church.

12 Many of them were sorely grieved for the wickedness which they saw had begun to be among their people.

13 For they saw and beheld with great sorrow that the people of the church began to be lifted up in the pride of their eyes, and to set their hearts upon riches and upon the vain things of the world, 14that they began to be scornful, one toward another, and they began to persecute those that did not believe according to their own will and pleasure.

15 Thus in this eighth year of the reign of the judges, there began to be great contentions among the people of the church.

16 There were envyings, and strifes, and malice, and persecutions, and pride, even to exceed the pride of those who did not belong to the church of God.

17 And thus ended the eighth year of the reign of the judges; and the wickedness of the church was a great stumbling block to those who did not belong to the church; and thus the church began to fail in its progress.

18 In the commencement of the ninth year, Alma saw the wickedness of the church, and he saw also that the example of the church began to lead those who were unbelievers on

from one piece of iniquity to another, thus bringing on the destruction of the people.

19 He saw great inequality among the people, some lifting themselves up with their pride, despising others, turning their backs upon the needy, and the naked, and those who were hungry, and those who were thirsty, and those who were sick and afflicted.

20 Now this was a great cause for lamentations among the people, while others were abasing themselves, succoring those who stood in need of their succor, such as imparting their substance to the poor and the needy, feeding the hungry, and suffering all manner of afflictions for Christ's sake, who should come according to the spirit of prophecy, looking forward to that day, thus retaining a remission of their sins, 21being filled with great joy because of the resurrection of the dead, according to the will, and power, and deliverance of Jesus Christ from the bands of death.

22 Now it came to pass that Alma, having seen the afflictions of the humble followers of God, and the persecutions which were heaped upon them by the remainder of his people, and seeing all their inequality, began to be very sorrowful; nevertheless, the Spirit of the Lord did not fail him.

23 And he selected a wise man who was among the elders of the church, and gave him power according to the voice of the people that he might have power to enact laws according to the laws which had been given, and to put them in force according to the wickedness and the crimes of the people.

24 This man's name was Nephihah, and he was appointed chief judge; and he sat in the judgment seat to judge and to govern the people.

25 Now Alma did not grant him the office of being high priest over the church, but he retained the office of high priest to himself; but he delivered the judgment seat to Nephihah.

26 And this he did that he himself might go forth among his people, or among the people of Nephi, that he might preach the word of God to them, to stir them up in remembrance of their duty, 27and that he might pull down, by the word of God, all the pride and craftiness, and all the contentions which were among his people, seeing no way that he might reclaim them save it were in bearing down in pure testimony against them.

28 Thus in the commencement of the ninth year of the reign of the judges over the people of Nephi, Alma delivered up the judgment seat to Nephihah, and confined himself wholly to the high priesthood of the holy order of God, to the testimony of the word, according to the spirit of revelation and prophecy.

CHAPTER 3

The words which Alma, the high priest according to the holy order of God, delivered to the people in their cities and villages throughout the land.

NOW Alma began to deliver the word of God to the people, first in the land of Zarahemla, then throughout all the land.

2 And these are the words which he spoke to the people in the church which was established in the city of Zarahemla, according to his own record, saying:

3 "I, Alma, having been consecrated by my father Alma to be a high priest over the church of God, he having power and authority from God to do these things, behold, I say to you that he began to establish a church in the land which was in the borders of Nephi, 4the land which was called the land of Mormon; and he baptized his brethren in the waters of Mormon.

5 "And, behold, I say to you, They were delivered out of the hands of the people of King Noah by the mercy and power of God.

6 "And, behold, after that, they were brought into bondage by the hands of the Lamanites in the wilderness; they were in captivity, and again the Lord delivered them out of bondage by the power of his word.

7 "And we were brought into this land, and here we began to establish the church of God throughout this land also.

8 "Now, behold, I say to you, my brethren, you that belong to this church, Have you sufficiently retained in remembrance the captivity of your fathers?

9 "Have you sufficiently retained in remembrance his mercy and long-suffering toward them?

10 "And moreover, have you sufficiently retained in remembrance that he has delivered their souls from hell?

11 "Behold, he changed their hearts; he awakened them out of a deep sleep, and they awoke to God.

12 "Behold, they were in the midst of darkness; nevertheless, their souls were illuminated by the light of the everlasting word.

13 "They were encircled by the bands of death, and the chains of hell, and an everlasting destruction awaited them.

14 "Now I ask of you, my brethren, Were they destroyed?

15 "Behold, I say to you, They were not.

16 "Again I ask, Were the bands of death broken, and the chains of hell which encircled them, were they loosed?

17 "I say to you, They were loosed, and their souls expanded, and they sang redeeming love.

18 "And I say to you that they are saved.

19 "Now I ask of you, On what conditions are they saved? What grounds had they to hope for salvation?

20 "What is the cause of their being loosed from the bands of death, and also the chains of hell?

21 "Behold, I can tell you: Did not my father Alma believe in the words which were delivered by the mouth of Abinadi? And was he not a holy prophet?

22 "Did he not speak the words of God, and my father Alma believe them?

23 "And according to his faith there was a mighty change wrought in his heart.

24 "Behold, I say to you that this is all true.

25 "And, behold, he preached the word to your fathers, and a mighty change was also wrought in their hearts; and they humbled themselves and put their trust in the true and living God.

26 "And, behold, they were faithful until the end; therefore they were saved.

27 "And now, behold, I ask of you, my brethren of the church, Have you spiritually been born of God?

28 "Have you received his image in your countenances?

29 "Have you experienced this mighty change in your hearts?

30 "Do you exercise faith in the redemption of him who created you?

31 "Do you look forward with an eye of faith, and view this mortal body raised in immortality, and this corruption raised in incorruption, to stand before God, to be judged according to the deeds which have been done in the mortal body?

32 "I say to you, Can you imagine to yourselves that you hear the voice of the Lord saying to you, in that day, 'Come to me ye blessed, for, behold, your works have been the works of righteousness upon the face of the earth'?

33 "Or do you imagine to yourselves that you can lie to the Lord in that day, and say, 'Lord, our works have been righteous works upon the face of the earth,' and that he will save you?

34 "Or otherwise, can you imagine yourselves brought before the tribunal of God, with your souls filled with guilt and remorse, having a remembrance of all your guilt, [35]a perfect remembrance of all your wickedness, a remembrance that you have set at defiance the commandments of God?

36 "I say to you, Can you look up to God at that day with a pure heart and clean hands?

37 "I say to you, Can you look up, having the image of God engraved upon your countenances?

38 "I say to you, Can you think of being saved when you have yielded yourselves to become subject to the devil?

149

39 "I say to you, You will know at that day that you cannot be saved; for there can no man be saved except his garments are washed white.

40 "His garments must be purified until they are cleansed from all stain through the blood of him of whom it has been spoken by our fathers who should come to redeem his people from their sins.

41 "And now I ask of you, my brethren, How will any of you feel, if you shall stand before the bar of God, having your garments stained with blood and all manner of filthiness?

42 "Behold, what will these things testify against you?

43 "Behold, will they not testify that you are murderers, and also that you are guilty of all manner of wickedness?

44 "Behold, my brethren, do you suppose that such a one can have a place to sit down in the kingdom of God, with Abraham, with Isaac, and with Jacob, and also all the holy prophets whose garments are cleansed, and are spotless, pure, and white?

45 "I say to you, Except you make our Creator a liar from the beginning, or suppose that he is a liar from the beginning, you cannot suppose that such can have place in the kingdom of heaven, but they shall be cast out, for they are the children of the kingdom of the devil.

46 "Now, behold, I say to you, my brethren, If you have experienced a change of heart, and if you have felt to sing the song of redeeming love, I would ask, Can you feel so now?

47 "Have you walked, keeping yourselves blameless before God?

48 "Could you say, if you were called to die at this time, within yourselves that you have been sufficiently humble, 49that your garments have been cleansed and made white, through the blood of Christ, who will come to redeem his people from their sins?

50 "Behold, are you stripped of pride? I say to you, If you are not, you are not prepared to meet God.

51 "Behold, you must prepare quickly, for the kingdom of heaven is soon at hand, and such a one has not eternal life.

52 "Behold, I say, Is there one among you who is not stripped of envy?

53 "I say to you, that such a one is not prepared, and I would that he should prepare quickly, for the hour is close at hand, and he knows not when the time shall come; for such a one is not found guiltless.

54 "And again I say to you, Is there one among you that makes a mock of his brother or that heaps upon him persecutions?

55 "Woe to such a one, for he is not prepared, and the time is at hand that he must repent, or he cannot be saved.

56 "Even woe to all you workers of iniquity; repent, repent, for the Lord God has spoken it.

57 "Behold, he sends an invitation to all men; for the arms of mercy are extended toward them; and he says, 'Repent, and I will receive you.'

58 "He says, 'Come to me and ye shall partake of the fruit of the tree of life; ye shall eat and drink of the bread and the waters of life freely.

59 "'Come to me and bring forth works of righteousness, and ye shall not be hewn down and cast into the fire; 60for, behold, the time is at hand that whoever bringeth forth not good fruit, or whoever doeth not the works of righteousness, the same has cause to wail and mourn.'

61 "O you workers of iniquity; you that are puffed up in the vain things of the world; you that have professed to have known the ways of righteousness, nevertheless have gone astray as sheep having no shepherd, notwithstanding a shepherd has called after you and is still calling after you, you will not hearken to his voice.

62 "Behold, I say to you that the good shepherd does call you; and in his own name he calls you, which is the name of Christ.

63 "And if you will not hearken to the voice of the good shepherd, to the name by which you are called, behold, you are not the sheep of the good shepherd.

64 "And now if you are not the sheep of the good shepherd, of what fold are you?

65 "Behold, I say to you that the devil is your shepherd, and you are

of his fold; and now who can deny this?

66 "Behold, I say to you, Whoever denies this is a liar and a child of the devil.

67 "For I say to you that whatever is good comes from God, and whatever is evil comes from the devil.

68 "Therefore, if a man brings forth good works, he hearkens to the voice of the good shepherd and he follows him.

69 "But whoever brings forth evil works, the same becomes a child of the devil; for he hearkens to his voice and follows him.

70 "And whoever does this must receive his wages of him; therefore, for his wages he receives death as to things pertaining to righteousness, being dead to all good works.

71 "Now, my brethren, I would that you should hear me, for I speak in the energy of my soul.

72 "For, behold, I have spoken to you plainly, that you cannot err, or have spoken according to the commandments of God.

73 "For I am called to speak after this manner according to the holy order of God, which is in Christ Jesus.

74 "I am commanded to stand and testify to this people the things which have been spoken by our fathers concerning the things which are to come.

75 "And this is not all. Do you not suppose that I know of these things myself?

76 "Behold, I testify to you that I do know that these things whereof I have spoken are true.

77 "And how do you suppose that I know of their surety?

78 "Behold, I say to you, They are made known to me by the Holy Spirit of God.

79 "Behold, I have fasted and prayed many days that I might know these things of myself.

80 "Now I do know of myself that they are true; for the Lord God has made them manifest to me by his Holy Spirit; and this is the spirit of revelation which is in me.

81 "Moreover, I say to you that as it has thus been revealed to me that the words which have been spoken by our fathers are true, [82]even so according to the spirit of prophecy which is in me, which is also by the manifestation of the Spirit of God, I say to you that I know of myself that whatever I shall say to you concerning that which is to come, is true.

83 "And I say to you that I know that Jesus Christ shall come; even the Son, the only begotten of the Father, full of grace, and mercy, and truth.

84 "And, behold, it is he that comes to take away the sins of the world; even the sins of every man who steadfastly believes on his name.

85 "Now I say to you that this is the order after which I am called to preach to my beloved brethren, and everyone that dwells in the land; [86]to preach to all, both old and young, both bond and free, the aged, and also the middle aged, and the rising generation, to cry to them that they must repent and be born again.

87 "Thus says the Spirit, 'Repent all ye ends of the earth, for the kingdom of heaven is soon at hand; the Son of God cometh in his glory, in his might, majesty, power and dominion.'

88 "My beloved brethren, I say to you that the Spirit says, 'Behold, the glory of the King of all the earth, and also the King of heaven, shall very soon shine forth among all the children of men.'

89 "And also the Spirit says to me, even cries to me with a mighty voice, saying, 'Go forth and say to this people, Repent, for except ye repent, ye can in no wise inherit the kingdom of heaven.'

90 "Again I say to you, the Spirit says, 'Behold, the ax is laid at the root of the tree; therefore every tree that bringeth not forth good fruit shall be hewn down and cast into the fire, a fire which cannot be consumed, even an unquenchable fire.

91 "Behold, and remember, the Holy One has spoken it.

92 "And now, my beloved brethren, I say to you, Can you withstand these sayings; can you lay aside these things and trample the Holy One under your feet?

93 "Can you be puffed up in the pride of your hearts; will you still persist in the wearing of costly ap-

parel and setting your hearts upon the vain things of the world, upon your riches?

94 "Will you persist in supposing that you are better one than another?

95 "Will you persist in the persecutions of your brethren who humble themselves and walk after the holy order of God wherewith they have been brought into this church, having been sanctified by the Holy Spirit, and they bring forth works which are meet for repentance?

96 "And will you persist in turning your backs upon the poor and the needy, and in withholding your substance from them?

97 "Finally, all you that will persist in your wickedness, I say to you that these are they who shall be hewn down and cast into the fire except they speedily repent.

98 "Now I say to you, all you that are desirous to follow the voice of the good shepherd, Come out from the wicked, and be separate, and touch not their unclean things.

99 "And, behold, their names shall be blotted out, that the names of the wicked shall not be numbered among the names of the righteous, that the word of God may be fulfilled which says, 'The names of the wicked shall not be mingled with the names of my people; [100]for the names of the righteous shall be written in the book of life; and to them will I grant an inheritance at my right hand.'

101 "Now, my brethren, What have you to say against this?

102 "I say to you, If you speak against it, it matters not, for the word of God must be fulfilled.

103 "For what shepherd is there among you who having many sheep does not watch over them that the wolves enter not and devour his flock?

104 "And, behold, if a wolf enter his flock, does he not drive him out? And at the last, if he can, he will destroy him.

105 "Now I say to you that the good shepherd calls after you; and if you will hearken to his voice, he will bring you into his fold, and you are his sheep.

106 "And he commands you that you suffer no ravenous wolf to enter among you, that you may not be destroyed.

107 "Now, I, Alma, command you in the language of him who has commanded me, that you observe to do the words which I have spoken to you.

108 "I speak by way of command to you that belong to the church; and to those who do not belong to the church, I speak by way of invitation, saying, Come, and be baptized unto repentance, that you also may be partakers of the fruit of the tree of life."

CHAPTER 4

AFTER Alma had made an end of speaking to the people of the church which was established in the city of Zarahemla, he ordained priests and elders, by laying on his hands according to the order of God, to preside and watch over the church.

2 And those who did not belong to the church who repented of their sins were baptized unto repentance and were received into the church.

3 And those who belonged to the church but did not repent of their wickedness and humble themselves before God [4](I mean those who were lifted up in the pride of their hearts), the same were rejected, and their names were blotted out that their names were not numbered among those of the righteous. And thus they began to establish the order of the church in the city of Zarahemla.

5 Now I would that you should understand that the word of God was liberal to all, that none were deprived of the privilege of assembling themselves together to hear the word of God.

6 Nevertheless, the children of God were commanded that they should gather themselves together often, and join in fasting and mighty prayer in behalf of the welfare of the souls of those who knew not God.

7 When Alma had made these regulations, he departed from them, from the church which was in the city of Zarahemla, [8]and went over upon the east of the river Sidon into the valley of Gideon, there having been a city built which was called the city of Gideon, which was in the valley that

was called Gideon, being called after the man who was slain by the hand of Nehor with the sword.

9 And Alma began to declare the word of God to the church which was established in the valley of Gideon, according to the revelation of the truth of the word which had been spoken by his fathers, 10and according to the spirit of prophecy which was in him, according to the testimony of Jesus Christ, the Son of God, who should come to redeem his people from their sins, and the holy order by which he was called. Thus it is written. Amen.

CHAPTER 5

The words of Alma which he delivered to the people in Gideon, according to his own record.

BEHOLD, my beloved brethren, seeing that I have been permitted to come to you, therefore I attempt to address you in my language, 2by my own mouth, seeing that it is the first time that I have spoken to you by the words of my mouth, having been wholly confined to the judgment seat, having had much business that I could not come to you.

3 "And even I could not have come now at this time, were it not that the judgment seat has been given to another to reign in my stead; and the Lord in much mercy has granted that I should come to you.

4 "And, behold, I have come, having great hopes and much desire that I should find that you had humbled yourselves before God, and that you had continued in the supplicating of his grace, that I should find that you were blameless before him, 5that I should find that you were not in the awful dilemma that our brethren were in at Zarahemla.

6 "But blessed be the name of God that he has given me the exceedingly great joy of knowing that they are established again in the way of his righteousness.

7 "And I trust, according to the Spirit of God which is in me, that I shall also have joy over you.

8 "Nevertheless, I do not desire that my joy over you should come by the cause of so much afflictions and sorrow which I have had for the brethren at Zarahemla; 9for, behold, my joy comes over them after wading through many afflictions and much sorrow.

10 "But, behold, I trust that you are not in a state of so much unbelief as were your brethren.

11 "I trust that you are not lifted up in the pride of your hearts; I trust that you have not set your hearts upon riches and the vain things of the world.

12 "I trust that you do not worship idols, but that you worship the true and the living God and that you look forward for the remission of your sins with an everlasting faith which is to come.

13 "For, behold, I say to you, There are many things to come; and, behold, there is one thing which is of more importance than they all; 14for, behold, the time is not far distant that the Redeemer will live and come among his people.

15 "Behold, I do not say that he will come among us at the time of his dwelling in his mortal tabernacle; for, behold, the Spirit has not said to me that this should be the case.

16 "Now as to this thing I do not know; but this much I do know, that the Lord God has power to do all things which are according to his word.

17 "But, behold, the Spirit has said this much to me: 'Cry unto this people, saying, Repent ye, repent ye and prepare the way of the Lord and walk in his paths which are strait.

18 "For, behold, the kingdom of heaven is at hand, and the Son of God is coming upon the face of the earth.

19 "And, behold, he shall be born of Mary at Jerusalem, which is the land of our forefathers, she being a virgin, a precious and chosen vessel, who shall be overshadowed, and conceive by the power of the Holy Ghost, and bring forth a son, even the Son of God.

20 "And he shall go forth, suffering pains and afflictions and temptations of every kind; 21and this that the word might be fulfilled which says, 'He will take upon him the pains and the sicknesses of his people; and he will take upon him death, that he may loose the bands of death which bind his people.

22 "'And he will take upon him their infirmities that his bowels may be filled with mercy, according to the flesh, that he may know according to the flesh how to succor his people according to their infirmities.'

23 "Now the Spirit knows all things; nevertheless the Son of God suffers according to the flesh, that he might take upon him the sins of his people, that he might blot out their transgressions according to the power of his deliverance; and now, behold, this is the testimony which is in me.

24 "I say to you, that you must repent and be born again: for the Spirit says, 'If ye are not born again, ye cannot inherit the kingdom of heaven.'

25 "Therefore, come and be baptized unto repentance, that you may be washed from your sins, that you may have faith on the Lamb of God, who takes away the sins of the world, who is mighty to save and to cleanse from all unrighteousness.

26 "I say to you, Come and fear not, and lay aside every sin which easily besets you, which binds you down to destruction.

27 "Come and go forth, and show to your God that you are willing to repent of your sins, and enter into a covenant with him to keep his commandments, and witness it to him this day by going into the waters of baptism.

28 "And whoever does this, and keeps the commandments of God thenceforth, the same will remember that I have said to him that he shall have eternal life, according to the testimony of the Holy Spirit which testifies in me.

29 "Now, my beloved brethren, do you believe these things?

30 "Behold, I say to you, I know that you believe them; and the way that I know that you believe them is

by the manifestation of the Spirit which is in me.

31 "And because your faith is strong concerning the things which I have spoken, great is my joy.

32 "For as I said to you from the beginning that I had much desire that you were not in the state of dilemma like your brethren, even so I have found that my desires have been gratified.

33 "For I perceive that you are in the paths of righteousness; I perceive that you are in the path which leads to the kingdom of God.

34 "I perceive that you are making his paths strait, and I perceive that it has been made known to you by the testimony of his word that he cannot walk in crooked paths.

35 "Neither does he vary from that which he has said; neither has he a shadow of turning from the right to the left, nor from that which is right to that which is wrong; therefore, his course is one eternal round.

36 "And he does not dwell in unholy temples; neither can filthiness nor anything which is unclean be received into the kingdom of God.

37 "Therefore I say to you, The time shall come, and it shall be at the last day, that he who is filthy shall remain in his filthiness.

38 "And now, my beloved brethren, I have said these things to you that I might awaken you to a sense of your duty to God, that you may walk blameless before him, that you may walk after the holy order of God after which you have been received.

39 "And I would that you should be humble, and be submissive, and gentle; easy to be entreated; full of patience and long-suffering; being temperate in all things; being diligent in keeping the commandments of God at all times; 40asking for whatever things you stand in need, both spiritual and temporal; always returning thanks to God for whatever things you do receive.

41 "And see that you have faith, hope and charity, and then you will always abound in good works.

42 "May the Lord bless you and keep your garments spotless, that you may at last be brought to sit down with Abraham, Isaac and Jacob, and

the holy prophets who have been ever since the world began, having your garments spotless even as their garments are spotless in the kingdom of heaven, to go no more out.

43 "Now, my beloved brethren, I have spoken these words to you according to the Spirit which testifies in me; and my soul rejoices exceedingly because of the exceeding diligence and heed which you have given to my word.

44 "May the peace of God rest upon you, and upon your houses and lands, and upon your flocks and herds, and all that you possess, and upon your women and your children, according to your faith and good works, from this time forth and forever. Thus I have spoken. Amen."

CHAPTER 6

ALMA returned from the land of Gideon after having taught the people of Gideon many things which cannot be written, having established the order of the church according as he had before done in the land of Zarahemla.

2 He returned to his own house at Zarahemla to rest himself from the labors which he had performed.

3 And thus ended the ninth year of the reign of the judges over the people of Nephi.

4 In the commencement of the tenth year of the reign of the judges over the people of Nephi, Alma departed thence and took his journey over into the land of Melek, on the west of the river Sidon, on the west by the borders of the wilderness.

5 And he began to teach the people in the land of Melek, according to the holy order of God by which he had been called; and he began to teach the people throughout all the land of Melek.

6 And the people came to him throughout all the borders of the land which was by the wilderness side.

7 And they were baptized throughout all the land, so that when he had finished his work at Melek, he departed thence and traveled three days' journey on the north of the land of Melek; and he came to a city which was called Ammonihah.

8 (Now it was the custom of the people of Nephi to call their lands, and their cities, and their villages, even all their small villages, after the name of him who first possessed them; and thus it was with the land of Ammonihah.)

9 When Alma had come to the city of Ammonihah, he began to preach the word of God to them.

10 Now Satan had gotten great hold upon the hearts of the people of the city of Ammonihah; therefore they would not hearken to the words of Alma.

11 Nevertheless, Alma labored much in the spirit, wrestling with God in mighty prayer that he would pour out his Spirit upon the people who were in the city, that he would also grant that he might baptize them unto repentance.

12 But they hardened their hearts, saying to him, "Behold, we know that you are Alma; and we know that you are high priest over the church which you have established in many parts of the land, according to your tradition.

13 "We are not of your church, and we do not believe in such foolish traditions.

14 "And we know that because we are not of your church, you have no power over us.

15 "And you have delivered up the judgment seat to Nephihah; therefore you are not the chief judge over us."

16 Now when the people had said this, and had withstood all his words, and reviled him, and spit upon him, and caused that he should be cast out of their city, he departed thence and took his journey toward the city which was called Aaron.

17 While he was journeying there, being weighed down with sorrow, wading through much tribulation and anguish of soul because of the wickedness of the people who were in the city of Ammonihah, 18an angel of the Lord appeared to him, saying, "Blessed art thou, Alma; therefore lift up thy head and rejoice, for thou hast great cause to rejoice.

19 "For thou hast been faithful in keeping the commandments of God from the time when thou received thy first message from him.

20 "Behold, I am he that delivered

155

it to you; and, behold, I am sent to command thee that thou return to the city of Ammonihah and preach again to the people of the city.

21 "Say to them, except they repent, the Lord God will destroy them.

22 "For, behold, they do study at this time that they may destroy the liberty of thy people (for thus saith the Lord), which is contrary to the statutes and judgments and commandments which he has given to his people."

23 Now after Alma had received his message from the angel of the Lord, he returned speedily to the land of Ammonihah.

24 And he entered the city by another way, by the way which is on the south of the city of Ammonihah.

25 As he entered the city he was hungry, and he said to a man, "Will you give to an humble servant of God something to eat?"

26 And the man said to him, "I am a Nephite, and I know that you are a holy prophet of God, for you are the man whom an angel said in a vision, 'Thou shalt receive.'

27 "Therefore go with me into my house, and I will impart to thee of my food; and I know that you will be a blessing to me and my house."

28 And the man received him into his house; and the man was called Amulek; and he brought forth bread and meat, and set them before Alma.

29 And Alma ate bread and was filled; and he blessed Amulek and his house, and he gave thanks to God.

30 After he had eaten and was filled, he said to Amulek, "I am Alma, and am the high priest over the church of God throughout the land.

31 "And, behold, I have been called to preach the word of God among all this people, according to the spirit of revelation and prophecy.

32 "I was in this land, and they would not receive me, but they cast me out, and I was about to set my back toward this land forever.

33 "But, behold, I have been commanded that I should turn again and prophesy to this people, and to testify against them concerning their iniquities.

34 "Now, Amulek, because you fed me and took me in, you are blessed; for I was hungry, for I had fasted many days."

35 And Alma tarried many days with Amulek before he began to preach to the people.

36 And it came to pass that the people waxed more gross in their iniquities.

37 And the word came to Alma, saying, "Go; and also say to my servant Amulek, Go forth and prophesy to this people, saying, Repent ye, for thus saith the Lord, 'Except ye repent, I will visit this people in my anger; and I will not turn my fierce anger away.'"

38 Alma went forth, and also Amulek, among the people to declare the words of God to them; and they were filled with the Holy Ghost.

39 And they had power given to them, insomuch that they could not be confined in dungeons; neither was it possible that any man could slay them.

40 Nevertheless they did not exercise their power until they were bound in bands and cast into prison.

41 Now this was done that the Lord might show forth his power in them.

42 And they went forth and began to preach and to prophesy to the people according to the spirit and power which the Lord had given them.

CHAPTER 7

The words of Alma and also the words of Amulek which were declared to the people who were in the land of Ammonihah. Also they are cast into prison and delivered by the miraculous power of God which was in them, according to the record of Alma.

AGAIN: I, Alma, having been commanded of God that I should take Amulek and go forth and preach again to this people, or the people who were in the city of Ammonihah, it came to pass as I began to preach to them, they began to contend with me, saying, "Who are you?

2 "Suppose you that we shall believe the testimony of one man, although he should preach to us that the earth should pass away?"

3 Now they understood not the words which they spoke, for they knew not that the earth should pass away.

4 And they said also, "We will not believe your words, if you should prophesy that this great city should be destroyed in one day."

5 Now they knew not that God could do such marvelous works, for they were a hardhearted and stiffnecked people.

6 And they said, "Who is God, that sends no more authority than one man among this people to declare to them the truth of such great and marvelous things?"

7 And they stood forth to lay their hands on me; but, behold, they did not.

8 And I stood with boldness to declare to them, and I boldly testified to them, saying: "Behold, O you wicked and perverse generation, how have you forgotten the tradition of your fathers; how soon you have forgotten the commandments of God.

9 "Do you not remember that our father Lehi was brought out of Jerusalem by the hand of God?

10 "Do you not remember that they were all led by him through the wilderness?

11 "And have you forgotten so soon how many times he delivered our fathers out of the hands of their enemies and preserved them from being destroyed, even by the hands of their own brethren?

12 "And if it had not been for his matchless power, and his mercy, and his long-suffering toward us, we should unavoidably have been cut off from the face of the earth, long before this period of time, and perhaps been consigned to a state of endless misery and woe.

13 "Behold, now I say to you that he commands you to repent; and except you repent, you can in no wise inherit the kingdom of God.

14 "But, behold, this is not all; he

has commanded you to repent, or he will utterly destroy you from the face of the earth; he will visit you in his anger, and in his fierce anger he will not turn away.

15 "Behold, do you not remember the words which he spoke to Lehi, saying, 'Inasmuch as ye shall keep my commandments ye shall prosper in the land'?

16 "And again it is said, 'Inasmuch as ye will not keep my commandments, ye shall be cut off from presence of the Lord.'

17 "Now I would that you should remember that inasmuch as the Lamanites have not kept the commandments of God they have been cut off from the presence of the Lord.

18 "And we see that the word of the Lord has been verified in this thing, and the Lamanites have been cut off from his presence from the beginning of their transgressions in the land.

19 "Nevertheless, I say to you that it shall be more tolerable for them in the day of judgment than for you, if you remain in your sins; 20and even more tolerable for them in this life than for you except you repent, for there are many promises which are extended to the Lamanites.

21 "For it is because of the traditions of their fathers that they remain in their state of ignorance; therefore the Lord will be merciful to them and prolong their existence in the land.

22 "And at some period of time they will be brought to believe in his word, and to know of the incorrectness of the traditions of their fathers; 23and many of them will be saved, for the Lord will be merciful to all who call on his name.

24 "But, behold, I say to you that if you persist in your wickedness, your days shall not be prolonged in the land, for the Lamanites shall be sent upon you.

25 "And if you repent not, they shall come in a time when you know not, and you shall be visited with utter destruction.

26 "And it shall be according to the fierce anger of the Lord; for he will not suffer you that you shall live in your iniquities to destroy his people.

27 "I say to you, No; he would

rather suffer that the Lamanites might destroy all this people who are called the people of Nephi, if it were possible that they could fall into sins and transgressions after having had so much light and so much knowledge given to them of the Lord their God; 28after having been such a highly favored people of the Lord; after having been favored above every other nation, kindred, tongue or people; 29after having had all things made known to them, according to their desires, and their faith, and prayers, of that which has been, and which is, and which is to come; 30having been visited by the Spirit of God; having conversed with angels, and having been spoken to by the voice of the Lord; 31and having the spirit of prophecy, and the spirit of revelation, and also many gifts—the gift of speaking with tongues, and the gift of preaching, and the gift of the Holy Ghost, and the gift of translation— 32and after having been delivered of God out of the land of Jerusalem by the hand of the Lord; 33having been saved from famine, and from sickness, and all manner of diseases of every kind; 34and they having been made strong in battle that they might not be destroyed, having been brought out of bondage time after time, and having been kept and preserved until now; and they have been prospered until they are rich in all manner of things.

35 "Now, behold, I say to you that if this people, who have received so many blessings from the hand of the Lord, should transgress, contrary to the light and knowledge which they do have; 36I say to you, that if this be the case, that they should fall into transgression, it would be far more tolerable for the Lamanites than for them.

37 "For, behold, the promises of the Lord are extended to the Lamanites, but they are not to you if you transgress.

38 "For has not the Lord expressly promised and firmly decreed that if you rebel against him you shall utterly be destroyed from the face of the earth?

39 "Now for this cause, that you may not be destroyed, the Lord has sent his angel to visit many of his people, declaring to them that they must go forth and cry mightily to this people, saying, 'Repent ye, repent ye, for the kingdom of heaven is nigh at hand.

40 "'And not many days hence, the Son of God shall come in his glory; and his glory shall be the glory of the only begotten of the Father, full of grace, equity and truth, full of patience, mercy, and long-suffering, quick to hear the cries of his people, and to answer their prayers.

41 "'Behold, he cometh to redeem those who will be baptized unto repentance, through faith on his name.

42 "'Therefore prepare ye the way of the Lord, for the time is at hand that all men shall reap a reward of their works according to that which they have been.

43 "'If they have been righteous, they shall reap the salvation of their souls, according to the power and deliverance of Jesus Christ; 44and if they have been evil, they shall reap the damnation of their souls, according to the power and captivation of the devil.'

45 "Now, behold, this is the voice of the angel crying to the people.

46 "And now, my beloved brethren (for you are my brethren and you ought to be beloved), you ought to bring forth works which are meet for repentance, seeing that your hearts have been grossly hardened against the word of God, and seeing that you are a lost and a fallen people."

47 When I, Alma, had spoken these words, behold, the people were angry with me because I said to them that they were a hardhearted and a stiff-necked people.

48 And also because I said to them that they were a lost and a fallen people, they were angry with me and sought to lay their hands upon me that they might cast me into prison.

49 But the Lord did not suffer them that they should take me at that time and cast me into prison.

50 And it came to pass that Amulek went and stood forth, and began to preach to them also.

51 Now the words of Amulek are not all written; nevertheless, a part of his words are written in this book.

CHAPTER 8

NOW these are the words which Amulek preached to the people who were in the land of Ammonihah, saying: "I am Amulek; I am the son of Giddonah, who was the son of Ishmael, who was a descendant of Aminadi.

2 "It was the same Aminadi who interpreted the writing which was upon the wall of the temple, which was written by the finger of God.

3 "And Aminadi was a descendant of Nephi, who was the son of Lehi, who came out of the land of Jerusalem, who was a descendant of Manasseh, who was the son of Joseph, who was sold into Egypt by the hands of his brethren.

4 "Behold, I am also a man of no small reputation among all those who know me.

5 "And, behold, I have many kindred and friends, and I have also acquired much riches by the hand of my industry; 6nevertheless, after all this, I never have known much of the ways of the Lord and his mysteries and marvelous power.

7 "I said I never had known much of these things; but, behold, I err, for I have seen much of his mysteries and his miraculous power, even in the preservation of the lives of this people.

8 "Nevertheless, I hardened my heart, for I was called many times, and I would not hear; therefore I knew concerning these things, yet I would not know.

9 "Therefore I went on rebelling against God in the wickedness of my heart, even until the fourth day of this seventh month, which is in the tenth year of the reign of the judges.

10 "As I was journeying to see a very near kindred, behold, an angel of the Lord appeared to me and said, 'Amulek, return to thine own house, for thou shalt feed a prophet of the Lord, a holy man, who is a chosen man of God.

11 "'For he has fasted many days because of the sins of this people, and he is hungry, and thou shalt receive him into thy house and feed him, and he shall bless thee and thy house;

and the blessing of the Lord shall rest upon thee and thy house.'

12 "I obeyed the voice of the angel and returned toward my house.

13 "And as I was going there, I found the man of whom the angel said to me, 'Thou shalt receive into thy house'; and, behold, it was this same man who has been speaking to you concerning the things of God.

14 "And the angel said to me, 'He is a holy man'; wherefore I know he is a holy man because it was said by an angel of God.

15 "Again, I know that the things whereof he has testified are true; for, behold, I say to you that as the Lord lives, even so he has sent his angel to make these things manifest to me; and this he has done while this Alma has dwelt at my house.

16 "For, behold, he has blessed my house, he has blessed me, and my women, and my children, and my father, and my kinfolk; 17even all my kindred has he blessed, and the blessing of the Lord has rested upon us according to the words which he spoke."

18 When Amulek had spoken these words, the people began to be astonished, seeing there was more than one witness who testified of the things whereof they were accused, and also of the things which were to come, according to the spirit of prophecy which was in them.

19 Nevertheless, there were some among them who thought to question them, that by their cunning devices they might catch them in their words, that they might find witness against them, that they might deliver them to the judges, 20that they might be judged according to the law, and that they might be slain or cast into prison, according to the crime which they could make appear or witness against them.

21 Now it was those men who sought to destroy them, who were lawyers, who were hired or appointed by the people to administer the law at their times of trials, or at the trials of the crimes of the people, before the judges.

22 These lawyers were learned in all the arts and cunning of the people; and this was to enable them that they

might be skillful in their profession.

23 And they began to question Amulek, that thereby they might make him cross his words, or contradict the words which he should speak.

24 Now they knew not that Amulek could know of their designs.

25 But as they began to question him, he perceived their thoughts, and he said to them, "O you wicked and perverse generation; you lawyers and hypocrites; you are laying the foundations of the devil.

26 "For you are laying traps and snares to catch the holy ones of God; you are laying plans to pervert the ways of the righteous and to bring down the wrath of God upon your heads, even to the utter destruction of this people.

27 "Well did Mosiah say, who was our last king, when he was about to deliver up the kingdom, having no one to confer it upon, causing that this people should be governed by their own voices; 28well did he say that if the time should come that the voice of this people should choose iniquity—that is, if the time should come that this people should fall into transgression—they would be ripe for destruction.

29 "And now I say to you, that well does the Lord judge of your iniquities; well does he cry to this people by the voice of his angels, 'Repent ye, repent, for the kingdom of heaven is at hand.'

30 "Well does he cry by the voice of his angels, 'I will come down among my people, with equity and justice in my hands.'

31 "And I say to you that if it were not for the prayers of the righteous, who are now in the land, you would even now be visited with utter destruction.

32 "Yet it would not be by flood, as were the people in the days of Noah, but it would be by famine, and by pestilence, and by the sword.

33 "But it is by the prayers of the righteous that you are spared; now therefore if you will cast out the righteous from among you, then the Lord will not stay his hand, but in his fierce anger he will come out against you.

34 "Then you shall be smitten by famine, and by pestilence, and by the sword; and the time is soon at hand, except you repent."

35 Now the people were more angry with Amulek, and they cried out, saying, "This man reviles against our laws, which are just, and our wise lawyers whom we have selected."

36 But Amulek stretched forth his hand, and cried the louder to them, saying: "O you wicked and perverse generation; why has Satan got such great hold upon your hearts?

37 "Why will you yield yourselves to him that he may have power over you, to blind your eyes that you will not understand the words which are spoken according to their truth?

38 "For, behold, have I testified against your law?

39 "You do not understand; you say that I have spoken against your law; but I have not. I have spoken in favor of your law, to your condemnation.

40 "And now, behold, I say to you that the foundation of the destruction of this people is beginning to be laid by the unrighteousness of your lawyers and your judges."

41 When Amulek had spoken these words, the people cried out against him, saying, "Now we know that this man is a child of the devil, for he has lied to us; for he has spoken against our law.

42 "And now he says that he has not spoken against it.

43 "Again, he has reviled against our lawyers and our judges."

44 And it came to pass that the lawyers put it into their hearts that they should remember these things against him.

45 And there was one among them whose name was Zeezrom.

46 He was the foremost to accuse Amulek and Alma, he being one of the most expert among them, having much business to do among the people.

47 Now the object of these lawyers was to get gain, and they got gain according to their employ.

48 For it was in the law of Mosiah that every man who was a judge of the law, or those who were appointed to be judges, should receive wages according to the time which they la-

bored to judge those who were brought before them to be judged.

49 If a man owed another and he would not pay that which he owed, he was complained of to the judge; 50and the judge executed authority and sent forth officers that the man should be brought before him.

51 And he judged the man according to the law and the evidences which were brought against him, and thus the man was compelled to pay that which he owed, or be stripped, or be cast out from among the people as a thief and a robber.

52 And the judge received for his wages according to his time: a senine of gold for a day, or a senum of silver, which is equal to a senine of gold; and this is according to the law which was given.

53 Now these are the names of the different pieces of their gold and of their silver, according to their value.

54 And the names are given by the Nephites; for they did not reckon after the manner of the Jews who were at Jerusalem; neither did they measure after the manner of the Jews.

55 But they altered their reckoning and their measure according to the minds and the circumstances of the people in every generation until the reign of the judges, they having been established by King Mosiah.

56 Now the reckoning is thus: a senine of gold, a seon of gold, a shum of gold, and a limnah of gold.

57 A senum of silver, an amnor of silver, an ezrom of silver, and an onti of silver.

58 A senum of silver was equal to a senine of gold; and either for a measure of barley, and also for a measure of every kind of grain.

59 The amount of a seon of gold was twice the value of a senine; and a shum of gold was twice the value of a seon; and a limnah of gold was the value of them all.

60 And an amnor of silver was as great as two senums; and an ezrom of silver was as great as four senums; and an onti was as great as them all.

61 Now this is the value of the lesser numbers of their reckoning: a shiblon is half of a senum; therefore a shiblon for half a measure of barley;

and a shiblum is a half of a shiblon; and a leah is the half of a shiblum.

62 And an antion of gold is equal to three shiblons.

63 Now this is their number according to their reckoning.

64 Now it was the sole purpose of the lawyers to get gain, because they received their wages according to their employ; 65therefore they stirred up the people to riotings, and all manner of disturbances and wickedness that they might have more employ, 66that they might get money according to the suits which were brought before them; therefore they stirred up the people against Alma and Amulek.

67 And this Zeezrom began to question Amulek, saying: "Will you answer me a few questions which I shall ask you?"

68 Now Zeezrom was a man who was expert in the devices of the devil, that he might destroy that which was good; therefore he said to Amulek, "Will you answer the questions which I shall put to you?"

69 And Amulek said to him, "I will if it be according to the Spirit of the Lord which is in me; for I shall say nothing which is contrary to the Spirit of the Lord."

70 And Zeezrom said to him, "Behold, here are six onties of silver, and all these will I give you if you will deny the existence of a supreme being."

71 Now Amulek said, "O you child of hell, why tempt me?

72 "Do you not know that the righteous yield to no such temptations?

73 "Do you believe that there is no God?

74 "I say to you, No; you know that there is a God, but you love that lucre more than him.

75 "And now you have lied before God to me.

76 "You said to me, 'Behold these six onties which are of great worth, I will give to you,' when you had it in your heart to retain them from me.

77 "And it was only your desire that I should deny the true and living God that you might have cause to destroy me.

78 "Now, behold, for this great evil you shall have your reward."

79 And Zeezrom said to him, "You say there is a true and living God?"

80 And Amulek said, "Yes, there is a true and a living God."

81 Now Zeezrom said, "Is there more than one God?"

82 And he answered, "No."

83 Then Zeezrom said to him again, "How do you know these things?"

84 And he said, "An angel has made them known to me."

85 Zeezrom said again, "Who is he that shall come? Is it the Son of God?"

86 And he said to him, "Yes."

87 And Zeezrom said again, "Shall he save his people in their sins?"

88 Amulek answered and said to him, "I say to you he shall not, for it is impossible for him to deny his word."

89 Now Zeezrom said to the people, "See that you remember these things; for he said there is but one God; yet he said that the Son of God shall come, but he shall not save his people, as though he had authority to command God."

90 But Amulek said again to him, "Behold, you have lied, for you said that I spoke as though I had authority to command God because I said he shall not save his people in their sins.

91 "And I say to you again that he cannot save them in their sins; for I cannot deny his word, and he has said that no unclean thing can inherit the kingdom of heaven.

92 "Therefore how can you be saved except you inherit the kingdom of heaven? Therefore you cannot be saved in your sins."

93 Now Zeezrom said again to him, "Is the Son of God the very eternal Father?"

94 And Amulek said to him, "He is the very eternal Father of heaven and of earth, and of all things which in them are.

95 "He is the beginning and the end, the first and the last.

96 "And he shall come into the world to redeem his people, and he shall take upon him the transgressions of those who believe on his name; and these are they that shall have eternal life, and salvation comes to no one else.

97 "Therefore the wicked remain as though there had been no redemption made except it be the loosing of the bands of death.

98 "For, behold, the day will come that all shall rise from the dead and stand before God and be judged according to their works.

99 "Now there is a death which is called a temporal death, and the death of Christ shall loose the bands of this temporal death, that all shall be raised from this temporal death.

100 "The spirit and the body shall be reunited in its perfect form, both limb and joint shall be restored to its proper frame even as we now are at this time.

101 "And we shall be brought to stand before God, knowing even as we know now, and have a bright recollection of all our guilt.

102 "Now this restoration shall come to all, both old and young, both bond and free, both male and female, both the wicked and the righteous.

103 "And even there shall not so much as a hair of their heads be lost; but all things shall be restored to their perfect frame, as it is now, or in the body, 104and shall be brought and be arraigned before the bar of Christ the Son, and God the Father, and the Holy Spirit, which is one eternal God, to be judged according to their works, whether they be good or whether they be evil.

105 "Now, behold, I have spoken to you concerning the death of the mortal body and also concerning the resurrection of the mortal body.

106 "I say to you that this mortal body is raised to an immortal body—that is, from death, even from the first death, to life, that they can die no more; their spirits uniting with their bodies, never to be divided; 107thus the whole becoming spiritual and immortal, that they can no more see corruption."

108 When Amulek had finished these words, the people began again to be astonished, and also Zeezrom began to tremble.

109 Thus ended the words of Amulek, or this is all that I have written.

CHAPTER 9

NOW Alma, seeing that the words of Amulek had silenced Zeezrom, for he beheld that Amulek had caught him in his lying and deceiving to destroy him, and seeing that he began to tremble under a consciousness of his guilt, opened his mouth and began to speak to him, and to establish the words of Amulek, and to explain things beyond, or to unfold the scriptures beyond that which Amulek had done.

2 The words that Alma spoke to Zeezrom were heard by the people round about; for the multitude was great, and he spoke on this wise:

3 "Now, Zeezrom, you have been taken in your lying and craftiness, for you have not lied to men only, but you have lied to God.

4 "For, behold, he knows all your thoughts; and you see that your thoughts are made known to us by his Spirit.

5 "And you see that we know that your plan was a very subtle plan, as to the subtlety of the devil, to lie and to deceive this people, that you might set them against us, to revile us and to cast us out.

6 "This was a plan of your adversary, and he has exercised his power in you.

7 "Now I would that you should remember that what I say to you, I say to all.

8 "And, behold, I say to you all that this was a snare of the adversary which he has laid to catch this people, 9that he might bring you into subjection to him, that he might encircle you about with his chains, that he might chain you down to everlasting destruction according to the power of his captivity."

10 When Alma had spoken these words, Zeezrom began to tremble more exceedingly, for he was convinced more and more of the power of God.

11 And he was also convinced that Alma and Amulek had a knowledge of him, for he was convinced that they knew the thoughts and intents of his heart; 12for power was given to them that they might know of these things according to the spirit of prophecy.

13 And Zeezrom began to inquire of them diligently that he might know more concerning the kingdom of God.

14 And he said to Alma, "What does this mean which Amulek has spoken concerning the resurrection of the dead, that all shall rise from the dead, both the just and the unjust, and are brought to stand before God to be judged according to their works?"

15 Alma began to expound these things to him, saying: "It is given to many to know the mysteries of God.

16 "Nevertheless, they are laid under a strict command that they shall impart only according to the portion of his word which he grants to the children of men, according to the heed and diligence which they give to him.

17 "Therefore, he that will harden his heart, the same will receive the lesser portion of the word.

18 "And he that will not harden his heart, to him is given the greater portion of the word, until it is given to him to know the mysteries of God until he knows them in full.

19 "And they that will harden their hearts, to them is given the lesser portion of the word, until they know nothing concerning his mysteries; 20and then they are taken captive by the devil and led by his will down to destruction.

21 "Now this is what is meant by the chains of hell. And Amulek has spoken plainly concerning death, and being raised from this mortality to a state of immortality, and being brought before the bar of God to be judged according to our works.

22 "Then if our hearts have been hardened, if we have hardened our hearts against the word insomuch that it has not been found in us, then will our state be awful, for then we shall be condemned.

23 "For our words will condemn us, and all our works will condemn us; we shall not be found spotless.

24 "And our thoughts will also condemn us; and in this awful state we shall not dare look up to our God; 25and we would be glad if we could command the rocks and the moun-

tains to fall upon us, to hide us from his presence.

26 "But this cannot be; we must come forth and stand before him in his glory, and in his power, and in his might, majesty, and dominion, and acknowledge to our everlasting shame that all his judgments are just, [27]that he is just in all his works, and that he is merciful to the children of men, and that he has all power to save every man that believes on his name and brings forth fruit meet for repentance.

28 "And now, behold, I say to you, then will come a death, even a second death, which is a spiritual death.

29 "Then is a time that whoever dies in his sins, as to a temporal death, shall also die a spiritual death; he shall die as to things pertaining to righteousness.

30 "Then is the time when their torments shall be as a lake of fire and brimstone, whose flames ascend up for ever and ever.

31 "And then is the time that they shall be chained down to an everlasting destruction according to the power and captivity of Satan, he having subjected them according to his will.

32 "Then, I say to you, they shall be as though there had been no redemption made; for they cannot be redeemed according to God's justice; and they cannot die, seeing there is no more corruption."

33 When Alma had made an end of speaking these words, the people began to be more astonished.

34 But there was one, Antionah, who was a chief ruler among them, that came forth and said to him, "What is this that you have said, that man should rise from the dead and be changed from this mortal to an immortal state, that the soul can never die?

35 "What does the scripture mean which says that God placed cherubims and a flaming sword on the east of the garden of Eden lest our first parents should enter and partake of the fruit of the tree of life and live forever?

36 "And thus we see that there was no possible chance that they should live forever."

37 Now Alma said to him, "This is the thing which I was about to explain.

38 "We see that Adam fell by the partaking of the forbidden fruit, according to the word of God; and thus we see that by his fall all mankind became a lost and a fallen people.

39 "And now, behold, I say to you that if it had been possible for Adam to have partaken of the fruit of the tree of life at that time, there would have been no death, and the word would have been void, making God a liar; for he said, 'If thou eat, thou shalt surely die.'

40 "And we see that death comes upon mankind, even the death which has been spoken of by Amulek, which is the temporal death; nevertheless there was a space granted to man in which he might repent.

41 "Therefore this life became a probationary state, a time to prepare to meet God, a time to prepare for that endless state which has been spoken of by us, which is after the resurrection of the dead.

42 "Now if it had not been for the plan of redemption, which was laid from the foundation of the world, there could have been no resurrection of the dead.

43 "But there was a plan of redemption laid which shall bring to pass the resurrection of the dead, of which has been spoken.

44 "And now, behold, if it were possible that our first parents could have gone forth and partaken of the tree of life, they would have been forever miserable, having no preparatory state; [45]and thus the plan of redemption would have been frustrated, and the word of God would have been void, taking no effect.

46 "But, behold, it was not so; but it was appointed to man that they must die; and after death, they must come to judgment, even that same judgment of which we have spoken, which is the end.

47 "And after God had appointed that these things should come to man, behold, then he saw that it was expedient that man should know concerning the things whereof he had appointed to them; [48]therefore he sent

angels to converse with them, who caused men to behold of his glory.

49 "And they began from that time forth to call on his name; therefore God conversed with men and made known to them the plan of redemption which had been prepared from the foundation of the world.

50 "This he made known to them according to their faith and repentance, and their holy works.

51 "Wherefore he gave commandments to men, they having first transgressed the first commandments as to things which were temporal, and becoming as gods, knowing good from evil, placing themselves in a state to act, or being placed in a state to act according to their wills and pleasures, whether to do evil or to do good.

52 "Therefore God gave them commandments, after having made known to them the plan of redemption, that they should not do evil, the penalty thereof being a second death which was an everlasting death as to things pertaining to righteousness; 53for on such the plan of redemption could have no power, for the works of justice could not be destroyed, according to the supreme goodness of God.

54 "But God called on men in the name of his Son (this being the plan of redemption which was laid), saying: 'If ye will repent and harden not your hearts, then will I have mercy upon you, through mine only begotten Son.

55 "'Therefore, whoever repenteth and hardeneth not his heart, he shall have claim on mercy through mine only begotten Son to a remission of his sins; and these shall enter into my rest.

56 "'And whoever will harden his heart and will do iniquity, behold, I swear in my wrath that he shall not enter into my rest.'

57 "And now, my brethren, behold, I say to you that if you will harden your hearts, you shall not enter into the rest of the Lord.

58 "Therefore your iniquity provokes him, that he sends down his wrath upon you as in the first provocation, 59according to his word in the last provocation as well as the first, to the everlasting destruction of your souls; therefore, according to his word, to the last death as well as the first.

60 "And now, my brethren, seeing we know these things, and they are true, let us repent and harden not our hearts, that we provoke not the Lord our God to pull down his wrath upon us in these his second commandments which he has given to us.

61 "But let us enter into the rest of God, which is prepared according to his word.

62 "Again, my brethren, I would cite your minds forward to the time which the Lord God gave these commandments to his children.

63 "And I would that you should remember that the Lord God ordained priests after his holy order, which was after the order of his Son, to teach these things to the people.

64 "And those priests were ordained after the order of his Son, in a manner that thereby the people might know in what manner to look forward to his Son for redemption.

65 "And this is the manner after which they were ordained: being called and prepared from the foundation of the world, according to the foreknowledge of God, on account of their exceeding faith and good works; in the first place being left to choose good or evil; 66therefore they, having chosen good, and exercising exceeding great faith, are called with a holy calling, even with that holy calling which was prepared with, and according to, a preparatory redemption for such.

67 "Thus they have been called to this holy calling on account of their faith, while others would reject the Spirit of God on account of the hardness of their hearts and blindness of their minds, while, if it had not been for this, they might have had as great privilege as their brethren.

68 "Or in fine: in the first place they were on the same standing with their brethren; thus this holy calling was prepared from the foundation of the world for such as would not harden their hearts, being in and through the atonement of the only begotten Son, who was prepared; 69and thus they were called by his holy calling, and ordained to the high

priesthood of the holy order of God to teach his commandments to the children of men that they also might enter into his rest.

70 "This high priesthood was after the order of his Son, which order was from the foundation of the world, 71or in other words, being without beginning of days or end of years, being prepared from eternity to all eternity, according to his foreknowledge of all things.

72 "Now they were ordained after this manner: Being called with a holy calling, and ordained with a holy ordinance, and taking upon them the high priesthood of the holy order, which calling, and ordinance, and high priesthood is without beginning or end; 73thus they become high priests forever, after the order of the Son, the only begotten of the Father, who is without beginning of days or end of years, who is full of grace, equity, and truth. And thus it is. Amen."

CHAPTER 10

NOW as I said concerning the holy order of this high priesthood, there were many who were ordained and became high priests of God.

2 "And it was on account of their exceeding faith, and repentance, and their righteousness before God, they choosing to repent and work righteousness rather than to perish.

3 "Therefore they were called after this holy order and were sanctified, and their garments were washed white through the blood of the Lamb.

4 "Now they, after being sanctified by the Holy Ghost, having their garments made white, being pure and spotless before God, could not look upon sin except with abhorrence.

5 "And there were many, an exceedingly great many, who were made pure and entered into the rest of the Lord their God.

6 "Now, my brethren, I would that you should humble yourselves before God and bring forth fruit meet for repentance, that you may also enter into that rest.

7 "Humble yourselves even as the people in the days of Melchisedec,

who was also a high priest after this same order which I have spoken, who also took upon him the high priesthood forever.

8 "It was this same Melchisedec to whom Abraham paid tithes; even our father Abraham paid tithes of one tenth part of all that he possessed.

9 "Now these ordinances were given after this manner, that thereby the people might look forward on the Son of God, it being a type of his order, or it being his order; 10and this, that they might look forward to him for a remission of their sins, that they might enter into the rest of the Lord.

11 "Now this Melchisedec was a king over the land of Salem; and his people had waxed strong in iniquity and abominations; they had all gone astray; they were full of all manner of wickedness.

12 "But Melchisedec, having exercised mighty faith and received the office of the high priesthood according to the holy order of God, preached repentance to his people.

13 "And, behold, they repented, and Melchisedec established peace in the land in his days; 14therefore he was called the prince of peace, for he was the king of Salem, and he reigned under his father.

15 "There were many before him, and also there were many afterwards, but none were greater; therefore of him they have more particularly made mention.

16 "Now I need not rehearse the matter; what I have said may suffice.

17 "Behold, the scriptures are before you; if you will wrest them it shall be to your own destruction."

18 Now it came to pass that when Alma had said these words to them, he stretched forth his hand to them and cried with a mighty voice, saying, "Now is the time to repent, for the day of salvation draws nigh.

19 "The voice of the Lord, by the mouth of angels, declares it to all nations; even declares it that they may have glad tidings of great joy.

20 "And he sounds these glad tidings among all his people, even to them that are scattered abroad upon the face of the earth; wherefore they have come to us.

21 "And they are made known to us in plain terms that we may understand that we cannot err, and this because of our being wanderers in a strange land.

22 "Therefore we are thus highly favored, for we have these glad tidings declared to us in all parts of our vineyard.

23 "For, behold, angels are declaring it to many at this time in our land; and this is for the purpose of preparing the hearts of the children of men to receive his word at the time of his coming in his glory.

24 "And now we only wait to hear the joyful news of his coming declared to us by the mouth of angels; for the time will come, we know not how soon.

25 "Would to God that it might be in my day; but let it be sooner or later, in it I will rejoice.

26 "And it shall be made known to just and holy men by the mouth of angels at the time of his coming, that the words of our fathers may be fulfilled according to that which they have spoken concerning him, which was according to the spirit of prophecy which was in them.

27 "Now, my brethren, I wish from the inmost part of my heart, with great anxiety, even to pain, that you would hearken to my words and cast off your sins, and not procrastinate the day of your repentance, 28and humble yourselves before the Lord, and call on his holy name, and watch and pray continually that you may not be tempted above that which you can bear, and thus be led by the Holy Spirit, becoming humble, meek, submissive, patient, full of love and all long-suffering, having faith on the Lord, 29having a hope that you shall receive eternal life, having the love of God always in your hearts, that you may be lifted up at the last day, and enter into his rest.

30 "May the Lord grant you repentance, that you may not bring down his wrath upon you, that you may not be bound down by the chains of hell, that you may not suffer the second death."

31 And Alma spoke many more words to the people which are not written in this book.

32 After he had made an end of speaking to the people, many of them believed on his words and began to repent and to search the scriptures.

33 But the greater part of them were desirous that they might destroy Alma and Amulek; for they were angry with Alma because of the plainness of his words to Zeezrom.

34 And they also said that Amulek had lied to them and had reviled against their law and also against their lawyers and judges.

35 They were also angry with Alma and Amulek because they had testified so plainly against their wickedness, and they sought to put them away privily.

36 But it came to pass that they did not; but they took them and bound them with strong cords, and took them before the chief judge of the land.

37 And the people went forth and witnessed against them, testifying that they had reviled against the law and their lawyers and judges of the land, and also all the people that were in the land, 38and also testified that there was but one God, and that he should send his Son among the people, but he should not save them. Many such things did the people testify against Alma and Amulek.

39 Now this was done before the chief judge of the land.

40 Zeezrom was astonished at the words which had been spoken; and he also knew concerning the blindness of the minds which he had caused among the people by his lying words.

41 And his soul began to be harrowed up under a consciousness of his own guilt; and he began to be encircled by the pains of hell.

42 He began to cry to the people, saying: "Behold, I am guilty, and these men are spotless before God."

43 And he began to plead for them from that time forth; but they reviled him, saying: "Are you also possessed with the devil?"

44 And they spit upon him and cast him out from among them, and also all those who believed in the words which had been spoken by Alma and Amulek; and they cast them out and sent men to cast stones at them.

45 And they brought their wives and children together, and whoever believed or had been taught to believe in the word of God, they caused that he should be cast into the fire.

46 They also brought forth their records, which contained the holy scriptures, and cast them into the fire also, that they might be burned and destroyed by fire.

47 And they took Alma and Amulek and carried them forth to the place of martydom that they might witness the destruction of those who were consumed by fire.

48 When Amulek saw the pains of the women and children who were being consumed in the fire, he was also pained; and he said to Alma, "How can we witness this awful scene?

49 "Therefore let us stretch forth our hands and exercise the power of God which is in us and save them from the flames."

50 But Alma said to him, "The Spirit constrains me that I must not stretch forth my hand; for, behold, the Lord receives them up to himself in glory.

51 "And he suffers that they may do this thing, or that the people may do this thing to them according to the hardness of their hearts, that the judgments which he shall exercise upon them in his wrath may be just.

52 "The blood of the innocent shall stand as a witness against them and cry mightily against them at the last day."

53 Now Amulek said to Alma, "Behold, perhaps they will burn us also."

54 And Alma said, "Be it according to the will of the Lord. But, behold, our work is not finished; therefore they burn us not."

55 When the bodies of those who had been cast into the fire were consumed, and also the records which were cast in with them, the chief judge of the land came and stood before Alma and Amulek, as they were bound.

56 And he smote them with his hand upon their cheeks and said to them, "After what you have seen, will you preach again to this people

that they shall be cast into a lake of fire and brimstone?

57 "Behold, you see that you had not power to save these who have been cast into the fire; neither has God saved them because they were of your faith."

58 And the judge smote them upon their cheeks and asked, "What say you for yourselves?"

59 Now this judge was after the order and faith of Nehor, who slew Gideon.

60 Alma and Amulek answered him nothing; and he smote them again and delivered them to the officers to be cast into prison.

61 When they had been cast into prison three days, there came many lawyers, and judges, and priests, and teachers, who were of the profession of Nehor.

62 And they came in to the prison to see them, and they questioned them about many words; but they answered them nothing.

63 And the judge stood before them, and said, "Why do you not answer the words of this people?

64 "Know you not that I have power to deliver you up to the flames?"

65 And he commanded them to speak, but they answered nothing.

66 And they departed and went their ways, but came again on the morrow; and the judge also smote them again on their cheeks.

67 And many came forth also and smote them, saying, "Will you stand again and judge this people and condemn our law?

68 "If you have such great power, why do you not deliver yourselves?"

69 Many such things they said to them, gnashing their teeth upon them, and spitting upon them, and saying, "How shall we look when we are damned?"

70 And many such things, even all manner of such things they said to them; and thus they mocked them for many days.

71 And they withheld food from them that they might hunger, and water that they might thirst.

72 They also took from them their clothes that they were naked, and

thus they were bound with strong cords and confined in prison.

73 After they had thus suffered for many days (and it was on the twelfth day, in the tenth month, in the tenth year of the reign of the judges over the people of Nephi), the chief judge over the land of Ammonihah, and many of their teachers and their lawyers, went in to the prison where Alma and Amulek were bound with cords.

74 And the chief judge stood before them and smote them again, and said to them, "If you have the power of God, deliver yourselves from these bands, and then we will believe that the Lord will destroy this people according to your words."

75 And they all went forth and smote them, saying the same words, even until the last.

76 When the last had spoken to them, the power of God was upon Alma and Amulek, and they arose and stood upon their feet; and Alma cried, saying, "How long shall we suffer these great afflictions, O Lord?

77 "O Lord, give us strength according to our faith which is in Christ, even to deliverance." And they broke the cords with which they were bound; and when the people saw this, they began to flee, for the fear of destruction had come upon them.

78 And so great was their fear that they fell to the earth and did not reach the outer door of the prison.

79 The earth shook mightily, and the walls of the prison were rent in twain, so that they fell to the earth.

80 And the chief judge, and the lawyers, and priests, and teachers who smote upon Alma and Amulek were slain by the fall thereof.

81 And Alma and Amulek came forth out of the prison, and they were not hurt; for the Lord had granted to them power according to their faith which was in Christ.

82 They straightway came forth out of the prison, and they were loosed from their bands.

83 And the prison had fallen to the earth, and every soul within the walls thereof was slain, save it were Alma and Amulek; and they straightway came forth into the city.

84 Now the people, having heard a great noise, came running together by multitudes to know the cause of it.

85 When they saw Alma and Amulek coming forth out of the prison, and the walls thereof had fallen to the earth, they were struck with great fear and fled from the presence of Alma and Amulek, even as a goat flees with her young from two lions; and thus they fled from the presence of Alma and Amulek.

86 And it came to pass that Alma and Amulek were commanded to depart out of that city; and they departed and came out even into the land of Sidom.

87 And, behold, there they found all the people who had departed out of the land of Ammonihah, who had been cast out and stoned because they believed in the words of Alma.

88 They related to them all that had happened to their wives and children, and also concerning themselves and of their power of deliverance.

89 Also Zeezrom lay sick at Sidom with a burning fever, which was caused by the great tribulations of his mind on account of his wickedness, for he supposed that Alma and Amulek were no more; and he supposed that they had been slain because of his iniquity.

90 And this great sin, and his many other sins, harrowed up his mind until it became exceedingly sore, having no deliverance; therefore he began to be scorched with a burning heat.

91 Now when he heard that Alma and Amulek were in the land of Sidom, his heart began to take courage; and he sent a message immediately to them, desiring them to come to him.

92 They went immediately, obeying the message which he had sent to them; and they went into the house to Zeezrom.

93 And they found him upon his bed sick, being very low with a burning fever; and his mind also was exceedingly sore because of his iniquities.

94 When he saw them he stretched forth his hand and besought them that they would heal him.

95 Alma said to him, taking him

by the hand, "Do you believe in the power of Christ to salvation?"

96 He answered and said, "Yes, I believe all the words that you have taught."

97 And Alma said, "If you believe in the redemption of Christ, you can be healed."

98 And he said, "I believe according to your words."

99 Then Alma cried to the Lord, saying, "O Lord our God, have mercy on this man and heal him according to his faith which is in Christ."

100 When Alma had said these words, Zeezrom leaped upon his feet and began to walk.

101 This was done to the great astonishment of all the people; and the knowledge of this went forth throughout all the land of Sidom.

102 And Alma baptized Zeezrom unto the Lord; and he began from that time forth to preach to the people.

103 And Alma established a church in the land of Sidom, and consecrated priests and teachers in the land to baptize unto the Lord those who were desirous to be baptized.

104 And they were many; for they flocked in from all the region round about Sidom and were baptized.

105 But as to the people that were in the land of Ammonihah, they yet remained a hardhearted and a stiff-necked people.

106 They repented not of their sins, ascribing all the power of Alma and Amulek to the devil; for they were of the profession of Nehor and did not believe in the repentance of their sins.

107 And now as to Alma and Amulek: Amulek had forsaken all his gold, and silver, and his precious things, which were in the land of Ammonihah, for the word of God, he being rejected by those who were once his friends, and also by his father and his kindred.

108 And Alma, after having established the church at Sidom, saw that the people were checked as to the pride of their hearts, and began to humble themselves before God, 109and began to assemble themselves together at their sanctuaries to worship God before the altar, watching and praying continually that they might be delivered from Satan, and from death, and from destruction.

110 Alma, having seen all these things, took Amulek and came over to the land of Zarahemla, and took him to his own house, and administered to him in his tribulations, and strengthened him in the Lord.

111 Thus ended the tenth year of the reign of the judges over the people of Nephi.

CHAPTER 11

IN the eleventh year of the reign of the judges over the people of Nephi, on the fifth day of the second month (there having been much peace in the land of Zarahemla, there having been no wars nor contentions for a certain number of years, even until the fifth day of the second month, in the eleventh year), there was a cry of war heard throughout the land.

2 For, behold, the armies of the Lamanites had come in upon the wilderness side into the borders of the land, even into the city of Ammonihah, and had begun to slay the people and to destroy the city.

3 And before the Nephites could raise a sufficient army to drive them out of the land, they had destroyed the people who were in the city of Ammonihah, and also some around the borders of Noah, taking others captive into the wilderness.

4 Now the Nephites were desirous to obtain those who had been carried away captive into the wilderness.

5 And he that had been appointed chief captain over the armies of the Nephites was named Zoram, and he had two sons, Lehi and Aha.

6 Zoram and his two sons, knowing that Alma was high priest over the church and having heard that he had the spirit of prophecy, 7went to him and desired of him to know whether the Lord would that they should go into the wilderness in search of their brethren who had been taken captive by the Lamanites.

8 Alma inquired of the Lord concerning the matter.

9 And Alma returned and said to them, "Behold, the Lamanites will

cross the river Sidon in the south wilderness, away up beyond the borders of the land of Manti.

10 "And, behold, there you shall meet them on the east of the river Sidon, and there the Lord will deliver to you your brethren who have been taken captive by the Lamanites."

11 Zoram and his sons crossed over the river Sidon with their armies, and marched away beyond the borders of Manti into the south wilderness, which was on the east side of the river Sidon.

12 And they came upon the armies of the Lamanites, and the Lamanites were scattered and driven into the wilderness; and they took their brethren who had been taken captive by the Lamanites, and there was not one soul of them who had been lost that were taken captive.

13 And they were brought by their brethren to possess their own lands.

14 Thus ended the eleventh year of the judges, the Lamanites having been driven out of the land, and the people of Ammonihah being destroyed.

15 Every living soul of the Ammonihahites had been destroyed, and also their great city, which they said God could not destroy because of its greatness.

16 But, behold, in one day it was left desolate; and the carcasses were mangled by dogs and wild beasts of the wilderness.

17 Nevertheless, after many days, their dead bodies were heaped up upon the face of the earth, and they were covered with a shallow covering.

18 Now so great was the scent thereof that the people did not go in to possess the land of Ammonihah for many years.

19 And it was called Desolation of Nehors; for they who were slain were of the profession of Nehor, and their lands remained desolate.

20 And the Lamanites did not come again to war against the Nephites until the fourteenth year of the reign of the judges over the people of Nephi.

21 Thus for three years the people of Nephi had continual peace in all the land.

22 And Alma and Amulek went forth preaching repentance to the people in their temples, and in their sanctuaries, and also in their synagogues, which were built after the manner of the Jews.

23 And as many as would hear their words, to them they imparted the word of God, without any respect of persons, continually.

24 Thus Alma and Amulek went forth, and also many more who had been chosen for the work, to preach the word throughout all the land.

25 And the establishment of the church became general throughout the land, in all the region round about, among all the people of the Nephites.

26 And there was no inequality among them, for the Lord poured out his Spirit on all the face of the land to prepare the minds of the children of men or to prepare their hearts to receive the word which should be taught among them at the time of his coming, 27that they might not be hardened against the word, that they might not be unbelieving and go on to destruction, 28but that they might receive the word with joy, and as a branch be grafted into the true vine, that they might enter into the rest of the Lord their God.

29 Now those priests who went forth among the people preached against all lyings, and deceivings, and envyings, and strifes, and malice, and revilings, and stealing, robbing, plundering, murdering, committing adultery, and all manner of lasciviousness, crying that these things ought not to be so; 30holding forth things which must shortly come, even the coming of the Son of God, his sufferings and death, and also the resurrection of the dead.

31 And many of the people inquired concerning the place where the Son of God should come; and they were taught that he would appear to them after his resurrection; and this the people heard with great joy and gladness.

32 And after the church had been established throughout all the land, having got the victory over the devil, the word of God was preached in its

purity in all the land and the Lord poured out his blessings upon the people.

33 Thus ended the fourteenth year of the reign of the judges over the people of Nephi.

CHAPTER 12

An account of the sons of Mosiah, who rejected their rights to the kingdom for the word of God, and went up to the land of Nephi to preach to the Lamanites. Their sufferings and deliverance according to the record of Alma.

AS Alma was journeying from the land of Gideon southward, away to the land of Manti, behold, to his astonishment, he met the sons of Mosiah journeying toward the land of Zarahemla.

2 Now these sons of Mosiah were with Alma at the time the angel first appeared to him; therefore Alma rejoiced exceedingly to see his brethren.

3 What added more to his joy, they were still his brethren in the Lord; and they had waxed strong in the knowledge of the truth; 4for they were men of a sound understanding, and they had searched the scriptures diligently that they might know the word of God.

5 But this is not all: they had given themselves to much prayer and fasting, therefore they had the spirit of prophecy and the spirit of revelation, and when they taught, they taught with power and authority, even as with the power and authority of God.

6 And they had been teaching the word of God for the space of fourteen years among the Lamanites, having had much success in bringing many to the knowledge of the truth.

7 By the power of their words, many were brought before the altar of God to call on his name and confess their sins before him.

8 Now these are the circumstances which attended them in their journeyings, for they had many afflictions:

9 They suffered much, both in body and in mind, such as hunger, thirst, and fatigue, and also much labor in the spirit.

10 Now these were their journeyings: Having taken leave of their father, Mosiah, in the first year of the reign of the judges, having refused the kingdom which their father was desirous to confer upon them (and also

this was the mind of the people), 11they departed out of the land of Zarahemla, and took their swords, and their spears, and their bows, and their arrows, and their slings.

12 And this they did that they might provide food for themselves while in the wilderness.

13 Thus they departed into the wilderness, with their numbers which they had selected, to go up to the land of Nephi to preach the word of God to the Lamanites.

14 And they journeyed many days in the wilderness, and they fasted much and prayed much that the Lord would grant to them a portion of his Spirit to go with them and abide with them, 15that they might be an instrument in the hands of God, to bring, if it were possible, their brethren, the Lamanites, to the knowledge of the truth, 16to the knowledge of the baseness of the traditions of their fathers, which were not correct.

17 And the Lord visited them with his Spirit and said to them, "Be comforted"; and they were comforted.

18 And the Lord said to them also, "Go forth among the Lamanites, thy brethren, and establish my word.

19 "Be patient in long-suffering and afflictions, that ye may show forth good examples to them in me, and I will make an instrument of thee in my hands to the salvation of many souls."

20 And it came to pass that the hearts of the sons of Mosiah, and also those who were with them, took courage to go forth to the Lamanites to declare to them the word of God.

21 When they had arrived in the borders of the land of the Lamanites, they separated themselves and departed one from another, trusting in the Lord that they should meet again at the close of their harvest; for they

supposed that great was the work which they had undertaken.

22 And assuredly it was great, for they had undertaken to preach the word of God to a wild, and a hardened, and a ferocious people—a people who delighted in murdering the Nephites, and robbing and plundering them.

23 Their hearts were set upon riches, or upon gold, and silver, and precious stones; 24yet they sought to obtain these things by murdering and plundering that they might not labor for them with their own hands.

25 Thus they were a very indolent people, many of whom worshiped idols, and the curse of God had fallen upon them because of the traditions of their fathers; notwithstanding, the promises of the Lord were extended to them on the conditions of repentance.

26 And this was the cause for which the sons of Mosiah had undertaken the work, that perhaps they might bring them to repentance, that perhaps they might bring them to know of the plan of redemption.

27 Therefore they separated themselves one from another and went forth among them, every man alone, according to the word and power of God which was given to him.

28 Now Ammon was the chief among them, or rather he ministered to them; and he departed from them after having blessed them according to their several stations, having imparted the word of God to them, or administered to them before his departure; and thus they took their several journeys throughout the land.

29 And Ammon went to the land of Ishmael, the land being called after the sons of Ishmael who also became Lamanites.

30 And as Ammon entered the land of Ishmael, the Lamanites took him and bound him, as was their custom to bind all the Nephites who fell into their hands and carry them before the king.

31 Thus it was left to the pleasure of the king to slay them, or to retain them in captivity, or to cast them into prison, or to cast them out of his land according to his will and pleasure.

32 Thus Ammon was carried before the king who was over the land of Ishmael; his name was Lamoni, and he was a descendant of Ishmael.

33 The king inquired of Ammon if it were his desire to dwell in the land among the Lamanites or among his people.

34 And Ammon said to him, "I desire to dwell among this people for a time, perhaps until the day I die."

35 King Lamoni was much pleased with Ammon and caused that his bands should be loosed; and he would that Ammon should take one of his daughters to wife.

36 But Ammon said to him, "No, but I will be your servant"; therefore Ammon became a servant to King Lamoni.

37 And he was set, among other servants, to watch the flocks of Lamoni according to the custom of the Lamanites.

38 After he had been in the service of the king three days, as he was with the Lamanitish servants going forth with their flocks to the place of water which was called the water of Sebus (and all the Lamanites drive their flocks hither, that they may have water), 39behold, a certain number of the Lamanites, who had been with their flocks to water, stood and scattered the flocks of Ammon and the servants of the king, and they scattered them insomuch that they fled many ways.

40 Now the servants of the king began to murmur, saying, "Now the king will slay us as he has our brethren because their flocks were scattered by the wickedness of these men."

41 And they began to weep exceedingly, saying, "Behold, our flocks are scattered already."

42 Now they wept because of the fear of being slain.

43 When Ammon saw this, his heart was swollen within him with joy; for, said he, "I will show forth my power to these my fellow servants, or the power which is in me, in restoring these flocks to the king, that I may win the hearts of these my fellow servants, that I may lead them to believe in my words."

44 Now these were the thoughts of Ammon when he saw the afflictions

of those whom he termed to be his brethren.

45 And he flattered them by his words, saying, "My brethren, be of good cheer and let us go in search of the flocks, and we will gather them together and bring them back to the place of water.

46 "Thus we will preserve the flocks to the king, and he will not slay us."

47 And they went in search of the flocks, and they followed Ammon, and they rushed forth with much swiftness and headed the flocks of the king and gathered them again to the place of water.

48 And those men again stood to scatter their flocks; but Ammon said to his brethren, "Encircle the flocks that they flee not, and I will go and contend with these men who scatter our flocks."

49 Therefore they did as Ammon commanded them, and he went forth and stood to contend with those who stood by the waters of Sebus.

50 And they were in number not a few; therefore they did not fear Ammon, for they supposed that one of their men could slay him according to their pleasure, for they knew not that the Lord had promised Mosiah that he would deliver his sons out of their hands; neither did they know anything concerning the Lord.

51 Therefore they delighted in the destruction of their brethren; and for this cause they stood to scatter the flocks of the king.

52 But Ammon stood forth and began to cast stones at them with his sling; with mighty power he slung stones among them.

53 Thus he slew a certain number of them, insomuch that they began to be astonished at his power.

54 Nevertheless they were angry because of the slain of their brethren, and they were determined that he should fall.

55 Therefore, seeing that they could not hit him with their stones, they came forth with clubs to slay him.

56 But, behold, every man that lifted his club to smite Ammon, he smote off his arm with his sword.

57 For he withstood their blows by smiting their arms with the edge of his sword, insomuch that they began to be astonished and began to flee before him.

58 And they were not few in number; and he caused them to flee by the strength of his arm.

59 Now six of them had fallen by the sling, but he slew none, save it were their leader, with his sword; and he smote off as many of their arms as were lifted against him, and they were not a few.

60 When he had driven them afar off, he returned, and they watered their flocks and returned them to the pasture of the king, and then went in to the king, bearing the arms which had been cut off by the sword of Ammon of those who sought to slay him.

61 And they were carried to the king for a testimony of the things which they had done.

62 And King Lamoni caused that his servants should stand forth and testify to all the things which they had seen, concerning the matter.

63 When they had all testified to the things which they had seen, and he had learned of the faithfulness of Ammon in preserving his flocks, and also of his great power in contending against those who sought to slay him, he was astonished exceedingly, and said, "Surely this is more than a man.

64 "Behold, is not this the Great Spirit who sends such great punishments upon this people because of their murders?"

65 And they answered the king, and said, "Whether he be the Great Spirit or a man, we know not; but this much we do know, that he cannot be slain by the enemies of the king.

66 "Neither can they scatter the king's flock when he is with us because of his expertness and great strength; therefore, we know that he is a friend to the king.

67 "And now, O king, we do not believe that a man has such great power, for we know that he cannot be slain."

68 When the king heard these words, he said to them, "Now I know that it is the Great Spirit; and he has come down at this time to preserve your lives, that I might not slay you as I did your brethren.

69 "This is the Great Spirit of whom our fathers have spoken."

70 Now this was the tradition of Lamoni, which he had received from his father, that there was a Great Spirit.

71 Notwithstanding they believed in a Great Spirit, they supposed that whatever they did was right.

72 Nevertheless Lamoni began to fear exceedingly, lest he had done wrong in slaying his servants; 73for he had slain many of them because their brethren had scattered their flocks at the place of water; and thus because their flocks had been scattered, they were slain.

74 Now it was the practice of the Lamanites to stand by the waters of Sebus to scatter the flocks of the people, that thereby they might drive many that were scattered away to their own land, it being a practice of plunder among them.

75 And King Lamoni inquired of his servants, saying, "Where is this man that has such great power?"

76 And they said to him, "Behold, he is feeding your horses."

77 Now the king had commanded his servants previous to the time of the watering of their flocks that they should prepare his horses and chariots and conduct him forth to the land of Nephi; 78for there had been a great feast appointed at the land of Nephi by the father of Lamoni, who was king over all the land.

79 And when King Lamoni heard that Ammon was preparing his horses and his chariots, he was more astonished because of the faithfulness of Ammon, saying:

80 "Surely, there has not been any servant among all my servants, that has been so faithful as this man; for he remembers all my commandments, to execute them.

81 "Now I surely know that this is the Great Spirit; and I would desire him that he come to me, but I dare not."

82 When Ammon had made ready the horses and the chariots for the king and his servants, he went in to the king, and he saw that the countenance of the king was changed; therefore he was about to return out of his presence.

83 And one of the king's servants said to him, "Rabbanah," which is, being interpreted, powerful or great king, considering their kings to be powerful; 84"Rabbanah, the king desireth thee to stay."

85 Therefore Ammon turned himself to the king and said to him, "What wilt thou that I should do for thee, O king!"

86 But the king answered him not for the space of an hour, according to their time, for he knew not what he should say to him.

87 And Ammon said to him again, "What desirest thou of me?" But the king answered him not.

88 And it came to pass that Ammon was filled with the Spirit of God, therefore he perceived the thoughts of the king.

89 And he said to him, "Is it because thou hast heard that I defended thy servants and thy flocks, and slew seven of their brethren with the sling and with the sword, and smote off the arms of others in order to defend thy flocks and thy servants; behold, is it this that causeth thy marvelings?

90 "I say to you, What is it that thy marvelings are so great?

91 "Behold, I am a man and am thy servant; therefore, whatever thou desirest which is right, that will I do."

92 Now when the king had heard these words, he marveled again, for he beheld that Ammon could discern his thoughts.

93 But notwithstanding this, King Lamoni opened his mouth and said to him, "Who art thou? Art thou that Great Spirit who knoweth all things?"

94 Ammon answered and said to him, "I am not."

95 And the king said, "How do you know the thoughts of my heart?

96 "You may speak boldly and tell me concerning these things, and also tell me by what power you slew and smote off the arms of my brethren that scattered my flocks.

97 "And now if you will tell me concerning these things, whatever you desire, I will give you.

98 "And if it were needed, I would guard you with my armies; but I know that you are more powerful than all they; nevertheless, whatever

you desire of me, I will grant it to you."

99 Ammon, being wise yet harmless, said to Lamoni, "Wilt thou hearken to my words if I tell thee by what power I do these things? This is the thing that I desire of thee."

100 And the king answered him and said, "I will believe all your words." Thus he was caught with guile.

101 And Ammon began to speak to him with boldness, and said to him, "Believest thou that there is a God?"

102 The king answered and said to him, "I do not know what that means."

103 Then Ammon said, "Believest thou that there is a Great Spirit?"

104 And he said, "Yes."

105 And Ammon said, "This is God."

106 Ammon said to him again, "Believest thou that this Great Spirit, who is God, created all things which are in heaven and in the earth?"

107 And he said, "I believe that he created all things which are in the earth; but I do not know the heavens."

108 And Ammon said to him, "Heaven is a place where God dwells, and all his holy angels."

109 And King Lamoni said, "Is it above the earth?"

110 And Ammon said, "Yea, and he looketh down upon all the children of men, and he knoweth all the thoughts and intents of the heart; for by his hand were they all created from the beginning."

111 And King Lamoni said, "I believe all these things which you have spoken. Are you sent from God?"

112 Ammon said to him, "I am a man; and man in the beginning was created after the image of God, and I am called by his Holy Spirit to teach these things to this people that they may be brought to a knowledge of that which is just and true.

113 "And a portion of that Spirit dwelleth in me, which giveth me knowledge, and also power, according to my faith and desires which are in God."

114 Now when Ammon had said these words, he began at the creation of the world, and also the creation of Adam, and told him all the things concerning the fall of man.

115 And he rehearsed and laid before him the records and the holy scriptures of the people which had been spoken by the prophets, even down to the time that their father Lehi left Jerusalem.

116 He also rehearsed to them (for it was to the king and to his servants) all the journeyings of their fathers in the wilderness, and all their sufferings with hunger and thirst, and their travel.

117 And he also rehearsed to them concerning the rebellions of Laman and Lemuel and the sons of Ishmael, even all their rebellions he related to them.

118 And he expounded to them all the records and scriptures from the time that Lehi left Jerusalem down to the present time.

119 But this is not all; for he expounded to them the plan of redemption which was prepared from the foundation of the world.

120 He also made known to them concerning the coming of Christ; and all the works of the Lord he made known to them.

121 After he had said all these things and expounded them to the king, the king believed all his words.

122 And he began to cry to the Lord, saying: O Lord, have mercy; according to thy abundant mercy which thou hast had upon the people of Nephi, have upon me and my people."

123 When he had said this, he fell to the earth as if he were dead.

124 His servants took him and carried him in to his wife, and laid him upon a bed; and he lay as if he were dead for the space of two days and two nights.

125 And his wife, and his sons, and his daughters mourned over him, after the manner of the Lamanites, greatly lamenting his loss.

126 And after two days and two nights, they were about to take his body and lay it in a sepulcher which they had made for the purpose of burying their dead.

127 Now the queen having heard of the fame of Ammon, therefore she

sent and desired that he should come to her.

128 Ammon did as he was commanded, and went to the queen and desired to know what she would that he should do.

129 And she said to him, "The servants of my husband have made it known to me that you are a prophet of a holy God, and that you have power to do many mighty works in his name.

130 "Therefore, if this is the case, I would that you should go in and see my husband, for he has been laid upon his bed for the space of two days and two nights; 131and some say that he is not dead, but others say that he is dead, and that he stinks, and that he ought to be placed in a sepulcher; but as for myself, to me he does not stink."

132 Now this was what Ammon desired, for he knew that King Lamoni was under the power of God.

133 He knew that the dark veil of unbelief was cast away from his mind, and the light which lighted up his mind was the light of the glory of God, which was a marvelous light of his goodness.

134 And this light had infused such joy into his soul, the cloud of darkness having been dispelled, that the light of everlasting light was lighted up in his soul.

135 He knew that this had overcome his natural frame, and he was carried away in God; therefore, what the queen desired of him was his only desire.

136 Therefore he went in to see the king according as the queen had desired him; and he saw the king, and he knew that he was not dead.

137 And he said to the queen, "He is not dead, but he sleepeth in God, and on the morrow he shall rise again; therefore bury him not."

138 And Ammon said to her, "Believest thou this?"

139 She said to him, "I have had no witness save your word and the word of our servants; nevertheless, I believe that it shall be according as you have said."

140 And Ammon said to her, "Blessed art thou because of thy exceeding faith; I say to thee, woman, there has not been such great faith among all the people of the Nephites."

141 She watched over the bed of her husband from that time, even until that time on the morrow which Ammon had appointed that he should rise.

142 And he arose according to the words of Ammon; and as he arose, he stretched forth his hand to the woman, and said, "Blessed be the name of God, and blessed are you.

143 "For as surely as you live, behold, I have seen my Redeemer; and he shall come forth and be born of a woman, and he shall redeem all mankind who believe on his name."

144 When he had said these words, his heart was swollen within him, and he sank again with joy; and the queen also sank down, being overpowered by the Spirit.

145 Now Ammon, seeing the Spirit of the Lord poured out according to his prayers upon the Lamanites, his brethren, who had been the cause of so much mourning among the Nephites, or among all the people of God, because of their iniquities and their traditions, 146fell upon his knees and began to pour out his soul in prayer and thanksgiving to God for what he had done for his brethren.

147 And he was also overpowered with joy; and thus they all three had sunk to the earth.

148 Now when the servants of the king saw that they had fallen, they also began to cry to God, for the fear of the Lord had come upon them also.

149 For it was they who had stood before the king and testified to him concerning the great power of Ammon.

150 They called on the name of the Lord in their might, even till they had all fallen to the earth save it were one of the Lamanitish women, whose name was Abish, she having been converted to the Lord for many years on account of a remarkable vision of her father; thus having been converted to the Lord, she never had made it known.

151 Therefore when she saw that all the servants of Lamoni had fallen to the earth, and also her mistress, the queen, and the king and Ammon lay

prostrate upon the earth, she knew that it was the power of God.

152 And supposing that this was an opportunity to make known to the people what had happened among them, and that beholding this scene would cause them to believe in the power of God, 153therefore she ran forth from house to house making it known to the people; and they began to assemble themselves together to the house of the king.

154 And there came a multitude, and to their astonishment they beheld the king, and the queen, and their servants, prostrate upon the earth, and they all lay there as though they were dead.

155 They also saw Ammon, and beheld he was a Nephite.

156 Now the people began to murmur among themselves, some saying that it was a great evil that had come upon them, or upon the king and his house, because he had suffered that the Nephite should remain in the land.

157 But others rebuked them, saying, "The king has brought this evil upon his house because he slew his servants who had had their flocks scattered at the waters of Sebus."

158 And they were also rebuked by those men who had stood at the waters of Sebus and scattered the flocks which belonged to the king, 159for they were angry with Ammon because of the number which he had slain of their brethren at the waters of Sebus, while defending the flocks of the king.

160 Now one of them, whose brother had been slain with the sword of Ammon, being exceedingly angry with Ammon, drew his sword and went forth that he might let it fall upon Ammon to slay him; and as he lifted the sword to smite him, behold, he fell dead.

161 Thus we see that Ammon could not be slain, for the Lord had said to Mosiah, his father, "I will spare him, and it shall be to him according to thy faith"; therefore Mosiah trusted him to the Lord.

162 When the multitude beheld that the man who lifted the sword to slay Ammon had fallen dead, fear came upon them all, and they dared not put forth their hands to touch him, or any of those who had fallen.

163 And they began to marvel again among themselves what could be the cause of this great power, or what all these things could mean.

164 There were many among them who said that Ammon was the Great Spirit, and others said he was sent by the Great Spirit.

165 But others rebuked them all, saying that he was a monster who had been sent from the Nephites to torment them.

166 And there were some who said that Ammon was sent by the Great Spirit to afflict them because of their iniquities, and that it was the Great Spirit that had always attended the Nephites who had ever delivered them out of their hands.

167 And they said that it was this Great Spirit who had destroyed so many of their brethren, the Lamanites; and thus the contention began to be exceedingly sharp among them.

168 While they were thus contending, the woman servant who had caused the multitude to be gathered together came; and when she saw the contention which was among the multitude, she was exceedingly sorrowful, even to tears.

169 And she went and took the queen by the hand, that perhaps she might raise her from the ground; and as soon as she touched her hand, she arose and stood upon her feet and cried with a loud voice, saying:

170 "O blessed Jesus, who has saved me from an awful hell! O blessed God, have mercy upon this people."

171 When she had said this, she clapped her hands, being filled with joy, speaking many words which were not understood.

172 And when she had done this, she took the king, Lamoni, by the hand, and, behold, he arose and stood upon his feet.

173 And he immediately, seeing the contention among his people, went forth and began to rebuke them and to teach them the words which he had heard from the mouth of Ammon; and as many as heard his words believed, and were converted to the Lord.

174 But there were many among them who would not hear his words; therefore they went their way.

175 When Ammon arose, he also administered to them, as also did all the servants of Lamoni.

176 And they all declared to the people the selfsame thing: that their hearts had been changed, that they had no more desire to do evil.

177 And, behold, many declared to the people that they had seen angels and had conversed with them, and thus they had told them things of God and of his righteousness.

178 There were many that believed in their words; and as many as believed were baptized; and they became a righteous people, and they established a church among them.

179 Thus the work of the Lord commenced among the Lamanites; thus the Lord began to pour out his Spirit upon them.

180 And we see that his arm is extended to all people who will repent and believe on his name.

181 When they had established a church in that land, King Lamoni desired that Ammon should go with him to the land of Nephi, that he might show him to his father.

182 And the voice of the Lord came to Ammon, saying, "Thou shalt not go up to the land of Nephi, for, behold, the king will seek thy life; but thou shalt go to the land of Middoni; for, behold, thy brother Aaron and also Muloki and Ammah are in prison."

183 Now when Ammon had heard this, he said to Lamoni, "Behold, my brother and brethren in prison at Middoni, and I go that I may deliver them."

184 And Lamoni said to Ammon, "I know that, in the strength of the Lord, you can do all things. But, behold, I will go with you to the land of Middoni, for the king of the land of Middoni, whose name is Antiomno, is a friend to me.

185 "Therefore I go to the land of Middoni that I may flatter the king of the land; and he will cast your brethren out of prison."

186 Now Lamoni said to him, "Who told you that your brethren were in prison?"

187 And Ammon said to him, "No one has told me, save it be God; and he said to me, 'Go and deliver thy brethren, for they are in prison in the land of Middoni.'"

188 When Lamoni heard this, he caused that his servants should make ready his horses and his chariots.

189 And he said to Ammon, "Come, I will go with you down to the land of Middoni, and there I will plead with the king, that he will cast your brethren out of prison."

190 And it came to pass that as Ammon and Lamoni were journeying, they met the father of Lamoni, who was king over all the land.

191 And, behold, the father of Lamoni said to him, "Why did you not come to the feast on that great day when I made a feast to my sons and to my people?"

192 He also said, "Where are you going with this Nephite, who is one of the children of a liar?"

193 And Lamoni rehearsed to him where he was going, for he feared to offend him.

194 He also told him all the cause of his tarrying in his own kingdom, that he did not go to his father to the feast which he had prepared.

195 When Lamoni had rehearsed to him all these things, behold, to his astonishment his father was angry with him, and said, "Lamoni, are you going to deliver these Nephites, who are sons of a liar?

196 "Behold, he robbed our fathers; and now his children are also come among us that they may, by their cunning and their lyings, deceive us, that they again may rob us of our property."

197 Now the father of Lamoni commanded him that he should slay Ammon with the sword.

198 And he also commanded him that he should not go to the land of Middoni, but that he should return with him to the land of Ishmael.

199 But Lamoni said to him, "I will not slay Ammon, neither will I return to the land of Ishmael, but I go to the land of Middoni that I may release the brethren of Ammon, for I know that they are just men, and holy prophets of the true God."

200 When his father heard these words, he was angry with him, and he drew his sword that he might smite him to the earth.

201 But Ammon stood forth and said to him, "Behold, thou shalt not slay thy son; nevertheless, it were better that he should fall than thee; [202]for, behold, he has repented of his sins; but if thou shouldst fall at this time in thine anger, thy soul could not be saved.

203 "And again, it is expedient that thou shouldst forbear; for if thou shouldst slay thy son (he being an innocent man), his blood would cry from the ground to the Lord his God for vengeance to come upon thee; and perhaps thou wouldst lose thy soul."

204 Now when Ammon had said these words to him, he answered him, saying, "I know that if I should slay my son, I should shed innocent blood; for it is you that have sought to destroy him"; and he stretched forth his hand to slay Ammon.

205 But Ammon withstood his blows, and also smote his arm that he could not use it.

206 Now when the king saw that Ammon could slay him, he began to plead with Ammon that he would spare his life.

207 But Ammon raised his sword and said to him, "Behold, I will smite thee except thou wilt grant to me that my brethren may be cast out of prison."

208 The king, fearing that he should lose his life, said, "If you will spare me, I will grant to you whatever you ask, even to the half of the kingdom."

209 When Ammon saw that he had wrought upon the old king according to his desire, he said to him, "If thou wilt grant that my brethren may be cast out of prison, and also that Lamoni may retain his kingdom, and that ye be not displeased with him, but grant that he may do according to his own desires in whatever thing he thinketh, then will I spare thee; otherwise I will smite thee to the earth."

210 Now when Ammon had said these words, the king began to rejoice because of his life.

211 And when he saw that Ammon had no desire to destroy him, and when he also saw the great love he had for his son, Lamoni, he was astonished exceedingly, and said:

212 "Because this is all that you have desired, that I would release your brethren, and suffer that my son Lamoni should retain his kingdom, behold, I will grant to you that my son may retain his kingdom from this time and forever, and I will govern him no more.

213 "And I will also grant you that your brethren may be cast out of prison, and you and your brethren may come to me in my kingdom; for I shall greatly desire to see you."

214 For the king was greatly astonished at the words which Ammon had spoken, and also at the words which had been spoken by his son Lamoni; therefore he was desirous to learn them.

215 And it came to pass that Ammon and Lamoni proceeded on their journey toward the land of Middoni.

216 And Lamoni found favor in the eyes of the king of the land; therefore the brethren of Ammon were brought forth out of prison.

217 When Ammon met them, he was exceedingly sorrowful, for, behold, they were naked, and their skins were worn exceedingly because of being bound with strong cords.

218 And they also had suffered hunger, thirst, and all kinds of affliction; nevertheless they were patient in all their sufferings.

219 As it happened, it was their lot to have fallen into the hands of a more hardened and a more stiff-necked people; [220]therefore they would not hearken to their words, and they had cast them out, and had smitten them, and had driven them from house to house, and from place to place, even until they had arrived to the land of Middoni.

221 There they were taken and cast into prison, and bound with strong cords, and kept in prison for many days, and were delivered by Lamoni and Ammon.

CHAPTER 13

An account of the preaching of Aaron and Muloki and their brethren to the Lamanites.

NOW when Ammon and his brethren separated themselves in the borders of the land of the Lamanites, behold, Aaron took his journey toward the land which was called, by the Lamanites, Jerusalem; calling it after the land of their fathers' nativity; and it was away joining the borders of Mormon.

2 And the Lamanites, and the Amalekites, and the people of Amulon had built a great city, which was also called Jerusalem.

3 Now the Lamanites, of themselves, were sufficiently hardened, but the Amalekites and the Amulonites were still harder; therefore they caused the Lamanites that they should harden their hearts, that they should wax strong in wickedness and their abominations.

4 And it came to pass that Aaron came to the city of Jerusalem and first began to preach to the Amalekites.

5 And he began to preach to them in their synagogues, for they had built synagogues after the order of the Nehors; for many of the Amalekites and the Amulonites were after the order of the Nehors.

6 Therefore, as Aaron entered into one of their synagogues to preach to the people, and as he was speaking to them, behold, there arose an Amalekite and began to contend with him, saying:

7 "What is that you have testified? Have you seen an angel? Why do not angels appear to us? Behold, are not this people as good as your people? You also said, except we repent, we shall perish.

8 "How do you know the thought and intent of our heart? How do you know that we have cause to repent? How do you know that we are not a righteous people?

9 "Behold, we have built sanctuaries, and we assemble ourselves together to worship God. We believe that God will save all men."

10 Now Aaron said to him, "Do you believe that the Son of God will come to redeem mankind from their sins?"

11 And the man said to him, "We do not believe that you know any such thing. We do not believe in these foolish traditions.

12 "We do not believe that you know of things to come, neither do we believe that your fathers, and also that our fathers, knew concerning the things which they spoke of that which is to come."

13 Now Aaron began to open the scriptures to them concerning the coming of Christ, and also concerning the resurrection of the dead, and that there could be no redemption for mankind, save it were through the death and sufferings of Christ and the atonement of his blood.

14 As he began to expound these things to them, they were angry with him and began to mock him; and they would not hear the words which he spoke.

15 Therefore, when he saw that they would not hear his words, he departed out of their synagogue and came over to a village which was called Ani-anti, and there he found Muloki preaching the word to them; and he also found Ammah and his brethren. And they contended with many about the word.

16 And it came to pass that they saw that the people would harden their hearts; therefore they departed and came over into the land of Middoni.

17 And they preached the word to many, but few believed on the words which they taught.

18 Nevertheless, Aaron and a certain number of his brethren were taken and cast into prison, and the remainder of them fled out of the land of Middoni to the regions round about.

19 And those who were cast into prison suffered many things, but they were delivered by the hand of Lamoni and Ammon; and they were fed and clothed.

20 And they went forth again to declare the word; and thus they were delivered for the first time out of prison; and thus they had suffered.

21 They went forth wherever they were led by the Spirit of the Lord, preaching the word of God in every synagogue of the Amalekites, or in every assembly of the Lamanites where they were admitted.

22 And the Lord began to bless them, insomuch that they brought many to the knowledge of the truth; they convinced many of their sins and that the traditions of their fathers were not correct.

23 And it came to pass that Ammon and Lamoni returned from the land of Middoni to the land of Ishmael, which was the land of their inheritance.

24 And King Lamoni would not suffer that Ammon should serve him or be his servant, but he caused that there should be synagogues built in the land of Ishmael; and he caused that his people, or the people who were under his reign, should assemble themselves together.

25 And he rejoiced over them, and he taught them many things.

26 He also declared to them that they were a people who were under him, and that they were a free people, that they were free from the oppressions of the king, his father; for his father had granted to him that he might reign over the people who were in the land of Ishmael and in all the land round about.

27 And he also declared to them that they might have the liberty of worshiping the Lord their God according to their desires, in whatever place they were in, if it were in the land which was under the reign of King Lamoni.

28 And Ammon preached to the people of King Lamoni, and he taught them concerning things pertaining to righteousness.

29 And he exhorted them daily with all diligence; and they gave heed to his word, and they were zealous for keeping the commandments of God.

30 Now as Ammon was thus teaching the people of Lamoni continually, we will return to the account

of Aaron and his other brethren.

31 After Aaron departed from the land of Middoni, he was led by the Spirit to the land of Nephi, even to the house of the king who was over all the land, save it were the land of Ishmael, and he was the father of Lamoni.

32 He went in to him into the king's palace with his brethren and bowed himself before the king, and said to him, "Behold, O king, we are the brethren of Ammon, whom thou hast delivered out of prison. And now, O king, if thou wilt spare our lives, we will be thy servants."

33 And the king said to them, "Arise, for I will grant to you your lives, and I will not suffer that you shall be my servants; but I will insist that you administer to me.

34 "For I have been somewhat troubled in mind because of the generosity and the greatness of the words of thy brother Ammon, and I desire to know the cause why he has not come up out of Middoni with you."

35 And Aaron said to the king, "Behold, the Spirit of the Lord has called him another way; he has gone to the land of Ishmael to teach the people of Lamoni."

36 Now the king said to them, "What is this that you have said concerning the Spirit of the Lord? Behold, this is the thing which troubles me.

37 "Also, what is this that Ammon said: 'If ye will repent ye shall be saved, and if ye will not repent, ye shall be cast off at the last day'?"

38 And Aaron answered him and said to him, "Believest thou that there is a God?"

39 And the king said, "I know that the Amalekites say that there is a God, and I have granted them that they should build sanctuaries that they may assemble themselves together to worship him. And if now you say there is a God, behold, I will believe."

40 When Aaron heard this, his heart began to rejoice, and he said, "Behold, assuredly as thou livest, O king, there is a God."

41 And the king said, "Is God that Great Spirit that brought our fathers out of the land of Jerusalem?"

42 And Aaron said to him, "He is that Great Spirit, and he created all things, both in heaven and in earth. Believest thou this?"

43 And he said, "I believe that the Great Spirit created all things, and I desire that you should tell me concerning all these things, and I will believe your words."

44 When Aaron saw that the king would believe his words, he began from the creation of Adam, reading the scriptures to the king—how God created man after his own image, and that God gave him commandments, and that because of transgression man had fallen.

45 And Aaron expounded to him the scriptures from the creation of Adam, laying the fall of man before him, and his carnal state, and also the plan of redemption which was prepared from the foundation of the world through Christ, for all who would believe on his name.

46 Since man had fallen, he could not merit anything of himself; but the sufferings and death of Christ atone for their sins, through faith and repentance; ⁴⁷and he breaks the bands of death, that the grave shall have no victory, and that the sting of death should be swallowed up in the hopes of glory. And Aaron expounded all these things to the king.

48 After Aaron had expounded these things to him, the king said, "What shall I do that I may have this eternal life of which you have spoken?

49 "What shall I do that I may be born of God, having this wicked spirit rooted out of my breast, and receive his Spirit that I may be filled with joy, that I may not be cast off at the last day?

50 "Behold," said he, "I will give up all that I possess. I will forsake my kingdom that I may receive this great joy."

51 But Aaron said to him, "If thou desirest this thing, if thou wilt bow down before God, if thou wilt repent of all thy sins, and will bow down before God and call on his name in faith, believing that ye shall receive, then shalt thou receive the hope which thou desirest."

52 And when Aaron had said these words, the king bowed down before the Lord upon his knees; he prostrated himself upon the earth and cried mightily, saying, "O God, Aaron hath told me that there is a God; ⁵³and if there is a God, and if thou art God, wilt thou make thyself known to me, and I will give away all my sins to know thee, and that I may be raised from the dead and be saved at the last day."

54 Now when the king had said these words, he was struck as if he were dead.

55 And his servants ran and told the queen all that had happened to the king.

56 She came to the king, and when she saw him lie as if he were dead, and also Aaron and his brethren standing as though they had been the cause of his fall, she was angry with them and commanded that her servants, or the servants of the king, should take them and slay them.

57 Now the servants had seen the cause of the king's fall, therefore they dared not lay their hands on Aaron and his brethren.

58 And they pleaded with the queen, saying, "Why commandest thou that we should slay these men, when, behold, one of them is mightier than us all? Therefore we shall fall before them."

59 When the queen saw the fear of the servants, she also began to fear exceedingly lest there should some evil come upon her.

60 And she commanded her servants that they should go and call the people that they might slay Aaron and his brethren.

61 When Aaron saw the determination of the queen, and also knowing the hardness of the hearts of the people, he feared lest a multitude should assemble themselves together, and there should be a great contention and a disturbance among them.

62 Therefore he put forth his hand and raised the king from the earth and said to him, "Stand"; and he stood upon his feet, receiving his strength.

63 This was done in the presence of the queen and many of the servants. And when they saw it, they

greatly marveled and began to fear.

64 And the king stood forth and began to minister to them. And he ministered to them insomuch that his whole household were converted to the Lord.

65 Now there was a multitude gathered together because of the commandment of the queen, and there began to be great murmurings among them because of Aaron and his brethren.

66 But the king stood forth among them and administered to them. And they were pacified toward Aaron and those who were with him.

67 When the king saw that the people were pacified, he caused that Aaron and his brethren should stand forth in the midst of the multitude, and that they should preach the word to them.

68 And the king sent a proclamation throughout all the land, among all his people who were in all his land who were in all the regions round about, which was bordering even to the sea on the east and on the west, and which was divided from the land of Zarahemla by a narrow strip of wilderness ⁶⁹which ran from the sea east even to the sea west, and round about on the borders of the seashore and the borders of the wilderness which was on the north by the land of Zarahemla, through the borders of Manti by the head of the river Sidon, running from the east toward the west; and thus were the Lamanites and the Nephites divided.

70 Now the more idle part of the Lamanites lived in the wilderness and dwelt in tents, and they were spread through the wilderness on the west in the land of Nephi, ⁷¹and also on the west of the land of Zarahemla, in the borders by the seashore, and on the west in the land of Nephi in the place of their fathers' first inheritance, and thus bordering along by the seashore.

72 And also there were many Lamanites on the east by the seashore, where the Nephites had driven them. Thus the Nephites were nearly surrounded by the Lamanites.

73 Nevertheless the Nephites had taken possession of all the northern

parts of the land bordering on the wilderness at the head of the river Sidon, from the east to the west, round about on the wilderness side on the north, even until they came to the land which they called Bountiful.

74 And it bordered upon the land which they called Desolation, it being so far northward that it came into the land which had been peopled (and whose people had been destroyed, of whose bones we have spoken), which was discovered by the people of Zarahemla, it being the place of their first landing. And they came from there up into the south wilderness.

75 Thus the land on the northward was called Desolation, and the land on the southward was called Bountiful; it being the wilderness which is filled with all manner of wild animals of every kind, a part of which had come from the land northward for food.

76 Now it was only the distance of a day and a half's journey for a Nephite, on the line Bountiful and the land Desolation, from the east to the west sea.

77 And thus the land of Nephi and the land of Zarahemla were nearly surrounded by water, there being a small neck of land between the land northward and the land southward.

78 And the Nephites had inhabited the land bountiful from the east to the west sea.

79 Thus the Nephites in their wisdom, with their guards and their armies, had hemmed in the Lamanites on the south, that thereby they should have no more possession on the north, that they might not overrun the land northward.

80 Therefore the Lamanites could have no more possessions only in the land of Nephi and the wilderness round about.

81 Now this was wisdom in the Nephites, as the Lamanites were an enemy to them, that they would not suffer their afflictions on every hand, and also that they might have a country where they might flee according to their desires.

82 And now I, after having said this, return again to the account of

Ammon, and Aaron, Omner, and Himni, and their brethren.

CHAPTER 14

BEHOLD, now the king of the Lamanites sent a proclamation among all his people, that they should not lay their hands on Ammon, or Aaron, or Omner, or Himni, nor any of their brethren who should go forth preaching the word of God, in whatever place they should be in any part of their land.

2 He sent a decree among them that they should not lay their hands on them to bind them or to cast them into prison; neither should they spit upon them, nor smite them, nor cast them out of their synagogues, nor scourge them; ³neither should they cast stones at them, but that they should have free access to their houses, and also their temples and their sanctuaries.

4 Thus they might go forth and preach the word according to their desires, for the king had been converted to the Lord, and all his household.

5 Therefore he sent this proclamation throughout the land to his people, that the word of God might have no obstruction, but that it might go forth throughout all the land, that his people might be convinced concerning the wicked traditions of their fathers, ⁶and that they might be convinced that they were all brethren, and that they ought not to murder, nor to plunder, nor to steal, nor to commit adultery, nor to commit any manner of wickedness.

7 When the king had sent forth this proclamation, Aaron and his brethren went forth from city to city and from one house of worship to another, ⁸establishing churches, and consecrating priests and teachers throughout the land among the Lamanites to preach and to teach the word of God among them; and thus they began to have great success.

9 And thousands were brought to the knowledge of the Lord; thousands were brought to believe in the traditions of the Nephites; and they were taught the records and the prophecies which were handed down, even to the present time.

10 And as surely as the Lord lives, so surely as many as believed, or as many as were brought to the knowledge of the truth through the preaching of Ammon and his brethren, according to the spirit of revelation and of prophecy and the power of God working miracles in them, ¹¹and were converted to the Lord never did fall away, for they became a righteous people.

12 They laid down the weapons of their rebellion, that they did not fight against God any more, neither against any of their brethren.

13 Now these are they who were converted to the Lord: The people of the Lamanites who were in the land of Ishmael, and also of the people of the Lamanites who were in the land of Middoni, and also of the people of the Lamanites who were in the city of Nephi, and also of the people of the Lamanites who were in the land of Shilom, and who were in the land of Shemlon, and in the city of Lemuel, and in the city of Shimnilom.

14 And these are the names of the cities of the Lamanites which were converted to the Lord; and these are they that laid down the weapons of their rebellion, even all their weapons of war; and they were all Lamanites.

15 And the Amalekites were not converted, save only one; neither were any of the Amulonites; but they hardened their hearts, and also the hearts of the Lamanites in that part of the land where they dwelt, and all their villages and all their cities.

16 Therefore we have named all the cities of the Lamanites in which they repented and came to the knowledge of the truth, and were converted.

17 Now it came to pass that the king and those who were converted were desirous that they might have a name, that thereby they might be distinguished from their brethren.

18 Therefore the king consulted with Aaron and many of their priests concerning the name that they should take upon them that they might be distinguished.

185   **90–77 B. C.**

19 And they called their name Anti-Nephi-Lehies; and they were called by this name, and were no more called Lamanites.

20 They began to be a very industrious people, and they were friendly with the Nephites; therefore they opened a correspondence with them, and the curse of God no more followed them.

21 And it came to pass that the Amalekites, and the Amulonites, and the Lamanites who were in the land of Amulon, and also in the land of Helam, and who were in the land of Jerusalem, and in fine, in all the land round about who had not been converted and had not taken upon them the name of Anti-Nephi-Lehi were stirred up by the Amalekites and by the Amulonites to anger against their brethren.

22 And their hatred became exceedingly sore against them, even insomuch that they began to rebel against their king, insomuch that they would not that he should be their king; therefore they took up arms against the people of Anti-Nephi-Lehi.

23 Now the king conferred the kingdom upon his son and he called his name Anti-Nephi-Lehi.

24 And the king died in that selfsame year that the Lamanites began to make preparations for war against the people of God.

25 Now when Ammon and his brethren, and all those who had come up with him, saw the preparations of the Lamanites to destroy their brethren, they came forth to the land of Midian, and there Ammon met all his brethren.

26 And from there they came to the land of Ishmael, that they might hold a council with Lamoni, and also with his brother Anti-Nephi-Lehi, on what they should do to defend themselves against the Lamanites.

27 Now there was not one soul among all the people who had been converted to the Lord that would take up arms against his brethren.

28 They would not even make any preparations for war; and also their king commanded them that they should not.

29 Now these are the words which he said to the people concerning the matter: "I thank my God, my beloved people, that our great God has in goodness sent these our brethren, the Nephites, to us to preach to us and to convince us of the wickedness of the traditions of our fathers.

30 "And, behold, I thank my great God that he has given us a portion of his Spirit to soften our hearts, that we have opened a correspondence with these brethren, the Nephites.

31 "And, behold, I also thank my God that by opening this correspondence we have been convinced of our sins and of the many murders which we have committed.

32 "I also thank my God, my great God, that he has granted us that we might repent of these things, and also that he has forgiven us of those our many sins and murders which we have committed, and has taken away the guilt from our hearts through the merits of his Son.

33 "And now, behold, my brethren, it has been all that we could do (as we were the most lost of all mankind) to repent of all our sins and the many murders which we have committed, and to get God to take them away from our hearts, for it was all we could do to repent sufficiently before God that he would take away our stain.

34 "Now, my best beloved brethren, since God has taken away our stains, and our swords have become bright, then let us stain our swords no more with the blood of our brethren.

35 "Behold, I say to you, Let us retain our swords that they be not stained with the blood of our brethren; ³⁶for perhaps if we should stain our swords again, they could no more be washed bright through the blood of the Son of our great God, which shall be shed for the atonement of our sins.

37 "And the great God has had mercy on us and has made these things known to us, that we might not perish.

38 "And he has made these things known to us beforehand because he loves our souls as well as he loves our children; therefore in his mercy he visits us by his angels, that the

plan of salvation might be made known to us as well as to future generations. Oh, how merciful is our God!

39 "And now, behold, since it has been as much as we could do to get our stains taken away from us, and our swords are made bright, [40]let us hide them away that they may be kept bright, as a testimony to our God at the last day, or at the day that we shall be brought to stand before him to be judged, that we have not stained our swords in the blood of our brethren since he imparted his word to us and has made us clean thereby.

41 "Now, my brethren, if our brethren seek to destroy us, behold, we will hide away our swords, even we will bury them deep in the earth that they may be kept bright as a testimony at the last day that we have never used them; and if our brethren destroy us, behold, we shall go to our God and shall be saved."

42 When the king had made an end of these sayings, and all the people were assembled together, they took their swords and all the weapons which were used for the shedding of man's blood, and they buried them deep in the earth.

43 This they did, it being in their view a testimony to God, and also to men, that they never would use weapons again for the shedding of man's blood.

44 And this they did, vouching and covenanting with God that rather than shed the blood of their brethren they would give up their own lives; [45]and rather than take away from a brother, they would give to him; and rather than spend their days in idleness, they would labor abundantly with their hands.

46 Thus we see that when these Lamanites were brought to believe and to know the truth, they were firm and would suffer even to death rather than commit sin.

47 And thus we see that they buried the weapons of peace, or they buried the weapons of war for peace.

48 And it came to pass that their brethren, the Lamanites, made preparations for war and came up to the land of Nephi, for the purpose of destroying the king, and to place another in his stead, and also of destroying the people of Anti-Nephi-Lehi out of the land.

49 Now when the people saw that they were coming against them, they went out to meet them and prostrated themselves before them to the earth and began to call on the name of the Lord.

50 Thus they were in this attitude when the Lamanites began to fall upon them and began to slay them with the sword. And thus without meeting any resistance they slew a thousand and five of them; and we know that they are blessed, for they have gone to dwell with their God.

51 Now when the Lamanites saw that their brethren would not flee from the sword, neither would they turn aside to the right hand nor to the left, but that they would lie down and perish, and praise God even in the very act of perishing under the sword, they forbore from slaying them.

52 And there were many whose hearts had swollen in them for those of their brethren who had fallen under the sword, for they repented of the things which they had done.

53 And they threw down their weapons of war, and they would not take them again, for they were stung for the murders which they had committed; and they came down, even as their brethren, relying upon the mercies of those whose arms were lifted to slay them.

54 And the people of God were joined that day by more than the number who had been slain; and those who had been slain were righteous people, therefore we have no reason to doubt that they are saved.

55 There was not a wicked man slain among them; but there were more than a thousand brought to the knowledge of the truth; thus we see that the Lord works in many ways to the salvation of his people.

56 Now the greatest number of those of the Lamanites who slew so many of their brethren were Amalekites and Amulonites, the greatest number of whom were after the order of the Nehors.

57 And among those who joined the people of the Lord, there were none who were Amalekites or Amulonites or who were of the order of Nehor, but they were actual descendants of Laman and Lemuel.

58 Thus we can plainly discern that after a people have been once enlightened by the Spirit of God, and have had great knowledge of things pertaining to righteousness, and then have fallen away into sin and transgression, they become more hardened; and thus their state becomes worse than though they had never known these things.

59 And, behold, now those Lamanites were more angry because they had slain their brethren; therefore they swore vengeance upon the Nephites.

60 And they no more attempted to slay the people of Anti-Nephi-Lehi at that time; but they took their armies and went over into the borders of the land of Zarahemla, and fell upon the people who were in the land of Ammonihah and destroyed them.

61 After that, they had many battles with the Nephites in which they were driven and slain.

62 Among the Lamanites who were slain were almost all the seed of Amulon and his brethren who were the priests of Noah, and they were slain by the hands of the Nephites.

63 And the remainder, having fled into the east wilderness and having usurped the power and authority over the Lamanites, caused that many of the Lamanites should perish by fire because of their belief.

64 For many of them, after having suffered much loss and so many afflictions, began to be stirred up in remembrance of the words which Aaron and his brethren had preached to them in their land; 65therefore they began to disbelieve the traditions of their fathers and to believe in the Lord, and that he gave great power to the Nephites; thus there were many of them converted in the wilderness.

66 And it came to pass that those rulers who were the remnant of the children of Amulon caused that they should be put to death, even all those that believed in these things.

67 Now this martyrdom caused that many of their brethren should be stirred up to anger, and there began to be contention in the wilderness; and the Lamanites began to hunt the seed of Amulon and his brethren and began to slay them, and they fled into the east wilderness.

68 And, behold, they are hunted at this day by the Lamanites; thus the words of Abinadi were brought to pass which he said concerning the seed of the priests who caused that he should suffer death by fire.

69 For he said to them, "What you shall do to me shall be a type of things to come."

70 Now Abinadi was the first that suffered death by fire because of his belief in God; and this is what he meant, that many should suffer death by fire according as he had suffered.

71 And he said to the priests of Noah that their seed should cause many to be put to death in the like manner as he was, and that they should be scattered abroad and slain, even as the sheep having no shepherd is driven and slain by wild beasts.

72 Now, behold, these words were verified, for they were driven by the Lamanites and they were hunted, and they were smitten.

73 When the Lamanites saw that they could not overpower the Nephites, they returned again to their own land; and many of them came over to dwell in the land of Ishmael and the land of Nephi, and joined themselves to the people of God, who were the people of Anti-Nephi-Lehi.

74 And they also buried their weapons of war according as their brethren had, and they began to be a righteous people; and they walked in the ways of the Lord and observed to keep his commandments and his statutes, and they kept the law of Moses; for it was expedient that they should keep the law of Moses as yet, for it was not all fulfilled.

75 But notwithstanding the law of Moses, they looked forward to the coming of Christ, considering that the law of Moses was a type of his coming and believing that they must keep those outward performances

188

until the time that he should be revealed to them.

76 Now they did not suppose that salvation came by the law of Moses, but the law of Moses served to strengthen their faith in Christ.

77 Thus they retained a hope through faith to eternal salvation, relying upon the spirit of prophecy which spoke of those things to come.

78 And now, behold, Ammon, and Aaron, and Omner, and Himni, and their brethren rejoiced exceedingly for the success which they had had among the Lamanites, seeing that the Lord had granted to them according to their prayers, and that he had also verified his word to them in every particular.

79 Now these are the words of Ammon to his brethren, which say thus: "My brothers and my brethren, behold, I say to you, How great reason have we to rejoice; for could we have supposed, when we started from the land of Zarahemla, that God would have granted us such great blessings?

80 "And now I ask, What great blessings has he bestowed upon us? Can you tell?

81 "Behold, I answer for you; for our brethren, the Lamanites, were in darkness, even in the darkest abyss; but, behold, how many of them are brought to behold the marvelous light of God!

82 "And this is the blessing which has been bestowed upon us, that we have been made instruments in the hands of God to bring about this great work.

83 "Behold, thousands of them rejoice, and have been brought into the fold of God.

84 "Behold, the field was ripe, and you are blessed, for you thrust in the sickle and reaped with your mights, even all the day long you labored.

85 "And behold the number of your sheaves. They shall be gathered into the garners, that they are not wasted; they shall not be beaten down by the storm at the last day.

86 "Neither shall they be harrowed up by the whirlwinds; but when the storm comes, they shall be gathered together in their place, that the storm cannot penetrate to them; neither

shall they be driven with fierce winds wherever the enemy lists to carry them.

87 "But, behold, they are in the hands of the Lord of the harvest, and they are his; and he will raise them up at the last day.

88 "Blessed be the name of our God; let us sing to his praise, let us give thanks to his holy name, for he works righteousness forever.

89 "For if we had not come up out of the land of Zarahemla, these, our dearly beloved brethren, who have so dearly loved us, would still have been racked with hatred against us, and they would also have been strangers to God."

90 When Ammon had said these words, his brother Aaron rebuked him, saying: "Ammon, I fear that your joy carries you away to boasting."

91 But Ammon said to him, "I do not boast in my own strength or in my own wisdom; but, behold, my joy is full, my heart is brimming with joy, and I will rejoice in my God.

92 "I know that I am nothing; as to my strength, I am weak; therefore I will not boast of myself, but I will boast of my God; for in his strength I can do all things; behold, many mighty miracles we have wrought in this land, for which we will praise his name forever.

93 "Behold, how many thousands of our brethren has he loosed from the pains of hell, and they are brought to sing redeeming love; and this because of the power of his word which is in us; therefore have we not great reason to rejoice?

94 "We have reason to praise him forever, for he is the most high God, and has loosed our brethren from the chains of hell.

95 "They were encircled with everlasting darkness and destruction; but, behold, he has brought them into his everlasting light, into everlasting salvation; and they are encircled with the matchless bounty of his love.

96 "And we have been instruments in his hands for doing this great and marvelous work; therefore let us glory in the Lord; we will rejoice, for our joy is full; we will praise our God forever.

97 "Behold, who can glory too much in the Lord? Who can say too much of his great power, and of his mercy, and of his long-suffering toward the children of men? Behold, I say to you, I cannot say the smallest part which I feel.

98 "Who could have supposed that our God would have been so merciful as to have snatched us from our awful, sinful, and polluted state?

99 "Behold, we went forth even in wrath, with mighty threatenings to destroy his church. Oh, then, why did he not consign us to an awful destruction; why did he not let the sword of his justice fall upon us and doom us to eternal despair?

100 "Oh, my soul almost, as it were, flees at the thought.

101 "Behold, he did not exercise his justice upon us, but in his great mercy he has brought us over that everlasting gulf of death and misery, even to the salvation of our souls.

102 "And now, behold, my brethren, what natural man is there that knows these things? I say to you there is none that knows these things, save it be the penitent.

103 "He that repents and exercises faith, and brings forth good works, and prays continually without ceasing, to such it is given to know the mysteries of God; to such it shall be given to reveal things which never have been revealed.

104 "And it shall be given to such to bring thousands of souls to repentance, even as it has been given to us to bring these our brethren to repentance.

105 "Now do you remember, my brethren, that we said to our brethren in the land of Zarahemla, 'We go up to the land of Nephi to preach to our brethren, the Lamanites,' and they laughed us to scorn?

106 "For they said to us, 'Do you suppose that you can bring the Lamanites to the knowledge of the truth?

107 "'Do you suppose that you can convince the Lamanites of the incorrectness of the traditions of their fathers, as stiffnecked a people as they are, whose hearts delight in the shedding of blood, whose days have been spent in the grossest iniquity, whose ways have been the ways of a transgressor from the beginning?'

108 "Now, my brethren, you remember that this was their language.

109 "And moreover they said, 'Let us take up arms against them, that we destroy them and their iniquity out of the land, lest they overrun us and destroy us.'

110 "But, behold, the Lord my beloved brethren, we came into the wilderness not with the intent to destroy our brethren, but with the intent that perhaps we might save some few of their souls.

111 "Now when our hearts were depressed, and we were about to turn back, behold, the Lord comforted us and said, 'Go among thy brethren, the Lamanites, and bear with patience thine afflictions, and I will give you success.'

112 "And now, behold, we have come and have gone forth among them; and we have been patient in our sufferings, and we have suffered every privation; we traveled from house to house, relying upon the mercies of the world; not upon the mercies of the world alone, but upon the mercies of God.

113 "We have entered into their houses and taught them, and we have taught them in their streets; and we taught them upon their hills; and we have also entered into their temples and their synagogues and taught them.

114 "We have been cast out, and mocked, and spit upon, and smote upon our cheeks; and we have been stoned, and taken and bound with strong cords, and cast into prison; and through the power and wisdom of God, we have been delivered again.

115 "And we have suffered all manner of afflictions, and all this that perhaps we might be the means of saving some soul; and we supposed that our joy would be full if perhaps we could be the means of saving some.

116 "Now, behold, we can look forth and see the fruits of our labors; and are they few?

117 "I say to you, They are many; and we can witness of their sincerity because of their love toward their brethren, and also toward us.

118 "For, behold, they had rather sacrifice their lives than even to take the life of their enemy, and they have buried their weapons of war deep in the earth because of their love toward their brethren.

119 "Now, behold, I say to you, Has there been so great love in all the land?

120 "Behold, I say to you, There has not, even among the Nephites.

121 "For, behold, they would take up arms against their brethren; they would not suffer themselves to be slain.

122 "But, behold, how many of these have laid down their lives; and we know that they have gone to their God because of their love, and of their hatred to sin.

123 "Now have we not reason to rejoice? I say to you, There never were men that had so great reason to rejoice as we, since the world began.

124 "And my joy is carried away, even to boasting in my God; for he has all power, all wisdom, and all understanding; he comprehends all things, and he is a merciful being, even to salvation, to those who will repent and believe on his name.

125 "Now if this is boasting, even so will I boast; for this is my life and my light, my joy and my salvation, and my redemption from everlasting woe.

126 "Blessed is the name of my God, who has been mindful of this people who are a branch of the tree of Israel and have been lost from its body in a strange land; I say, Blessed be the name of my God who has been mindful of us wanderers in a strange land.

127 "Now, my brethren, we see that God is mindful of every people in whatever land they may be; he numbers his people, and his bowels of mercy are over all the earth.

128 "This is my joy and my great thanksgiving; and I will give thanks to my God forever. Amen."

CHAPTER 15

WHEN those Lamanites who had gone to war against the Nephites found, after their many struggles to destroy them, that it was in vain to seek their destruction, they returned again to the land of Nephi.

2 And the Amalekites, because of their loss, were exceedingly angry.

3 When they saw that they could not get revenge from the Nephites, they began to stir up the people in anger against their brethren, the people of Anti-Nephi-Lehi; therefore they began again to destroy them.

4 Now this people again refused to take up their arms, and they suffered themselves to be slain according to the desires of their enemies.

5 When Ammon and his brethren saw this work of destruction among those whom they so dearly loved, and among those who had so dearly loved them (for they were treated as though they were angels sent from God to save them from everlasting destruction) 6they were moved with compassion, and they said to the king, "Let us gather together this people of the Lord, and let us go down to the land of Zarahemla to our brethren, the Nephites, and flee out of the hands of our enemies, that we be not destroyed."

7 But the king said to them, "Behold, the Nephites will destroy us because of the many murders and sins we have committed against them."

8 And Ammon said, "I will go and inquire of the Lord, and if he says to us, 'Go down to your brethren,' will you go?"

9 And the king said to him, "If the Lord says to us, 'Go,' we will go down to our brethren, and we will be their slaves until we repair to them the many murders and sins which we have committed against them."

10 But Ammon said to him, "It is against the law of our brethren, which was established by my father, that there should be any slaves among them; therefore let us go down and rely upon the mercies of our brethren."

11 But the king said to him, "Inquire of the Lord, and if he says to us, 'Go,' we will go; otherwise we will perish in the land."

12 And Ammon went and inquired of the Lord, and the Lord said to

191

him, "Get this people out of this land that they perish not, for Satan has great hold on the hearts of the Amalekites who stir up the Lamanites to anger against their brethren to slay them; therefore get thee out of this land; and blessed are this people in this generation; for I will preserve them."

13 Ammon went and told the king all the words which the Lord had said to him.

14 And they gathered together all their people, even all the people of the Lord, and gathered together all their flocks and herds, and departed out of the land, and came into the wilderness which divided the land of Nephi from the land of Zarahemla, and came over near the borders of the land.

15 And Ammon said to them, "Behold, I and my brethren will go forth into the land of Zarahemla, and you shall remain here until we return; and we will try the hearts of our brethren, whether they will that you shall come into their land."

16 As Ammon was going forth into the land, he and his brethren met Alma over in the place of which has been spoken; and, behold, this was a joyful meeting.

17 Now the joy of Ammon was so great that he was full, he was swallowed up in the joy of his God, even to the exhausting of his strength; and he fell again to the earth.

18 Was not this exceeding joy? Behold, this is joy which none receive save it be the truly penitent and humble seeker of happiness.

19 Now the joy of Alma in meeting his brethren was truly great, and also the joy of Aaron, of Omner, and Himni; but, behold, their joy was not that to exceed their strength.

20 And Alma conducted his brethren back to the land of Zarahemla, even to his own house.

21 And they went and told the chief judge all the things that had happened to them in the land of Nephi among their brethren, the Lamanites.

22 And it came to pass that the chief judge sent a proclamation throughout all the land, desiring the voice of the people concerning the admitting of their brethren who were the people of Anti-Nephi-Lehi.

23 The voice of the people came, saying: "Behold, we will give up the land of Jershon, which is on the east by the sea, which joins the land Bountiful, which is on the south of the land Bountiful; and this land Jershon is the land which we will give to our brethren for an inheritance.

24 "And, behold, we will set our armies between the land Jershon and the land Nephi, that we may protect our brethren in the land Jershon.

25 "This we do for our brethren on account of their fear to take up arms against their brethren lest they should commit sin, and this their great fear came because of their sore repentance which they had on account of their many murders and their awful wickedness.

26 "And now, behold, this will we do to our brethren that they may inherit the land Jershon; and we will guard them from their enemies with our armies, on condition they will give us a portion of their substance to assist us that we may maintain our armies."

27 When Ammon had heard this he returned to the people of Anti-Nephi-Lehi, and also Alma with him, into the wilderness where they had pitched their tents, and made known to them all these things.

28 And Alma also related to them his conversion with Ammon, and Aaron and his brethren, and it caused great joy among them.

29 And they went down into the land of Jershon and took possession of the land of Jershon; and they were called by the Nephites the people of Ammon.

30 Therefore they were distinguished by that name ever after; and they were among the people of Nephi, and also numbered among the people who were of the church of God.

31 And they were also distinguished for their zeal toward God, and also toward men; for they were perfectly honest and upright in all things; and they were firm in the faith of Christ, even to the end.

32 They looked upon shedding the blood of their brethren with the greatest abhorrence; and they never

could be prevailed upon to take up arms against their brethren.

33 And they never looked upon death with any degree of terror for their hope and views of Christ and the resurrection; therefore death was swallowed up to them by the victory of Christ over it.

34 Therefore they would suffer death in the most aggravating and distressing manner which could be inflicted by their brethren before they would take the sword or the cimeter to smite them.

35 Thus they were a zealous and beloved people, a highly favored people of the Lord.

36 And now it came to pass that after the people of Ammon were established in the land of Jershon, and a church was also established in the land of Jershon, and the armies of the Nephites were set round about the land of Jershon and in all the borders round about the land of Zarahemla, behold, the armies of the Lamanites followed their brethren into the wilderness.

37 Thus there was a tremendous battle, even such a one as never had been known among all the people in the land from the time Lehi left Jerusalem; and tens of thousands of the Lamanites were slain and scattered abroad.

38 And also there was a tremendous slaughter among the people of Nephi; nevertheless the Lamanites were driven and scattered, and the people of Nephi returned again to their land.

39 Now this was a time that there was a great mourning and lamentation heard throughout all the land among all the people of Nephi, 40the cry of widows mourning for their husbands, and also of fathers mourning for their sons, and the daughter for the brother, and the brother for the father.

41 And thus the cry of mourning was heard among them, every one mourning for his kindred who had been slain.

42 Now surely this was a sorrowful day, a time of solemnity and a time of much fasting and prayer. And thus ended the fifteenth year of the reign of the judges of the people of Nephi.

43 And this is the account of Ammon and his brethren, their journeyings in the land of Nephi, their sufferings in the land, their sorrows, and their afflictions, and their incomprehensive joy, and the reception and safety of the brethren in the land of Jershon.

44 May the Lord, the Redeemer of all men, bless their souls forever.

45 And this is the account of the wars and contentions among the Nephites, and also the wars between the Nephites and the Lamanites; and the fifteenth year of the reign of the judges is ended.

46 And from the first year to the fifteenth has brought to pass the destruction of many thousand lives; it has brought to pass an awful scene of bloodshed.

47 The bodies of many thousands are laid low in the earth, while the bodies of many thousands are mouldering in heaps upon the face of the earth.

48 And many thousands are mourning for the loss of their kindred because they have reason to fear, according to the promises of the Lord, that they are consigned to a state of endless woe.

49 While many thousands of others truly mourn for the loss of their kindred, yet they rejoice and exult in the hope, and even know according to the promises of the Lord that they are raised to dwell at the right hand of God in a state of never ending happiness.

50 Thus we see how great the inequality of man is because of sin and transgression, and the power of the devil which comes by the cunning plans which he has devised to ensnare the hearts of men.

51 And thus we see the great call of the diligence of men to labor in the vineyards of the Lord; and thus we see the great reason of sorrow, and also of rejoicing—sorrow because of death and destruction among men, and joy because of the light of Christ unto life.

52 Oh, that I were an angel, and could have the wish of my heart, that I might go forth and speak with the trump of God, with a voice to shake

the earth, and cry repentance to every people.

53 I would declare to every soul, as with the voice of thunder, repentance and the plan of redemption, that they should repent and come to our God, that there might be no more sorrow upon all the face of the earth.

54 But, behold, I am a man and do sin in my wish, for I ought to be content with the things which the Lord has allotted to me.

55 I ought not to harrow up in my desires the firm decree of a just God, for I know that he grants to men according to their desire, whether it be to death or to life; I know that he allots to men, even decrees to them decrees which are unalterable according to their wills; whether they be to salvation or to destruction.

56 And I know that good and evil have come before all men, or he that knows not good from evil is blameless; but he that knows good and evil, to him it is given according to his desires, whether he desires good or evil, life or death, joy or remorse of conscience.

57 Now seeing that I know these things, why should I desire more than to perform the work to which I have been called?

58 Why should I desire to be an angel that I could speak to all the ends of the earth?

59 For, behold, the Lord grants to all nations, those of their own nation and tongue, to teach his word, in wisdom, all that he sees fit that they should have; therefore we see that the Lord counsels in his wisdom according to that which is just and true.

60 I know that which the Lord has commanded me, and I glory in it; I do not glory of myself, but I glory in that which the Lord has commanded me.

61 And this is my glory, that perhaps I may be an instrument in the hands of God to bring some soul to repentance; and this is my joy.

62 And, behold, when I see many of my brethren truly penitent and coming to the Lord their God, then is my soul filled with joy; then do I remember what the Lord has done for me, even that he has heard my prayer; then do I remember his merciful arm which he extended toward me.

63 I also remember the captivity of my fathers; for I surely do know that the Lord delivered them out of bondage, and by this established his church; the Lord God—the God of Abraham, the God of Isaac, and the God of Jacob—delivered them out of bondage.

64 I have always remembered the captivity of my fathers; and that same God who delivered them out of the hands of the Egyptians delivered them out of bondage; and that same God established his church among them.

65 And that same God has called me by a holy calling to preach the word to this people, and has given me much success, in which my joy is full. But I do not joy in my own success alone, but my joy is fuller because of the success of my brethren, who have been up to the land of Nephi.

66 Behold, they have labored exceedingly and have brought forth much fruit, and how great shall be their reward.

67 Now when I think of the success of these my brethren, my soul is carried away, even to the separation of it from the body, as it were, so great is my joy.

68 And now may God grant these my brethren that they may sit down in the kingdom of God; and also all those who are the fruit of their labors that they may go out no more, but that they may praise him forever.

69 And may God grant that it may be done according to my words, even as I have spoken. Amen.

CHAPTER 16

BEHOLD, now it came to pass that after the people of Ammon were established in the land of Jershon, and also after the Lamanites were driven out of the land, and their dead were buried by the people of the land 2(now their dead were not numbered, because of the greatness of their numbers, neither were the dead of the Nephites numbered), 3and also after the days of fasting, and mourning, and prayer (and it was in the sixteenth year of the reign of the judges over the people of Nephi), there began to be continual peace throughout all the land and the people observed to keep the commandments of the Lord.

4 And they were strict in observing the ordinances of God according to the law of Moses; for they were taught to keep the law of Moses until it should be fulfilled.

5 Thus the people had no disturbance in all the sixteenth year of the reign of the judges over the people of Nephi.

6 And in the seventeenth year of the reign of the judges there was continual peace.

7 But in the latter end of the seventeenth year, there came a man into the land of Zarahemla; and he was antichrist, for he began to preach to the people against the prophecies which had been spoken by the prophets concerning the coming of Christ.

8 Now there was no law against a man's belief; for it was strictly contrary to the commands of God that there should be a law which should bring men on to unequal grounds.

9 For thus says the scripture, "Choose ye this day whom ye will serve."

10 Now if a man desired to serve God, it was his privilege; or rather, if he believed in God, it was his privilege to serve him; but if he did not believe in him, there was no law to punish him.

11 But if he murdered, he was punished to death; and if he robbed, he was also punished; and if he stole, he was also punished; and if he committed adultery, he was also punished; for all this wickedness, they were punished; for there was a law that men should be judged according to their crimes.

12 Nevertheless, there was no law against a man's belief; therefore a man was punished only for the crimes which he had done; therefore all men were on equal grounds.

13 And this antichrist, whose name was Korihor (and the law could have no hold upon him) began to preach to the people that there should be no Christ.

14 And after this manner he preached, saying: "O you that are bound down under a foolish and a vain hope, why do you yoke yourselves with such foolish things? Why do you look for a Christ? For no man can know of anything which is to come.

15 "Behold, these things which you call prophecies, which you say are handed down by holy prophets, behold, they are foolish traditions of your fathers. How do you know of their surety?

16 "Behold, you cannot know of things which you do not see; therefore you cannot know that there shall be a Christ.

17 "You look forward and say that you see a remission of your sins. But, behold, it is the effect of a frenzied mind; and this derangement of your minds comes because of the traditions of your fathers which lead you away into a belief of things which are not so."

18 And many more such things he said to them, telling them that there could be no atonement made for the sins of men, but every man fared in this life according to the management of the creature; therefore every man prospered according to his genius, and every man conquered according to his strength; and whatever a man did was no crime.

19 Thus he preached to them, leading away the hearts of many, causing them to lift up their heads in their wickedness, leading away many women and also men to commit whoredoms, telling them that when a man was dead that was the end thereof.

20 Now this man went over to the land of Jershon also, to preach these things among the people of Ammon, who were once the people of the Lamanites.

21 But, behold, they were more wise than many of the Nephites; for they took him, and bound him, and carried him before Ammon, who was a high priest over that people.

22 And Ammon caused that he should be carried out of the land.

23 And he came over into the land of Gideon and began to preach to them also; and here he did not have much success, for he was taken and

bound, and carried before the high priest, and also the chief judge over the land.

24 And the high priest said to him, "Why do you go about perverting the ways of the Lord?

25 "Why do you teach this people that there shall be no Christ, to interrupt their rejoicings?

26 "Why do you speak against all the prophecies of the holy prophets?"

27 (Now the high priest's name was Giddonah.)

28 And Korihor said to him, "Because I do not teach the foolish traditions of your fathers, and because I do not teach this people to bind themselves down under the foolish ordinances and performances which are laid down by ancient priests to usurp power and authority over them, to keep them in ignorance that they may not lift up their heads, but be brought down according to your words.

29 "You say that this people are a free people. Behold, I say they are in bondage.

30 "You say that those ancient prophecies are true. Behold, I say that you do not know that they are true.

31 "You say that this people are a guilty and a fallen people because of the transgression of a parent. Behold, I say that a child is not guilty because of its parents.

32 "You also say that Christ shall come. But, behold, I say that you do not know that there shall be a Christ.

33 "And you say also that he shall be slain for the sins of the world; and thus you lead away this people after the foolish traditions of your fathers and according to your own desires.

34 "And you keep them down, even as it were, in bondage, that you may glut yourselves with the labors of their hands, that they dare not look up with boldness, and that they dare not enjoy their rights and privileges.

35 "They dare not make use of that which is their own lest they should offend their priests, who yoke them according to their desires, and have brought them to believe by their traditions, and their dreams, and their whims, and their visions, and their pretended mysteries that they should, if they did not do according to their words, offend some unknown being who they say is God—a being who never has been seen nor known, who never was nor ever will be."

36 Now when the high priest and chief judge saw the hardness of his heart, when they saw that he would revile even against God, they would not make any reply to his words.

37 But they caused that he should be bound, and they delivered him up into the hands of the officers and sent him to the land of Zarahemla that he might be brought before Alma and the chief judge who was governor over all the land.

38 When he was brought before Alma and the chief judge, he went on in the same manner as he did in the land of Gideon; he went on to blaspheme.

39 And he rose up in great swelling words before Alma, and reviled against the priests and teachers, accusing them of leading away the people after the silly traditions of their fathers for the sake of glutting on the labors of the people.

40 Now Alma said to him, "You know that we do not glut ourselves on the labors of this people; for, behold, I have labored even from the commencement of the reign of the judges until now, with my own hands, for my support, notwithstanding my many travels round about the land to declare the word of God to my people.

41 "And notwithstanding the many labors which I have performed in the church, I have never received so much as even one senine for my labor; neither have any of my brethren, save it were in the judgment seat; and then we have received only according to law for our time.

42 "Now if we do not receive anything for our labors in the church, what does it profit us to labor in the church, save it were to declare the truth that we may have rejoicings in the joy of our brethren?

43 "Then why do you say that we preach to this people to get gain, when you of yourself know that we receive no gain?

44 "And now, do you believe that

we deceive this people, that causes such joy in their hearts?"

45 And Korihor answered him, "Yes."

46 Then Alma said to him, "Do you believe that there is a God?" And he answered, "No."

47 Now Alma said to him, "Will you deny again that there is a God, and also deny the Christ? For, behold, I say to you, I know there is a God, and also that Christ shall come.

48 "What evidence have you that there is no God, or that Christ comes not? I say to you that you have none, save it be your word only.

49 "But, behold, I have all things as a testimony that these things are true; and you also have all things as a testimony to you that they are true, and will you deny them?

50 "Do you believe that these things are true?

51 "Behold, I know that you believe, but you are possessed with a lying spirit, and you have put off the Spirit of God that it may have no place in you; but the devil has power over you, and he carries you about, working devices that he may destroy the children of God."

52 Now Korihor said to Alma, "If you will show me a sign that I may be convinced that there is a God, and show me that he has power, then will I be convinced of the truth of your words."

53 But Alma said to him, "You have had signs enough; will you tempt your God? Will you say, 'Show me a sign,' when you have the testimony of all these your brethren, and also all the holy prophets?

54 "The scriptures are laid before you, and all things denote there is a God, even the earth and all things that are upon the face of it, and its motion.

55 "Also all the planets which move in their regular form witness that there is a Supreme Creator; and yet you go about, leading away the hearts of this people, testifying to them there is no God. Will you deny against all these witnesses?"

56 And Korihor said, "I will deny except you shall show me a sign."

57 Then Alma said to him, "Behold, I am grieved because of the hardness of your heart, that you will still resist the spirit of the truth, that your soul may be destroyed.

58 "But, behold, it is better that your soul should be lost than that you should be the means of bringing many souls down to destruction by your lying and by your flattering words.

59 "Therefore if you shall deny again, behold, God shall smite you, that you shall become dumb, that you shall never open your mouth any more, that you shall not deceive this people any more."

60 Now Korihor said to him, "I do not deny the existence of a God, but I do not believe that there is a God; and I say also that you do not know that there is a God; and except you show me a sign, I will not believe."

61 And Alma said to him, "This will I give to you for a sign, that you shall be struck dumb according to my words; and I say that, in the name of God, you shall be struck dumb, that you shall no more have utterance."

62 When Alma had said these words, Korihor was struck dumb, that he could not have utterance.

63 When the chief judge saw this, he put forth his hand and wrote to Korihor, saying: "Are you convinced of the power of God?

64 "In whom did you desire that Alma should show forth his sign? Would you that he should afflict others to show to you a sign?

65 "Behold, he has showed to you a sign; and now will you dispute more?"

66 And Korihor put forth his hand and wrote, saying: "I know that I am dumb, for I cannot speak; and I know that nothing, save it were the power of God, could bring this upon me; and I also knew that there was a God.

67 "But, behold, the devil has deceived me; for he appeared to me in the form of an angel and said to me, 'Go and reclaim this people, for they have all gone astray after an unknown God.'

68 "And he said to me, 'There is no God'; and he taught me that which I should say. And I have taught his

74 B. C.

words; and I taught them because they were pleasing to the carnal mind.

69 "And I taught them until I had much success, insomuch that I verily believed that they were true; and for this cause I withstood the truth, even until I have brought this great curse upon me."

70 Now when he had said this, he besought that Alma should pray to God that the curse might be taken from him.

71 But Alma said to him, "If this curse should be taken from you, you would again lead away the hearts of this people; therefore, it shall be to you, even as the Lord will."

72 And it came to pass that the curse was not taken off Korihor; but he was cast out, and went about from house to house, begging for his food.

73 Now the knowledge of what had happened to Korihor was immediately published throughout all the land; and the proclamation was sent forth by the chief judge to all the people in the land, declaring to those who had believed in the words of Korihor that they must speedily repent lest the same judgments come to them.

74 And it came to pass that they were all convinced of the wickedness of Korihor, therefore they were all converted again to the Lord; and this put an end to the iniquity after the manner of Korihor.

75 And Korihor went about from house to house, begging food for his support.

76 And as he went forth among the people, among a people who had separated themselves from the Nephites and called themselves Zoramites, being led by a man whose name was Zoram, behold, he was run upon, and trodden down until he was dead.

77 Thus we see the end of him who perverts the ways of the Lord; and thus we see that the devil will not support his children at the last day, but speedily drags them down to hell.

78 Now after the end of Korihor, Alma, having received tidings that the Zoramites were perverting the ways of the Lord and that Zoram, who was their leader, was leading the hearts of the people to bow down to dumb idols, again began to sicken because of the iniquity of the people.

79 For it was the cause of great sorrow to Alma to know of iniquity among his people; therefore his heart was exceedingly sorrowful because of the separation of the Zoramites from the Nephites.

80 Now the Zoramites had gathered themselves together in a land which they called Antionum, which was east of the land of Zarahemla, which lay nearly bordering upon the seashore, which was south of the land of Jershon, which also bordered upon the wilderness south, which wilderness was full of the Lamanites.

81 The Nephites greatly feared that the Zoramites would enter into a correspondence with the Lamanites, and that it would be the means of great loss on the part of the Nephites.

82 And now, as the preaching of the word had had a greater tendency to lead the people to do that which was just and had more powerful effect upon the minds of the people than the sword or anything else which had happened to them, therefore Alma thought it was expedient that they should try the virtue of the word of God.

83 Therefore he took Ammon, and Aaron, and Omner; and Himni he left in the church in Zarahemla; but the former three he took with him, and also Amulek and Zeezrom who were at Melek; and he also took two of his sons.

84 But the eldest of his sons he did not take with him, and his name was Helaman; but the names of those whom he took with him were Shiblon and Corianton; and these are the names of those who went with him among the Zoramites to preach to them the word.

85 Now the Zoramites were dissenters from the Nephites; therefore they had the word of God preached to them.

86 But they had fallen into great errors for they would not observe to keep the commandments of God, and his statutes according to the law of Moses.

87 Neither would they observe the performances of the church, to continue in prayer and supplication to God daily that they might not enter into temptation; in fine, they per-

verted the ways of the Lord in very many instances; therefore Alma and his brethren went into the land to preach the word to them.

88 Now when they came into the land, behold, to their astonishment, they found that the Zoramites had built synagogues, and that they gathered themselves together on one day of the week, which day they called the day of the Lord.

89 And they worshiped after a manner which Alma and his brethren had never beheld; for they had a place built up in the center of their synagogue, a place for standing, which was high above the head; and the top thereof would only admit one person.

90 Therefore, whoever desired to worship must go forth and stand upon the top thereof, and stretch forth his hands toward heaven, and cry with a loud voice, saying: "Holy, holy God; we believe that thou art God, and we believe that thou art holy, and that thou wast a spirit, and that thou art a spirit, and that thou wilt be a spirit forever.

91 "Holy God, we believe that thou hast separated us from our brethren; and we do not believe in the tradition of our brethren which was handed down to them by the childishness of their fathers; but we believe that thou hast elected us to be thy holy children.

92 "And also thou hast made it known unto us that there shall be no Christ; but thou art the same, yesterday, today, and forever; and thou hast elected us that we shall be saved, whilst all around us are elected to be cast by thy wrath down to hell; for which holiness, O God, we thank thee.

93 "We also thank thee that thou hast elected us that we may not be led away after the foolish traditions of our brethren, which doth bind them down to a belief of Christ, which doth lead their hearts to wander far from thee, our God.

94 "And again we thank thee, O God, that we are a chosen and a holy people. Amen."

95 After Alma and his brethren and his sons had heard these prayers, they were astonished beyond all measure.

96 For, behold every man went forth and offered up the same prayers.

97 Now the place was called by them Rameumptom, which, being interpreted, is the Holy Stand.

98 From this stand they offered up, every man, the selfsame prayer to God, thanking their God that they were chosen of him, and that he did not lead them away after the tradition of their brethren, and that their hearts were not stolen away to believe in things to come which they knew nothing about.

99 And after the people had all offered up thanks after this manner, they returned to their homes, never speaking of their God again until they had assembled themselves together again to the holy stand to offer up thanks after their manner.

100 Now when Alma saw this, his heart was grieved; for he saw that they were a wicked and a perverse people; he saw that their hearts were set upon gold, and upon silver, and upon all manner of fine goods.

101 He also saw that their hearts were lifted up to great boasting in their pride.

102 And he lifted up his voice to heaven and cried, saying: "Oh, how long, O Lord, wilt thou suffer that thy servants shall dwell here below in the flesh to behold such gross wickedness among the children of men.

103 "Behold, O God, they cry unto thee, and yet their hearts are swallowed up in their pride.

104 "Behold, O God, they cry unto thee with their mouths, while they are puffed up even to greatness with the vain things of the world.

105 "Behold, O my God, their costly apparel, and their ringlets, and their bracelets, and their ornaments of gold, and all their precious things which they are ornamented with.

106 "And, behold, their hearts are set upon them, and yet they cry unto thee and say, 'We thank thee, O God, for we are a chosen people unto thee, while others shall perish.'

107 "And they say that thou hast made it known unto them that there shall be no Christ.

108 "O Lord God, how long wilt thou suffer that such wickedness and iniquity shall be among this people?

109 "O Lord, wilt thou give me strength that I may bear with my infirmities. For I am infirm, and such wickedness among this people doth pain my soul.

110 "O Lord, my heart is exceedingly sorrowful; wilt thou comfort my soul in Christ.

111 "O Lord, wilt thou grant me that I may have strength, that I may suffer with patience these afflictions which shall come upon me because of the iniquity of this people.

112 "O Lord, wilt thou comfort my soul and give me success, and also my fellow laborers who are with me; Ammon, and Aaron, and Omner, and also Amulek and Zeezrom, and also my two sons, even all these wilt thou comfort, O Lord. Wilt thou comfort their souls in Christ.

113 "Wilt thou grant them that they may have strength that they may bear their afflictions which shall come upon them because of the iniquities of this people.

114 "O Lord, wilt thou grant us that we may have success in bringing them again to thee, in Christ.

115 "Behold, O Lord, their souls are precious, and many of them are our near brethren, therefore give us, O Lord, power and wisdom that we may bring these, our brethren, again to thee."

116 When Alma had said these words, he clapped his hands upon all them who were with him.

117 And, behold, as he clapped his hands upon them, they were filled with the Holy Spirit.

118 And after that they separated themselves one from another, taking no thought for themselves what they should eat, or what they should drink, or what they should put on.

119 And the Lord provided for them that they should hunger not, neither should they thirst; and he also gave them strength that they should suffer no manner of afflictions, save it were swallowed up in the joy of Christ.

120 Now this was according to the prayer of Alma, and this because he prayed in faith.

121 And they went forth and began to preach the word of God to the people, entering into their synagogues

and into their houses; and they even preached the word in their streets.

122 After much labor among them, they began to have success among the poor class of people; for, behold, they were cast out of the synagogues because of the coarseness of their apparel.

123 Therefore the people were not permitted to enter into their synagogues to worship God, being esteemed as filthiness; therefore they were poor; they were esteemed by their brethren as dross; therefore they were poor as to things of the world, and also they were poor in heart.

124 Now as Alma was teaching and speaking to the people upon the hill Onidah, there came a great multitude to him, who were those of whom we have been speaking who were poor in heart because of their poverty as to the things of the world.

125 And they came to Alma; and the one who was the foremost among them said to him, "Behold, what shall these my brethren do? For they are despised of all men because of their poverty; and more especially by our priests.

126 "For they have cast us out of our synagogues, which we have labored abundantly to build with our own hands; and they have cast us out because of our exceeding poverty, and we have no place to worship our God; and, behold, what shall we do?"

127 When Alma heard this, he turned his face immediately toward him, and he beheld with great joy; for he beheld that their afflictions had truly humbled them, and that they were prepared to hear the word.

128 Therefore he said no more to the other multitude, but he stretched forth his hand and cried to those whom he beheld who were truly penitent, and said to them, "I behold that you are lowly in heart; and if so, you are blessed.

129 "Behold, your brother has said, 'What shall we do? For we are cast out of our synagogues that we cannot worship our God.'

130 "Behold, I say to you, Do you suppose that you cannot worship God, save it be in your synagogues only?

131 "And moreover I would ask,

Do you suppose that you must worship God only once in a week?

132 "I say to you, It is well that you are cast out of your synagogues, that you may be humble, and that you may learn wisdom; for it is necessary that you should learn widsom.

133 "For it is because you are cast out, that you are despised of your brethren, because of your exceeding poverty that you are brought to a lowliness of heart; for you are necessarily brought to be humble.

134 "And now because you are compelled to be humble, blessed are you; for a man sometimes, if he is compelled to be humble, seeks repentance.

135 "Now surely, whoever repents shall find mercy; and he that finds mercy and endures to the end, the same shall be saved.

136 "And as I said to you that because you were compelled to be humble you were blessed, do you not suppose that they are more blessed who truly humble themselves because of the word?

137 "He that truly humbles himself and repents of his sins, and endures to the end, the same shall be blessed, much more blessed than they who are compelled to be humble because of their exceeding poverty; therefore blessed are they who humble themselves without being compelled to be humble.

138 "In other words, Blessed is he that believes in the word of God and is baptized without stubbornness of heart, without being brought to know the word, or even compelled to know, before he will believe.

139 "There are many who say, 'If you will show us a sign from heaven, then we shall know of a surety; then we shall believe.'

140 "Now I ask, Is this faith? Behold, I say to you, No; for if a man knows a thing, he has no cause to believe, for he knows it.

141 "And now how much more cursed is he that knows the will of God and does it not, than he that only believes, or only has cause to believe, and falls into transgression. Now of this thing, you must judge.

142 "Behold, I say to you that it is on the one hand even as it is on the other; and it shall be to every man according to his work.

143 "Now as I said concerning faith: Faith is not to have a perfect knowledge of things; therefore if you have faith, you hope for things which are not seen, which are true.

144 "Behold, I say to you, and I would that you should remember, that God is merciful to all who believe on his name; therefore he desires, in the first place, that you should believe, even on his word.

145 "He imparts his word by angels to men; and not only men, but to women also.

146 "And this is not all; little children have words given to them many times which confound the wise and the learned.

147 "And now, my beloved brethren, you have desired to know of me what you shall do because you are afflicted and cast out: now I do not desire that you should suppose that I mean to judge you only according to that which is true.

148 "For I do not mean that all of you have been compelled to humble yourselves; for I verily believe that there are some among you who would humble themselves, let them be in whatever circumstances they might.

149 "Now as I said concerning faith—that it was not a perfect knowledge—even so it is with my words.

150 "You cannot know of their surety at first to perfection, any more than faith is a perfect knowledge.

151 "But, behold, if you will awake and arouse your faculties, even to an experiment upon my words, and exercise a particle of faith, even if ye can no more than desire to believe, let this desire work in you even until you believe in a manner that you can give place for a portion of my words.

152 "Now we will compare the word to a seed.

153 "If you give place that a seed may be planted in your heart, behold, if it be a true seed, or a good seed, and if you do not cast it out by your unbelief that you will resist the Spirit of the Lord, behold, it will begin to swell within your breasts.

154 "And when you feel these swelling motions, you will begin to say within yourselves, 'It must be a good

seed, or that the word is good, for it begins to enlarge my soul; it begins to enlighten my understanding; and it begins to be delicious to me.'

155 "Now, behold, would not this increase your faith? I say to you, Yes; nevertheless it has not grown up to a perfect knowledge.

156 "But, behold, as the seed swells and sprouts and begins to grow, then you must say that the seed is good; for, behold, it swells and sprouts and begins to grow.

157 "And now, behold, will not this strengthen your faith? It will strengthen your faith, for you will say, 'I know that this is a good seed, for, behold, it sprouts and begins to grow.'

158 "And now, behold, are you sure that this is a good seed? I say to you, Yes; for every seed brings forth its own likeness; therefore, if a seed grows, it is good, but if it grows not, behold, it is not good; therefore it is cast away.

159 "And because you have tried the experiment and planted the seed, and it swells and sprouts and begins to grow, you must know that the seed is good.

160 "But is your knowledge perfect? Your knowledge is perfect in that thing, and your faith is dormant.

161 "This is because you know; for you know that the word has swelled your souls, and you also know that it has sprouted up, that your understanding begins to be enlightened and your mind begins to expand.

162 "Oh, then, is not this real? I say to you, Yes; because it is light; and whatever is light is good, because it is discernible; therefore you must know that it is good.

163 "And after you have tasted this light, is your knowledge perfect? Behold, I say to you, No; neither must you lay aside your faith, for you have only exercised your faith to plant the seed, that you might try the experiment to know if the seed was good.

164 "And, behold, as the tree begins to grow, you will say, 'Let us nourish it with great care, that it may get root, that it may grow up and bring forth fruit to us.'

165 "And if you nourish it with much care, it will get root, and grow up, and bring forth fruit.

166 "But if you neglect the tree and take no thought for its nourishment, behold, it will not get any root; and when the heat of the sun comes and scorches it, because it has no root it withers away, and you pluck it up and cast it out.

167 "Now this is not because the seed was not good, neither is it because the fruit thereof would not be desirable.

168 "But it is because your ground is barren, and you will not nourish the tree; therefore you cannot have the fruit thereof.

169 "And thus it is if you will not nourish the word, looking forward with an eye of faith to the fruit thereof, you can never pluck the fruit of the tree of life.

170 "But if you will nourish the word, nourish the tree as it begins to grow, by your faith with great diligence and with patience, looking forward to the fruit thereof, it shall take root; and, behold, it shall be a tree springing up to everlasting life.

171 "And because of your diligence, and your faith, and your patience with the word in nourishing it that it may take root in you, behold, by and by you shall pluck the fruit thereof, which is most precious, which is sweet above all that is sweet, white above all that is white, and pure above all that is pure.

172 "And you shall feast upon this fruit, even until you are filled, that you hunger not, neither shall you thirst.

173 "Then, my brethren, you shall reap the rewards of your faith, and your diligence and patience and long-suffering, waiting for the tree to bring forth fruit to you."

174 After Alma had spoken these words, they sent forth to him desiring to know whether they should believe in one God, that they might obtain this fruit of which he had spoken, or how they should plant the seed, or the word of which he had spoken, which he said must be planted in their hearts, or in what manner they should begin to exercise their faith.

175 And Alma said to them, "Behold, you have said that you could

not worship your God because you are cast out of your synagogues.

176 "But, behold, I say to you, If you suppose that you cannot worship God, you do greatly err, and you ought to search the scriptures; if you suppose that they have taught you this, you do not understand them.

177 "Do you remember to have read what Zenos, the prophet of old, has said concerning prayer or worship?

178 "He said, 'Thou art merciful, O God, for thou hast heard my prayer, even when I was in the wilderness; thou wast merciful when I prayed concerning those who were mine enemies, and thou didst turn them to me.

179 "'O God, thou wast merciful to me when I did cry to thee in my field; when I did cry to thee in my prayer, and thou didst hear me.

180 "'And again, O God, when I did turn to my house thou didst hear me in my prayer.

181 "'And when I did turn to my closet, O Lord, and prayed to thee, thou didst hear me; yea, thou art merciful to thy children when they cry to thee to be heard of thee and not of men, and thou wilt hear them.

182 "'O God, thou hast been merciful to me and heard my cries in the midst of thy congregations; and thou hast also heard me when I have been cast out and have been despised by mine enemies.

183 "'Thou didst hear my cries, and wast angry with mine enemies, and thou didst visit them in thine anger with speedy destruction; and thou didst hear me because of mine afflictions and my sincerity.

184 "'And it is because of thy Son that thou hast been thus merciful to me; therefore I will cry to thee in all mine afflictions; for in thee is my joy, for thou hast turned thy judgments away from me because of thy Son.'"

185 Then Alma said to them, "Do you believe those scriptures which have been written by them of old?

186 "Behold, if you do, you must believe what Zenos said; for, behold, he said, 'Thou has turned away thy judgments, because of thy Son.'

187 "Behold, my brethren, I would ask if you have read the scriptures.

If you have, how can you disbelieve on the Son of God?

188 "For it is not written that Zenos alone spoke of these things, but Zenock also spoke of these things; for, behold, he said, 'Thou art angry, O Lord, with this people because they will not understand of thy mercies which thou hast bestowed upon them because of thy Son.'

189 "And now, my brethren, you see that a second prophet of old has testified of the Son of God; and because the people would not understand his words, they stoned him to death.

190 "But, behold, this is not all; these are not the only ones who have spoken concerning the Son of God.

191 "Behold, he was spoken of by Moses; and, behold, a type was raised up in the wilderness that whoever would look upon it might live. And many did look and live.

192 "But few understood the meaning of those things, and this because of the hardness of their hearts.

193 "And there were many who were so hardened that they would not look; therefore they perished.

194 "Now the reason they would not look was that they did not believe it would heal them.

195 "O my brethren, if you could be healed by merely casting about your eyes that you might be healed, would you not behold quickly, or would you rather harden your hearts in unbelief, and be slothful, that you would not cast about your eyes, that you might perish?

196 "If so, woe shall come upon you; but if not so, then cast about your eyes and begin to believe in the Son of God, that he will come to redeem his people, and that he shall suffer and die to atone for their sins.

197 "Believe that he shall rise again from the dead, which shall bring to pass the resurrection, that all men shall stand before him to be judged at the last and judgment day, according to their works.

198 "And now, my brethren, I desire that you shall plant this word in your hearts, and as it begins to swell, even so nourish it by your faith.

199 "And, behold, it will become

a tree springing up in you to everlasting life.

200 "Then may God grant you that your burdens may be light through the joy of his Son. And even all this can you do, if you will. Amen."

201 After Alma had spoken these words to them, he sat down upon the ground, and Amulek arose and began to teach them, saying, "My brethren, I think that it is impossible that you should be ignorant of the things which have been spoken concerning the coming of Christ, who is taught by us to be the Son of God.

202 "I know that these things were taught to you bountifully before your dissension from among us. As you have desired of my beloved brother that he should make known to you what you should do because of your afflictions, he has spoken somewhat to you to prepare your minds; and he has exhorted you to faith and to patience, [203]even that you would have so much faith as to plant the word in your hearts, that you may try the experiment of its goodness; and we have beheld that the great question which is in your minds is whether the word be in the Son of God, or whether there shall be no Christ.

204 "And you also beheld that my brother has proved to you, in many instances, that the word is in Christ unto salvation.

205 "My brother has called upon the words of Zenos that redemption comes through the Son of God, and also upon the words of Zenock, and also he has appealed to Moses to prove that these things are true.

206 "And now, behold, I will testify to you of myself that these things are true.

207 "Behold, I say to you that I know that Christ shall come among the children of men to take upon him the transgressions of his people, and that he shall atone for the sins of the world; for the Lord God has spoken it.

208 "For it is expedient that an atonement should be made; for according to the great plan of the eternal God, there must be an atonement made, or else all mankind must unavoidably perish.

209 "All are hardened; all are fallen, and are lost, and must perish except it be through the atonement which it is expedient should be made.

210 "For it is expedient that there should be a great and last sacrifice; not a sacrifice of man (for it shall not be a human sacrifice), neither of beast, neither of any manner of fowl; but it must be an infinite and eternal sacrifice.

211 "Now there is not any man that can sacrifice his own blood which will atone for the sins of another.

212 "And if a man murders, behold, will our law, which is just, take the life of his brother? I say to you, No.

213 "But the law requires the life of him who has murdered; therefore there can be nothing which is short of an infinite atonement which will suffice for the sins of the world; therefore it is expedient that there should be a great and last sacrifice.

214 "Then shall there be, or it is expedient there should be, a stop to the shedding of blood; then shall the law of Moses be fulfilled; it shall all be fulfilled, every jot and tittle, and none shall have passed away.

215 "And, behold, this is the whole meaning of the law, every whit pointing to that great and last sacrifice; and that great and last sacrifice will be the Son of God, infinite and eternal; and thus he shall bring salvation to all those who shall believe on his name.

216 "This is the intent of this last sacrifice, to bring about the bowels of mercy which overpowers justice and brings about means to men that they may have faith unto repentance.

217 "Thus mercy satisfies the demands of justice and encircles them in the arms of safety, while he that exercises no faith unto repentance is exposed to the whole law of the demands of justice; therefore, only to him that has faith unto repentance is brought about the great and eternal plan of redemption.

218 "Therefore may God grant you, my brethren, that you may begin to exercise your faith unto repentance, that you begin to call upon his holy name, that he would have mercy upon you; cry to him for mercy, for he is mighty to save.

219 "Humble yourselves, and continue in prayer to him; cry to him when you are in your fields, and over all your flocks; cry to him in your houses, and over all your household, morning, midday, and evening; cry to him against the power of your enemies; cry to him against the devil, who is an enemy to all righteousness.

220 "Cry to him over the crops of your fields, that you may prosper in them; cry over the flocks of your fields that they may increase.

221 "But this is not all: you must pour out your souls in your closets, and your secret places, and in your wilderness.

222 "And when you do not cry to the Lord, let your hearts be full, drawn out in prayer to him continually for your welfare, and also for the welfare of those who are around you.

223 "Now, behold, my brethren, I say to you, Do not suppose that this is all; for after you have done all these things, if you turn away the needy and the naked, and visit not the sick and afflicted, and impart not of your substance if you have, to those who stand in need, 224behold, your prayer is vain, and avails you nothing, and you are as hypocrites who deny the faith.

225 "Therefore, if you do not remember to be charitable, you are as dross which the refiners cast out (it being of no worth), and it is trodden under foot of men.

226 "And now, my brethren, I would that, after you have received so many witnesses, seeing that the holy scriptures testify of these things, you come forth and bring fruit unto repentance.

227 "I would that you would come forth and harden not your hearts any longer; for, behold, now is the time and the day of your salvation; therefore, if you will repent and harden not your hearts, immediately shall the great plan of redemption be brought about unto you.

228 "For, behold, this life is the time for men to prepare to meet God; behold, the day of this life is the day for men to perform their labors.

229 "And now as I said to you before, as you have had so many witnesses, therefore I beseech of you that you do not procrastinate the day of your repentance until the end.

230 "For after this day of life, which is given us to prepare for eternity, behold, if we do not improve our time while in this life, then comes the night of darkness wherein there can be no labor performed.

231 "You cannot say, when you are brought to that awful crisis, 'I will repent, I will return to my God.'

232 "No, you cannot say this, for that same spirit which possesses your bodies at the time that you go out of this life will have power to possess your body in that eternal world.

233 "For, behold, if you have procrastinated the day of your repentance even until death, behold, you have become subjected to the spirit of the devil, and he seals you his.

234 "Therefore the Spirit of the Lord has withdrawn from you and has no place in you, and the devil has all power over you; and this is the final state of the wicked.

235 "And this I know because the Lord has said he dwells not in unholy temples, but in the hearts of the righteous does he dwell.

236 "He has also said that the righteous shall sit down in his kingdom to go no more out, but their garments should be made white through the blood of the Lamb.

237 "And now, my beloved brethren, I desire that you should remember these things, and that you should work out your salvation with fear before God, and that you should no more deny the coming of Christ; that you contend no more against the Holy Ghost, but that you receive it and take upon you the name of Christ; that you humble yourselves even to the dust and worship God in whatever place you may be in, in spirit and in truth.

238 "And I desire that you live in thanksgiving daily for the many mercies and blessings which he bestows upon you. And I also exhort you, my brethren, that you be watchful to pray continually, that you may not be led away by the temptation of the devil, that he may not overpower you, that you may not become his subjects at the last day; for, be-

hold, he rewards you no good thing.

239 "Now, my beloved brethren, I would exhort you to have patience, and that you bear with all manner of afflictions; that you do not revile against those who cast you out because of your exceeding poverty, lest you become sinners like them; but that you have patience, and bear with those afflictions, with a firm hope that you shall one day rest from all your afflictions."

240 After Amulek had made an end of these words, they withdrew themselves from the multitude and came over into the land of Jershon.

241 And the rest of the brethren, after they had preached the word to the Zoramites, also came over into the land of Jershon.

242 After the more popular part of the Zoramites had consulted together concerning the words which had been preached to them, they were angry because of the word, for it destroyed their craft; therefore they would not hearken to the words.

243 And they sent and gathered together all the people throughout all the land, and consulted with them concerning the words which had been spoken.

244 Now their rulers, and their priests, and their teachers did not let the people know concerning their desires; therefore they found out privily the minds of all the people.

245 After they had found out the minds of all the people, those who were in favor of the words which had been spoken by Alma and his brethren were cast out of the land; and they were many, and they came over also into the land of Jershon.

246 And Alma and his brethren ministered to them.

247 Now the people of the Zoramites were angry with the people of Ammon who were in Jershon, and the chief ruler of the Zoramites, being a very wicked man, sent over to the people of Ammon desiring them that they should cast out of their land all those who came over from them into their land.

248 And he breathed out many threatenings against them.

249 Now the people of Ammon did not fear his words, therefore they did not cast them out, but they received all the poor of the Zoramites that came over to them.

250 And they nourished them, and clothed them, and gave to them lands for their inheritance; and they administered to them according to their wants.

251 This stirred up the Zoramites to anger against the people of Ammon, and they began to mix with the Lamanites and to stir them up also to anger against them.

252 Thus the Zoramites and the Lamanites began to make preparations for war against the people of Ammon, and also against the Nephites.

253 And thus ended the seventeenth year of the reign of the judges over the people of Nephi.

254 And the people of Ammon departed out of the land of Jershon, and went over into the land of Melek, and gave place in the land of Jershon for the armies of the Nephites, that they might contend with the armies of the Lamanites and the armies of the Zoramites.

255 Thus commenced a war between the Lamanites and the Nephites in the eighteenth year of the reign of the judges; and an account shall be given of their wars hereafter.

256 And Alma and Ammon and their brethren, and also the two sons of Alma, returned to the land of Zarahemla after having been instruments in the hands of God of bringing many of the Zoramites to repentance; and as many as were brought to repentance were driven out of their land.

257 But they have lands for their inheritance in the land of Jershon, and they have taken up arms to defend themselves, and their wives, and children, and their lands.

258 Now Alma, being grieved for the iniquity of his people, for the wars, and the bloodsheds, and the contentions which were among them, and having been sent to declare the word among all the people in every city, 259and seeing that the hearts of the people began to wax hard, and that they began to be offended because of the strictness of the word, was exceedingly sorrowful.

260 Therefore, he caused that his sons should be gathered together that he might give to them every one his charge, separately, concerning the things pertaining to righteousness.

261 And we have an account of his commandments which he gave to them according to his own record.

CHAPTER 17

The commandments of Alma to his son, Helaman.

MY SON, give ear to my words; for I swear to you, that inasmuch as you shall keep the commandments of God you shall prosper in the land.

2 I would that you should do as I have done in remembering the captivity of our fathers; for they were in bondage, and none could deliver them, except it was the God of Abraham, Isaac, and Jacob; and he surely delivered them in their afflictions.

3 Now, O my son Helaman, behold, you are in your youth, therefore I beseech of you that you will hear my words and learn of me; for I know that whoever shall put his trust in God shall be supported in his trials and troubles and afflictions, and shall be lifted up at the last day.

4 And I would not have you think that I know of myself—not of the temporal, but of the spiritual; not of the carnal mind, but of God.

5 Now, behold, I say to you, If I had not been born of God, I should not have known these things; but God has, by the mouth of his holy angel, made these things known to me, not of any worthiness of myself, for I went about with the sons of Mosiah seeking to destroy the church of God; but, behold, God sent his holy angel to stop us by the way.

6 And he spoke to us, as it were with the voice of thunder, and the whole earth trembled beneath our feet, and we all fell to the earth, for the fear of the Lord came upon us.

7 But, behold, the voice said to me, "Arise." And I arose and stood up, and beheld the angel. And he said to me, "If thou wilt not of thyself be destroyed, seek no more to destroy the church of God."

8 And I fell to the earth; and it was for the space of three days and three nights that I could not open my mouth; neither had I the use of my limbs.

9 And the angel spoke more things to me which were heard by my brethren, but I did not hear them; for when I heard the words, "If thou wilt not of thyself be destroyed, seek no more to destroy the church of God," I was struck with such great fear and amazement lest perhaps I should be destroyed that I fell to the earth, and I heard no more.

10 But I was racked with eternal torment; for my soul was harrowed up to the greatest degree, and racked with all my sins. And I remembered all my sins and iniquities for which I was tormented with the pains of hell.

11 I saw that I had rebelled against my God, and that I had not kept his holy commandments; and I had murdered many of his children, or rather led them away to destruction.

12 And in fine, so great had been my iniquities that the very thoughts of coming into the presence of my God racked my soul with inexpressible horror.

13 Oh, thought I, that I could be banished and become extinct both soul and body, that I might not be brought to stand in the presence of my God to be judged of my deeds.

14 And for three days and for three nights I was racked, even with the pains of a damned soul.

15 As I was thus racked with torment, while I was harrowed up by the memory of my many sins, behold, I remembered also to have heard my father prophesy to the people concerning the coming of one Jesus Christ, a Son of God, to atone for the sins of the world.

16 Now as my mind caught hold upon this thought, I cried within my heart, "O Jesus, thou Son of God, have mercy on me who am in the gall of bitterness, and am encircled by the everlasting chains of death."

17 And now, behold, when I

thought this, I could remember my pains no more; I was harrowed up by the memory of my sins no more.

18 Oh, what joy and what marvelous light I beheld; my soul was filled with joy as exceeding as was my pain; I say to you, my son, that there could be nothing so exquisite and so bitter as were my pains.

19 And again I say to you, my son, that on the other hand, there can be nothing so exquisite and sweet as was my joy.

20 I thought I saw, even as our father Lehi saw, God sitting upon his throne, surrounded with numberless concourses of angels in the attitude of singing and praising their God; and my soul longed to be there.

21 But, behold, my limbs received their strength again, and I stood upon my feet and manifested to the people that I had been born of God.

22 And from that time even until now, I have labored without ceasing that I might bring souls to repentance, that I might bring them to taste of the exceeding joy of which I tasted, that they might also be born of God and be filled with the Holy Ghost.

23 And now, behold, O my son, the Lord gives me exceedingly great joy in the fruit of my labors; for because of the word which he has imparted to me, behold, many have been born of God, and have tasted as I have tasted, and have seen eye to eye as I have seen.

24 Therefore they know of these things of which I have spoken as I know; and the knowledge which I have is of God.

25 I have been supported under trials and troubles of every kind, and in all manner of afflictions; God has delivered me from prison, and from bonds, and from death; and I put my trust in him, and he will still deliver me.

26 And I know that he will raise me up at the last day to dwell with him in glory; and I will praise him forever, for he has brought our fathers out of Egypt, and he has swallowed up the Egyptians in the Red Sea, and he led them by his power into the promised land.

27 And he has delivered them out of bondage and captivity from time to time; and he has also brought our fathers out of the land of Jerusalem; and he has also by his everlasting power delivered them out of bondage and captivity from time to time, even down to the present day.

28 And I have always retained in remembrance their captivity; and you also ought to retain in remembrance, as I have done, their captivity.

29 But, behold, my son, this is not all; for you ought to know, as I know, that inasmuch as you shall keep the commandments of God, you shall prosper in the land.

30 And you ought to know also that inasmuch as you will not keep the commandments of God, you shall be cut off from his presence. This is according to his word.

31 And now, my son Helaman, I command you that you take the records which have been entrusted with me; and I also command you that you keep a record of this people, according as I have done, upon the plates of Nephi, and keep all these things sacred which I have kept, even as I have kept them; for it is for a wise purpose that they are kept.

32 And these plates of brass which contain these engravings, which have the records of the holy scriptures upon them, have the genealogy of our forefathers, even from the beginning.

33 And, behold, it has been prophesied by our fathers that they should be kept and handed down from one generation to another, and be kept and preserved by the hand of the Lord until they should go forth to every nation, kindred, tongue, and people, that they shall know of the mysteries contained thereon.

34 Now, behold, if they are kept, they must retain their brightness; and they will retain their brightness, and so shall all the plates which contain that which is holy writ.

35 You may suppose that this is foolishness in me; but, behold, I say to you that by small and simple things are great things brought to pass; and small means, in many instances, confound the wise.

36 And the Lord God works by means to bring about his great and eternal purposes; and by very small means the Lord confounds the wise,

and brings about the salvation of many souls.

37 And now it has hitherto been wisdom in God that these things should be preserved; for, behold, they have enlarged the memory of this people, and convinced many of the error of their ways and brought them to the knowledge of their God, to the salvation of their souls.

38 I say to you, were it not for these things that these records contain, which are on these plates, Ammon and his brethren could not have convinced so many thousands of the Lamanites of the incorrect tradition of their fathers.

39 These records and their words brought them to repentance; that is, they brought them to the knowledge of the Lord their God and to rejoice in Jesus Christ their Redeemer.

40 And who knows but that they will be the means of bringing many thousands of them, and also many thousands of our stiff-necked brethren, the Nephites, who are now hardening their hearts, in sins and iniquities, to the knowledge of their Redeemer.

41 Now these mysteries are not yet fully made known to me; therefore I shall forbear.

42 And it may suffice if I only say they are preserved for a wise purpose, which purpose is known to God; for he counsels in wisdom over all his works, and his paths are straight and his course is one eternal round.

43 O remember, remember, my son Helaman, how strict are the commandments of God.

44 And he said, "If ye will keep my commandments, ye shall prosper in the land; but if ye keep not my commandments, ye shall be cut off from my presence."

45 And now remember, my son, that God has entrusted you with these things which are sacred, which he has kept sacred, and also which he will keep and preserve for a wise purpose in him that he may show forth his power to future generations.

46 And now, behold, I tell you by the spirit of prophecy that if you transgress the commandments of God, behold, these things which are sacred shall be taken away from you by the power of God, and ye shall be delivered up to Satan, that he may sift you as chaff before the wind.

47 But if you keep the commandments of God, and do with these things which are sacred according to that which the Lord commands you (for you must appeal to the Lord for all things whatever you must do with them), behold, no power of earth or hell can take them from you, for God is powerful to the fulfilling of all his words.

48 For he will fulfill all his promises which he shall make to you, for he has fulfilled his promises which he has made to our fathers.

49 For he promised them that he would reserve these things for a wise purpose in him, that he might show forth his power to future generations.

50 And now, behold, one purpose has he fulfilled, even to the restoration of many thousands of the Lamanites to the knowledge of the truth; and he has shown forth his power in them, and he will also still show forth his power in them to future generations; therefore they shall be preserved.

51 Therefore I command you, my son Helaman, that you be diligent in fulfilling all my words, and that you be diligent in keeping the commandments of God as they are written.

52 And now I will speak to you concerning those twenty-four plates, that you keep them, that the mysteries and the works of darkness, and their secret works, or the secret works of those people, who have been destroyed, may be made manifest to this people; 53even all their murders, and robbings, and their plunderings, and all their wickedness, and abominations may be made manifest to this people; and that you preserve these directors.

54 For, behold, the Lord saw that his people began to work in darkness, to work secret murders and abominations; therefore the Lord said that if they did not repent, they should be destroyed from off the face of the earth.

55 And the Lord said, "I will prepare to my servant, Gazelem, a stone which shall shine forth in darkness unto light, that I may reveal to my people who serve me the works of their brethren, their secret works,

their works of darkness, and their wickedness and abominations."

56 And now, my son, these directors were prepared that the word of God might be fulfilled which he spoke, saying: "I will bring forth out of darkness unto light all their secret works and their abominations.

57 "And except they repent, I will destroy them from off the face of the earth; and I will bring to light all their secrets and abominations to every nation that shall hereafter possess the land."

58 Now, my son, we see that they did not repent; therefore they have been destroyed; and thus far the word of God has been fulfilled; their secret abominations have been brought out of darkness and made known to us.

59 And now, my son, I command you that you retain all their oaths, and their covenants, and their agreements in their secret abominations; and all their signs and their wonders you shall retain from this people, that they know them not, lest peradventure they should fall into darkness also, and be destroyed.

60 For, behold, there is a curse upon all this land, that destruction shall come upon all those workers of darkness, according to the power of God, when they are fully ripe; therefore I desire that this people might not be destroyed.

61 Therefore you shall keep these secret plans of their oaths and their covenants from this people, and only their wickedness, and their murders, and their abominations, shall you make known to them.

62 And you shall teach them to abhor such wickedness, and abominations, and murders; and you shall also teach them that these people were destroyed on account of their wickedness, and abominations, and their murders.

63 For, behold, they murdered all the prophets of the Lord who came among them to declare to them concerning their iniquities; and the blood of those whom they murdered cried to the Lord their God for vengeance upon those who were their murderers.

64 Thus the judgments of God came upon these workers of darkness and secret combinations; and cursed

be the land for ever and ever to those workers of darkness and secret combinations, even to destruction, except they repent before they are fully ripe.

65 And now, my son, remember the words which I have spoken to you; trust not those secret plans to this people, but teach them an everlasting hatred against sin and iniquity.

66 Preach to them repentance and faith on the Lord Jesus Christ; teach them to humble themselves, and to be meek and lowly in heart; teach them to withstand every temptation of the devil, with their faith on the Lord Jesus Christ.

67 Teach them never to be weary of good works, but to be meek and lowly in heart; for such shall find rest to their souls.

68 O remember, my son, and learn wisdom in your youth; learn in your youth to keep the commandments of God, and cry to God for all your support.

69 Let all your doings be unto the Lord, and wherever you go, let it be in the Lord; let your thoughts be directed to the Lord; let the affections of your heart be placed upon the Lord forever; counsel with the Lord in all your doings, and he will direct you for good.

70 When you lie down at night, lie down unto the Lord, that he may watch over you in your sleep; and when you rise in the morning, let your heart be full of thanks to God; and if you do these things, you shall be lifted up at the last day.

71 And now, my son, I have somewhat to say concerning the thing which our fathers call a ball, or director; or our fathers called it liahona, which is, being interpreted, a compass; and the Lord prepared it.

72 Behold, there cannot any man work after the manner of so curious a workmanship.

73 And, behold, it was prepared to show to our fathers the course which they should travel in the wilderness, and it worked for them according to their faith in God.

74 Therefore, if they had faith to believe that God could cause that those spindles should point the way they should go, behold, it was done;

therefore they had this miracle and also many other miracles wrought by the power of God, day by day.

75 Nevertheless, because those miracles were worked by small means, it showed them marvelous works.

76 They were slothful, and forgot to exercise their faith and diligence, and then those marvelous works ceased, and they did not progress in their journey.

77 Therefore they tarried in the wilderness, or did not travel a direct course, and were afflicted with hunger and thirst because of their transgressions.

78 And now, my son, I would that you should understand that these things are not without a shadow; for as our fathers were slothful to give heed to this compass (now these things were temporal), they did not prosper; even so it is with things which are spiritual.

79 For, behold, it is as easy to give heed to the word of Christ, which will point to you a straight course to eternal bliss, as it was for our fathers to give heed to this compass which would point to them a straight course to the promised land.

80 And now I say, Is there not a type in this thing? For just as surely as this director brought our fathers, by following its course, to the promised land, so shall the words of Christ, if we follow their course, carry us beyond this vale of sorrow into a far better land of promise.

81 O my son, do not let us be slothful because of the easiness of the way; for so was it with our fathers; for it was prepared for them that if they would look they might live; even so it is with us.

82 The way is prepared, and if we will look, we may live forever.

83 And now, my son, see that you take care of these sacred things; see that you look to God and live.

84 Go to this people, and declare the word, and be sober. My son, farewell.

CHAPTER 18

The commandments of Alma to his son, Shiblon.

MY SON, give ear to my words; for I say to you, even as I said to Helaman, that inasmuch as you shall keep the commandments of God you shall prosper in the land; and inasmuch as you will not keep the commandments of God you shall be cast off from his presence.

2 And now, my son, I trust that I shall have great joy in you because of your steadiness and your faithfulness to God; for as you have commenced in your youth to look to the Lord your God, even so I hope that you will continue in keeping his commandments; for blessed is he that endures to the end.

3 I say to you, my son, that I have had great joy in you already because of your faithfulness, and your diligence, and your patience, and your long-suffering among the people of the Zoramites.

4 For I knew that you were in bonds; and I also knew that you were stoned for the word's sake; and you bore all these things with patience because the Lord was with you; and now you know that the Lord delivered you.

5 And now, my son Shiblon, I would that you should remember that asmuch as you shall put your trust in God, even so much you shall be delivered out of your trials, and your troubles, and your afflictions; and you shall be lifted up at the last day.

6 Now, my son, I would not that you should think that I know these things of myself, but it is the Spirit of God which is in me which makes these things known to me; for if I had not been born of God, I would not have known these things.

7 But, behold, the Lord in his great mercy sent his angel to declare to me that I must stop the work of destruction among his people.

8 And I have seen an angel face to face; and he spoke with me, and his voice was as thunder, and it shook the whole earth.

9 I was three days and three nights in the most bitter pain and anguish of soul; and never until I cried out to the Lord Jesus Christ for mercy did I receive a remission of my sins.

10 But, behold, I cried to him, and I found peace to my soul.

11 And now, my son, I have told you this that you may learn wisdom, that you may learn of me that there is no other way nor means whereby man can be saved only in and through Christ.

12 Behold, he is the life and the light of the world. Behold, he is the word of truth and righteousness.

13 And now, as you have begun to teach the word, even so I would that you should continue to teach; and I would that you would be diligent and temperate in all things.

14 See that you are not lifted up to pride: see that you do not boast in your own wisdom, nor of your much strength; use boldness, but not over-bearance.

15 And also see that you bridle all your passions that you may be filled with love; see that you refrain from idleness. Do not pray as the Zoramites do, for you have seen that they pray to be heard of men and to be praised for their wisdom.

16 Do not say, "O God, I thank thee that we are better than our brethren"; but rather say, "O Lord, forgive my unworthiness, and remember my brethren in mercy"; and acknowledge your unworthiness before God at all times.

17 And may the Lord bless your soul and receive you at the last day into his kingdom to sit down in peace.

18 Now go, my son, and teach the word to this people. Be sober. My son, farewell.

CHAPTER 19

The commandments of Alma to his son, Corianton.

AND now, my son, I have somewhat more to say to you than I said to your brother; for, behold, have you not observed the steadiness of your brother, his faithfulness, and his diligence in keeping the commandments of God?

2 Behold, has he not set a good example for you?

3 For you did not give so much heed to my words as did your brother, among the people of the Zoramites.

4 Now this is what I have against you: you went on boasting in your strength, and your wisdom.

5 And this is not all, my son. You did that which was grievous to me; for you forsook the ministry and went over into the land of Siron, among the borders of the Lamanites, after the harlot Isabel; she stole away the hearts of many, but this was no excuse for you, my son.

6 You should have tended to the ministry wherewith you were entrusted.

7 Know you not, my son, that these things are an abomination in the sight of the Lord, even most abominable above all sins, save it be the shedding of innocent blood or denying the Holy Ghost?

8 For, behold, if you deny the Holy Ghost when it once has had place in you, and you know that you deny it, behold, this is a sin which is unpardonable.

9 And whoever murders against the light and knowledge of God, it is not easy for him to obtain forgiveness; I say to you, my son, that it is not easy for him to obtain a forgiveness.

10 And now, my son, I would to God that you had not been guilty of so great a crime.

11 I would not dwell upon your crimes, to harrow up your soul, if it were not for your good.

12 But, behold, you cannot hide your crimes from God; and except you repent, they will stand as a testimony against you at the last day.

13 Now, my son, I would that you should repent, and forsake your sins, and go no more after the lusts of your eyes, but cross yourself in all these things; for except you do this you can in no wise inherit the kingdom of God.

212

14 O remember, and take it upon you, and cross yourself in these things.

15 And I command you to take it upon you to counsel with your elder brothers in your undertakings; for, behold, you are in your youth, and you stand in need to be nourished by your brothers.

16 Give heed to their counsel; suffer not yourself to be led away by any vain or foolish thing; suffer not that the devil lead away your heart again after those wicked harlots.

17 Behold, O my son, how great iniquity you brought upon the Zoramites; for when they saw your conduct, they would not believe in my words.

18 And now the Spirit of the Lord says to me, "Command thy children to do good, lest they lead away the hearts of many people to destruction."

19 Therefore I command you, my son, in the fear of God, that you refrain from your iniquities; that you turn to the Lord with all your mind, might, and strength; that you lead away the hearts of no more to do wickedly.

20 But rather return to them and acknowledge your faults, and acknowledge that wrong which you have done; seek not after riches nor the vain things of this world; for, behold, you cannot carry them with you.

21 And now, my son, I would say somewhat to you concerning the coming of Christ.

22 Behold, I say to you that it is he that surely shall come to take away the sins of the world; he comes to declare glad tidings of salvation to his people.

23 And now, my son, this was the ministry to which you were called: to declare these glad tidings to this people, to prepare their minds, or rather that salvation might come to them that they may prepare the minds of their children to hear the word at the time of his coming.

24 And now I will ease your mind somewhat on this subject. Behold, you marvel why these things should be known so long beforehand.

25 Behold, I say to you, Is not a soul at this time as precious to God as a soul will be at the time of his coming?

26 Is it not as necessary that the plan of redemption should be made known to this people as to their children?

27 Is it not as easy at this time for the Lord to send his angel to declare these glad tidings to us as to our children, or as after the time of his coming?

28 Now, my son, here is somewhat more I would say to you; for I perceive that your mind is worried concerning the resurrection of the dead.

29 Behold, I say to you that there is no resurrection—that this mortal does not put on immortality, this corruption does not put on incorruption—until after the coming of Christ.

30 Behold, he brings to pass the resurrection of the dead. But, behold, my son, the resurrection is not yet.

31 Now I unfold to you a mystery; nevertheless, there are many mysteries, which are kept, that no one knows save God himself.

32 But I show you one thing which I have inquired diligently of God that I might know—that is, concerning the resurrection.

33 Behold, there is a time appointed that all shall come forth from the dead.

34 Now when this time will come, no one knows; but God knows the time which is appointed.

35 Whether there shall be one time, or a second time, or a third time that men shall come forth from the dead, it matters not; for God knows all these things; and it suffices me to know that this is the case, that there is a time appointed that all shall rise from the dead.

36 Now there needs be a space between the time of death and the time of the resurrection.

37 And now I would inquire what becomes of the souls of men from this time of death to the time appointed for the resurrection?

38 Now whether there is more than one time appointed for men to rise, it matters not; for all do not die at once, and this matters not; all is as one day with God; and time only is measured to men.

39 Therefore there is a time appointed to men that they shall rise from the dead, and there is a space

between the time of death and the resurrection.

40 And now concerning this space of time: What becomes of the souls of men is the thing which I have inquired diligently of the Lord to know; and this is the thing of which I do know.

41 When the time comes when all shall rise, then shall they know that God knows all the times which are appointed to man.

42 Now concerning the state of the soul between death and the resurrection:

43 Behold, it has been made known to me by an angel that the spirits of all men, as soon as they are departed from this mortal body, whether they be good or evil, are taken home to that God who gave them life.

44 Then shall it come to pass that the spirits of those who are righteous are received into a state of happiness which is called paradise, a state of rest, a state of peace, where they shall rest from all their troubles, and from all care, and sorrow.

45 And then shall it come to pass that the spirits of the wicked, those who are evil—for, behold, they have no part nor portion of the Spirit of the Lord, for, behold, they choose evil works, rather than good, therefore the spirit of the devil enters into them and takes possession of their house— 46shall be cast out into outer darkness; there shall be weeping, and wailing, and gnashing of teeth; and this because of their own iniquity, being led captive by the will of the devil.

47 Now this is the state of the souls of the wicked, in darkness, and a state of awful, fearful looking for the fiery indignation of the wrath of God upon them; thus they remain in this state, as well as the righteous in paradise, until the time of their resurrection.

48 Now there are some who have understood that this state of happiness, and this state of misery of the soul, before the resurrection, was a first resurrection.

49 I admit it may be termed a resurrection—the raising of the spirit of the soul, and its consignation to happiness or misery—according to the words which have been spoken.

50 And, behold, again it has been spoken that there is a first resurrection—a resurrection of all those who have been, or who are, or who shall be, down to the resurrection of Christ from the dead.

51 Now we do not suppose that this first resurrection, which is spoken of in this manner, can be the resurrection of the souls, and their consignation to happiness or misery. You cannot suppose that this is what it means.

52 Behold, I say to you, No; but it means the reuniting of the soul with the body of those from the days of Adam down to the resurrection of Christ.

53 Now whether the souls and the bodies of those of whom we have spoken shall all be reunited at once, the wicked as well as the righteous, I do not say.

54 Let it suffice that I say that they all come forth; or in other words, their resurrection comes to pass before the resurrection of those who die after the resurrection of Christ.

55 Now, my son, I do not say that their resurrection comes at the resurrection of Christ; but, behold, I give it as my opinion that the souls and the bodies of the righteous are reunited at the resurrection of Christ and his ascension into heaven.

56 But whether it be at his resurrection or after, I do not say; but this much I say, there is a space between death and the resurrection of the body, and a state of the soul in happiness or in misery, until the time which is appointed of God that the dead shall come forth and be reunited, both soul and body, and be brought to stand before God, and be judged according to their works.

57 This brings about the restoration of those things which have been spoken by the mouths of the prophets.

58 The soul shall be restored to the body, and the body to the soul; and every limb and joint shall be restored to its body; even a hair of the head shall not be lost, but all things shall be restored to their proper and perfect frame.

59 Now, my son, this is the restoration which has been spoken of by the mouths of the prophets. And then shall the righteous shine forth in the kingdom of God.

60 But, behold, an awful death comes upon the wicked; for they die as to things pertaining to righteousness; for they are unclean, and no unclean thing can inherit the kingdom of God.

61 But they are cast out and consigned to partake of the fruits of their labors, or their works, which have been evil; and they drink the dregs of a bitter cup.

62 And now, my son, I have somewhat to say concerning the restoration which has been spoken of; for, behold, some have wrested the scriptures and have gone far astray because of this thing.

63 And I perceive that your mind has been worried also concerning this thing. But, behold, I will explain it to you.

64 I say to you, my son, that the plan of restoration is requisite with the justice of God; for it is requisite that all things should be restored to their proper order.

65 Behold, it is requisite and just, according to the power and resurrection of Christ, that the soul of man should be restored to its body, and that every part of the body should be restored to itself.

66 And it is requisite with the justice of God that men should be judged according to their works; and if their works were good in this life, and the desires of their hearts were good, they should also, at the last day, be restored to that which is good.

67 And if their works are evil, they shall be restored to him for evil; therefore, all things shall be restored to their proper order, everything to its natural frame, mortality raised to immortality, corruption to incorruption, raised to endless happiness to inherit the kingdom of God, or to endless misery to inherit the kingdom of the devil; 68the one on the one hand, the other on the other; the one raised to happiness according to his desires of happiness, or good according to his desires of good; and the other to evil according to his desires of evil; for as he has desired to do evil all the day long, even so shall he have his reward of evil when the night comes.

69 And so it is on the other hand. If he has repented of his sins and desired righteousness until the end of his days, even so shall he be rewarded to righteousness.

70 These are they that are redeemed of the Lord; these are they that are taken out, that are delivered from that endless night of darkness; and thus they stand or fall; for, behold, they are their own judges whether to do good or do evil.

71 Now the decrees of God are unalterable; therefore the way is prepared that whoever will may walk therein and be saved.

72 And now, behold, my son, do not risk one more offense against your God upon those points of doctrine which you have hitherto risked to commit sin.

73 Do not suppose, because it has been spoken concerning restoration, that you shall be restored from sin to happiness.

74 Behold, I say to you, Wickedness never was happiness.

75 All men that are in a state of nature, or I would say in a carnal state, are in the gall of bitterness and in the bonds of iniquity; they are without God in the world, and they have gone contrary to the nature of God; therefore they are in a state contrary to the nature of happiness.

76 And now, behold, is the meaning of the word "restoration" to take a thing of a natural state and place it in an unnatural state, or to place it in a state opposite to its nature?

77 O my son, this is not the case; but the meaning of the word "restoration" is to bring back again evil for evil, or carnal for carnal, or devilish for devilish, good for that which is good, righteous for that which is righteous, just for that which is just, merciful for that which is merciful.

78 Therefore, my son, see that you are merciful to your brethren; deal justly, judge righteously, and do good continually; and if you do all these things, then shall you receive your reward.

79 You shall have mercy restored to you again; you shall have justice restored to you again; you shall have a righteous judgment restored to you again.

80 And you shall have good rewarded to you again; for that which

you send out shall return to you again, and be restored; therefore the word "restoration" more fully condemns the sinner and justifies him not at all.

81 And now, my son, I perceive there is somewhat more which worries your mind, which you cannot understand, which is concerning the justice of God in the punishment of the sinner; for you try to suppose that it is injustice that the sinner should be consigned to a state of misery.

82 Now, my son, I will explain this thing to you; for, behold, after the Lord God sent our first parents forth from the garden of Eden to till the ground whence they were taken, he drew out the man, and he placed at the east end of the garden of Eden cherubim, and a flaming sword which turned every way to keep the tree of life.

83 Now we see that the man had become as God, knowing good and evil; and lest he should put forth his hand and take also of the tree of life, and eat, and live forever, the Lord God placed cherubim and the flaming sword that he should not partake of the fruit.

84 Thus we see that there was a time granted man to repent, a probationary time, a time to repent and serve God.

85 For, behold, if Adam had put forth his hand immediately and partaken of the tree of life, he would have lived forever, according to the word of God, having no space for repentance.

86 And also the word of God would have been void, and the great plan of salvation would have been frustrated.

87 But, behold, it was appointed to man to die; therefore as they were cut off from the tree of life, they should be cut off from the face of the earth; and mankind became lost forever; they became fallen man.

88 And now we see by this that our first parents were cut off, both temporally and spiritually, from the presence of the Lord; and thus we see they became subjects to follow after their own will.

89 Now, behold, it was not expedient that man should be reclaimed from this temporal death, for that

would destroy the great plan of happiness.

90 Therefore, as the soul could never die, and the fall had brought upon all mankind a spiritual death as well as a temporal one—that is, they were cut off from the presence of the Lord—it was expedient that mankind should be reclaimed from this spiritual death.

91 Therefore, as they had been carnal, sensual, and devilish by nature, this probationary state became a state for them to prepare; it became a preparatory state.

92 And now remember, my son, if it were not for the plan of redemption (laying it aside), as soon as they were dead their souls were miserable, being cut off from the presence of the Lord.

93 There was no means to reclaim men from this fallen state which man had brought upon himself because of his own disobedience.

94 Therefore, according to justice, the plan of redemption could be brought about only on conditions of repentance of men in this probationary state, this preparatory state; for except it were for these conditions, mercy could not take effect except it should destroy the work of justice.

95 Now the work of justice could not be destroyed; if so, God would cease to be God.

96 Thus we see that all mankind were fallen, and they were in the grasp of justice—the justice of God, which consigned them forever to be cut off from his presence.

97 And now the plan of mercy could not be brought about except an atonement should be made; therefore God himself atones for the sins of the world, to bring about the plan of mercy, to appease the demands of justice, that God might be a perfect, just God, and a merciful God also.

98 Now repentance could not come to men except there were a punishment, which also was as eternal as the life of the soul should be, affixed opposite to the plan of happiness, which was as eternal also as the life of the soul.

99 Now how could a man repent except he should sin? How could he sin if there was no law? How could

there be a law save there was a punishment?

100 But there was a punishment affixed, and a just law given which brought remorse of conscience to man.

101 Now if there was no law given that if a man murdered he should die, would he be afraid he should die if he should murder?

102 And also, if there was no law given against sin, men would not be afraid to sin.

103 And if there was no law given if men sinned, what could justice do, or mercy either, for they would have no claim upon the creature.

104 But there is a law given and a punishment affixed, and repentance granted; which repentance, mercy claims; otherwise, justice claims the creature and executes the law, and the law inflicts the punishment; if not so, the works of justice would be destroyed, and God would cease to be God.

105 But God ceases not to be God, and mercy claims the penitent, and mercy comes because of the atonement; and the atonement brings to pass the resurrection of the dead; and the resurrection of the dead brings back men into the presence of God.

106 Thus they are restored into his presence to be judged according to their works, according to the law and justice. For, behold, justice exercises all his demands, and also mercy claims all which is her own; and thus, none but the truly penitent are saved.

107 What, do you suppose that mercy can rob justice? I say to you, No; not one whit. If so, God would cease to be God.

108 Thus God brings about his great and eternal purposes which were prepared from the foundation of the world.

109 And thus comes about the salvation and redemption of men, and also their destruction and misery; therefore, O my son, whoever will come, may come and partake of the waters of life freely.

110 And whoever will not come, the same is not compelled to come; but in the last day it shall be restored to him, according to his deeds.

111 If he has desired to do evil and has not repented in his days, behold, evil shall be done to him, according to the restoration of God.

112 And now, my son, I desire that you should let these things trouble you no more, and only let your sins trouble you, with that trouble which shall bring you down to repentance.

113 O my son, I desire that you should deny the justice of God no more.

114 Do not endeavor to excuse yourself in the least point because of your sins, by denying the justice of God, but let the justice of God, and his mercy, and his long-suffering have full sway in your heart; let it bring you down to the dust in humility.

115 And now, O my son, you are called of God to preach the word to this people.

116 Go your way, declare the word with truth and soberness, that you may bring souls to repentance, that the great plan of mercy may have claim upon them.

117 And may God grant to you even according to my words. Amen.

CHAPTER 20

AND now it came to pass that the sons of Alma went forth among the people to declare the word to them. And Alma himself could not rest, and he also went forth.

2 We shall say no more concerning their preaching, except that they preached the word and the truth according to the spirit of prophecy and revelation; and they preached after the holy order of God by which they were called.

3 Now I return to an account of the wars between the Nephites and the Lamanites in the eighteenth year of the reign of the judges.

4 For, behold, it came to pass that the Zoramites became Lamanites; therefore in the commencement of the eighteenth year, the people of the Nephites saw that the Lamanites were coming upon them; therefore they made preparations for war; and they gathered together their armies in the land of Jershon.

5 And the Lamanites came with their thousands; and they came into the land of Antionum, which was the

land of the Zoramites; and a man by the name of Zerahemnah was their leader.

6 As the Amalekites were of a more wicked and murderous disposition than the Lamanites were, in and of themselves, therefore Zerahemnah appointed chief captains over the Lamanites, and they were all the Amalekites and the Zoramites.

7 This he did that he might preserve their hatred toward the Nephites, that he might bring them into subjection to the accomplishment of his designs.

8 For, behold, his designs were to stir up the Lamanites to anger against the Nephites; this he did that he might usurp great power over them, and also that he might gain power over the Nephites by bringing them into bondage.

9 Now the design of the Nephites was to support their lands, and their houses, and their wives and their children, that they might preserve them from the hands of their enemies, and also that they might preserve their rights and their privileges, 10and also their liberty, that they might worship God according to their desires; for they knew that if they should fall into the hands of the Lamanites, whoever should worship God in spirit and in truth, the true and the living God, the Lamanites would destroy.

11 And they also knew the extreme hatred of the Lamanites toward their brethren who were the people of Anti-Nephi-Lehi, who were called the people of Ammon, 12and they would not take up arms—they had entered into a covenant and they would not break it—therefore if they should fall into the hands of the Lamanites, they would be destroyed.

13 And the Nephites would not suffer that they should be destroyed; therefore they gave them lands for their inheritance.

14 And the people of Ammon gave to the Nephites a large portion of their substance to support their armies.

15 Thus the Nephites were compelled, alone, to withstand the Lamanites, who were a compound of Laman and Lemuel, and the sons of Ishmael, and all those who had dissented from the Nephites, who were Amalekites, and Zoramites, and the descendants of the priests of Noah.

16 Now those descendants were as numerous, nearly, as were the Nephites; and thus the Nephites were obliged to contend with their brethren even to bloodshed.

17 And it came to pass as the armies of the Lamanites had gathered together in the land of Antionum, behold, the armies of the Nephites were prepared to meet them in the land of Jershon.

18 Now the leader of the Nephites, or the man who had been appointed to be the chief captain over the Nephites, took the command of all the armies of the Nephites; and his name was Moroni.

19 And Moroni took all the command, and the government of their wars. And he was only twenty-five years old when he was appointed chief captain over the armies of the Nephites.

20 He met the Lamanites in the borders of Jershon, and his people were armed with swords, and with cimeters, and all manner of weapons of war.

21 And the armies of the Lamanites saw that the people of Nephi, had been prepared by Moroni with breastplates, and with arm shields, and also shields to defend their heads; and also they were dressed with thick clothing.

22 Now the army of Zerahemnah was not prepared with any such thing.

23 They had only their swords, and their cimeters, their bows and their arrows, their stones and their slings; and they were naked, save it were a skin which was girded about their loins; all were naked, save it were the Zoramites and the Amalekites.

24 But they were not armed with breastplates nor shields; therefore they were exceedingly afraid of the armies of the Nephites because of their armor, notwithstanding their number being so much greater than the Nephites.

25 And they dared not come against the Nephites in the borders of Jershon; therefore they departed out of the land of Antionum into the wilderness, and took their journey round about in the wilderness away by the head of the river Sidon, that they might come into the land of Manti and take possession

of the land; for they did not suppose that the armies of Moroni would know where they had gone.

26 But as soon as they had departed into the wilderness, Moroni sent spies into the wilderness to watch their camp; and Moroni also, knowing of the prophecies of Alma, sent certain men to him desiring him that he should inquire of the Lord where the armies of the Nephites should go to defend themselves against the Lamanites.

27 The word of the Lord came to Alma, and Alma informed the messenger of Moroni that the armies of the Lamanites were marching round about in the wilderness, that they might come over into the land of Manti, that they might commence an attack upon the weaker part of the people.

28 And those messengers went and delivered the message to Moroni.

29 Now Moroni, leaving a part of his army in the land of Jershon, lest by any means a part of the Lamanites should come into that land and take possession of the city, took the remaining part of his army and marched over into the land of Manti.

30 And he caused that all the people in that quarter of the land should gather themselves together to battle against the Lamanites to defend their lands and their country, their rights and their liberties; therefore they were prepared against the time of the coming of the Lamanites.

31 Moroni also caused that his army should be secreted in the valley which was near the bank of the river Sidon, which was on the west of the river Sidon, in the wilderness.

32 And Moroni placed spies round about that he might know when the camp of the Lamanites should come.

33 Now Moroni knew the intention of the Lamanites, that it was their intention to destroy their brethren or to subject them and bring them into bondage that they might establish a kingdom to themselves over all the land.

34 And he also knew that it was the only desire of the Nephites to preserve their lands, their liberty, and their church, therefore he thought it no sin that he should defend them by stratagem; therefore he found by his spies which course the Lamanites were to take.

35 Therefore he divided his army, and brought a part over into the valley, and concealed them on the east and on the south of the hill Riplah; and the remainder he concealed in the west valley on the west of the river Sidon, and so down into the borders of the land Manti.

36 Thus having placed his army according to his desire, he was prepared to meet them.

37 And it came to pass that the Lamanites came up on the north of the hill where a part of the army of Moroni was concealed.

38 As the Lamanites passed the hill Riplah and came into the valley, and began to cross the river Sidon, the army which was concealed on the south of the hill, which was led by a man whose name was Lehi, went forth and encircled the Lamanites on the east in their rear.

39 And the Lamanites, when they saw the Nephites coming upon them in their rear, turned about and began to contend with the army of Lehi; and the work of death commenced on both sides.

40 But it was more dreadful on the part of the Lamanites; for their nakedness was exposed to the heavy blows of the Nephites, with their swords and their cimeters, which brought death almost at every stroke; while on the other hand, only now and then a man fell among the Nephites by their swords and the loss of blood; ⁴¹for they were shielded from the more vital parts of the body, or the more vital parts of the body were shielded from the strokes of the Lamanites by their breastplates, and their arm shields, and their headplates; thus the Nephites carried on the work of death among the Lamanites.

42 And the Lamanites became frightened because of the great destruction among them, even until they began to flee toward the river Sidon.

43 They were pursued by Lehi and his men, and they were driven by Lehi into the waters of Sidon; and they crossed the waters of Sidon.

44 And Lehi retained his armies upon the bank of the river Sidon that they should not cross.

45 Moroni and his army met the Lamanites in the valley on the other side of the river Sidon and began to fall upon them, and to slay them.

46 And the Lamanites fled again before them toward the land of Manti, and they were met again by the armies of Moroni.

47 Now in this case, the Lamanites fought exceedingly well; never had the Lamanites been known to fight with such exceedingly great strength and courage, not even from the beginning.

48 And they were inspired by the Zoramites and the Amalekites who were their chief captains and leaders, and by Zerahemnah who was their chief captain, or their chief leader and commander.

49 They fought like dragons, and many of the Nephites were slain by their hands; for they smote in two many of their headplates; and they pierced many of their breastplates; and they smote off many of their arms; thus the Lamanites smote in their fierce anger.

50 Nevertheless, the Nephites were inspired by a better cause; for they were not fighting for monarchy nor power. But they were fighting for their homes, and their liberties, their wives, and their children, and their all, and for their rites of worship and their church.

51 And they were doing that which they felt was the duty which they owed to their God; for the Lord had said to them, and also to their fathers, "Inasmuch as ye are not guilty of the first offense, neither the second, ye shall not suffer yourselves to be slain by the hands of your enemies."

52 And again, the Lord has said, "Ye shall defend your families, even to bloodshed"; therefore were the Nephites contending with the Lamanites, to defend themselves, and their families, and their lands, their country, and their rights, and their religion.

53 When the men of Moroni saw the fierceness and the anger of the Lamanites, they were about to shrink and flee from them.

54 But Moroni, perceiving their intent, sent forth and inspired their hearts with these thoughts, the thoughts of their lands, their liberty, and their freedom from bondage.

55 And they turned upon the Lamanites, and they cried with one voice to the Lord their God for their liberty and their freedom from bondage.

56 And they began to stand against the Lamanites with power; and in the selfsame hour that they cried to the Lord for their freedom, the Lamanites began to flee before them, and they fled even to the waters of Sidon.

57 Now the Lamanites were more numerous, by more than double the number of the Nephites; nevertheless, they were driven insomuch that they were gathered together in one body in the valley upon the bank by the river Sidon.

58 Therefore the armies of Moroni encircled them, even on both sides of the river; for, behold, on the east were the men of Lehi.

59 And when Zerahemnah saw the men of Lehi on the east of the river Sidon and the armies of Moroni on the west of the river Sidon, that they were encircled by the Nephites, they were struck with terror.

60 Now Moroni, when he saw their terror, commanded his men that they should stop shedding their blood.

61 And it came to pass that they stopped, and withdrew a pace from them.

62 And Moroni said to Zerahemnah, "Behold, Zerahemnah, that we do not desire to be men of blood.

63 "You know that you are in our hands, yet we do not desire to slay you.

64 "Behold, we have not come out to battle against you, that we might shed your blood, for power; neither do we desire to bring any one to the yoke of bondage.

65 "But this is the very cause for which you have come against us; and you are angry with us because of our religion.

66 "But now you behold that the Lord is with us; and you behold that he has delivered you into our hands.

67 "And now I would that you should understand that this is done to us because of our religion and our faith in Christ. And now you see that you cannot destroy our faith.

68 "Now you see that this is the

true faith of God; you see that God will support, and keep, and preserve us, as long as we are faithful to him, and to our faith, and our religion.

69 "And never will the Lord suffer that we shall be destroyed except we should fall into transgression and deny our faith.

70 "Now, Zerahemnah, I command you in the name of that all-powerful God, who has strengthened our arms that we have gained power over you by our faith, by our religion, and by our rites of worship, and by our church, and by the sacred support which we owe to our wives and our children, by that liberty which binds us to our lands and our country, and also by the maintenance of the sacred word of God to which we owe all our happiness, [71]and all that is most dear to us, and this is not all—I command you by all the desires which you have for life that you deliver up your weapons of war to us, and we will seek not your blood, but we will spare your lives if you will go your way and come not again to war against us.

72 "And now if you do not this, behold, you are in our hands, and I will command my men that they shall fall upon you and inflict the wounds of death in your bodies that you may become extinct.

73 "Then we shall see who shall have power over this people; we shall see who will be brought into bondage."

74 When Zerahemnah had heard these sayings, he came forth and delivered up his sword, and his cimeter, and his bow into the hands of Moroni, and said to him:

75 "Behold, here are our weapons of war; we will deliver them up to you, but we will not suffer ourselves to take an oath to you which we know that we shall break, and also our children; but take our weapons of war and suffer that we may depart into the wilderness; otherwise we will retain our swords and we will perish or conquer.

76 "Behold, we are not of your faith; we do not believe that it is God that has delivered us into your hands; but we believe that it is your cunning that has preserved you from our swords.

77 "Behold, it is your breastplates and your shields that have preserved you."

78 When Zerahemnah had made an end of speaking these words, Moroni returned the sword, and the weapons of war which he had received, to Zerahemnah, saying, "Behold, we will end the conflict.

79 "Now I cannot retract the words which I have spoken; therefore as the Lord lives, you shall not depart except you depart with an oath that you will not return again against us to war.

80 "Now as you are in our hands, we will spill your blood upon the ground, or you shall submit to the conditions which I have proposed."

81 When Moroni had said these words, Zerahemnah retained his sword, and he was angry with Moroni and he rushed forward that he might slay Moroni.

82 But as he raised his sword, behold, one of Moroni's soldiers smote it even to the earth, and it broke by the hilt; and he also smote Zerahemnah, that he took off his scalp, and it fell to the earth.

83 And Zerahemnah withdrew from before them into the midst of his soldiers.

84 And the soldier who stood by, who smote off the scalp of Zerahemnah, took up the scalp from the ground by the hair, and laid it upon the point of his sword, and he stretched it forth to them, saying to them with a loud voice:

85 "Even as this scalp has fallen to the earth, which is the scalp of your chief, so shall you fall to the earth except you will deliver up your weapons of war and depart with a covenant of peace."

86 Now there were many, when they heard these words and saw the scalp which was upon the sword, that were struck with fear, and many came forth and threw down their weapons of war at the feet of Moroni and entered into a covenant of peace.

87 And as many as entered into a covenant were suffered to depart into the wilderness.

88 Zerahemnah was exceedingly angry, and he stirred up the remainder of his soldiers to anger, to contend

more powerfully against the Nephites.

89 And now Moroni was angry because of the stubbornness of the Lamanites; therefore he commanded his people that they should fall upon them and slay them.

90 They began to slay them; and the Lamanites contended with their swords and their mights.

91 But, behold, their naked skins and their bare heads were exposed to the sharp swords of the Nephites; and, behold, they were pierced and smitten, ⁹²and fell exceedingly fast before the swords of the Nephites; and they began to be swept down, even as the soldier of Moroni had prophesied.

93 Now Zerahemnah, when he saw that they were all about to be destroyed, cried mightily to Moroni, promising that he and his people would covenant with them, if they would spare the lives of the remainder, that they never would come to war against them.

94 And Moroni caused that the work of death should cease again among the people.

95 And he took the weapons of war from the Lamanites; and after they had entered into a covenant of peace with him, they were suffered to depart into the wilderness.

96 Now their dead were not numbered, because of the greatness of the number; but the number of dead was exceedingly great, both of the Nephites and of the Lamanites.

97 And they cast their dead into the waters of Sidon; and they have gone forth, and are buried in the depths of the sea.

98 And the armies of the Nephites, or of Moroni, returned and came to their houses and their lands.

99 Thus ended the eighteenth year of the reign of the judges over the people of Nephi.

100 And thus ended the record of Alma, which was written upon the plates of Nephi.

CHAPTER 21

The account of the people of Nephi, and their wars and dissensions in the days of Helaman, according to the record of Helaman, which he kept in his days.

BEHOLD, the people of Nephi were exceedingly rejoiced because the Lord had again delivered them out of the hands of their enemies.

2 Therefore they gave thanks to the Lord their God; and they fasted much and prayed much, and they worshiped God with exceedingly great joy.

3 In the nineteenth year of the reign of the judges over the people of Nephi, Alma came to his son Helaman and said to him, "Do you believe the words which I spoke to you concerning those records which have been kept?"

4 And Helaman said to him, "I believe."

5 Alma said again, "Do you believe in Jesus Christ, who shall come?" And he said, "I believe all the words which you have spoken."

6 And Alma said to him again, "Will you keep my commandments?" And he said, "I will keep your commandments with all my heart."

7 Then Alma said to him, "You are blessed; and the Lord shall prosper you in this land.

8 "But, behold, I have somewhat to prophesy to you; but what I prophesy to you, you shall not make known; what I prophesy to you shall not be made known even until the prophecy is fulfilled; therefore write the words which I shall say.

9 "And these are the words: Behold, I perceive that this very people, the Nephites, according to the spirit of revelation which is in me, in four hundred years from the time that Jesus Christ shall manifest himself to them, shall dwindle in unbelief.

10 "And then shall they see wars and pestilences, famines and bloodshed, even until the people of Nephi shall become extinct; ¹¹and this because they shall dwindle in unbelief, and fall into the works of darkness, and lasciviousness, and all manner of iniquities.

12 "I say to you that, because

they shall sin against so great light
and knowledge, from that day, even
the fourth generation shall not all pass
away before this great iniquity shall
come.

13 "And when that great day
comes, behold, the time will very
soon come that those who are now,
or the seed of those who are now,
numbered among the people of the
Nephites shall no more be numbered
among the people of Nephi.

14 "But whoever remains, and is
not destroyed in that great and
dreadful day, shall be numbered
among the Lamanites and shall become like them, all except a few who
shall be called the disciples of the
Lord.

15 "And them shall the Lamanites
pursue, even until they shall become
extinct. And now, because of iniquity, this prophecy shall be fulfilled."

16 After Alma had said these
things to Helaman, he blessed him,
and also his other sons; and he also
blessed the earth for the righteous'
sake.

17 And he said, "Thus says the
Lord God: 'Cursed shall be the land,
even this land, to every nation,
kindred, tongue, and people which
do wickedly, unto destruction when
they are fully ripe.'

18 "As I have said, so shall it be,
for this is the cursing and the blessing
of God upon the land, for the Lord
cannot look upon sin with the least
degree of allowance."

19 When Alma had said these
words, he blessed the church, even all
those who should stand fast in the
faith from that time henceforth.

20 And when Alma had done this,
he departed out of the land of
Zarahemla as if to go into the land
of Melek. And it came to pass that
he was never heard of more; as to his
death or burial we know not.

21 Behold, this we know, that he
was a righteous man; and the saying
went abroad in the church that he
was taken up by the Spirit, or buried
by the hand of the Lord, even as
Moses.

22 But, behold, the scripture says
the Lord took Moses to himself; and
we suppose that he has also received

Alma, in the spirit, to himself; but
we know nothing concerning his
death and burial.

23 In the commencement of the
nineteenth year of the reign of the
judges over the people of Nephi,
Helaman went forth among the
people to declare the word to them.

24 For, behold, because of their
wars with the Lamanites, and the
many little dissensions and disturbances which had been among the
people, it became expedient that the
word of God should be declared
among them, and that a regulation
should be made throughout the
church.

25 Therefore Helaman and his
brethren went forth to establish
the church again in all the land, in
every city throughout all the land
which was possessed by the people
of Nephi.

26 And they appointed priests and
teachers throughout all the land over
all the churches.

27 And now it came to pass that
after Helaman and his brethren had
appointed priests and teachers over
the churches, there arose a dissension
among them, and they would not
give heed to the words of Helaman
and his brethren.

28 But they grew proud, being
lifted up in their hearts because of
their exceedingly great riches; therefore they grew rich in their own eyes
and would not give heed to their
words to walk uprightly before God.

29 And as many as would not
hearken to the words of Helaman
and his brethren were gathered together against their brethren.

30 And, behold, they were exceedingly angry, insomuch that they were
determined to slay them.

31 Now the leader of those who
were angry against their brethren
was a large and a strong man; and
his name was Amalickiah.

32 And Amalickiah was desirous
to be a king; and those people who
were angry were also desirous that
he should be their king; and they
were, the greater part of them, the
lower judges of the land; and they
were seeking for power.

33 And they had been led by the
flatteries of Amalickiah, that, if they

would support him and establish him to be their king, he would make them rulers over the people.

34 Thus they were led away by Amalickiah to dissensions, notwithstanding the preaching of Helaman and his brethren, and notwithstanding their exceedingly great care over the church, for they were high priests over the church.

35 And there were many in the church who believed in the flattering words of Amalickiah, therefore they dissented even from the church.

36 Thus were the affairs of the people of Nephi exceedingly precarious and dangerous, notwithstanding their great victory which they had had over the Lamanites, and their great rejoicings which they had had because of their deliverance by the hands of the Lord.

37 Thus we see how quickly the children of men forget the Lord their God, and how quick to do iniquity and to be led away by the evil one; and we also see the great wickedness one very wicked man can cause to take place among the children of men.

38 We see that Amalickiah, because he was a man of cunning devices and a man of many flattering words, led away the hearts of many people to do wickedly, 39and to seek to destroy the church of God and to destroy the foundation of liberty which God had granted them, or which blessing God had sent upon the face of the land for the righteous' sake.

40 When Moroni, who was the chief commander of the armies of the Nephites, heard of these dissensions, he was angry with Amalickiah.

41 And he rent his coat; and he took a piece thereof and wrote upon it, "In memory of our God, our religion and freedom, and our peace, our wives, and our children"; and he fastened it upon the end of a pole.

42 And he fastened on his headplate, and his breastplate, and his shields, and girded on his armor about his loins; and he took the pole which had on the end thereof his rent coat which he called by the title of liberty.

43 And he bowed himself to the earth, and he prayed mightily to his God for the blessings of liberty to rest upon his brethren as long as a band of Christians should remain to possess the land.

44 For thus were all the true believers of Christ, who belonged to the church of God, called by those who did not belong to the church; and those who did belong to the church were faithful.

45 All those who were true believers in Christ took upon them gladly the name of Christ, or Christians, as they were called because of their belief in Christ, who should come; and therefore, at this time, Moroni prayed that the cause of the Christians and the freedom of the land might be favored.

46 When he had poured out his soul to God, he dedicated all the land which was south of the land Desolation, in fine, all the land, both on the north and south, as a chosen land and the land of liberty.

47 And he said, "Surely God shall not suffer that we who are despised because we take upon us the name of Christ shall be trodden down and destroyed, until we bring it upon us by our own transgressions."

48 When Moroni had said these words, he went forth among the people, waving the rent of his garment in the air, that all might see the writing which he had written upon the rent, and crying with a loud voice, saying:

49 "Behold, all who will maintain this title upon the land, let them come forth in the strength of the Lord and enter into a covenant that they will maintain their rights and their religion, that the Lord God may bless them."

50 When Moroni had proclaimed these words, behold, the people came running together, with their armor girded about their loins, rending their garments in token, or as a covenant, that they would not forsake the Lord their God.

51 Or, in other words, if they should transgress the commandments of God, or fall into transgression, and be ashamed to take upon them the name of Christ, the Lord should rend them even as they had rent their garments.

52 Now this was the covenant which they made, and they cast their garments at the feet of Moroni, saying, "We covenant with our God that we shall be destroyed, even as our brethren in the land northward, if we should fall into transgression.

53 "He may cast us at the feet of our enemies, even as we have cast our garments at your feet, to be trodden under foot, if we shall fall into transgression."

54 Moroni said to them, "Behold, we are a remnant of the seed of Jacob; we are a remnant of the seed of Joseph whose coat was rent by his brethren into many pieces.

55 "And now, behold, let us remember to keep the commandments of God, or our garments shall be rent by our brethren, and we be cast into prison, or be sold, or be slain. Let us preserve our liberty, as a remnant of Joseph.

56 "Let us remember the words of Jacob before his death; for, behold, he saw that a part of the remnant of the coat of Joseph was preserved, and had not decayed.

57 "And he said, 'Even as this remnant of garment of my son has been preserved, so shall a remnant of the seed of my sons be preserved by the hand of God, and be taken to himself, while the remainder of the seed of Joseph shall perish even as the remnant of his garment.

58 "'Behold, this gives my soul sorrow; nevertheless, my soul has joy in my son because of that part of his seed which shall be taken unto God.'

59 "Now, behold, this was the language of Jacob.

60 "And now, who knows but that the remnant of the seed of Joseph, which shall perish as his garment, are those who have dissented from us; and even it shall be us, if we do not stand fast in the faith of Christ."

61 When Moroni had said these words, he went forth, and also sent forth in all the parts of the land where there were dissensions, and gathered together all the people who were desirous to maintain their liberty, to stand against Amalickiah

and those who had dissented who were called Amalickiahites.

62 And when Amalickiah saw that the people of Moroni were more numerous than the Amalickiahites, and he also saw that his people were doubtful concerning the justice of the cause which they had undertaken, therefore, fearing that he should not gain the point, he took those of his people who would, and departed into the land of Nephi.

63 Now Moroni thought it was not expedient that the Lamanites should have any more strength; therefore he thought to cut off the people of Amalickiah, or to take them and bring them back, and put Amalickiah to death.

64 For he knew that they would stir up the Lamanites to anger against them and cause them to come to battle against them; and this he knew that Amalickiah would do that he might achieve his purposes.

65 Therefore Moroni thought it was expedient that he should take his armies, who had gathered together and armed themselves and entered into a covenant to keep the peace.

66 And he took his army and marched out into the wilderness to cut off the course of Amalickiah in the wilderness.

67 And he did according to his desires, and marched forth into the wilderness, and headed the armies of Amalickiah.

68 And Amalickiah fled with a small number of his men, and the remainder were delivered up into the hands of Moroni and were taken back into the land of Zarahemla.

69 Now Moroni was a man who was appointed by the chief judges and the voice of the people, therefore he had power according to his will, with the armies of the Nephites, to establish and to exercise authority over them.

70 And it came to pass that all of the Amalickiahites that would not enter into a covenant to support the cause of freedom, that they might maintain a free government, he caused to be put to death; and there were but few who denied the covenant of freedom.

71 And he caused the title of liberty to be hoisted upon every tower which was in all the land which was possessed by the Nephites; and thus Moroni planted the standard of liberty among the Nephites.

72 They began to have peace again in the land; and thus they maintained peace in the land until nearly the end of the nineteenth year of the reign of the judges.

73 And Helaman and the high priests also maintained order in the church; even for the space of four years they had much peace and rejoicing in the church.

74 And it came to pass that there were many who died, firmly believing that their souls were redeemed by the Lord Jesus Christ; thus they went out of the world rejoicing.

75 There were some who died with fevers, which at some seasons of the year were very frequent in the land; 76but not so much so with fevers, because of the excellent qualities of the many plants and roots which God had prepared to remove the cause of diseases to which man was subject by the nature of the climate.

77 But there were many who died with old age; and those who died in the faith of Christ are happy in him, as we must suppose.

78 Now we will return in our record to Amalickiah and those who had fled with him into the wilderness; for, behold, he had taken those who went with him, and had gone up into the land of Nephi among the Lamanites, and stirred up the Lamanites to anger against the people of Nephi, insomuch that the king of the Lamanites sent a proclamation throughout all his land, among all his people, that they should gather themselves together again to go to battle against the Nephites.

79 When the proclamation had gone forth among them, they were exceedingly afraid; they feared to displease the king, and they also feared to go to battle against the Nephites lest they should lose their lives.

80 And they would not, or the greater part of them would not, obey the commandments of the king.

81 The king was angry because of their disobedience; therefore he gave Amalickiah the command of that part of his army which was obedient to his commands, and commanded him that he should go forth and compel them to arms.

82 Now, behold, this was the desire of Amalickiah; for being a very subtle man to do evil, therefore he laid the plan in his heart to dethrone the king of the Lamanites.

83 And now he had got the command of those parts of the Lamanites who were in favor of the king, and he sought to gain favor of those who were not obedient.

84 Therefore he went forward to the place which was called Onidah, for there had all the Lamanites fled; for they discovered the army coming, and supposing that they were coming to destroy them, therefore they fled to Onidah, to the place of arms.

85 And they had appointed a man to be a king and a leader over them, being fixed in their minds with a determined resolution that they would not be subjected to go against the Nephites.

86 And they had gathered themselves together upon the top of the mount which was called Antipas in preparation to battle.

87 Now it was not Amalickiah's intention to give them battle according to the commandments of the king; but, behold, it was his intention to gain favor with the armies of the Lamanites, that he might place himself at their head, and dethrone the king, and take possession of the kingdom.

88 And, behold, it came to pass that he caused his army to pitch their tents in the valley which was near the mount Antipas.

89 And when it was night, he sent a secret embassy into the mount Antipas, desiring that the leader of those who were upon the mount, whose name was Lehonti, should come down to the foot of the mount, for he desired to speak with him.

90 When Lehonti received the message, he dared not go down to the foot of the mount.

91 And Amalickiah sent again the second time, desiring him to come

down. And Lehonti would not; and he sent again the third time.

92 When Amalickiah found that he could not get Lehonti to come down from the mount, he went up into the mount, nearly to Lehonti's camp; and he sent again the fourth time his message to Lehonti, desiring that he would come down, and that he would bring his guards with him.

93 When Lehonti had come down with his guards to Amalickiah, Amalickiah desired him to come down with his army in the night time, and surround those men in their camp over whom the king had given him command, and he would deliver them into Lehonti's hands if he would make him (Amalickiah) a second leader over the whole army.

94 Lehonti came down with his men and surrounded the men of Amalickiah, so that, before they awoke at the dawn of the day, they were surrounded by the armies of Lehonti.

95 When they saw they were surrounded, they pleaded with Amalickiah that he would suffer them to fall in with their brethren that they might not be destroyed.

96 Now this was the very thing which Amalickiah desired. And he delivered his men, contrary to the commands of the king.

97 This was the thing that Amalickiah desired, that he might accomplish his designs in dethroning the king.

98 Now it was the custom among the Lamanites, if their chief leader was killed, to appoint the second leader to be their chief leader.

99 And Amalickiah caused that one of his servants should administer poison by degrees to Lehonti, that he died.

100 When Lehonti was dead, the Lamanites appointed Amalickiah to be their leader and chief commander.

101 And Amalickiah marched with his armies (for he had gained his desires) to the land of Nephi, to the city of Nephi, which was the chief city.

102 And the king came out to meet him with his guards; for he supposed that Amalickiah had ful-

filled his commands, and that Amalickiah had gathered together so great an army to go against the Nephites to battle.

103 But, behold, as the king came out to meet him, Amalickiah caused that his servants should go forth to meet the king.

104 And they went and bowed themselves before the king as if to reverence him because of his greatness.

105 The king put forth his hand to raise them, as was the custom with the Lamanites, as a token of peace, which custom they had taken from the Nephites.

106 And when he had raised the first from the ground, behold, he stabbed the king to the heart, and he fell to the earth.

107 Now the servants of the king fled; and the servants of Amalickiah raised a cry, saying, "Behold, the servants of the king have stabbed him to the heart, and he has fallen, and they have fled; behold, come and see."

108 Amalickiah commanded that his armies should march forth and see what had happened to the king.

109 And when they had come to the spot, and found the king lying in his gore, Amalickiah pretended to be angry and said, "Whoever loved the king, let him go forth and pursue his servants, that they may be slain."

110 All who loved the king, when they heard these words, came forth and pursued after the servants of the king.

111 Now when the servants of the king saw an army pursuing after them, they were frightened again, and fled into the wilderness, and came over in the land of Zarahemla, and joined the people of Ammon.

112 And the army which pursued after them returned, having pursued after them in vain; and thus Amalickiah, by his fraud, gained the hearts of the people.

113 On the morrow, he entered the city Nephi, with his armies, and took possession of the city.

114 Now when the queen heard that the king was slain; for Amalickiah had sent an embassy to the queen informing her that the king had been

slain by his servants, that he had pursued them with his army, but it was in vain, and they had made their escape.

115 Therefore when the queen had received this message, she sent to Amalickiah, desiring him that he would spare the people of the city; and she also desired him that he should come to her; and she also desired him that he should bring witnesses with him to testify concerning the death of the king.

116 Amalickiah took the same servant that slew the king, and all they who were with him, and went to the queen, to the place where she sat.

117 And they all testified to her that the king was slain by his own servants; and they said also, "They have fled; does not this testify against them?"

118 Thus they satisfied the queen concerning the death of the king.

119 Amalickiah sought the favor of the queen and took her to wife; thus by his fraud, and by the assistance of his cunning servants, he obtained the kingdom.

120 And he was acknowledged king throughout all the land, among all the people of the Lamanites, who were composed of the Lamanites, and the Lemuelites, and the Ishmaelites, and all the dissenters of the Nephites, from the reign of Nephi down to the present time.

121 Now these dissenters had the same instruction and the same information as the Nephites, having been instructed in the same knowledge of the Lord; nevertheless, it is strange to relate, not long after their dissensions they became more hardened and impenitent, and more wild, wicked, and ferocious than the Lamanites, [122]drinking in the traditions of the Lamanites, giving way to indolence and all manner of lasciviousness, entirely forgetting the Lord their God.

123 Now as soon as Amalickiah had obtained the kingdom, he began to inspire the hearts of the Lamanites against the people of Nephi; and he appointed men to speak to the Lamanites from their towers against the Nephites.

124 And thus he inspired their hearts against the Nephites insomuch that in the latter end of the nineteenth year of the reign of the judges, having accomplished his designs thus far, and having been made king over the Lamanites, he sought also to reign over all the land, [125]and all the people who were in the land, the Nephites as well as the Lamanites. Therefore he had accomplished his design, for he had hardened the hearts of the Lamanites, and blinded their minds, and stirred them up to anger, insomuch that he had gathered together a numerous host to go to battle against the Nephites, for he was determined, because of the greatness of the number of his people, to overpower the Nephites and to bring them into bondage.

126 Thus he appointed chief captains of the Zoramites, they being most acquainted with the strength of the Nephites, and their places of resort, and the weakest parts of their cities; therefore he appointed them to be chief captains over his armies.

127 And it came to pass that they took their camp and moved forth toward the land of Zarahemla, in the wilderness.

128 Now while Amalickiah had thus been obtaining power by fraud and deceit, Moroni, on the other hand, had been preparing the minds of the people to be faithful to the Lord their God.

129 He had been strengthening the armies of the Nephites, and erecting small forts, or places of resort, throwing up banks of earth round about to enclose his armies, and also building walls of stone to encircle their cities and the borders of their lands, all round about the land.

130 And in their weakest fortifications, he placed the greatest number of men; and thus he fortified and strengthened the land which was possessed by the Nephites.

131 Thus he was preparing to support their liberty, their lands, their wives, and their children, and their peace, that they might live to the Lord their God, and that they might maintain that which was called by their enemies the cause of Christians.

132 And Moroni was a strong and a mighty man; he was a man of a

perfect understanding, a man who did not delight in bloodshed, a man whose soul rejoiced in the liberty and the freedom of his country and his brethren from bondage and slavery.

133 He was a man whose heart swelled with thanksgiving to his God for the many privileges and blessings which he bestowed upon his people, a man who labored exceedingly for the welfare and safety of his people.

134 And he was a man who was firm in the faith of Christ, and he had sworn with an oath to defend his people, his rights, and his country, and his religion, even to the loss of his blood.

135 Now the Nephites were taught to defend themselves against their enemies, even to the shedding of blood, if it were necessary.

136 And they were also taught never to give an offense, and never to raise the sword except it were against an enemy to preserve their lives.

137 And this was their faith, that by so doing God would prosper them in the land; or in other words, if they were faithful in keeping the commandments of God, he would prosper them in the land, and warn them to flee, or to prepare for war according to their danger, 138and also that God would make it known to them where they should go to defend themselves against their enemies; and by so doing, the Lord would deliver them; and this was the faith of Moroni.

139 And his heart gloried in it, not in the shedding of blood, but in doing good, in preserving his people, in keeping the commandments of God, and resisting iniquity.

140 Verily, verily I say to you, if all men had been, and were, and ever would be like Moroni, behold, the very powers of hell would have been shaken forever, and the devil would never have power over the hearts of the children of men.

141 Behold, he was a man like Ammon, the son of Mosiah, and even the other sons of Mosiah, and also Alma and his sons, for they were all men of God.

142 Now, behold, Helaman and his brethren were no less serviceable to the people than was Moroni; for they preached the word of God, and

they baptized unto repentance all men who would hearken to their words.

143 Thus they went forth, and the people humbled themselves because of their words, insomuch that they were highly favored of the Lord; and thus they were free from wars and contentions among themselves, even for the space of four years.

144 But, as I have said, in the latter end of the nineteenth, notwithstanding their peace among themselves, they were compelled reluctantly to contend with their brethren, the Lamanites.

145 And in fine, their wars never ceased for the space of many years with the Lamanites, notwithstanding their much reluctance.

146 Now they were sorry to take up arms against the Lamanites because they did not delight in the shedding of blood; and this was not all, they were sorry to be the means of sending so many of their brethren out of this world into an eternal world unprepared to meet their God.

147 Nevertheless, they could not suffer that their wives and their children should be massacred by the barbarous cruelty of those who were once their brethren, and had dissented from their church, and had left them, and had gone to destroy them by joining the Lamanites.

148 They could not bear that their brethren should rejoice over the blood of the Nephites as long as there were any who should keep the commandments of God, for the promise of the Lord was that if they should keep his commandments, they should prosper in the land.

149 In the eleventh month of the nineteenth year, on the tenth day of the month, the armies of the Lamanites were seen approaching toward the land of Ammonihah.

150 And, behold, the city had been rebuilt, and Moroni had stationed an army by the borders of the city, and they had cast up dirt round about to shield them from the arrows and the stones of the Lamanites; for, behold, they fought with stones and with arrows.

151 Behold, I said that the city of Ammonihah had been rebuilt. I meant to say that it was in part rebuilt;

and because the Lamanites had destroyed it once because of the iniquity of the people, they supposed that it would again become an easy prey for them.

152 But, behold, how great was their disappointment; for, behold, the Nephites had dug up a ridge of earth round about them which was so high that the Lamanites could not cast their stones and arrows at them, that they might take effect, neither could they come upon them, save it was by their place of entrance.

153 Now at this time, the chief captains of the Lamanites were astonished exceedingly because of the wisdom of the Nephites in preparing their places of security.

154 The leaders of the Lamanites had supposed, because of the greatness of their numbers, that they should be privileged to come upon them as they had hitherto done.

155 And they had also prepared themselves with shields and with breastplates; and they had also prepared themselves with garments of skins, very thick garments, to cover their nakedness.

156 Being thus prepared, they supposed that they should easily overpower and subject their brethren to the yoke of bondage, or slay and massacre them according to their pleasure.

157 But, behold, to their utter astonishment, the Nephites were prepared for them in a manner which never had been known among all the children of Lehi.

158 Now they were prepared for the Lamanites, to battle after the manner of the instructions of Moroni.

159 And it came to pass that the Lamanites, or the Amalickiahites, were exceedingly astonished at their manner of preparation for war.

160 Now if King Amalickiah had come down out of the land of Nephi at the head of his army, perhaps he would have caused the Lamanites to attack the Nephites at the city of Ammonihah; for, behold, he cared not for the blood of his people.

161 But, behold, Amalickiah himself did not come down to battle.

162 And, behold, his chief captains dared not attack the Nephites at the

city of Ammonihah, for Moroni had altered the management of affairs among the Nephites insomuch that the Lamanites were disappointed in their places of retreat, and they could not come upon them.

163 Therefore they retreated into the wilderness, and took their camp, and marched toward the land of Noah, supposing that to be the next best place for them to come against the Nephites.

164 For they knew not that Moroni had fortified or had built forts of security for every city in all the land round about.

165 Therefore they marched forward to the land of Noah with a firm determination; and their chief captains came forward and took an oath that they would destroy the people of that city.

166 But, behold, to their astonishment, the city of Noah, which had hitherto been a weak place, had now, by the means of Moroni, become strong, even to exceed the strength of the city Ammonihah.

167 And now, behold, this was wisdom in Moroni; for he had supposed that they would be frightened at the city Ammonihah; and as the city of Noah had hitherto been the weakest part of the land, therefore they would march there to battle; and thus it was, according to his desires.

168 And, behold, Moroni had appointed Lehi to be chief captain over the men of that city; and it was that same Lehi who fought with the Lamanites in the valley on the east of the river Sidon.

169 When the Lamanites found that Lehi commanded the city, they were again disappointed, for they feared Lehi exceedingly; nevertheless, their chief captains had sworn with an oath to attack the city; therefore they brought up their armies.

170 Now, behold, the Lamanites could not get into their forts of security by any other way save by the entrance, because of the highness of the bank which had been thrown up and the depth of the ditch which had been dug round about.

171 And thus were the Nephites prepared to destroy all such as should attempt to climb up to enter

the fort by any other way, by casting over stones and arrows at them.

172 Thus they were prepared, a body of their strongest men with their swords and their slings, to smite down all who should attempt to come into their place of security by the place of entrance; and thus were they prepared to defend themselves against the Lamanites.

173 And it came to pass that the captains of the Lamanites brought up their armies before the place of entrance and began to contend with the Nephites to get into their place of security.

174 But, behold, they were driven back from time to time, insomuch that they were slain with an immense slaughter.

175 Now when they found that they could not gain power over the Nephites by the pass, they began to dig down their banks of earth, that they might obtain a pass to their armies, that they might have an equal chance to fight.

176 But, behold, in these attempts, they were swept off by the stones and the arrows which were thrown at them; and instead of filling up their ditches by pulling down the banks of earth, they were filled up in a measure with their dead and wounded bodies.

177 Thus the Nephites had all power over their enemies; and thus the Lamanites attempted to destroy the Nephites, until their chief captains were all slain.

178 And more than a thousand of the Lamanites were slain, while on the other hand there was not a single soul of the Nephites which was slain.

179 There were about fifty who were wounded, who had been exposed to the arrows of the Lamanites through the pass, but they were shielded by their shields, and their breastplates, and their headplates, insomuch that their wounds were upon their legs, many of which were very severe.

180 When the Lamanites saw that their chief captains were all slain, they fled into the wilderness.

181 And they returned to the land of Nephi to inform their king, Amal-ickiah, who was a Nephite by birth, concerning their great loss.

182 And he was exceedingly angry with his people because he had not obtained his desire over the Nephites; he had not subjected them to the yoke of bondage.

183 He was exceedingly angry, and he cursed God, and also Moroni, swearing with an oath that he would drink his blood; and this because Moroni had kept the commandments of God in preparing for the safety of his people.

184 On the other hand, the people of Nephi thanked the Lord their God because of his matchless power in delivering them from the hands of their enemies.

185 Thus ended the nineteenth year of the reign of the judges over the people of Nephi; and there was continual peace among them and exceedingly great prosperity in the church because of their heed and diligence which they gave to the word of God, which was declared to them by Helaman, and Shiblon, and Corianton, and Ammon, and his brethren, [186]and by all those who had been ordained by the holy order of God, being baptized unto repentance, and sent forth to preach among the people.

CHAPTER 22

NOW Moroni did not stop making preparations for war and to defend his people against the Lamanites; for he caused that his armies should commence in the twentieth year of the reign of the judges to dig up heaps of earth round about all the cities throughout all the land which was possessed by the Nephites.

2 And upon the top of these ridges of earth he caused that there should be timbers, even works of timbers built up to the height of a man, round about the cities.

3 And he caused that upon those works of timbers there should be a frame of pickets built round about; and they were strong and high; and he caused towers to be erected that overlooked those works of pickets.

4 And he caused places of security to be built upon those towers that

the stones and the arrows of the Lamanites could not hurt them.

5 They were prepared that they could cast stones from the top thereof, according to their pleasure and their strength, and slay him who should attempt to approach near the walls of the city.

6 Thus Moroni prepared strongholds against the coming of their enemies round about every city in all the land.

7 And it came to pass that Moroni caused that his armies should go forth into the east wilderness; and they went forth and drove all the Lamanites who were in the east wilderness into their own lands which were south of the land of Zarahemla.

8 And the land of Nephi ran in a straight course from the east sea to the west.

9 When Moroni had driven all the Lamanites out of the east wilderness, which was north of the lands of their own possessions, he caused that the inhabitants who were in the land of Zarahemla, and in the land round about, should go forth into the east wilderness, even to the borders by the seashore, and possess the land.

10 And he also placed armies on the south, in the borders of their possessions, and caused them to erect fortifications that they might secure their armies and their people from the hands of their enemies.

11 Thus he cut off all the strongholds of the Lamanites in the east wilderness, and also on the west, fortifying the line between the Nephites and the Lamanites, between the land of Zarahemla and the land of Nephi, from the west sea, running by the head of the river Sidon, 12the Nephites possessing all the land northward, even all the land which was northward of the land Bountiful, according to their pleasure.

13 Thus Moroni, with his armies which increased daily because of the assurance of protection which his works brought forth to them, sought to cut off the strength and the power of the Lamanites from the lands of their possessions, that they should have no power upon the lands of their possessions.

14 And it came to pass that the Nephites began the foundation of a city; and they called the name of the city Moroni, and it was by the east sea, and it was on the south by the line of the possessions of the Lamanites.

15 And they also began a foundation for a city between the city of Moroni and the city of Aaron, joining the borders of Aaron and Moroni; and they called the name of the city, or the land, Nephihah.

16 And they also began, in that same year, to build many cities on the north, one in a particular manner which they called Lehi, which was by the borders of the seashore. And thus ended the twentieth year.

17 In these prosperous circumstances were the people of Nephi in the commencement of the twenty-first year of the reign of the judges over the people of Nephi.

18 And they prospered exceedingly, and they became exceedingly rich; and they multiplied and waxed strong in the land.

19 Thus we see how merciful and just are all the dealings of the Lord to the fulfilling of all his words to the children of men.

20 We can behold that his words are verified, even at this time, which he spoke to Lehi, saying, "Blessed art thou and thy children, and they shall be blessed; inasmuch as they shall keep my commandments, they shall prosper in the land.

21 "But remember, inasmuch as they will not keep my commandments, they shall be cut off from the presence of the Lord."

22 And we see that these promises have been verified to the people of Nephi; for it has been their quarrelings and their contentions, their murderings and their plunderings, their idolatry, their whoredoms, and their abominations, which were among themselves, which brought upon them their wars and their destructions.

23 And those who were faithful in keeping the commandments of the Lord were delivered at all times, while thousands of their wicked brethren have been consigned to bondage, or to perish by the sword, or to dwindle in unbelief and mingle with the Lamanites.

24 But, behold, there never was

a happier time among the people of Nephi since the days of Nephi than in the days of Moroni, even at this time in the twenty-first year of the reign of the judges.

25 And the twenty-second year of the reign of the judges also ended in peace, and also the twenty-third year.

26 In the commencement of the twenty-fourth year of the reign of the judges, there would also have been peace among the people of Nephi had it not been for a contention which took place among them concerning the land of Lehi and the land of Morianton, which joined on the borders of Lehi, both of which were on the borders by the seashore.

27 For, behold, the people who possessed the land of Morianton claimed a part of the land of Lehi; therefore there began to be a warm contention between them, insomuch that the people of Morianton took up arms against their brethren, and they were determined to slay them by the sword.

28 But, behold, the people who possessed the land of Lehi fled to the camp of Moroni and appealed to him for assistance; for, behold, they were not in the wrong.

29 When the people of Morianton, who were led by a man whose name was Morianton, found that the people of Lehi had fled to the camp of Moroni, they were exceedingly fearful lest the army of Moroni should come upon them and destroy them.

30 Therefore Morianton put it into their hearts that they should flee to the land which was northward, which was covered with large bodies of water, and take possession of the land which was northward.

31 And they would have carried this plan into effect (which would have been a cause to be lamented), but Morianton, being a man of much passion, was angry with one of his maidservants, and he fell upon her and beat her much.

32 And she fled and came over to the camp of Moroni, and told Moroni all things concerning the matter, and also concerning their intentions to flee into the land northward.

33 Now the people who were in the land Bountiful, or rather Moroni, feared that they would hearken to the words of Morianton and unite with his people, and thus he would obtain possession of those parts of the land, which would lay a foundation for serious consequences among the people of Nephi, which consequences would lead to the overthrow of their liberty.

34 Therefore Moroni sent an army, with their camp, to head the people of Morianton, to stop their flight into the land northward.

35 But they did not head them until they had come to the borders of the land Desolation; and there they headed them by the narrow pass which led by the sea into the land northward, by the sea on the west and on the east.

36 And the army which was sent by Moroni, which was led by a man whose name was Teancum, met the people of Morianton.

37 And so stubborn were the people of Morianton (being inspired by his wickedness and his flattering words) that a battle commenced between them in which Teancum slew Morianton, and defeated his army, and took them prisoners, and returned to the camp of Moroni.

38 Thus ended the twenty-fourth year of the reign of the judges over the people of Nephi. And thus were the people of Morianton brought back.

39 Upon their covenanting to keep the peace, they were restored to the land of Morianton, and a union took place between them and the people of Lehi; and they were also restored to their lands.

40 In the same year that the people of Nephi had peace restored to them, Nephihah, the second chief judge, died, having filled the judgment seat with perfect uprightness before God.

41 Nevertheless, he had refused Alma to take possession of those records and those things which were esteemed by Alma and his fathers to be most sacred; therefore Alma had conferred them upon his son Helaman.

42 Behold, it came to pass that the son of Nephihah was appointed to fill the judgment seat in the stead

of his father; he was appointed chief judge and governor over the people, with an oath and sacred ordinance to judge righteously, and to keep the peace and the freedom of the people, and to grant to them their sacred privileges to worship the Lord their God, ⁴³to support and maintain the cause of God all his days, and to bring the wicked to justice according to their crime. Now, behold, his name was Pahoran.

44 And Pahoran filled the seat of his father and commenced his reign in the end of the twenty-fourth year over the people of Nephi.

CHAPTER 23

IN the commencement of the twenty-fifth year of the reign of the judges over the people of Nephi, they had established peace between the people of Lehi and the people of Morianton concerning their lands, and had commenced the twenty-fifth year in peace.

2 Nevertheless, they did not long maintain an entire peace in the land, for there began to be a contention among the people concerning their chief judge, Pahoran; for, behold, there were a part of the people who desired that a few particular points of the law should be altered.

3 But, behold, Pahoran would not alter, nor suffer the law to be altered; therefore he did not hearken to those who had sent in their voices, with their petitions, concerning the altering of the law.

4 Therefore those who were desirous that the law should be altered were angry with him and desired that he should no longer be chief judge over the land; therefore there arose a warm dispute concerning the matter, but not to bloodshed.

5 Those who were desirous that Pahoran should be dethroned from the judgment seat were called king-men, for they were desirous that the law should be altered in a manner to overthrow the free government and to establish a king over the land.

6 And those who were desirous that Pahoran should remain chief judge over the land took upon them the name of freemen, and thus was the division among them; for the freemen had sworn or covenanted to maintain their rights and the privileges of their religion by a free government

7 And it came to pass that this matter of their contention was settled by the voice of the people.

8 The voice of the people came in favor of the freemen, and Pahoran retained the judgment seat, which caused much rejoicing among the brethren of Pahoran, and also many of the people of liberty; which also put the king-men to silence that they dared not oppose, but were obliged to maintain the cause of freedom.

9 Now those who were in favor of kings were those of high birth, and they sought to be kings, and they were supported by those who sought power and authority over the people.

10 But, behold, this was a critical time for such contentions to be among the people of Nephi; for, behold, Amalickiah had again stirred up the hearts of the people of the Lamanites against the people of the Nephites, and he was gathering soldiers from all parts of his land, and arming them and preparing for war with all diligence; for he had sworn to drink the blood of Moroni.

11 But, behold, we shall see that his promise which he made was rash; nevertheless, he prepared himself and his armies to come to battle against the Nephites.

12 Now his armies were not so great as they had hitherto been because of the many thousands who had been slain by the hand of the Nephites.

13 But notwithstanding their great loss, Amalickiah had gathered together a wonderfully great army, insomuch that he feared not to come down to the land of Zarahemla.

14 And Amalickiah himself came down at the head of the Lamanites.

15 It was in the twenty-fifth year of the reign of the judges; and it was at the same time that they had begun to settle the affairs of their contentions concerning the chief judge, Pahoran.

16 When the men who were called king-men had heard that the Lamanites were coming down to battle against them, they were glad in their

hearts, and they refused to take up arms; for they were so angry with the chief judge, and also with the people of liberty, that they would not take up arms to defend their country.

17 When Moroni saw this, and also saw that the Lamanites were coming into the borders of the land, he was exceedingly angry because of the stubbornness of those people with whom he had labored with so much diligence to preserve; he was exceedingly angry; his soul was filled with anger against them.

18 And he sent a petition, with the voice of the people, to the governor of the land, desiring that he should read it and give him (Moroni) power to compel those dissenters to defend their country, or to put them to death.

19 For it was his first care to put an end to such contentions and dissensions among the people; for, behold, this had been hitherto a cause of all their destruction.

20 And it came to pass that it was granted according to the voice of the people.

21 Moroni commanded that his army should go against those king-men, to pull down their pride and their nobility, and level them with the earth, or they should take up arms and support the cause of liberty.

22 And the armies marched forth against them; and they pulled down their pride and their nobility insomuch that as they lifted their weapons of war to fight against the men of Moroni, they were hewn down and leveled to the earth.

23 There were four thousand of those dissenters who were hewn down by the sword; and those of their leaders who were not slain in battle were taken and cast into prison, for there was no time for their trials at this period.

24 And the remainder of those dissenters, rather than be smitten down to the earth by the sword, yielded to the standard of liberty, and were compelled to hoist the title of liberty upon their towers and in their cities, and to take up arms in defense of their country.

25 Thus Moroni put an end to those king-men, that there were not any known by the appellation of king-men; and thus he put an end to the stubbornness and the pride of those people who professed the blood of nobility.

26 But they were brought down to humble themselves like their brethren and to fight valiantly for their freedom from bondage.

27 While Moroni was thus breaking down the wars and contentions among his own people, and subjecting them to peace and civilization, and making regulations to prepare for war against the Lamanites, behold, the Lamanites had come into the land of Moroni, which was in the borders by the seashore.

28 And the Nephites were not sufficiently strong in the city of Moroni; therefore Amalickiah drove them, slaying many.

29 And Amalickiah took possession of the city; even possession of all their fortifications.

30 And those who fled out of the city of Moroni came to the city of Nephihah; and also the people of the city of Lehi gathered themselves together and made preparations, and were ready to receive the Lamanites to battle.

31 But Amalickiah would not suffer the Lamanites to go against the city of Nephihah to battle, but kept them down by the seashore, leaving men in every city to maintain and defend it.

32 And thus he went on, taking possession of many cities: the city of Moroni, and the city of Lehi, and the city of Morianton, and the city of Omner, and the city of Gid, and the city of Mulek, all of which were on the east borders by the seashore.

33 Thus had the Lamanites obtained, by the cunning of Amalickiah and by their numberless hosts, so many cities, all of which were strongly fortified after the manner of the fortifications of Moroni, all of which afforded strongholds for the Lamanites.

34 And they marched to the borders of the land Bountiful, driving the Nephites before them and slaying many.

35 But they were met by Teancum, who had slain Morianton and had headed his people in his flight.

36 And he headed Amalickiah also

as he was marching forth with his numerous army that he might take possession of the land Bountiful, and also the land northward.

37 But, behold, he met with a disappointment by being repulsed by Teancum and his men, for they were great warriors; for the men of Teancum exceeded the Lamanites in their strength and in their skill of war, insomuch that they gained advantage over the Lamanites.

38 They harassed them, and they slew them even until it was dark.

39 And Teancum and his men pitched their tents in the borders of the land Bountiful; and Amalickiah pitched his tents in the borders on the beach by the seashore, and after this manner were they driven.

40 When the night had come, Teancum and his servant stole forth and went out by night into the camp of Amalickiah; and, behold, sleep had overpowered them because of their much fatigue which was caused by the labors and heat of the day.

41 And Teancum stole privily into the tent of the king and put a javelin into his heart; and he caused the death of the king immediately, that he did not awake his servants.

42 And he returned again privily to his own camp, and, behold, his men were asleep; and he awakened them and told them all the things that he had done.

43 And he caused that his armies should stand in readiness lest the Lamanites had awakened, and should come upon them.

44 Thus ended the twenty-fifth year of the reign of the judges over the people of Nephi; and thus ended the days of Amalickiah.

CHAPTER 24

IN the twenty-sixth year of the reign of the judges over the people of Nephi, behold, when the Lamanites awoke on the first morning of the first month, they found that Amalickiah was dead in his own tent; and they also saw that Teancum was ready to give them battle on that day.

2 Now when the Lamanites saw this, they were affrighted; and they abandoned their design in marching into the land northward, and retreated with all their army into the city of Mulek, and sought protection in their fortifications.

3 The brother of Amalickiah was appointed king over the people, and his name was Ammoron; thus King Ammoron, the brother of King Amalickiah, was appointed to reign in his stead.

4 And he commanded that his people should maintain those cities which they had taken by the shedding of blood; for they had not taken any cities save they had lost much blood.

5 Now Teancum saw that the Lamanites were determined to maintain those cities which they had taken, and those parts of the land of which they had obtained possession.

6 And also seeing the enormity of their number, Teancum thought it was not expedient that he should attempt to attack them in their forts; but he kept his men round about, as if making preparations for war.

7 And truly he was preparing to defend himself against them by casting up walls round about and preparing places of resort.

8 He kept thus preparing for war until Moroni had sent a large number of men to strengthen his army.

9 And Moroni also sent orders to him that he should retain all the prisoners who fell into his hands; for as the Lamanites had taken many prisoners, he should retain all the prisoners of the Lamanites as a ransom for those whom the Lamanites had taken.

10 He also sent orders to him that he should fortify the land Bountiful and secure the narrow pass which led into the land northward, lest the Lamanites should obtain that point and should have power to harass them on every side.

11 And Moroni also sent to him desiring him that he would be faithful in maintaining that quarter of the land, and that he would seek every opportunity to scourge the Lamanites in that quarter, as much as was in his power, 12that perhaps he might take again, by stratagem or some other way, those cities which had been taken out of their hands;

and that he also would fortify and
strengthen the cities round about
which had not fallen into the hands
of the Lamanites.

13 He also said to him, "I would
come to you, but, behold, the Lamanites are upon us in the borders of the
land by the west sea; and, behold, I go
against them, therefore I cannot
come to you."

14 Now the king (Ammoron) had
departed out of the land of Zarahemla, and had made known to the
queen concerning the death of his
brother, and had gathered together
a large number of men, and had
marched forth against the Nephites,
on the borders by the west sea.

15 And thus he was endeavoring
to harass the Nephites and to draw
away a part of their forces to that
part of the land, while he had commanded those whom he had left to
possess the cities which he had taken,
that they should also harass the
Nephites on the borders by the east
sea, and should take possession of
their lands as much as it was in their
power according to the power of
their armies.

16 Thus were the Nephites in those
dangerous circumstances in the ending of the twenty-sixth year of the
reign of the judges over the people
of Nephi.

17 But in the twenty-seventh year
of the reign of the judges, Teancum
had established armies to protect the
south and the west borders of the
land, by the command of Moroni
who had begun his march toward
the land Bountiful that he might
assist Teancum with his men in re-
taking the cities which they had lost.

18 Teancum had received orders
to make an attack upon the city of
Mulek and retake it if it were possible.

19 And Teancum made preparations to make an attack upon the city
of Mulek and to march forth with
his army against the Lamanites; but
he saw that it was impossible that
he could overpower them while they
were in their fortifications.

20 Therefore he abandoned his
designs and returned again to the city
Bountiful to wait for the coming of
Moroni, that he might receive
strength to his army.

21 Moroni arrived with his army
to the land of Bountiful in the latter
end of the twenty-seventh year of the
reign of the judges over the people
of Nephi.

22 And in the commencement of
the twenty-eighth year, Moroni and
Teancum and many of the chief
captains held a council of war on
what they should do to cause the
Lamanites to come out against them
to battle, ²³or that they might by
some means flatter them out of their
strongholds, that they might gain
advantage over them and take again
the city of Mulek.

24 And they sent embassies to the
army of the Lamanites which protected the city of Mulek, to their
leader, whose name was Jacob, desiring him that he would come out with
his armies to meet them upon the
plains between the two cities.

25 But, behold, Jacob, who was a
Zoramite, would not come out with
his army to meet them upon the
plains.

26 Moroni, having no hopes of
meeting them upon fair grounds, resolved upon a plan that he might
decoy the Lamanites out of their
strongholds.

27 Therefore he caused that Teancum should take a small number of
men and march down near the seashore; and Moroni and his army, by
night, marched into the wilderness
on the west of the city Mulek.

28 Thus, on the morrow, when the
guards of the Lamanites had discovered Teancum, they ran and told
it to Jacob, their leader.

29 And the armies of the Lamanites marched forth against Teancum,
supposing by their numbers to overpower Teancum because of the
smallness of his numbers.

30 As Teancum saw the armies of
the Lamanites coming out against
him, he began to retreat down by the
seashore northward.

31 When the Lamanites saw that
he began to flee, they took courage
and pursued them with vigor.

32 And while Teancum was thus
leading away the Lamanites who were
pursuing them in vain, behold, Moroni commanded that a part of his
army who were with him should

march forth into the city and take possession of it.

33 Thus they did, and slew all those who had been left to protect the city, all those who would not yield up their weapons of war.

34 And thus Moroni had obtained possession of the city Mulek with a part of his army, while he marched with the remainder to meet the Lamanites when they should return from the pursuit of Teancum.

35 The Lamanites pursued Teancum until they came near the city Bountiful, and then they were met by Lehi and a small army which had been left to protect the city Bountiful.

36 And, behold, when the chief captains of the Lamanites beheld Lehi with his army coming against them, they fled in much confusion lest perhaps they should not reach the city Mulek before Lehi should overtake them; for they were wearied because of their march, and the men of Lehi were fresh.

37 Now the Lamanites did not know that Moroni was in their rear with his army; and all they feared was Lehi and his men.

38 Now Lehi was not desirous to overtake them till they should meet Moroni and his army.

39 And before the Lamanites had retreated far, they were surrounded by the Nephites, by the men of Moroni on one hand and the men of Lehi on the other, all of whom were fresh and full of strength; but the Lamanites were wearied because of their long march.

40 And Moroni commanded his men that they should fall upon them, until they gave up their weapons of war.

41 Jacob, being their leader, being also a Zoramite, and having an unconquerable spirit, led the Lamanites forth to battle with exceeding fury against Moroni.

42 Moroni being in their course of march, therefore Jacob was determined to slay them and cut his way through to the city of Mulek.

43 But, behold, Moroni and his men were more powerful; therefore they did not give way before the Lamanites.

44 They fought on both hands with exceeding fury, and there were many slain on both sides; and Moroni was wounded, and Jacob was killed.

45 And Lehi pressed upon their rear with such fury with his strong men that the Lamanites in the rear delivered up their weapons of war; and the remainder of them, being much confused, knew not whether to go or to strike.

46 Now Moroni, seeing their confusion, said to them, "If you will bring forth your weapons of war and deliver them up, behold, we will forbear shedding your blood."

47 When the Lamanites heard these words, their chief captains, all those who were not slain, came forth and threw down their weapons of war at the feet of Moroni, and also commanded their men that they should do the same.

48 But, behold, there were many that would not; and those who would not deliver up their swords were taken and bound, and their weapons of war were taken from them, and they were compelled to march with their brethren forth into the land Bountiful.

49 Now the number of prisoners who were taken exceeded more than the number of those who had been slain, even more than those who had been slain on both sides.

50 And they set guards over the prisoners of the Lamanites, and compelled them to go forth and bury their dead, and also the dead of the Nephites who were slain; and Moroni placed men over them to guard them while they should perform their labor.

51 And Moroni went to the city of Mulek with Lehi and took command of the city, and gave it to Lehi.

52 Now, behold, this Lehi was a man who had been with Moroni in the greater part of all his battles, and he was a man like Moroni; and they rejoiced in each other's safety; they were beloved by each other and also beloved by all the people of Nephi.

53 And it came to pass that after the Lamanites had finished burying their dead and also the dead of the Nephites, they were marched back into the land Bountiful.

54 And Teancum, by the orders of Moroni, caused that they should

commence laboring in digging a ditch round about the land, or the city Bountiful.

55 He caused that they should build a breastwork of timbers upon the inner bank of the ditch; and they cast up dirt out of the ditch against the breastwork of timbers.

56 Thus he caused the Lamanites to labor until they had encircled the city of Bountiful with a strong wall of timbers and earth to an exceeding height.

57 And this city became an exceeding stronghold ever after; and in this city they guarded the prisoners of the Lamanites, even within a wall which they had caused them to build with their own hands.

58 Now Moroni was compelled to cause the Lamanites to labor because it was easy to guard them while at their labor, and he desired all his forces when he should make an attack upon the Lamanites.

59 Moroni had thus gained a victory over one of the greatest of the armies of the Lamanites, and had obtained possession of the city Mulek, which was one of the strongest holds of the Lamanites in the land of Nephi; and thus he had also built a stronghold to retain his prisoners.

60 He no more attempted a battle with the Lamanites in that year, but he employed his men in preparing for war, and in making fortifications to guard against the Lamanites, and also delivering their women and their children from famine and affliction, and providing food for their armies.

61 Now the armies of the Lamanites on the west bank, south, while in the absence of Moroni on account of some intrigue among the Nephites which caused dissensions among them, had gained some ground over the Nephites, insomuch that they had obtained possession of a number of their cities in that part of the land.

62 Thus because of their iniquity and because of dissension and intrigue among themselves, they were placed in the most dangerous circumstances.

63 And now, behold, I have somewhat to say concerning the people of Ammon, who in the beginning were Lamanites; but by Ammon and his brethren, or rather by the power and word of God, they had been converted to the Lord.

64 They had been brought down into the land of Zarahemla, and had ever since been protected by the Nephites; and because of their oath, they had been kept from taking up arms against their brethren.

65 For they had taken an oath that they nevermore would shed blood; and according to their oath, they would have perished; they would have suffered themselves to fall into the hands of their brethren had it not been for the pity and the exceeding love which Ammon and his brethren had had for them.

66 And for this cause, they were brought down into the land of Zarahemla, and they ever had been protected by the Nephites.

67 But when they saw the danger, and the many afflictions and tribulations which the Nephites bore for them, they were moved with compassion and were desirous to take up arms in defense of their country.

68 But, behold, as they were about to take their weapons of war, they were overpowered by the persuasions of Helaman and his brethren, for they were about to break the oath which they had made.

69 And Helaman feared lest by so doing they should lose their souls; therefore all those who had entered into this covenant were compelled to behold their brethren wade through their afflictions in their dangerous circumstances at this time.

70 But, behold, it came to pass they had many sons, who had not entered into a covenant that they would not take their weapons of war to defend themselves against their enemies; [71]therefore they assembled themselves together at this time, as many as were able to take up arms; and they called themselves Nephites.

72 And they entered into a covenant to fight for the liberty of the Nephites, to protect the land unto the laying down of their lives.

73 They even covenanted that they never would give up their liberty, but they would fight in all cases to protect the Nephites and themselves from bondage.

74 Now, behold, there were two

thousand of those young men who entered into this covenant and took their weapons of war to defend their country.

75 And as they never had hitherto been a disadvantage to the Nephites, they became at this period of time a great support, for they took their weapons of war, and they would that Helaman should be their leader.

76 And they were all young men, and they were exceedingly valiant for courage, and also for strength and activity; but, behold, this was not all: they were men who were true at all times in whatever thing they were entrusted.

77 They were men of truth and soberness, for they had been taught to keep the commandments of God and to walk uprightly before him.

78 Helaman marched at the head of his two thousand stripling soldiers to the support of the people in the borders of the land on the south by the west sea.

79 And thus ended the twenty-eighth year of the reign of the judges over the people of Nephi.

CHAPTER 25

NOW it came to pass in the twenty-ninth year of the judges that Ammoron sent to Moroni desiring that he would exchange prisoners.

2 Moroni felt to rejoice exceedingly at this request, for he desired the provisions which were imparted for the support of the Lamanite prisoners, for the support of his own people; and he also desired his own people for the strengthening of his army.

3 Now the Lamanites had taken many women and children; and there was not a woman nor a child among all the prisoners of Moroni, or the prisoners whom Moroni had taken.

4 Therefore Moroni resolved upon a stratagem to obtain as many prisoners of the Nephites from the Lamanites as it was possible. Therefore he wrote an epistle and sent it by the servant of Ammoron, the same who had brought an epistle to Moroni.

5 These are the words which he wrote to Ammoron, saying, "Behold, Ammoron, I have written to you

somewhat concerning this war which you have waged against my people, or rather which your brother has waged against them and which you are still determined to carry on after his death.

6 "Behold, I would tell you something concerning the justice of God, and the sword of his Almighty wrath which hangs over you except you repent and withdraw your armies into your own lands, or the lands of your possessions, which is the land of Nephi; I would tell you these things, if you were capable of hearkening to them.

7 "I would tell you concerning that awful hell that awaits to receive such murderers as you and your brother have been, except you repent and withdraw your murderous purposes, and return with your armies to your own lands.

8 "But as you have once rejected these things and have fought against the people of the Lord, even so I may expect you will do it again.

9 "And now, behold, we are prepared to receive you; and except you withdraw your purposes, behold, you will pull down the wrath of that God whom you have rejected upon you, even to your utter destruction.

10 "But as the Lord lives, our armies shall come upon you except you withdraw, and you shall soon be visited with death, for we will retain our cities and our lands; and we will maintain our religion and the cause of our God.

11 "But, behold, I suppose that I talk to you concerning these things in vain; or I suppose that you are a child of hell; therefore, I will close my epistle by telling you that I will not exchange prisoners, save it be on conditions that you will deliver up a man, and his wife, and his children, for one prisoner; if this be the case that you will do it, I will exchange.

12 "And, behold, if you do not this, I will come against you with my armies; I will arm my women and my children, and I will come against you, and I will follow you even into your own land, which is the land of our first inheritance; and it shall be blood for blood, life for life; and I will give you battle, even until you

are destroyed from the face of the earth.

13 "Behold, I am in my anger, so also are my people; you have sought to murder us, and we have only sought to defend ourselves.

14 "But if you seek to destroy us any more, we will seek to destroy you; and we will seek our land, the lands of our first inheritance.

15 "Now I close my epistle. I am Moroni; I am a leader of the people of the Nephites."

16 When Ammoron received this epistle, he was angry; and he wrote another epistle to Moroni; and these are the words which he wrote, saying, "I am Ammoron the king of the Lamanites; I am the brother of Amalickiah, whom you have murdered.

17 "Behold, I will avenge his blood upon you; and I will come upon you with my armies, for I fear not your threatenings.

18 "For, behold, your fathers wronged their brethren, insomuch that they robbed them of their right to the government when it rightly belonged to them.

19 "And now, if you will lay down your arms and subject yourselves to be governed by those to whom the government rightly belongs, then will I cause that my people shall lay down their weapons and shall be at war no more.

20 "Behold, you have breathed out many threatenings against me and my people; but, behold, we fear not your threatenings.

21 "Nevertheless, I will grant to exchange prisoners according to your request, gladly, that I may preserve my food for my men of war.

22 "And we will wage a war which shall be eternal, either to subjecting the Nephites to our authority, or to their eternal extinction.

23 "And as concerning that God whom you say we have rejected, behold, we know not such a being; neither do you; but if it so be that there is such a being, we know not but that he has made us as well as you.

24 "And if it so be that there is a devil and a hell, behold, will he not send you there to dwell with my brother, whom you have murdered,

who you have hinted has gone to such a place? But, behold, these things matter not.

25 "I am Ammoron, and a descendant of Zoram, whom your fathers pressed and brought out of Jerusalem. And, behold, now, I am a bold Lamanite.

26 "Behold, this war has been waged to avenge their wrongs, and to maintain and to obtain their rights to the government; and I close my epistle to Moroni."

27 When Moroni received this epistle, he was more angry because he knew that Ammoron had a perfect knowledge of his fraud; he knew that Ammoron knew that it was not a just cause that had caused him to wage a war against the people of Nephi.

28 And he said, "Behold, I will not exchange prisoners with Ammoron, save he will withdraw his purpose, as I have stated in my epistle; for I will not grant him that he shall have any more power than he now has.

29 "I know the place where the Lamanites guard my people whom they have taken prisoners; and as Ammoron would not grant me my epistle, behold, I will give him according to my words; I will seek death among them until they shall sue for peace."

30 When Moroni had said these words, he caused that a search should be made among his men, that perhaps he might find a man who was a descendant of Laman among them.

31 And they found one, whose name was Laman, and he was one of the servants of the king who was murdered by Amalickiah.

32 Now Moroni caused that Laman and a small number of his men should go forth to the guards who were over the Nephites.

33 Now the Nephites were guarded in the city of Gid; therefore Moroni appointed Laman and caused that a small number of men should go with him.

34 And when it was evening, Laman went to the guards who were over the Nephites, and, behold, they saw him coming and they hailed him.

35 But he said to them, "Fear not. Behold, I am a Lamanite. Behold,

we have escaped from the Nephites, and they sleep; and, behold, we have taken of their wine and brought with us."

36 When the Lamanites heard these words, they received him with joy. And they said to him, "Give us of your wine, that we may drink; we are glad that you have thus taken wine with you, for we are weary."

37 But Laman said to them, "Let us keep of our wine till we go against the Nephites to battle." But this saying only made them more desirous to drink of the wine.

38 For, said they, "We are weary, therefore let us take of the wine, and by and by we shall receive wine for our rations, which will strengthen us to go against the Nephites." And Laman said to them, "You may do according to your desires."

39 And they took of the wine freely; and it was pleasant to their taste; therefore they took of it more freely; and it was strong, having been prepared in its strength.

40 And they drank and were merry, and by and by they were all drunken.

41 When Laman and his men saw that they were all drunken and were in a deep sleep, they returned to Moroni and told him all the things that had happened. And now this was according to the design of Moroni.

42 And Moroni prepared his men with weapons of war; and he sent them to the city of Gid, while the Lamanites were in a deep sleep and drunken, and they cast the weapons of war in to the prisoners, insomuch that they were all armed, even their women, and all those of their children as were able to use a weapon of war.

43 All those things were done in a profound silence. But had they awakened the Lamanites, behold, they were drunken, and the Nephites could have slain them.

44 But, behold, this was not the desire of Moroni. He did not delight in murder or bloodshed; but he delighted in the saving of his people from destruction; so that he might not bring upon him injustice, he would not fall upon the Lamanites and destroy them in their drunkenness.

45 But he had obtained his desires; for he had armed those prisoners who were within the wall of the city and had given them power to gain possession of those parts which were within the walls.

46 Then he caused the men who were with him to withdraw a pace from them and surround the armies of the Lamanites.

47 Now, behold, this was done in the nighttime, so that when the Lamanites awoke in the morning, they beheld that they were surrounded by the Nephites without, and that their prisoners were armed within.

48 Thus they saw that the Nephites had power over them; and in these circumstances they found that it was not expedient that they should fight with the Nephites.

49 Therefore their chief captains demanded their weapons of war, and they brought them forth and cast them at the feet of the Nephites, pleading for mercy. Now, behold, this was the desire of Moroni.

50 He took them prisoners of war, and took possession of the city, and caused that all the prisoners should be liberated who were Nephites; and they joined the army of Moroni and were a great strength to his army.

51 And he caused the Lamanites whom he had taken prisoners to commence a labor in strengthening the fortifications round about the city Gid.

52 When he had fortified the city Gid according to his desires, he caused that his prisoners should be taken to the city Bountiful.

53 And he also guarded that city with an exceedingly strong force.

54 And they, notwithstanding all the intrigues of the Lamanites, kept and protected all the prisoners whom they had taken, and also maintained all the ground and the advantage which they had retaken.

55 And the Nephites began again to be victorious and to reclaim their rights and their privileges.

56 Many times the Lamanites attempted to encircle them by night, but in these attempts they lost many prisoners.

57 And many times they attempted

to administer of their wine to the Nephites that they might destroy them with poison or with drunkenness.

58 But, behold, the Nephites were not slow to remember the Lord their God in this their time of affliction.

59 They could not be taken in such snares; they would not partake of their wine; they would not partake of wine save they had first given to some of the Lamanite prisoners.

60 And they were thus cautious that no poison should be administered among them; for if their wine would poison a Lamanite, it would also poison a Nephite; and thus they tried all their liquors.

61 And now it came to pass that it was expedient for Moroni to make preparations to attack the city Morianton.

62 For, behold, the Lamanites had, by their labors, fortified the city of Morianton until it had become an exceedingly great stronghold; and they were continually bringing new forces into that city and also new supplies of provisions.

63 Thus ended the twenty-ninth year of the reign of the judges over the people of Nephi.

CHAPTER 26

IN the commencement of the thirtieth year of the reign of the judges, in the second day of the first month, Moroni received an epistle from Helaman stating the affairs of the people in that quarter of the land.

2 And these are the words which he wrote, saying, "My dearly beloved brother, Moroni, as well in the Lord as in the tribulations of our warfare; behold, my beloved brother, I have somewhat to tell you concerning our warfare in this part of the land.

3 "Behold, two thousand of the sons of those men whom Ammon brought down out of the land of Nephi 4(now you have known that these were descendants of Laman, who was the eldest son of our father Lehi, 5and I need not rehearse to you concerning their traditions or their unbelief, for you know concerning all these things) have taken their weapons of war and would that I

should be their leader; and we have come forth to defend our country.

6 "And now you also know concerning the covenant which their fathers made that they would not take up their weapons of war against their brethren to shed blood.

7 "But in the twenty-sixth year, when they saw our afflictions and our tribulations for them, they were about to break the covenant which they had made and take up their weapons of war in our defense.

8 "But I would not suffer them that they should break this covenant which they had made, supposing that God would strengthen us insomuch that we should not suffer more because of their fulfilling the oath which they had taken.

9 "But, behold, here is one thing in which we may have great joy.

10 "For, behold, in the twenty-sixth year, I, Helaman, marched at the head of these two thousand young men to the city of Judea to assist Antipus, whom you had appointed a leader over the people of that part of the land.

11 "And I joined my two thousand sons (for they are worthy to be called sons) to the army of Antipus, in which strength Antipus rejoiced exceedingly; for, behold, his army had been reduced by the Lamanites because their forces had slain a vast number of our men, for which cause we have to mourn.

12 "Nevertheless, we may console ourselves in this point: that they have died in the cause of their country and of their God, and they are happy.

13 "And the Lamanites had also retained many prisoners, all of whom are chief captains; for no others have they spared alive.

14 "And we suppose that they are now at this time in the land of Nephi; it is so if they are not slain.

15 "And now these are the cities which the Lamanites have obtained possession by the shedding of the blood of so many of our valiant men: The land of Manti, or the city of Manti, and the city of Zeezrom, and the city of Cumeni, and the city of Antiparah.

16 "And these are the cities which they possessed when I arrived at the

city of Judea; and I found Antipus and his men toiling with their mights to fortify the city.

17 "They were depressed in body as well as in spirit; for they had fought valiantly by day and toiled by night to maintain their cities, and thus they had suffered great afflictions of every kind.

18 "And they were determined to conquer in this place, or die; therefore you may well suppose that this little force which I brought with me, those sons of mine, gave them great hopes and much joy.

19 "Now it came to pass that when the Lamanites saw that Antipus had received a greater strength to his army, they were compelled, by the orders of Ammoron, not to come against the city of Judea, or against us, to battle.

20 "Thus were we favored of the Lord; for had they come upon us in this our weakness, they might have destroyed our little army; but thus were we preserved.

21 "They were commanded by Ammoron to maintain those cities which they had taken. And thus ended the twenty-sixth year.

22 "And in the commencement of the twenty-seventh year, we had prepared our city and ourselves for defense.

23 "Now we were desirous that the Lamanites should come upon us; for we were not desirous to make an attack upon them in their strongholds.

24 "And we kept spies out round about to watch the movements of the Lamanites that they might not pass us by night, nor by day, to make an attack upon our other cities which were on the northward.

25 "For we knew in those cities they were not sufficiently strong to meet them; therefore we were desirous, if they should pass by us, to fall upon them in their rear, and thus bring them up in the rear at the same time they were met in the front.

26 "We supposed that we could overpower them; but, behold, we were disappointed in this our desire.

27 "They dared not pass by us with their whole army; neither dared they with a part, lest they should

not be sufficiently strong and they should fall.

28 "Neither dared they march down against the city of Zarahemla; neither dared they cross the head of Sidon over to the city of Nephihah.

29 "And thus, with their forces, they were determined to maintain those cities which they had taken.

30 "In the second month of this year, there were brought to us many provisions from the fathers of those my two thousand sons.

31 "And also there were sent two thousand men to us from the land of Zarahemla.

32 "Thus we were prepared with ten thousand men and provisions for them, and also for their wives and their children.

33 "And the Lamanites, thus seeing our forces increase daily and provisions arrive for our support, began to be fearful, and began to sally forth, if it were possible, to put an end to our receiving provisions and strength.

34 "Now when we saw that the Lamanites began to grow uneasy on this wise, we were desirous to bring a stratagem into effect upon them.

35 "Therefore Antipus ordered that I should march forth with my little sons, as if we were carrying provisions to a neighboring city.

36 "And we were to march near the city of Antiparah, as if we were going to the city beyond in the borders by the seashore.

37 "We marched forth as if with our provisions, to go to that city.

38 "And Antipus marched forth with a part of his army, leaving the remainder to maintain the city.

39 "But he did not march forth until I had gone forth with my little army and had come near the city Antiparah.

40 "And now in the city Antiparah was stationed the strongest army of the Lamanites, and the most numerous.

41 "When they had been informed by their spies, they came forth with their army and marched against us.

42 "And it came to pass that we fled before them, northward.

43 "Thus we led away the most

powerful army of the Lamanites, even to a considerable distance, insomuch that when they saw the army of Antipus pursuing them with their mights, they did not turn to the right nor to the left, but pursued their march in a straight course after us.

44 "And we suppose it was their intent to slay us before Antipus should overtake them, and this that they might not be surrounded by our people.

45 "Now Antipus, beholding our danger, speeded the march of his army.

46 "But, behold, it was night; therefore they did not overtake us, neither did Antipus overtake them; therefore we camped for the night.

47 "And before the dawn of the morning, behold, the Lamanites were pursuing us.

48 "Now we were not sufficiently strong to contend with them; and I would not suffer that my little sons should fall into their hands; therefore we continued our march, and we took our march into the wilderness.

49 "They dared not turn to the right nor to the left lest they should be surrounded; neither would I turn to the right nor to the left lest they should overtake me, and we could not stand against them, but be slain, and they would make their escape; thus we fled all that day into the wilderness, even until it was dark.

50 "And again when the light of the morning came, we saw the Lamanites upon us, and we fled before them.

51 "But they did not pursue us far before they halted; and it was in the morning of the third day of the seventh month.

52 "Whether they were overtaken by Antipus, we knew not; but I said to my men, 'Behold, we know not but they have halted for the purpose that we should come against them, that they might catch us in their snare; therefore what say you, my sons, will you go against them to to battle?'

53 "And now I say to you, my beloved brother, Moroni, that never had I seen so great courage, no, not among all the Nephites.

54 "For as I had ever called them my sons (for they were all of them

very young), even so they said to me, 'Father, behold, our God is with us, and he will not suffer that we shall fall; then let us go forth.

55 "'We would not slay our brethren, if they would let us alone; therefore let us go, lest they should overpower the army of Antipus.'

56 "Now they never had fought, yet they did not fear death; and they thought more upon the liberty of their fathers than they did upon their lives; and they had been taught by their mothers that if they did not doubt, God would deliver them.

57 "And they rehearsed to me the words of their mothers, saying, 'We do not doubt our mothers knew.'

58 "And it came to pass that I returned with my two thousand against these Lamanites who had pursued us.

59 "Now, behold, the armies of Antipus had overtaken them and a terrible battle had commenced.

60 "The army of Antipus, being weary because of their long march in so short a space of time, were about to fall into the hands of the Lamanites; and had I not returned with my two thousand, they would have attained their purpose.

61 "For Antipus had fallen by the sword, and also many of his leaders, because of their weariness which was occasioned by the speed of their march; therefore the men of Antipus, being confused because of the loss of their leaders, began to give way before the Lamanites.

62 "And the Lamanites took courage, and began to pursue them; and thus were the Lamanites pursuing them with great vigor, when we came upon their rear with our two thousand and began to slay them exceedingly, insomuch that the whole army of the Lamanites halted and turned upon us.

63 "Now when the people of Antipus saw that the Lamanites had turned them about, they gathered together their men and came again upon the rear of the Lamanites.

64 "And now we, the people of Nephi, the people of Antipus, and I with my two thousand, surrounded the Lamanites and slew them, insomuch that they were compelled to

deliver up their weapons of war, and also themselves as prisoners of war.

65 "When they had surrendered themselves to us, behold, I numbered those young men who had fought with me, fearing lest there were many of them slain.

66 "But, behold, to my great joy, there had not one soul of them fallen to the earth, and they had fought as if with the strength of God. Never were men known to have fought with such miraculous strength.

67 "And with such mighty power they fell upon the Lamanites that they frightened them; and for this cause the Lamanites delivered themselves up as prisoners of war.

68 "As we had no place for our prisoners that we could guard them to keep them from the armies of the Lamanites, therefore we sent them to the land of Zarahemla, and a part of those men who were not slain of Antipus with them.

69 "The remainder I took and joined them to my stripling Ammonites, and we took our march back to the city of Judea.

70 "Now it came to pass that I received an epistle from Ammoron, the king, stating that if I would deliver up those prisoners of war whom we had taken, he would deliver up the city of Antiparah to us.

71 "But I sent an epistle to the king that we were sure our forces were sufficient to take the city of Antiparah by our force; and by delivering up the prisoners for that city, we should suppose ourselves unwise, and that we would only deliver up our prisoners on exchange.

72 "And Ammoron refused my epistle, for he would not exchange prisoners; therefore we began to make preparations to go against the city of Antiparah.

73 "But the people of Antiparah left the city and fled to their other cities of which they had possession, to fortify them; thus the city of Antiparah fell into our hands.

74 "And thus ended the twenty-eighth year of the reign of the judges.

75 "In the commencement of the twenty-ninth year, we received a supply of provisions, and also an addition to our army, from the land of Zarahemla and from the land round about, to the number of six thousand men, besides sixty of the sons of the Ammonites who had come to join their brethren, my little band of two thousand.

76 "Now, behold, we were strong; and we had also plenty of provisions brought to us.

77 "And it came to pass that it was our desire to wage a battle with the army which was placed to protect the city Cumeni.

78 "And now, behold, I will show you that we soon accomplished our desire; with our strong force, or with a part of our strong force, we surrounded by night the city Cumeni, a little before they were to receive a supply of provisions.

79 "We camped round about the city for many nights; but we slept upon our swords, and kept guards that the Lamanites could not come upon us by night and slay us, which they attempted many times; but as many times as they attempted this, their blood was spilt.

80 "At length their provisions arrived, and they were about to enter the city by night.

81 "And we, instead of being Lamanites, were Nephites; therefore, we took them and their provisions.

82 "Notwithstanding the Lamanites being cut off from their support after this manner, they were still determined to maintain the city.

83 "Therefore it became expedient that we should take those provisions and send them to Judea and our prisoners to the land of Zarahemla.

84 "And not many days passed before the Lamanites began to lose all hopes of succor; therefore they yielded up the city into our hands; and thus we had accomplished our designs in obtaining the city Cumeni.

85 "But our prisoners were so numerous that, notwithstanding the enormity of our numbers, we were obliged to employ all our force to keep them, or to put them to death.

86 "For, behold, they would break out in great numbers, and would fight with stones and with clubs, or whatever things they could get into their hands, insomuch that we slew upwards of two thousand of them

after they had surrendered themselves prisoners of war.

87 "Therefore it became expedient for us that we should put an end to their lives, or guard them, sword in hand, down to the land of Zarahemla.

88 "Also our provisions were not any more than sufficient for our own people, notwithstanding that which we had taken from the Lamanites.

89 "And now in those critical circumstances, it became a very serious matter to determine concerning these prisoners of war; nevertheless, we resolved to send them down to the land of Zarahemla.

90 "Therefore we selected a part of our men and gave them charge over our prisoners, to go down to the land of Zarahemla. But on the morrow, they returned.

91 "And now, behold, we did not inquire of them concerning the prisoners; for, behold, the Lamanites were upon us, and they returned in season to save us from falling into their hands.

92 "For, behold, Ammoron had sent to their support a new supply of provisions and also a numerous army of men.

93 "And those men whom we sent with the prisoners arrived in season to check them as they were about to overpower us.

94 "But, behold, my little band of two thousand and sixty fought most desperately; they were firm before the Lamanites and administered death to all those who opposed them.

95 "And as the remainder of our army were about to give way before the Lamanites, behold, those two thousand and sixty were firm and undaunted; and they obeyed and observed to perform every word of command with exactness.

96 "And even according to their faith, it was done to them; and I remembered the words which they said to me that their mothers had taught them.

97 "Now, behold, it was these, my sons, and those men who had been selected to convey the prisoners to whom we owe this great victory; for it was they who beat the Lamanites; therefore they were driven back to the city of Manti.

98 "And we retained our city Cumeni and were not all destroyed by the sword; nevertheless, we had suffered great loss.

99 "After the Lamanites had fled, I immediately gave orders that my men who had been wounded should be taken from among the dead, and caused that their wounds should be dressed.

100 "There were two hundred, out of my two thousand and sixty, who had fainted because of the loss of blood.

101 "Nevertheless, according to the goodness of God, and to our great astonishment, and also the joy of our whole army, there was not one soul of them who had perished; and neither was there one soul among them who had not received many wounds.

102 "Now their preservation was astonishing to our whole army, that they should be spared while there were a thousand of our brethren who were slain.

103 "And we do justly ascribe it to the miraculous power of God because of their exceeding faith in that which they had been taught to believe, that there was a just God and that whoever did not doubt should be preserved by his marvelous power.

104 "Now this was the faith of these of whom I have spoken; they are young and their minds are firm, and they put their trust in God continually.

105 "After we had thus taken care of our wounded men and had buried our dead, and also the dead of the Lamanites, who were many, behold, we inquired of Gid concerning the prisoners with whom they had started to go down to the land of Zarahemla.

106 "Now Gid was the chief captain over the band which was appointed to guard them down to the land.

107 "And these are the words which Gid said to me, 'Behold, we started to go down to the land of Zarahemla with our prisoners.

108 "'And we met the spies of our armies who had been sent out to watch the camp of the Lamanites.

109 "'And they cried to us, saying, "Behold, the armies of the Lamanites are marching toward the city of Cumeni; and, behold, they will fall

upon them, and will destroy our people."

110 "'Our prisoners heard their cries, which caused them to take courage; and they rose up in rebellion against us.

111 "'And because of their rebellion, we caused that our swords should come upon them.

112 "'And they, in a body, ran upon our swords, in which the greater number of them were slain; the remainder of them broke through and fled from us.

113 "'And, behold, when they had fled, and we could not overtake them, we took our march with speed toward the city Cumeni; and, behold, we arrived in time that we might assist our brethren in preserving the city.

114 "'And, behold, we are again delivered out of the hands of our enemies.

115 "'And blessed is the name of our God; for, behold, it is he that has delivered us, that has done this great thing for us.'

116 "When I, Helaman, had heard these words of Gid, I was filled with exceeding joy because of the goodness of God in preserving us that we might not all perish.

117 "And I trust that the souls of them who have been slain have entered into the rest of their God.

118 "Our next object was to obtain the city of Manti; but there was no way that we could lead them out of the city by our small bands.

119 "For, behold, they remembered that which we had hitherto done; therefore we could not decoy them away from their strongholds.

120 "And they were so much more numerous than our army that we dared not go forth and attack them in their strongholds.

121 "And it became expedient that we should employ our men to the maintaining those parts of the land which we had retained of our possessions.

122 "Therefore it became expedient that we should wait, that we might receive more strength from the land of Zarahemla and also a new supply of provisions.

123 "I thus sent an embassy to the governor of our land to acquaint him concerning the affairs of our people.

124 "And we waited to receive provisions and strength from the land of Zarahemla.

125 "But, behold, this profited us but little; for the Lamanites were also receiving great strength from day to day, and also many provisions; and thus were our circumstances at this period of time.

126 "And the Lamanites were sallying forth against us from time to time, resolving by stratagem to destroy us; nevertheless, we could not come to battle with them because of their retreats and their strongholds.

127 "We waited in these difficult circumstances for the space of many months, even until we were about to perish for want of food.

128 "But it came to pass that we received food, which was guarded to us by an army of two thousand men, to our assistance.

129 "And this is all the assistance which we received to defend ourselves and our country from falling into the hands of our enemies, and to contend with an enemy which was innumerable.

130 "Now the cause of these our embarrassments, or the cause why they did not send more strength to us, we knew not; therefore we were grieved, and also filled with fear lest by any means the judgments of God should come upon our land, to our overthrow and utter destruction.

131 "Therefore we poured out our souls in prayer to God, that he would strengthen us and deliver us out of the hands of our enemies, and also give us strength that we might retain our cities, and our lands, and our possessions, for the support of our people.

132 "And it came to pass that the Lord our God visited us with assurances that he would deliver us, insomuch that he spoke peace to our souls, and granted to us great faith, and caused us that we should hope for our deliverance in him.

133 "And we took courage with our small force which we had received, and were fixed with a determination to conquer our enemies and to maintain our lands, and our pos-

sessions, and our wives, and our children, and the cause of our liberty.

134 "Thus we went forth with all our might against the Lamanites who were in the city of Manti; and we pitched our tents by the wilderness side which was near to the city.

135 "On the morrow, when the Lamanites saw that we were in the borders by the wilderness which was near the city, they sent out their spies round about us that they might discover the number and the strength of our army.

136 "When they saw that we were not strong according to our numbers, and fearing that we should cut them off from their support except they should come out to battle against us and kill us, 137and also supposing that they could easily destroy us with their numerous hosts, therefore they began to make preparations to come out against us to battle.

138 "And when we saw that they were making preparations to come out against us, behold, I caused that Gid and a small number of men should secrete themselves in the wilderness, and that Teomner and a small number of men should secrete themselves also in the wilderness.

139 "Now Gid and his men were on the right, and the others on the left; and when they had thus secreted themselves, behold, I remained with the remainder of my army, in that same place where we had first pitched our tents, against the time that the Lamanites should come out to battle.

140 "And it came to pass that the Lamanites came out with their numerous army against us.

141 "When they had come and were about to fall upon us with the sword, I caused that my men, those who were with me, should retreat into the wilderness.

142 "And the Lamanites followed us with great speed, for they were exceedingly desirous to overtake us that they might slay us; therefore they followed us into the wilderness.

143 "And we passed by in the midst of Gid and Teomner, insomuch that they were not discovered by the Lamanites.

144 "When the Lamanites had passed by, or when the army had passed by, Gid and Teomner rose up from their secret places and cut off the spies of the Lamanites that they should not return to the city.

145 "When they had cut them off, they ran to the city and fell upon the guards who were left to guard the city, insomuch that they destroyed them and took possession of the city.

146 "Now this was done because the Lamanites suffered their whole army, save a few guards only, to be led away into the wilderness.

147 "And Gid and Teomner, by this means, had obtained possession of their strongholds.

148 "And it came to pass that we took our course, after having traveled much in the wilderness, toward the land of Zarahemla.

149 "When the Lamanites saw that they were marching toward the land of Zarahemla, they were exceedingly afraid, lest there was a plan laid to lead them on to destruction; therefore they began to retreat into the wilderness again, even back by the same way which they had come.

150 "And, behold, it was night, and they pitched their tents; for the chief captains of the Lamanites had supposed that the Nephites were weary because of their march; and supposing that they had driven their whole army, therefore they took no thought concerning the one city of Manti.

151 "Now when it was night, I caused that my men should not sleep, but that they should march forward by another way toward the land of Manti.

152 "And because of our march in the nighttime, behold, on the morrow we were beyond the Lamanites, insomuch that we arrived before them to the city of Manti.

153 "Thus by this stratagem we took possession of the city of Manti without the shedding of blood.

154 "When the armies of the Lamanites arrived near the city and saw that we were prepared to meet them, they were astonished exceedingly and struck with great fear, insomuch that they fled into the wilderness.

155 "And it came to pass that the

armies of the Lamanites fled out of all this quarter of the land.

156 "But, behold, they have carried with them many women and children out of the land.

157 "And those cities which had been taken by the Lamanites, all of them, are at this period of time in our possession; and our fathers, and our women, and our children are returning to their homes, all save it be those who have been taken prisoners and carried off by the Lamanites.

158 "But, behold, our armies are small to maintain so great a number of cities and so great possessions.

159 "But, behold, we trust our God, who has given us victory over those lands, insomuch that we have obtained those cities and those lands which were our own.

160 "Now we do not know the cause that the government does not grant us more strength; neither do those men who came up to us know why we have not received greater strength.

161 "Behold, we do not know but that you are unsuccessful, and you have drawn away the forces into that quarter of the land; if so, we do not desire to murmur.

162 "And if it is not so, behold, we fear that there is some faction in the government that they do not send more men to our assistance; for we know that they are more numerous than that which they have sent.

163 "But, behold, it matters not; we trust God will deliver us, notwithstanding the weakness of our armies, and deliver us out of the hands of our enemies.

164 "Behold, this is the twenty-ninth year, in the latter end, and we are in possession of our lands; and the Lamanites have fled to the land of Nephi.

165 "And those sons of the people of Ammon, of whom I have so highly spoken, are with me in the city of Manti; and the Lord has supported them and kept them from falling by the sword, insomuch that not even one soul has been slain.

166 "But, behold, they have received many wounds; nevertheless they stand fast in that liberty wherewith God has made them free.

167 "And they are strict to remember the Lord their God from day to day; they observe to keep his statutes, and his judgments, and his commandments continually; and their faith is strong in the prophecies concerning that which is to come.

168 "Now, my beloved brother Moroni, may the Lord our God, who has redeemed us and made us free, keep you continually in his presence.

169 "And may he favor this people, even that you may have success in obtaining the possession of all that which the Lamanites have taken from us, which was for our support.

170 "And now, behold, I close my epistle. I am Helaman, the son of Alma."

CHAPTER 27

IN the thirtieth year of the reign of the judges over the people of Nephi, after Moroni had received and had read Helaman's epistle, he rejoiced exceedingly because of the welfare and the exceeding success which Helaman had had in obtaining those lands which were lost.

2 And he made it known to all his people in all the land round about in that part where he was, that they might rejoice also.

3 He immediately sent an epistle to Pahoran, desiring that he should cause men to be gathered together to strengthen Helaman, or the armies of Helaman, insomuch that he might with ease maintain that part of the land which he had been so miraculously prospered in retaining.

4 When Moroni had sent this epistle to the land of Zarahemla, he began again to lay a plan that he might obtain the remainder of those possessions and cities which the Lamanites had taken from them.

5 While Moroni was thus making preparations to go against the Lamanites to battle, behold, the people of Nephihah who were gathered together from the city of Moroni, and the city of Lehi, and the city of Morianton were attacked by the Lamanites.

6 Even those who had been compelled to flee from the land of Manti and from the land round about had

come over and joined the Lamanites in this part of the land.

7 Thus being exceedingly numerous, and receiving strength from day to day by the command of Ammoron, they came forth against the people of Nephihah and began to slay them with an exceedingly great slaughter.

8 And their armies were so numerous that the remainder of the people of Nephihah were obliged to flee before them; and they came even and joined the army of Moroni.

9 Now as Moroni had supposed that there should be men sent to the city of Nephihah to the assistance of the people to maintain that city, and knowing that it was easier to keep the city from falling into the hands of the Lamanites than to retake it from them, he supposed that they would easily maintain that city; [10]therefore he retained all his force to maintain those places which he had recovered.

11 And when Moroni saw that the city of Nephihah was lost, he was exceedingly sorrowful and began to doubt, because of the wickedness of the people, whether they should not fall into the hands of their brethren.

12 Now this was the case with all his chief captains. They doubted and marveled also because of the wickedness of the people, and this because of the success of the Lamanites over them.

13 Moroni was angry with the government because of their indifference concerning the freedom of their country.

14 And he wrote again to the governor of the land, who was Pahoran, and these are the words which he wrote, saying, "Behold, I direct my epistle to Pahoran, in the city of Zarahemla, who is the chief judge and the governor over the land, and also to all those who have been chosen by this people to govern and manage the affairs of this war.

15 "For, behold, I have somewhat to say to them by the way of condemnation; for, behold, you yourselves know that you have been appointed to gather together men and to arm them with swords, and with cimeters, and all manner of weapons of war of every kind, and send them forth against the Lamanites in whatever parts they should come into our land.

16 "And now, behold, I say to you that I myself, and also my men, and also Helaman and his men, have suffered exceedingly great sufferings, even hunger, thirst, and fatigue, and all manner of afflictions of every kind.

17 "But, behold, were this all we had suffered, we would not murmur nor complain; but, behold, great has been the slaughter among our people.

18 "Thousands have fallen by the sword, while it might have been otherwise if you had rendered to our armies sufficient strength and succor for them.

19 "Great has been your neglect toward us. And now, behold, we desire to know the cause of this exceedingly great neglect; we desire to know the cause of your thoughtless state.

20 "Can you think to sit upon your thrones in a state of thoughtless stupor while your enemies are spreading the work of death around you, [21]while they are murdering thousands of your brethren, even they who have looked up to you for protection and have placed you in a situation that you might have succored them?

22 "You might have sent armies to them to have strengthened them and have saved thousands of them from falling by the sword!

23 "But, behold, this is not all, you have withheld your provisions from them, insomuch that many have fought and bled out their lives because of their great desires which they had for the welfare of this people.

24 "And this they have done when they were about to perish with hunger because of your exceedingly great neglect toward them.

25 "Now, my beloved brethren— for you ought to be beloved—you ought to have stirred yourselves more diligently for the welfare and the freedom of this people; [26]but you have neglected them, insomuch that the blood of thousands shall come upon your heads for vengeance; for known to God were all their cries and all their sufferings.

27 "Behold, could you suppose that you could sit upon your thrones and because of the exceeding goodness of

God you could do nothing and he would deliver you? Behold, if you have supposed this, you have supposed in vain.

28 "Do you suppose that so many of your brethren have been killed because of their wickedness? I say to you, If you have supposed this, you have supposed in vain; for I say to you, There are many who have fallen by the sword.

29 "It is to your condemnation; for the Lord suffers the righteous to be slain that his justice and judgment may come upon the wicked; therefore you need not suppose that the righteous are lost because they are slain; but, behold, they enter into the rest of the Lord their God.

30 "And now, behold, I say to you, I fear exceedingly that the judgments of God will come upon this people because of their exceedingly great slothfulness, even the slothfulness of our government and their exceedingly great neglect toward their brethren, those who have been slain.

31 "For were it not for the wickedness which first commenced at our head, we could have withstood our enemies. They could have gained no power over us had it not been for the war which broke out among ourselves.

32 "Were it not for those king-men, who caused so much bloodshed at the time we were contending among ourselves, and if we had united our strength as we hitherto had done; ³³and had those king-men not desired power and authority over us, but united with us and gone forth against our enemies instead of taking up their swords against us; ³⁴and if we had gone forth in the strength of the Lord, we should have dispersed our enemies; for it would have been done according to the fulfilling of his word.

35 "But, behold, now the Lamanites are coming upon us, taking possession of our lands, and murdering our people with the sword, even our women and our children; and also carrying them away captive, causing them that they should suffer all manner of afflictions; and this because of the great wickedness of those who are seeking for power and authority, even those king-men.

36 "But why should I say much concerning this matter, for we know not but what you yourselves are seeking for authority. We know not but what you are also traitors to your country.

37 "Or is it that you have neglected us because you are in the heart of our country and you are surrounded by security that you do not cause food to be sent to us, and also men to strengthen our armies?

38 "Have you forgotten the commandments of the Lord your God? Have you forgotten the captivity of our fathers?

39 "Have you forgotten the many times we have been delivered out of the hands of our enemies?

40 "Or do you suppose that the Lord will still deliver us while we sit upon our thrones and do not make use of the means which the Lord has provided for us?

41 "Will you sit in idleness, surrounded with thousands, even tens of thousands, who do also sit in idleness, while there are thousands round about in the borders of the land who are falling by the sword, wounded and bleeding?

42 "Do you suppose that God will look upon you as guiltless, while you sit still and behold these things? Behold, I say to you, No.

43 "Now I would that you should remember that God has said that the inward vessel shall be cleansed first, and then shall the outer vessel be cleansed also.

44 "Except you repent of that which you have done, and begin to be up and doing, and send forth food and men to us, and also to Helaman that he may support those parts of our country which he has retained, and that we may also recover the remainder of our possessions in these parts, behold, it will be expedient that we contend no more with the Lamanites until we have first cleansed our inward vessel, even the great head of our government.

45 "And except you grant my epistle, and come out and show to me a true spirit of freedom, and strive to strengthen and fortify our armies, and grant them food for their support, behold, I will leave a part of my freemen to maintain this part of

our land, and I will leave the strength and the blessings of God upon them, that no other power can operate against them, and this because of their exceeding faith and their patience in their tribulations; 46and I will come to you, and if there be any among you that has a desire for freedom, if there be even a spark of freedom remaining, behold, I will stir up insurrections among you, even until those who have desires to usurp power and authority shall become extinct.

47 "Behold, I do not fear your power nor your authority, but it is my God whom I fear, and it is according to his commandments that I take my sword to defend the cause of my country, and it is because of your iniquity that we have suffered so much loss.

48 "Behold, it is time that except you bestir yourselves in the defense of your country and your little ones, the sword of justice will hang over you, and it shall fall upon you and visit you even to your utter destruction.

49 "I wait for assistance from you, and except you administer to our relief, behold, I will come to you, even into the land of Zarahemla, and smite you with the sword, insomuch that you can have no more power to impede the progress of this people in the cause of our freedom.

50 "For, behold, the Lord will not suffer that you shall live and wax strong in your iniquities to destroy his righteous people.

51 "Can you suppose that the Lord will spare you and come out in judgment against the Lamanites when it is the tradition of their fathers that has caused their hatred?

52 "And it has been redoubled by those who have dissented from us, while your iniquity is because of your love of glory and the vain things of the world.

53 "You know that you transgress the laws of God, and you know that you trample them under your feet.

54 "Behold, the Lord said to me, 'If those whom ye have appointed your governors do not repent of their sins and iniquities, ye shall go up to battle against them.'

55 "And now, behold, I Moroni, am constrained according to the cove-

nant which I have made to keep the commandments of my God; therefore I would that you should adhere to the word of God and send speedily to me of your provisions and of your men, and also to Helaman.

56 "And, behold, if you will not do this, I come to you speedily; for, behold, God will not suffer that we should perish with hunger; therefore he will give us of your food, even if it must be by the sword.

57 "Now see that you fulfill the word of God.

58 "I am Moroni, your chief captain. I seek not for power, but to pull it down.

59 "I seek not for honor of the world, but for the glory of my God and the freedom and welfare of my country. And thus I close my epistle."

CHAPTER 28

SOON after Moroni had sent his epistle to the chief governor, he received an epistle from Pahoran, the chief governor.

2 And these are the words which he received: "I, Pahoran, who am the chief governor of this land, send these words to Moroni, the chief captain over the army: Behold, I say to you, Moroni, that I do not joy in your great afflictions; it grieves my soul.

3 "Behold, there are those who do joy in your afflictions; insomuch that they have risen up in rebellion against me, and also those of my people who are freemen; and those who have risen up are exceedingly numerous.

4 "And it is those who have sought to take away the judgment seat from me that have been the cause of this great iniquity.

5 "For they have used great flattery; and they have led away the hearts of many people, which will be the cause of sore affliction among us; they have withheld our provisions and have daunted our freemen that they have not come to you.

6 "And, behold, they have driven me out before them, and I have fled to the land of Gideon with as many men as it was possible that I could get.

7 "I have sent a proclamation throughout this part of the land;

and, behold, they are flocking to us daily, to their arms, to defend their country and their freedom, and to avenge our wrongs.

8 "And they have come to us, insomuch that those who have risen up in rebellion against us are set at defiance, insomuch that they fear us and dare not come out against us to battle.

9 "They have taken possession of the land, or the city of Zarahemla; they have appointed a king over them, and he has written to the king of the Lamanites, in which he has joined an alliance with him.

10 "In this alliance, he has agreed to maintain the city of Zarahemla, which maintenance he supposes will enable the Lamanites to conquer the remainder of the land, and he shall be placed king over this people when they shall be conquered under the Lamanites.

11 "And now, in your epistle you have censured me; but it matters not; I am not angry but rejoice in the greatness of your heart.

12 "I, Pahoran, do not seek for power save only to retain my judgment seat, that I may preserve the rights and the liberty of my people.

13 "My soul stands fast in that liberty in which God has made us free.

14 "And now, behold, we will resist wickedness even to bloodshed.

15 "We would not shed the blood of the Lamanites if they would stay in their own land.

16 "We would not shed the blood of our brethren if they would not rise up in rebellion and take the sword against us.

17 "We would subject ourselves to the yoke of bondage if it were requisite with the justice of God, or if he should command us so to do.

18 "But, behold, he does not command us that we shall subject ourselves to our enemies, but that we should put our trust in him and he will deliver us.

19 "Therefore, my beloved brother Moroni, let us resist evil; and whatever evil we cannot resist with our words, such as rebellions and dissensions, let us resist them with our swords, that we may retain our freedom, that we may rejoice in the great privilege of our church and in the cause of our Redeemer and our God.

20 "Come to me speedily with a few of your men, and leave the remainder in the charge of Lehi and Teancum; give them power to conduct the war in that part of the land according to the Spirit of God, which is also the spirit of freedom which is in them.

21 "Behold, I have sent a few provisions to them that they may not perish until you can come to me.

22 "Gather together whatever force you can upon your march here, and we will go speedily against those dissenters in the strength of our God according to the faith which is in us.

23 "And we will take possession of the city of Zarahemla that we may obtain more food to send forth to Lehi and Teancum; and we will go forth against them in the strength of the Lord, and we will put an end to this great iniquity.

24 "Now, Moroni, I joy in receiving your epistle; for I was somewhat worried concerning what we should do, whether it should be just in us to go against our brethren.

25 "But you have said, Except they repent, the Lord has commanded you that you should go against them.

26 "See that you strengthen Lehi and Teancum in the Lord; tell them to fear not, for God will deliver them, and also all those who stand fast in that liberty wherewith God has made them free.

27 "And now I close my epistle to my beloved brother Moroni."

CHAPTER 29

WHEN Moroni had received this epistle, his heart took courage, and was filled with exceedingly great joy because of the faithfulness of Pahoran, that he was not also a traitor to the freedom and cause of his country.

2 But he also mourned exceedingly because of the iniquity of those who had driven Pahoran from the judgment seat and, in fine, because of those who had rebelled against their country and also their God.

3 And Moroni took a small number of men according to the desire of

Pahoran, and gave Lehi and Teancum command over the remainder of his army, and took his march toward the land of Gideon.

4 And he raised the standard of liberty in whatever place he entered, and gained whatever force he could in all his march toward the land of Gideon.

5 Thousands flocked to his standard and took up their swords in the defense of their freedom that they might not come into bondage.

6 Thus when Moroni had gathered together whatever men he could in all his march, he came to the land of Gideon; and he united his forces with that of Pahoran, and they became exceedingly strong, even stronger than the men of Pachus, who was the king of those dissenters who had driven the freemen out of the land of Zarahemla and had taken possession of the land.

7 And it came to pass that Moroni and Pahoran went down with their armies into the land of Zarahemla, and went forth against the city, and met the men of Pachus, insomuch that they came to battle.

8 And, behold, Pachus was slain and his men were taken prisoners, and Pahoran was restored to his judgment seat.

9 And the men of Pachus received their trial according to the law, and also those king-men who had been taken and cast into prison; and they were executed according to the law.

10 Those men of Pachus and those king-men, those who would not take up arms in the defense of their country, but would fight against it, were put to death.

11 And thus it became expedient that this law should be strictly observed for the safety of their country; and whoever was found denying freedom was speedily executed according to the law.

12 Thus ended the thirtieth year of the reign of the judges over the people of Nephi: Moroni and Pahoran having restored peace to the land of Zarahemla among their own people, having inflicted death upon all those who were not true to the cause of freedom.

13 In the commencement of the thirty-first year of the reign of the

judges over the people of Nephi, Moroni immediately caused that provisions, and also an army of six thousand men, should be sent to Helaman to assist him in preserving that part of the land.

14 And he also caused that an army of six thousand men, with a sufficient quantity of food, should be sent to the armies of Lehi and Teancum.

15 This was done to fortify the land against the Lamanites.

16 And it came to pass that Moroni and Pahoran, leaving a large body of men in the land of Zarahemla, took their march with a large body of men toward the land of Nephihah, being determined to overthrow the Lamanites in that city.

17 As they were marching toward the land, they took a large body of men of the Lamanites and slew many of them, and took their provisions and their weapons of war.

18 And after they had taken them, they caused them to enter into a covenant that they would no more take up their weapons of war against the Nephites.

19 When they had entered into this covenant, they sent them to dwell with the people of Ammon; and they were in number about four thousand who had not been slain.

20 And when they had sent them away, they pursued their march toward the land of Nephihah.

21 And when they had come to the city Nephihah, they pitched their tents in the plains of Nephihah, which is near the city Nephihah.

22 Now Moroni was desirous that the Lamanites should come out upon the plains to battle against them; but the Lamanites, knowing of their exceeding great courage and beholding the greatness of their numbers, dared not come out against them; therefore they did not come to battle in that day.

23 When the night came, Moroni went forth in the darkness of the night and came upon the top of the wall to spy out in what part of the city the Lamanites camped with their army.

24 And they were on the east by the entrance; and they were all asleep.

25 Now, Moroni returned to his army and caused that they should prepare in haste strong cords and ladders to be let down from the top of the wall into the inner part of the wall.

26 And Moroni caused that his men should march forth and come upon the top of the wall and let themselves down into that part of the city, even on the west, where the Lamanites did not camp with their armies.

27 They were all let down into the city by night by the means of their strong cords and their ladders; thus when the morning came, they were all within the walls of the city.

28 When the Lamanites awoke and saw that the armies of Moroni were within the walls, they were frightened exceedingly, insomuch that they fled out by the pass.

29 And when Moroni saw that they were fleeing before him, he caused that his men should march forth against them, and they slew many and surrounded many others and took them prisoners; and the remainder of them fled into the land of Moroni, which was in the borders of the seashore.

30 Thus had Moroni and Pahoran obtained the possession of the city of Nephihah without the loss of one of their men; and there were many of the Lamanites who were slain.

31 Now it came to pass that many of the Lamanites who were prisoners were desirous to join the people of Ammon and become a free people.

32 And as many as were desirous, to them it was granted according to their desires; therefore all the prisoners of the Lamanites joined the people of Ammon, and began to labor exceedingly, tilling the ground, raising all manner of grain, and flocks, and herds of every kind.

33 Thus were the Nephites relieved from a great burden; they were relieved from all the prisoners of the Lamanites.

34 After Moroni had obtained possession of the city of Nephihah, having taken many prisoners, which reduced the armies of the Lamanites exceedingly, and having regained many of the Nephites who had been taken prisoners, which strengthened his army exceedingly, he went forth from the land of Nephihah to the land of Lehi.

35 When the Lamanites saw that Moroni was coming against them, they were again frightened and fled before the army of Moroni.

36 And Moroni and his army pursued them from city to city, until they were met by Lehi and Teancum; and the Lamanites fled from Lehi and Teancum, even down upon the borders by the seashore, until they came to the land of Moroni.

37 And the armies of the Lamanites were all gathered together, insomuch that they were all in one body in the land of Moroni.

38 Now Ammoron, the king of the Lamanites, was also with them.

39 And Moroni, and Lehi, and Teancum encamped with their armies round about in the borders of the land of Moroni, insomuch that the Lamanites were encircled in the borders by the wilderness on the south, and in the borders by the wilderness on the east; thus they encamped for the night.

40 For, behold, the Nephites and the Lamanites also were weary because of the greatness of the march; therefore they did not resolve upon any stratagem in the nighttime, save Teancum.

41 For he was exceedingly angry with Ammoron, insomuch that he considered that Ammoron and Amalickiah, his brother, had been the cause of this great and lasting war between them and the Lamanites, which had been the cause of so much war and bloodshed, and so much famine.

42 And Teancum in his anger went forth into the camp of the Lamanites, and let himself down over the walls of the city.

43 And he went forth with a cord, from place to place, until he found the king; and he cast a javelin at him, which pierced him near the heart.

44 But, behold, the king awakened his servant before he died, insomuch that he pursued Teancum and slew him.

45 Now when Lehi and Moroni knew that Teancum was dead, they

were exceedingly sorrowful; for, behold, he had been a man who fought valiantly for his country, even a true friend to liberty; and he had suffered very many exceedingly sore afflictions.

46 But, behold, he was dead, and had gone the way of all the earth.

47 Moroni marched forth on the morrow, and came upon the Lamanites, insomuch that his men slew them with a great slaughter, and drove them out of the land; and they fled, even that they did not return at that time against the Nephites.

48 Thus ended the thirty-first year of the reign of the judges over the people of Nephi; and thus they had had wars, and bloodsheds, and famine, and affliction for the space of many years.

49 And there had been murders, and contentions, and dissensions, and all manner of iniquity among the people of Nephi; nevertheless, for the righteous' sake, because of the prayers of the righteous, they were spared.

50 But, behold, because of the exceedingly great length of the war between the Nephites and the Lamanites, many had become hardened.

51 And many were softened because of their afflictions, insomuch that they humbled themselves before God, even in the depth of humility.

52 After Moroni had fortified those parts of the land which were most exposed to the Lamanites until they were sufficiently strong, he returned to the city of Zarahemla, and also Helaman returned to the place of his inheritance; and there was once more peace established among the people of Nephi.

53 And Moroni yielded up the command of his armies into the hands of his son whose name was Moronihah, and he retired to his own house that he might spend the remainder of his days in peace.

54 Pahoran returned to his judgment seat; and Helaman took upon him again to preach to the people the word of God; for, because of so many wars and contentions, it had become expedient that a regulation should be made again in the church.

55 Therefore Helaman and his brethren went forth and declared the word of God with much power to the convincing of many people of their wickedness, which caused them to repent of their sins and to be baptized unto the Lord their God.

56 And it came to pass that they established again the church of God throughout all the land; and regulations were made concerning the law.

57 And their judges and their chief judges were chosen.

58 And the people of Nephi began to prosper again in the land and began to multiply and to wax exceedingly strong again in the land.

59 And they began to grow exceedingly rich; but not withstanding their riches, or their strength, or their prosperity, they were not lifted up in pride of their eyes; neither were they slow to remember the Lord their God; but they humbled themselves exceedingly before him.

60 They remembered how great things the Lord had done for them, that he had delivered them from death, and from bonds, and from prisons, and from all manner of afflictions; and he had delivered them out of the hands of their enemies.

61 And they prayed to the Lord their God continually, insomuch that the Lord blessed them according to his words, so that they waxed strong and prospered in the land.

62 And it came to pass that all these things were done.

63 And Helaman died in the thirty-fifth year of the reign of the judges over the people of Nephi.

CHAPTER 30

IN the commencement of the thirty-sixth year of the reign of the judges over the people of Nephi, Shiblon took possession of those sacred things which had been delivered to Helaman by Alma.

2 And he was a just man, and he walked uprightly before God; and he observed to do good continually, to keep the commandments of the Lord his God, as also did his brother.

3 And it came to pass that Moroni died also.

4 Thus ended the thirty-sixth year of the reign of the judges.

5 In the thirty-seventh year of the reign of the judges, a large company, even to the amount of five thousand and four hundred men, with their wives and their children, departed out of the land of Zarahemla into the land which was northward.

6 And Hagoth, he being an exceedingly curious man, went forth and built him an exceedingly large ship on the borders of the land Bountiful by the land Desolation, and launched it forth into the west sea by the narrow neck which led into the land northward.

7 And, behold, there were many of the Nephites who entered therein and sailed forth with many provisions, and also with many women and children; and they took their course northward.

8 Thus ended the thirty-seventh year.

9 And in the thirty-eighth year, this man built other ships.

10 And the first ship returned, and many more people entered into it; and they also took many provisions and set out again to the land northward.

11 They were never heard of more, and we suppose that they were drowned in the depths of the sea.

12 One other ship also sailed forth; and where it went we know not.

13 And in this year, there were many people who went forth into the land northward. Thus ended the thirty-eighth year.

14 In the thirty-ninth year of the reign of the judges, Shiblon died also, and Corianton had gone forth to the land northward in a ship, to carry forth provisions to the people who had gone forth into that land.

15 Therefore it became expedient for Shiblon to confer those sacred things before his death upon the son of Helaman, who was called Helaman after the name of his father.

16 Now, behold, all those engravings which were in the possession of Helaman were written and sent forth among the children of men throughout all the land, save those parts which had been commanded by Alma should not go forth.

17 Nevertheless these things were to be kept sacred and handed down from one generation to another; therefore, in this year they had been conferred upon Helaman before the death of Shiblon.

18 Also in this year, there were some dissenters who went forth to the Lamanites; and they were stirred up again to anger against the Nephites.

19 And also in this same year, they came down with a numerous army to war against the people of Moronihah, or against the army of Moronihah, in which they were beaten and driven back again to their own lands, suffering great loss.

20 Thus ended the thirty-ninth year of the reign of the judges over the people of Nephi.

21 And thus ended the account of Alma, and Helaman his son, and also Shiblon, who was his son.

THE BOOK OF HELAMAN

CHAPTER 1

An account of the Nephites. Their wars and contentions, and their dissensions. Also the prophecies of many holy prophets before the coming of Christ, according to the record of Helaman who was the son of Helaman, and also according to the records of his sons, even down to the coming of Christ. And also many of the Lamanites are converted. An account of their conversion. An account of the righteousness of the Lamanites, and the wickedness and abominations of the Nephites, according to the record of Helaman and his sons, even down to the coming of Christ, which is called the book of Helaman.

AND now, behold, in the commencement of the fortieth year of the reign of the judges over the people of Nephi, there began to be a serious difficulty among the people of the Nephites.

2 For, behold, Pahoran had died and gone the way of all the earth; therefore there began to be a serious contention concerning who should have the judgment seat among the brethren who were the sons of Pahoran.

3 Now these are their names who contended for the judgment seat, who also caused the people to contend: Pahoran, Paanchi, and Pacumeni.

4 These are not all the sons of Pahoran (for he had many), but these are they who contended for the judgment seat; therefore, they caused three divisions among the people.

5 Nevertheless, it came to pass that Pahoran was appointed by the voice of the people to be chief judge and a governor over the people of Nephi.

6 And Pacumeni, when he saw that he could not obtain the judgment seat, united with the voice of the people.

7 But Paanchi, and that part of the people that were desirous he should be their governor, was exceedingly angry, therefore he was about to flatter away those people to rise up in rebellion against their brethren.

8 And as he was about to do this, behold, he was taken and was tried according to the voice of the people, and condemned to death; for he had raised up in rebellion, and sought to destroy the liberty of the people.

9 Now when those people who were desirous that he should be their governor saw that he was condemned to death, they were angry; and, behold, they sent forth one Kishkumen, even to the judgment seat of Pahoran, and he murdered Pahoran as he sat upon the judgment seat.

10 And he was pursued by the servants of Pahoran; but, behold, so speedy was the flight of Kishkumen that no man could overtake him.

11 He went to those that sent him, and they all entered into a covenant, swearing by their everlasting Maker that they would tell no man that Kishkumen had murdered Pahoran; therefore Kishkumen was not known among the people of Nephi, for he was in disguise at the time that he murdered Pahoran.

12 And Kishkumen and his band who had covenanted with him mingled themselves among the people in a manner that all could not be found; but as many as were found were condemned to death.

13 Now, behold, Pacumeni was appointed according to the voice of the people to be a chief judge and a governor over the people to reign in the stead of his brother Pahoran; and it was according to his right.

14 And all this was done in the fortieth year of the reign of the judges; and it had an end.

15 In the forty-first year of the reign of the judges, the Lamanites

gathered an innumerable army of men and armed them with swords, and with cimeters, and with bows, and with arrows, and with headplates, and with breastplates, and with all manner of shields of every kind; and they came down again that they might pitch battle against the Nephites.

16 And they were led by a man whose name was Coriantumr, a descendant of Zarahemla; and he was a dissenter from among the Nephites; and he was a large and a mighty man.

17 The king of the Lamanites, whose name was Tubaloth, who was the son of Ammoron, supposed that Coriantumr, being a mighty man, could stand against the Nephites with his strength, and also his great wisdom, and that by sending him forth he should gain power over the Nephites.

18 Therefore he stirred them up to anger, and gathered together his armies, appointed Coriantumr to be their leader, and caused that they should march down to the land of Zarahemla to battle against the Nephites.

19 And it came to pass that because of so much contention and so much difficulty in the government, the Nephites had not kept sufficient guards in the land of Zarahemla; for they had supposed that the Lamanites dared not come into the heart of their lands to attack that great city Zarahemla.

20 But Coriantumr marched forth at the head of his numerous host and came upon the inhabitants of the city, and their march was with such exceedingly great speed that there was no time for the Nephites to gather together their armies.

21 Therefore Coriantumr cut down the watch by the entrance of the city and marched forth with his whole army into the city, and they slew every one who opposed them, insomuch that they took possession of the whole city.

22 Pacumeni, who was the chief judge, fled before Coriantumr, even to the walls of the city.

23 And Coriantumr smote him against the wall, insomuch that he died. And thus ended the days of Pacumeni.

24 Now when Coriantumr saw that he was in possession of the city of Zarahemla and that the Nephites had fled before them and were slain or were taken and cast into prison, and that he had obtained possession of the strongest hold in all the land, his heart took courage insomuch that he was about to go forth against all the land.

25 He did not tarry in the land of Zarahemla, but he marched forth with a large army even toward the city of Bountiful; for it was his determination to go forth and cut his way through with the sword that he might obtain the north parts of the land.

26 And supposing that the Nephites' greatest strength was in the center of the land, therefore he marched forth, giving them no time to assemble themselves together save in small bodies; and in this manner they fell upon them and cut them down to the earth.

27 But this march of Coriantumr through the center of the land gave Moronihah great advantage over them, notwithstanding the greatness of the number of the Nephites who were slain.

28 For Moronihah supposed that the Lamanites dared not come into the center of the land, but that they would attack the cities round about in the borders as they had hitherto done; therefore Moronihah caused that their strong armies should maintain those parts round about by the borders.

29 But the Lamanites were not frightened according to his desire; but they had come into the center of the land and had taken the capital city, which was the city of Zarahemla, and were marching through the most populous parts of the land, slaying the people with a great slaughter, men, women and children, taking possession of many cities and of many strongholds.

30 When Moronihah had discovered this, he immediately sent forth Lehi with an army round about to head them before they should come to the land Bountiful.

31 And this he did; and he headed them before they came to the land

Bountiful and gave them battle insomuch that they began to retreat toward the land of Zarahemla.

32 Moronihah headed them in their retreat, and gave them battle insomuch that it became an exceedingly bloody battle, and many were slain; and among the number who were slain, Coriantumr was also found.

33 And now, behold, the Lamanites could not retreat either way, neither on the north, nor on the south, nor on the east, nor on the west; for they were surrounded on every hand by the Nephites.

34 Thus had Coriantumr plunged the Lamanites into the midst of the Nephites, insomuch that they were in the power of the Nephites, and he himself was slain, and the Lamanites yielded themselves into the hands of the Nephites.

35 And Moronihah took possession of the city of Zarahemla again and caused that the Lamanites who had been taken prisoners should depart out of the land in peace.

36 Thus ended the forty-first year of the reign of the judges.

37 In the forty-second year of the reign of the judges, after Moronihah had established peace again between the Nephites and the Lamanites, behold, there was no one to fill the judgment seat; therefore there began to be a contention among the people concerning who should fill the judgment seat.

38 And Helaman, who was the son of Helaman, was appointed by the voice of the people to fill the judgment seat.

39 But, behold, Kishkumen, who had murdered Pahoran, laid in wait to destroy Helaman also; and he was upheld by his band, who had entered into a covenant that no one should know his wickedness.

40 For there was one Gadianton who was exceedingly expert in many words, and also in his craft, to carry on the secret work of murder and of robbery; therefore he became the leader of the band of Kishkumen.

41 He flattered them, and also Kishkumen, that if they would place him in the judgment seat, he would grant those who belonged to his band

that they should be placed in power and authority among the people; therefore Kishkumen sought to destroy Helaman.

42 As he went forth toward the judgment seat to destroy Helaman, behold, one of the servants of Helaman, having been out by night, and having obtained through disguise a knowledge of those plans which had been laid by his band to destroy Helaman, [43]met Kishkumen and gave him a sign; therefore Kishkumen made known to him the object of his desire, that he would conduct him to the judgment seat that he might murder Helaman.

44 When the servant of Helaman had known all the heart of Kishkumen and that it was his object to murder, and also that it was the object of all those who belonged to his band, to murder, and to rob, and to gain power (and this was their secret plan and their combination), the servant of Helaman said to Kishkumen, "Let us go forth to the judgment seat."

45 Now this pleased Kishkumen exceedingly, for he supposed that he should accomplish his design; but, behold, as they were going forth to the judgment seat, the servant of Helaman stabbed Kishkumen even to the heart that he fell dead without a groan.

46 And he ran and told Helaman all the things which he had seen, and heard, and done.

47 And Helaman sent forth to take this band of robbers and secret murderers that they might be executed according to the law.

48 But, behold, when Gadianton had found that Kishkumen did not return, he feared lest he should be destroyed; therefore he caused that his band should follow him.

49 And they took their flight out of the land, by a secret way, into the wilderness; and thus when Helaman sent forth to take them, they could nowhere be found. And more of this Gadianton shall be spoken hereafter.

50 Thus ended the forty-second year of the reign of the judges over the people of Nephi.

51 And, behold, in the end of this

book, you shall see that this Gadianton proved the overthrow, even almost the entire destruction of the people of Nephi.

52 Behold, I do not mean the end of the book of Helaman, but I mean the end of the book of Nephi from which I have taken all the account which I have written.

CHAPTER 2

IN the forty-third year of the reign of the judges, there was no contention among the people of Nephi, save it were a little pride which was in the church, which caused some little dissensions among the people, which affairs were settled in the ending of the forty-third year.

2 And there was no contention among the people in the forty-fourth year; neither was there much contention in the forty-fifth year.

3 But in the forty-sixth, there were many contentions and many dissensions, in which there were an exceedingly great many who departed out of the land of Zarahemla and went forth to the land northward to inherit the land.

4 And they traveled to an exceedingly great distance, insomuch that they came to large bodies of water and many rivers.

5 And even they spread forth into all parts of the land, into whatever parts had not been rendered desolate and without timber because of the many inhabitants who had before inherited the land.

6 Now no part of the land was desolate save it were for timber; but because of the greatness of the destruction of the people who before had inhabited the land, it was called desolate.

7 There being little timber upon the face of the land, the people who went forth became exceedingly expert in the working of cement; therefore they built houses of cement in which they dwelt.

8 And it came to pass that they multiplied and spread, and went forth from the land southward to the land northward, and spread insomuch that they began to cover the face of the whole earth, from the sea south to the sea north, from the sea west to the sea east.

9 And the people who were in the land northward dwelt in tents and in houses of cement, and they suffered whatever tree should spring up upon the face of the land, that it should grow up, that in time they might have timber to build their houses, their cities, and their temples, and their synagogues, and their sanctuaries, and all manner of their buildings.

10 As timber was exceedingly scarce in the land northward, they sent forth much by the way of shipping; and thus they enabled the people in the land northward that they might build many cities, both of wood and of cement.

11 And it came to pass that many of the people of Ammon who were Lamanites by birth also went forth into this land.

12 Now there are many records kept of the proceedings of this people, by many of this people, which are particular and very large, concerning them.

13 But a hundredth part of the proceedings of this people, the account of the Lamanites and of the Nephites, and their wars, and contentions, and dissensions, and their preaching, and their prophecies, and their shipping, and their building of ships, and their building of temples and of synagogues, and their sanctuaries, and their righteousness, and their wickedness, and their murders, and their robbings, and their plundering, and all manner of abominations and whoredoms, cannot be contained in this work.

14 But, behold, there are many books and many records of every kind, and they have been kept chiefly by the Nephites. And they have been handed down from one generation to another by the Nephites, even until they have fallen into transgression, and have been murdered, plundered and hunted, and driven forth, and slain, and scattered upon the face of the earth, and mixed with the Lamanites until they are no more called the Nephites, becoming wicked, and wild, and ferocious, even becoming Lamanites.

15 Now I return again to my

account; therefore what I have spoken had passed after there had been great contentions, and disturbances, and wars, and dissensions among the people of Nephi.

16 The forty-sixth year of the reign of the judges ended.

17 And there were still great contentions in the land, even in the forty-seventh year, and also in the forty-eighth year.

18 Nevertheless, Helaman filled the judgment seat with justice and equity; he observed to keep the statutes, and the judgments, and the commandments of God; and he did that which was right in the sight of God continually; and he walked after the ways of his father, insomuch that he prospered in the land.

19 And it came to pass that he had two sons. He gave to the eldest the name of Nephi and to the youngest the name of Lehi. And they began to grow up unto the Lord.

20 And the wars and contentions began to cease in a small degree among the people of the Nephites in the latter end of the forty-eighth year of the reign of the judges over the people of Nephi.

21 In the forty-ninth year of the reign of the judges, there was continual peace established in the land, save for the secret combinations which Gadianton the robber had established in the more settled parts of the land, which combinations at that time were not known to those who were at the head of government; therefore they were not destroyed out of the land.

22 In this same year there was exceedingly great prosperity in the church, insomuch that there were thousands who joined themselves to the church and were baptized unto repentance.

23 So great was the prosperity of the church, and so many the blessings which were poured out upon the people, that even the high priests and the teachers were themselves astonished beyond measure.

24 And the work of the Lord prospered unto the baptizing and uniting to the church of God many souls, even tens of thousands.

25 Thus we may see that the Lord is merciful to all who will in the sincerity of their hearts call upon his holy name. Thus we see that the gate of heaven is open to all, even to those who will believe on the name of Jesus Christ, who is the son of God, [26]those who will lay hold upon the word of God, which is quick and powerful, which shall divide asunder all the cunning, and the snares, and the wiles of the devil, and lead the man of Christ in a straight and narrow course across that everlasting gulf of misery which is prepared to engulf the wicked, and land his soul, even his immortal soul, at the right hand of God in the kingdom of heaven, to sit down with Abraham, and Isaac, and with Jacob, and with all our holy fathers, to go no more out.

27 In this year there was continual rejoicing in the land of Zarahemla and in all the regions round about, even in all the land which was possessed by the Nephites.

28 And there were peace and exceedingly great joy in the remainder of the forty-ninth year; and also there were continual peace and great joy in the fiftieth year of the reign of the judges.

29 In the fifty-first year of the reign of the judges, there was peace also, save for the pride which began to enter into the church—not into the church of God, but into the hearts of the people who professed to belong to the church of God—and some were lifted up in pride, even to the persecution of many of their brethren.

30 Now this was a great evil, which caused the more humble part of the people to suffer great persecutions and to wade through much affliction.

31 Nevertheless, they fasted and prayed often, and waxed stronger and stronger in their humility, and firmer and firmer in the faith of Christ, to the filling of their souls with joy and consolation, even to the purifying and the sanctifying of their hearts, which sanctification comes because of their yielding their hearts to God.

32 And the fifty-second year ended in peace also, save for the exceedingly great pride which had gotten into the hearts of the people; and it

was because of their exceedingly great riches and their prosperity in the land; and it grew upon them from day to day.

33 In the fifty-third year of the reign of the judges, Helaman died, and his eldest son Nephi began to reign in his stead.

34 And he filled the judgment seat with justice and equity; he kept the commandments of God and walked in the ways of his father.

35 And it came to pass in the fifty-fourth year, there were many dissensions in the church, and there was also a contention among the people, insomuch that there was much bloodshed; and the rebellious part were slain and driven out of the land, and they went to the king of the Lamanites.

36 And they endeavored to stir up the Lamanites to war against the Nephites; but, behold, the Lamanites were exceedingly afraid, insomuch that they would not hearken to the words of those dissenters.

37 But in the fifty-sixth year of the reign of the judges, there were dissenters who went up from the Nephites to the Lamanites, and they succeeded with those others in stirring them up to anger against the Nephites; and they were all that year preparing for war.

38 And in the fifty-seventh year, they came down against the Nephites to battle; and they commenced the work of death, insomuch that in the fifty-eighth year of the reign of the judges, they succeeded in obtaining possession of the land of Zarahemla, and also all the lands, even to the land which was near the land Bountiful.

39 And the Nephites and the armies of Moronihah were driven even into the land of Bountiful; and there they fortified against the Lamanites, from the west sea even to the east, it being a day's journey for a Nephite on the line which they had fortified and stationed their armies to defend their north country.

40 Thus those dissenters of the Nephites, with the help of a numerous army of the Lamanites, had obtained all the possession of the Nephites which was in the land southward.

41 And all this was done in the fifty-eighth and ninth years of the reign of the judges.

42 In the sixtieth year of the reign of the judges, Moronihah succeeded with his armies in obtaining many parts of the land; and they regained many cities which had fallen into the hands of the Lamanites.

43 And in the sixty-first year of the reign of the judges, they succeeded in regaining even the half of all their possessions.

44 Now this great loss of the Nephites and the great slaughter which was among them would not have happened had it not been for their wickedness and their abomination which was among them; and it was among those also who professed to belong to the church of God.

45 And it was because of the pride of their hearts because of their exceeding riches, because of their oppression to the poor, withholding their food from the hungry, withholding their clothing from the naked, and smiting their humble brethren upon the cheek, making a mock of that which was sacred, denying the spirit of prophecy and of revelation, their murderings, plunderings, lying, stealing, committing adultery, rising up in great contentions, and deserting away into the land of Nephi, among the Lamanites.

46 And because of this their great wickedness and their boastings in their own strength, they were left in their own strength; therefore they did not prosper, but were afflicted and smitten, and driven before the Lamanites, until they had lost possession of almost all their lands.

47 But, behold, Moronihah preached many things to the people because of their iniquity, and also Nephi and Lehi, who were the sons of Helaman, preached many things to the people, [48]and prophesied many things to them concerning their iniquities and what should come to them if they did not repent of their sins.

49 And it came to pass that they repented, and inasmuch as they repented they began to prosper.

50 For when Moronihah saw that

they repented, he ventured to lead them forth from place to place, and from city to city, even until they had regained the half of their property and the half of all their lands.

51 Thus ended the sixty-first year of the reign of the judges.

52 In the sixty-second year of the reign of the judges, Moronihah could obtain no more possessions from the Lamanites.

53 Therefore they abandoned their design to regain the remainder of their lands, for so numerous were the Lamanites that it became impossible for the Nephites to obtain more power over them; therefore Moronihah employed all his armies in maintaining those parts which he had taken.

54 And because of the greatness of the number of the Lamanites, the Nephites were in great fear lest they should be overpowered, and trodden down, and slain, and destroyed.

55 They began to remember the prophecies of Alma, and also the words of Mosiah; and they saw that they had been a stiffed-necked people, and that they had set at nought the commandments of God; 56and that they had altered and trampled under their feet the laws of Mosiah, or that which the Lord commanded him to give the people.

57 Thus they saw that their laws had become corrupted, and that they had become a wicked people, insomuch that they were wicked even like the Lamanites.

58 And because of their iniquity, the church had begun to dwindle; and they began to disbelieve in the spirit of prophecy and in the spirit of revelation; and the judgments of God stared them in the face.

59 And they saw that they had become weak like their brethren, the Lamanites, and that the Spirit of the Lord no more preserved them, because the Spirit of the Lord does not dwell in unholy temples.

60 Therefore the Lord ceased to preserve them by his miraculous and matchless power, for they had fallen into a state of unbelief and awful wickedness; and they saw that the Lamanites were exceedingly more numerous than they, and except they should cleave to the Lord their God, they must unavoidably perish.

61 For, behold, they saw that the strength of the Lamanites was as great as their strength, even man for man.

62 And thus had they fallen into this great transgression; thus had they become weak, because of their transgression, in the space of not many years.

63 In this same year, behold, Nephi delivered up the judgment seat to a man whose name was Cezoram.

64 For as their laws and their governments were established by the voice of the people, and they who chose evil were more numerous than they who chose good, therefore they were ripening for destruction, for the laws had become corrupted.

65 And this was not all; they were a stiff-necked people, insomuch that they could not be governed by the law nor justice, save it were to their destruction.

66 Nephi had become weary because of their iniquity; and he yielded up the judgment seat and took it upon him to preach the word of God all the remainder of his days, and his brother Lehi also, all the remainder of his days; for they remembered the words which their father Helaman spoke to them.

67 And these are the words which he spoke: "Behold, my sons, I desire that you should remember to keep the commandments of God; and I would that you should declare to the people these words.

68 "Behold, I have given you the names of our first parents who came out of the land of Jerusalem; and this I have done that when you remember your names you may remember them; and when you may remember them, you may remember their works; and when you remember their works, you may know how that it is said, and also written, that they were good.

69 "Therefore, my sons, I would that you should do that which is good, that it may be said of you, and also written, even as it has been said and written of them.

70 "And now, my sons, behold, I have somewhat more to desire of you,

which desire is that you may not do these things that you may boast, but that you may do these things to lay up for yourselves a treasure in heaven, which is eternal and which fades not away; that you may have that precious gift of eternal life which we have reason to suppose has been given to our fathers.

71 "O remember, remember, my sons, the words which King Benjamin spoke to his people; remember that there is no other way nor means whereby man can be saved only through the atoning blood of Jesus Christ, who shall come; and remember that he comes to redeem the world.

72 "And remember also the words which Amulek spoke to Zeezrom in the city of Ammonihah; for he said to him that the Lord surely should come to redeem his people; but that he should not come to redeem them in their sins, but to redeem them from their sins.

73 "And he has power given to him from the Father to redeem them from their sins, because of repentance; therefore he has sent his angels to declare the tidings of the conditions of repentance, which brings to them the power of the Redeemer to the salvation of their souls.

74 "Now, my sons, remember, remember that it is upon the rock of our redeemer, who is Christ, the Son of God, that you must build your foundation, that when the devil shall send forth his mighty winds and his shafts in the whirlwind, 75when all his hail and his mighty storm shall beat upon you, it shall have no power over you to drag you down to the gulf of misery and endless woe, because of the rock upon which you are built, which is a sure foundation, a foundation whereon if men build, they cannot fall."

76 These were the words which Helaman taught to his sons; he taught them many things which are not written and also many things which are written.

77 And they remembered his words, and therefore they went forth, keeping the commandments of God, to teach the word of God among all the people of Nephi, beginning at the city Bountiful, and thence to the city of Gid, and from the city of Gid to the city of Mulek; 78and even from one city to another, until they had gone forth among all the people of Nephi who were in the land southward, and thence into the land of Zarahemla among the Lamanites.

79 And they preached with great power, insomuch that they confounded many of those dissenters who had gone over from the Nephites, insomuch that they came forth and confessed their sins and were baptized unto repentance and immediately returned to the Nephites to endeavor to repair them the wrongs which they had done.

80 And Nephi and Lehi preached to the Lamanites with great power and authority, for they had power and authority given to them that they might speak; and they also had what they should speak given unto them.

81 Therefore they spoke to the great astonishment of the Lamanites and to the convincing of them, insomuch that there were eight thousand of the Lamanites, who were in the land of Zarahemla and round about, baptized unto repentance and convinced of the wickedness of the traditions of their fathers.

82 And it came to pass that Nephi and Lehi proceeded thence to go to the land of Nephi.

83 And they were taken by an army of the Lamanites and cast into prison, even in that same prison in which Ammon and his brethren were cast by the servants of Limhi.

84 After they had been cast into prison many days without food, behold, the Lamanites went forth into the prison to take them that they might slay them.

85 And Nephi and Lehi were encircled as if by fire, even insomuch that they dared not lay their hands upon them for fear lest they should be burned.

86 Nevertheless, Nephi and Lehi were not burned; and they were as if standing in the midst of fire and were not burned.

87 When they saw that they were encircled with a pillar of fire and that it burned them not, their hearts took courage.

88 For they saw that the Lamanites dared not lay their hands upon them; neither dared they come near them, but stood as if they were struck dumb with amazement.

89 Nephi and Lehi stood forth and began to speak to them, saying, "Fear not, for, behold, it is God that has shown you this marvelous thing in which is shown you that you cannot lay your hands on us to slay us."

90 And when they had said these words, the earth shook exceedingly, and the walls of the prison shook as if they were about to tumble to the earth, but they did not fall.

91 And, behold, they that were in the prison were Lamanites and Nephites who were dissenters.

92 And it came to pass that they were overshadowed with a cloud of darkness, and an awful, solemn fear came upon them.

93 And there came a voice, as if it were above the cloud of darkness, saying, "Repent ye, repent ye, and seek no more to destroy my servants whom I have sent to you to declare good tidings."

94 When they heard this voice— and beheld that it was not a voice of thunder, neither was it a voice of a great tumultuous noise, but, behold, it was a still voice of perfect mildness, as if it had been a whisper—it pierced even to the very soul.

95 Notwithstanding the mildness of the voice, behold, the earth shook exceedingly, and the walls of the prison trembled again as if they were about to tumble to the earth; and, behold, the cloud of darkness which had overshadowed them did not disperse.

96 And, behold, the voice came again, saying, "Repent ye, repent ye, for the kingdom of heaven is at hand; and seek no more to destroy my servants."

97 And the earth shook again, and the walls trembled; and also again the third time the voice came and spoke to them marvelous words which cannot be uttered by man; and the walls trembled again, and the earth shook as if it were about to divide asunder.

98 And the Lamanites could not flee because of the cloud of darkness which overshadowed them; and also they were immovable because of the fear which came upon them.

99 Now there was one among them who was a Nephite by birth who had once belonged to the church of God but had dissented from it.

100 He turned about and, behold, he saw through the cloud of darkness the faces of Nephi and Lehi; and, behold, they shone exceedingly, even as the faces of angels.

101 And he beheld that they lifted their eyes to heaven; and they were in the attitude as if talking or lifting their voices to some being whom they beheld.

102 This man cried to the multitude that they might turn and look.

103 And, behold, there was power given to them that they turned and looked, and they beheld the faces of Nephi and Lehi.

104 And they said to the man, "Behold, what do all these things mean, and who is it with whom these men converse?"

105 Now the man's name was Aminadab. And Aminadab said to them, "They converse with the angels of God."

106 And the Lamanites said to him, "What shall we do that this cloud of darkness may be removed from overshadowing us?"

107 Aminadab said to them, "You must repent and cry to the voice, even until you shall have faith in Christ, who was taught to you by Alma, and Amulek, and Zeezrom; and when you shall do this, the cloud of darkness shall be removed from overshadowing you."

108 And all began to cry to the voice of him who had shaken the earth; they cried even until the cloud of darkness was dispersed.

109 When they cast their eyes about and saw that the cloud of darkness was dispersed from overshadowing them, behold, they saw that they were encircled, every soul, by a pillar of fire.

110 And Nephi and Lehi were in the midst of them; and they were encircled as if in the midst of a flaming fire, yet it did not harm them,

neither did it take hold upon the walls of the prison; and they were filled with that joy which is unspeakable and full of glory.

111 And, behold, the Holy Spirit of God came down from heaven and entered into their hearts, and they were filled as if with fire; and they could speak forth marvelous words.

112 And there came a voice to them, a pleasant voice, as if it were a whisper, saying, "Peace, peace be to' you because of your faith in my well beloved, who was from the foundation of the world."

113 When they heard this, they cast up their eyes as if to behold whence the voice came; and, behold, they saw the heavens open; and angels came down out of heaven and ministered to them.

114 And there were about three hundred souls who saw and heard these things; and they were bid to go forth and marvel not, neither should they doubt.

115 And they went forth and ministered to the people, declaring throughout all the regions round about all the things which they had heard and seen, insomuch that the greater part of the Lamanites were convinced of them because of the greatness of the evidences which they had received.

116 And as many as were convinced laid down their weapons of war, and also their hatred and the tradition of their fathers.

117 And they yielded up to the Nephites the lands of their possession.

118 When the sixty-second year of the reign of the judges had ended, all these things had happened, and the Lamanites had become, the greater part of them, a righteous people, insomuch that their righteousness exceeded that of the Nephites because of their firmness and their steadiness in the faith.

119 For, behold, there were many of the Nephites who had become hardened, and impenitent, and grossly wicked, insomuch that they rejected the word of God, and all the preaching and prophesying which came among them.

120 Nevertheless the people of the church had great joy because of the conversion of the Lamanites, and because of the church of God which had been established among them.

121 And they fellowshiped one with another, and rejoiced one with another, and had great joy.

122 And it came to pass that many of the Lamanites came down into the land of Zarahemla, and declared to the people of the Nephites the manner of their conversion, and exhorted them to faith and repentance.

123 And many preached with exceedingly great power and authority, to the bringing down many of them into the depths of humility to be the humble followers of God and the Lamb.

124 And it came to pass that many of the Lamanites went into the land northward; and also Nephi and Lehi went into the land northward to preach to the people.

125 Thus ended the sixty-third year.

126 And, behold, there was peace in all the land, insomuch that the Nephites went into whatever part of the land they would, whether among the Nephites or the Lamanites.

127 The Lamanites also went wherever they would, whether it was among the Lamanites or among the Nephites; and thus they had free intercourse one with another, to buy, and to sell, and to get gain according to their desire.

128 And they became exceedingly rich, both the Lamanites and the Nephites; and they had plenty of gold, and of silver, and of all manner of precious metals, both in the land south and in the land north.

129 Now the land south was called Lehi, and the land north was called Mulek, which was after the son of Zedekiah; for the Lord brought Mulek into the land north and Lehi into the land south.

130 And, behold, there was all manner of gold in both these lands, and of silver, and of precious ore of every kind; and there were also curious workmen, who worked all kinds of ore, and refined it; and thus they became rich.

131 They raised grain in abundance, both in the north and in the south. And they flourished exceed-

ingly, both in the north and in the south.

132 And they multiplied and waxed exceedingly strong in the land. And they raised many flocks and herds, and many fatlings.

133 Behold, their women toiled and spun, and made all manner of cloth, of fine twined linen, and cloth of every kind, to clothe their nakedness.

134 Thus the sixty-fourth year passed away in peace.

135 And in the sixty-fifth year, they also had great joy and peace, and much preaching, and many prophecies concerning that which was to come. And thus passed away the sixty-fifth year.

136 In the sixty-sixth year of the reign of the judges, behold, Cezoram was murdered by an unknown hand, as he sat upon the judgment seat.

137 And in the same year his son, who had been appointed by the people in his stead, was also murdered. Thus ended the sixty-sixth year.

138 In the commencement of the sixty-seventh year, the people began to grow exceedingly wicked again.

139 For, behold, the Lord had blessed them so long with the riches of the world that they had not been stirred up to anger, to wars, nor to bloodsheds; therefore they began to set their hearts upon their riches.

140 They began to seek to get gain that they might be lifted up one above another; therefore they began to commit secret murders, and to rob and to plunder that they might get gain.

141 And now, behold, those murderers and plunderers were a band who had been formed by Kishkumen and Gadianton.

142 And there were many of Gadianton's band even among the Nephites. But, behold, they were more numerous among the more wicked part of the Lamanites.

143 And they were called Gadianton's robbers and murderers; and it was they who murdered the chief judge Cezoram and his son while they were in the judgment seat; and, behold, they were not found.

144 When the Lamanites found that there were robbers among them, they were exceedingly sorrowful; and they used every means in their power to destroy them off the face of the earth.

145 But, behold, Satan stirred up the hearts of the greater part of the Nephites, insomuch that they united with those bands of robbers and entered into their covenants and their oaths that they would protect and preserve one another in whatever difficult circumstances they should be placed, that they should not suffer for their murders, and their plunderings, and their stealings.

146 And they had their signs, their secret signs, and their secret words; and this that they might distinguish a brother who had entered into the covenant that whatever wickedness his brother should do, he should not be injured by his brother, nor by those who belonged to his band who had taken this covenant.

147 Thus they might murder, and plunder, and steal, and commit whoredoms, and all manner of wickedness contrary to the laws of their country and also the laws of their God.

148 And whoever of those who belonged to their band and should reveal to the world of their wickedness and their abominations should be tried, not according to the laws of their country, but according to the laws of their wickedness which had been given by Gadianton and Kishkumen.

149 Now, behold, it is these secret oaths and covenants which Alma commanded his son should not go forth to the world, lest they should be a means of bringing down the people to destruction.

150 Now those secret oaths and covenants did not come forth to Gadianton from the records which were delivered to Helaman.

151 But they were put into the heart of Gadianton by that same being who enticed our first parents to partake of the forbidden fruit, that same being who plotted with Cain that if he would murder his brother Abel it should not be known to the world.

152 And he plotted with Cain and his followers from that time forth.

153 Also it is that same being who put it into the hearts of the people to build a tower sufficiently high that they might get to heaven.

154 And it is that same being who led on the people who came from that tower into this land, who spread the works of darkness and abominations over all the face of the land, until he dragged the people down to an entire destruction and to an everlasting hell.

155 It is that same being who put it into the heart of Gadianton to still carry on the work of darkness and of secret murder; and he has brought it forth from the beginning of man, even down to this time.

156 And, behold, it is he who is the author of all sin. And, behold, he carries on his works of darkness and secret murder, and hands down their plots, and their oaths, and their covenants, and their plans of awful wickedness from generation to generation, according as he can get hold upon the hearts of the children of men.

157 Now, behold, he had got great hold upon the hearts of the Nephites, insomuch that they had become exceedingly wicked.

158 The greater part of them had turned out of the way of righteousness, and trampled under their feet the commandments of God, and turned to their own ways, and built up to themselves idols of their gold and their silver.

159 And all these iniquities came to them in the space of not many years, insomuch that a larger part had come to them in the sixty-seventh year of the reign of the judges over the people of Nephi.

160 They grew in their iniquities in the sixty-eighth year also, to the great sorrow and lamentation of the righteous.

161 And thus we see that the Nephites began to dwindle in unbelief and to grow in wickedness and abominations, while the Lamanites began to grow exceedingly in the knowledge of their God; they began to keep his statutes and commandments and to walk in truth and uprightness before him.

162 Thus we see that the Spirit of the Lord began to withdraw from the Nephites because of the wickedness and the hardness of their hearts, 163that the Lord began to pour out his Spirit upon the Lamanites because of their easiness and willingness to believe in his word.

164 And it came to pass that the Lamanites hunted the band of robbers of Gadianton; and they preached the word of God among the more wicked part of them, insomuch that this band of robbers was utterly destroyed from among the Lamanites.

165 On the other hand, the Nephites built them up and supported them, beginning at the more wicked part of them, until they had overspread all the land of the Nephites, and had seduced the greater part of the righteous until they had come down to believe in their works, and to partake of their spoils, and to join with them in their secret murders and combinations.

166 Thus they obtained the sole management of the government, insomuch that they trampled under their feet, and smote, and rent, and turned their backs upon the poor, and the meek, and the humble followers of God.

167 And thus we see that they were in an awful state and ripening for an everlasting destruction.

168 Thus ended the sixty-eighth year of the reign of the judges over the people of Nephi.

CHAPTER 3

The prophecy of Nephi, the son of Helaman. God threatens the people of Nephi, that he will visit them in his anger to their utter destruction except they repent of their wickedness. God smites the people of Nephi with pestilence; they repent and turn to him. Samuel, a Lamanite, prophesies to the Nephites.

BEHOLD, now it came to pass in the sixty-ninth year of the reign of the judges over the people of the Nephites that Nephi, the son of Helaman, returned to the land of Zarahemla from the land northward; for he had been among the people who were in the land northward, and preached the word of God to them and prophesied many things to them;

2 And they rejected all his words, insomuch that he could not stay among them, but returned again to the land of his nativity.

3 And he saw the people in a state of such awful wickedness, and those Gadianton robbers filling the judgment seats, having usurped the power and authority of the land, laying aside the commandments of God and not in the least aright before him, doing no justice to the children of men, condemning the righteous because of their righteousness, letting the guilty and the wicked go unpunished because of their money, ⁴and being held in office at the head of government to rule and do according to their wills that they might get gain and glory of the world, and moreover that they might the more easily commit adultery, and steal, and kill, and do according to their own wills.

5 Now this great iniquity had come upon the Nephites in the space of not many years; and when Nephi saw it, his heart was swollen with sorrow within his breast.

6 And he exclaimed in the agony of his soul, "Oh, that I could have had my days in the days when my father Nephi first came out of the land of Jerusalem, that I could have rejoiced with him in the promised land.

7 "Then were his people easy to be entreated, firm to keep the commandments of God, and slow to be led to do iniquity; and they were quick to hearken to the words of the Lord.

8 "If my days could have been in those days, then would my soul have had joy in the righteousness of my brethren.

9 "But, behold, I am resigned that these are my days, and that my soul shall be filled with sorrow because of the wickedness of my brethren."

10 Now it was upon a tower which was in the garden of Nephi, which was by the highway which led to the chief market which was in the city of Zarahemla, ¹¹that Nephi bowed himself. The tower which was in his garden was near the garden gate which led by the highway.

12 And there were certain men passing by who saw Nephi as he was pouring out his soul to God upon the tower, and they ran and told the people what they had seen, and the people came together in multitudes that they might know the cause of so great mourning for the wickedness of the people.

13 When Nephi arose he beheld the multitudes of people who had gathered together.

14 And he opened his mouth and said to them, "Behold, why have you gathered yourselves together? That I may tell you of your iniquities?

15 "Because I have got upon my tower that I might pour out my soul to my God because of the exceeding sorrow of my heart, which is because of your iniquities?

16 "And because of my mourning and lamentation, you have gathered yourselves together and do marvel; and you have great need to marvel.

17 "You ought to marvel because you are given away that the devil has got so great hold upon your hearts. How could you have given away to the enticing of him who is seeking to hurl your souls down to everlasting misery and endless woe?

18 "O repent, repent! Why will you die? Turn you, turn you to the Lord your God. Why has he forsaken you?

19 "It is because you have hardened your hearts; you will not hearken to the voice of the Good Shepherd; and you have provoked him to anger against you.

20 "And, behold, instead of gathering you, except you will repent, behold, he shall scatter you forth that you shall become meat for dogs and wild beasts.

21 "Oh, how could you have forgotten your God in the very day that he has delivered you?

22 "But, behold, it is to get gain, to be praised of men, and that you might get gold and silver.

23 "And you have set your hearts upon the riches and the vain things of this world, for which you murder, and plunder, and steal, and bear false witness against your neighbor, and do all manner of iniquity; and for this cause woe shall come to you except you shall repent.

24 "For if you will not repent, behold, this great city, and also all those great cities which are round about which are in the land of our possession, shall be taken away that you shall have no place in them, for, behold, the Lord will not grant to you strength, as he has hitherto done, to withstand your enemies.

25 "For, behold, thus says the Lord, 'I will not show to the wicked of my strength, to one more than the other, save it be to those who repent of their sins and hearken to my words.'

26 "Now therefore I would that you should behold, my brethren, that it shall be better for the Lamanites than for you except you shall repent; for, behold, they are more righteous than you, for they have not sinned against that great knowledge which you have received.

27 "Therefore the Lord will be merciful to them; he will lengthen out their days and increase their seed, even when you shall be utterly destroyed, except you shall repent.

28 "Woe be to you because of that great abomination which has come among you; and you have united yourselves to it, even to that secret band which was established by Gadianton.

29 "Woe shall come to you because of that pride which you have suffered to enter your hearts, which has lifted you up beyond that which is good because of your exceedingly great riches; woe be to you because of your wickedness and abominations.

30 "And except you repent, you shall perish; even your lands shall be taken from you, and you shall be destroyed from off the face of the earth.

31 "Behold, now I do not say of myself that these things shall be, because it is not of myself that I know these things; but, behold, I know that these things are true because the Lord God has made them known to me; therefore I testify that they shall be."

32 When Nephi had said these words, behold, there were men who were judges who also belonged to the secret band of Gadianton, and they were angry, 33and they cried out against him, saying to the people, "Why do you not seize upon this man and bring him forth that he may be condemned according to the crime which he has done?

34 "Why do you see this man and hear him revile against this people and against our law?"

35 For, behold, Nephi had spoken to them concerning the corruptness of their law; even many things Nephi spoke which cannot be written; and nothing did he speak which was contrary to the commandments of God.

36 And those judges were angry with him because he spoke plainly to them concerning their secret works of darkness; nevertheless they dared not lay their own hands upon him; for they feared the people, lest they should cry out against them; therefore they cried to the people, saying, "Why do you suffer this man to revile against us?

37 "For, behold, he condemns all this people, even to destruction, and also says that these our great cities shall be taken from us that we shall have no place in them.

38 "Now we know that this is impossible; for, behold, we are powerful, and our cities are great; therefore our enemies can have no power over us."

39 And thus they stirred up the

people to anger against Nephi, and raised contentions among them; for there were some who cried out, "Let this man alone, for he is a good man, and those things which he says will surely come to pass except we repent.

40 "Behold, all the judgments will come upon us which he has testified to us; for we know that he has testified aright to us concerning our iniquities.

41 "And, behold, they are many; and he knows as well all things which shall befall us as he knows of our iniquities; and, behold, if he had not been a prophet he could not have testified concerning those things."

42 And those people who sought to destroy Nephi were compelled because of their fear that they did not lay their hands on him.

43 Therefore he began again to speak to them, seeing that he had gained favor in the eyes of some, insomuch that the remainder of them feared.

44 Therefore he was constrained to speak more to them, saying, "Behold, my brethren, have you not read that God gave power to one man, even Moses, to smite upon the waters of the Red Sea, and they parted insomuch that the Israelites, who were our fathers, came through upon dry ground, and the waters closed upon the armies of the Egyptians and swallowed them up?

45 "Now, behold, if God gave to this man such power, then why should you dispute among yourselves and say that he has given me no power whereby I may know concerning the judgments that shall come upon you except you repent?

46 "But, behold, you not only deny my words, but you also deny all the words which have been spoken by our fathers, and also the words which were spoken by this man, Moses, who had such great power given him, even the words which he has spoken concerning the coming of the Messiah.

47 "Did he not bear record that the Son of God should come? And as he lifted up the brazen serpent in the wilderness, even so shall he be lifted up who should come.

48 "And as many as should look upon that serpent should live, even so as many as should look upon the Son of God, with faith, having a contrite spirit, might live, even to that life which is eternal.

49 "Now, behold, not only did Moses testify of these things, but also all the holy prophets from his days even to the days of Abraham.

50 "Behold, Abraham saw his coming, and was filled with gladness, and rejoiced.

51 "And, behold, I say to you that not only Abraham knew of these things, but there were many before the days of Abraham who were called by the order of God, even after the order of his Son; 52and this that it should be shown to the people a great many thousand years before his coming that even redemption should come to them.

53 "Now I would that you should know that, even since the days of Abraham, there have been many prophets that have testified these things; and, behold, the prophet Zenos testified boldly, for which he was slain, 54and also Zenock, and also Ezaias, and also Isaiah, and Jeremiah (Jeremiah being that same prophet who testified of the destruction of Jerusalem).

55 "And now we know that Jerusalem was destroyed according to the words of Jeremiah. Oh, then, why not the Son of God come according to his prophecy?

56 "And now will you dispute that Jerusalem was destroyed? Will you say that the sons of Zedekiah were not slain, all except Mulek?

57 "And do you not behold that the seed of Zedekiah are with us, and they were driven out of the land of Jerusalem?

58 "But, behold, this is not all. Our father Lehi was driven out of Jerusalem because he testified of these things.

59 "Nephi also testified of these things, and also almost all of our fathers, even down to this time; they have testified of the coming of Christ, and have looked forward, and have rejoiced in his day which is to come.

60 "And, behold, he is God, and he is with them, and he manifested himself to them that they were redeemed by him; and they gave

to him glory because of that which is to come.

61 "And now seeing you know these things and cannot deny them, except you shall lie, therefore in this you have sinned, for you have rejected all these things, notwithstanding so many evidences which you have received.

62 "Even you have received all things, both things in heaven, and all things which are in the earth, as a witness that they are true.

63 "But, behold, you have rejected the truth and rebelled against your holy God; and even at this time, instead of laying up for yourselves treasures in heaven where nothing corrupts, and where nothing can come which is unclean, you are heaping up for yourselves wrath against the day of judgment.

64 "Even at this time you are ripening, because of your murders, and your fornication and wickedness, for everlasting destruction; and except you repent, it will come to you soon.

65 "Behold, it is now even at your doors; go in to the judgment seat and search; and, behold, your judge is murdered, and he lies in his blood; and he has been murdered by his brother, who seeks to sit in the judgment seat.

66 "And, behold, they both belong to your secret band, whose author is Gadianton and the evil one who seeks to destroy the souls of men."

67 Behold, when Nephi had spoken these words, certain men who were among them ran to the judgment seat; even there were five who went.

68 And they said among themselves as they went, "Behold, now we will know of a surety whether this man be a prophet, and that God has commanded him to prophesy such marvelous things to us.

69 "Behold, we do not believe that he has; we do not believe that he is a prophet; nevertheless, if this thing which he has said concerning the chief judge be true, that he be dead, then will we believe that the other words which he has spoken are true."

70 And they ran in their might and came in to the judgment seat; and,

behold, the chief judge had fallen to the earth and lay in his blood.

71 When they saw this, they were astonished exceedingly, insomuch that they fell to the earth; for they had not believed the words which Nephi had spoken concerning the chief judge.

72 But now when they saw, they believed, and fear came upon them lest all the judgments which Nephi had spoken should come upon the people; therefore they quaked and fell to the earth.

73 Now immediately when the judge had been murdered (he being stabbed by his brother in a garb of secrecy, and he fled), the servants ran and told the people, raising the cry of murder among them.

74 And, behold, the people gathered to the place of the judgment seat; and, behold, to their astonishment, they saw those five men who had fallen to the earth.

75 Now, behold, the people knew nothing concerning the multitude which had gathered together at the garden of Nephi; therefore they said among themselves, "These men are they who have murdered the judge, and God has smitten them that they could not flee from us."

76 And they laid hold on them, and bound them, and cast them into prison.

77 And there was a proclamation sent abroad that the judge was slain, and that the murderers had been taken, and were cast into prison.

78 On the morrow, the people assembled themselves together to mourn and to fast at the burial of the great chief judge who had been slain.

79 And those judges who were at the garden of Nephi and heard his words were also gathered together at the burial.

80 And they inquired among the people, saying, "Where are the five who were sent to inquire concerning the chief judge whether he was dead?"

81 And they answered and said, "Concerning this five whom you say you have sent, we know not; but there are five, who are the murderers, whom we have cast into prison."

82 The judges desired that they

should be brought; and they were brought, and, behold, they were the five who were sent.

83 And, behold, the judges inquired of them to know concerning the matter, and they told them all that they had done, saying,"We ran and came to the place of the judgment seat, and when we saw all things, even as Nephi had testified, we were astonished, insomuch that we fell to the earth; and when we were recovered from our astonishment, behold, they cast us into prison.

84 "As for the murder of this man, we know not who has done it, and only this much we know, we ran and came according as you desired, and, behold, he was dead according to the words of Nephi."

85 Now the judges expounded the matter to the people and cried out against Nephi, saying, "Behold, we know that this Nephi must have agreed with someone to slay the judge, and then he might declare it to us that he might convert us to his faith, that he might raise himself to be a great man, chosen of God, and a prophet.

86 "And now, behold, we will detect this man, and he shall confess his fault and make known to us the true murderer of this judge."

87 And it came to pass that the five were liberated on the day of the burial.

88 Nevertheless, they rebuked the judges in the words which they had spoken against Nephi and contended with them one by one, insomuch that they confounded them.

89 The judges caused that Nephi should be taken and bound and brought before the multitude, and they began to question him in divers ways, that they might cross him, that they might accuse him to death.

90 And they said to him, "You are a confederate; who is this man that has done this murder? Now tell us and acknowledge your fault," and "Behold, here is money; and also we will grant you your life if you will tell us and acknowledge the agreement which you have made with him."

91 But Nephi said to them, "O you fools, you uncircumcised of heart, you blind, and you stiff-necked people, do you know how long the Lord your God will suffer you that you shall go on in your way of sin?

92 "You ought to begin to howl and mourn because of the great destruction at this time which awaits you except you shall repent.

93 "Behold, you say that I have agreed with a man that he should murder Seezoram, our chief judge.

94 "But, behold, I say to you that this is because I have testified to you that you might know concerning this thing, even for a witness to you that I knew of the wickedness and abominations which are among you.

95 "And because I have done this, you say that I have agreed with a man that he should do this thing; because I showed you this sign, you are angry with me and seek to destroy my life.

96 "And now, behold, I will show you another sign and see if you will in this thing seek to destroy me.

97 "Behold, I say to you, Go to the house of Seantum, who is the brother of Seezoram, and say to him, 'Has Nephi, the pretended prophet, who prophesies so much evil concerning this people, agreed with you, in which you have murdered Seezoram, who is your brother?' And, behold, he shall say to you, 'No.'

98 "And you shall say to him, 'Have you murdered your brother?' And he shall stand with fear and know not what to say.

99 "And, behold, he shall deny to you; and he shall make as if he were astonished; nevertheless, he shall declare to you that he is innocent.

100 "But, behold, you shall examine him, and you shall find blood upon the skirts of his cloak.

101 "And when you have seen this, you shall say, 'Whence comes this blood? Do we not know that it is the blood of your brother?' And then shall he tremble and shall look pale, even as if death had come upon him.

102 "Then shall you say, 'Because of this fear and this paleness which has come upon your face, behold, we know that you are guilty.'

103 "Then shall greater fear come

upon him; and then shall he confess to you and deny no more that he has done this murder.

104 "And then shall he say to you that I, Nephi, knew nothing concerning the matter save it were given to me by the power of God.

105 "And then shall you know that I am an honest man, and that I am sent to you from God."

106 And it came to pass that they went and did even according as Nephi had said to them.

107 And, behold, the words which he had said were true; for according to the words, he denied; and also according to the words, he confessed.

108 And he was brought to prove that he himself was the very murderer, insomuch that the five were set at liberty, and also was Nephi.

109 There were some of the Nephites who believed on the words of Nephi; and there were some also who believed because of the testimony of the five, for they had been converted while they were in prison.

110 And there were some among the people who said that Nephi was a prophet; and there were others who said, "Behold, he is a god, for except he was a god, he could not know of all things.

111 "For, behold, he has told us the thoughts of our hearts, and also has told us things; and even he has brought to our knowledge the true murderer of our chief judge."

112 And there arose a division among the people, insomuch that they divided and went their ways, leaving Nephi alone as he was standing in the midst of them.

113 And Nephi went his way toward his own house, pondering upon the things which the Lord had shown him.

114 As he was thus pondering, being much cast down because of the wickedness of the people of the Nephites, their secret works of darkness, and their murderings, and their plunderings, and all manner of iniquities, behold, a voice came to him, saying:

115 "Blessed art thou, Nephi, for those things which thou hast done; for I have beheld how thou hast with

unwearyingness declared the word which I have given thee for this people.

116 "And thou hast not feared them, and hast not sought thine own life, but hast sought my will and to keep my commandments.

117 "Now because thou hast done this with such unwearyingness, behold, I will bless thee forever; and I will make thee mighty in word and in deed, in faith and in works; even that all things shall be done to thee according to thy word, for thou shalt not ask that which is contrary to my will.

118 "Behold, thou art Nephi, and I am God.

119 "I declare it to thee in the presence of mine angels, that ye shall have power over this people and shall smite the earth with famine, and with pestilence and destruction, according to the wickedness of this people.

120 "Behold, I give thee power that whatever thou shalt seal on earth shall be sealed in heaven; and whatever thou shalt loose on earth shall be loosed in heaven; and thus shall ye have power among this people.

121 "And thus if ye shall say of this temple, 'It shall be rent in twain,' it shall be done.

122 "And if ye shall say to this mountain, 'Be thou cast down and become smooth,' it shall be done.

123 "And, behold, if ye shall say, 'God shall smite this people,' it shall come to pass.

124 "Now, behold, I command thee that thou shalt go and declare to this people, 'Thus saith the Lord God, who is Almighty, Except ye repent, ye shall be smitten, even to destruction.'"

125 When the Lord had spoken these words, Nephi stopped and did not go to his own house, but returned to the multitudes who were scattered upon the face of the land, and began to declare to them the word of the Lord which had been spoken to him concerning their destruction if they did not repent.

126 Now, behold, notwithstanding that great miracle which Nephi had done in telling them concerning the death of the chief judge, they hard-

ened their hearts, and did not hearken to the words of the Lord.

127 Therefore Nephi declared to them the word of the Lord, saying, "Except ye repent, thus saith the Lord, Ye shall be smitten, even to destruction."

128 And when Nephi had declared to them the word, behold, they still hardened their hearts, and would not hearken to his words; therefore they reviled against him and sought to lay their hands upon him that they might cast him into prison.

129 But, behold, the power of God was with him, and they could not take him to cast him into prison, for he was taken by the Spirit and conveyed away out of the midst of them.

130 And he went forth in the Spirit, from multitude to multitude, declaring the word of God, even until he had declared it to them all, or sent it forth among all the people.

131 And it came to pass that they would not hearken to his words; and there began to be contentions, insomuch that they were divided against themselves and began to slay one another with the sword.

132 Thus ended the seventy-first year of the reign of the judges over the people of Nephi.

CHAPTER 4

IN the seventy-second year of the reign of the judges, the contentions increased, insomuch that there were wars throughout all the land among all the people of Nephi.

2 And it was this secret band of robbers who carried on this work of destruction and wickedness.

3 This war lasted all that year. And in the seventy-third year it also lasted.

4 And it came to pass that in this year Nephi cried to the Lord, saying, "O Lord, do not suffer that this people shall be destroyed by the sword; but, O Lord, rather let there be a famine in the land to stir them up in remembrance of the Lord their God, and perhaps they will repent and turn to thee."

5 And so it was done according to the words of Nephi. And there was a great famine upon the land among all the people of Nephi.

6 Thus, in the seventy-fourth year, the famine continued, and the work of destruction ceased by the sword, but became sore by famine.

7 And this work of destruction also continued in the seventy-fifth year.

8 For the earth was smitten, that it was dry and did not yield forth grain in the season of grain; and the whole earth was smitten, even among the Lamanites as well as among the Nephites, so that they were smitten that they perished by thousands in the more wicked parts of the land.

9 And it came to pass that the people saw that they were about to perish by famine, and they began to remember the Lord their God; and they began to remember the words of Nephi.

10 And the people began to plead with their chief judges and their leaders that they would say to Nephi, "Behold, we know that you are a man of God, therefore cry to the Lord our God that he turn away from us this famine, lest all the words which you have spoken concerning our destruction be fulfilled."

11 And the judges said to Nephi according to the words which had been desired.

12 When Nephi saw that the people had repented and humbled themselves in sackcloth, he cried again to the Lord, saying, "O Lord, behold this people repenteth.

13 "They have swept away the band of Gadianton from amongst them, insomuch that they have become extinct, and they have concealed their secret plans in the earth.

14 "Now, O Lord, because of this their humility, wilt thou turn away thine anger, and let thine anger be appeased in the destruction of those wicked men whom thou hast already destroyed.

15 "O Lord, wilt thou turn away thine anger, thy fierce anger, and cause that this famine may cease in this land.

16 "O Lord, wilt thou hearken to me, and cause that it may be done according to my words, and send forth rain upon the face of the earth that she may bring forth her fruit and her grain in the season of grain.

17 "O Lord, thou didst hearken to my words when I said, 'Let there be a famine, that the pestilence of the sword might cease'; and I know that thou wilt even at this time hearken to my words, for thou saidst that if this people repent, 'I will spare them.'

18 "O Lord, thou seest that they have repented because of the famine, and the pestilence and destruction which have come to them.

19 "And now, O Lord, wilt thou turn away thine anger and try again if they will serve thee? And if so, O Lord, thou canst bless them according to thy words which thou hast said."

20 And in the seventy-sixth year, the Lord turned away his anger from the people and caused that rain should fall upon the earth, insomuch that the earth brought forth her fruit in the season of her fruit.

21 And she brought forth her grain in the season of her grain.

22 And, behold, the people rejoiced, and glorified God, and the whole face of the land was filled with rejoicing; and they no more sought to destroy Nephi, but they esteemed him as a great prophet, and a man of God having great power and authority given him from God.

23 And, behold, Lehi, his brother, was not a whit behind him as to things pertaining to righteousness.

24 Thus it came to pass that the people of Nephi began to prosper again in the land, and began to build up their waste places, and began to multiply and spread even until they covered the whole face of the land, both on the northward and on the southward, from the sea west to the sea east.

25 And the seventy-sixth year ended in peace.

26 And the seventy-seventh year began in peace; and the church spread throughout the face of all the land; and the greater part of the people, both the Nephites and the Lamanites, belonged to the church; and they had exceedingly great peace in the land; and thus ended the seventy-seventh year.

27 Also they had peace in the seventy-eighth year, save it were a few contentions concerning the points of doctrine which had been laid down by the prophets.

28 And in the seventy-ninth year, there began to be much strife.

29 But Nephi and Lehi, and many of their brethren who knew concerning the true points of doctrine, having had many revelations daily, preached to the people insomuch that they put an end to their strife in that same year.

30 And in the eightieth year of the reign of the judges over the people of Nephi, there were a certain number of the dissenters from the people of Nephi who had some years before gone over to the Lamanites and had taken upon themselves the name of Lamanites, 31and also a certain number who were real descendants of the Lamanites who were stirred up to anger by those dissenters; therefore they commenced a war with their brethren.

32 They would commit murder and plunder; then they would retreat back into the mountains, and into the wilderness, and into secret places, hiding themselves that they could not be discovered, receiving daily an addition to their numbers inasmuch as there were dissenters that went forth to them.

33 Thus in time, even in the space of not many years, they became an exceedingly great band of robbers; and they searched out all the secret plans of Gadianton; and thus they became robbers of Gadianton.

34 Now, behold, these robbers made great havoc, even great destruction among the people of Nephi, and also among the people of the Lamanites.

35 And it came to pass that it was expedient that a stop should be put to this work of destruction; therefore they sent an army of strong men into the wilderness and upon the mountains to search out this band of robbers and to destroy them.

36 But, behold, it came to pass that in that same year they were driven back even into their own lands.

37 And thus ended the eightieth year of the reign of the judges over the people of Nephi.

38 In the commencement of the

eighty-first year, they went forth again against this band of robbers and destroyed many.

39 But they were also visited with much destruction, and they were again obliged to return out of the wilderness and out of the mountains to their own lands because of the exceeding greatness of the numbers of those robbers who infested the mountains and the wilderness.

40 And thus ended this year. And the robbers still increased and waxed strong, insomuch that they defied the whole armies of the Nephites and also of the Lamanites; and they caused great fear to come on the people upon all the face of the land.

41 For they visited many parts of the land and did great destruction to them, killed many, and carried away others captive into the wilderness, more especially their women and their children.

42 Now this great evil which came to the people because of their iniquity stirred them up again in remembrance of the Lord their God.

43 And thus ended the eighty-first year of the reign of the judges.

44 In the eighty-second year they began again to forget the Lord their God.

45 And in the eighty-third year they began to wax strong in iniquity.

46 And in the eighty-fourth year they did not mend their ways.

47 And in the eighty-fifth year, they waxed stronger and stronger in their pride and in their wickedness; and thus they were ripening again for destruction. And thus ended the eighty-fifth year.

48 Thus we can behold how false and unsteady are the hearts of the children of men; and we can see that the Lord in his great, infinite goodness blesses and prospers those who put their trust in him.

49 And we may see at the very time when he prospers his people, in the increase of their fields, their flocks, and their herds, and in gold, and in silver, and in all manner of precious things of every kind, and art, 50sparing their lives, and delivering them out of the hands of their enemies, softening the hearts of their enemies that they should not declare wars against them, and in fine, doing all things for the welfare and happiness of his people, 51then is the time that they harden their hearts, and forget the Lord their God, and trample under their feet the Holy One, and this because of their ease and their exceedingly great prosperity.

52 And thus we see that except the Lord chastens his people with many afflictions, except he visits them with death, and with terror, and with famine, and with all manner of pestilences, they will not remember him.

53 Oh, how foolish, and how vain, and how evil and devilish, and how quick to do iniquity, and how slow to do good are the children of men; 54how quick to hearken to the words of the evil one and to set their hearts upon the vain things of the world; how quick to be lifted up in pride; how quick to boast and do all manner of that which is iniquity; 55and how slow are they to remember the Lord their God and to give ear to his counsels; how slow to walk in wisdom's paths!

56 Behold, they do not desire that the Lord their God, who has created them, should rule and reign over them; notwithstanding his great goodness and his mercy toward them, they set at nought his counsels, and they will not that he should be their guide.

57 Oh, how great is the nothingness of the children of men; even they are less than the dust of the earth.

58 For, behold, the dust of the earth moves here and there, to the dividing asunder at the command of our great and everlasting God.

59 Behold, at his voice the hills and the mountains tremble and quake; and by the power of his voice they are broken up and become smooth, even like a valley.

60 By the power of his voice the whole earth shakes; by the power of his voice the foundations rock, even to the very center.

61 And if he says to the earth, "Move," it is moved; if he says to the earth, "Thou shalt go back," that it lengthen out the day for many

hours, it is done; [62]and thus according to his word, the earth goes back, and it appears to man that the sun stands still; and, behold, this is so, for surely it is the earth that moves, and not the sun.

63 Also, if he says to the waters of the great deep, "Be thou dried up," it is done.

64 Behold, if he says to this mountain, "Be thou raised up, and come over and fall upon that city that it be buried up," behold, it is done.

65 And, behold, if a man hide a treasure in the earth, and the Lord shall say, "Let it be accursed because of the iniquity of him who hath hid it up," behold, it shall be accursed.

66 And if the Lord shall say, "Be thou accursed, that no man shall find thee from this time henceforth and forever," behold, no man gets it henceforth and forever.

67 And, behold, if the Lord shall say to a man, "Because of thine iniquities thou shalt be accursed forever," it shall be done.

68 And if the Lord shall say, "Because of thine iniquities, thou shalt be cut off from my presence," he will cause that it shall be so.

69 Woe to him to whom he shall say this, for it shall be to him that will do iniquity, and he cannot be saved; therefore, for this cause, that men might be saved, repentance has been declared.

70 Therefore blessed are they who will repent and hearken to the voice of the Lord their God; for these are they that shall be saved.

71 And may God grant in his great fullness that men might be brought to repentance and good works, that they might be restored to grace, for grace according to their works.

72 And I would that all men might be saved. But we read that in that great and last day there are some who shall be cast out, who shall be cast off from the presence of the Lord, [73]who shall be consigned to a state of endless misery, fulfilling the words which say, "They that have done good shall have everlasting life, and they that have done evil shall have everlasting damnation." And thus it is. Amen.

CHAPTER 5

The prophecy of Samuel, the Lamanite, to the Nephites.

IN the eighty-sixth year, the Nephites still remained in wickedness, even in great wickedness, while the Lamanites observed strictly to keep the commandments of God according to the law of Moses.

2 And it came to pass that in this year there was one Samuel, a Lamanite, who came into the land of Zarahemla and began to preach to the people.

3 And he preached repentance many days, to the people, and they cast him out, and he was about to return to his own land.

4 But, behold, the voice of the Lord came to him that he should return and prophesy to the people whatever things should come into his heart.

5 And it came to pass that they would not suffer that he should enter into the city; therefore he got upon the wall thereof, and stretched forth his hand, and cried with a loud voice, and prophesied to the people whatever things the Lord put into his heart.

6 And he said to them, "Behold, I, Samuel, a Lamanite, speak the words of the Lord which he puts into my heart; and, behold, he has put it into my heart to say to this people that the sword of justice hangs over this people; and four hundred years pass not away save the sword of justice will fall upon this people.

7 "Heavy destruction awaits this people, and it surely will come to this people, and nothing can save this people save it be repentance and faith on the Lord Jesus Christ, who surely shall come into the world, and shall suffer many things, and shall be slain for his people.

8 "Behold, an angel of the Lord

has declared it to me, and he brought glad tidings to my soul.

9 "And, behold, I was sent to you to declare it to you also, that you might have glad tidings; but, behold, you would not receive me.

10 "Therefore thus says the Lord, 'Because of the hardness of the hearts of the people of the Nephites, except they repent, I will take away my word from them, and I will withdraw my Spirit from them, and I will suffer them no longer, and I will turn the hearts of their brethren against them.

11 "'Four hundred years shall not pass away before I will cause that they shall be smitten; I will visit them with the sword, and with famine, and with pestilence.

12 "'I will visit them in my fierce anger, and there shall be those of the fourth generation of your enemies who shall live to behold your utter destruction.

13 "'And this shall surely come except ye repent,' saith the Lord, 'and those of the fourth generation shall visit your destruction.

14 "'But if ye will repent and return to the Lord your God, I will turn away mine anger,' saith the Lord; thus saith the Lord, 'Blessed are they who will repent and turn to me, but woe to him that repenteth not.

15 "'Woe to this great city of Zarahemla; for, behold, it is because of those who are righteous that it is saved.

16 "'Woe to this great city, for I perceive,' saith the Lord, 'that there are many, even the larger part of this great city that will harden their hearts against me,' saith the Lord. 'But blessed are they who will repent, for them will I spare.

17 "'But, behold, if it were not for the righteous who are in this great city, behold, I would cause that fire should come down out of heaven and destroy it. But, behold, it is for the righteous' sake that it is spared.

18 "'But, behold, the time cometh,' saith the Lord, 'that when ye shall cast out the righteous from among you, then shall ye be ripe for destruction.

19 "'Woe be to this great city be-

cause of the wickedness and abominations which are in her.

20 "'And woe be to the city of Gideon for the wickedness and abominations which are in her.

21 "'And woe be to all the cities which are in the land round about, which are possessed by the Nephites, because of the wickedness and abominations which are in them.

22 "'Behold, a curse shall come upon the land,' saith the Lord of Hosts, 'because of the people's sake who are upon the land, because of their wickedness and their abominations.

23 "'And it shall come to pass,' saith the Lord of Hosts, even our great and true God, 'that whoever shall hide treasures in the earth shall find them again no more, because of the great curse of the land, save he be a righteous man and shall hide it up unto the Lord.

24 "'For I will,' saith the Lord, 'that they shall hide their treasures unto me; and cursed be they who hide not their treasures unto me; for none hideth their treasures unto me save it be the righteous.

25 "'And he that hideth not his treasures unto me, cursed is he and also the treasure, and none shall redeem it because of the curse of the land.

26 "'And the day shall come that they shall hide their treasures because they have set their hearts upon riches.

27 "'And because they have set their hearts upon their riches, and will hide their treasures when they shall flee before their enemies, because they will not hide them unto me, cursed be they and also their treasures; and in that day shall they be smitten,' saith the Lord.

28 "Behold, you people of this great city, and hearken to my words; hearken to the words which the Lord said; for, behold, he said that you are cursed because of your riches.

29 "And also are your riches cursed because you have set your hearts upon them and have not hearkened to the words of him who gave them to you.

30 "You do not remember the Lord your God in the things which he has blessed you, but you do always remember your riches, and

do not thank the Lord your God for them.

31 "Your hearts are not drawn out to the Lord, but they swell with great pride unto boasting and unto great swelling, envyings, strifes, malice, persecutions, murders, and all manner of iniquities.

32 "For this has the Lord God caused that a curse should come upon the land and also upon your riches, and this because of your iniquities.

33 "Woe to this people because of this time which has arrived that you cast out the prophets, and mock them, and cast stones at them, and slay them, and do all manner of iniquity to them, even as they did of old time.

34 "And now when you talk, you say, 'If our days had been in the days of our fathers of old, we would not have slain the prophets; we would not have stoned them and cast them out.'

35 "Behold, you are worse than they; for as the Lord lives, if a prophet comes among you and declares to you the word of the Lord, which testifies of your sins and iniquities, you are angry with him, and cast him out, and seek all manner of ways to destroy him.

36 "You will say that he is a false prophet, and that he is a sinner and of the devil because he testifies that your deeds are evil.

37 "But, behold, if a man shall come among you and shall say, 'Do this, and there is no iniquity; do that, and you shall not suffer'; and will say, 'Walk after the pride of your own hearts; walk after the pride of your eyes and do whatever your heart desires,' if a man shall come among you and say this, you will receive him, and you will say that he is a prophet.

38 "You will lift him up, and you will give him of your substance; you will give him of your gold and of your silver, and you will clothe him with costly apparel.

39 "And because he speaks flattering words to you, and he says that all is well, then you will not find fault with him.

40 "O you wicked and perverse generation, you hardened and stiff-necked people, how long will you suppose that the Lord will suffer you, how long will you suffer yourselves, to be led by foolish and blind guides? How long will you choose darkness rather than light?

41 "Behold, the anger of the Lord is already kindled against you; behold, he has cursed the land because of your iniquity; and, behold, the time will come that he will curse your riches, that they become slippery, that you cannot hold them.

42 "And in the days of your poverty, you cannot retain them; and in the days of your poverty, you shall cry to the Lord; and in vain shall you cry, for your desolation is already come upon you, and your destruction is made sure.

43 "'Then shall ye weep and howl in that day,' saith the Lord of Hosts.

44 "And then shall you lament, and say, 'Oh, that I had repented, and had not killed the prophets, and stoned them, and cast them out.'

45 "In that day you shall say, 'Oh, that we had remembered the Lord our God in the day that he gave us our riches, and then they would not have become slippery that we should lose them; for, behold, our riches are gone from us.

46 "'Behold, we lay a tool here, and on the morrow it is gone; and, behold, our swords are taken from us in the day we have sought them for battle.

47 "'We have hid our treasures, and they have slipped away from us because of the curse of the land.

48 "'Oh, that we had repented in the day that the word of the Lord came to us; for, behold, the land is cursed, and all things have become slippery, and we cannot hold them.

49 "'Behold we are surrounded by demons, we are encircled by the angels of him who has sought to destroy our souls.

50 "'Behold, our iniquities are great. O Lord, canst thou not turn away thine anger from us?' And this shall be your language in those days.

51 "But, behold, your days of probation are past; you have procrastinated the day of your salvation until it is everlastingly too late, and your destruction is made sure.

52 "For you have sought all the

days of your lives for that which you could not obtain; and you have sought for happiness in doing iniquity, which thing is contrary to the nature of that righteousness which is in our great and Eternal Head.

53 "O you people of the land, that you would hear my words. And I pray that the anger of the Lord be turned away from you, and that you would repent and be saved."

54 And now Samuel, the Lamanite, prophesied a great many more things which cannot be written.

55 And, behold, he said to them, "Behold, I give you a sign: five years more will come, and, behold, then will come the Son of God to redeem all those who shall believe on his name.

56 "And, behold, this will I give you for a sign at the time of his coming; for, behold, there shall be great lights in heaven, insomuch that in the night before he comes, there shall be no darkness, insomuch that it shall appear to man as if it were day.

57 "Therefore there shall be one day and a night and a day, as if it were one day and there were no night; and this shall be to you for a sign; for you shall know of the rising of the sun, and also of its setting.

58 "You shall know of a surety that there shall be two days and a night; nevertheless the night shall not be darkened, and it shall be the night before he is born.

59 "And, behold, there shall be a new star arise, such a one as you never have beheld; and this also shall be a sign to you.

60 "And, behold, this is not all: there shall be many signs and wonders in heaven.

61 "It shall come to pass that you shall be amazed and wonder, insomuch that you shall fall to the earth.

62 "And it shall come to pass that whoever shall believe on the son of God, the same shall have everlasting life.

63 "Behold, thus has the Lord commanded me, by his angel, that I should come and tell this thing to you; he has commanded that I should prophesy these things to you; he has said to me, 'Cry to this people,

Repent and prepare the way of the Lord.'

64 "And now because I am a Lamanite and have spoken to you the words which the Lord has commanded me, and because it was hard against you, you are angry with me and seek to destroy me, and have cast me out from among you.

65 "But you shall hear my words, for, for this intent I have come upon the walls of this city, that you might hear and know of the judgments of God which await you because of your iniquities, and also that you might know the conditions of repentance; 66and also that you might know of the coming of Jesus Christ, the Son of God, the Father of heaven and of earth, the Creator of all things from the beginning; and that you might know of the signs of his coming, to the intent that you might believe on his name.

67 "And if you believe on his name, you will repent of all your sins, that thereby you may have a remission of them through his merits.

68 "And, behold, again, another sign I give you, even a sign of his death; for, behold, he surely must die, that salvation may come.

69 "It behooves him and becomes expedient that he die to bring to pass the resurrection of the dead, that thereby men may be brought into the presence of the Lord.

70 "Behold, this death brings to pass the resurrection and redeems all mankind from the first death— that spiritual death for all mankind, by the fall of Adam—which is being cut off from the presence of the Lord, or considered as dead, both as to things temporal and to things spiritual.

71 "But, behold, the resurrection of Christ redeems mankind, even all mankind, and brings them back into the presence of the Lord.

72 "And it brings to pass the conditions of repentance, that whoever repents, the same is not hewn down and cast into the fire.

73 "But whoever repents not, is hewn down and cast into the fire, and there comes upon him again a spiritual death, a second death, for he is cut off again as to things pertaining to righteousness.

74 "Therefore, repent, repent, lest by knowing these things and not doing them, you shall suffer yourselves to come under condemnation, and you are brought down to this second death.

75 "But, behold, as I said to you concerning another sign, a sign of his death, behold, in that day that he shall suffer death, the sun shall be darkened and refuse to give his light to you; and also the moon and the stars.

76 "And there shall be no light upon the face of this land, even from the time that he shall suffer death, for the space of three days, to the time that he shall rise again from the dead.

77 "At the time that he shall yield up the ghost, there shall be thunderings and lightnings for the space of many hours, and the earth shall shake and tremble, and the rocks which are upon the face of the earth, which are both above the earth and beneath, which you know at this time is solid, or the greater part of it is one solid mass, shall be broken up.

78 "They shall be rent in twain, and shall ever after be found in seams, and in cracks, and in broken fragments upon the face of the whole earth, both above the earth and beneath.

79 "And, behold, there shall be great tempests, and there shall be many mountains laid low, like a valley, and there shall be many places which are now called valleys which shall become mountains, whose height is great.

80 "And many highways shall be broken up, and many cities shall become desolate, and many graves shall be opened and shall yield up many of their dead; and many saints shall appear to many.

81 "Behold, thus has the angel spoken to me; for he said to me that there should be thunderings and lightnings for the space of many hours.

82 "And he said to me that while the thunder and the lightning lasted, and the tempest, these things should be, and darkness should cover the face of the whole earth for the space of three days.

83 "And the angel said to me that many shall see greater things than these, to the intent that they might believe that these signs and these wonders should come to pass upon all the face of this land, to the intent that there should be no cause for unbelief among the children of men; [84]and this to the intent that whoever will believe, might be saved, and that those who will not believe might have a righteous judgment come upon them; and also if they are condemned, they bring upon themselves their own condemnation.

85 "Now remember, remember, my brethren, that whoever perishes, perishes unto himself; and whoever does iniquity, does it unto himself; for, behold, you are free; you are permitted to act for yourselves; for, behold, God has given to you a knowledge, and he has made you free.

86 "He has given to you that you might know good from evil, and he has given to you that you might choose life or death, and you can do good and be restored to that which is good, or have that which is good restored to you; or you can do evil, and have that which is evil restored to you.

87 "And now, my beloved brethren, behold, I declare to you that except you shall repent, your houses shall be left to you desolate; except you repent, your women shall have great cause to mourn in the day they shall give suck.

88 "For you shall attempt to flee, and there shall be no place for refuge; and woe to them which are with child, for they shall be heavy, and cannot flee; therefore they shall be trodden down and shall be left to perish.

89 "Woe to this people, who are called the people of Nephi, except they shall repent when they shall see all these signs and wonders which shall be shown to them.

90 "For, behold, they have been a chosen people of the Lord; the people of Nephi has he loved, and also has he chastened them; in the days of their iniquities has he chastened them because he loves them.

91 "But, behold, my brethren, the Lamanites, has he hated because their

deeds have been evil continually, and this because of the iniquity of the tradition of their fathers.

92 "But, behold, salvation has come to them through the preaching of the Nephites; and for this intent has the Lord prolonged their days.

93 "And I would that you should behold that the greater part of them are in the path of their duty, and they walk circumspectly before God, and they observe to keep his commandments, and his statutes, and his judgments according to the law of Moses.

94 "I say to you that the greater part of them are doing this, and they are striving with unwearied diligence that they may bring the remainder of their brethren to the knowledge of the truth; therefore there are many who add to their numbers daily.

95 "And, behold, you know of yourselves, for you have witnessed it, that as many of them as are brought to the knowledge of the truth, and to know of the wicked and abominable traditions of their fathers, and are led to believe the holy scriptures, 96even the prophecies of the holy prophets which are written, which leads them to have faith on the Lord and to repentance, which faith and repentance bring a change of heart to them, 97are firm and steadfast in the faith and in the things wherewith they have been made free.

98 "And you know also that they have buried their weapons of war, and they fear to take them up lest by any means they should sin. You can see that they fear to sin; 99for, behold, they will suffer themselves that they be trodden down and slain by their enemies and will not lift their swords against them, and this because of their faith in Christ.

100 "Now because of their steadfastness, when they do believe, in that thing which they do believe, and because of their firmness when they are once enlightened, behold, the Lord shall bless them and prolong their days, notwithstanding their iniquity.

101 "Even if they should dwindle in unbelief, the Lord shall prolong their days until the time shall come which has been spoken of by our fathers, and also by the prophet Zenos and many other prophets, concerning the restoration of our brethren, the Lamanites, again, to the knowledge of the truth.

102 "I say to you that in the latter times the promises of the Lord have been extended to our brethren, the Lamanites.

103 "Notwithstanding the many afflictions which they shall have, and notwithstanding they shall be driven to and fro upon the face of the earth, and be hunted, and shall be smitten and scattered abroad, having no place for refuge, the Lord shall be merciful to them.

104 "And this is according to the prophecy that they shall again be brought to the true knowledge, which is the knowledge of their Redeemer, and their great and true Shepherd, and be numbered among his sheep.

105 "Therefore I say to you, It shall be better for them than for you, except you repent.

106 "For, behold, had the mighty works been shown to them which have been shown to you, even to them who have dwindled in unbelief because of the traditions of their fathers, you can see for yourselves that they never would again have dwindled in unbelief.

107 "Therefore says the Lord, 'I will not utterly destroy them, but I will cause that in the day of my wisdom, they shall return again to me.'

108 "And now, behold, says the Lord concerning the people of the Nephites, 'If they will not repent and observe to do my will, I will utterly destroy them because of their unbelief, notwithstanding the many mighty works which I have done among them'; and as surely as the Lord liveth, shall these things be."

109 Now it came to pass that there were many who heard the words of Samuel, the Lamanite, which he spoke upon the walls of the city.

110 And as many as believed on his words went forth and sought for Nephi; and when they had found him, they confessed to him their sins and denied not, desiring that they might be baptized unto the Lord.

111 But as many as there were who did not believe in the words of Samuel

were angry with him; and they cast stones at him upon the wall, and also many shot arrows at him as he stood upon the wall.

112 But the Spirit of the Lord was with him, insomuch that they could not hit him with their stones, neither with their arrows.

113 Now when they saw that they could not hit him, there were many more who believed on his words, insomuch that they went away to Nephi to be baptized.

114 For, behold, Nephi was baptizing, and prophesying, and preaching, crying repentance to the people, showing signs and wonders, working miracles among the people that they might know that the Christ must shortly come, [115]telling them of things which must shortly come, that they might know and remember at the time of their coming that these things had been made known to them beforehand to the intent that they might believe.

116 Therefore as many as believed on the words of Samuel went forth to him to be baptized, for they came repenting and confessing their sins.

117 But the greater part of them did not believe in the words of Samuel; therefore, when they saw that they could not hit him with their stones and their arrows, they cried out to their captains, saying, "Take this fellow and bind him, for, behold, he has a devil.

118 "And because of the power of the devil which is in him, we cannot hit him with our stones and our arrows; therefore take him and bind him, and away with him."

119 As they went forth to lay their hands on him, behold, he cast himself down from the wall, and fled out of their lands to his own country, and began to preach and to prophesy among his own people.

120 And, behold, he was never heard of more among the Nephites; and thus were the affairs of the people.

121 Thus ended the eighty-sixth year of the reign of the judges over the people of Nephi.

122 And thus ended also the eighty-seventh year of the reign of the judges, the greater part of the people remaining in their pride and wickedness, and the lesser part walking more circumspectly before God.

123 And these were the conditions also in the eighty-eighth year of the reign of the judges.

124 And there was but little alteration in the affairs of the people, save that the people began to be more hardened in iniquity and to do more and more of that which was contrary to the commandments of God, in the eighty-ninth year of the reign of the judges.

125 But in the ninetieth year of the reign of the judges, there were great signs given the people, and wonders; and the words of the prophets began to be fulfilled.

126 Angels appeared to men, wise men, and declared to them glad tidings of great joy; thus in this year the scriptures began to be fulfilled.

127 Nevertheless, the people began to harden their hearts, all save it were the most believing part of them, both of the Nephites and also of the Lamanites, and began to depend upon their own strength and upon their own wisdom, saying:

128 "Some things they may have guessed right among so many; but, behold, we know that all these great and marvelous works cannot come to pass of which have been spoken."

129 And they began to reason and to contend among themselves, saying, "It is not reasonable that such a being as a Christ shall come.

130 "If so, and he be the Son of God, the father of heaven and of earth, as it has been spoken, why will he not show himself to us, as well as to them who shall be at Jerusalem?

131 "Why will he not show himself in this land, as well as in the land at Jerusalem?

132 "But, behold, we know that this is a wicked tradition which has been handed down to us by our fathers to cause us that we should believe in some great and marvelous thing which should come to pass, but not among us, but in a land which is far distant, a land which we know not.

133 "Therefore they can keep us in ignorance, for we cannot witness with our own eyes that they are true.

134 "And they will, by the cunning and the mysterious arts of the evil one,

work some great mystery which we cannot understand, which will keep us down to be servants to their words, and also servants to them, for we depend upon them to teach us the word.

135 "Thus will they keep us in ignorance, if we will yield ourselves to them all the days of our lives."

136 And many more things the people imagined in their hearts, which were foolish and vain.

137 And they were much disturbed, for Satan stirred them up to do iniquity continually; he went about spreading rumors and contentions upon all the face of the land that he might harden the hearts of the people against that which was good and against that which should come.

138 Notwithstanding the signs and the wonders which were wrought among the people of the Lord and the many miracles which they did, Satan got great hold upon the hearts of the people upon all the face of the land.

139 Thus ended the ninetieth year of the reign of the judges over the people of Nephi.

140 And thus ended the book of Helaman, according to the record of Helaman and his sons.

THIRD BOOK OF NEPHI

THE SON OF NEPHI, WHO WAS THE SON OF HELAMAN

CHAPTER 1

And Helaman was the son of Helaman, who was the son of Alma, who was the son of Alma, being a descendant of Nephi who was the son of Lehi, who came out of Jerusalem in the first year of the reign of Zedekiah, the king of Judah.

NOW the ninety-first year had passed away; and it was six hundred years from the time that Lehi left Jerusalem; and it was in the year that Lachoneus was the chief judge and the governor over the land.

2 And Nephi, the son of Helaman, had departed out of the land of Zarahemla, giving charge to his son, Nephi, who was his eldest son, concerning the plates of brass, and all the records which had been kept, and all those things which had been kept sacred, from the departure of Lehi out of Jerusalem.

3 Then he departed out of the land, and where he went, no man knows; and his son Nephi kept the record of this people in his stead.

4 And in the commencement of the ninety-second year, behold, the prophecies of the prophets began to be fulfilled more fully; for there began to be greater signs and greater miracles wrought among the people.

5 But there were some who began to say that the time was past for the words to be fulfilled which were spoken by Samuel, the Lamanite.

6 And they began to rejoice over their brethren, saying, "Behold, the time is past, and the words of Samuel are not fulfilled; therefore, your joy and your faith concerning this thing have been vain."

7 And they made a great uproar throughout the land; and the people who believed began to be very sorrowful, lest by any means those things which had been spoken might not come to pass.

8 But, behold, they watched steadfastly for that day, and that night, and that day, which should be as one day,

as if there were no night, that they might know that their faith had not been vain.

9 Now it came to pass that there was a day set apart by the unbelievers that all those who believed in those traditions should be put to death except the sign should come to pass which had been given by Samuel the prophet.

10 And when Nephi, the son of Nephi, saw this wickedness of his people, his heart was exceedingly sorrowful.

11 And he went out and bowed himself down upon the earth and cried mightily to his God in behalf of his people, those who were about to be destroyed because of their faith in the tradition of their fathers.

12 And he cried mightily to the Lord all that day; and, behold, the voice of the Lord came to him, saying, "Lift up your head and be of good cheer, for, behold, the time is at hand, and on this night shall the sign be given.

13 "On the morrow come I into the world to show the world that I will fulfill all that which I have caused to be spoken by the mouth of my holy prophets.

14 "Behold, I come to my own to fulfill all things which I have made known to the children of men from the foundation of the world, and to do the will both of the Father and of the Son, of the Father because of me, and of the Son because of my flesh.

15 "And, behold, the time is at hand, and this night shall the sign be given."

16 And the words which came to Nephi were fulfilled according as they had been spoken; 17for, behold, at the going down of the sun, there was no darkness; and the people began to be astonished because there was no darkness when the night came.

18 And there were many who had not believed the words of the prophets, who fell to the earth and became as if they were dead, for they knew that the great plan of destruction which they had laid for those who believed in the words of the prophets had been frustrated, for the sign which had been given was already at hand; and they began to know that the Son of God must shortly appear.

19 All the people upon the face of the whole earth, from the west to the east, both in the land north and in the land south, were so exceedingly astonished that they fell to the earth; 20for they knew that the prophets had testified of these things for many years and that the sign which had been given was already at hand; and they began to fear because of their iniquity and their unbelief.

21 And there was no darkness in all that night, but it was as light as though it was midday.

22 And the sun rose in the morning again according to its proper order; and they knew that it was the day that the Lord should be born, because of the sign which had been given.

23 It had come to pass, even all things, every whit, according to the words of the prophets.

24 And it came to pass also that a new star did appear, according to the word.

25 From this time forth there began to be lyings sent forth among the people by Satan to harden their hearts, to the intent that they might not believe in those signs and wonders which they had seen.

26 But notwithstanding those lyings and deceivings, the greater part of the people believed and were converted to the Lord.

27 And it came to pass that Nephi went forth among the people, and also many others, baptizing unto repentance, in which there was a great remission of sins.

28 Thus the people began again to have peace in the land; and there were no contentions, save that a few began to preach, endeavoring to prove by the scriptures that it was no more expedient to observe the law of Moses.

29 Now in this thing they erred, not having understood the scriptures.

30 But they soon became converted and were convinced of the error which they were in; for it was made known to them that the law was not yet fulfilled and that it must be fulfilled in every whit.

31 The word came to them that it must be fulfilled; that one jot or tittle should not pass away till it should all

be fulfilled; therefore in this same year, they were brought to a knowledge of their error and confessed their faults.

32 And thus the ninety-second year passed away, bringing glad tidings to the people because of the signs which came to pass according to the words of the prophecy of all the holy prophets.

33 And the ninety-third year also passed away in peace, save for the Gadianton robbers, who dwelt upon the mountains and who infested the land.

34 So strong were their holds and their secret places that the people could not overpower them, therefore they committed many murders and did much slaughter among the people.

35 And in the ninety-fourth year, they began to increase in a great degree because there were many dissenters of the Nephites who fled to them, which caused much sorrow to those Nephites who remained in the land.

36 There was also a cause of much sorrow among the Lamanites, for, behold, they had many children who grew up and began to wax strong in years, and they became agents for themselves and were led away by some who were Zoramites, by their lyings and their flattering words, to join those Gadianton robbers.

37 Thus were the Lamanites afflicted also and began to decrease as to their faith and righteousness because of the wickedness of the rising generation.

38 And thus passed away the ninety-fifth year also, and the people began to forget those signs and wonders which they had heard and began to be less and less astonished at a sign or a wonder from heaven, 39insomuch that they began to be hard in their hearts and blind in their minds, and began to disbelieve all which they had heard and seen, imagining up some vain thing in their hearts, that it was wrought by men, and by the power of the devil, to lead away and deceive the hearts of the people.

40 Thus Satan got possession of the hearts of the people again, insomuch that he blinded their eyes and led them away to believe that the doctrine of Christ was a foolish and a vain thing.

41 And it came to pass that the people began to wax strong in wickedness and abominations; and they did not believe that there should be any more signs or wonders given.

42 And Satan went about, leading away the hearts of the people, tempting them and causing them that they should do great wickedness in the land.

43 And thus passed away the ninety-sixth year, and also the ninety-seventh year, and also the ninety-eighth year, and also the ninety-ninth year, and also a hundred years had passed away since the days of Mosiah who was the last king over the people of the Nephites.

44 And six hundred and nine years had passed away since Lehi left Jerusalem; and nine years had passed away from the time when the sign was given, which was spoken of by the prophets, that Christ should come into the world.

45 Now the Nephites began to reckon their time from this period when the sign was given, or from the coming of Christ; 46therefore, nine years had passed away, and Nephi, who was the father of Nephi who had the charge of the records, did not return to the land of Zarahemla and could nowhere be found in all the land.

47 And the people still remained in wickedness, notwithstanding the much preaching and prophesying which was done among them; and thus passed away the tenth year also; and the eleventh year also passed away in iniquity.

48 In the thirteenth year there began to be wars and contentions throughout all the land; for the Gadianton robbers had become so numerous, and had slain so many of the people, and laid waste so many cities, and spread so much death and carnage throughout the land, that it became expedient that all the people, both the Nephites and the Lamanites, should take up arms against them.

49 Therefore all the Lamanites who had become converted to the Lord united with their brethren, the Nephites, and were compelled, for the

safety of their lives, and their women, and their children, to take up arms against those Gadianton robbers; [50]and also to maintain their rites, and their privileges of their church, and of their worship, and their freedom, and their liberty.

51 Before this thirteenth year had passed away, the Nephites were threatened with utter destruction because of this war, which had become exceedingly sore.

52 And it came to pass that those Lamanites who had united with the Nephites were numbered among the Nephites; and their curse was taken from them and their skin became white like the Nephites.

53 And their young men and their daughters became exceedingly fair, and they were numbered among the Nephites and were called Nephites. And thus ended the thirteenth year.

54 In the commencement of the fourteenth year, the war between the robbers and the people of Nephi continued and became exceedingly sore.

55 Nevertheless, the people of Nephi gained some advantage of the robbers, insomuch that they drove them back out of their lands into the mountains and into their secret places. And thus ended the fourteenth year.

56 And in the fifteenth year they came forth again against the people of Nephi; and because of the wickedness of the people of Nephi, and their many contentions and dissensions, the Gadianton robbers gained many advantages over them.

57 Thus ended the fifteenth year, and thus were the people in a state of many afflictions; and the sword of destruction hung over them, insomuch that they were about to be smitten down by it, and this because of their iniquity.

CHAPTER 2

NOW in the sixteenth year from the coming of Christ, Lachoneus, the governor of the land, received an epistle from the leader and the governor of this band of robbers.

2 And these are the words which were written, saying: "Lachoneus, most noble and chief governor of the land, behold, I write this epistle to you,

and give you exceedingly great praise because of your firmness, and also the firmness of your people, in maintaining that which you suppose to be your right and liberty.

3 "You stand well, as if you were supported by the hand of a god in the defense of your liberty, and your property, and your country, or that which you call so.

4 "And it seems a pity to me, most noble Lachoneus, that you should be so foolish and vain as to suppose that you can stand against so many brave men who are at my command, who now at this time stand in their arms and await with great anxiety for the word, 'Go down upon the Nephites and destroy them.'

5 "And I know of their unconquerable spirit, having proved them in the field of battle, and I know of their everlasting hatred toward you because of the many wrongs which you have done to them, therefore if they should come down against you, they would visit you with utter destruction.

6 "Therefore I have written this epistle, sealing it with my own hand, feeling for your welfare because of your firmness in that which you believe to be right, and your noble spirit in the field of battle.

7 "Therefore I write to you desiring that you would yield to my people, your cities, your lands, and your possessions, rather than that they should visit you with the sword, and that destruction should come upon you.

8 "In other words, yield yourselves to us, and unite with us, and become acquainted with our secret works, and become our brethren, that you may be like us; not our slaves, but our brethren and partners of all our substance.

9 "And, behold, I swear to you with an oath that if you will do this you shall not be destroyed; but if you will not do this, I swear to you with an oath that on the morrow month, I will command that my armies shall come down against you.

10 "And they shall not stay their hand and shall spare not, but shall slay you and shall let fall the sword upon you, even until you shall become extinct.

11 "Behold, I am Giddianhi; and I am the governor of this the secret society of Gadianton; which society and the works thereof, I know to be good; and they are of ancient date, and they have been handed down to us.

12 "And I write this epistle to you, Lachoneus, and I hope that you will deliver up your lands and your possessions without the shedding of blood, that my people may recover their rights and government who have dissented away from you because of your wickedness in retaining from them their rights of government; and except you do this, I will avenge their wrongs. I am Giddianhi."

13 When Lachoneus received this epistle, he was exceedingly astonished because of the boldness of Giddianhi in demanding the possession of the land of the Nephites, ¹⁴and also in threatening the people to avenge the wrong of those that had received no wrong save they had wronged themselves by dissenting away to those wicked and abominable robbers.

15 Now, behold, this Lachoneus, the governor, was a just man and could not be frightened by the demands and the threatenings of a robber.

16 Therefore he did not hearken to the epistle of Giddianhi, the governor of the robbers, but he caused that his people should cry to the Lord for strength against the time that the robbers should come down against them.

17 He sent a proclamation among all the people that they should gather together their women and their children, their flocks and their herds, and all their substance, save their land, to one place.

18 And he caused that fortifications should be built round about them, and the strength thereof should be exceedingly great.

19 And he caused that armies, both of the Nephites and of the Lamanites, or of all them who were numbered among the Nephites, should be placed as guards round about, to watch them and to guard them from the robbers day and night.

20 He said to them, "As the Lord lives, except you repent of all your iniquities and cry to the Lord, you can in no wise be delivered out of the hands of those Gadianton robbers."

21 And so great and marvelous were the words and prophecies of Lachoneus that they caused fear to come upon all the people, and they exerted themselves in their might to do according to the words of Lachoneus.

22 And Lachoneus appointed chief captains over all the armies of the Nephites to command them at the time that the robbers should come down out of the wilderness against them.

23 Now the chiefest among all the chief captains, and the great commander of all the armies of the Nephites, was appointed, and his name was Gidgiddoni.

24 Now it was the custom among all the Nephites to appoint for their chief captains, save in their times of wickedness, someone that had the spirit of revelation, and also prophecy; and this Gidgiddoni was a great prophet among them, and also was the chief judge.

25 And the people said to Gidgiddoni, "Pray to the Lord and let us go up on the mountains and into the wilderness, that we may fall upon the robbers and destroy them in their own lands."

26 But Gidgiddoni said to them, "The Lord forbid; for if we should go up against them, the Lord would deliver us into their hands.

27 "Therefore we will prepare ourselves in the center of our lands, and we will gather all our armies together, and we will not go against them, but we will wait till they shall come against us.

28 "As the Lord lives, if we do this, he will deliver them into our hands."

29 And in the seventeenth year, in the latter end of the year, the proclamation of Lachoneus had gone forth throughout all the face of the land.

30 And they had taken their horses, and their chariots, and their cattle, and all their flocks, and their herds, and their grain, and all their substance, ³¹and marched forth by thousands, and by tens of thousands, until they had all gone forth to the place which had been appointed that they should gather themselves together to

291   A. D. 16–17

defend themselves against their enemies.

32 The land which was appointed was the land of Zarahemla and the land which was between the land of Zarahemla and the land Bountiful, to the line which was between the land Bountiful and the land Desolation.

33 And there were a great many thousand people who were called Nephites who gathered themselves together in this land.

34 Now Lachoneus caused that they should gather themselves together in the land southward because of the great curse which was upon the land northward; and they fortified themselves against their enemies.

35 And they dwelt in one land and in one body, and they feared the words which had been spoken by Lachoneus insomuch that they repented of all their sins.

36 And they put up their prayers to the Lord their God that he would deliver them in the time that their enemies should come down against them to battle.

37 And they were exceedingly sorrowful because of their enemy.

38 And Gidgiddoni caused that they should make weapons of war, of every kind, that they should be strong with armor, and with shields, and with bucklers, after the manner of his instructions.

39 In the latter end of the eighteenth year, those armies of robbers had prepared for battle, and began to come down, and to sally forth from the hills, and out of the mountains, and the wilderness, and their strongholds, and their secret places.

40 And they began to take possession of the lands which were in the land south, and which were in the land north, and began to take possession of all the lands which had been deserted by the Nephites and the cities which had been left desolate.

41 But, behold, there were no wild beasts nor game in those lands which had been deserted by the Nephites, and there was no game for the robbers, save in the wilderness.

42 And the robbers could not exist, save in the wilderness, for the want of food; for the Nephites had left their lands desolate, and had gathered their flocks, and their herds and all their substance, and they were in one body.

43 Therefore there was no chance for the robbers to plunder and to obtain food save to come up in open battle against the Nephites.

44 And the Nephites being in one body, and having so great a number, had reserved for themselves provisions, and horses, and cattle, and flocks of every kind, that they might subsist for the space of seven years, 45in which time they hoped to destroy the robbers from the face of the land. And thus the eighteenth year passed away.

46 In the nineteenth year Giddianhi found that it was expedient that he should go up to battle against the Nephites, for there was no way that they could subsist save to plunder, and rob, and murder.

47 And they dared not spread themselves upon the face of the land, so that they could raise grain, lest the Nephites should come upon them and slay them.

48 Therefore Giddianhi gave commandment to his armies that in this year they should go up to battle against the Nephites.

49 And they came up to battle; and it was in the sixth month; and, behold, great and terrible was the day that they came up to battle.

50 And they were girded about after the manner of robbers; and they had lambskins which were dyed in blood about their loins; and their heads were shorn; and they had headplates upon them.

51 And great and terrible was the appearance of the armies of Giddianhi because of their armor, and because of its being dyed in blood.

52 The armies of the Nephites, when they saw the appearance of the army of Giddianhi, had all fallen to the earth, and they lifted their cries to the Lord their God that he would spare them and deliver them out of the hands of their enemies.

53 When the armies of Giddianhi saw this, they began to shout with a loud voice because of their joy; for they supposed that the Nephites had fallen with fear because of the terror of their armies.

54 But in this thing they were disappointed, for the Nephites did not fear them; but they feared their God, and supplicated him for protection.

55 Therefore when the armies of Giddianhi rushed upon them, they were prepared to meet them; and in the strength of the Lord they received them; and the battle commenced in this the sixth month.

56 Great and terrible was the battle; and great and terrible was the slaughter thereof, insomuch that there never was known so great a slaughter among all the people of Lehi since he left Jerusalem.

57 And notwithstanding the threatenings and the oaths which Giddianhi had made, behold, the Nephites beat them insomuch that they fell back from before them.

58 And Gidgiddoni commanded that his armies should pursue them as far as the borders of the wilderness and that they should not spare any that should fall into their hands by the way.

59 Thus they pursued them, and slew them, to the borders of the wilderness, even until they had fulfilled the commandment of Gidgiddoni.

60 And Giddianhi, who had stood and fought with boldness, was pursued as he fled; and being weary because of his much fighting, he was overtaken and slain. And thus was the end of Giddianhi, the robber.

61 And it came to pass that the armies of the Nephites returned again to their place of security.

62 And this nineteenth year passed away, and the robbers did not come again to battle; neither did they come in the twentieth year.

63 And in the twenty-first year they did not come up to battle, but they came up on all sides to lay siege round about the people of Nephi; 64for they supposed that if they should cut off the people of Nephi from their lands and should hem them in on every side, and if they should cut them off from all their outward privileges, they could cause them to yield themselves up according to their wishes.

65 Now they had appointed to themselves another leader, whose name was Zemnarihah; therefore it was Zemnarihah that caused that this siege should take place.

66 But, behold, this was an advantage to the Nephites; for it was impossible for the robbers to lay siege sufficiently long to have any effect upon the Nephites because of their greater provisions which they had laid up in store, and because of the scantiness of provisions among the robbers; 67for, behold, they had nothing save it were meat for their subsistence, which meat they obtained in the wilderness.

68 And it came to pass that the wild game became scarce in the wilderness, insomuch that the robbers were about to perish with hunger.

69 And the Nephites were continually marching out by day and by night, and falling upon their armies, and cutting them off by thousands and by tens of thousands.

70 Thus it became the desire of the people of Zemnarihah to withdraw from their design because of the great destruction which came upon them by night and by day.

71 And it came to pass that Zemnarihah gave command to his people that they should withdraw themselves from the siege and march into the farthermost parts of the land northward.

72 Gidgiddoni, being aware of their design and knowing of their weakness because of the want of food and the great slaughter which had been made among them, sent out his armies in the nighttime, and cut off the way of their retreat, and placed his armies in the way of their retreat.

73 This they did in the nighttime and got on their march beyond robbers, so that on the morrow, when the robbers began their march, they were met by the armies of the Nephites, both in their front and in their rear.

74 And the robbers who were on the south were also cut off in their places of retreat. And all these things were done by command of Gidgiddoni.

75 There were many thousands who yielded themselves up prisoners to the Nephites, and the remainder of

them were slain; and their leader Zemnarihah was taken and hanged upon a tree, even upon the top thereof, until he was dead.

76 When he was dead, they felled the tree to the earth, and cried with a loud voice, saying, "May the Lord preserve his people in righteousness and in holiness of heart, that they may cause to be felled to the earth all who shall seek to slay them because of power and secret combinations, even as this man has been felled to the earth."

77 And they rejoiced and cried again with one voice, saying, "May the God of Abraham, and the God of Isaac, and the God of Jacob protect this people in righteousness as long as they shall call on the name of their God for protection."

78 And they broke forth, all as one, in singing and praising their God for the great thing which he had done for them in preserving them from falling into the hands of their enemies.

79 And they cried, "Hosanna to the Most High God"; and they cried, "Blessed be the name of the Lord God Almighty, the Most High God."

80 And their hearts were swollen with joy, to the gushing out of many tears, because of the great goodness of God in delivering them out of the hands of their enemies.

81 They knew it was because of their repentance and their humility that they had been delivered from an everlasting destruction.

82 And now, behold, there was not a living soul among all the people of the Nephites who doubted in the least the words of all the holy prophets who had spoken.

83 For they knew that they must be fulfilled; and they knew that Christ had come because of the many signs which had been given according to the words of the prophets.

84 And because of the things which had come to pass already, they knew that it must be that all things should come to pass according to that which had been spoken.

85 Therefore they forsook all their sins, and their abominations, and their whoredoms, and served God with all diligence day and night.

86 Now when they had taken all the robbers prisoners, insomuch that none escaped who were not slain, they cast their prisoners into prison and caused the word of God to be preached to them.

87 And as many as would repent of their sins and enter into a covenant that they would murder no more were set at liberty.

88 But as many as would not enter into a covenant, and who still continued to have those secret murders in their hearts, and as many as were found breathing out threatenings against their brethren were condemned and punished according to the law.

89 And thus they put an end to all those wicked, and secret, and abominable combinations in which there was so much wickedness and so many murders committed.

90 Thus had the twenty-second year passed away, and the twenty-third year also, and the twenty-fourth, and the twenty-fifth.

91 And thus had twenty-five years passed away, and many things had transpired which, in the eyes of some, would be great and marvelous.

92 Nevertheless, they cannot all be written in this book; for this book cannot contain even a hundredth part of what was done among so many people in the space of twenty-five years.

93 But, behold, there are records which do contain all the proceedings of this people; and a shorter but a true account was given by Nephi.

94 Therefore I have made my record of these things according to the record of Nephi, which was engraved on the plates which were called the plates of Nephi.

95 And, behold, I make this record on plates which I have made with my own hands.

96 And, behold, I am called Mormon, being called after the land of Mormon, the land in which Alma established the church among this people, even the first church which was established among them after their transgression.

97 Behold, I am a disciple of Jesus Christ, the Son of God. I have been called of him to declare his word

among his people, that they might have everlasting life.

98 And it has become expedient that I (according to the will of God that the prayers of those who have gone hence, who were the holy ones, should be fulfilled according to their faith) should make a record of these things which have been done, ⁹⁹a small record of that which has taken place from the time that Lehi left Jerusalem even down until the present time.

100 Therefore I make my record from the accounts which have been given by those who were before me until the commencement of my day; and then will I make a record of the things which I have seen with my own eyes.

101 And I know the record which I make to be a just and a true record; nevertheless there are many things which, according to our language, we are not able to write.

102 And now I make an end of my saying which is of myself and proceed to give my account of the things which have been before me. I am Mormon, and a pure descendant of Lehi.

103 I have reason to bless my God and my Savior Jesus Christ, that he brought our fathers out of the land of Jerusalem (and no one knew it save himself and those whom he brought out of that land), and that he has given me and my people so much knowledge to the salvation of our souls.

104 Surely he has blessed the house of Jacob and has been merciful to the seed of Joseph.

105 And insomuch as the children of Lehi have kept his commandments, he has blessed them and prospered them according to his word.

106 And surely he shall again bring a remnant of the seed of Joseph to the knowledge of the Lord their God.

107 And as surely as the Lord lives will he gather in from the four quarters of the earth all the remnant of the seed of Jacob, who are scattered abroad upon all the face of the earth.

108 And as he has covenanted with all the house of Jacob, even so shall the covenant wherewith he has covenanted with the house of Jacob be fulfilled in his own due time to the restoring all the house of Jacob to the knowledge of the covenant that he has covenanted with them.

109 And then shall they know their Redeemer, who is Jesus Christ, the Son of God; and then shall they be gathered in from the four quarters of the earth to their own lands, whence they have been dispersed; as the Lord lives, so shall it be. Amen.

CHAPTER 3

NOW it came to pass that the people of the Nephites all returned to their own lands in the twenty-sixth year, every man with his family, his flocks and his herds, his horses and his cattle, and all things that belonged to him.

2 They had not eaten all their provisions, therefore they took with them all that they had not devoured of all their grain of every kind, and their gold, and their silver, and all their precious things; ³and they returned to their own lands and their possessions, both on the north and on the south, both on the land northward and on the land southward.

4 And they granted to those robbers who had entered into a covenant to keep the peace of the land, who were desirous to remain Lamanites, lands according to their numbers, that they might have, with their labors, wherewith to subsist upon; and thus they established peace in all the land.

5 And they began again to prosper and to wax great; and the twenty-sixth and seventh years passed away, and there was great order in the land; and they had formed their laws according to equity and justice.

6 Now there was nothing in all the land to hinder the people from prospering continually except they should fall into transgressions.

7 And it was Gidgiddoni, and the judge Lachoneus, and those who had been appointed leaders, who had established this great peace in the land.

8 And it came to pass that there were many cities built anew, and

there were many old cities repaired, and there were many highways cast up, and many roads made which led from city to city, and from land to land, and from place to place.

9 Thus passed away the twenty-eighth year, and the people had continual peace.

10 But in the twenty-ninth year, there began to be some disputings among the people.

11 Some were lifted up to pride and boastings because of their exceedingly great riches, even to great persecutions; for there were many merchants in the land, and also many lawyers and many officers.

12 And the people began to be distinguished by ranks according to their riches and their chances for learning; 13some were ignorant because of their poverty, and others received great learning because of their riches.

14 Some were lifted up in pride, and others were exceedingly humble; some returned railing for railing, while others would receive railing, and persecution, and all manner of afflictions, and would not turn and revile again, but were humble and penitent before God.

15 Thus there became a great inequality in all the land, insomuch that the church began to be broken up; insomuch that in the thirtieth year the church was broken up in all the land, save among a few of the Lamanites who were converted to the true faith.

16 And they would not depart from it, for they were firm, and steadfast, and immovable, willing with all diligence to keep the commandments of the Lord.

17 Now the cause of this iniquity of the people was this: Satan had great power, even to the stirring up of the people to do all manner of iniquity, and to the puffing them up with pride, tempting them to seek for power, and authority, and riches, and the vain things of the world.

18 Thus Satan led away the hearts of the people to do all manner of iniquity; therefore they had enjoyed peace but a few years.

19 And thus in the commencement of the thirtieth year—the people hav-ing been delivered up for the space of a long time, to be carried about by the temptations of the devil wherever he desired to carry them, and to do whatever iniquity he desired they should—they were in a state of awful wickedness.

20 Now they did not sin ignorantly, for they knew the will of God concerning them, for it had been taught to them; therefore they willfully rebelled against God.

21 And it was in the days of Lachoneus, the son of Lachoneus, for Lachoneus filled the seat of his father and governed the people that year.

22 And there began to be men inspired from heaven, and sent forth, standing among the people in all the land, preaching and testifying boldly of the sins and iniquities of the people, 23and testifying to them concerning the redemption which the Lord would make for his people, or in other words, the resurrection of Christ; and they testified boldly of his death and sufferings.

24 Now there were many of the people who were exceedingly angry because of those who testified of these things.

25 And those who were angry were chiefly the chief judges, and they who had been high priests and lawyers.

26 All those who were lawyers were angry with those who testified of these things.

27 Now there was no lawyer, nor judge, nor high priest that could have power to condemn any one to death save his condemnation was signed by the governor of the land.

28 But there were many of those who testified of the things pertaining to Christ, who testified boldly, who were taken and put to death secretly by the judges, that the knowledge of their death came not to the governor of the land until after their death.

29 Now, behold, this was contrary to the laws of the land that any man should be put to death except power was given from the governor of the land.

30 Therefore a complaint came to the land of Zarahemla, to the governor of the land, against these

judges who had condemned the prophets of the Lord to death, but not according to the law.

31 And they were taken and brought up before the judge, to be judged of the crime which they had done, according to the law which had been given by the people.

32 Now those judges had many friends and kindreds; and the remainder, even almost all the lawyers and the high priests, gathered themselves together and united with the kindreds of those judges who were to be tried according to the law.

33 And they entered into a covenant one with another, even into that covenant which was given by them of old, which covenant was given and administered by the devil, to combine against all righteousness.

34 Therefore they combined against the people of the Lord and entered into a covenant to destroy them, and to deliver those who were guilty of murder from the grasp of justice which was about to be administered according to the law.

35 And they set at defiance the law and the rights of their country; and they covenanted one with another to destroy the governor and to establish a king over the land, that the land should no more be at liberty, but should be subject to kings.

36 Now, behold, I will show you that they did not establish a king over the land; but in this same year, the thirtieth year, they destroyed upon the judgment seat, even murdered, the chief judge of the land.

37 And the people were divided one against another; and they separated one from another into tribes, every man according to his family, and his kindred, and his friends; and thus they destroyed the government of the land.

38 Every tribe appointed a chief, or a leader, over them; and thus they became tribes and leaders of tribes.

39 Now, behold, there was no man among them save he had a large family and many kindred and friends; therefore their tribes became exceedingly great.

40 Now all this was done and there were no wars as yet among them; and all this iniquity had come upon the people because they yielded themselves to the power of Satan.

41 And the regulations of the government were destroyed because of the secret combination of the friends and kindreds of those who murdered the prophets.

42 And they caused a great contention in the land, insomuch that they had nearly all become wicked; and there were but few righteous men among them.

43 Thus six years had not passed away since the greater part of the people had turned from their righteousness, like the dog to his vomit, or like the sow to her wallowing in the mire.

44 Now this secret combination, which had brought so great iniquity upon the people, gathered themselves together and placed at their head a man whom they called Jacob; and they called him their king.

45 Therefore he became a king over this wicked band, and he was one of the chiefest who had given his voice against the prophets who testified of Jesus.

46 And they were not so strong in number as the tribes of the people who were united together, save that their leaders established their laws, each one according to his tribe.

47 Nevertheless they were enemies, notwithstanding they were not a righteous people; yet they were united in the hatred of those who had entered into a covenant to destroy the government.

48 Therefore Jacob, seeing that their enemies were more numerous than they and being the king of the band, commanded his people that they should take their flight into the northernmost part of the land, 49and there build up to themselves a kingdom until they were joined by dissenters (for he flattered them that there would be many dissenters) and became sufficiently strong to contend with the tribes of the people.

50 And they did so; and so speedy was their march that it could not be impeded until they had gone forth out of the reach of the people.

51 Thus ended the thirtieth year; and thus were the affairs of the people of Nephi.

52 And in the thirty-first year, they were divided into tribes, every man according to his family, kindred, and friends.

53 Nevertheless they had come to an agreement that they would not go to war one with another; but they were not united as to their laws and their manner of government, for they were established according to the minds of those who were their chiefs and their leaders.

54 But they established very strict laws that one tribe should not trespass against another, insomuch that in some degree they had peace in the land.

55 Nevertheless, their hearts were turned from the Lord their God, and they stoned the prophets and cast them out from among them.

56 And it came to pass that Nephi, having been visited by angels, and also having heard the voice of the Lord, having seen angels and being eyewitness, and having had power given him that he might know concerning the ministry of Christ, and also being eyewitness to their quick return from righteousness to their wickedness and abominations, 57and being grieved for the hardness of their hearts and the blindness of their minds, went forth among them in that same year and began to testify boldly of repentance and remission of sins through faith on the Lord Jesus Christ.

58 And he ministered many things to them, and all of them cannot be written, and a part of them would not suffice; therefore they are not written in this book. And Nephi ministered with power and with great authority.

59 And it came to pass that they were angry with him because he had greater power than they, for it was not possible that they could disbelieve his words, for so great was his faith on the Lord Jesus Christ that angels ministered to him daily.

60 And in the name of Jesus he cast out devils and unclean spirits; and even his brother he raised from the dead, after he had been stoned and had suffered death by the people.

61 And the people saw it, and witnessed of it, and were angry with him because of his power; and he also did many more miracles in the sight of the people in the name of Jesus.

62 And the thirty-first year passed away, and there were but few who were converted to the Lord.

63 But as many as were converted truly signified to the people that they had been visited by the power and Spirit of God, which was in Jesus Christ in whom they believed.

64 And as many as had devils cast out of them, and were healed of their sicknesses and their infirmities, truly manifested to the people that they had been wrought upon by the Spirit of God and had been healed.

65 And they showed forth signs also and did some miracles among the people.

66 Thus passed away the thirty-second year also.

67 And Nephi cried to the people in the commencement of the thirty-third year, and he preached to them repentance and remission of sins.

68 Now I would have you remember also that there were none who were brought to repentance who were not baptized with water.

69 Therefore there were ordained of Nephi men to this ministry, that all such as should come to them should be baptized with water, and this as a witness and a testimony before God and to the people that they had repented and received a remission of their sins.

70 And there were many in the commencement of this year that were baptized to repentance; and thus the greater part of the year passed away.

CHAPTER 4

NOW it came to pass that according to our record (and we know our record to be true, for, behold, it was a just man who kept the record; for he truly did many miracles in the name of Jesus; 2and there was not any man who could do a miracle in the name of Jesus, save he were cleansed every whit from his iniquity), 3and if there was no mistake made in the reckoning of our time, the thirty-third year had passed away, and the people began to look with great earnestness for the sign which had been given by the prophet Samuel, the Lamanite, 4for the time that there should be darkness for the space of three days over the face of the land.

5 And there began to be great doubtings and disputations among the people, notwithstanding so many signs had been given.

6 And in the thirty-fourth year, in the first month, in the fourth day of the month, there arose a great storm, such a one as never had been known in all the land.

7 There was also a great and terrible tempest; and there was terrible thunder, insomuch that it shook the whole earth as if it was about to divide asunder; and there were exceedingly sharp lightnings, such as never had been known in all the land.

8 And the city of Zarahemla took fire; and the city of Moroni sank into the depths of the sea, and the inhabitants thereof were drowned.

9 And the earth was carried up upon the city of Moronihah, that in the place of the city there became a great mountain; and there was a great and terrible destruction in the land southward.

10 But, behold, there was a greater and more terrible destruction in the land northward; for, behold, the whole face of the land was changed because of the tempests, and the whirlwinds, and the thunderings, and the lightnings, and the exceedingly great quaking of the whole earth.

11 And the highways were broken up, and the level roads were spoiled, and many smooth places became rough, and many great and notable cities were sunk, and many were burned, and many were shaken till the buildings thereof had fallen to the earth, and the inhabitants thereof were slain, and the places were left desolate.

12 There were some cities which remained; but the damage thereof was exceedingly great, and there were many in them who were slain.

13 And there were some who were carried away in the whirlwind; and and where they went, no man knows, save they know that they were carried away.

14 Thus the face of the whole earth became deformed because of the tempests, and the thunderings, and the lightnings, and the quaking of the earth.

15 And, behold, the rocks were rent in two; they were broken up upon the face of the whole earth, insomuch that they were found in broken fragments, and in seams, and in cracks upon all the face of the land.

16 And it came to pass that when the thunderings, and the lightnings, and the storm, and the tempest, and the quakings of the earth ceased (for, behold, they lasted for about the space of three hours, and it was said by some that the time was greater; 17nevertheless, all these great and terrible things were done in about the space of three hours), then, behold, there was darkness upon the face of the land.

18 And it came to pass that there was thick darkness upon all the face of the land, insomuch that the inhabitants thereof who had not fallen could feel the vapor of darkness.

19 And there could be no light because of the darkness, neither candles, neither torches; neither could there be fire kindled with their fine and exceedingly dry wood, so that there could not be any light at all.

20 And there was not any light seen, neither fire, nor glimmer, neither the sun, nor the moon, nor the stars, so great were the mists of darkness which were upon the face of the land.

21 For the space of three days there was no light seen; and there was great mourning, and howling, and weeping among all the people continually.

22 And great were the groanings of the people because of the darkness and the great destruction which had come upon them.

23 In one place they were heard to cry, saying, "Oh, that we had repented before this great and terrible day, then would our brethren have been spared, and they would not have been burned in that great city Zarahemla."

24 And in another place they were heard to cry and mourn, saying, "Oh,

299   A. D. 34

that we had repented before this great and terrible day, and had not killed and stoned the prophets, and cast them out.

25 "Then would our mothers, and our fair daughters, and our children have been spared, and not have been buried up in that great city Moronihah." Thus were the howlings of the people great and terrible.

26 And it came to pass that there was a voice heard among all the inhabitants of the earth upon all the face of this land, crying, "Woe, woe, woe to this people; woe to the inhabitants of the whole earth, except they shall repent.

27 "For the devil laughs, and his angels rejoice because of the slain of the fair sons and daughters of my people; and it is because of their iniquity and abominations that they are fallen.

28 "Behold, that great city Zarahemla have I burned with fire, and the inhabitants thereof.

29 "And that great city Moroni have I caused to be sunk in the depths of the sea, and the inhabitants thereof to be drowned.

30 "And that great city Moronihah have I covered with earth, and the inhabitants thereof, to hide their iniquities and their abominations from before my face, that the blood of the prophets and of the saints shall not come up any more to me against them.

31 "And, behold, the city of Gilgal have I caused to be sunk, and the inhabitants thereof to be buried in the depths of the earth; 32and the city of Onihah, and the inhabitants thereof, and the city of Mocum, and the inhabitants thereof, and the city of Jerusalem, and the inhabitants thereof, and waters have I caused to come up in the stead thereof, 33to hide their wickedness and abominations from before my face, that the blood of the prophets and the saints shall not come up any more to me against them.

34 "And, behold, the city of Gadiandi, and the city of Gadiomnah, and the city of Jacob, and the city Gimgimno, all these have I caused to be sunk, and made hills and valleys in the places thereof.

35 "And the inhabitants thereof have I buried up in the depths of the earth, to hide their wickedness and abominations from before my face, that the blood of the prophets and the saints should not come up any more to me against them.

36 "And, behold, that great city Jacobugath, which was inhabited by the people of the king of Jacob, have I caused to be burned with fire because of their sins and their wickedness, which was above all the wickedness of the whole earth, because of their secret murders and combinations.

37 "For it was they that destroyed the peace of my people and the government of the land; therefore I caused them to be burned, to destroy them from before my face, that the blood of the prophets and the saints should not come up to me any more against them.

38 "And, behold, the city of Laman, and the city of Josh, and the city of Gad, and the city of Kishkumen have I caused to be burned with fire, and the inhabitants thereof, because of their wickedness in casting out the prophets and stoning those whom I sent to declare to them concerning their wickedness and their abominations.

39 "Because they cast them all out that there were none righteous among them, I sent down fire and destroyed them, that their wickedness and abominations might be hid from before my face, that the blood of the prophets and the saints whom I sent among them might not cry to me from the ground against them.

40 "And many great destructions have I caused to come upon this land and upon this people because of their wickedness and their abominations.

41 "O all ye that are spared because ye were more righteous than they, will ye not now return unto me, and repent of your sins, and be converted that I may heal you?

42 "Verily I say unto you, If ye will come unto me, ye shall have eternal life.

43 "Behold, mine arm of mercy is extended towards you, and whosoever will come, him will I receive;

and blessed are those who come unto me.

44 "Behold, I am Jesus Christ, the Son of God. I created the heavens and the earth, and all things that in them are.

45 "I was with the Father from the beginning. I am in the Father, and the Father in me; and in me hath the Father glorified his name.

46 "I came unto my own, and my own received me not. And the scriptures concerning my coming are fulfilled.

47 "And as many as have received me, to them have I given to become the sons of God; and even so will I to as many as shall believe on my name, for, behold, by me redemption cometh and in me is the law of Moses fulfilled.

48 "I am the light and the life of the world. I am Alpha and Omega, the beginning and the end.

49 "And ye shall offer unto me no more the shedding of blood; your sacrifices and your burnt offerings shall be done away, for I will accept none of your sacrifices and your burnt offerings; and ye shall offer for a sacrifice unto me a broken heart and a contrite spirit.

50 "Whoso cometh unto me with a broken heart and a contrite spirit, him will I baptize with fire and with the Holy Ghost, even as the Lamanites, because of their faith in me at the time of their conversion, were baptized with fire and with the Holy Ghost, and they knew it not.

51 "Behold, I have come to the world to bring redemption to the world, to save the world from sin; therefore whoso repenteth and cometh to me as a little child, him will I receive; for of such is the kingdom of God.

52 "For such I have laid down my life and have taken it up again; therefore repent, and come unto me, ye ends of the earth, and be saved."

53 And all the people of the land heard these sayings and witnessed of it.

54 And after these sayings there was silence in the land for the space of many hours; for so great was the astonishment of the people that they ceased lamenting and howling for the loss of their kindred which had been slain, therefore there was silence in all the land for the space of many hours.

55 And there came a voice again to the people, and all the people heard, and witnessed of it, saying: "O ye people of these great cities which have fallen, who are descendants of Jacob, who are of the house of Israel. O ye people of the house of Israel, how oft have I gathered you as a hen gathereth her chickens under her wings, and have nourished you.

56 "And again, how oft would I have gathered you as a hen gathereth her chickens under her wings, O ye people of the house of Israel, who have fallen.

57 "O ye people of the house of Israel, ye that dwell at Jerusalem as well as ye that have fallen, how oft would I have gathered you as a hen gathereth her chickens, and ye would not.

58 "O ye house of Israel, whom I have spared, how oft will I gather you as a hen gathereth her chickens under her wings, if ye will repent and return to me with full purpose of heart.

59 "But if not, O house of Israel, the places of your dwellings shall become desolate until the time of the fulfilling of the covenant to your fathers."

60 After the people had heard these words, behold, they began to weep and to howl again because of the loss of their kindred and friends.

61 And thus the three days passed away.

62 And it was in the morning, and the darkness dispersed from off the face of the land, and the earth ceased to tremble, and the rocks ceased to rend, and the dreadful groanings ceased, and all the tumultuous noises passed away.

63 The earth cleaved together again, that it stood, and the mourning, and the weeping, and the wailing of the people who were spared alive ceased.

64 And their mourning was turned into joy, and their lamentations into the praise and thanksgiving to the Lord Jesus Christ, their Redeemer.

65 Thus far were the scriptures

fulfilled which had been spoken by the prophets.

66 And it was the more righteous part of the people who were saved, and it was they who received the prophets and stoned them not; and it was they who had not shed the blood of the saints who were spared.

67 They were spared, and were not sunk and buried up in the earth; and they were not drowned in the depths of the sea; and they were not burned by fire, neither were they fallen upon and crushed to death.

68 And they were not carried away in the whirlwind; neither were they overpowered by the vapor of smoke and of darkness.

69 Now whoever reads, let him understand; he that has the scriptures, let him search them and see and behold if all these deaths and destructions by fire, and by smoke, and by tempests, and by whirlwinds, and by the opening of the earth to receive them, and all these things are not to the fulfilling of the prophecies of many of the holy prophets.

70 Behold, I say to you, many have testified of these happenings at the coming of Christ, and were slain because they testified of these things.

71 The prophet Zenos testified of these things, and also Zenock spoke concerning these things, because they testified particularly concerning us, who are the remnant of their seed.

72 Behold, our father Jacob also testified concerning a remnant of the seed of Joseph. And, behold, are not we a remnant of the seed of Joseph?

73 And these things which testify of us, are they not written upon the plates of brass which our father Lehi brought out of Jerusalem?

74 And in the ending of the thirty-fourth year, behold, I will show you that the people of Nephi who were spared, and also those who had been called Lamanites who had been spared, had great favors shown them and great blessings poured out upon their heads, insomuch that soon after the ascension of Christ into heaven, he truly manifested himself to them, showing his body to them and ministering to them.

75 An account of his ministry shall be given hereafter. Therefore for this time I make an end of my sayings.

CHAPTER 5

Jesus Christ shows himself to the people of Nephi, as the multitude were gathered together in the land Bountiful, and ministers to them; and on this wise he showed himself to them.

NOW it came to pass that there were a great multitude gathered together, of the people of Nephi, round about the temple which was in the land Bountiful.

2 And they were marveling and wondering one with another, and were showing one to another the great and marvelous change which had taken place.

3 And they were also conversing about this Jesus Christ of whom the sign had been given concerning his death.

4 While they were thus conversing one with another, they heard a voice as if it came out of heaven; and they cast their eyes round about, for they understood not the voice which they heard.

5 It was not a harsh voice, neither was it a loud voice; nevertheless, and notwithstanding it being a small voice, it pierced them that heard to the center, insomuch that there was no part of their frame that it did not cause to quake; it pierced them to the very soul and caused their hearts to burn.

6 Again they heard the voice, and they understood it not; and again the third time they heard the voice and opened their ears to hear it.

7 And their eyes were toward the sound thereof; and they looked steadfastly toward heaven whence the sound came; and, behold, the third time they understood the voice which they heard.

8 And it said to them, "Behold

my beloved Son, in whom I am well pleased, in whom I have glorified my name, hear ye him."

9 As they understood, they cast their eyes up again toward heaven; and, behold, they saw a man descending out of heaven.

10 He was clothed in a white robe, and he came down and stood in the midst of them; and the eyes of the whole multitude were turned upon him, and they dared not open their mouths, even one to another, and knew not what it meant, for they thought it was an angel that had appeared to them.

11 And he stretched forth his hand and spoke to the people, saying, "Behold, I am Jesus Christ, of whom the prophets testified should come into the world.

12 "I am the light and the life of the world, and I have drunk out of that bitter cup which the Father hath given me and have glorified the Father in taking upon me the sins of the world, in which I have suffered the will of the Father in all things from the beginning."

13 When Jesus had spoken these words, the whole multitude fell to the earth, for they remembered that it had been prophesied among them that Christ should show himself to them after his ascension into heaven.

14 And the Lord spoke to them, saying, "Arise and come forth to me, that ye may thrust your hands into my side, and also that ye may feel the prints of the nails in my hands and in my feet, that ye may know that I am the God of Israel, and the God of the whole earth, and have been slain for the sins of the world."

15 And the multitude went forth, and thrust their hands into his side, and felt the prints of the nails in his hands and in his feet.

16 This they did, going forth one by one until they had all gone forth, and they saw with their eyes, and felt with their hands, and knew of a surety, and bore record that it was he, of whom it was written by the prophets, who should come.

17 When they had all gone forth and had witnessed for themselves, they cried out with one accord, saying, "Hosanna! Blessed be the name of the Most High God!" And they fell down at the feet of Jesus and worshiped him.

18 And it came to pass that he spoke to Nephi (for Nephi was among the multitude) and commanded him to come forth.

19 And Nephi arose and went forth, and bowed himself before the Lord, and he kissed his feet.

20 And the Lord commanded him that he should arise. And he arose and stood before him.

21 And the Lord said to him, "I give to you power that ye shall baptize this people when I am again ascended into heaven."

22 Again the Lord called others and said to them likewise; and he gave to them power to baptize.

23 And he said to them, "On this wise shall ye baptize; and there shall be no disputations among you.

24 "Verily I say unto you that whoso repenteth of his sins through your words, and desireth to be baptized in my name, on this wise shall ye baptize him: Behold, ye shall go down and stand in the water, and in my name shall ye baptize him.

25 "And now, behold, these are the words which ye shall say, calling each by name, saying: 'Having authority given me of Jesus Christ, I baptize you in the name of the Father, and of the Son, and of the Holy Ghost. Amen.'

26 "Then shall ye immerse him in the water and come forth again out of the water.

27 "And after this manner shall ye baptize in my name, for, behold, verily I say to you that the Father, and the Son, and the Holy Ghost are one; and I am in the Father, and the Father in me, and the Father and I are one.

28 "And according as I have commanded you, thus shall ye baptize.

29 "And there shall be no disputations among you, as there hath hitherto been; neither shall there be disputations among you concerning the points of my doctrine, as there hath hitherto been.

30 "For verily, verily I say to you, He that hath the spirit of contention is not of me, but is of the devil, who is the father of contention, and he stirreth

up the hearts of men to contend with anger one with another.

31 "Behold, this is not my doctrine, to stir up the hearts of men with anger one against another; but this is my doctrine, that such things should be done away.

32 "Behold, verily, verily I say to you, I will declare to you my doctrine. And this is my doctrine, and it is the doctrine which the Father hath given to me.

33 "And I bear record of the Father, and the Father beareth record of me, and the Holy Ghost beareth record of the Father and me, and I bear record that the Father commandeth all men, everywhere, to repent and believe in me.

34 "And whoso believeth in me and is baptized, the same shall be saved; and they shall inherit the kingdom of God.

35 "And whoso believeth not in me, and is not baptized, shall be damned.

36 "Verily, verily I say to you that this is my doctrine; and I bear record of it from the Father; and whoso believeth in me, believeth in the Father also.

37 "Unto him will the Father bear record of me; for he will visit him with fire and with the Holy Ghost.

38 "Thus will the Father bear record of me; and the Holy Ghost will bear record to him of the Father and me; for the Father, and I, and the Holy Ghost are one.

39 "Again I say to you, Ye must repent, and become as a little child, and be baptized in my name, or ye can in no wise receive these things.

40 "And again I say to you, Ye must repent, and be baptized in my name, and become as a little child, or ye can in nowise inherit the kingdom of God.

41 "Verily, verily I say to you that this is my doctrine; and whoso buildeth upon this, buildeth upon my rock; and the gates of hell shall not prevail against him.

42 "And whoso shall declare more or less than this and establish it for my doctrine, the same cometh of evil and is not built upon my rock, but he buildeth upon a sandy foundation, and the gates of hell standeth open

to receive such, when the floods come, and the winds beat upon them.

43 "Therefore go forth to this people and declare the words which I have spoken, to the ends of the earth."

44 When Jesus had spoken these words to Nephi, and to those who had been called (now the number of them who had been called and received power and authority to baptize were twelve), 45behold, he stretched forth his hand to the multitude and cried to them, saying, "Blessed are ye if ye shall give heed to the words of these twelve whom I have chosen from among you to minister unto you and to be your servants.

46 "And to them I have given power that they may baptize you with water, and after ye are baptized with water, behold, I will baptize you with fire and with the Holy Ghost.

47 "Therefore blessed are ye, if ye shall believe in me and be baptized, after ye have seen me and know that I am.

48 "And again, more blessed are they who shall believe in your words because ye shall testify that ye have seen me, and that ye know that I am.

49 "Blessed are they who shall believe in your words, and come down into the depths of humility, and be baptized; for they shall be visited with fire and with the Holy Ghost and shall receive a remission of their sins.

50 "Blessed are the poor in spirit who come unto me, for theirs is the kingdom of heaven.

51 "And again, blessed are all they that mourn, for they shall be comforted.

52 "And blessed are the meek, for they shall inherit the earth.

53 "And blessed are all they who do hunger and thirst after righteousness, for they shall be filled with the Holy Ghost.

54 "And blessed are the merciful, for they shall obtain mercy.

55 "And blessed are all the pure in heart, for they shall see God.

56 "And blessed are all the peacemakers, for they shall be called children of God.

57 "And blessed are all they who

are persecuted for my name's sake, for theirs is the kingdom of heaven.

58 "And blessed are ye when men shall revile you, and persecute, and shall say all manner of evil against you falsely for my sake.

59 "For ye shall have great joy and be exceedingly glad, for great shall be your reward in heaven; for so persecuted they the prophets who were before you.

60 "Verily, verily I say to you, I give to you to be the salt of the earth; but if the salt shall lose its savor, wherewith shall the earth be salted? The salt shall be thenceforth good for nothing, but to be cast out and to be trodden under foot of men.

61 "Verily, verily I say to you, I give unto you to be the light of this people. A city that is set on a hill cannot be hid.

62 "Behold, do men light a candle and put it under a bushel? No, but on a candlestick; and it giveth light to all that are in the house.

63 "Therefore let your light so shine before this people that they may see your good works and glorify your Father who is in heaven.

64 "Think not that I am come to destroy the law or the prophets. I am not come to destroy, but to fulfill.

65 "For verily I say to you, Not one jot nor one tittle hath passed away from the law, but in me it hath all been fulfilled.

66 "And, behold, I have given you the law and the commandments of my Father, that ye shall believe in me, and that ye shall repent of your sins and come to me with a broken heart and a contrite spirit.

67 "Behold, ye have the commandments before you, and the law is fulfilled; therefore come to me and be ye saved.

68 "For verily I say to you that except ye shall keep my commandments which I have commanded you at this time, ye shall in no case enter into the kingdom of heaven.

69 "Ye have heard that it hath been said by them of old time, and it is also written before you, that thou shalt not kill; and whosoever shall kill shall be in danger of the judgment of God.

70 "But I say to you that whoso-ever is angry with his brother shall be in danger of his judgment. And whosoever shall say to his brother 'Raca' shall be in danger of the council; and whosoever shall say 'Thou fool' shall be in danger of hell fire.

71 "Therefore, if ye shall come unto me, or shall desire to come unto me, and rememberest that thy brother hath aught against thee, [72]go thy way unto thy brother, and first be reconciled to thy brother, and then come unto me with full purpose of heart, and I will receive you.

73 "Agree with thine adversary quickly, while thou art in the way with him, lest at any time he shall get thee, and thou shalt be cast into prison.

74 "Verily, verily I say to thee, Thou shalt by no means come out thence until thou hast paid the uttermost senine.

75 "And while ye are in prison, can ye pay even one senine? Verily, verily I say to you, Nay.

76 "Behold, it is written by them of old time that thou shalt not commit adultery.

77 "But I say to you that whoso-ever looketh on a woman to lust after her hath committed adultery already in his heart.

78 "Behold, I give you a commandment that ye suffer none of these things to enter into your heart; for it is better that ye should deny yourselves of these things, wherein ye will take up your cross, than that ye should be cast into hell.

79 "It hath been written that who-soever shall put away his wife shall give her a writing of divorce-ment.

80 "Verily, verily I say to you that whosoever shall put away his wife, save for the cause of forni-cation, causeth her to commit adul-tery; and whoso shall marry her who is divorced committeth adultery.

81 "And again it is written, 'Thou shalt not forswear thyself, but shalt perform to the Lord thine oaths.'

82 "But verily, verily I say to you, Swear not at all; neither by heaven, for it is God's throne; nor by the earth, for it is his footstool; neither shalt thou swear by thy head,

because thou canst not make one hair black or white.

83 "But let your communication be Yea, yea; Nay, nay; for whatsoever cometh of more than these is evil.

84 "And, behold, it is written, 'An eye for an eye, and a tooth for a tooth.'

85 "But I say to you that ye shall not resist evil, but whosoever shall smite thee on thy right cheek, turn to him the other also.

86 "And if any man will sue thee at the law and take away thy coat, let him have thy cloak also.

87 "And whosoever shall compel thee to go a mile, go with him twain.

88 "Give to him that asketh thee, and from him that would borrow of thee, turn thou not away.

89 "And, behold, it is written also that thou shalt love thy neighbor and hate thine enemy.

90 "But, behold, I say to you, Love your enemies, bless them that curse you, do good to them that hate you, and pray for them who despitefully use you and persecute you, 91that ye may be the children of your Father who is in heaven; for he maketh his sun to rise on the evil and on the good; therefore those things which were of old time, which were under the law, in me are all fulfilled.

92 "Old things are done away, and all things have become new; therefore I would that ye should be perfect even as I and your Father who is in heaven are perfect.

93 "Verily, verily, I say that I would that ye should do alms to the poor; but take heed that ye do not your alms before men to be seen of them; otherwise ye have no reward of your Father who is in heaven.

94 "Therefore when ye shall do your alms, do not sound a trumpet before you, as hypocrites do in the synagogues and in the streets that they may have glory of men. Verily, I say to you, They have their reward.

95 "But when thou doest alms, let not thy left hand know what thy right hand doeth, 96that thine alms may be in secret; and thy Father, who seeth in secret, himself shall reward thee openly.

97 "And when thou prayest, thou shalt not do as the hypocrites, for they love to pray standing in the synagogues and in the corners of the streets, that they may be seen of men. Verily, I say to you, They have their reward.

98 "But thou, when thou prayest, enter into thy closet, and when thou hast shut thy door, pray to thy Father who is in secret; and thy Father, who seeth in secret, shall reward thee openly.

99 "But when ye pray, use not vain repetitions as do the heathen, for they think that they shall be heard for their much speaking.

100 "Be not ye therefore like them, for your Father knoweth what things ye have need of before ye ask him.

101 "After this manner therefore pray ye:

102 "Our Father who art in heaven, hallowed be thy name.

103 "Thy will be done on earth as it is in heaven.

104 "And forgive us our debts, as we forgive our debtors.

105 "And lead us not into temptation, but deliver us from evil.

106 "For thine is the kingdom, and the power, and the glory, forever. Amen.

107 "For if ye forgive men their trespasses, your heavenly Father will also forgive you; but if ye forgive not men their trespasses, neither will your Father forgive your trespasses.

108 "Moreover, when ye fast, be not as the hypocrites, of a sad countenance, for they disfigure their faces that they may appear to men to fast. Verily, I say to you, They have their reward.

109 "But thou, when thou fastest, anoint thy head and wash thy face, that thou appear not to men to fast, but to thy Father, who is in secret; and thy Father, who seeth in secret, shall reward thee openly.

110 "Lay not up for yourselves treasures upon earth, where moth and rust doth corrupt, and thieves break through and steal.

111 "But lay up for yourselves treasures in heaven, where neither moth nor rust doth corrupt, and where thieves do not break through nor steal.

112 "For where your treasure is, there will your heart be also.

113 "The light of the body is the eye, if therefore thine eye be single, thy whole body shall be full of light.

114 "But if thine eye be evil, thy whole body shall be full of darkness. If therefore the light that is in thee be darkness, how great is that darkness!

115 "No man can serve two masters, for either he will hate the one and love the other; or else he will hold to the one and despise the other. Ye cannot serve God and Mammon."

CHAPTER 6

WHEN Jesus had spoken these words, he looked upon the twelve whom he had chosen, and said to them, "Remember the words which I have spoken.

2 "For, behold, ye are they whom I have chosen to minister unto this people.

3 "Therefore I say to you, Take no thought for your life, what ye shall eat, or what ye shall drink; nor yet for your body, what ye shall put on. Is not the life more than meat, and the body than raiment?

4 "Behold the fowls of the air, for they sow not, neither do they reap, nor gather into barns; yet your heavenly Father feedeth them. Are ye not much better than they?

5 "Which of you by taking thought can add one cubit unto his stature?

6 "And why take ye thought for raiment? Consider the lilies of the field, how they grow; they toil not, neither do they spin; 7and yet I say unto you that even Solomon, in all his glory, was not arrayed like one of these.

8 "Wherefore, if God so clothe the grass of the field, which today is, and tomorrow is cast into the oven, even so will he clothe you, if ye are not of little faith.

9 "Therefore take no thought, saying, 'What shall we eat?' or 'What shall we drink?' or 'Wherewithal shall we be clothed?'

10 "For your heavenly Father knoweth that ye have need of all these things.

11 "But seek ye first the kingdom of God, and his righteousness, and all these things shall be added to you.

12 "Take therefore no thought for the morrow, for the morrow shall take thought for the things of itself. Sufficient is the day unto the evil thereof."

13 When Jesus had spoken these words, he turned again to the multitude and opened his mouth to them again, saying, "Verily, verily, I say to you, Judge not, that ye be not judged.

14 "For with what judgment ye judge, ye shall be judged; and with what measure ye mete, it shall be measured to you again.

15 "And why beholdest thou the mote that is in thy brother's eye, but considerest not the beam that is in thine own eye?

16 "Or how wilt thou say to thy brother, 'Let me pull the mote out of thine eye'; and, behold, a beam is in thine own eye?

17 "Thou hypocrite, first cast the beam out of thine own eye, and then shalt thou see clearly to cast the mote out of thy brother's eye.

18 "Give not that which is holy to the dogs, neither cast ye your pearls before swine, lest they trample them under their feet and turn again and rend you.

19 "Ask, and it shall be given to you; seek, and ye shall find; knock, and it shall be opened to you.

20 "For everyone that asketh, receiveth; and he that seeketh, findeth; and to him that knocketh, it shall be opened.

21 "Or what man is there of you, who, if his son ask bread, will give him a stone?

22 "Or if he ask a fish, will he give him a serpent?

23 "If ye then, being evil, know how to give good gifts to your children, how much more shall your Father who is in heaven give good things to them that ask him?

24 "Therefore all things whatsoever ye would that men should do to you, do ye even so to them, for this is the law and the prophets.

25 "Enter ye in at the strait gate; for wide is the gate and broad is the way that leadeth to destruction, and many there be who go in thereat.

26 "Because strait is the gate and narrow is the way which leadeth to life, and few there be that find it.

27 "Beware of false prophets who come to you in sheep's clothing, but inwardly they are ravening wolves.

28 "Ye shall know them by their fruits. Do men gather grapes of thorns, or figs of thistles?

29 "Even so every good tree bringeth forth good fruit; but a corrupt tree bringeth forth evil fruit.

30 "A good tree cannot bring forth evil fruit, neither can a corrupt tree bring forth good fruit.

31 "Every tree that bringeth not forth good fruit is hewn down and cast into the fire.

32 "Wherefore, by their fruits ye shall know them.

33 "Not everyone that saith to me, 'Lord, Lord,' shall enter into the kingdom of heaven, but he that doeth the will of my Father who is in heaven.

34 "Many will say to me in that day, 'Lord, Lord, have we not prophesied in thy name, and in thy name have we cast out devils, and in thy name done many wonderful works?'

35 "And then will I profess to them, 'I never knew you; depart from me, ye that work iniquity.'

36 "Therefore, whoso heareth these sayings of mine and doeth them, I will liken him to a wise man who built his house upon a rock; and the rain descended, and the floods came, and the winds blew, and beat upon that house, and it fell not; for it was founded upon a rock.

37 "And everyone that heareth these sayings of mine and doeth them not shall be likened to a foolish man who built his house upon the sand; and the rain descended, and the floods came, and the winds blew and beat upon that house, and it fell; and great was the fall of it."

CHAPTER 7

WHEN Jesus had ended these sayings, he cast his eyes round about on the multitude, and said to them, "Behold, ye have heard the things which I have taught before I ascended to my Father.

2 "Therefore whoso remembereth these sayings of mine and doeth them, him will I raise up at the last day."

3 When Jesus had said these words, he perceived that there were some among them who marveled and wondered what he would say concerning the law of Moses; for they understood not the saying that old things had passed away, and that all things had become new.

4 And he said to them, "Marvel not that I said to you that old things had passed away and that all things had become new.

5 "Behold, I say to you that the law is fulfilled that was given to Moses.

6 "Behold, I am he that gave the law, and I am he who covenanted with my people Israel; therefore, the law in me is fulfilled, for I have come to fulfill the law; therefore, it hath an end.

7 "Behold, I do not destroy the prophets, for as many as have not been fulfilled in me, verily, I say to you, shall all be fulfilled.

8 "And because I said to you that old things hath passed away, I do not destroy that which hath been spoken concerning things which are to come.

9 "For, behold, the covenant which I have made with my people is not all fulfilled; but the law which was given to Moses hath an end in me.

10 "Behold, I am the law and the light; look to me and endure to the end, and ye shall live; for to him that endureth to the end will I give eternal life.

11 "Behold, I have given you commandments; therefore keep my commandments.

12 "And this is the law and the prophets, for they truly testified of me."

13 When Jesus had spoken these words, he said to those twelve whom he had chosen, "Ye are my disciples; and ye are a light to this people who are a remnant of the house of Joseph.

14 "And, behold, this is the land of your inheritance, and the Father hath given it to you.

15 "And not at any time hath the Father given me commandment that

I should tell it to your brethren at Jerusalem; neither at any time hath the Father given me commandment that I should tell to them concerning the other tribes of the house of Israel, whom the Father hath led away out of the land.

16 "This much did the Father command me that I should tell to them, that other sheep I have, which are not of this fold; them also I must bring, and they shall hear my voice; and there shall be one fold and one shepherd.

17 "And now because of stiff-neckedness and unbelief, they understood not my word; therefore I was commanded to say no more of the Father concerning this thing to them.

18 "But, verily, I say to you that the Father hath commanded me, and I tell it to you, that ye were separated from among them because of their iniquity; therefore it is because of their iniquity that they know not of you.

19 "And, verily, I say to you again that the other tribes hath the Father separated from them; and it is because of their iniquity that they know not of them.

20 "And, verily, I say to you that ye are they of whom I said, 'Other sheep I have which are not of this fold; them also I must bring, and they shall hear my voice, and there shall be one fold and one shepherd.'

21 "And they understood me not, for they supposed it had been the Gentiles; for they understood not that the Gentiles should be converted through their preaching.

22 "And they understood me not that I said they shall hear my voice; and they understood me not that the Gentiles should not at any time hear my voice, that I should not manifest myself unto them save by the Holy Ghost.

23 "But, behold, ye have both heard my voice and seen me, and ye are my sheep, and ye are numbered among those whom the Father hath given me.

24 "And verily, verily I say to you that I have other sheep which are not of this land; neither of the land of Jerusalem; neither in any

parts of that land round about where I have been to minister.

25 "For they, of whom I speak, are they who have not as yet heard my voice; neither have I at any time manifested myself to them.

26 "But I have received a commandment of the Father, that I shall go to them, and that they shall hear my voice and shall be numbered among my sheep, that there may be one fold and one shepherd; therefore I go to show myself to them.

27 "And I command you that ye shall write these sayings after I am gone, that if it so be that my people at Jerusalem, they who have seen me and been with me in my ministry, do not ask the Father in my name that they may receive a knowledge of you by the Holy Ghost, and also of the other tribes whom they know not of, [28]that these sayings which ye shall write shall be kept and shall be manifested to the Gentiles, that through the fullness of the Gentiles the remnant of their seed, who shall be scattered forth upon the face of the earth because of their unbelief, may be brought in, or may be brought to a knowledge of me, their Redeemer.

29 "And then will I gather them in from the four quarters of the earth; and then will I fulfill the covenant which the Father hath made to all the people of the house of Israel.

30 "And blessed are the Gentiles because of their belief in me, in and of the Holy Ghost which witnesses to them of me and of the Father.

31 "'Behold, because of their belief in me,' saith the Father, 'and because of the unbelief of you, O house of Israel, in the latter day shall the truth come to the Gentiles, that the fullness of these things shall be made known to them.

32 "'But woe,' saith the Father, 'to the unbelieving of the Gentiles,' for notwithstanding they have come forth upon the face of this land and have scattered my people who are of the house of Israel, and my people who are of the house of Israel have been cast out from among them, and have been trodden under feet by them, [33]and because of the mercies of the Father to the Gentiles, and also the

judgments of the Father upon my people who are of the house of Israel, verily, verily, I say to you that after all this, I have caused my people who are of the house of Israel to be smitten, and to be afflicted, and to be slain, and to be cast out from among them, and to become hated by them, and to become a hiss and a byword among them.

34 "And thus commandeth the Father that I should say to you, 'At that day when the Gentiles shall sin against my gospel, and shall reject the fullness of my gospel, and shall be lifted up in the pride of their hearts above all nations and above all the people of the whole earth, and shall be filled with all manner of lyings, and of deceits, and of mischiefs, and all manner of hypocrisy, and murders, and priestcrafts, and whoredoms, and of secret abominations; 35and if they shall do all these things and shall reject the fullness of my gospel, behold,' saith the Father, 'I will bring the fullness of my gospel from among them.

36 "'And then will I remember my covenant which I have made to my people, O house of Israel, and I will bring my gospel to them.

37 "'And I will show thee, O house of Israel, that the Gentiles shall not have power over you, but I will remember my covenant to you, O house of Israel, and ye shall come to the knowledge of the fullness of my gospel.

38 "'But if the Gentiles will repent and return to me,' saith the Father, 'behold, they shall be numbered among my people, O house of Israel.

39 "'And I will not suffer my people, who are of the house of Israel, to go through among them and tread them down,' saith the Father.

40 "'But if they will not turn to me and hearken to my voice, I will suffer my people, O house of Israel, that they shall go through among them, and shall tread them down.

41 "'And they shall be as salt that hath lost its savor, which is thenceforth good for nothing but to be cast out and to be trodden under foot of my people, O house of Israel.'

42 "Verily, verily, I say to you,

Thus hath the Father commanded me that I should give to this people this land for their inheritance.

43 "And then the words of the prophet Isaiah shall be fulfilled, which say,

*Thy watchmen shall lift up the voice; with the voice together shall they sing, for they shall see eye to eye, when the Lord shall bring again Zion.

44 Break forth into joy; sing together, ye waste places of Jerusalem, for the Lord hath comforted his people, he hath redeemed Jerusalem.

45 The Lord hath made bare his holy arm in the eyes of all the nations; and all the ends of the earth shall see the salvation of God.

CHAPTER 8

WHEN Jesus had spoken these words, he looked round about again on the multitude, and he said to them, "Behold, my time is at hand.

2 "I perceive that ye are weak, that ye cannot understand all my words which I am commanded of the Father to speak to you at this time.

3 "Therefore, go ye to your homes, and ponder upon the things which I have said, and ask of the Father, in my name, that ye may understand; and prepare your minds for the morrow, and I come to you again.

4 "But now I go to the Father, and also to show myself to the lost tribes of Israel, for they are not lost to the Father, for he knoweth where he hath taken them."

5 When Jesus had thus spoken, he cast his eyes round about again on the multitude, and beheld they were in tears and looked steadfastly upon him as if they would ask him to tarry a little longer with them.

6 And he said to them, "Behold, my bowels are filled with compassion toward you. Have ye any that are sick among you, bring them here.

7 "Have ye any that are lame, or blind, or halt, or maimed, or leprous, or that are withered, or that are deaf,

---

*Isaiah 52:8, 9, 10

or that are afflicted in any manner, bring them here and I will heal them, for I have compassion upon you.

8 "My bowels are filled with mercy; for I perceive that ye desire that I should show you what I have done to your brethren at Jerusalem, for I see that your faith is sufficient that I should heal you."

9 When he had thus spoken, all the multitude with one accord went forth with their sick, and their afflicted, and their lame, and with their blind, and with their dumb, and with all those that were afflicted in any manner; and he healed them every one as they were brought forth to him.

10 And they all, both they who had been healed and they who were whole, bowed down at his feet and worshiped him.

11 And as many as could come, for the multitude, kissed his feet, insomuch that they bathed his feet with their tears.

12 And he commanded that their little children should be brought.

13 So they brought their little children and set them down upon the ground round about him, and Jesus stood in the midst; and the multitude gave way till they had all been brought to him.

14 When they had all been brought and Jesus stood in the midst, he commanded the multitude that they should kneel down upon the ground.

15 And when they had knelt upon the ground, Jesus groaned within himself and said, "Father, I am troubled because of the wickedness of the people of the house of Israel."

16 When he had said these words, he himself also knelt upon the earth, and, behold, he prayed to the Father, and the things which he prayed cannot be written, and the multitude bore record who heard him.

17 And after this manner they bore record: "The eye hath never seen, neither hath the ear heard, before, so great and marvelous things as we saw and heard Jesus speak unto the Father.

18 "And no tongue can speak, neither can there be written by any man, neither can the hearts of men conceive so great and marvelous things as we both saw and heard Jesus speak.

19 "And no one can conceive of the joy which filled our souls at the time we heard him pray for us to the Father."

20 When Jesus had made an end of praying to the Father, he arose; but so great was the joy of the multitude that they were overcome.

21 And Jesus spoke to them and bade them arise.

22 And they arose from the earth, and he said to them, "Blessed are ye because of your faith. And now, behold, my joy is full."

23 And when he had said these words, he wept, and the multitude bore record of it, and he took their little children, one by one, and blessed them, and prayed to the Father for them.

24 And when he had done this he wept again, and he spoke to the multitude and said to them, "Behold your little ones."

25 And as they looked to behold, they cast their eyes toward heaven, and they saw the heavens open, and they saw angels descending out of heaven, as it were in the midst of fire; and they came down and encircled those little ones.

26 And they were encircled with fire; and the angels ministered to them. And the multitude saw and heard and bore record; and they know that their record is true, for all of them saw and heard, every man for himself.

27 They were in number about two thousand and five hundred souls; and they consisted of men, women, and children.

28 And it came to pass that Jesus commanded his disciples that they should bring forth some bread and wine to him.

29 And while they were gone for bread and wine, he commanded the multitude that they should sit down upon the earth.

30 And when the disciples had come with bread and wine, he took of the bread, and broke and blessed it; and he gave to the disciples and commanded that they should eat.

31 And when they had eaten and

311   A. D. 34

were filled, he commanded that they should give to the multitude.

32 And when the multitude had eaten and were filled, he said to the disciples, "Behold, there shall one be ordained among you, and to him will I give power that he shall break bread, and bless it, and give it to the people of my church, to all those who shall believe and be baptized in my name.

33 "And this shall ye always observe to do, even as I have done, even as I have broken bread, and blessed it, and given it to you.

34 "And this shall ye do in remembrance of my body, which I have shown to you.

35 "And it shall be a testimony unto the Father that ye do always remember me.

36 "And if ye do always remember me, ye shall have my Spirit to be with you."

37 When he had said these words, he commanded his disciples that they should take of the wine of the cup, and drink of it, and that they should also give to the multitude that they might drink of it.

38 And they did so, and drank of it, and were filled; and they gave to the multitude, and they drank, and they were filled.

39 When the disciples had done this, Jesus said to them, "Blessed are ye for this thing which ye have done, for this is fulfilling my commandments, and this doth witness to the Father that ye are willing to do that which I have commanded you.

40 "And this shall ye always do unto those who repent and are baptized in my name; and ye shall do it in remembrance of my blood, which I have shed for you, that ye may witness to the Father that ye do always remember me.

41 "And if ye do always remember me, ye shall have my Spirit to be with you.

42 "And I give you a commandment that ye shall do these things.

43 "And if ye shall always do these things, blessed are ye, for ye are built upon my rock.

44 "But those among you who shall do more or less than these are not built upon my rock, but are built upon a sandy foundation.

45 "And when the rain descends, and the floods come, and the winds blow and beat upon them, they shall fall, and the gates of hell are already open to receive them.

46 "Therefore blessed are ye if ye shall keep my commandments, which the Father hath commanded me that I should give you.

47 "Verily, verily I say to you, Ye must watch and pray always, lest ye be tempted by the devil, and ye are led away captive by him.

48 "And as I have prayed among you, even so shall ye pray in my church, among my people who do repent and are baptized in my name.

49 "Behold, I am the light; I have set an example for you."

50 When Jesus had spoken these words to his disciples, he turned again to the multitude and said to them, "Behold, verily, verily I say to you, Ye must watch and pray always, lest ye enter into temptation.

51 "For Satan desireth to have you, that he may sift you as wheat; therefore ye must always pray to the Father in my name; and whatsoever ye shall ask the Father in my name, which is right, believing that ye shall receive, behold, it shall be given to you.

52 "Pray in your families to the Father, always in my name, that your wives and your children may be blessed.

53 "And, behold, ye shall meet together often and ye shall not forbid any man from coming to you when ye shall meet together, but suffer them that they may come to you, and forbid them not.

54 "Ye shall pray for them, and shall not cast them out; and if it so be that they come to you oft, ye shall pray for them to the Father in my name; therefore hold up your light that it may shine unto the world.

55 "Behold, I am the light which ye shall hold up; do that which ye have seen me do.

56 "Behold, ye see that I have prayed to the Father, and ye all have witnessed; and ye see that I have commanded that none of you should go away, but rather have com-

manded that ye should come to me that ye might feel and see.

57 "Even so shall ye do to the world; and whoever breaketh this commandment suffereth himself to be led into temptation."

58 When Jesus had spoken these words, he turned his eyes again upon the disciples whom he had chosen and said to them:

59 "Behold, verily, verily I say to you, I give you another commandment, and then I must go to my Father that I may fulfill other commandments which he hath given me.

60 "And now, behold, this is the commandment which I give to you, that ye shall not suffer anyone knowingly to partake of my flesh and blood unworthily, when ye shall minister it, for whoever eateth and drinketh my flesh and blood unworthily, eateth and drinketh damnation to his soul.

61 "Therefore if ye know that a man is unworthy to eat and drink of my flesh and blood, ye shall forbid him; nevertheless ye shall not cast him out from among you, but ye shall minister to him and shall pray for him to the Father in my name.

62 "And if it so be that he repenteth and is baptized in my name, then shall ye receive him, and shall minister to him of my flesh and blood.

63 "But if he repent not, he shall not be numbered among my people, that he may not destroy my people, for, behold, I know my sheep, and they are numbered.

64 "Nevertheless ye shall not cast him out of your synagogues, or your places of worship, for to such shall ye continue to minister.

65 "For ye know not but what he will return and repent, and come unto me with full purpose of heart, and I shall heal him, and ye shall be the means of bringing salvation to him.

66 "Therefore keep these sayings which I have commanded you, that ye come not under condemnation, for woe to him whom the Father condemneth.

67 "And I give you these commandments because of the disputations which have been among you.

68 "And blessed are ye if ye have no disputations among you.

69 "Now I go to the Father, because it is expedient that I should go to the Father for your sakes."

70 When Jesus had made an end of these sayings, he touched with his hand the disciples whom he had chosen, one by one, even until he had touched them all, and spoke to them as he touched them.

71 The multitude heard not the words which he spoke, therefore they did not bear record; but the disciples bore record that he gave them power to give the Holy Ghost.

72 And I will show to you hereafter that this record is true.

73 When Jesus had touched them all, there came a cloud and overshadowed the multitude that they could not see Jesus.

74 And while they were overshadowed, he departed from them and ascended into heaven.

75 And the disciples saw and bore record that he ascended again into heaven.

CHAPTER 9

NOW when Jesus had ascended into heaven, the multitude dispersed, and every man took his wife and his children and returned to his own home.

2 And it was noised abroad among the people immediately, before it was yet dark, that the multitude had seen Jesus, and that he had ministered to them, and that he would also show himself on the morrow to the multitude.

3 Even all the night it was noised abroad concerning Jesus; and so much did they send forth to the people, that an exceedingly great number labored exceedingly all that night that they might be on the morrow in the place where Jesus should show himself to the multitude.

4 On the morrow, when the multitude was gathered together, behold, Nephi and his brother whom he had raised from the dead, whose name was Timothy, and also his son, whose name was Jonas, and also Mathoni, and Mathonihah, his brother, and Kumen, and Kumenonhi, and Jere-

miah, and Shemnon, and Jonas, and Zedekiah, and Isaiah (now these were the names of the disciples whom Jesus had chosen) ⁵went forth and stood in the midst of the multitude.

6 And, behold, the multitude was so great that they caused that they should be separated into twelve bodies.

7 And the twelve taught the multitude and, behold, they caused that the multitude should kneel down upon the face of the earth and should pray to the Father in the name of Jesus.

8 And the disciples prayed to the Father also in the name of Jesus.

9 And they arose and ministered to the people.

10 And when they had ministered those same words which Jesus had spoken—nothing varying from the words which Jesus had spoken—behold, they knelt again and prayed to the Father in the name of Jesus, and they prayed for that which they most desired; and they desired that the Holy Ghost should be given to them.

11 When they had thus prayed, they went down to the water's edge, and the multitude followed them.

12 And Nephi went down into the water and was baptized.

13 And he came up out of the water and began to baptize. And he baptized all those whom Jesus had chosen.

14 When they were all baptized and had come up out of the water, the Holy Ghost fell upon them, and they were filled with the Holy Ghost and with fire.

15 And, behold, they were encircled as if with fire; and it came down from heaven, and the multitude witnessed it and bore record; and angels came down out of heaven and ministered to them.

16 While the angels were ministering to the disciples, behold, Jesus came and stood in the midst and ministered to them.

17 And he spoke to the multitude and commanded them that they should kneel down again upon the earth, and also that his disciples should kneel down upon the earth.

18 When they had all knelt down upon the earth, he commanded his disciples that they should pray.

19 And, behold, they began to pray; and they prayed to Jesus, calling him their Lord and their God.

20 And it came to pass that Jesus departed out of the midst of them and went a little way off from them and bowed himself to the earth, and he said, "Father, I thank thee that thou hast given the Holy Ghost to these whom I have chosen; and it is because of their belief in me that I have chosen them out of the world.

21 "Father, I pray thee that thou wilt give the Holy Ghost to all them that shall believe in their words.

22 "Father, thou hast given them the Holy Ghost because they believe in me, and thou seest that they believe in me, because thou hearest them, and they pray to me; and they pray to me because I am with them.

23 "And now, Father, I pray to thee for them, and also for all those who shall believe on their words, that they may believe in me, that I may be in them as thou, Father, art in me, that we may be one."

24 When Jesus had thus prayed to the Father, he came to his disciples, and, behold, they still continued without ceasing to pray to him; and they did not multiply many words, for it was given to them what they should pray, and they were filled with desire.

25 And Jesus beheld them, as they prayed to him, and his countenance smiled upon them, and the light of his countenance shone upon them, and, behold, they were as white as the countenance, and also as the garments, of Jesus.

26 And, behold, the whiteness thereof exceeded all whiteness, even there could be nothing upon earth so white as the whiteness thereof.

27 And Jesus said to them, "Pray on"; nevertheless they did not cease to pray.

28 He turned from them again, and went a little way off, and bowed himself to the earth; and he prayed again to the Father, saying, "Father, I thank thee that thou hast purified these whom I have chosen, because of their faith.

29 "And I pray for them, and also

for them who shall believe on their words, that they may be purified in me through faith on their words, even as they are purified in me.

30 "Father, I pray not for the world, but for those whom thou hast given me out of the world, because of their faith, that they may be purified in me, that I may be in them as thou, Father, art in me, that we may be one, that I may be glorified in them."

31 When Jesus had spoken these words, he came again to his disciples, and, behold, they prayed steadfastly without ceasing to him; and he smiled upon them again; and, behold, they were white, even as Jesus.

32 And he went again a little way off and prayed to the Father; and tongue cannot speak the words which he prayed, neither can be written by man the words which he prayed.

33 And the multitude heard and bore record, and their hearts were open, and they understood in their hearts the words which he prayed.

34 Nevertheless, so great and marvelous were the words which he prayed that they cannot be written, neither can they be uttered by man.

35 When Jesus had made an end of praying, he came again to the disciples and said to them, "So great faith have I never seen among all the Jews; wherefore I could not show to them so great miracles because of their unbelief.

36 "Verily I say to you, There are none of them that have seen so great things as ye have seen; neither have they heard so great things as ye have heard."

37 And he commanded the multitude that they should cease to pray, and also his disciples.

38 But he commanded them that they should not cease to pray in their hearts.

39 And he commanded them that they should arise and stand upon their feet. And they arose and stood upon their feet.

40 And he broke bread again, and blessed it, and gave to the disciples to eat.

41 When they had eaten he commanded them that they should break bread and give it to the multitude.

42 And when they had given to the multitude, he also gave them wine to drink and commanded them that they should give to the multitude.

43 Now there had been no bread, neither wine, brought by the disciples, neither by the multitude; but he truly gave them bread to eat, and also wine to drink.

44 And he said to them, "He that eateth this bread, eateth of my body to his soul, and he that drinketh of this wine, drinketh of my blood to his soul, and his soul shall never hunger nor thirst, but shall be filled."

45 Now when the multitude had all eaten and drunk, behold, they were filled with the Spirit, and they cried out with one voice and gave glory to Jesus, whom they both saw and heard.

46 When they had all given glory to Jesus, he said to them, "Behold, now I finish the commandment which the Father hath commanded me concerning this people who are a remnant of the house of Israel.

47 "Ye remember that I spoke to you, and said that when the words of Isaiah should be fulfilled (behold, they are written, ye have them before you; therefore search them), 48then is the fulfilling of the covenant which the Father hath made unto his people, 49O house of Israel. Then shall the remnants which shall be scattered abroad upon the face of the earth be gathered in from the east, and from the west, and from the south, and from the north; and they shall be brought to the knowledge of the Lord their God, who hath redeemed them.

50 "And the Father hath commanded me that I should give to you this land for your inheritance.

51 "And I say to you that if the Gentiles do not repent, after the blessing which they shall receive, after they have scattered my people, then shall ye who are a remnant of the house of Jacob go forth among them.

52 "And ye shall be in the midst of them, who shall be many; and ye shall be among them as a lion among the beasts of the forests, and as a young lion among the flocks of sheep,

who, if he goeth through, both treadeth down and teareth in pieces, and none can deliver.

53 "Thy hand shall be lifted up upon thine adversaries, and all thine enemies shall be cut off.

54 "And I will gather my people with whom the Father hath covenanted together as a man gathereth his sheaves into the floor, for I will make thy horn iron, and I will make thy hoofs brass.

55 "And thou shalt beat in pieces many people; and I will consecrate their gain to the Lord, and their substance to the Lord of the whole earth. And, behold, I am he who doeth it.

56 "'And it shall come to pass,' saith the Father, 'that the sword of my justice shall hang over them at that day; and except they repent, it shall fall upon them,' saith the Father, 'even upon all the nations of the Gentiles.

57 "'And it shall come to pass that I will establish my people, O house of Israel.

58 "'Behold, this people will I establish in this land, to the fulfilling of the covenant which I made with your father Jacob; and it shall be a new Jerusalem.

59 "'And the powers of heaven shall be in the midst of this people, even I will be in the midst of you.'

60 "Behold, I am he of whom Moses spoke, saying, 'A prophet shall the Lord your God raise up unto you of your brethren, like unto me; him shall ye hear in all things whatsoever he shall say to you.

61 "'And it shall come to pass that every soul who will not hear that prophet shall be cut off from among the people.'

62 "Verily, I say to you, Yea; and all the prophets from Samuel and those that follow after, as many as have spoken, have testified of me.

63 "And, behold, ye are the children of the prophets, and ye are of the house of Israel, and ye are of the covenant which the Father made with your fathers, saying to Abraham, 'And in thy seed shall all the kindreds of the earth be blessed,' 64the Father having raised me up to you first, and sent me to bless you in turning away every one of you from his iniquities, and this because ye are the children of the covenant.

65 "And after ye were blessed, then fulfilleth the Father the covenant which he made with Abraham, saying, 'In thy seed shall all the kindreds of the earth be blessed,' to the pouring out of the Holy Ghost through me upon the Gentiles, which blessing upon the Gentiles shall make them mighty above all, to the scattering of my people, O house of Israel; and they shall be a scourge to the people of this land.

66 "Nevertheless, when they shall have received the fullness of my gospel, then if they shall harden their hearts against me, 'I will return their iniquities upon their own heads,' saith the Father.

67 "'And I will remember the covenant which I have made with my people, and I have covenanted with them that I would gather them together in my own due time, 68that I would give to them again the land of their fathers for their inheritance, which is the land of Jerusalem, which is the promised land to them forever,' saith the Father.

69 "And the time cometh when the fullness of my gospel shall be preached to them, and they shall believe in me, that I am Jesus Christ, the Son of God, and shall pray to the Father in my name.

*70 Then shall their watchmen lift up their voice; and with the voice together shall they sing; for they shall see eye to eye.

71 Then will the Father gather them together again and give them Jerusalem for the land of their inheritance.

72 Then shall they break forth into joy; sing together ye waste places of Jerusalem; for the Father hath comforted his people, he hath redeemed Jerusalem.

73 The Father hath made bare his holy arm in the eyes of all the nations; and all the ends of the earth shall see the salvation of the Father; and the Father and I are one.

---

*Isaiah 52 (selected verses)

74 "And then shall be brought to pass that which is written:

*Awake, awake again, and put on thy strength, O Zion; put on thy beautiful garments, O Jerusalem, the holy city; for henceforth there shall no more come into thee the uncircumcised and the unclean.

75 Shake thyself from the dust; arise, sit down, O Jerusalem; loose thyself from the bands of thy neck, O captive daughter of Zion.

76 For thus saith the Lord, "Ye have sold yourselves for naught; and ye shall be redeemed without money.

77 "Verily, verily, I say to you that my people shall know my name; in that day they shall know that I am he that doth speak."

78 "And then shall they say,

*How beautiful upon the mountains are the feet of him that bringeth good tidings to them, that publisheth peace; that bringeth good tidings to them of good, that publisheth salvation: that saith to Zion, "Thy God reigneth!"

79 "And then shall a cry go forth,

*Depart ye, depart ye, go ye out from thence, touch not that which is unclean; go ye out of the midst of her; be ye clean that bear the vessels of the Lord.

80 For ye shall not go out with haste, nor go by flight; for the Lord will go before you, and the God of Israel shall be your rearward.

81 Behold, my servant shall deal prudently, he shall be exalted and extolled, and be very high.

82 As many were astonished at thee; his visage was so marred more than any man, and his form more than the sons of men.

83 So shall he sprinkle many nations; the kings shall shut their mouths at him; for that which had not been told them, shall they see; and that which they had not heard, shall they consider.

84 "Verily, verily, I say to you, All these things shall surely come, even as the Father hath commanded me.

85 "Then shall this covenant which the Father hath covenanted with his people be fulfilled; and then shall Jerusalem be inhabited again with my people, and it shall be the land of their inheritance.

86 "Verily, I say to you, I give you a sign that ye may know the time when these things shall be about to take place, that I shall gather in, from their long dispersion, my people, O house of Israel, and shall establish again among them my Zion.

87 "And, behold, this is the thing which I will give to you for a sign: When these things which I declare to you, and which I shall declare to you hereafter of myself and by the power of the Holy Ghost which shall be given to you of the Father, shall be made known of the Father to the Gentiles 88that they may know concerning this people who are a remnant of the house of Jacob and concerning this my people who shall be scattered by them, 89and shall come forth of the Father, from them to you (for it is wisdom in the Father that they should be established in this land 90and be set up as a free people by the power of the Father, that these things might come forth from them to a remnant of your seed, that the covenant of the Father may be fulfilled which he hath covenanted with his people, O house of Israel) 91—when these works and the work which shall be wrought among you hereafter shall come forth from the Gentiles to your seed which shall dwindle in unbelief because of iniquity 92(for thus it behooveth the Father that it should come forth from the Gentiles that he may show forth his power to the Gentiles for this cause: that the Gentiles, if they will not harden their hearts, may repent, and come to me, and be baptized in my name, and know of the true points of my doctrine, that they may be numbered among my people, O house of Israel) 93and thy seed shall begin to know these things—it shall be a sign to them that they may know that the work

A. D. 34

of the Father hath already commenced unto the fulfilling of the covenant which he hath made to the people who are of the house of Israel.

94 "And when that day shall come, kings shall shut their mouths; for that which had not been told them, shall they see; and that which they had not heard, shall they consider.

95 "For in that day, for my sake, shall the Father work a work which shall be a great and a marvelous work among them; and there shall be among them those who will not believe it, although a man shall declare it to them.

96 "But, behold, the life of my servant shall be in my hand; therefore they shall not hurt him, although he shall be marred because of them.

97 "Yet I will heal him, for I will show them that my wisdom is greater than the cunning of the devil.

98 "Therefore it shall come to pass that whosoever will not believe in my words—who am Jesus Christ—which the Father shall cause him to bring forth to the Gentiles and shall give to him power that he shall bring them forth to the Gentiles (it shall be done even as Moses said), he shall be cut off from among my people who are of the covenant.

99 "And my people who are a remnant of Jacob shall be among the Gentiles, in the midst of them as a lion among the beasts of the forest, as a young lion among the flocks of sheep, who, if he go through, both treadeth down and teareth in pieces, and none can deliver.

100 "Their hand shall be lifted up upon their adversaries, and all their enemies shall be cut off.

101 "'Woe be to the Gentiles except they repent, for it shall come to pass in that day,' saith the Father, 'that I will cut off thy horses out of the midst of thee, and I will destroy thy chariots, and I will cut off the cities of thy land and throw down all thy strongholds.

102 "'And I will cut off witchcrafts out of thy hand, and thou shalt have no more soothsayers.

103 "'Thy graven images I will also cut off, and thy standing images out of the midst of thee; and thou shalt no more worship the works of thy hands.

104 "'And I will pluck up thy groves out of the midst of thee; so will I destroy thy cities.

105 "'And it shall come to pass that all lyings, and deceivings, and envyings, and strifes, and priestcrafts, and whoredoms shall be done away.

106 " 'For it shall come to pass,' saith the Father, 'that at that day, those who will not repent and come unto my beloved Son will I cut off from among my people, O house of Israel, and I will execute vengeance and fury upon them, even as upon the heathen, such as they have not heard.'"

CHAPTER 10

BUT if they will repent, and hearken to my words, and harden not their hearts, I will establish my church among them, and they shall come in to the covenant and be numbered among this the remnant of Jacob to whom I have given this land for their inheritance; and they shall assist my people, the remnant of Jacob, ²and also, as many of the house of Israel as shall come, that they may build a city, which shall be called the New Jerusalem.

3 "Then shall they assist my people that they may be gathered in, who are scattered upon all the face of the land, to the New Jerusalem.

4 "And then shall the power of heaven come down among them; and I also will be in the midst, and then shall the work of the Father commence even at that day when this gospel shall be preached among the remnant of this people.

5 "Verily, I say to you, At that day shall the work of the Father commence among all the dispersed of my people, even the tribes which have been lost which the Father hath led away out of Jerusalem.

6 "The work shall commence with the Father among all the dispersed of my people to prepare the way whereby they may come to me, that they may call on the Father in my name.

7 "And then shall the work com-

mence with the Father among all nations in preparing the way whereby his people may be gathered home to the land of their inheritance.

8 "And they shall go out from all nations; and they shall not go out in haste, nor go by flight; for 'I will go before them,' saith the Father, 'and I will be their rearward.' And then shall that which is written come to pass:

*9 "Sing, O barren, thou that didst not bear; break forth into singing and cry aloud, thou that didst not travail with child; for more are the children of the desolate than the children of the married wife, saith the Lord.

10 "Enlarge the place of thy tent, and let the curtains of thy habitations stretch forth; spare not, lengthen thy cords, and strengthen thy stakes.

11 "For thou shalt break forth on the right hand and on the left; and thy seed shall inherit the Gentiles and make the desolate cities to be inhabited.

12 "Fear not, for thou shalt not be ashamed; neither be thou confounded, for thou shalt not be put to shame; for thou shalt forget the shame of thy youth and shalt not remember the reproach of thy widowhood any more.

13 "For thy maker, thy husband, the Lord of hosts is his name; and thy Redeemer, the Holy One of Israel, the God of the whole earth shall he be called.

14 "For the Lord hath called thee as a woman forsaken and grieved in spirit, and a wife of youth when thou wast refused, saith thy God.

15 "For a small moment have I forsaken thee; but with great mercies will I gather thee.

16 "In a little wrath I hid my face from thee for a moment; but with everlasting kindness will I have mercy on thee,' saith the Lord thy Redeemer.

17 "For this is like the waters of Noah to me, for as I have sworn that the waters of Noah should no more go over the earth, so have I

sworn that I would not be wroth with thee.

18 "For the mountains shall depart and the hills be removed; but my kindness shall not depart from thee, neither shall the covenant of my peace be removed, saith the Lord that hath mercy on thee.

19 "O thou afflicted, tossed with tempest, and not comforted! Behold, I will lay thy stones with fair colors and lay thy foundations with sapphires.

20 "And I will make thy windows of agates, and thy gates of carbuncles, and all thy borders of pleasant stones.

21 "And all thy children shall be taught of the Lord; and great shall be the peace of thy children.

22 "In righteousness shalt thou be established; thou shalt be far from oppression, for thou shalt not fear; and from terror, for it shall not come near thee.

23 "Behold, they shall surely gather against thee, but it is not by me; whoever shall gather against thee shall fall for thy sake.

24 "Behold, I have created the smith that bloweth the coals in the fire, and that bringeth forth an instrument for his work; and I have created the waster to destroy.

25 "No weapon that is formed against thee shall prosper, and every tongue that shall revile against thee in judgment thou shalt condemn. This is the heritage of the servants of the Lord, and their righteousness is of me, saith the Lord."

26 "Now, behold, I say to you that ye had ought to search these things.

27 "A commandment I give to you that ye search these things diligently; for great are the words of Isaiah.

28 "For surely he spoke as touching all things concerning my people which are of the house of Israel; therefore it must be that he must speak also to the Gentiles.

29 "And all things that he spoke hath been, and shall be, even according to the words which he spoke.

---

*Isaiah 54

319   A. D. 34

30 "Therefore give heed to my words; write the things which I have told you, and according to the time and the will of the Father, they shall go forth to the Gentiles.

31 "And whosoever will hearken unto my words, and repenteth, and is baptized, the same shall be saved.

32 "Search the prophets, for many there be that testify of these things."

33 When Jesus had said these words, he said to them again, after he had expounded all the scriptures to them which they had received, "Behold, other scriptures I would that ye should write, that ye have not."

34 And he said to Nephi, "Bring forth the record which ye have kept."

35 And when Nephi had brought forth the records and laid them before him, he cast his eyes upon them, and said,

36 "Verily, I say to you, I commanded my servant Samuel, the Lamanite, that he should testify to this people, that at the day that the Father should glorify his name in me, there were many saints who should arise from the dead, and should appear to many, and should minister to them."

37 And he said to them, "Were it not so?"

38 And his disciples answered him and said, "Yea, Lord, Samuel did prophesy according to thy words, and they were all fulfilled."

39 And Jesus said to them, "How be it that ye have not written this thing, that many saints should arise, and appear to many, and minister to them?"

40 And Nephi remembered that this thing had not been written.

41 And Jesus commanded that it should be written, therefore it was written according as he commanded.

CHAPTER 11

NOW when Jesus had expounded all the scriptures, in one, which they had written, he commanded them that they should teach the things which he had expounded to them.

2 And he commanded them that they should write the words which the Father had given to Malachi, which he should tell them.

3 And after they were written, he expounded them.

4 And these are the words which he told them, saying, "Thus said the Father to Malachi,

*"Behold, I will send my messenger, and he shall prepare the way before me, and the Lord, whom ye seek, shall suddenly come to his temple, even the messenger of the covenant, whom ye delight in; behold, he shall come, saith the Lord of hosts.

5 "But who may abide the day of his coming, and who shall stand when he appeareth? For he is like a refiner's fire and like fuller's soap.

6 "And he shall sit as a refiner and purifier of silver; and he shall purify the sons of Levi, and purge them as gold and silver, that they may offer to the Lord an offering in righteousness.

7 "Then shall the offering of Judah and Jerusalem be pleasant to the Lord as in the days of old and as in former years.

8 "And I will come near to you to judgment; and I will be a swift witness against the sorcerers, and against the adulterers, and against false swearers, and against those that oppress the hireling in his wages, the widow, and the fatherless, and that turn aside the stranger, and fear not me, saith the Lord of hosts.

9 "For I am the Lord I change not; therefore ye sons of Jacob are not consumed.

10 "Even from the days of your fathers ye are gone away from mine ordinances and have not kept them. Return to me, and I will return to you, saith the Lord of hosts. But ye said, 'Wherein shall we return?'

11 "Will a man rob God? Yet ye have robbed me. But ye say, 'Wherein have we robbed thee?' In tithes and offerings.

12 "Ye are cursed with a curse, for ye have robbed me, even this whole nation.

*Malachi 3

13 "Bring ye all the tithes into the storehouse, that there may be meat in my house, and prove me now herewith, saith the Lord of hosts, if I will not open you the windows of heaven, and pour you out a blessing, that there shall not be room enough to receive it.

14 "And I will rebuke the devourer for your sakes, and he shall not destroy the fruits of your ground; neither shall your vine cast her fruit before the time in the fields, saith the Lord of hosts.

15 "And all nations shall call you blessed, for ye shall be a delightsome land, saith the Lord of Hosts.

16 "Your words have been stout against me, saith the Lord. Yet ye say, 'What have we spoken against thee?'

17 "Ye have said, 'It is vain to serve God, and what doth it profit that we have kept his ordinances and that we have walked mournfully before the Lord of hosts?

18 "'And now we call the proud happy; even they that work wickedness are set up; they that tempt God are even delivered.'"

19 Then they that feared the Lord spoke often one to another, and the Lord hearkened and heard; and a book of remembrance was written before him for them that feared the Lord and that thought upon his name.

20 "And they shall be mine, saith the Lord of hosts, in that day when I make up my jewels; and I will spare them, as a man spareth his own son that serveth him.

21 "Then shall ye return and discern between the righteous and the wicked, between him that serveth God and him that serveth him not.

*22 "For, behold, the day cometh that shall burn as an oven; and all the proud, yea, and all that do wickedly shall be stubble; and the day that cometh shall burn them up, saith the Lord of hosts, that it shall leave them neither root nor branch.

23 "But unto you that fear my

name shall the Son of righteousness arise with healing in his wings; and ye shall go forth and grow up as calves of the stall.

24 "And ye shall tread down the wicked; for they shall be ashes under the soles of your feet in the day that I shall do this, saith the Lord of hosts.

25 "Remember ye the law of Moses, my servant, which I commanded him in Horeb for all Israel, with the statutes and judgments.

26 "Behold, I will send you Elijah, the prophet, before the coming of the great and dreadful day of the Lord.

27 "And he shall turn the hearts of the fathers to the children, and the hearts of the children to their fathers, lest I come and smite the earth with a curse."

28 When Jesus had told these things, he expounded them to the multitude, and he expounded all things to them, both great and small.

29 And he said, "These scriptures which ye had not with you, the Father commanded that I should give to you, for it was wisdom in him that they should be given to future generations."

30 And he expounded all things, even from the beginning until the time that he should come in his glory; 31even all things which should come upon the face of the earth, even until the elements should melt with fervent heat, and the earth should be wrapped together as a scroll, and the heavens and the earth should pass away; 32And even to the great and last day, when all people, and all kindreds, and all nations and tongues shall stand before God to be judged of their works, whether they be good or whether they be evil; 33if they be good, to the resurrection of everlasting life; and if they be evil, to the resurrection of damnation, being on a parallel, the one on the one hand and the other on the other hand, according to the mercy, and the justice, and the holiness which is in Christ who was before the world began.

---
*Malachi 4

CHAPTER 12

NOW there cannot be written in this book even a hundredth part of the things which Jesus truly taught to the people; but, behold, the plates of Nephi contain the greater part of the things which he taught the people.

2 And these things I have written are a lesser part of the things which he taught the people; and I have written them to the intent that they may be brought again to this people from the Gentiles, according to the words which Jesus has spoken.

3 When they shall have received this, which is expedient that they should have first to try their faith, and if it shall so be that they shall believe these things, then shall the greater things be made manifest to them.

4 And if it so be that they will not believe these things, then shall the greater things be withheld from them, to their condemnation.

5 Behold, I was about to write them all which were engraved upon the plates of Nephi, but the Lord forbade it, saying, "I will try the faith of my people"; therefore I, Mormon, write only the things which have been commanded me of the Lord.

6 Now I, Mormon, make an end of my sayings, and proceed to write the things which have been commanded me; therefore I would that you should behold that the Lord truly taught the people for the space of three days; and after that, he showed himself to them often, and broke bread often, and blessed it, and gave it to them.

7 And it came to pass that he taught and ministered to the children of the multitude of whom I have spoken, and he loosed their tongues, and they spoke to their fathers great and marvelous things, even greater than he had revealed to the people, and loosed their tongues that they could utter.

8 And after he had ascended into heaven the second time that he showed himself to them, and had gone to the Father after having healed all their sick, and their lame, and opened the eyes of their blind, and unstopped the ears of the deaf, and even had done all manner of cures among them, and had raised a man from the dead, and had shown forth his power to them, 9behold, on the morrow the multitude gathered themselves together, and they both saw and heard these children, even babes, open their mouths and utter marvelous things; and the things which they uttered were forbidden that any man should write them.

10 And the disciples whom Jesus had chosen began from that time forth to baptize and to teach as many as came to them; and as many as were baptized in the name of Jesus were filled with the Holy Ghost.

11 And many of them saw and heard unspeakable things, which are not lawful to be written; and they taught and ministered one to another; and they had all things common among them, every man dealing justly one with another.

12 And they did all things, even as Jesus had commanded them.

13 And they who were baptized in the name of Jesus were called the church of Christ.

14 And it came to pass that as the disciples of Jesus were journeying and were preaching the things which they had both heard and seen, and were baptizing in the name of Jesus, the disciples were gathered together and were united in mighty prayer and fasting.

15 And Jesus again showed himself to them, for they were praying to the Father in his name; and Jesus came, and stood in the midst of them, and said to them, "What will ye that I shall give to you?"

16 And they said to him, "Lord, we will that thou wouldst tell us the name whereby we shall call this church; for there are disputations among the people concerning this matter."

17 And the Lord said to them, "Verily, verily I say to you, Why is it that the people should murmur and dispute because of this thing?

18 "Have they not read the scriptures, which say, 'Ye must take upon you the name of Christ,' which is my name? For by this name shall ye

be called at the last day; and whoso taketh upon him my name and endureth to the end, the same shall be saved at the last day.

19 "Therefore, whatever ye shall do, ye shall do it in my name; therefore ye shall call the church in my name; and ye shall call upon the Father in my name, that he will bless the church for my sake; and how be it my church, save it be called in my name?

20 "For if a church be called in Moses' name, then it be Moses' church; or if it be called in the name of a man, then it be the church of a man; but if it be called in my name, then it is my church, if it so be that it is built upon my gospel.

21 "Verily I say to you that ye are built upon my gospel; therefore ye shall call whatever things ye do call in my name; therefore if ye call upon the Father for the church, if it be in my name, the Father will hear you.

22 "And if it so be that the church is built upon my gospel, then will the Father show forth his own works in it.

23 "But if it be not built upon my gospel, and is built upon the works of men or upon the works of the devil, verily I say to you, They have joy in their works for a season; but by and by the end cometh, and they are hewn down and cast into the fire, whence there is no return.

24 "For their works follow them, for it is because of their works that they are hewn down; therefore remember the things that I have told you.

25 "Behold, I have given to you my gospel, and this is the gospel which I have given to you, that I came into the world to do the will of my Father because my Father sent me.

26 "And my Father sent me that I might be lifted up upon the cross; and that after I had been lifted up upon the cross, I might draw all men unto me; [27]that as I have been lifted up by men, even so should men be lifted up by the Father, to stand before me to be judged of their works, whether they be good or whether they be evil.

28 "For this cause have I been lifted up; therefore, according to the power of the Father, I will draw all men unto me that they may be judged according to their works.

29 "And it shall come to pass that whoso repenteth and is baptized in my name shall be filled; and if he endureth to the end, behold, him will I hold guiltless before my Father at that day when I shall stand to judge the world.

30 "And he that endureth not to the end, the same is he that is also hewn down and cast into the fire, whence they can no more return, because of the justice of the Father; and this is the word which he hath given to the children of men.

31 "And for this cause he fulfilleth the words which he hath given, and he lieth not, but fulfilleth all his words; and no unclean thing can enter into his kingdom.

32 "Therefore none entereth into his rest save it be those who have washed their garments in my blood because of their faith, and the repentance of all their sins, and their faithfulness to the end.

33 "Now this is the commandment, Repent, all ye ends of the earth, and come to me, and be baptized in my name, that ye may be sanctified by the reception of the Holy Ghost, that ye may stand spotless before me at the last day.

34 "Verily, verily I say to you, This is my gospel; and ye know the things that ye must do in my church; for the works which ye have seen me do, that shall ye also do.

35 "For that which ye have seen me do, even that shall ye do; therefore if ye do these things, blessed are ye, for ye shall be lifted up at the last day."

CHAPTER 13

WRITE the things which ye have seen and heard, save it be those which are forbidden; write the works of this people, which shall be even as hath been written of that which hath been.

2 "For, behold, out of the books which have been written, and which shall be written, shall this people be

323   A. D. 34, 35

judged, for by them shall their works be known to men.

3 "And, behold, all things are written by the Father; therefore out of the books which shall be written shall the world be judged.

4 "And know ye that ye shall be judges of this people according to the judgment which I shall give to you, which shall be just.

5 "Therefore what manner of men ought ye to be? Verily I say to you, Even as I am. And now I go to the Father.

6 "And verily I say to you, Whatsoever things ye shall ask the Father in my name, it shall be given to you; therefore ask, and ye shall receive; knock, and it shall be opened to you; for he that asketh, receiveth, and to him that knocketh, it shall be opened.

7 "And now, behold, my joy is great, even to fullness, because of you, and also this generation; and even the Father rejoiceth, and also all the holy angels, because of you and this generation; for none of them are lost.

8 "Behold, I would that ye should understand; for I mean them who are now alive of this generation; and none of them are lost; and in them I have fullness of joy.

9 "But, behold, I sorrow because of the fourth generation from this generation, for they are led away captive by him, even as was the son of perdition; for they will sell me for silver, and for gold, and for that which moth doth corrupt, and which thieves can break through and steal.

10 "And in that day will I visit them, even in turning their works upon their own heads."

11 When Jesus had ended these sayings, he said to his disciples, "Enter ye in at the strait gate; for strait is the gate and narrow is the way that leads to life, and few there be that find it; but wide is the gate, and broad the way which leads to death, and many there be that travel therein until the night cometh wherein no man can work."

12 And when Jesus had said these words, he spoke to his disciples, one by one, saying to them, "What is it that ye desire of me after that I am gone to the Father?"

13 And they all spoke, save it were three, saying, "We desire that after we have lived to the age of man, our ministry wherein thou hast called us may have an end, that we may come speedily to thee, in thy kingdom."

14 And he said to them, "Blessed are ye because ye desire this thing of me; therefore after that ye are seventy-two years old, ye shall come to me in my kingdom, and with me ye shall find rest."

15 When he had spoken to them, he turned himself toward the three, and said to them, "What will ye that I should do to you when I am gone to the Father?"

16 And they sorrowed in their hearts, for they dared not speak to him the thing which they desired.

17 And he said to them, "Behold, I know your thoughts, and ye have desired the thing which John, my beloved, who was with me in my ministry before I was lifted up by the Jews, desired of me.

18 "Therefore more blessed are ye, for ye shall never taste of death, but ye shall live to behold all the doings of the Father to the children of men, even until all things shall be fulfilled according to the will of the Father, when I shall come in my glory with the powers of heaven.

19 "And ye shall never endure the pains of death; but when I shall come in my glory, ye shall be changed in the twinkling of an eye from mortality to immortality; and then shall ye be blessed in the kingdom of my Father.

20 "And again, ye shall not have pain while ye shall dwell in the flesh, neither sorrow, save it be for the sins of the world.

21 "All this will I do because of the thing which ye have desired of me, for ye have desired that ye might bring the souls of men to me while the world shall stand; and for this cause ye shall have fullness of joy; and ye shall sit down in the kingdom of my Father.

22 "And your joy shall be full, even as the Father hath given me fullness of joy; and ye shall be even as I am, and I am even as the Father; and the Father and I are one.

23 "And the Holy Ghost beareth record of the Father and me; and

the Father giveth the Holy Ghost to the children of men because of me."

24 When Jesus had spoken these words, he touched every one of them with his finger, save the three who were to tarry, and then he departed.

25 And, behold, the heavens were opened, and they were caught up into heaven and saw and heard unspeakable things.

26 And it was forbidden them that they should utter, neither was power given to them that they could utter, the things which they saw and heard.

27 And whether they were in the body or out of the body, they could not tell; for it seemed to them like a transfiguration of them, that they were changed from this body of flesh into an immortal state, that they could behold the things of God.

28 But it came to pass that they again ministered upon the face of the earth; nevertheless they did not minister of the things which they had heard and seen because of the commandment which was given them in heaven.

29 Now whether they were mortal or immortal from the day of their transfiguration, I know not; but this much I know, according to the record which has been given, they went forth upon the face of the land and ministered to all the people, uniting as many to the church as would believe in their preaching, baptizing them.

30 And as many as were baptized, received the Holy Ghost; and they were cast into prison by those who did not belong to the church.

31 And the prisons could not hold them, for they were rent in twain and they were cast down into the earth.

32 But they smote the earth with the word of God, insomuch that by his power they were delivered out of the depths of the earth; and therefore they could not dig pits sufficient to hold them.

33 Thrice they were cast into a furnace and received no harm.

34 And twice they were cast into a den of wild beasts; and, behold, they played with the beasts, as a child with a suckling lamb, and received no harm.

35 Thus they went forth among all the people of Nephi and preached the gospel of Christ to all people upon the face of the land.

36 And many were converted to the Lord and were united to the church of Christ, and thus the people of that generation were blessed according to the word of Jesus.

37 Now I, Mormon, make an end of speaking concerning these things for a time.

38 Behold, I was about to write the names of those who were never to taste of death; but the Lord forbade, therefore I write them not, for they are hid from the world.

39 But, behold, I have seen them, and they have ministered to me; and, behold, they will be among the Gentiles, and the Gentiles will know them not.

40 They will also be among the Jews, and the Jews will know them not.

41 And it shall come to pass, when the Lord sees fit in his wisdom, that they shall minister to all the scattered tribes of Israel and to all nations, kindreds, tongues and people, and shall bring out of them to Jesus many souls, that their desire may be fulfilled, and also because of the convincing power of God which is in them.

42 And they are as the angels of God, and if they shall pray to the Father in the name of Jesus, they can show themselves to whatever man it seems to them good.

43 Therefore great and marvelous works shall be wrought by them before the great and coming day when all people must surely stand before the judgment seat of Christ.

44 Even among the Gentiles shall there be a great and marvelous work wrought by them before that judgment day.

45 And if you had all the scriptures which give an account of all the marvelous works of Christ, you would, according to the words of Christ, know that these things must surely come.

46 And woe be to him that will not hearken to the words of Jesus and also to them whom he has chosen and sent among them.

47 For those who receive not the words of Jesus, and the words of

those whom he has sent, receive not him; and therefore he will not receive them at the last day; and it would be better for them if they had not been born.

48 For do you suppose that you can get rid of the justice of an offended God, who has been trampled under feet of men, that thereby salvation might come?

49 And now, behold, I spoke concerning those whom the Lord had chosen, even three who were caught up into the heavens, that I knew not whether they were cleansed from mortality to immortality.

50 But, behold, since I wrote, I have inquired of the Lord, and he has made it manifest to me that there must be a change wrought upon their bodies, or else it must be that they must taste of death.

51 Therefore that they might not taste of death, there was a change wrought upon their bodies that they might not suffer pain nor sorrow, save for the sins of the world.

52 Now this change was not equal to that which should take place at the last day; but there was a change wrought upon them insomuch that Satan could have no power over them, that he could not tempt them, and they were sanctified in the flesh that they were holy, and that the powers of the earth could not hold them.

53 And in this state they were to remain until the judgment day of Christ; and at that day they were to receive a greater change and to be received into the kingdom of the Father to go no more out, but to dwell with God eternally in the heavens.

54 Now, behold, I say to you that when the Lord shall see fit, in his wisdom, that these sayings shall come to the Gentiles according to his word, then you may know that the covenant which the Father has made with the children of Israel, concerning their restoration to the lands of their inheritance, is already beginning to be fulfilled.

55 And you may know that the words of the Lord which have been spoken by the holy prophets shall all be fulfilled; and you need not

say that the Lord delays his coming unto the children of Israel.

56 And you need not imagine in your hearts that the words which have been spoken are vain; for, behold, the Lord will remember his covenant which he has made to his people of the house of Israel.

57 And when you shall see these sayings coming forth among you, then you need not any longer spurn the doings of the Lord, for the sword of his justice is in his right hand, and at that day, if you shall spurn his doings, he will cause that it shall soon overtake you.

58 Woe to him that spurns the doings of the Lord; woe to him that shall deny the Christ and his works.

59 Woe to him that shall deny the revelations of the Lord, and that shall say, "The Lord no longer works by revelation, or by prophecy, or by gifts, or by tongues, or by healings, or by the power of the Holy Ghost."

60 And woe to him that shall say at that day, to get gain, that there can be no miracle wrought by Jesus Christ; for he that does this shall become like the son of perdition, for whom there was no mercy, according to the word of Christ.

61 And you need not any longer hiss, nor spurn, nor ridicule the Jews, nor any of the remnant of the house of Israel, for, behold, the Lord remembers his covenant to them, and he will do to them according to that which he has sworn.

62 Therefore you need not suppose that you can turn the right hand of the Lord to the left, that he may not execute judgment to the fulfilling of the covenant which he has made to the house of Israel.

CHAPTER 14

HEARKEN, O ye Gentiles, and hear the words of Jesus Christ, the Son of the living God, which he has commanded me that I should speak concerning you; for, behold, he commands me that I should write, saying:

2 "Turn, all ye Gentiles, from your wicked ways and repent of your evil doings, of your lyings, deceivings, and whoredoms, of your secret abom-

inations and idolatries, of your murders and priestcrafts, and your envyings and strifes, and from all your wickedness and abominations.

3 "And come to me, and be baptized in my name, that ye may receive a remission of your sins and be filled with the Holy Ghost, that ye may be numbered with my people who are of the house of Israel."

FOURTH BOOK OF NEPHI

WHO IS THE SON OF NEPHI, ONE OF THE DISCIPLES OF JESUS CHRIST

CHAPTER 1

An account of the people of Nephi, according to his record.

A ND the thirty-fourth year passed away and also the thirty-fifth, and, behold, the disciples of Jesus had formed a church of Christ in all the lands round about.

2 And as many as came to them and truly repented of their sins were baptized in the name of Jesus; and they also received the Holy Ghost.

3 And in the thirty-sixth year, the people were all converted to the Lord upon all the face of the land, both Nephites and Lamanites, and there were no contentions and disputations among them, and every man dealt justly one with another.

4 And they had all things common among them, therefore they were not rich and poor, bond and free, but they were all made free and partakers of the heavenly gift.

5 And the thirty-seventh year passed away also, and there still continued to be peace in the land.

6 And there were great and marvelous works wrought by the disciples of Jesus, insomuch that they healed the sick, and raised the dead, and caused the lame to walk, and the blind to receive their sight, and the deaf to hear.

7 And all manner of miracles did they work among the children of men, and in nothing did they work miracles, save it were in the name of Jesus.

8 Thus the thirty-eighth year passed away, and also the thirty-ninth, and the forty-first, and the forty-second, even until forty-nine years had passed away, and also the fifty-first, and the fifty-second, and even until fifty-nine years had passed away.

9 And the Lord prospered them exceedingly in the land, insomuch that they built cities again where there had been cities burned; even that great city Zarahemla they caused to be built again.

10 But there were many cities which had been sunk, and waters came up in the stead thereof; therefore these cities could not be renewed.

11 Now, behold, it came to pass that the people of Nephi waxed strong, and multiplied exceedingly fast, and became an exceedingly fair and delightsome people.

12 And they were married and given in marriage, and were blessed according to the multitude of the promises which the Lord had made to them.

13 And they did not walk any more after the performances and ordinances of the law of Moses, but they walked after the commandments which they had received from their

Lord and their God, continuing in fasting and prayer, and in meeting together often, both to pray and to hear the word of the Lord.

14 And it came to pass that there was no contention among all the people in all the land, but there were mighty miracles wrought among the disciples of Jesus.

15 And the seventy-first year passed away, and also the seventy-second year; and in fine, until the seventy-ninth year had passed away; and even a hundred years had passed away, and the disciples of Jesus, whom he had chosen, had all gone to the paradise of God, save the three who should tarry.

16 And there were other disciples ordained in their stead, and also many of that generation had passed away.

17 And it came to pass that there was no contention in the land because of the love of God which dwelt in the hearts of the people.

18 And there were no envyings, nor strifes, nor tumults, nor whoredoms, nor lyings, nor murders, nor any manner of lasciviousness.

19 And surely there could not be a happier people among all the people who had been created by the hand of God.

20 There were no robbers, nor murderers, neither were there Lamanites, nor any manner of "ites"; but they were in one, the children of Christ, and heirs to the kingdom of God.

21 And how blessed were they, for the Lord blessed them in all their doings; even they were blessed and prospered until a hundred and ten years had passed away; and the first generation from Christ had passed away, and there was no contention in all the land.

22 And it came to pass that Nephi, he that kept the last record (and he kept it upon the plates of Nephi), died, and his son Amos kept it in his stead; and he kept it upon the plates of Nephi also.

23 And he kept it eighty-four years, and there was still peace in the land, save it were a small part of the people who had revolted from the church and had taken upon them the name of Lamanites; therefore there began to be Lamanites again in the land.

24 And it came to pass that Amos died also (and it was a hundred and ninety-four years from the coming of Christ), and his son Amos kept the record in his stead; and he also kept it upon the plates of Nephi; and it was also written in the book of Nephi, which is this book.

25 And two hundred years had passed away, and the second generation had all passed away, save it were a few.

26 Now I, Mormon, would that you should know that the people had multiplied, insomuch that they were spread upon all the face of the land, and that they had become exceedingly rich because of their prosperity in Christ.

27 And now in this two hundred and first year, there began to be among them those who were lifted up in pride, such as the wearing of costly apparel, and all manner of fine pearls and of the fine things of the world.

28 And from that time forth they had their goods and their substance no more common among them, and they began to be divided into classes, and they began to build up churches to themselves, to get gain, and began to deny the true church of Christ.

29 And when two hundred and ten years had passed away, there were many churches in the land; there were many churches which professed to know the Christ, and yet they denied the more part of his gospel, insomuch that they received all manner of wickedness, and administered that which was sacred to him to whom it had been forbidden because of unworthiness.

30 And this church multiplied exceedingly because of iniquity and because of the power of Satan who got hold upon their hearts.

31 And again, there was another church which denied the Christ; and they persecuted the true church of Christ because of their humility and their belief in Christ, and they despised them because of the many miracles which were wrought among them.

32 Therefore they exercised power and authority over the disciples of Jesus who tarried with them, and they cast them into prison.

33 But by the power of the word of God, which was in them, the prisons were rent in twain, and they went forth doing mighty miracles among them.

34 Nevertheless, and notwithstanding all these miracles, the people hardened their hearts and sought to kill them, even as the Jews at Jerusalem sought to kill Jesus, according to his word.

35 And they cast them into furnaces of fire, and they came forth receiving no harm; and they also cast them into dens of wild beasts, and they played with the wild beasts even as a child with a lamb; and they came forth from among them receiving no harm.

36 Nevertheless, the people hardened their hearts, for they were led by many priests and false prophets to build up many churches and to do all manner of iniquity.

37 And they smote the people of Jesus; but the people of Jesus did not smite again.

38 Thus they dwindled in unbelief and wickedness from year to year, even until two hundred and thirty years had passed away.

39 Now it came to pass in this year, in the two hundred and thirty-first year, there was a great division among the people.

40 And in this year there arose a people who were called the Nephites, and they were true believers in Christ; and among them there were those who were called (by the Lamanites) Jacobites, and Josephites, and Zoramites.

41 Therefore the true believers in Christ and the true worshipers of Christ (among whom were the three disciples of Jesus who should tarry) were called Nephites, and Jacobites, and Josephites, and Zoramites.

42 And they who rejected the gospel were called Lamanites, and Lemuelites, and Ishmaelites; and they did not dwindle in unbelief, but they willfully rebelled against the gospel of Christ.

43 And they taught their children that they should not believe, even as their fathers, from the beginning.

44 And it was because of the wickedness and abominations of their fathers, even as it was in the beginning.

45 And they were taught to hate the children of God, even as the Lamanites were taught to hate the children of Nephi from the beginning.

46 And two hundred and forty-four years had passed away, and thus were the affairs of the people.

47 The more wicked part of the people waxed strong and became exceedingly more numerous than were the people of God.

48 And they still continued to build up churches to themselves and to adorn them with all manner of precious things.

49 Thus two hundred and fifty years passed away, and also two hundred and sixty years.

50 And it came to pass that the wicked part of the people began again to build up the secret oaths and combinations of Gadianton.

51 Also the people who were called the people of Nephi began to be proud in their hearts because of their exceeding riches, and became vain like their brethren, the Lamanites.

52 And from this time, the disciples began to sorrow for the sins of the world.

53 By the time three hundred years had passed away, both the people of Nephi and the Lamanites had become exceedingly wicked, one like another.

54 And the robbers of Gadianton spread over all the face of the land; and there were none that were righteous, save it were the disciples of Jesus.

55 And gold and silver they laid up in store in abundance and trafficked in all manner of traffic.

56 After three hundred and five years had passed away (and the people still remained in wickedness), Amos died, and his brother Ammoron kept the record in his stead.

57 And when three hundred and twenty years had passed away, Ammoron, being constrained by the Holy Ghost, hid up the records which were sacred; [58]even all the sacred

records which had been handed down from generation to generation, even until the three hundred and twentieth year from the coming of Christ.

59 And he hid them up unto the Lord, that they might come again to the remnant of the house of Jacob according to the prophecies and the promises of the Lord. And thus is the end of the record of Ammoron.

THE BOOK OF MORMON

CHAPTER 1

NOW I, Mormon, make a record of the things which I have both seen and heard, and call it the book of Mormon.

2 And about the time that Ammoron hid up the records to the Lord, he came to me (I being about ten years of age; and I began to be learned somewhat after the manner of the learning of my people), and said to me, "I perceive that you are a sober child and are quick to observe.

3 "Therefore when you are about twenty-four years old, I would that you should remember the things that you have observed concerning this people.

4 "And when you are of that age, go to the land of Antum, to a hill which shall be called Shim; and there have I deposited to the Lord all the sacred engravings concerning this people.

5 "And, behold, you shall take the plates of Nephi to yourself, and the remainder shall you leave in the place where they are; and you shall engrave upon the plates of Nephi all the things that you have observed concerning this people."

6 And I, Mormon, being a descendant of Nephi (and my father's name was Mormon), remembered the things which Ammoron commanded me.

7 And it came to pass that I, being eleven years old, was carried by my father into the land southward, even to the land of Zarahemla; the whole face of the land having become covered with buildings, and the people were as numerous, almost, as the sand of the sea.

8 And in this year, there began to be a war between the Nephites (who consisted of the Nephites, and the Jacobites, and the Josephites, and the Zoramites) and the Lamanites, and the Lemuelites, and the Ishmaelites.

9 Now the Lamanites, and the Lemuelites, and the Ishmaelites were called Lamanites; and the two parties were Nephites and Lamanites.

10 And the war began to be among them in the borders of Zarahemla by the waters of Sidon.

11 The Nephites had gathered together a great number of men, even to exceed the number of thirty thousand.

12 And they had in this same year a number of battles in which the Nephites beat the Lamanites and slew many of them.

13 And it came to pass that the Lamanites withdrew their design, and there was peace settled in the land, and peace remained for the space of about four years, that there was no blood shed.

14 But wickedness prevailed upon the face of the whole land, insomuch that the Lord took away his beloved disciples, and the work of miracles and of healing ceased, because of the iniquity of the people.

15 And there were no gifts from the Lord, and the Holy Ghost did not come upon any, because of their wickedness and unbelief.

16 And I, being fifteen years of age and being somewhat of a sober mind, was visited of the Lord, and tasted, and knew of the goodness of Jesus.

17 And I endeavored to preach

to this people, but my mouth was shut, and I was forbidden that I should preach to them; for, behold, they had willfully rebelled against their God, and the beloved disciples were taken away out of the land because of the people's iniquity.

18 I remained among them, but I was forbidden to preach to them because of the hardness of their hearts; and because of the hardness of their hearts, the land was cursed for their sake.

19 And the Gadianton robbers, who were among the Lamanites, infested the land, insomuch that the inhabitants thereof began to hide their treasures in the earth; and they became slippery because the Lord had cursed the land, that they could not hold them nor regain them again.

20 And it came to pass that there were sorceries, and witchcrafts, and magics; and the power of the evil one was wrought upon all the face of the land even to the fulfilling of all the words of Abinadi, and also Samuel the Lamanite.

21 In that same year, there began to be a war again between the Nephites and the Lamanites.

22 And notwithstanding I was young, I was large in stature, therefore the people of Nephi appointed me that I should be their leader, or the the leader of their armies.

23 Therefore in my sixteenth year I went forth at the head of an army of the Nephites against the Lamanties; therefore three hundred and twenty-six years had passed away.

24 And in the three hundred and twenty-seventh year, the Lamanites came upon us with exceedingly great power, insomuch that they frightened my armies; therefore they would not fight, and they began to retreat toward the north countries.

25 And we came to the city of Angola, and we took possession of the city and made preparations to defend ourselves against the Lamanites.

26 We fortified the city with our mights; but notwithstanding all our fortifications, the Lamanites came upon us and drove us out of the city.

27 And they also drove us forth out of the land of David. And we marched forth and came to the land of Joshua, which was in the borders west by the seashore.

28 And we gathered in our people as fast as it were possible, that we might get them together in one body.

29 But, behold, the land was filled with robbers and with Lamanites; and notwithstanding the great destruction which hung over my people, they did not repent of their evil doings.

30 Therefore there was blood and carnage spread throughout all the face of the land, both on the part of the Nephites and on the part of the Lamanites; and it was one complete revolution throughout all the face of the land.

31 Now the Lamanites had a king whose name was Aaron, and he came against us with an army of forty-four thousand.

32 And, behold, I withstood him with forty-two thousand. And I beat him with my army and he fled before me.

33 And, behold, all this was done and three hundred and thirty years had passed away.

34 And it came to pass that the Nephites began to repent of their iniquity, and began to cry even as had been prophesied by Samuel the prophet; for, behold, no man could keep that which was his own because of the thieves, and the robbers, and the murderers, and the magic art and the witchcraft which was in the land.

35 Thus there began to be a mourning and a lamentation in all the land because of these things, and more especially among the people of Nephi.

36 And when I, Mormon, saw their lamentations, and their mourning, and their sorrowing before the Lord, my heart began to rejoice within me, knowing the mercies and the long-suffering of the Lord, therefore supposing that he would be merciful to them, that they would again become a righteous people.

37 But, behold, my joy was vain, for their sorrowing was not unto repentance because of the goodness of God, but it was rather the sorrowing of the damned because the Lord

would not always suffer them to take happiness in sin.

38 And they did not come to Jesus with broken hearts and contrite spirits, but they cursed God and wished to die.

39 Nevertheless they would struggle with the sword for their lives.

40 And my sorrow returned to me again, and I saw that the day of grace was past with them, both temporally and spiritually, for I saw thousands of them hewn down in open rebellion against their God and heaped up as dung upon the face of the land.

41 Thus three hundred and forty-four years had passed away.

42 And in the three hundred and forty-fifth year, the Nephites began to flee before the Lamanites, and they were pursued until they came even to the land of Jashon before it was possible to stop them in their retreat.

43 Now the city of Jashon was near the land where Ammoron had deposited the records unto the Lord that they might not be destroyed.

44 And, behold, I had gone according to the word of Ammoron and taken the plates of Nephi, and made a record according to the words of Ammoron.

45 Upon the plates of Nephi I made a full account of all the wickedness and abominations; but upon these plates I forbore to make a full account of their wickedness and abominations, for, behold, a continual scene of wickedness and abominations has been before my eyes ever since I have been sufficient to behold the ways of man.

46 And woe is me because of their wickedness, for my heart has been filled with sorrow because of their wickedness all my days; nevertheless, I know that I shall be lifted up at the last day.

47 And in this year the people of Nephi again were hunted and driven.

48 We were driven forth until we had come northward to the land which was called Shem.

49 And we fortified the city of Shem, and we gathered in our people as much as it were possible, that perhaps we might save them from destruction.

50 And in the three hundred and forty-sixth year, they began to come upon us again.

51 And I spoke to my people, and urged them with great energy that they would stand boldly before the Lamanites, and fight for their wives and their children, and their houses and their homes.

52 My words aroused them somewhat to vigor, insomuch that they did not flee from before the Lamanites, but stood with boldness against them.

53 And we contended with an army of thirty thousand against an army of fifty thousand.

54 And we stood before them with such firmness that they fled before us.

55 And when they had fled, we pursued them with our armies, and met them again, and beat them.

56 Nevertheless the strength of the Lord was not with us; we were left to ourselves, that the Spirit of the Lord did not abide in us; therefore we had become weak like our brethren.

57 And my heart sorrowed because of this the great calamity of my people, because of their wickedness and their abominations.

58 But, behold, we went forth against the Lamanites and the robbers of Gadianton until we had again taken possession of the lands of our inheritance.

59 And the three hundred and forty-ninth year had passed away.

60 And in the three hundred and fiftieth year, we made a treaty with the Lamanites and the robbers of Gadianton in which we got the lands of our inheritance divided.

61 The Lamanites gave to us the land northward, even to the narrow passage which led into the land southward.

62 And we gave to the Lamanites all the land southward.

63 And the Lamanites did not come to battle again until ten years more had passed away.

64 Behold, I had employed my people, the Nephites, in preparing their lands and their arms against the time of battle.

65 And it came to pass that the Lord said to me, "Cry to this people,

Repent ye, and come to me, and be ye baptized, and build up again my church, and ye shall be spared."

66 And I cried to this people; but it was in vain, and they did not realize that it was the Lord that had spared them and granted them a chance for repentance.

67 And, behold, they hardened their hearts against the Lord their God.

68 And after this tenth year had passed away, making, in the whole, three hundred and sixty years from the coming of Christ, the king of the Lamanites sent an epistle to me which gave me to know that they were preparing to come again to battle against us.

69 And it came to pass that I caused my people to gather themselves together at the land Desolation, to a city which was in the borders by the narrow pass which led into the land southward.

70 There we placed our armies, that we might stop the armies of the Lamanites, that they might not get possession of any of our lands; therefore we fortified against them with all our force.

71 And in the three hundred and sixty-first year, the Lamanites came down to the city of Desolation to battle against us; and in that year we beat them insomuch that they returned to their own lands again.

72 And in the three hundred and sixty-second year, they came down again to battle.

73 And we beat them again and slew a great number of them, and their dead were cast into the sea.

74 Now because of this great thing which my people, the Nephites, had done, they began to boast in their own strength and began to swear before the heavens that they would avenge themselves of the blood of their brethren who had been slain by their enemies.

75 And they swore by the heavens, and also by the throne of God, that they would go up to battle against their enemies and would cut them off from the face of the land.

76 And I, Mormon, utterly refused from this time forth to be a commander and a leader of this people because of their wickedness and abomination.

77 Behold, notwithstanding their wickedness, I had led them many times to battle and had loved them, according to the love of God which was in me, with all my heart.

78 And my soul had been poured out in prayer to my God all the day long for them; nevertheless, it was without faith because of the hardness of their hearts.

79 Thrice have I delivered them out of the hands of their enemies, and they have repented not of their sins.

80 And when they had sworn by all that had been forbidden them by our Lord and Savior Jesus Christ that they would go up to their enemies to battle and avenge themselves of the blood of their brethren, behold, the voice of the Lord came to me, saying, "Vengeance is mine, and I will repay; and because this people repented not after I had delivered them, behold, they shall be cut off from the face of the earth."

81 And I utterly refused to go up against my enemies; and I did even as the Lord had commanded me; and I stood as an idle witness to manifest to the world the things which I saw and heard, according to the manifestations of the Spirit which had testified of things to come.

82 Therefore I write to you, Gentiles, and also to you, house of Israel, when the work shall commence, that you shall be about to prepare to return to the land of your inheritance.

83 Behold, I write to all the ends of the earth; even to you, twelve tribes of Israel, who shall be judged according to your works by the twelve whom Jesus chose to be his disciples in the land of Jerusalem.

84 And I write also to the remnant of this people, who shall also be judged by the twelve whom Jesus chose in this land; and they shall be judged by the other twelve whom Jesus chose in the land of Jerusalem.

85 These things does the Spirit manifest to me; therefore I write to all of you.

86 And for this cause I write to you, that you may know that you

must all stand before the judgment seat of Christ, even every soul who belongs to the whole human family of Adam.

87 You must stand to be judged of your works, whether they be good or evil; and also that you may believe the gospel of Jesus Christ which you shall have among you; 88and also that the Jews, the covenant people of the Lord, shall have other witnesses besides him whom they saw and heard, that Jesus whom they slew was the very Christ and the very God.

89 And I would that I could persuade all you ends of the earth to repent and prepare to stand before the judgment seat of Christ.

CHAPTER 2

IN the three hundred and sixty-third year, the Nephites went up with their armies to battle against the Lamanites out of the land of Desolation.

2 And it came to pass that the armies of the Nephites were driven back again to the land of Desolation.

3 And while they were yet weary, a fresh army of the Lamanites came upon them; and they had a sore battle, insomuch that the Lamanites took possession of the city Desolation and slew many of the Nephites, and took many prisoners; and the remainder fled and joined the inhabitants of the city Teancum.

4 Now the city Teancum lay in the borders by the seashore; and it was also near the city Desolation.

5 And it was because the armies of the Nephites went up to the Lamanites that they began to be smitten; for were it not for that, the Lamanites could have had no power over them.

6 But, behold, the judgments of God will overtake the wicked; and it is by the wicked that the wicked are punished, for it is the wicked that stir up the hearts of the children of men to bloodshed.

7 And it came to pass that the Lamanites made preparation to come against the city Teancum.

8 And in the three hundred and sixty-fourth year, the Lamanites came against the city Teancum that they might take possession of the city Teancum also.

9 But they were repulsed and driven back by the Nephites.

10 And when the Nephites saw that they had driven the Lamanites, they again boasted of their own strength, and they went forth in their own might and took possession again of the city Desolation.

11 Now all these things had been done, and there had been thousands slain on both sides, both the Nephites and the Lamanites.

12 And the three hundred and sixty-sixth year passed away, and the Lamanites came again upon the Nephites to battle; and yet the Nephites repented not of the evil they had done, but persisted in their wickedness continually.

13 It is impossible for the tongue to describe or for man to write a perfect description of the horrible scene of the blood and carnage which was among the people, both of the Nephites and of the Lamanites; and every heart was hardened so that they delighted in the shedding of blood continually.

14 And there never had been so great wickedness among all the children of Lehi, nor even among all the house of Israel, according to the words of the Lord, as was among this people.

15 And it came to pass that the Lamanites took possession of the city Desolation, and this because their number exceeded the number of the Nephites.

16 They also marched forward against the city Teancum, and drove the inhabitants out of her, and took many prisoners of both women and children, and offered them up as sacrifices to their idol gods.

17 In the three hundred and sixty-seventh year, the Nephites, being angry because the Lamanites had sacrificed their women and their children, went against the Lamanites with exceedingly great anger, insomuch that they beat again the Lamanites, and drove them out of their lands.

18 And the Lamanites did not come again against the Nephites

until the three hundred and seventy-fifth year.

19 In this year they came down against the Nephites with all their powers; and they were not numbered because of the greatness of their number.

20 And from this time forth the Nephites gained no power over the Lamanites, but began to be swept off by them even as a dew before the sun.

21 And it came to pass that the Lamanites came down against the city Desolation; and there was an exceedingly sore battle fought in the land Desolation, in which they beat the Nephites.

22 And the Nephites fled again from before them, and they came to the city Boaz; and there they stood against the Lamanites with exceeding boldness, insomuch that the Lamanites did not beat them until they had come again the second time.

23 When they had come the second time, the Nephites were driven and slaughtered with an exceedingly great slaughter; and their women and their children were again sacrificed to idols.

24 And the Nephites again fled before them, taking all the inhabitants with them, both in towns and villages.

25 Now I, Mormon, seeing that the Lamanites were about to overthrow the land, went to the hill Shim, and took up all the records which Ammoron had hid unto the Lord.

26 And I went forth among the Nephites and repented of the oath which I had made that I would no more assist them, and they gave me command again of their armies; for they looked upon me as though I could deliver them from their afflictions.

27 But, behold, I was without hopes, for I knew the judgments of the Lord which should come upon them; for they repented not of their iniquities, but struggled for their lives without calling upon that being who created them.

28 And it came to pass that the Lamanites came against us as we fled to the city of Jordan; but, behold, they were driven back that they did not take the city at that time.

29 And they came against us again, and we maintained the city.

30 There were also other cities which were maintained by the Nephites, which strongholds cut them off that they could not get into the country which lay before us to destroy the inhabitants of our land.

31 But it came to pass that whatever lands we had passed by, and the inhabitants thereof were not gathered in, were destroyed by the Lamanites; and their towns, and villages, and cities were burned with fire; and thus the three hundred and seventy-nine years passed away.

32 In the three hundred and eightieth year, the Lamanites came again against us to battle, and we stood against them boldly; but it was all in vain; for so great were their numbers that they trod the people of the Nephites under their feet.

33 And we again took to flight, and those whose flight was swifter than the Lamanites' escaped, and those whose flight did not exceed the Lamanites' were swept down and destroyed.

34 Now, behold, I, Mormon, do not desire to harrow up the souls of men in casting before them such an awful scene of blood and carnage as was laid before my eyes.

35 But I, knowing that these things must surely be made known, and that all things which are hid must be revealed upon the housetops, and also that a knowledge of these things must come to the remnant of these people, and also to the Gentiles who the Lord has said should scatter this people, and this people should be counted as nought among them; [36]therefore I write a small abridgment, daring not to give a full account of the things which I have seen because of the commandment which I have received, and also that you might not have too great sorrow because of the wickedness of this people.

37 Now, behold, this I speak to their seed, and also to the Gentiles who have care for the house of Israel, that realize and know from whom their blessings come.

38 For I know that such will sorrow for the calamity of the house of Israel; they will sorrow for the destruction of this people; they will

sorrow that this people had not repented, that they might have been clasped in the arms of Jesus.

39 Now these things are written to the remnant of the house of Jacob; and they are written after this manner because it is known of God that wickedness will not bring them forth to them; and they are to be hid up unto the Lord that they may come forth in his own due time.

40 And this is the commandment which I have received; and, behold, they shall come forth according to the commandment of the Lord, when he shall see fit in his wisdom.

41 And, behold, they shall go to the unbelieving of the Jews; and for this intent shall they go, that they may be persuaded that Jesus is the Christ, the Son of the living God; 42that the Father may bring about, through his most beloved, his great and eternal purpose, in restoring the Jews, or all the house of Israel, to the land of their inheritance, which the Lord their God has given them to the fulfilling of his covenant; 43and also that the seed of this people may more fully believe his gospel, which shall go forth to them from the Gentiles.

44 For this people shall be scattered and shall become a dark, a filthy, and a loathsome people beyond the description of that which has ever been among us, or even that which has been among the Lamanites, and this because of their unbelief and idolatry.

45 For, behold, the Spirit of the Lord has already ceased to strive with their fathers, and they are without Christ and God in the world, and they are driven about as chaff before the wind.

46 They were once a delightsome people, and they had Christ for their Shepherd; they were led even by God, the Father.

47 But now, behold, they are led about by Satan, even as chaff is driven before the wind, or as a vessel is tossed about upon the waves without sail or anchor or without anything wherewith to steer her; and even as she is, so are they.

48 And, behold, the Lord has reserved their blessings, which they might have received in the land, for the Gentiles who shall possess the land.

49 But, behold, it shall come to pass that they shall be driven and scattered by the Gentiles; and after they have been driven and scattered by the Gentiles, behold, then will the Lord remember the covenant which he made to Abraham, and to all the house of Israel.

50 Also the Lord will remember the prayers of the righteous which have been put up to him for them.

51 And then, O you Gentiles, how can you stand before the power of God, except you shall repent and turn from your evil ways!

52 Know you not that you are in the hands of God?

53 Know you not that he has all power, and at his great command the earth shall be rolled together as a scroll?

54 Therefore repent and humble yourselves before him, lest he shall come out in justice against you, lest a remnant of the seed of Jacob shall go forth among you as a lion and tear you in pieces, and there is none to deliver.

CHAPTER 3

NOW I finish my record concerning the destruction of my people, the Nephites.

2 It came to pass that we marched forth before the Lamanites.

3 And I, Mormon, wrote an epistle to the king of the Lamanites and desired that he would grant us that we might gather our people to the land of Cumorah, by a hill which was called Cumorah, and there we would give them battle.

4 And the king of the Lamanites granted me the thing which I desired.

5 And it came to pass that we marched forth to the land of Cumorah, and we pitched our tents round about the hill Cumorah; and it was in a land of many waters, rivers and fountains; and here we had hope to gain advantage over the Lamanites.

6 When three hundred and eighty-four years had passed away, we had gathered all the remainder of our people to the land Cumorah.

7 And when we had gathered in

all our people in one to the land of Cumorah, behold, I, Mormon, began to be old; and knowing it to be the last struggle of my people and having been commanded of the Lord that I should not suffer the records which had been handed down by our fathers, which were sacred, to fall into the hands of the Lamanites (for the Lamanites would destroy them), ⁸therefore I made this record out of the plates of Nephi and hid up in the hill Cumorah all the records which had been entrusted to me by the hand of the Lord, save these few plates which I gave to my son Moroni.

9 And it came to pass that my people, with their wives and their children, now beheld the armies of the Lamanites marching toward them; and with that awful fear of death which fills the breasts of all the wicked, they waited to receive them.

10 They came to battle against us, and every soul was filled with terror because of the greatness of their numbers.

11 And they fell upon my people with the sword, and with the bow, and with the arrow, and with the ax, and with all manner of weapons of war.

12 My men were hewn down, even my ten thousand who were with me, and I fell wounded in the midst, and they passed by me that they did not put an end to my life.

13 And when they had gone through and hewn down all my people, save twenty-four of us (among whom was my son Moroni), ¹⁴and having survived the dead of our people, we beheld on the morrow, when the Lamanites had returned to their camps, from the top of the hill Cumorah the ten thousand of my people who were hewn down, being led in the front by me; and we also beheld the ten thousand of my people who were led by my son, Moroni.

15 And, behold, the ten thousand of Gidgiddonah had fallen, and he also in the midst; and Lamah had fallen with his ten thousand; and Gilgal had fallen with his ten thousand; and Limhah had fallen with his ten thousand; and Jeneum had fallen with his ten thousand; and Cumenihah, and Moronihah, and Antionum, and Shiblom, and Shem, and Josh had fallen with their ten thousand each.

16 And there were ten more who fell by the sword with their ten thousand each; even all my people had fallen, save it were those twenty-four who were with me, and also a few who had escaped into the south countries and a few who had deserted over to the Lamanites.

17 And their flesh, and bones, and blood lay upon the face of the earth, being left by the hands of those who slew them, to moulder upon the land and to crumble and to return to their mother earth.

18 And my soul was rent with anguish because of the slain of my people, and I cried, O you fair ones, how could you have departed from the ways of the Lord! O you fair ones, how could you have rejected that Jesus who stood with open arms to receive you!

19 Behold, if you had not done this, you would not have fallen. But, behold, you are fallen, and I mourn your loss.

20 O you fair sons and daughters, you fathers and mothers, you husbands and wives, you fair ones, how is it that you could have fallen!

21 But, behold, you are gone, and my sorrows cannot bring your return; and the day soon cometh that your mortal must put on immortality, and these bodies which are now mouldering in corruption must soon become incorruptible bodies.

22 Then you must stand before the judgment seat of Christ to be judged according to your works; and if it so be that you are righteous, then are you blessed with your fathers who have gone before you.

23 Oh, that you had repented before this great destruction had come upon you. But, behold, you are gone, and the Father, even the eternal Father of heaven, knows your state; and he will do with you according to his justice and mercy.

24 Now, behold, I would speak somewhat to the remnant of this people who are spared, if it so be that God may give them my words that they may know of the things of their fathers; I speak to you, a

remnant of the house of Israel; and these are the words which I speak, Know you that you are of the house of Israel.

25 Know you that you must come unto repentance, or you cannot be saved.

26 Know you that you must lay down your weapons of war and delight no more in the shedding of blood, and take them not again save it be that God shall command you.

27 Know you that you must come to the knowledge of your fathers, and repent of all your sins and iniquities, and believe in Jesus Christ, that he is the Son of God, and that he was slain by the Jews and by the power of the Father he has risen again, whereby he has gained the victory over the grave; and also in him is the sting of death swallowed up.

28 And he brings to pass the resurrection of the dead, whereby man must be raised to stand before his judgment seat.

29 And he has brought to pass the redemption of the world, whereby he that is found guiltless before him at the judgment day has it given to him to dwell in the presence of God in his kingdom, to sing ceaseless praises with the choirs above, to the Father, and to the Son, and to the Holy Ghost, which are one God, in a state of happiness which has no end.

30 Therefore repent, and be baptized in the name of Jesus, and lay hold upon the gospel of Christ which shall be set before you, not only in this record, but also in the record which shall come to the Gentiles from the Jews, which record shall come from the Gentiles to you.

31 For, behold, this is written for the intent that you may believe that; and if you may believe that, you will believe this also; and if you believe this, you will know concerning your fathers, and also the marvelous works which were wrought by the power of God among them.

32 And you will also know that you are a remnant of the seed of Jacob; therefore you are numbered among the people of the first covenant.

33 And if it so be that you believe in Christ, and are baptized, first with water, then with fire and with the Holy Ghost, following the example of our Savior according to that which he has commanded us, it shall be well with you in the day of judgment. Amen.

CHAPTER 4

BEHOLD, I Moroni, finish the record of my father Mormon. Behold, I have but few things to write, which things I have been commanded of my father.

2 Now after the great and tremendous battle at Cumorah, behold, the Nephites who had escaped into the country southward were hunted by the Lamanites until they were all destroyed; and my father also was killed by them; and I remain alone to write the sad tale of the destruction of my people.

3 But, behold, they are gone, and I fulfill the commandment of my father.

4 And whether they will slay me, I know not; therefore I will write and hide the records in the earth, and where I go it matters not.

5 Behold, my father has made this record, and he has written the intent thereof.

6 And, behold, I would write it also if I had room upon the plates, but I have not; and ore I have none, for I am alone; my father has been slain in battle, and all my kinfolk, and I have not friends, nor where to go; and how long the Lord will suffer that I may live, I know not.

7 Behold, four hundred years have passed since the coming of our Lord and Savior.

8 And the Lamanites have hunted down my people, the Nephites, from city to city and from place to place, even until they are no more, and great has been their fall; and great and marvelous is the destruction of my people, the Nephites.

9 And, behold, it is the hand of the Lord which has done it.

10 Also, the Lamanites are at war one with another; and the whole face of this land is one continual round of murder and bloodshed; and no one knows the end of the war.

11 And now, behold, I say no

more concerning them, for there are none, save it be the Lamanites and robbers, that exist upon the face of the land.

12 And there are none that know the true God, save it be the disciples of Jesus, who tarried in the land until the wickedness of the people was so great that the Lord would not suffer them to remain with the people; and whether they be upon the face of the land, no man knows.

13 But, behold, my father and I have seen them, and they have ministered to us.

14 And whoever receives this record and shall not condemn it because of the imperfections which are in it, the same shall know of greater things than these.

15 Behold, I am Moroni; and were it possible, I would make all things known to you.

16 Behold, I make an end of speaking concerning this people.

17 I am the son of Mormon, and my father was a descendant of Nephi; and I am the same who hides up this record unto the Lord; the plates thereof are of no worth, because of the commandment of the Lord.

18 For he truly said that no one shall have them to get gain; but the record thereof is of great worth; and whoever shall bring it to light, him will the Lord bless.

19 For no one can have power to bring it to light, save it be given him of God; for God wills that it shall be done with an eye single to his glory, or the welfare of the ancient and long dispersed covenant people of the Lord.

20 And blessed is he who shall bring this thing to light; for it shall be brought out of darkness to light according to the word of God.

21 It shall be brought out of the earth, and it shall shine forth out of darkness and come to the knowledge of the people; and it shall be done by the power of God; and if there be faults, they be faults of a man.

22 But, behold, we know no fault; nevertheless, God knows all things; therefore he that condemns, let him beware lest he shall be in danger of hell fire.

23 And he that says, "Show to me or you shall be smitten," let him beware lest he commands that which is forbidden of the Lord.

24 For, behold, the same that judges rashly shall be judged rashly again; for according to his works shall his wages be; therefore, he that smites, shall be smitten again of the Lord.

25 Behold what the scripture says: "Man shall not smite, neither shall he judge; for judgment is mine, saith the Lord; and vengeance is mine also, and I will repay."

26 And he that shall breathe out wrath and strifes against the work of the Lord, and against the covenant people of the Lord who are the house of Israel, and shall say, "We will destroy the work of the Lord, and the Lord will not remember his covenant which he has made to the house of Israel," the same is in danger to be hewn down and cast into the fire; for the eternal purposes of the Lord shall roll on until all his promises shall be fulfilled.

27 Search the prophecies of Isaiah. Behold, I cannot write them.

28 Behold, I say to you that those saints who have gone before me, who have possessed this land, shall cry, even from the dust will they cry to the Lord; and as the Lord lives, he will remember the covenant which he has made with them.

29 He knows their prayers, that they were in behalf of their brethren.

30 And he knows their faith; for in his name could they remove mountains; and in his name could they cause the earth to shake; and by the power of his word they caused prisons to tumble to the earth; [31]even the fiery furnace could not harm them, neither wild beasts nor poisonous serpents, because of the power of his word.

32 And, behold, their prayers were also in behalf of him whom the Lord should suffer to bring these things forth.

33 And no one need say, "They shall not come," for they surely shall, for the Lord has spoken it; for out of the earth shall they come by the hand of the Lord, and none can stay it.

34 It shall come in a day when it

shall be said that miracles are done away, and it shall come even as if one should speak from the dead.

35 And it shall come in a day when the blood of the saints shall cry to the Lord because of secret combinations and the works of darkness.

36 It shall come in a day when the power of God shall be denied, and churches become defiled and shall be lifted up in the pride of their hearts, even in a day when leaders of churches, and teachers, in the pride of their hearts envy them who belong to their churches.

37 It shall come in a day when there shall be heard of fires, and tempests, and vapors of smoke in foreign lands; and there shall also be heard of wars, and rumors of wars, and earthquakes in divers places.

38 It shall come in a day when there shall be great pollutions upon the face of the earth.

39 There shall be murders and robbing, and lying, and deceivings, and whoredoms, and all manner of abominations, when there shall be many who will say, "Do this, or do that, and it matters not, for the Lord will uphold such at the last day."

40 But woe to such, for they are in the gall of bitterness and in the bonds of iniquity.

41 It shall come in a day when there shall be churches built up that shall say, "Come to me, and for your money you shall be forgiven of your sins."

42 O you wicked and perverse, and stiff-necked people, why have you built up churches to yourselves to get gain?

43 Why have you transfigured the holy word of God that you might bring damnation upon your souls?

44 Behold, look to the revelations of God. For, behold, the time will come at that day when all these things must be fulfilled.

45 Behold, the Lord has shown to me great and marvelous things concerning that which must shortly come at that day when these things shall come forth among you.

46 Behold, I speak to you as if you were present, and yet you are not.

47 But, behold, Jesus Christ has shown you to me, and I know your doing; and I know that you walk in the pride of your hearts.

48 And there are none, save a few only, who do not lift themselves up in the pride of their hearts, to the wearing of very fine apparel, to envying, and strifes, and malice, and persecutions, and all manner of iniquity.

49 And your churches, even every one, have become polluted because of the pride of your hearts.

50 For, behold, you love money, and your substance, and your fine apparel, and the adorning of your churches more than you love the poor and the needy, the sick and the afflicted.

51 O you pollutions, you hypocrites, you teachers who sell yourselves for that which will canker, why have you polluted the holy church of God?

52 Why are you ashamed to take upon you the name of Christ?

53 Why do you not think that greater is the value of an endless happiness than that misery which never dies, because of the praise of the world?

54 Why do you adorn yourselves with that which has no life, and yet suffer the hungry, and the needy, and the naked, and the sick, and the afflicted to pass by you and notice them not?

55 Why do you build up your secret abominations to get gain and cause that widows should mourn before the Lord, and also orphans to mourn before the Lord, and also the blood of their fathers and their husbands to cry to the Lord from the ground for vengeance upon your heads?

56 Behold, the sword of vengeance hangs over you; and the time will soon come that he avenges the blood of the saints upon you, for he will not suffer their cries any longer.

57 Now I speak also concerning those who do not believe in Christ.

58 Behold, will you believe in the day of your visitation, when the Lord shall come, even that great day when the earth shall be rolled together as a scroll, and the elements shall melt with fervent heat?

59 In that great day when you shall be brought to stand before the Lamb of God, then will you say that there is no God?

60 Then will you longer deny the Christ, or can you behold the Lamb of God?

61 Do you suppose that you shall dwell with him under a consciousness of your guilt?

62 Do you suppose that you could be happy to dwell with that holy being when your souls are racked with a consciousness of your guilt that you have ever abused his laws?

63 Behold, I say to you that you would be more miserable to dwell with a holy and just God under a consciousness of your filthiness before him than you would to dwell with the damned souls in hell.

64 For, behold, when you shall be brought to see your nakedness before God, and also the glory of God and the holiness of Jesus Christ, it will kindle a flame of unquenchable fire upon you.

65 O then you unbelieving, turn to the Lord; cry mightily to the Father in the name of Jesus that perhaps you may be found spotless, pure, fair, and white, having been cleansed by the blood of the Lamb at that great and last day.

66 Again I speak to you who deny the revelations of God and say that they are done away, that there are no revelations, nor prophecies, nor gifts, nor healing, nor speaking with tongues and the interpretation of tongues.

67 Behold, I say to you, He that denies these things, knows not the gospel of Christ; he has not read the scriptures; if so, he does not understand them.

68 For do we not read that God is the same yesterday, today, and forever; and in him there is no variableness, neither shadow of changing.

69 And now, if you have imagined to yourselves a god who does vary, and in whom there is shadow of changing, then you have imagined to yourselves a god who is not a god of miracles.

70 But, behold, I will show to you a God of miracles, even the God of Abraham, and the God of Isaac, and the God of Jacob; and it is that same God who created the heavens and the earth, and all things that in them are.

71 Behold, he created Adam; and by Adam came the fall of man. And because of the fall of man, came Jesus Christ, even the Father and the Son; and because of Jesus Christ came the redemption of man.

72 And because of the redemption of man, which came by Jesus Christ, they are brought back into the presence of the Lord; this is wherein all men are redeemed because the death of Christ brings to pass the resurrection, which brings to pass a redemption from an endless sleep, from which sleep all men shall be awakened by the power of God when the trump shall sound.

73 And they shall come forth, both small and great, and all shall stand before his bar, being redeemed and loosed from this eternal band of death, which death is a temporal death.

74 Then comes the judgment of the Holy One upon them; and then comes the time that he that is filthy shall be filthy still, and he that is righteous shall be righteous still; he that is happy shall be happy still; and he that is unhappy shall be unhappy still.

75 Now, O all you that have imagined to yourselves a god who can do no miracles, I would ask of you, Have all these things passed of which I have spoken? Has the end come yet?

76 Behold, I say to you, No; and God has not ceased to be a God of miracles.

77 Behold, are not the things that God has wrought marvelous in our eyes? And who can comprehend the marvelous works of God?

78 Who shall say that it was not a miracle that by his word the heaven and the earth should be; and by the power of his word man was created of the dust of the earth; and by the power of his word have miracles been wrought?

79 And who shall say that Jesus Christ did not do many mighty miracles?

80 There were many mighty mira-

cles wrought by the hands of the apostles.

81 And if there were miracles wrought, then why has God ceased to be a God of miracles and yet be an unchangeable being?

82 Behold, I say to you, He changes not; if so, he would cease to be God; but he ceases not to be God, but is a God of miracles.

83 And the reason he ceases to do miracles among the children of men is that they dwindle in unbelief, and depart from the right way, and know not the God in whom they should trust.

84 Behold, I say to you that whoever believes in Christ, doubting nothing, whatever he shall ask the Father in the name of Christ, it shall be granted him; and this promise is to all, even to the ends of the earth.

85 For, behold, thus says Jesus Christ, the Son of God, to his disciples who should tarry, and also to his disciples in the hearing of the multitude:

86 "Go ye into all the world and preach the gospel to every creature; and he that believeth and is baptized shall be saved, but he that believeth not shall be damned.

87 "And these signs shall follow them that believe: in my name shall they cast out devils; they shall speak with new tongues; they shall take up serpents; and if they drink any deadly thing, it shall not hurt them; they shall lay hands on the sick, and they shall recover.

88 "And whoever shall believe in my name, doubting nothing, to him will I confirm all my words, even to the ends of the earth."

89 Now, behold, who can stand against the works of the Lord? Who can deny his sayings?

90 Who will rise up against the almighty power of the Lord? Who will despise the works of the Lord? Who will despise the children of Christ?

91 Behold, all you who are despisers of the works of the Lord, for you shall wonder and perish.

92 O then despise not and wonder not, but hearken to the words of the Lord, and ask the Father in the name of Jesus for whatever things you shall stand in need.

93 Doubt not, but be believing, and begin as in times of old, and come to the Lord with all your hearts, and work out your own salvation with fear and trembling before him.

94 Be wise in the days of your probation; strip yourselves of all uncleanness; ask not that you may consume it on your lusts; but ask with a firmness unshaken, that you will yield to no temptation, but that you will serve the true and living God.

95 See that you are not baptized unworthily; see that you partake not of the sacrament of Christ unworthily; but see that you do all things in worthiness and do them in the name of Jesus Christ, the Son of the living God; and if you do this and endure to the end, you will in no wise be cast out.

96 Behold, I speak to you as though I spoke from the dead; for I know that you shall have my words.

97 Condemn me not because of my imperfections, neither my father because of his imperfection, neither them who have written before him; but rather give thanks to God that he has made manifest to you our imperfections, that you may learn to be more wise than we have been.

98 Now, behold, we have written this record according to our knowledge in the characters which are called among us the reformed Egyptian, being handed down and altered by us according to our manner of speech.

99 And if our plates had been sufficiently large, we should have written in the Hebrew; but the Hebrew has been altered by us also; and if we could have written in the Hebrew, behold, you would have had no imperfection in our record.

100 But the Lord knows the things which we have written, and also that no other people know our language; and because no other people know our language, therefore he has prepared means for the interpretation thereof.

101 And these things are written that we may rid our garments of the blood of our brethren who have dwindled in unbelief.

102 Behold, these things which we have desired concerning our brethren, even their restoration to the knowledge of Christ, are according to the prayers of all the saints who have dwelt in the land.

103 May the Lord Jesus Christ grant that their prayers may be answered according to their faith; and may God the Father remember the covenant which he has made with the house of Israel; and may he bless them forever through faith on the name of Jesus Christ. Amen.

BOOK OF ETHER

CHAPTER 1

NOW I, Moroni, proceed to give an account of those ancient inhabitants who were destroyed by the hand of the Lord upon the face of this north country.

2 And I take my account from the twenty-four plates which were found by the people of Limhi, which is called the book of Ether.

3 And as I suppose that the first part of this record which speaks concerning the creation of the world, and also of Adam, and an account from that time even to the great tower, and whatever things transpired among the children of men until that time, is had among the Jews, ⁴therefore I do not write those things which transpired from the days of Adam until that time; but they are had upon the plates; and whoever finds them, the same will have power that he may get the full account.

5 But, behold, I give not the full account, but a part of the account I give, from the tower down until they were destroyed. And on this wise do I give the account.

6 He that wrote this record was Ether, and he was a descendant of Coriantor; and Coriantor was the son of Moron; and Moron was the son of Ethem; and Ethem was the son of Ahah; and Ahah was the son of Seth; and Seth was the son of Shiblom; and Shiblom was the son of Com; and Com was the son of Coriantum; and Coriantum was the son of Amnigaddah; and Amnigaddah was the son of Aaron; and Aaron was a descendant of Heth, who was the son of Hearthom; and Hearthom was the son of Lib; and Lib was the son of Kish; and Kish was the son of Corom; and Corom was the son of Levi; and Levi was the son of Kim; and Kim was the son of Morianton; and Morianton was a descendant of Riplakish; and Riplakish was the son of Shez; and Shez was the son of Heth; and Heth was the son of Com; and Com was son of Coriantum; and Coriantum was the son of Emer; and Emer was the son of Omer; and Omer was the son of Shule; and Shule was the son of Kib; and Kib was the son of Orihah, who was the son of Jared; ⁷which Jared came forth with his brother and their families, with some others and their families, from the great tower at the time the Lord confounded the language of the people and swore in his wrath that they should be scattered upon all the face of the earth, and according to the word of the Lord the people were scattered.

8 The brother of Jared was a large and a mighty man, and being a man highly favored of the Lord, Jared his brother said to him, "Cry to the Lord that he will not confound us that we may not understand our words."

9 And the brother of Jared cried to the Lord, and the Lord had compassion upon Jared; therefore he did not confound the language of Jared, and Jared and his brother were not confounded.

10 Then Jared said to his brother,

343   C. 3000–2000 B. C.

"'Cry again to the Lord, and it may be that he will turn away his anger from them who are our friends, that he confound not their language."

11 And the brother of Jared cried to the Lord, and the Lord had compassion upon their friends, and also their families that they were not confounded.

12 And Jared spoke again to his brother, saying, "Go and inquire of the Lord whether he will drive us out of the land, and if he will drive us out of the land, cry to him where we shall go.

13 "Who knows but the Lord will carry us forth into a land which is choice above all the earth.

14 "And if it so be, let us be faithful to the Lord, that we may receive it for our inheritance."

15 The brother of Jared cried to the Lord according to that which had been spoken by the mouth of Jared.

16 And the Lord heard the brother of Jared, and had compassion upon him, and said to him, "Go to and gather thy flocks, both male and female, of every kind, and also of the seed of the earth of every kind, and thy family, and also Jared thy brother and his family, and also thy friends and their families, and the friends of Jared and their families.

17 "And when thou hast done this, thou shalt go at the head of them down into the valley, which is northward.

18 "And there will I meet thee, and I will go before thee into a land which is choice above all the land of the earth.

19 "There will I bless thee and thy seed and raise up to me of thy seed and of the seed of thy brother, and they who shall go with thee, a great nation.

20 "And there shall be none greater than the nation which I will raise up to me of thy seed, upon all the face of the earth.

21 "And this I will do to thee because this long time ye have cried to me."

22 And it came to pass that Jared, and his brother, and their families, and also the friends of Jared and his brother and their families went down into the valley which was northward

(and the name of the valley was Nimrod, being called after the mighty hunter), with their flocks which they had gathered, male and female, of every kind.

23 They also laid snares and caught fowls of the air, and they also prepared a vessel in which they carried with them the fish of the waters.

24 And they also carried with them deseret, which, by interpretation, is a honey bee; and thus they carried with them swarms of bees, and all manner of that which was upon the face of the land, seeds of every kind.

25 When they had come down into the valley of Nimrod, the Lord came down and talked with the brother of Jared; and he was in a cloud, and the brother of Jared saw him not.

26 And the Lord commanded them that they should go forth into the wilderness, into that quarter where there never had man been.

27 And it came to pass that the Lord went before them, and talked with them as he stood in a cloud, and gave directions where they should travel.

28 And they traveled in the wilderness, and built barges in which they crossed many waters, being directed continually by the hand of the Lord.

29 And the Lord would not suffer that they should stop beyond the sea in the wilderness, but he would that they should come forth even to the land of promise, which was choice above all other lands, which the Lord God had preserved for a righteous people.

30 He had sworn in his wrath to the brother of Jared that those who should possess this land of promise, from that time henceforth and forever, should serve him, the true and only God, or they should be swept off when the fullness of his wrath should come upon them.

31 Now we can behold the decrees of God concerning this land, that it is a land of promise, and whatever nation shall possess it shall serve God, or they shall be swept off when the fullness of his wrath shall come upon them.

32 And the fullness of his wrath

will come upon them when they are ripened in iniquity; for, behold, this is a land which is choice above all other lands; wherefore he that possesses it shall serve God or shall be swept off; for it is the everlasting decree of God.

33 And it is not until the fullness of iniquity among the children of the land that they are swept off.

34 This comes to you, O Gentiles, that you may know the decrees of God, that you may repent and not continue in your iniquities until the fullness come, that you may not bring down the fullness of the wrath of God upon you as the inhabitants of the land have hitherto done.

35 Behold, this is a choice land, and whatever nation shall possess it shall be free from bondage, and from captivity, and from all other nations under heaven, if they will but serve the God of the land, who is Jesus Christ who has been manifested by the things which we have written.

36 Now I proceed with my record; for, behold, it came to pass that the Lord brought Jared and his brethren forth even to that great sea which divides the lands.

37 And as they came to the sea, they pitched their tents; and they called the name of the place Moriancumer; and they dwelt in tents upon the seashore for the space of four years.

38 At the end of four years the Lord came again to the brother of Jared and stood in a cloud and talked with him.

39 For the space of three hours the Lord talked with the brother of Jared and chastened him because he remembered not to call upon the name of the Lord.

40 And the brother of Jared repented of the evil which he had done and called upon the name of the Lord for his brethren who were with him.

41 And the Lord said to him, "I will forgive thee and thy brethren of their sins; but thou shalt not sin any more, for ye shall remember that my Spirit will not always strive with man; wherefore if ye will sin until ye are fully ripe, ye shall be cut off from the presence of the Lord.

42 "These are my thoughts upon the land which I shall give you for your inheritance, for it shall be a land choice above all other lands."

43 And the Lord said, "Go to work and build after the manner of barges which ye have hitherto built."

44 And it came to pass that the brother of Jared went to work, and also his brethren, and built barges after the manner which they had built, according to the instructions of the Lord.

45 They were small, and they were light upon the water, even like the lightness of a fowl upon the water; and they were built after a manner that they were exceedingly tight, even that they would hold water like a dish.

46 And the bottom thereof was tight like a dish; and the sides were tight like a dish; and the ends were peaked; and the top was tight like a dish; and the length was the length of a tree; and the door, when it was shut, was tight like a dish.

47 And it came to pass that the brother of Jared cried to the Lord, saying, "O Lord, I have performed the work which thou hast commanded me, and I have made the barges according as thou hast directed me.

48 "And, behold, O Lord, in them there is no light; where shall we steer?

49 "Also we shall perish, for in them we cannot breathe save it is the air which is in them; therefore we shall perish."

50 And the Lord said to the brother of Jared, "Behold, thou shalt make a hole in the top, and also in the bottom; and when thou shalt suffer for air, thou shalt unstop the hole and receive air.

51 "And if it so be that the water come in upon thee, behold, ye shall stop the hole, that ye may not perish in the flood."

52 And the brother of Jared did according as the Lord had commanded.

53 And he cried again to the Lord, saying, "O Lord, behold, I have done even as thou hast commanded me; and I have prepared the vessels for my people, and, behold, there is no light in them.

54 "Behold, O Lord, wilt thou

suffer that we shall cross this great water in darkness?"

55 And the Lord said to the brother of Jared, "What will ye that I should do that ye may have light in your vessels?

56 "For, behold, ye cannot have windows, for they will be dashed in pieces; neither shall ye take fire with you, for ye shall not go by the light of fire; for, behold, ye shall be as a whale in the midst of the sea; for the mountainous waves shall dash upon you.

57 "Nevertheless, I will bring you up again out of the depths of the sea; for the winds have gone forth out of my mouth, and also the rains and the floods have I sent forth.

58 "Behold, I prepare you against these things; for howbeit, ye cannot cross this great deep, save I prepare you against the waves of the sea, and the winds which have gone forth, and the floods which shall come.

59 "Therefore what will ye that I should prepare for you, that ye may have light when ye are swallowed up in the depths of the sea?"

60 And it came to pass that the brother of Jared (now the number of the vessels which had been prepared was eight) went forth to the mount which they called the mount Shelem because of its exceeding height, and smelted out of a rock sixteen small stones.

61 And they were white and clear, even as transparent glass, and he carried them in his hands upon the top of the mount and cried again to the Lord, saying, "O Lord, thou hast said that we must be encompassed about by the floods.

62 "Now, behold, O Lord, and do not be angry with thy servant because of his weakness before thee; for we know that thou art holy and dwellest in the heavens, and that we are unworthy before thee.

63 "Because of the fall, our natures have become evil continually; nevertheless, O Lord, thou hast given us a commandment that we must call upon thee that from thee we may receive according to our desires.

64 "Behold, O Lord, thou hast smitten us because of our iniquity and hath driven us forth, and for this many years we have been in the wilderness; nevertheless, thou hast been merciful to us.

65 "O Lord, look upon me in pity, and turn away thine anger from this thy people, and suffer not that they shall go forth across this raging deep in darkness, but behold these things which I have smelted out of the rock.

66 "And I know, O Lord, that thou hast all power and can do whatever thou wilt for the benefit of man; therefore touch these stones, O Lord, with thy finger and prepare them that they may shine forth in darkness; and they shall shine forth to us in the vessels which we have prepared that we may have light while we shall cross the sea.

67 "Behold, O Lord, thou canst do this. We know that thou art able to show forth great power which looks small to the understanding of men."

68 When the brother of Jared had said these words, behold, the Lord stretched forth his hand and touched the stones, one by one, with his finger.

69 And the veil was taken from the eyes of the brother of Jared, and he saw the finger of the Lord; and it was as the finger of a man, like flesh and blood; and the brother of Jared fell down before the Lord, for he was struck with fear.

70 The Lord saw that the brother of Jared had fallen to the earth, and the Lord said to him, "Arise, why hast thou fallen?"

71 And he said to the Lord, "I saw the finger of the Lord and I feared lest he should smite me; for I knew not that the Lord had flesh and blood."

72 And the Lord said to him, "Because of thy faith thou hast seen that I shall take upon me flesh and blood; and never has man come before me with such exceeding faith as thou hast; for were it not so, ye could not have seen my finger. Sawest thou more than this?"

73 He answered, "Nay, Lord, show thyself to me."

74 And the Lord said to him, "Believest thou the words which I shall speak?"

75 And he answered, "Yea, Lord, I know that thou speakest the truth, for thou art a God of truth and canst not lie."

76 When he had said these words, behold, the Lord showed himself to him and said, "Because thou knowest these things, ye are redeemed from the fall; therefore ye are brought back into my presence; therefore I show myself to you.

77 "Behold, I am he who was prepared from the foundation of the world to redeem my people. Behold, I am Jesus Christ. I am the Father and the Son.

78 "In me shall all mankind have life, and that eternally, even they who shall believe on my name; and they shall become my sons and my daughters.

79 "And never have I showed myself to man whom I have created, for never has man believed in me as thou hast.

80 "Seest thou that ye are created after my own image? Even all men were created in the beginning after my own image.

81 "Behold, this body which ye now behold is the body of my spirit; and man have I created after the body of my spirit; and even as I appear to thee to be in the spirit, will I appear to my people in the flesh."

82 Now as I, Moroni, said I could not make a full account of these things which are written, therefore it suffices me to say that Jesus showed himself to this man in the spirit after the manner and in the likeness of the same body, even as he showed himself to the Nephites.

83 And he ministered to him even as he ministered to the Nephites; and all this, that this man knew that he was God, because of the many great works which the Lord had showed to him.

84 And because of the knowledge of this man, he could not be kept from beholding within the veil; and he saw the finger of Jesus; and when he saw it, he fell with fear, for he knew that it was the finger of the Lord.

85 And he had faith no longer, for he knew, doubting nothing;

wherefore, having this perfect knowledge of God, he could not be kept from within the veil; therefore he saw Jesus, who ministered to him.

86 And it came to pass that the Lord said to the brother of Jared, "Behold, thou shalt not suffer these things which ye have seen and heard to go forth to the world until the time cometh that I shall glorify my name in the flesh; wherefore, ye shall treasure up the things which ye have seen and heard and show them to no man.

87 "And, behold, when ye shall come to me, ye shall write them and shall seal them up, that no one can interpret them; for ye shall write them in a language that they cannot be read.

88 "And, behold, these two stones will I give thee, and ye shall seal them up also with the things which ye shall write.

89 "For, behold, the language which ye shall write, I have confounded; wherefore I will cause in my own due time that these stones shall magnify to the eyes of men these things which ye shall write."

90 When the Lord had said these words, he showed to the brother of Jared all the inhabitants of the earth which had been, and also all that would be; and the Lord withheld them not from his sight, even to the ends of the earth.

91 For the Lord had said to him in times before that if he would believe in him, believe that he could show to him all things, they should be shown him; therefore the Lord could not withhold anything from him, for he knew that the Lord could show him all things.

92 And the Lord said to him, "Write these things and seal them up, and I will show them in my own due time to the children of men."

93 And it came to pass that the Lord commanded him that he should seal up the two stones which he had received, and show them not, until the Lord should show them to the children of men.

94 And the Lord commanded the brother of Jared to go down out of the mount from the presence of the Lord and write the things which he

had seen; and they were forbidden to come to the children of men until after he should be lifted up upon the cross.

95 For this cause King Mosiah kept them that they should not come to the world until after Christ should show himself to his people.

96 And after Christ truly had shown himself to his people, he commanded that they should be made manifest.

97 Now, after that, they have all dwindled in unbelief, and there is none save it be the Lamanites, and they have rejected the gospel of Christ; therefore I am commanded that I should hide them again in the earth.

98 Behold, I have written upon these plates the very things which the brother of Jared saw; and there never were greater things made manifest than were made manifest to the brother of Jared; wherefore, the Lord has commanded me to write them, and I have written them.

99 And he commanded me that I should seal them up, and he also has commanded that I should seal up the interpretation thereof; wherefore I have sealed up the interpreters according to the commandment of the Lord.

100 For the Lord said to me, "They shall not go forth to the Gentiles until the day that they shall repent of their iniquity and become clean before the Lord.

101 "And in that day that they shall exercise faith in me," saith the Lord, "even as the brother of Jared did, that they may become sanctified in me, then will I manifest to them the things which the brother of Jared saw, even to the unfolding to them all my revelations," saith Jesus Christ, the Son of God, the Father of the heavens and of the earth, and all things that in them are.

102 "And he that will contend against the word of the Lord, let him be accursed; and he that shall deny these things, let him be accursed; for to them will I show no greater things," saith Jesus Christ, "for I am he who speaketh.

103 "At my command the heavens are opened and are shut; and at my word the earth shall shake; and at my command the inhabitants thereof shall pass away, even so as by fire.

104 "And he that believeth not my words, believeth not my disciples; and if it so be that I do not speak, judge ye; for ye shall know that it is I that speaketh at the last day.

105 "But he that believeth these things which I have spoken, him will I visit with the manifestations of my Spirit; and he shall know and bear record.

106 "For because of my Spirit, he shall know that these things are true, for it persuadeth men to do good; and whatever thing persuadeth men to do good is of me, for good cometh of none, save it be of me.

107 "I am the same that leadeth men to all good; he that will not believe my words will not believe me, that I am; and he that will not believe me will not believe the Father who sent me.

108 "For, behold, I am the Father, I am the light, and the life, and the truth of the world.

109 "Come to me, O ye Gentiles, and I will show you the greater things, the knowledge which is hid up because of unbelief.

110 "Come to me, O ye house of Israel, and it shall be made manifest to you how great things the Father hath laid up for you from the foundation of the world; and it hath not come to you, because of unbelief.

111 "Behold, when ye shall rend that veil of unbelief which causes you to remain in your awful state of wickedness and hardness of heart and blindness of mind, then shall the great and marvelous things which have been hid up from the foundation of the world be revealed to you.

112 "When ye shall call upon the Father in my name, with a broken heart and a contrite spirit, then shall ye know that the Father hath remembered the covenant which he made to your fathers, O house of Israel.

113 "And then shall my revelations which I have caused to be written by my servant John be unfolded in the eyes of all the people.

114 "Remember, when ye see these

things, ye shall know that the time is at hand that they shall be made manifest in very deed; therefore, when ye shall receive this record, ye may know that the work of the Father has commenced upon all the face of the land.

115 "Therefore, repent all ye ends of the earth, and come to me, and believe in my gospel, and be baptized in my name; for he that believeth and is baptized shall be saved; but he that believeth not shall be damned, and signs shall follow them that believe in my name.

116 "And blessed is he that is found faithful to my name at the last day, for he shall be lifted up to dwell in the kingdom prepared for him from the foundation of the world.

117 "And, behold, it is I that hath spoken it. Amen."

CHAPTER 2

NOW I, Moroni, have written the words which were commanded me, according to my memory; and I have told you the things which I have sealed up; therefore touch them not, in order that you may translate; for that thing is forbidden you, except by and by it shall be wisdom in God.

2 Behold, you may be privileged that you may show the plates to those who shall assist to bring forth this work; and to three shall they be shown by the power of God, wherefore they shall know of a surety that these things are true.

3 And in the mouth of three witnesses shall these things be established; and the testimony of three, and this work in which shall be shown forth the power of God, and also his word, of which the Father, and the Son, and the Holy Ghost beareth record, shall stand as a testimony against the world at the last day.

4 And if it so be that they repent and come to the Father in the name of Jesus, they shall be received into the kingdom of God.

5 Now if I have no authority for these things, judge you, for you shall know that I have authority when you

shall see me, and we shall stand before God at the last day. Amen.

CHAPTER 3

AND now I, Moroni, proceed to give the record of Jared and his brother.

2 For it came to pass after the Lord had prepared the stones which the brother of Jared had carried up into the mount, the brother of Jared came down out of the mount, and he put the stones into the vessels which were prepared, one in each end; and, behold, they gave light to the vessels.

3 Thus the Lord caused stones to shine in darkness to give light to men, women and children, that they might not cross the great waters in darkness.

4 And it came to pass that they had prepared all manner of food, that thereby they might subsist upon the water, and also food for their flocks, and herds, and whatever beast, or animal, or fowl that they should carry with them.

5 When they had done all these things, they got aboard their vessels, or barges, and set forth into the sea, commending themselves to the Lord their God.

6 And it came to pass that the Lord God caused that there should a furious wind blow upon the face of the waters toward the promised land, and thus they were tossed upon the waves of the sea before the wind.

7 They were many times buried in the depths of the sea because of the mountainous waves which broke upon them, and also the great and terrible tempests which were caused by the fierceness of the wind.

8 And when they were buried in the deep, there was no water that could hurt them, their vessels being tight like a dish, and also they were tight like the ark of Noah.

9 Therefore when they were encompassed about by many waters, they cried to the Lord, and he brought them forth again upon the top of the waters.

10 And the wind never ceased to blow toward the promised land while they were upon the waters, and thus

they were driven forth before the wind.

11 And they sang praises to the Lord; and the brother of Jared sang praises to the Lord, and he thanked and praised the Lord all the day long; and when the night came, they did not cease to praise the Lord.

12 Thus they were driven forth; and no monster of the sea could break them, neither whale that could mar them; and they had light continually, whether it was above the water or under the water.

13 And thus they were driven forth three hundred and forty-four days upon the water, and they landed upon the shore of the promised land.

14 And when they had set their feet upon the shores of the promised land, they bowed themselves down upon the face of the land, and humbled themselves before the Lord, and shed tears of joy before the Lord because of the multitude of his tender mercies over them.

15 And it came to pass that they went forth upon the face of the land and began to till the earth.

16 And Jared had four sons; and they were called Jacom, and Gilgah, and Mahah, and Orihah.

17 And the brother of Jared also begot sons and daughters.

18 And the friends of Jared and his brother were in number twenty-two souls, and they also begot sons and daughters before they came to the promised land, and therefore they began to be many.

19 And they were taught to walk humbly before the Lord, and they were also taught from on high.

20 And it came to pass that they began to spread upon the face of the land, and to multiply and to till the earth; and they waxed strong in the land.

21 The brother of Jared began to be old and saw that he must soon go down to the grave; wherefore he said to Jared, "Let us gather together our people that we may number them, that we may know of them what they will desire of us before we go down to our graves."

22 And accordingly the people were gathered together.

23 Now the number of the sons and the daughters of the brother of Jared were twenty-two souls; and the number of the sons and daughters of Jared were twelve, he having four sons.

24 And it came to pass that they numbered their people; and after they had numbered them, they desired of them the things which they would that they should do before they went down to their graves.

25 And the people desired of them that they should anoint one of their sons to be a king over them.

26 Now, behold, this was grievous to them.

27 And the brother of Jared said to them, "Surely, this thing leads into captivity."

28 But Jared said to his brother, "Suffer them that they may have a king"; and therefore he said to them, "Choose from among our sons a king, even whom you will."

29 And they chose the first-born of the brother of Jared, and his name was Pagag.

30 But he refused and would not be their king.

31 And the people would that his father should constrain him, but his father would not; and he commanded them that they should constrain no man to be their king.

32 And it came to pass that they chose all the brothers of Pagag, but they would not.

33 And neither would the sons of Jared, even all save one; and Orihah was anointed to be king over the people.

34 And he began to reign, and the people began to prosper, and they became exceedingly rich.

35 And it came to pass that Jared died, and his brother also.

36 And Orihah walked humbly before the Lord, and remembered what great things the Lord had done for his father, and also taught his people how great were the things the Lord had done for their fathers.

37 And Orihah executed judgment upon the land in righteousness all his days, whose days were exceedingly many.

38 And he begot sons and daughters; he begot thirty-one, among whom were twenty-three sons.

39 He also begot Kib in his old age.

40 And Kib reigned in his stead; and Kib begot Corihor.

41 When Corihor was thirty-two years old, he rebelled against his father and went over and dwelt in the land of Nehor; and he begot sons and daughters, and they became exceedingly fair, wherefore Corihor drew away many people after him.

42 And when he had gathered together an army, he came up to the land of Moron where the king dwelt and took him captive, which brought to pass the saying of the brother of Jared that they would be brought into captivity.

43 Now the land of Moron where the king dwelt was near the land which is called Desolation by the Nephites.

44 And Kib and his people dwelt in captivity under Corihor his son until he became exceedingly old; nevertheless Kib begot Shule in his old age, while he was yet in captivity.

45 And it came to pass that Shule was angry with his brother; and Shule waxed strong and became mighty as to the strength of a man, and he was also mighty in judgment.

46 Wherefore he came to the hill Ephraim, and he smelted ore out of the hill and made swords out of steel for those whom he had drawn away with him; and after he had armed them with swords, he returned to the city Nehor and gave battle to his brother Corihor, by which means he obtained the kingdom and restored it to his father Kib.

47 Now because of the thing which Shule had done, his father bestowed upon him the kingdom; therefore he began to reign in the stead of his father.

48 And he executed judgment in righteousness; and he spread his kingdom upon all the face of the land, for the people had become exceedingly numerous.

49 Shule also begot many sons and daughters.

50 And Corihor repented of the many evils which he had done, wherefore Shule gave him power in his kingdom.

51 And Corihor had many sons and daughters.

52 Among the sons of Corihor there was one whose name was Noah.

53 And it came to pass that Noah rebelled against Shule, the king, and also against his father Corihor, and drew away Cohor his brother, and also all his brethren and many of the people.

54 And he gave battle to Shule the king in which he obtained the land of their first inheritance; and he became a king over that part of the land.

55 And he gave battle again to Shule the king; and he took Shule the king and carried him away captive into Moron.

56 As he was about to put him to death, the sons of Shule crept into the house of Noah by night and slew him, and broke down the door of the prison and brought out their father and placed him upon his throne in his own kingdom; wherefore the son of Noah built up his kingdom in his stead.

57 Nevertheless they did not gain power any more over Shule the king, and the people who were under the reign of Shule the king prospered exceedingly and waxed great.

58 And the country was divided, and there were two kingdoms, the kingdom of Shule and the kingdom of Cohor, the son of Noah.

59 And Cohor, the son of Noah, caused that his people should give battle to Shule, in which Shule beat them, and slew Cohor.

60 Now Cohor had a son who was called Nimrod; and Nimrod gave up the kingdom of Cohor to Shule, and he gained favor in the eyes of Shule; wherefore Shule bestowed great favors upon him, and he did in the kingdom of Shule according to his desires.

61 Also in the reign of Shule there came prophets among the people, who were sent from the Lord, prophesying that the wickedness and idolatry of the people were bringing a curse upon the land, and that they should be destroyed if they did not repent.

62 And it came to pass that the people reviled against the prophets and mocked them.

63 And King Shule executed judg-

ment against all those who reviled against the prophets; and he executed a law throughout all the land which gave power to the prophets that they should go wherever they would, and by this cause the people were brought to repentance.

64 And because the people repented of their iniquities and idolatries, the Lord spared them, and they began to prosper again in the land.

65 And Shule begot sons and daughters in his old age.

66 And there were no more wars in the days of Shule, and he remembered the great things that the Lord had done for his fathers in bringing them across the great deep into the promised land; wherefore he executed judgment in righteousness all his days.

67 And he begot Omer, and Omer reigned in his stead.

68 And Omer begot Jared; and Jared begot sons and daughters.

69 And Jared rebelled against his father and came and dwelt in the land of Heth.

70 And he flattered many people because of his cunning words, until he had gained the half of the kingdom.

71 When he had gained the half of the kingdom, he gave battle to his father, and he carried away his father into captivity and made him serve in captivity.

72 Now in the days of the reign of Omer, he was in captivity the half of his days.

73 And he begot sons and daughters, among whom were Esrom and Coriantumr; and they were exceedingly angry because of the doings of Jared their brother, insomuch that they raised an army and gave battle to Jared.

74 And they gave battle to him by night.

75 And when they had slain the army of Jared, they were about to slay him also; and he pleaded with them that they would not slay him, and he would give up the kingdom to his father.

76 And they granted him his life.

77 Now Jared became exceedingly sorrowful because of the loss of the kingdom, for he had set his heart upon the kingdom and upon the glory of the world.

78 The daughter of Jared, being exceedingly expert and seeing the sorrow of her father, thought to devise a plan whereby she could redeem the kingdom to her father.

79 Now the daughter of Jared was exceedingly fair. And it came to pass that she talked with her father and said to him, "Whereby has my father so much sorrow?

80 "Has he not read the record which our fathers brought across the great deep?

81 "Behold, is there not an account concerning them of old, that they by their secret plans obtained kingdoms and great glory?

82 "And now therefore, let my father send for Akish, the son of Kimnor; and, behold, I am fair, and I will dance before him, and I will please him that he will desire me to wife; wherefore if he shall desire of thee that you shall give me to him to wife, then shall you say, 'I will give her if you will bring to me the head of my father the king.' "

83 Now Omer was a friend to Akish, wherefore when Jared had sent for Akish, the daughter of Jared danced before him, that she pleased him insomuch that he desired her to wife.

84 And he said to Jared, "Give her to me to wife."

85 And Jared said to him, "I will give her to you if you will bring to me the head of my father the king."

86 And it came to pass that Akish gathered in to the house of Jared all his kinfolk and said to them, "Will you swear to me that you will be faithful to me in the thing which I shall desire of you?"

87 They all swore to him by the God of heaven, and also by the heavens, and also by the earth, and by their heads, that whoever should vary from the assistance which Akish desired should lose his head.

88 And whoever should divulge whatever thing Akish made known to them, the same should lose his life. And it came to pass that thus they agreed with Akish.

89 And Akish administered to them the oaths which were given by

them of old, who also sought power which had been handed down even from Cain, who was a murderer from the beginning.

90 And they were kept up by the power of the devil to administer these oaths to the people, to keep them in darkness, to help such as sought power, to gain power, and to murder, and to plunder, and to lie, and to commit all manner of wickedness and whoredoms.

91 And it was the daughter of Jared who put it into his heart to search up these things of old, and Jared put it into the heart of Akish; wherefore Akish administered it to his kindred and friends, leading them away by fair promises to do whatever thing he desired.

92 And it came to pass that they formed a secret combination, even as they of old; which combination is most abominable and wicked above all, in the sight of God.

93 For the Lord works not in secret combinations, neither does he will that man should shed blood, but in all things has forbidden it from the beginning of man.

94 Now I, Moroni, do not write the manner of their oaths and combinations, for it has been made known to me that they are had among all people, and they are had among the Lamanites, and they have caused the destruction of this people of whom I am now speaking, and also the destruction of the people of Nephi.

95 And whatever nation shall uphold such secret combinations to get power and gain, until they shall spread over the nation, behold, they shall be destroyed, for the Lord will not suffer that the blood of his saints, which shall be shed by them, shall always cry to him from the ground for vengeance upon them, and yet he avenge them not.

96 Wherefore, O Gentiles, it is wisdom in God that these things should be shown to you, that thereby you may repent of your sins, and suffer not that these murderous combinations shall get above you, which are built up to get power and gain, and the work of destruction come upon you.

97 Even the sword of the justice of the eternal God shall fall upon you to your overthrow and destruction if you shall suffer these things to be.

98 Wherefore the Lord commands you, when you shall see these things come among you, that you shall awake to a sense of your awful situation because of this secret combination which shall be among you, or woe be to it because of the blood of them who have been slain; for they cry from the dust for vengeance upon it, and also upon those who build it up.

99 For it will come to pass that whoever builds it will seek to overthrow the freedom of all lands, nations and countries.

100 And it will bring to pass the destruction of all people, for it is built up by the devil, who is the father of all lies, even that same liar who beguiled our first parents; [101]even that same liar who has caused man to commit murder from the beginning, who has hardened the hearts of men that they have murdered the prophets, and stoned them, and cast them out from the beginning.

102 Wherefore I, Moroni, am commanded to write these things that evil may be done away, and that the time may come that Satan may have no power upon the hearts of the children of men, but that they may be persuaded to do good continually, that they may come to the fountain of all righteousness and be saved.

CHAPTER 4

NOW I, Moroni, proceed with my record.

2 Therefore it came to pass that because of the secret combinations of Akish and his friends, behold, they overthrew the kingdom of Omer; nevertheless the Lord was merciful to Omer, and also to his sons and to his daughters who did not seek his destruction.

3 And the Lord warned Omer in a dream that he should depart out of the land; wherefore Omer departed out of the land with his family, and traveled many days, and came over and passed by the hill of Shim, [4]and came over by the place where the

Nephites were destroyed, and thence eastward, and came to a place which was called Ablom, by the seashore, and there he pitched his tent, as also did his sons, and his daughters, and all his household, save Jared and his family.

5 And it came to pass that Jared was anointed king over the people by the hand of wickedness, and he gave to Akish his daughter to wife.

6 And it came to pass that Akish sought the life of his father-in-law, and he applied to those whom he had sworn by the oath of the ancients, and they obtained the head of his father-in-law as he sat upon his throne giving audience to his people.

7 For so great had been the spreading of this wicked and secret society that it had corrupted the hearts of all the people; therefore Jared was murdered upon his throne, and Akish reigned in his stead.

8 And Akish began to be jealous of his son, therefore he shut him up in prison and kept him upon little or no food until he had suffered death.

9 Now the brother of him that suffered death (and his name was Nimrah) was angry with his father because of that which his father had done to his brother.

10 And it came to pass that Nimrah gathered together a small number of men, and fled out of the land, and came over and dwelt with Omer.

11 And Akish begot other sons, and they won the hearts of the people, notwithstanding they had sworn to him to do all manner of iniquity according to that which he desired.

12 Now the people of Akish were desirous for gain, even as Akish was desirous for power; wherefore the sons of Akish offered them money, by which means they drew away the greater part of the people after them.

13 And there began to be a war between the sons of Akish and Akish, which lasted for the space of many years, even to the destruction of nearly all the people of the kingdom; 14even all, save thirty souls and they who fled with the house of Omer; wherefore Omer was restored again to the land of his inheritance.

15 And Omer began to be old; nevertheless, in his old age he begot Emer, and he anointed Emer to be king to reign in his stead.

16 After that he had anointed Emer to be king, he saw peace in the land for the space of two years, and he died, having seen exceedingly many days which were full of sorrow.

17 And Emer reigned in his stead and filled the steps of his father.

18 And the Lord began again to take the curse from the land, and the house of Emer prospered exceedingly under the reign of Emer.

19 And in the space of sixty-two years, they had become exceedingly strong, insomuch that they became exceedingly rich, having all manner of fruit, and of grain, and of silks, and of fine linen, and of gold, and of silver, and of precious things, 20and also all manner of cattle, of oxen and cows, and of sheep, and of swine, and of goats, and also many other kinds of animals which were useful for the food of man.

21 They also had horses and asses, and there were elephants, and cureloms, and cumoms, all of which were useful to man, and more especially the elephants, and cureloms, and cumoms.

22 Thus the Lord poured out his blessings upon this land, which was choice above all other lands; and he commanded that those who should possess the land should possess it unto the Lord, or they should be destroyed when they were ripened in iniquity; for upon such, says the Lord, "I will pour out the fullness of my wrath."

23 And Emer executed judgment in righteousness all his days, and he begot many sons and daughters; and he begot Coriantum, and he anointed Coriantum to reign in his stead.

24 After he had anointed Coriantum to reign in his stead, he lived four years, and he saw peace in the land; and he even saw the Son of righteousness, and rejoiced and gloried in his day; and he died in peace.

25 And Coriantum walked in the steps of his father, and built many mighty cities, and administered that which was good to his people in all his days.

26 And he had no children, even until he was exceedingly old.

27 And his wife died, being a hundred and two years old.

28 And it came to pass that Coriantum took to wife in his old age a young maid, and begot sons and daughters; wherefore he lived until he was a hundred and forty-two years old.

29 And he begot Com, and Com reigned in his stead; and he reigned forty-nine years, and he begot Heth; and he also begot other sons and daughters.

30 The people had spread again over all the face of the land, and there began again to be an exceedingly great wickedness upon the face of the land, and Heth began to embrace the secret plans again of old, to destroy his father.

31 And it came to pass that he dethroned his father; for he slew him with his own sword, and he reigned in his stead.

32 And there came prophets in the land again, crying repentance to them; that they must prepare the way of the Lord, or there should come a curse upon the face of the land; even there should be a great famine in which they should be destroyed if they did not repent.

33 But the people believed not the words of the prophets, but they cast them out; and some of them they cast into pits and left them to perish.

34 And they did all these things according to the commandment of the king Heth.

35 And there began to be a great drought upon the land, and the inhabitants began to be destroyed exceedingly fast because of the drought, for there was no rain upon the face of the earth; and there came forth poisonous serpents also upon the face of the land and poisoned many people.

36 And their flocks began to flee before the poisonous serpents toward the land southward, which was called Zarahemla by the Nephites.

37 And there were many of them who perished by the way; nevertheless, there were some which fled into the land southward.

38 And it came to pass that the Lord caused the serpents that they should pursue them no more, but that they should hedge up the way that the people could not pass; that whoever should attempt to pass might fall by the poisonous serpents.

39 And the people followed the course of the beasts and devoured the carcasses of them which fell by the way, until they had devoured them all.

40 Now when the people saw that they must perish, they began to repent of their iniquities and to cry to the Lord.

41 And when they had humbled themselves sufficiently before the Lord, he sent rain upon the face of the earth, and the people began to revive again, and there began to be fruit in the north countries and in all the countries round about, 42and the Lord showed forth his power to them in preserving them from famine.

43 And it came to pass that Shez, who was a descendant of Heth (for Heth had perished by the famine, and all his household save Shez), began to build up again a broken people.

44 And Shez remembered the destruction of his fathers, and he built up a righteous kingdom, for he remembered what the Lord had done in bringing Jared and his brother across the deep; and he walked in the ways of the Lord, and he begot sons and daughters.

45 His eldest son, whose name was Shez, rebelled against him; nevertheless, Shez was smitten by the hand of a robber because of his exceeding riches, which brought peace again to his father.

46 And it came to pass that his father built up many cities upon the face of the land, and the people began again to spread over all the face of the land.

47 And Shez lived to an exceedingly old age; and he begot Riplakish, and he died. And Riplakish reigned in his stead.

48 And it came to pass that Riplakish did not do that which was right in the sight of the Lord, for he had many wives and concubines, and laid that upon men's shoulders which was grievous to be borne; he taxed them with heavy taxes, and with the taxes he built many spacious buildings.

49 And he erected for himself an exceedingly beautiful throne; and he built many prisons, and whoever would not be subject to taxes, he cast into prison; and whoever was not able to pay taxes, he cast into prison.

50 And he caused that they should labor continually for their support; and whoever refused to labor, he caused to be put to death; wherefore he obtained all his fine work, even his fine gold he caused to be refined in prison, and all manner of fine workmanship he caused to be wrought in prison.

51 He afflicted the people with his whoredoms and abominations; and when he had reigned for the space of forty-two years, the people raised up in rebellion against him, and there began to be war again in the land, insomuch that Riplakish was killed and his descendants were driven out of the land.

52 And after the space of many years, Morianton (he being a descendant of Riplakish) gathered together an army of outcasts, and went forth and gave battle to the people; and he gained power over many cities.

53 And the war became exceedingly sore, and lasted for the space of many years, and he gained power over all the land and established himself king over all the land.

54 After he had established himself king, he eased the burden of the people, by which he gained favor in the eyes of the people, and they anointed him to be their king.

55 And he did justice to the people, but not to himself because of his many whoredoms; wherefore he was cut off from the presence of the Lord.

56 And it came to pass that Morianton built up many cities, and the people became exceedingly rich under his reign, in buildings, and in gold, and in silver, and in raising grain, and in flocks, and herds, and such things which had been restored to them.

57 And Morianton lived to an exceedingly great age, and then he begot Kim; and Kim reigned in the stead of his father; and he reigned eight years, and his father died.

58 And it came to pass that Kim did not reign in righteousness, wherefore he was not favored of the Lord.

59 And his brother raised up in rebellion against him, by which the brother brought him into captivity; and he remained in captivity all his days; and he begot sons and daughters in captivity; and in his old age he begot Levi, and he died.

60 And Levi served in captivity after the death of his father for the space of forty-two years.

61 And he made war against the king of the land by which he obtained to himself the kingdom.

62 After he had obtained to himself the kingdom, he did that which was right in the sight of the Lord; and the people prospered in the land, and he lived to a good old age and begot sons and daughters; and he also begot Corom, whom he anointed king in his stead.

63 And Corom did that which was good in the sight of the Lord all his days; and he begot many sons and daughters; and after he had seen many days, he passed away, even like the rest of the earth; and Kish reigned in his stead.

64 And it came to pass that Kish passed away also, and Lib reigned in his stead.

65 And Lib also did that which was good in the sight of the Lord.

66 In the days of Lib the poisonous serpents were destroyed; wherefore they went into the land southward to hunt food for the people of the land; for the land was covered with animals of the forest.

67 And Lib also himself became a great hunter.

68 And the people built a great city by the narrow neck of land, by the place where the sea divides the land.

69 And they preserved the land southward for a wilderness to get game.

70 The whole face of the land northward was covered with inhabitants; and they were exceedingly industrious, and they bought and sold, and trafficked one with another that they might get gain.

71 They worked in all manner of ore, and they made gold, and silver, and iron, and brass, and all manner of metals; and they dug it out of the

earth; wherefore they cast up mighty heaps of earth to get ore, of gold, and of silver, and of iron, and of copper.

72 And they worked all manner of fine work.

73 They had silks and fine twined linen; and they worked all manner of cloth that they might clothe themselves from their nakedness.

74 They made all manner of tools to till the earth, to plow and to sow, to reap and to hoe, and also to thresh.

75 And they made all manner of tools with which they worked their beasts.

76 And they made all manner of weapons of war.

77 And they worked all manner of work of exceedingly curious workmanship.

78 Never could be a people more blessed than were they, and more prospered by the hand of the Lord.

79 And they were in a land that was choice above all lands, for the Lord had spoken it.

80 And Lib lived many years and begot sons and daughters; and he also begot Hearthom.

81 And Hearthom reigned in the stead of his father.

82 When Hearthom had reigned twenty-four years, behold, the kingdom was taken away from him; 83and he served many years in captivity, even all the remainder of his days.

84 And he begot Heth, and Heth lived in captivity all his days.

85 And Heth begot Aaron, and Aaron dwelt in captivity all his days; and he begot Amnigaddah, and Amnigaddah also dwelt in captivity all his days; and he begot Coriantum, and Coriantum dwelt in captivity all his days; and he begot Com.

86 And it came to pass that Com drew away the half of the kingdom.

87 And he reigned over the half of the kingdom forty-two years; and he went to battle against the king Amgid, and they fought for the space of many years, during which time Com gained power over Amgid and obtained power over the remainder of the kingdom.

88 And in the days of Com there began to be robbers in the land; and they adopted the old plans, and administered oaths after the manner of the ancients, and sought again to destroy the kingdom.

89 Now Com fought much against them; nevertheless he did not prevail against them.

90 There came also in the days of Com many prophets who prophesied of the destruction of that great people, except they should repent and turn to the Lord and forsake their murders and wickedness.

91 And it came to pass that the prophets were rejected by the people, and they fled to Com for protection, for the people sought to destroy them; and they prophesied to Com many things; and he was blessed all the remainder of his days.

92 And he lived to a good old age and begot Shiblom; and Shiblom reigned in his stead.

93 And the brother of Shiblom rebelled against him; and there began to be an exceedingly great war in all the land.

94 And it came to pass that the brother of Shiblom caused that all the prophets who prophesied of the destruction of the people should be put to death.

95 And there was great calamity in all the land, for they had testified that a greater curse should come upon the land, and also upon the people, and that there should be a great destruction among them, such a one as never had been upon the face of the earth; 96and their bones should become as heaps of earth upon the face of the land, except they should repent of their wickedness.

97 But they hearkened not to the voice of the Lord because of their wicked combinations; wherefore there began to be wars and contentions in all the land, and also many famines and pestilences, insomuch that there was a great destruction, such a one as never had been known upon the face of the earth, and all this came to pass in the days of Shiblom.

98 And the people began to repent of their iniquity; and inasmuch as they did, the Lord had mercy on them.

99 And it came to pass that Shiblom was slain, and Seth was brought into captivity and dwelt in captivity all his days.

100 And Ahab, his son, obtained the kingdom; and he reigned over the people all his days.

101 And he did all manner of iniquity in his days, by which he caused the shedding of much blood; and few were his days.

102 And Ethem, being a descendant of Ahah, obtained the kingdom; and he also did that which was wicked in his days.

103 And in the days of Ethem, there came many prophets who prophesied again to the people; they prophesied that the Lord would utterly destroy them from the face of the earth, except they repented of their iniquities.

104 But the people hardened their hearts, and would not hearken to their words; and the prophets mourned and withdrew from among the people.

105 And Ethem executed judgment in wickedness all his days; and he begot Moron; 106and Moron reigned in his stead; and Moron did that which was wicked before the Lord.

107 And there arose a rebellion among the people because of that secret combination which was built up to get power and gain; and there arose a mighty man among them in iniquity who gave battle to Moron, in which he overthrew the half of the kingdom; and he maintained the half of the kingdom for many years.

108 And it came to pass that Moron overthrew him and obtained the kingdom again.

109 And it came to pass that there arose another mighty man; and he was a descendant of the brother of Jared.

110 And he overthrew Moron and obtained the kingdom; wherefore Moron dwelt in captivity all the remainder of his days; and he begot Coriantor.

111 And Coriantor dwelt in captivity all his days.

112 In the days of Coriantor there also came many prophets who prophesied of great and marvelous things and cried repentance to the people, and that except they should repent, the Lord God would execute judgment against them to their utter de-

struction, 113 and would send or bring forth another people to possess the land by his power, after the manner which he brought their fathers.

114 And they rejected all the words of the prophets because of their secret society and wicked abominations.

115 And Coriantor begot Ether, and he died, having dwelt in captivity all his days.

CHAPTER 5

THE days of Ether were in the days of Coriantumr; and Coriantumr was king over all the land.

2 And Ether was a prophet of the Lord; wherefore Ether came forth in the days of Coriantumr and began to prophesy to the people, for he could not be restrained because of the Spirit of the Lord which was in him.

3 For he cried from the morning until the going down of the sun, exhorting the people to believe in God unto repentance lest they should be destroyed, saying to them that by faith all things are fulfilled.

4 Wherefore, whoever believes in God may with surety hope for a better world, even a place at the right hand of God, which hope comes of faith and makes an anchor to the souls of men which would make them sure and steadfast, always abounding in good works, being led to glorify God.

5 And it came to pass that Ether prophesied great and marvelous things to the people which they did not believe because they saw them not.

6 Now I, Moroni, would speak somewhat concerning these things; I would show to the world that faith is things which are hoped for and not seen.

7 Wherefore, dispute not because you see not, for you receive no witness until after the trial of your faith, for it was by faith that Christ showed himself to our fathers, after he had risen from the dead.

8 And he showed not himself to them until after they had faith in him; wherefore, it must be that some had faith in him, for he showed himself not to the world.

9 But because of the faith of men, he has shown himself to the world,

and glorified the name of the Father, and prepared a way that thereby others might be partakers of the heavenly gift, that they might hope for those things which they have not seen.

10 Wherefore you may also have hope and be partakers of the gift, if you will but have faith.

11 Behold, it was by faith that they of old were called after the holy order of God; wherefore, by faith was the law of Moses given.

12 But in the gift of his Son has God prepared a more excellent way, and it is by faith that it has been fulfilled.

13 For if there be no faith among the children of men, God can do no miracle among them; wherefore he showed not himself until after their faith.

14 Behold, it was the faith of Alma and Amulek that caused the prison to tumble to the earth.

15 Behold, it was the faith of Nephi and Lehi that wrought the change upon the Lamanites, that they were baptized with fire and with the Holy Ghost.

16 Behold, it was the faith of Ammon and his brethren which wrought so great a miracle among the Lamanites; and even all they who wrought miracles wrought them by faith, even those who were before Christ, and also them who were after.

17 And it was by faith that the three disciples obtained a promise that they should not taste of death, and they obtained not the promise until after their faith.

18 Neither at any time have any wrought miracles until after their faith; wherefore they first believed in the Son of God.

19 And there were many whose faith was so exceedingly strong even before Christ came that they could not be kept from within the veil, but truly saw with their eyes the things which they had beheld with an eye of faith, and they were glad.

20 Behold, we have seen in this record that one of these was the brother of Jared; for so great was his faith in God that when God put forth his finger, he could not hide it from the sight of the brother of Jared, because of his word which he had

spoken to him, which word he had obtained by faith.

21 And after the brother of Jared had beheld the finger of the Lord, because of the promise which the brother of Jared had obtained by faith, the Lord could not withhold anything from his sight; wherefore he showed him all things, for he could no longer be kept without the veil.

22 And it is by faith that my fathers have obtained the promise that these things should come to their brethren through the Gentiles; therefore the Lord has commanded me, even Jesus Christ.

23 And I said to him, "Lord, the Gentiles will mock at these things because of our weakness in writing; for, Lord, thou hast made us mighty in word by faith, but thou hast not made us mighty in writing.

24 "For thou hast made all this people that they could speak much because of the Holy Ghost which thou hast given them; and thou hast made us that we could write but little because of the awkwardness of our hands.

25 "Behold, thou hast not made us mighty in writing like the brother of Jared, for thou madest him that the things which he wrote were mighty, even as thou art, to the overpowering of man to read them.

26 "Thou hast also made our words powerful and great, even that we cannot write them; wherefore, when we write, we behold our weakness and stumble because of the placing of our words; and I fear lest the Gentiles shall mock at our words."

27 And when I had said this, the Lord spoke to me, saying, "Fools mock, but they shall mourn; and my grace is sufficient for the meek that they shall take no advantage of your weakness; and if men come to me, I will show them their weakness.

28 "I give to men weakness that they may be humble; and my grace is sufficient for all men that humble themselves before me; for if they humble themselves before me and have faith in me, then will I make weak things become strong to them.

29 "Behold, I will show the Gen-

tiles their weakness, and I will show them that faith, hope, and charity bringeth unto me, the fountain of all righteousness."

30 And I, Moroni, having heard these words, was comforted, and said, "O Lord, thy righteous will be done, for I know that thou workest to the children of men according to their faith; for the brother of Jared said to the mountain Zerin, 'Remove,' and it was removed.

31 "And if he had not had faith, it would not have moved; wherefore thou workest after men have faith; for thus didst thou manifest thyself to thy disciples.

32 "For after they had faith and spoke in thy name, thou didst show thyself to them in great power; and I also remember that thou hast said that thou hast prepared a house for man, even among the mansions of thy Father, in which man might have a more excellent hope; wherefore man must hope, or he cannot receive an inheritance in the place which thou hast prepared.

33 "And again I remember that thou hast said that thou hast loved the world, even unto the laying down of thy life for the world, that thou mightest take it again to prepare a place for the children of men.

34 "Now I know that this love which thou hast had for the children of men is charity; wherefore, except men shall have charity, they cannot inherit that place which thou hast prepared in the mansions of thy Father.

35 "Wherefore, I know by this thing which thou hast said that if the Gentiles have not charity, because of our weakness, thou wilt prove them and take away their talent, even that which they have received, and give to them who shall have more abundantly."

36 And it came to pass that I prayed to the Lord that he would give the Gentiles grace that they might have charity.

37 And the Lord said to me, "If they have not charity, it mattereth not to thee, thou hast been faithful; wherefore thy garments shall be made clean.

38 "And because thou hast seen thy weakness, thou shalt be made strong, even to the sitting down in the place which I have prepared in the mansions of my Father."

39 Now I, Moroni, bid farewell to the Gentiles, and also to my brethren whom I love, until we shall meet before the judgment seat of Christ where all men shall know that my garments are not spotted with your blood.

40 Then shall you know that I have seen Jesus, and that he has talked with me face to face, and that he told me in plain humility, even as a man tells another in his own language, concerning these things; and only a few have I written because of my weakness in writing.

41 Now I would commend you to seek this Jesus of whom the prophets and apostles have written, that the grace of God the Father, and also the Lord Jesus Christ, and the Holy Ghost, which bears record of them, may be and abide in you forever. Amen.

CHAPTER 6

NOW I, Moroni, proceed to finish my record concerning the destruction of the people of whom I have been writing.

2 For, behold, they rejected all the words of Ether; for he truly told them of all things from the beginning of man, and that after the waters had receded from off the face of this land, it became a choice land above all other lands, a chosen land of the Lord; 3wherefore the Lord would have all men serve him who dwell upon the face thereof; and that it was the place of the New Jerusalem, which should come down out of heaven, and the holy sanctuary of the Lord.

4 Behold, Ether saw the days of Christ, and he spoke concerning a new Jerusalem upon this land; and he spoke also concerning the house of Israel and the Jerusalem from whence Lehi should come; after it should be destroyed, it should be built up again a holy city unto the Lord; 5wherefore it could not be a New Jerusalem, for it had been in a time of old, but it should be built up

again and become a holy city of the Lord; and it should be built up to the house of Israel; ⁶and that a New Jerusalem should be built upon this land to the remnant of the seed of Joseph, for which things there has been a type; for as Joseph brought his father down into the land of Egypt, even so he died there; ⁷wherefore the Lord brought a remnant of the seed of Joseph out of the land of Jerusalem that he might be merciful to the seed of Joseph, that they should perish not, even as he was merciful to the father of Joseph that he should perish not.

8 Wherefore the remnant of the house of Joseph shall be built upon this land, and it shall be a land of their inheritance; and they shall build up a holy city to the Lord, like the Jerusalem of old; and they shall no more be confounded until the end come when the earth shall pass away.

9 And there shall be a new heaven and a new earth; and they shall be like the old, save the old have passed away, and all things have become new.

10 Then will come the New Jerusalem; and blessed are they who dwell therein, for it is they whose garments are white through the blood of the lamb; and they are they who are numbered among the remnant of the seed of Joseph who were of the house of Israel.

11 And then also will come the Jerusalem of old; and the inhabitants thereof, blessed are they, for they have been washed in the blood of the Lamb.

12 And they are they who were scattered and gathered in from the four quarters of the earth and from the north countries, and are partakers of the fulfilling of the covenant which God made with their father Abraham.

13 When these things come, it will bring to pass the scripture which says "There are they who were first, who shall be last; and there are they who were last, who shall be first."

14 I was about to write more, but I am forbidden. Great and marvelous were the prophecies of Ether, but they esteemed him as

nought and cast him out, and he hid himself in the cavity of a rock by day, and by night he went forth viewing the things which should come upon the people.

15 And as he dwelt in the cavity of a rock, he made the remainder of this record, viewing by night the destructions which came upon the people.

16 In that same year which he was cast out from among the people, there began to be a great war among the people, for there were many mighty men who rose up and sought to destroy Coriantumr by their secret plans of wickedness, of which has been spoken.

17 And now Coriantumr, having studied all the arts of war and all the cunning of the world, therefore he gave battle to them who sought to destroy him.

18 But he repented not, neither did his fair sons nor daughters, neither the fair sons and daughters of Cohor, neither the fair sons and daughters of Corihor; and in fine, there were none of the fair sons and daughters upon the face of the whole earth who repented of their sins.

19 Wherefore it came to pass that in the first year that Ether dwelt in the cavity of a rock, there were many people who were slain by the sword of those secret combinations fighting against Coriantumr that they might obtain the kingdom.

20 And it came to pass that the sons of Coriantumr fought much and bled much.

21 In the second year, the word of the Lord came to Ether that he should go and prophesy to Coriantumr that if he and all his household would repent, the Lord would give him his kingdom and spare the people.

22 Otherwise they should be destroyed and all his household, save himself, and he should only live to see the fulfilling of the propechies which had been spoken concerning another people receiving the land for their inheritance; ²³and Coriantumr should receive a burial by them; and every soul should be destroyed save Coriantumr.

24 But Coriantumr repented not,

neither his household, neither the people; and the wars ceased not; and they sought to kill Ether, but he fled from before them and hid again in the cavity of the rock.

25 And it came to pass that there arose Shared, and he also gave battle to Coriantumr; and he beat him, insomuch that in the third year he brought him into captivity.

26 And the sons of Coriantumr in the fourth year beat Shared and obtained the kingdom again to their father.

27 Now there began to be a war upon all the face of the land, every man with his band fighting for that which he desired.

28 And there were robbers, and in fine, all manner of wickedness upon all the face of the land.

29 And it came to pass that Coriantumr was exceedingly angry with Shared, and he went against him with his armies to battle, and they met in great anger in the valley of Gilgal; and the battle became exceedingly sore.

30 And Shared fought against him for the space of three days; ³¹and Coriantumr beat him and pursued him until he came to the plains of Heshlon.

32 And Shared gave him battle again upon the plains; and, behold, he beat Coriantumr and drove him back again to the valley of Gilgal.

33 And Coriantumr gave Shared battle again in the valley of Gilgal, in which he beat Shared and slew him.

34 And Shared wounded Coriantumr in his thigh so that he did not go to battle again for the space of two years, in which time all the people upon all the face of the land were shedding blood, and there was none to restrain them.

35 Now there began to be a great curse upon the land because of the iniquity of the people, in which, if a man should lay his tool or his sword upon the shelf, or upon the place where he would keep it, behold, upon the morrow, he could not find it, so great was the curse upon the land.

36 Wherefore every man cleaved to that which was his own with his hands and would not borrow, neither

would he lend; and every man kept the hilt of his sword in his right hand in the defense of his property, and his own life and that of his wives and children.

37 After the space of two years and after the death of Shared, behold, there arose the brother of Shared, and he gave battle to Coriantumr, in which Coriantumr beat him and pursued him to the wilderness of Akish.

38 And the brother of Shared gave battle to him in the wilderness of Akish; and the battle became exceedingly sore, and many thousands fell by the sword.

39 And it came to pass that Coriantumr laid siege to the wilderness, and the brother of Shared marched forth out of the wilderness by night and slew a part of the army of Coriantumr as they were drunken.

40 And he came forth to the land of Moron and placed himself upon the throne of Coriantumr.

41 And Coriantumr dwelt with his army in the wilderness for the space of two years, in which he received great strength to his army.

42 Now the brother of Shared, whose name was Gilead, also received great strength to his army because of secret combinations.

43 And it came to pass that his high priest murdered him as he sat upon his throne.

44 And one of the secret combinations murdered him (the high priest) in a secret pass and obtained for himself the kingdom, and his name was Lib; and Lib was a man of great stature, more than any other man among all the people.

45 In the first year of Lib, Coriantumr came up to the land of Moron and gave battle to Lib.

46 And he fought with Lib, in which Lib smote upon his arm that he was wounded; nevertheless, the army of Coriantumr pressed forward upon Lib, that he fled to the borders upon the seashore.

47 And Coriantumr pursued him; and Lib gave battle to him upon the seashore.

48 And Lib smote the army of Coriantumr, that they fled again to the wilderness of Akish.

49 And Lib pursued him until he came to the plains of Agosh.

50 Coriantumr had taken all the people with him, as he fled before Lib, to that quarter of the land where he fled.

51 And when he had come to the plains of Agosh, he gave battle to Lib, and he smote upon him until he died; nevertheless, the brother of Lib came against Coriantumr in his stead and the battle became exceedingly sore, in which Coriantumr fled again before the army of the brother of Lib.

52 Now the name of the brother of Lib was Shiz.

53 And Shiz pursued Coriantumr, and he overthrew many cities, and he slew both women and children, and he burned the cities thereof.

54 And there went a fear of Shiz throughout all the land; and a cry went forth throughout the land, "Who can stand before the army of Shiz? Behold, he sweeps the earth before him!"

55 And the people began to flock together in armies throughout all the face of the land.

56 But they were divided, and a part of them fled to the army of Shiz, and a part of them fled to the army of Coriantumr.

57 So great and lasting had been the war, and so long had been the scene of bloodshed and carnage, that the whole face of the land was covered with the bodies of the dead.

58 And so swift and speedy was the war that there were none left to bury the dead, but they marched forth from the shedding of blood to the shedding of blood, leaving the bodies of men, women, and children strewed upon the face of the land to become a prey to the worms of the flesh.

59 And the scent went forth upon the face of the land, even upon all the face of the land; wherefore the people became troubled by day and by night because of the scent.

60 Nevertheless, Shiz did not cease to pursue Coriantumr, for he had sworn to avenge himself upon Coriantumr of the blood of his brother who had been slain, and the word of the Lord came to Ether that Coriantumr should not fall by the sword.

61 Thus we see that the Lord visited them in the fullness of his wrath, and their wickedness and abominations had prepared a way for their everlasting destruction.

62 And it came to pass that Shiz pursued Coriantumr eastward, even to the borders of the seashore, and there he gave battle to Shiz for the space of three days.

63 And so terrible was the destruction among the armies of Shiz that the people began to be frightened and began to flee before the armies of Coriantumr.

64 They fled to the land of Corihor and swept off the inhabitants before them, all they that would not join them; and they pitched their tents in the valley of Corihor.

65 And Coriantumr pitched his tents in the valley of Shurr.

66 Now the valley of Shurr was near the hill Comnor; wherefore Coriantumr gathered his armies together upon the hill Comnor and sounded a trumpet to the armies of Shiz to invite them forth to battle.

67 And they came forth, but were driven again; and they came the second time, and they were driven again the second time.

68 They came again the third time, and the battle became exceedingly sore.

69 And Shiz smote upon Coriantumr that he gave him many deep wounds.

70 And Coriantumr, having lost his blood, fainted and was carried away as though he were dead.

71 Now the loss of men, women, and children on both sides was so great that Shiz commanded his people that they should not pursue the armies of Coriantumr; wherefore they returned to their camp.

72 When Coriantumr had recovered of his wounds, he began to remember the words which Ether had spoken to him.

73 He saw that there had been slain by the sword already nearly two millions of his people, and he began to sorrow in his heart; for there had been slain two millions of mighty men, and also their wives and their children.

74 He began to repent of the evil

which he had done; he began to remember the words which had been spoken by the mouth of all the prophets, and he saw them that they were fulfilled thus far, every whit, and his soul mourned and refused to be comforted.

75 And it came to pass that he wrote an epistle to Shiz, desiring him that he would spare the people, and he would give up the kingdom for the sake of the lives of the people.

76 When Shiz had received his epistle, he wrote an epistle to Coriantumr that if he would give himself up, that Shiz might slay him with his own sword, he would spare the lives of the people.

77 But the people repented not of their iniquity; and the people of Coriantumr were stirred up to anger against the people of Shiz.

78 And the people of Shiz were stirred up to anger against the people of Coriantumr; wherefore the people of Shiz gave battle to the people of Coriantumr.

79 When Coriantumr saw that he was about to fall, he fled again before the people of Shiz.

80 And he came to the waters of Ripliancum, which, by interpretation, is large, or to exceed all; wherefore, when they came to these waters, they pitched their tents; and Shiz also pitched his tents near them; and on the morrow they came to battle.

81 They fought an exceedingly sore battle, in which Coriantumr was wounded again, and he fainted from the loss of blood.

82 And the armies of Coriantumr pressed upon the armies of Shiz, that they beat them, and caused them to flee before them; and they fled southward and pitched their tents in a place which was called Ogath.

83 And the army of Coriantumr pitched their tents by the hill Ramah, and it was that same hill where my father Mormon hid up to the Lord the records which were sacred.

84 And they gathered together all the people upon all the face of the land who had not been slain, save it was Ether.

85 And it came to pass that Ether beheld all the doings of the people; and he beheld that the people who were for Coriantumr were gathered into the army of Coriantumr; and the people who were for Shiz were gathered into the army of Shiz.

86 Wherefore they were for the space of four years gathering together the people that they might get all who were upon the face of the land and that they might receive all the strength which it was possible that they could receive.

87 And it came to pass that when they were all gathered together, every one to the army which he would, with their wives and their children (men, women, and children being armed with weapons of war, having shields, and breastplates, and head-plates, and being clothed after the manner of war), they marched forth one against another to battle; and they fought all that day and conquered not.

88 When it was night, they were weary and retired to their camps; and after they had retired to their camps, they took up a howling and a lamentation for the loss of the slain of their people; and so great were their cries, their howlings and lamentations, that it rent the air exceedingly.

89 And on the morrow they went again to battle, and great and terrible was that day.

90 Nevertheless they conquered not, and when the night came again, they rent the air with their cries, and their howlings, and their mournings for the loss of the slain of their people.

91 And Coriantumr wrote again an epistle to Shiz desiring that he would not come again to battle, but that he would take the kingdom, and spare the lives of the people.

92 But, behold, the Spirit of the Lord had ceased striving with them, and Satan had full power over the hearts of the people, for they were given up to the hardness of their hearts and the blindness of their minds, that they might be destroyed; wherefore they went again to battle.

93 And they fought all that day; and when the night came, they slept upon their swords; and on the morrow they fought even until the night came.

94 And when the night came, they were drunken with anger, even as a

man who is drunken with wine; and they slept again upon their swords; and on the morrow they fought again.

95 And when the night came, they had all fallen by the sword save fifty-two of the people of Coriantumr and sixty-nine of the people of Shiz.

96 They slept upon their swords that night, and on the morrow they fought again, and they contended in their mights with their swords and with their shields all that day.

97 And when the night came, there were thirty-two of the people of Shiz and twenty-seven of the people of Coriantumr.

98 And they ate and slept, and prepared for death on the morrow.

99 And they were large and mighty men, as to the strength of men.

100 On the morrow they fought for the space of three hours, and they fainted with the loss of blood.

101 And when the men of Coriantumr had received sufficient strength that they could walk, they were about to flee for their lives, but, behold, Shiz arose, and also his men, and he swore in his wrath that he would slay Coriantumr, or he would perish by the sword.

102 Wherefore he pursued them, and on the morrow he overtook them; and they fought again with the sword.

103 And it came to pass that they all fell by the sword save Coriantumr and Shiz, and, behold, Shiz had fainted with the loss of blood.

104 When Coriantumr had leaned upon his sword that he rested a little he smote off the head of Shiz.

105 And after he smote off the head of Shiz, Shiz raised upon his hands and fell; and after he had struggled for breath, he died.

106 And Coriantumr fell to the earth and became as if he had no life.

107 And the Lord spoke to Ether and said to him, "Go forth."

108 And he went forth and beheld that the words of the Lord had all been fulfilled; and he finished his records (and the hundredth part I have not written), and he hid them in a manner that the people of Limhi found them.

109 Now the last words which are written by Ether are these: "Whether the Lord will that I be translated, or that I suffer the will of the Lord in the flesh, it matters not, if it so be that I am saved in the kingdom of God. Amen."

THE BOOK OF MORONI

CHAPTER 1

NOW I, Moroni, after having made an end of abridging the account of the people of Jared, had supposed not to write more; but I have not as yet perished, and I make not myself known to the Lamanites, lest they should destroy me.

2 For, behold, their wars are exceedingly fierce among themselves; and because of their hatred, they put to death every Nephite that will not deny the Christ.

3 And I, Moroni, will not deny the Christ; wherefore, I wander wherever I can for the safety of my own life.

4 Wherefore I write a few more things, contrary to that which I had supposed; for I had supposed not to write any more; but I write a few more things that perhaps they may be of worth to my brethren the Lamanites in some future day according to the will of the Lord.

CHAPTER 2

THE words of Christ, which he spoke to his disciples, the twelve whom he had chosen, as he laid his hands upon them:

2 He called them by name, saying,

"Ye shall call on the Father in my name in mighty prayer; and after ye have done this, ye shall have power that on him whom ye shall lay your hands, ye shall give the Holy Ghost; and in my name shall ye give it, for thus do mine apostles."

3 Now Christ spoke these words to them at the time of his first appearing; and the multitude heard it not, but the disciples heard it, and on as many as they laid their hands fell the Holy Ghost.

CHAPTER 3

THE manner which the disciples, who were called the elders of the church, ordained priests and teachers:

2 After they had prayed to the Father in the name of Christ, they laid their hands upon them, and said, "In the name of Jesus Christ I ordain you to be a priest (or if he be a teacher, I ordain you to be a teacher) to preach repentance and remission of sins through Jesus Christ by the endurance of faith on his name to the end. Amen."

3 And after this manner they ordained priests and teachers, according to the gifts and callings of God to men; and they ordained them by the power of the Holy Ghost, which was in them.

CHAPTER 4

THE manner of their elders and priests administering the flesh and blood of Christ to the church:

2 They administered it according to the commandments of Christ; wherefore we know the manner to be true, and the elder or priest administered it:

3 And they knelt down with the church and prayed to the Father in the name of Christ, saying,

4 "O God, the eternal Father, we ask thee in the name of thy Son Jesus Christ, to bless and sanctify this bread to the souls of all those who partake of it, that they may eat in remembrance of the body of thy Son, and witness unto thee, O God the eternal Father, that they are willing to take upon them the name of thy

Son, and always remember him, and keep his commandments which he has given them, that they may always have his Spirit to be with them. Amen."

CHAPTER 5

THE manner of administering the wine:

2 Behold, they took the cup, and said,

3 "O God, the eternal Father, we ask thee, in the name of thy Son Jesus Christ, to bless and sanctify this wine to the souls of all those who drink of it, that they may do it in remembrance of the blood of thy Son which was shed for them, that they may witness unto thee, O God, the eternal Father, that they do always remember him, that they may have his Spirit to be with them. Amen."

CHAPTER 6

AND now I speak concerning baptism.

2 Behold, elders, priests, and teachers were baptized; and they were not baptized save they brought forth fruit worthy of it, neither did they receive any unto baptism save they came forth with a broken heart and a contrite spirit, and witnessed to the church that they truly repented of all their sins.

3 And none were received unto baptism save they took upon them the name of Christ, having a determination to serve him to the end.

4 After they had been received in baptism, and were wrought upon and cleansed by the power of the Holy Ghost, they were numbered among the people of the church of Christ.

5 And their names were taken that they might be remembered and nourished by the good word of God to keep them in the right way, to keep them continually watchful unto prayer, relying alone upon the merits of Christ who was the author and the finisher of their faith.

6 And the church met together often to fast and to pray, and to speak one with another concerning the welfare of their souls; and they met together often to partake of bread and

wine in remembrance of the Lord Jesus.

7 They were strict to observe that there should be no iniquity among them; and whoever was found to commit iniquity, and three witnesses of the church condemned them before the elders, [8]and if they repented not and confessed not, their names were blotted out, and they were not numbered among the people of Christ; but as often as they repented and sought forgiveness with real intent, they were forgiven.

9 Their meetings were conducted by the church after the manner of the working of the Spirit, and by the power of the Holy Ghost; for as the power of the Holy Ghost led them whether to preach or exhort, or to pray, or to supplicate, or to sing, even so it was done.

CHAPTER 7

NOW I, Moroni, write a few of the words of my father Mormon, which he spoke concerning faith, hope and charity; for after this manner he spoke to the people as he taught them in the synagogue which they had built for the place of worship:

2 "I, Mormon, speak to you, my beloved brethren; and it is by the grace of God, the Father, and our Lord Jesus Christ, and his holy will, because of the gift of his calling to me, that I am permitted to speak to you at this time.

3 "Wherefore I would speak to you that are of the church, that are the peaceable followers of Christ, and that have obtained a sufficient hope by which you can enter into the rest of the Lord from this time henceforth until you shall rest with him in heaven.

4 "And now, my brethren, I judge these things of you because of your peaceable walk with the children of men; for I remember the word of God, which says, 'By their works ye shall know them; for if their works be good, then they are good also.'

5 "For, behold, God has said that a man being evil, cannot do that which is good; for if he offers a gift or prays to God, except he shall do it with real intent, it profits him noth-

ing; [6]for it is not counted to him for righteousness.

7 "For, behold, if a man, being evil, gives a gift, he does it grudgingly; wherefore it is counted to him the same as if he had retained the gift; wherefore he is counted evil before God.

8 "And likewise also is it counted evil to a man if he shall pray without real intent of heart, and it profits him nothing; for God receives none such; wherefore a man, being evil, cannot do that which is good; neither will he give a good gift.

9 "For, behold, a bitter fountain cannot bring forth good water; neither can a good fountain bring forth bitter water; wherefore a man, being a servant of the devil, cannot follow Christ; and if he follow Christ, he cannot be a servant of the devil.

10 "Wherefore, all things which are good come of God; and that which is evil comes of the devil; for the devil is an enemy to God and fights against him continually, and invites and entices to sin and to do that which is evil continually.

11 "But, behold, that which is of God invites and entices to do good continually; wherefore, everything which invites and entices to do good, and to love God, and to serve him is inspired of God.

12 "Wherefore take heed, my beloved brethren, that you do not judge that which is evil to be of God or that which is good and of God to be of the devil.

13 "For, behold, my brethren, it is given to you to judge, that you may know good from evil; and the way to judge is as plain, that you may know with a perfect knowledge, as the daylight is from the dark night.

14 "For the Spirit of Christ is given to every man that he may know good from evil; wherefore I show to you the way to judge: for everything which invites to do good, and persuades to believe in Christ is sent forth by the power and gift of Christ.

15 "Wherefore, you may know with a perfect knowledge it is of God; but whatever persuades men to do evil and believe not in Christ, and to deny him, and serve not God,

then you may know with a perfect knowledge it is of the devil.

16 "For after this manner does the devil work, for he persuades no man to do good, no, not one; neither do his angels; neither do they who subject themselves to him.

17 "And now, my brethren, seeing that you know the light by which you may judge, which light is the light of Christ, see that you do not judge wrongfully; for with that same judgment which you judge, you shall also be judged.

18 "Wherefore I beseech of you, brethren, that you should search diligently in the light of Christ that you may know good from evil; and if you will lay hold upon every good thing and condemn it not, you certainly will be a child of Christ.

19 "And now, my brethren, how is it possible that you can lay hold upon every good thing?

20 "Now I come to that faith of which I said I would speak; and I will tell you the way whereby you may lay hold on every good thing.

21 "For, behold, God, knowing all things, being from everlasting to everlasting, sent angels to minister to the children of men, to make manifest concerning the coming of Christ; and in Christ there should come every good thing.

22 "And God also declared to prophets by his own mouth that Christ should come.

23 "And, behold, there were divers ways that he manifested things to the children of men, which were good; and all things which are good come of Christ, otherwise men were fallen, and there could no good thing come to them.

24 "Wherefore, by the ministering of angels, and by every word which proceeded out of the mouth of God, men began to exercise faith in Christ; and thus by faith they laid hold upon every good thing; and thus it was until the coming of Christ.

25 "And after he came, men also were saved by faith in his name; and by faith they became the sons of God.

26 "And as sure as Christ lives, he spoke these words to our fathers, saying, 'Whatsoever thing ye shall ask the Father in my name, which is good,

in faith believing that ye shall receive, behold, it shall be done to you.'

27 "Wherefore, my beloved brethren, have miracles ceased because Christ has ascended into heaven and has sat down on the right hand of God, to claim of the Father his rights of mercy which he has upon the children of men?

28 "For he has answered the ends of the law, and he claims all those who have faith in him; and they who have faith in him will cleave to every good thing; wherefore he advocates the cause of the children of men; and he dwells eternally in the heavens.

29 "And because he has done this, my beloved brethren, have miracles ceased?

30 "Behold, I say to you, No; neither have angels ceased to minister to the children of men.

31 "For, behold, they are subject to him, to minister according to the word of his command, showing themselves to them of strong faith and a firm mind in every form of godliness.

32 "And the office of their ministry is to call men to repentance, and to fulfill and to do the work of the covenants of the Father which he has made to the children of men, to prepare the way among the children of men by declaring the word of Christ to the chosen vessels of the Lord, that they may bear testimony of him.

33 "And by so doing, the Lord God prepares the way that the residue of men may have faith in Christ, that the Holy Ghost may have place in their hearts according to the power thereof.

34 "And after this manner the Father brings to pass the covenants which he has made to the children of men.

35 "And Christ has said, 'If ye will have faith in me, ye shall have power to do whatever thing is expedient in me.'

36 "And he has said, 'Repent, all ye ends of the earth, and come to me, and be baptized in my name, and have faith in me, that ye may be saved.'

37 "Now, my beloved brethren, if

this be the case that these things are true which I have spoken to you, and God will show you with power and great glory at the last day that they are true; and if they are true, has the day of miracles ceased?

38 "Or have angels ceased to appear to the children of men?

39 "Or has he withheld the power of the Holy Ghost from them?

40 "Or will he, as long as time shall last, or the earth shall stand, or there shall be one man upon the face thereof to be saved?

41 "Behold, I say to you, No, for it is by faith that miracles are wrought; and it is by faith that angels appear and minister to men.

42 "Wherefore if these things have ceased, woe be to the children of men, for it is because of unbelief, and all is vain; for no man can be saved, according to the words of Christ, save they shall have faith in his name.

43 "Wherefore, if these things have ceased, then has faith ceased also; and awful is the state of men; for they are as though there had been no redemption made.

44 "But, behold, my beloved brethren, I judge better things of you, for I judge that you have faith in Christ because of your meekness; for if you have not faith in him, then you are not fit to be numbered among the people of his church.

45 "And again, my beloved brethren, I would speak to you concerning hope.

46 "How is it that you can attain to faith, save you shall have hope? And what is it that you shall hope for?

47 "Behold, I say to you that you shall have hope through the atonement of Christ and the power of his resurrection to be raised to life eternal; and this because of your faith in him according to the promise.

48 "Wherefore, if a man have faith, he must have hope; for without faith there cannot be any hope.

49 "And again, behold, I say to you that he cannot have faith and hope save he shall be meek and lowly of heart; if so, his faith and hope are vain, for none are acceptable before God, save the meek and lowly of heart.

50 "And if a man be meek and lowly in heart and confesses by the power of the Holy Ghost that Jesus is the Christ, he must have charity; for if he have not charity, he is nothing; wherefore he must have charity.

51 "Charity suffers long, and is kind, and envies not, and is not puffed up, seeks not her own, is not easily provoked, thinks no evil, and rejoices not in iniquity, but rejoices in the truth, bears all things, believes all things, hopes all things, endures all things; wherefore, my beloved brethren, if you have not charity, you are nothing, for charity never fails.

52 "Wherefore, cleave to charity, which is the greatest of all, for all things must fail; but charity is the pure love of Christ, and it endures forever; and whoever is found possessed of it at the last day, it shall be well with him.

53 "Wherefore, my beloved brethren, pray to the Father with all the energy of heart, that you may be filled with this love which he has bestowed upon all who are true followers of his Son Jesus Christ, that you may become the sons of God, that when he shall appear, we shall be like him (for we shall see him as he is), that we may have this hope, that we may be purified even as he is pure. Amen."

CHAPTER 8

AN epistle of my father Mormon, written to me, Moroni, soon after my calling to the ministry:

2 On this wise he wrote me, saying, "My beloved son, Moroni, I rejoice exceedingly that your Lord Jesus Christ has been mindful of you and has called you to his ministry, and to his holy work.

3 "I am mindful of you always in my prayers, continually praying to God the Father, in the name of his holy child, Jesus, that he, through his infinite goodness and grace, will keep you through the endurance of faith on his name to the end.

4 "And now, my son, I speak to you concerning that which grieves me exceedingly; for it grieves me that disputations should rise among you.

5 "For if I have learned the truth,

there have been disputations among you concerning the baptism of your little children.

6 "And now, my son, I desire that you should labor diligently that this gross error should be removed from among you; for, for this intent I have written this epistle.

7 "For immediately after I had learned these things of you, I inquired of the Lord concerning the matter.

8 "And the word of the Lord came to me by the power of the Holy Ghost, saying, 'Listen to the words of Christ, your Redeemer, your Lord, and your God.

9 "'Behold, I came into the world not to call the righteous, but sinners, to repentance; the whole need no physician, but they that are sick; wherefore little children are whole, for they are not capable of committing sin; wherefore the curse of Adam is taken from them in me that it hath no power over them; and the law of circumcision is done away in me.'

10 "And after this manner did the Holy Ghost manifest the word of God to me; wherefore, my beloved son, I know that it is solemn mockery before God that you should baptize little children.

11 "Behold, I say to you that this shall you teach: repentance and baptism to those who are accountable and capable of committing sin; teach parents that they must repent and be baptized, and humble themselves as their little children, and they shall be saved with their little children; and their little children need no repentance, neither baptism.

12 "Behold, baptism is unto repentance to the fulfilling the commandments unto the remission of sins.

13 "But little children are alive in Christ, even from the foundation of the world; if not so, God is a partial God, and also a changeable God and a respecter of persons; for how many little children have died without baptism.

14 "Wherefore, if little children could not be saved without baptism, these must have gone to an endless hell.

15 "Behold, I say to you that he that supposes that little children need baptism is in the gall of bitterness and in the bonds of iniquity; for he has neither faith, hope, nor charity; wherefore, should he be cut off while in the thought, he must go down to hell.

16 "For awful is the wickedness to suppose that God saves one child because of baptism, and the other must perish because he has no baptism.

17 "Woe be to them that shall pervert the ways of the Lord after this manner, for they shall perish except they repent.

18 "Behold, I speak with boldness, having authority from God; and I fear not what man can do; for perfect love casts out all fear; and I am filled with charity, which is everlasting love; wherefore all children are alike to me; wherefore I love little children with a perfect love; and they are all alike, and partakers of salvation.

19 "For I know that God is not a partial God, neither a changeable being; but he is unchangeable from all eternity to all eternity.

20 "Little children cannot repent; wherefore it is awful wickedness to deny the pure mercies of God to them, for they are all alive in him because of his mercy.

21 "And he that says that little children need baptism denies the mercies of Christ, and sets at naught the atonement of him and the power of his redemption.

22 "Woe to such, for they are in danger of death, hell, and an endless torment.

23 "I speak it boldly; God has commanded me.

24 "Listen to these words and give heed, or they stand against you at the judgment seat of Christ.

25 "For, behold, all little children are alive in Christ, and also all they that are without the law.

26 "For the power of redemption comes on all that have no law; wherefore, he that is not condemned, or he that is under no condemnation, cannot repent; and to such baptism avails nothing.

27 "But it is mockery before God,

denying the mercies of Christ and the power of his Holy Spirit and putting trust in dead works.

28 "Behold, my son, this thing ought not to be; for repentance is unto them that are under condemnation and under the curse of a broken law.

29 "And the firstfruits of repentance is baptism; and baptism comes by faith, to the fulfilling of the commandments; and the fulfilling of the commandments brings remission of sins; and the remission of sins brings meekness and lowliness of heart; and because of meekness and lowliness of heart comes the visitation of the Holy Ghost, which Comforter fills with hope and perfect love, which love endures by diligence unto prayer, until the end shall come, when all the saints shall dwell with God.

30 "Behold, my son, I will write you again if I go not out soon against the Lamanites.

31 "Behold, the pride of this nation, or the people of the Nephites, has proved their destruction, except they should repent.

32 "Pray for them, my son, that repentance may come to them.

33 "But, behold, I fear lest the Spirit has ceased striving with them; and in this part of the land they are also seeking to put down all power and authority which comes from God; and they are denying the Holy Ghost.

34 "And after rejecting so great a knowledge, my son, they must perish soon, to the fulfilling of the prophecies which were spoken by the prophets as well as the words of our Savior himself.

35 "Farewell, my son, until I shall write you or shall meet you again. Amen."

CHAPTER 9

The Second Epistle of Mormon to his son Moroni.

MY beloved son, I write you again that you may know that I am yet alive, but I write somewhat that which is grievous.

2 "For, behold, I have had a sore battle with the Lamanites, in which we did not conquer; and Archeantus has fallen by the sword, and also Luram and Emron; and we have lost a great number of our choice men.

3 "And now, behold, my son, I fear lest the Lamanites shall destroy this people, for they do not repent, and Satan stirs them up continually to anger, one with another.

4 "Behold, I am laboring with them continually; and when I speak the word of God with sharpness, they tremble and anger against me; and when I use no sharpness, they harden their hearts against it; wherefore I fear lest the Spirit of the Lord has ceased striving with them.

5 "For so exceedingly do they anger that it seems to me they have no fear of death; and they have lost their love, one toward another; and they thirst after blood and revenge continually.

6 "Now, my beloved son, notwithstanding their hardness, let us labor diligently; for if we should cease to labor, we should be brought under condemnation; for we have a labor to perform while in this tabernacle of clay, that we may conquer the enemy of all righteousness and rest our souls in the kingdom of God.

7 "And now I write somewhat concerning the sufferings of this people.

8 "For according to the knowledge which I have received from Amoron, behold, the Lamanites have many prisoners which they took from the tower of Sherrizah; and there were men, women, and children.

9 "And the husbands and fathers of those women and children they have slain; and they feed the women upon the flesh of their husbands and the children upon the flesh of their fathers; and no water, save a little, do they give to them.

10 "And notwithstanding this great abomination of the Lamanites, it does not exceed that of our people in Moriantum.

11 "For, behold, many of the daughters of the Lamanites have

they taken prisoners; and after depriving them of that which was most dear and precious above all things, which is chastity and virtue, they murdered them in a most cruel manner, torturing their bodies even to death; and after they have done this, they devour their flesh like wild beasts because of the hardness of their hearts; and they do it for a token of bravery.

12 "O my beloved son, how can a people like this, that are without civilization (and only a few years have passed away since they were a civil and a delightsome people), whose delight is in so much abomination, expect that God will stay his hand in judgment against them?

13 "Behold, my heart cries, Woe to this people.

14 "Come out in judgment, O God, and hide their sins, and wickedness, and abominations from before thy face.

15 "And again, my son, there are many widows and their daughters who remain in Sherrizah; and that part of the provisions which the Lamanites did not carry away, behold, the army of Zenephi has carried away, and left them to wander wherever they can for food; and many old women faint by the way and die.

16 "And the army which is with me is weak; and the armies of the Lamanites are between Sherrizah and me; and as many as have fled to the army of Aaron have fallen victims to their awful brutality.

17 "Oh, the depravity of my people! They are without order and without mercy.

18 "Behold, I am but a man, and I have but the strength of a man, and I cannot any longer enforce my commands; and they have become strong in their perversion.

19 "And they are alike brutal, sparing none, neither old nor young; and they delight in everything, save that which is good; and the sufferings of our women and our children upon all the face of this land exceeds everything; tongue cannot tell, neither can it be written.

20 "And now, my son, I dwell no longer upon this horrible scene.

21 "Behold, you know the wickedness of this people; you know that they are without principle and past feeling; and their wickedness exceeds that of the Lamanites.

22 "Behold, my son, I cannot recommend them to God lest he should smite me.

23 "But, behold, my son, I recommend you to God, and I trust in Christ that you will be saved; and I pray to God that he would spare your life to witness the return of his people to him, or their utter destruction.

24 "For I know that they must perish except they repent and return to him; and if they perish, it will be like the Jaredites, because of the willfulness of their hearts, seeking for blood and revenge.

25 "And if it so be that they perish, we know that many of our brethren have dissented over to the Lamanites, and many more will also dissent over to them.

26 "Wherefore, write a few things, if you are spared, and I should perish and not see you; but I trust that I may see you soon; for I have sacred records that I would deliver up to you.

27 "My son, be faithful in Christ; and may not the things which I have written grieve you, to weigh you down to death; but may Christ lift you up, and may his sufferings and death, and the showing of his body to our fathers, and his mercy and long-suffering, and the hope of his glory and of eternal life rest in your mind forever.

28 "And may the grace of God the Father, whose throne is high in the heavens, and of our Lord Jesus Christ, who sits on the right hand of his power until all things shall become subject to him, be, and abide with you forever. Amen."

CHAPTER 10

NOW I, Moroni, write somewhat as seems to me good; and I write to my brethren the Lamanites, and I would that they should know that more than four hundred and twenty years have passed away since the sign was given of the coming of Christ.

2 And I seal up these records after

I have spoken a few words by way of exhortation to you.

3 Behold, I would exhort you that when you shall read these things, if it be wisdom in God that you should read them, that you would remember how merciful the Lord has been to the children of men, from the creation of Adam even down until the time that you shall receive these things, and ponder it in your hearts.

4 And when you shall receive these things, I would exhort you that you would ask God the eternal Father, in the name of Christ, if these things are not true.

5 And if you shall ask with a sincere heart, with real intent, having faith in Christ, he will manifest the truth to you by the power of the Holy Ghost; and by the power of the Holy Ghost you may know the truth of all things.

6 Whatever thing is good, is just and true; wherefore, nothing that is good denies the Christ, but acknowledges that he is.

7 And you may know that he is, by the power of the Holy Ghost; wherefore I would exhort you that you deny not the power of God; for he works by power, according to the faith of the children of men, the same today and tomorrow, and forever.

8 Again I exhort you, my brethren, that you deny not the gifts of God, for they are many; and they come from the same God.

9 And there are different ways that these gifts are administered; but it is the same God who works all in all; and they are given by the manifestations of the Spirit of God to men, to profit them.

10 For, behold, to one is given by the Spirit of God that he may teach the word of wisdom; and to another, that he may teach the word of knowledge by the same Spirit; and to another exceedingly great faith; and to another, the gifts of healing by the same Spirit.

11 And again, to another, that he may work mighty miracles; and again, to another, that he may prophesy concerning all things; and again, to another, the beholding of angels and ministering spirits; and again, to another, all kinds of tongues; and again, to another, the interpretation of languages and of divers kinds of tongues.

12 And all these gifts come by the Spirit of Christ; and they come to every man severally, according as he will.

13 I would exhort you, my beloved brethren, that you remember that every good gift comes of Christ.

14 And I would exhort you, my beloved brethren, that you remember that he is the same yesterday, today, and forever, and that all these gifts of which I have spoken, which are spiritual, never will be done away, even as long as the world shall stand, only according to the unbelief of the children of men.

15 Wherefore, there must be faith; and if there must be faith, there must also be hope; and if there must be hope, there must also be charity; and except you have charity, you can in no wise be saved in the kingdom of God.

16 Neither can you be saved in the kingdom of God if you have not faith; neither can you if you have no hope; and if you have no hope, you must be in despair; and despair comes because of iniquity.

17 And Christ truly said to our fathers, "If ye have faith, ye can do all things which are expedient unto me."

18 Now I speak to all the ends of the earth, that if the day comes that the power and gifts of God shall be done away among you, it shall be because of unbelief.

19 And woe be to the children of men if this be the case; for there shall be none that do good among you, no, not one.

20 For if there be one among you that does good, he shall work by the power and gifts of God.

21 And woe to them who shall do away with these things and die, for they die in their sins, and they cannot be saved in the kingdom of God; and I speak it according to the words of Christ, and I lie not.

22 I exhort you to remember these things; for the time speedily comes that you shall know that I lie not, for you shall see me at the bar of God, and the Lord God will say to

you, "Did I not declare my words to you, which were written by this man, like as one crying from the dead?

23 "Even as one speaking out of the dust?"

24 I declare these things unto the fulfilling of the prophecies.

25 And, behold, they shall proceed forth out of the mouth of the everlasting God; and his word shall hiss forth from generation to generation.

26 And God shall show to you that that which I have written is true.

27 Again I would exhort you that you would come to Christ, and lay hold upon every good gift, and touch not the evil gift nor the unclean thing.

28 And awake, and arise from the dust, O Jerusalem; and put on your beautiful garments, O daughter of Zion, and strengthen your stakes, and enlarge your borders forever, that you may no more be confounded, that the covenants of the eternal Father which he has made to thee, O house of Israel, may be fulfilled.

29 Come to Christ, and be perfected in him, and deny yourselves of all ungodliness, and if you shall deny yourselves of all ungodliness, and love God with all your might, mind, and strength, then is his grace sufficient for you, that by his grace you may be perfect in Christ; and if by the grace of God ye are perfect in Christ, you can in no wise deny the power of God.

30 And again, if you, by the grace of God, are perfect in Christ and deny not his power, then are you sanctified in Christ by the grace of God, through the shedding of the blood of Christ, which is in the covenant of the Father, to the remission of your sins, that you become holy without spot.

31 Now I bid to all, farewell. I soon go to rest in the paradise of God until my spirit and body shall reunite, and I am brought forth triumphant through the air to meet you before the pleasing bar of the great Jehovah, the eternal Judge of both quick and dead. Amen.

The End

Proper Names Pronunciation Guide

(Also unusual common nouns)

â as in bâre; ā as in sāle; å as in Sabbåth; ă as in lămb; ä as in cälm; ȧ as in chȧotic. ĕ as in sĕt; ē as in hē; ê as in desêrve; ẽ as in markẽr; ḙ as in ḙlope. ĭ as in pĭn; ī as in sīgn; ḽ as in cḽtation. ŏ as in sŏck; ȯ as in kingdȯm; ô as in absôrb; ō as in rōll; ǒ as in mǒre. ū as in tūne; ŭ as in fŭn. (k) after a word indicates "ch" in the word is pronounced as a "k."

A		Ăm'mȯn	Mos 5:4, 7, 15; 11:203; A 12:28
Aâr'ŏn	Mos 11:203; 13:4, 5; 13:1	Ăm'mȯn ītes	A 26:69, 75
Ā'bĕl	He 2:151	Ăm mȯn i'häh	A 6:7; 11:14
Ȧ bĭn'ȧ dī	Mos 7:28, 39, 40, 41	Ăm mȯn i'häh ītes	A 11:15
Ȧ bĭn'ȧ dȯm	O 1:13, 18	Ăm'mō ron	A 24:3, 14; 25:1; 4 N 1:56-58; Mn 1:6
Ā'bĭsh	A 12:150		
Ăb'lȯm	E 4:4	Ăm'nĭ găd'däh	E 1:6; 4:85
Ā'brȧ hăm	1 N 2:4; 4:29; 5:132	Ăm'nĭ hū	A 1:70
Ā'gōsh	E 6:49, 51	Ăm'nôr	A 1:78
Ā'hă	A 11:5	Ăm'ō rŏn	Mi 9:8
Ā'häh	E 1:6; 4:100, 102	Ā'mȯs	4 N 1:22, 24, 56
Ā'hăz	2 N 9:14, 16; 10:50	Ā'mōz	2 N 8:17; 10:1
		Ăm'ū lĕk	A 6:28; 7:1; 8:10
Ā ī'ăth	2 N 9:109	Ăm'ū lŏn	Mos 11:35, 36; 13:2; 14:62
Ā'kĭsh	E 3:82, 83; 4:2		
Ăl'mȧ	Mos 9:2, 5, 28; A 2:5	Ăm'ū lŏn ītes	A 13:3; 14:15, 57
Ȧ măl'ĕ kī	O 1:18, 40, 52; WM 1:4; Mos 5:7	Ăn'a thŏth	2 N 9:111
		Ăn gō'lȧ	Mn 1:25
		Ăn'i-ăn'tī	A 13:15
Ȧ măl'ĕ kītes	A 13:2, 21; 14:15	Ăn tī'-Nē'phī-Lē'hī	A 14:19, 21,26
Ȧ măl'ĭc kī äh	A 21:31, 40, 61; 23:10; 24:1		
		Ăn'tī ŏm'nō	A 12:184
		ăn'tī ôn	A 8:62
Ȧ măl ĭc kī'ä hītes	A 21:61, 62, 70	Ăn tī ōn'äh	A 9:34
Ăm'ā rȯn	O 1:5, 6	Ăn tī ō'nŭm	Mn 3:15
Ăm'gĭd	E 4:87	Ăn tī pȧr'äh	A 26:73
Ȧ mĭn'ȧ dăb	H 2:105, 107	Ăn'tī pàs	A 21:86, 88, 89
Ȧ mĭn'ȧ dī	A 8:1, 2, 3	Ăn'tī pŭs	A 26:10, 35, 52
Ăm'lĭ cī	A 1:53, 54, 60	Ăn'tŭm	Mn 1:4
Ăm'lĭ cītes	A 1:64, 70, 92	Ȧr chē ăn'tus (k)	Mi 9:2
Ăm'mäh	A 12:182; 13:15	Ȧr'păd	2 N 9:90

B

Băb′y lŏn	1 N 1:12; 3:2, 6: 21; 2 N 11:18
Bă′shăn	2 N 8:29
Běn′jà mĭn	O 1:40; WM 1:4; Mos 1:1
Běth ăb′ă rä	1 N 3:11
Bō′ăz	Mn 2:22
Boun′tĭ fŭl	1 N 5:62; A 13: 73

C

Căl′nō	2 N 9:90
Cär chĕm′ĭsh (k)	2 N 9:90
Cē zō′răm	H 2:63, 136, 143
Chăl dē′ăns (k)	1 N 6:21, 27
Chĕm′ĭsh (k)	O 1:10, 11, 13
Cō′hôr	E 3:53, 60; 6:18
Côm	E 1:6; 4:85, 90
Côm′nôr	E 6:66
Cōr ĭ ăn′tŏn	A 16:84; 21:185; 30:14
Cōr′ĭ ăn′tôr	E 1:6; 4:110, 115
Cōr′ĭ ăn′tŭm	E 1:6; 4:23, 85
Cōr ĭ ăn′tŭ mr	H 1:16, 20, 32; O 1:36; E 5:1
Cōr′ĭ hŏr	E 3:40, 50; 6:18
Cō′rŏm	E 1:6 (misspelled for *corum*); 4: 62, 63
Cū mĕn′ĭ	A 26:15, 77, 98
Cū mĕn ĭ′hah	Mn 3:15
cū′mŏms	E 4:21
Cŭ mō′räh	Mn 3:3, 14; 4:1
cū rē′lŏm	E 4:21

D

Dā′vid	Mn 1:27
dĕs êr ĕt′	E 1:24
Dĕs′ō lā′tion	A 13:74; H 5:42

E

Ē′dĕn	2 N 5:73
Ē′dòm	2 N 9:129
Ē′gўpt	1 N 1:165; 2 N 2:16; A 8:3
Ē′lăm	2 N 9:126
Ē lī′jäh	3 N 11:26
Ē′mēr	E 1:6; 4:15, 23
Ĕm′rŏn	Mi 9:2
Ē′nŏs	Jb 5:45; En 1:1; Jm 1:1
ē′phäh	2 N 8:80
Ē′phrä ĭm	2 N 9:15; 81; 128
Ĕs′rŏm	E 3:73
Ē′thĕm	E 1:6; 4:102, 105
Ē′thēr	E 1:6; 4:115; 5:1
Ē zĭ′ás	H 3:54
ĕz′rŏm	A 8:57, 60

G

Găd	3 N 4:38
Găd ĭ ăn′dĭ	3 N 4:34
Găd ĭ ăn′tŏn	H 1:40; 2:21; 3: 28; 4:150
Găd ĭ ŏm′näh	3 N 4:34
Găl′lĭm	2 N 9:111
Gā′zĕ lĕm	A 17:55
Gē′bá	2 N 9:110
Gē′bĭm	2 N 9:112
Gĭb′ē äh	2 N 9:110
Gĭd	A 26:105, 116, 147
Gĭd′dĭ ăn′hĭ	3 N 2:11, 46, 60
Gĭd dō′näh	A 8:1; 16:27
Gĭd′eon	M 9:77; A 28:6
Gĭd gĭd dō′näh	Mn 3:15
Gĭd′gĭd dō′nĭ	3 N 2:23, 58; 3:7
Gĭl′ē ăd	E 6:42
Gĭl′gäh	E 3:16
Gĭl′găl	Mn 3:15
Gĭm gĭm′nō	3 N 4:34
Gò mõr′räh	2 N 10:19

H

Hā′gŏth	A 30:6
Hā′măth	2 N 9:90, 126
Heärth′ŏm	E 1:6; 4:80, 82
Hē′lăm	Mos 9:43; 11:22, 28
Hē′lă măn	A 16:84; 17:3; 21:3; H 1:38

Index

Aaron, city of, 155, 232.

Aaron, descendant of Heth, 343; dwells in captivity, 357.

Aaron, king of Lamanites, 331; defeated by army of Moroni, 331; brutality of army of, 372.

Aaron, son of Mosiah, 137; teaches people of Zarahemla, 137; refuses kingdom, 138; in prison at Middoni, 179, 181; released from prison, 180, 181; goes to Jerusalem, 181; teaches atonement, 181, 183; goes to Ani-Anti, 181; goes to Middoni, 181; goes to land of Nephi, 182; account of, 185; and brethren establish churches, 185; rejoices, 189; rebukes Ammon, 189; rejoices in meeting Alma, 192; goes with Alma to Zoramites, 198; goes to Jershon, 206; returns to Zarahemla, 206.

Abinadi, prophesies to people to Noah, 114, 115, 120, 122; brought bound before Noah, 115; cast into prison, 116, 121; ten commandments quoted by, 117; Isaiah quoted by, 120; Isaiah quoted to, 116; prophesies of Christ, 119; condemned to death by Noah, 121; suffers death by fire, 122; words of Alma blessed because of faith in, 134; words of, fulfilled, 188, 331.

Abinadom, 95.

Abish, conversion of, 177; raises queen, 178.

Ablom, Omner pitches tent at, 353, 354.

Abomination, of Lamanites and Nephites, 371.

Abraham, kindreds of earth blessed through, 20; seed of, to rejoice in Lord, 71; covenant with, 73; counted to be obedient, 82; tithes paid by, 166.

Abridgment of record of Mormon, 335.

Account of Nephi, 2.

Adam and Eve, plates of brass contain account of, 7.

Adam, and tree of life, 216; cut off from presence of God, 216; fall of man through, 341.

Agosh, Lib pursues Coriantumr to plains of, 363; gives battle to Lib, slays Lib, 363.

Aha, son of Zoram, 170.

Ahah, son of Seth, 343; becomes king, 358.

Akish, son of Kimnor, 352; daughter of Jared dances before, 352; swears kinfolks of Jared, 352; oaths administered by, 352, 353; overthrows kingdom of Omer, 353; marries daughter of Jared, 354; seeks life of Jared, 354; obtains kingdom, 354; causes death of son, 354; war between, and sons, 354.

Akish, wilderness of, Coriantumr pursues brother of Shared to, 362; army of Coriantumr flees to, 362.

All things common, among disciples of Christ, 322, 327.

Alma, believes words of Abinadi, 121; cast out, life sought by Noah, 121; teaches words of Abinadi, 122; flees to place of Mormon, 122; baptizes, 123; ordains priest, 123; teachings of, 123; discovered by King Noah, 124; departs into wilderness, 124, 129; declines to be king, 129; teachings of, 130; high priest, 130; consecrates priests and teachers, 130; people of, surrender to Lamanites, 130; and people oppressed by Amulon and people, 131; and people gather flocks, 132; departs into wilderness, 132; valley of, 132; and people arrive at Zarahemla, 132; records of, read by Mosiah, 132; preaches to people of Nephi, 133; baptizes people of Limhi, 133; permitted to establish churches, 133; dissenters brought before, 134; given authority over church by Mosiah, 134; receives direction from the Lord, 134; regulates all affairs of church, 135; church complains to, 135; son of, an unbeliever, 135; appoints son high priest, 141; dies, 141; age of, 141; founder of church, 141.

Alma, son of Alma, 135; seeks to destroy church, 135; angel appears to, 136; becomes dumb, 136; explains his conversion, 136; teaches people, 137; receives plates, records, and interpreters from Mosiah, 138; to keep records, 138; appointed chief judge, 141; appointed high priest by his father, 141; Nehor sentenced by, 142; head of armies of Nephites, 144; slays

381

Amoron, Mormon receives knowledge from, 371.

Amos, son of Amos, keeps record, 328; record of, written in Book of Nephi, 328; dies, 329.

Amos, son of Nephi, keeps record, 328; death of, 328.

Amulek, receives Alma, 156; preaches to preople of Ammonihah, 158; son of Giddonah, 159; angel appears to, 159; questioned by Zeezrom, 161; teaches restoration and resurrection, 162; bound, 167; smitten by chief judge, 168; breaks cords with which bound, 169; departs from Ammonihah, goes to Sidom, 169; rejected by kindred, 170; goes to Zarahemla, 170; preaches repentance, 171; goes to Zoramites, 198; preaches at Onidah, 204; testifies of Christ, 204; goes to Jershon, 206; returns to Zarahemla, 206.

Amulon, land of, 130; leader of priests of King Noah, 130; and brethren join Lamanites, 131; made king over people of Helam, 131; and brethren appointed teachers by king of Lamanites, 131; oppresses Alma and people, 54; descendants of, take name of Nephites, 133; people of, and others build city of Jerusalem, 181; seed of, 188; slain by Lamanites, 188.

Amulonites, harder than Lamanites, 181; after order of Nehors, 181; those not converted take up arms, 186; rebel against king of Anti-Nephi-Lehies, 186; seed of Amulon, 188; slain by Lamanites, 188.

Ancient inhabitants, Moroni gives account of, 343.

Angel, speaks to Laman and Lemuel, 5; to Nephi, 17; appears to Nephi, 13, 14, 15; makes things known to Nephi, 19; words of, concerning coming of Messiah, 29; speaks to Benjamin, 102; appears to Alma and sons of Mosiah, 136; appears to Alma, 155, 207, 211; appears to Amulek, 159; appears to Samuel, 281.

Angels, in Lehi's vision, 1; minister to Nephi, 42; speak with tongues of, 75, 76; to the devil, 81; minister to Jacob, 89; declare word to many, 167; appear to Lamanites, 179; visit people of Anti-Nephi-Lehi, 186, 187; declare tidings of repentance, 266; faces of Nephi and Lehi shine as, 267; minister to Nephites and Lamanites, 268; appear to wise men, 286; visit Nephi, 298; of devil rejoice in calamities of people, 300; minister to little children, 311; minister to twelve disciples, 314; three Nephite disciples as, 325; office and ministry of, 368.

Anger, people drunken with, 364, 365; of Nephites, 371.

Angola, Nephites fortify city of, Lamanites drive Nephites from, 331.

Ani-anti, Aaron goes to, 181; Muloki at, 181.

Animals, found in land of promise, 28; raised by people of Nephi, 43; to dwell in peace, 74; possessed by Jaredites, 354.

Antichrist, in Zarahemla, 195; in Gideon, 195, 196.

Anti-Nephi-Lehi, made king, 186; Ammon and brethren counsel with Lamoni and, 186; forbids people to go to war, 186.

Anti-Nephi-Lehies, name of Lamanites converted, 186; friendly with Nephites, 186; Amulonites, Amalekites, and Lamanites rebel against king of, 186; Anti-Nephi-Lehi made king of, 186; would not go to war, 186, 191; bury swords and other weapons, 187; prostrate themselves before Lamanites, 187; slain by Lamanites, 187; joined by Lamanites, 188; observe law of Moses, 188; Amalekites slay, 191; depart out of land, 192; commanded to remain in wilderness, 192; proclamation concerning, 192; land of Jershon given to, 192; protected by Nephites, 192; Alma visits, 192; take possession of Jershon, 192; hatred of Lamanites toward, 218; would not take up arms, 218.

Antiomno, king of Middoni, 179.

Antion, of gold, 161.

Antionah, ruler of people of Amnonihah, questions Alma, 164.

Antionum, settled by Zoramites, 198, 217, 218; east of Zarahemla, 198; Lamanites come into land of, 217, 218; Lamanites gathered in land of, 218; Lamanites depart from, 218; leader of ten thousand slain, 337.

Antiparah, city of, taken by Lamanites, 243; Lamanites march from, to attack Helaman, 244; Nephites regain city of, 246.

Antipas, Lamanites gather at mount of, 226; place of arms, 226.

Antipus, Helaman goes to assistance of, at Judea, 243; pursues Lamanites, 244, 245; overtakes Lamanites, 245; and leaders fall by sword, 245; Helaman and army rescue, 245, 246.

Antum, land of, sacred records deposited in, by Ammoron, 330.

Apostle of Lamb to write, 19

Apostles, Israel fights against, 14; all nations fight against, 14; judge tribes of Israel, 14; book goes forth by hand of, 16; record of, true, 17; one of, seen by Nephi, 19; writes of end of world, 19; things written about, just and true, 19; have power to give Holy Ghost, 366.

Archeantus, fallen by sword, 371.

Atonement, infinite, 48; claims of, 49; satisfies demands of justice, 49; all men lost without, 90; law of Moses avails nothing except through, 103, 118; prepared from foundation of world, 104; without, men shall perish, 118; preached by Amulek, 158, 162; taught by Aaron, 181, 183; taught by king of Anti-Nephi-Lehies, 186; Korihor preaches against, 195; God atones for sins of world, 216; bringeth mercy and resurrection, 217; no salvation outside of, 266.

Babylon, captives carried to, 2; to be destroyed, 65.

Ball of Brass, found by Lehi, 22; directions of, followed, 22, 23; pointers of, work according to faith, 23; compass ceased to work, 28; delivered to Mosiah by Benjamin, 99.

Baptism, prophet to administer, 11, 13; Holy Spirit follows, 13; all men must be obedient to, 49; of Lamb of God, 13, 75; commanded, 75; of fire and Holy Ghost, 75; gate by which to enter is repentance and, 75; taught and administered by Alma, 123, 133, 134, 135; administered in Sidon, 147; Alma teaches, 154; Alma baptizes at Melek, 155, at Sidom, 170; administered to Lamanites, 179; Helaman and brethren preach, 257; thousands enter church by, 263; of Nephites,

266; of eight thousand Lamanites, 266; by Nephi, 286; by Nephi and others, 288; of all who repented, 298; of fire and Holy Ghost promised by Christ, 301; Christ commands disciples to administer, 303; is immersion, 303; twelve given power to administer, 304; of twelve disciples, 314; brings salvation, 320; by disciples of Christ, 322; called church of Christ after, 322; commanded, 323; Gentiles commanded to receive, 327; in name of Jesus, 327; not to be administered to those unworthy, 342; commanded of Christ, 349; teaching concerning, 366; of little children gross error, 370; first-fruits of repentance, 371.

Barges, built by Jared and brother, 344, 345; description of, 345; number of, 346; people embark in, 349; driven before wind, 349; voyage of, 349, 350.

Barley, 161.

Beggar, not to petition in vain, 105.

Beggars, all are, 105.

Benjamin, reigns instead of Mosiah, 95; war in days of, 95; receives plates from Amaleki, 95; reign of, 96; plates handed down from reign of, 97; contentions among people of, 97; fights with sword of Laban, 97; drives out Lamanites, 97; establishes peace in land, 97; peace during remainder of days of, 98; sons of, 98; teaches sons language of fathers, 98; teaches sons, 98; words of, to Mosiah, 98; confers kingdom upon Mosiah, 99; gives Mosiah charge of records, plates, sword of Laban, and ball or director, 99; addresses his people, 99, 104; declares Mosiah king, 101; takes names of those entering into covenant, 107; consecrates son Mosiah to be king, 107; appoints priests to teach people, 107; death of, 107; words of, not understood by some, 133.

Bethabara, prophet to baptize at, 11.

Bible, Gentiles say there cannot be any more, 72; to proceed from Jews, 73; not to contain all the words of God, 73.

Boaz, Nephites flee to city of, 335; Nephites driven from, 335.

Book, given to Lehi, 2; Nephi writes in, 12; carried forth among Gentiles, 16; contains covenants of Lord, 16; of Lamb of God, 17; proceeding out of mouth of Jew, 19; Joseph's seed to hearken to words of, 41; words of righteous sealed up in, 68; to be sealed, 69; words of, to be brought forth, 69; to contain revelation from beginning to end of world, 69; words of, to be read upon housetops, 69; three witnesses of, 69; words of, delivered to learned, 70; learned unable to read, 70; unlearned to read words of, 70; sealed up again unto the Lord, 70; deaf to hear words of, 70; many to believe words of, 74.

Books, other, 17; sealed, 19; to come forth in their purity to house of Israel, 19; world to be judged out of, 73; world to be judged by words written in, 324.

Bountiful, land of, 24, 184; inhabited by Nephites, 184; appearance of Christ in, 303.

Bountiful, Nephites possess land north of, 232; Moroni and people in, 233; Lamanites drive Nephites to borders of, 235; Teancum's army at borders of, 235; Moroni orders Teancum to fortify, 236; Moroni marches to assist Teancum, 237; returns to city of, 237; Moroni and army arrive at, 237; Lehi meets Lamanites near, 238; Lamanite prisoners marched to, 238; Lamanites erect fortifications about city of, by order of Moroni, 238, 239; Lamanite prisoners caused to labor in, 239; Hagoth builds ship on borders of, 258; Coriantumr marches toward, 260; Lamanites obtain possession of lands near, 264; Nephi and Lehi begin preaching at, 266.

Breastplates, found by people of Limhi, 110.

Brother of Jared, man highly favored of the Lord, 343; language of, not confounded, 343; promised choice land, 344; seed of, and of brother to become great nation, 344; and brother go into Valley of Nimrod, 344; the Lord talks with, 344, 345; commanded to depart into wilderness, 344; chastened and repents, 345; smelts stones from Shelem, 346; sees finger of Lord, 346; sees the Lord, 347; could not be kept

from within the vail, 347; given two stones or interpreters, 347; commanded to write and seal up records, 347; commanded to write in a language confounded, 347; shown all inhabitants of earth, 347; to seal up two stones, 347; puts stones into vessels, 349; embarks for promised land, 349; and people reach promised land, 350; begets sons and daughters, 350; number of sons and daughters of, 350; Pagag, son of, chosen to be king, refuses, 350; other sons of, refuse to be king, 350; death of, 350; descendant of, subdues Moron, 358; commands mountain to be moved, 360.

Burnt offerings, offered by Lehi, 7, 9.

Cain, 352, 353.

Cement, expert in use of, 262.

Cezoram, Nephi delivers judgment seat to, 265; murdered, 269; son of, appointed judge and murdered, 270.

Charity, all men should have, 68; Nephi has, 77; defined, 369; cannot be saved without, 373.

Chastity, God delights in, 80.

Chemish, receives plates from Amaron, 94; writes in book of his brother, 94.

Chief, of tribe, 297.

Children, born in wilderness, 23; confidence of, lost, 81; husbands and wives love, 81; speak marvelous things to fathers, 322; baptism of little, a gross error, 370; little, alive in Christ, 370.

Christ, people believe in, 66; made alive in, 66; preach, talk, and write of, 66; life in, 66; law fulfilled in, 66; to show himself to children of Lehi, 66; Jews and Gentiles must be convinced of, 67; doctrine of, 75; name of, taken upon by baptism, 75; feasting upon word of, 76; no other name whereby man can be saved, 76; words of, 76, 77; prophets had hope of glory of, 82; coming of, foretold, 102; atonement and salvation only through, 103; to be called by name of, 106; resurrection through, 120, 148; death swallowed up in, 121; life and light of world, 121; church of, 123; Alma's prophecy concerning,

153; Amulek teaches concerning coming of, 162; Alma teaches concerning coming of, 167; to appear after his resurrection, 171; Ammon teaches Lamoni of, 176; Lamoni testifies of, 177; queen of Lamanites testifies of, 178; atonement of, taught by Aaron, 181; Antichrist speaks against, 195; Alma testifies of, 197, 213; denied by Zoramites, 199; spoken of by Moses, 203; Amulek testifies of, 204; only means of salvation, 212; bringeth to pass resurrection of dead, 213; atonement of, 216; believers in, called Christians by Moroni, 224; many died in faith of, 226; Moroni firm in faith of, 229; gate of heaven open to those who believe on, 263; atonement of, 266; to redeem from sins, 266; faith in, taught by Aminadab, 267; Holy Spirit bears witness of, 268; death of, redeems mankind, 283; signs of coming of and death of, 283, 284, 288; doctrine of, called foolish and vain, 289; nine years from birth of, 289; tenth, eleventh, thirteenth years from, 289; fourteenth, fifteenth, sixteenth year from coming of, 290; seventeenth year, 291; eighteenth year, 292; nineteenth year, 292, 293; twentieth and twenty-first years, 293; twenty-second, twenty-third, twenty-fourth, and twenty-fifth years, 294; twenty-sixth, twenty-seventh years, 295; twenty-eighth year, 296; twenty-ninth, 296; thirtieth, 296; death and resurrection of, testified of, 296; thirtieth year, 297; thirty-first year, 298; Nephi testifies of remission of sins through, 298; thirty-second year, 298; thirty-third year, 298; thirty-fourth year, 299; speaks to people after destruction of cities, 300, 301; law of Moses fulfilled in, 301; thirty-fourth year, 302; manifests himself to Nephites and Lamanites, 302; appearance and words of, 303; speaks to Nephi, 303; doctrine of, 303; calls twelve, 303, 304; instructs twelve disciples, 307, 308, 312; teaches the multitude, 307, 310, 312; law of Moses fulfilled in, 308; speaks concerning all nations of Gentiles, 309, 310, 315; to go to lost tribes of Israel, 310; heals the

afflicted, 311; blesses little children, 311; teaches disciples, 311–313; administers bread and wine, 311, 312, 315; commands one be ordained to administer bread and wine, 312; a light and an example, 312; forbids partaking of flesh and blood unworthily, 313; sheep of, known and numbered, 313; gives power to disciples to give Holy Ghost, 313; ascension of, 313; appears again to multitude, 314; commands disciples to pray, 314; prays to Father, 314, 315; speaks to multitude, 315; speaks to disciples, 315; spoken of by Moses, 316; commands twelve to write scriptures, 320; commands words of Samuel to be recorded, 320; expounds words of Malachi, 320; teachings of, contained on plates of Nephi, 322; shows himself often and breaks bread and administers, 322; administers to children, 322; heals afflicted, 322; raises man from dead, 322; disciples of, baptize, 322; all things common among disciples of, 322; those baptized called church of, 322; appears again, 322; church to be called in name of, 323; all things to be done in name of, 323; admonishes disciples, 324; speaks to disciples, 323, 324; three of disciples of, not to taste of death, 324, 325; touches all disciples save three, 325; ascension of, 325; disciples of, caught up into heaven, 325; disciples of, cast into furnace and den of wild beasts, 325; three disciples of, are changed, 326; Lamanites and Nephites all converted unto, 327; children of, 328; first generation from, passed away, 328; second generation after, 328; churches deny greater part of gospel of, 328; a church denies, 328; Nephites once had, for Shepherd, 336; Mormon exhorts house of Israel to believe in, 338; shows Gentile nations to Moroni, 340; results of faith in, 342; commission of, 342; words of, to twelve, 365; manner of administering flesh and blood of, 366; effects of faith in, 368; circumcision done away in, 370; little children alive in, 370; nothing which is good denies the, 373. (See Jesus Christ, and Messiah.)

Christians, believers in Christ called, 224; cause of, 224.

Church, great and abominable, 15; destroys saints of God, 15; takes from book plain and precious things, 16; founded by devil, etc., 18; utter destruction of, 18, 72; is whore of all the earth, 18; has dominion over all the earth, 18; gathered together to fight, 18; of Lamb of God, 18; numbers of, few, 18; wrath of God upon, 19; of Christ, 123; people of, to impart of substance, 123; Alma high priest of, 130; of God, those baptized belong to, 133; Alma regulates affairs of, 135; prosperity and persecution of, 135; murmurs, 135; nothing to overthrow it but transgression of people, 136; became rich, 143; wealthy and prosperous, 143; thirty-five hundred additions to, 147; people of, wax proud, 147; elders, priests, teachers of, consecrated, 147; evils of, 147, 148; in city of Zarahemla, 148; received into, after baptism, 152; transgressors cast out of, 152; established in city of Zarahemla, 152; commanded to fast and pray, 152; regulations of, made by Alma, 152; Alma establishes order of, in Gideon, 155; established at Sidom, 170; establishment of general, among Nephites, 171; established among Lamanites, 179, 268; of God, people of Ammon numbered with, 192; performances of, 198; Alma and brethren sought to destroy, 207; Alma blesses, 223; saying of, concerning Alma, 223; established by Helaman and brethren, 223; priests and teachers appointed over, 223; dissenters from, under Amalickiah, 224; established by Helaman and brethren, 257; pride and contention in, 262, 263; great prosperity in, 263; brethren of, persecuted, 263; fasting and praying of, 263; dissension in, 264; abominations in, 264; began to dwindle and disbelieve, 265; spread throughout face of land, 278; contention among members of, 278; broken up in all land, 296; to be established among Gentiles, 317, 318, 320; those baptized called, of Christ, 322; to be called by name of Christ, 323; to be built

upon gospel of Christ, 323; disciples of Christ unite people to, 325; all converted united with, 325; disciples form, in all lands round about, 327; all people converted unto, 327; began to deny true, 328; another, which denied the Christ, 328; of Christ, those baptized into, 366; meets together often, 366.

Churches, two only, 18; not unto the Lord, 71; to contend, to deny the Holy Ghost, 71; become corrupted, 71; rob the poor, persecute meek, 71; pride and wickedness of, 71; taught by precepts of men, 71; Alma permitted to establish, 133; seven, in land of Zarahemla, 133; established by Aaron and brethren, 185; built up, to themselves to get gain, 328; many churches, 328, 329; built up, to themselves— richly adorned, 329; to become defiled, 340; to forgive sins to get gain, 340; polluted by pride, 340.

Circumcision, done away in Christ, 370.

Cities, built in Zarahemla, 135; many, built, 232; many, built and repaired, 295, 296; destroyed, 299; built where formerly burned, 327.

Classes, among people, 328.

Cloth, woven by people of Zeniff, 112, 143, 269; made by Jaredites, 357.

Cohor, brother of Noah, drawn away by Noah, 351.

Cohor, son of Noah, kingdom of, 351; gives battle to Shule, slain, 351; kingdom of, given to Shule by Nimrod, 351; sons and daughters of, repent not, 351.

Com, son of Coriantum, 343; reigns as king, 355; dethroned by Heth, 355; reigns over half of kingdom, 357; subdues Amgid, 357; prophets flee to, for protection, 357.

Combinations, secret, plans to be kept from people, 210; judgments of God upon, 210; signs and words of, 269; wickedness of, 269; origin of, 269; plots handed down by devil—among all nations, 270; destroyed among Lamanites, 270; Nephites build up, 270, 276; control government, 271; judges included in, 272; chief judge slain because of, 274; war caused by, 277; war and destruction caused by, 278, 279, 289; leader of, slain, 293, 294; Nephites make end of,

294; judges enter into, against government, 297; destroy government, 297; gather together and appoint king, 297; people of, migrate northward to establish kingdom, 297; people again build up, 329; work to come forth in a day of, 340; built up, to get gain, 340; secret, 352; swearing of people into, 352; oaths of, handed down by Cain, 352, 353; abominable and wicked above all in sight of God, 353; Lord worketh not in, 353; cause destruction of Nephites and Jaredites, 353; Gentiles warned against, 353; built up by devil to destroy all nations, 353; Jared murdered by, 354; Heth embraces, 355; Com fights against, 357; people rebel because of, 358; reject words of prophets because of, 358; many of people of, slain, 361; Gilead receives strength from, 362; cause murder of Gilead, 362. (See Gadianton.)

Commandments, Lord prepares a way for accomplishment of, 4, 11, 24.

Comnor, hill, 363.

Compass, ceases working, 28, 211; again works, 28. (See Director, and Ball.)

Concubines, prohibited, 80, 81; and wives of King Noah, 113.

Contention forbidden, 123, 130; appears through Amlici, 144; in church, 147; among Lamanites because of Ammon, 178; cause of wars and destructions of Nephites, 232; concerning lands of Lehi and Morianton, 233; concerning law, 234; among Nephites, 257; in church, 262; among people, 262, 263, 264; Gadiantons stir up among Nephites, 272, 273; people divided by, 277; slay because of, 279; concerning doctrine, 278; ended by preaching of Nephi and Lehi, 278; concerning law of Moses, 288; caused by secret combinations, 297; not of Christ, 303, 304; no, in all the land, 327, 328.

Corianton, son of Alma, goes to Zoramites, 198; commandments of Alma to 212; called to preach, 217; declares word of God, 231; sails with provisions to people of land northward, 258.

Coriantor, Ether descendant from,

343; son of Moron, 343, 358; dwells in captivity, 358; begets Ether, 358; death of, 358.

Coriantum, son of Amnigaddah, 343; dwells in captivity, 357.

Coriantum, son of Emer, 343; anointed king by Emer, 354.

Coriantumr, account of people of, 95; discovered by people of Zarahemla, 95; son of Omer, 352; and Esrom defeat Jared, 352; king of Jaredites, 358; destruction sought, 361; fought against by secret combinations, 361; taken captive by Shared, 362; sons of, regain kingdom from Shared, 362; defeats Shared in battle, 362; defeated by Shared, 362; slays Shared in battle, wounded by Shared, 362; defeats brother of Shared; later Shared places himself upon throne of, 362; battles Lib, 362; wounded, 362, defeated by Lib, 362; flees to Agosh, 363; battles Shiz three days, 363; not to fall by sword, 363; gathers armies at hill Comnor, 363; wounded by Shiz, 363; repentance of, 363, 364; writes epistle to Shiz, 364; flees before Shiz, 364; comes to waters of Ripliancum, 364; wounded at Ripliancum, 364; defeats Shiz, 364; encamps at hill Ramah, 364; has final battle with Shiz, 365; slays Shiz, 365.

Coriantumr, led army of Lamanites, 260; takes city of Zarahemla, 260; slays Pacumeni, 260; marches toward Bountiful, 260; slain, 261.

Corihor, land of, Shiz flees to, 363.

Corihor, son of Kib, 351; rebels against father, 351; dwells in land of Nehor, 351; takes father captive in Moron, 351; given battle by Shule, 351; kingdom taken from, by Shule, 351; repents, given power by Shule, 351; Noah rebels against, 351; sons and daughters repent not, 361.

Corom, made king, 356; death of, 356.

Corum, son of Levi, 343.

Covenant, made to Abraham, 20; people enter into, 106; names of those entering into, 107; secret, of Kishkumen, 259.

Crime, Jacob speaks of grosser, 80.

Cross, Lamb of God lifted upon, 14.

Cumeni, city of, taken by Lamanites, 243; surrendered to Helaman, 246.

olive tree, 12; to receive fullness of gospel, 12; foundation of great and abominable church among, 15; waters divide, from seed of Nephi's brethren, 15; upon land of promise, 16; smite seed of Nephi's brethren, 16; described, 16; delivered from other nations, 16; prospered, 16; book carried among, 16; not to remain in blindness, 17; not to destroy seed of brethren, 17; to stumble, 17; plain and precious things to be restored to, 17; books from, to Jews, 17; Shepherd to manifest himself to, 18; to be numbered among seed of Israel, 18; promises to, 18; woe to, 18; fullness of gospel to come to, 20; seed of Lehi scattered by, 20; power of God manifested through, 20; promises to, 20; must be convinced that Jesus is the Christ, 67; smite seed of Lehi, 68; pride, greatness of stumbling block of, 68; build up many churches, 68; put down power and miracles of God, 68; preach their own learning, 68; grind upon face of poor, 68; secret combinations of, 68; and Jew alike to God, 69; will be drunken with iniquity, 69; to be visited with destructions from the Lord, 69; will deny God, 72; shall say cannot be any more Bible, 73; who repent are covenant people, 74; Nephi prophesies concerning, 74; book written to, 74; blessed because of belief in Christ, 309; abominations among, 310; promises and warnings to, 310; to be scourge to people of this land, 316; work to be brought forth among, 318; work of Christ to come forth among, 317, 320; to be a free people on this land, 317; promises to, 317; warnings concerning, 318; remnant of Jacob to tread down, 318; church to be established among, 318; three Nephite disciples to be among, 325; commanded to be baptized, 327; Mormon writes to, 333; spoken to by Mormon, 335; to receive blessing reserved for Nephites, 336; admonished to repent, 336; remnant of Jacob to tear, in pieces, 318, 336; warned by Mormon concerning decrees of God, 344; sealed records not to come forth in days of wickedness of, 348; warned

against secret combinations, 353; weakness of, to be shown to, 359, 360; Moroni bids farewell to, 360.

Gid, chief captain among Nephites, 247; and Teomner take city of Manti, 249.

Gid, city of, taken by Amalickiah, 235; Nephites guarded by Lamanites in, 241; Moroni arms prisoners in, 242; surrendered to Moroni, 242; Moroni causes Lamanites to erect fortifications about, 242; Nephi and Lehi preach at, 266.

Giddianhi, governor of society of Gidianton, 291; robbers of, take possession of lands vacated by Nephites, 292; orders robbers against Nephites, 292; slain by Nephites, 293.

Giddonah, Amulek son of, 159.

Giddonah, high priest of Gideon, 196.

Gideon, attacks King Noah, 124; searches for King Noah, 125; advises King Limhi, 128; a teacher, 142; withstands teaching of Nehor, 142; slain by Nehor, 142; valley of, 144; Alma declares word to church in valley of, 153; Alma establishes order of church in, 155; Korihor goes to land of, 195, 196; Giddonah, high priest of, 196; people of, send Korihor to Zarahemla, 196; Pahoran flees to land of, 253; Moroni joins Pahoran in, 255.

Gidgiddoni, chief captain of Nephites, 291; is great prophet and chief judge, 291; arms Nephites, 292; orders Nephites to pursue Gadianton robbers, 293; army of, destroys army of Gadianton robbers, 293; and Lachoneus establish peace, 295.

Gifts, different administrations of, 373; all good, of Christ, 373; not to be done away except because of sins, 373.

Gilead, brother of Shared, fights Coriantumr and is driven to Akish, 362; assumes throne of Coriantumr, 362; receives strength because of secret combinations, 362; murdered by his high priest, 362.

Gilgah, son of Jared, 350.

Gilgal, battle in valley of, 362; Coriantumr defeated by Shared at, 362; Coriantumr slays Shared in, 362.

Gilgal, city of, sunk, inhabitants buried, 300.

Gilgal, leader of ten thousand slain, 337.

Gimgimno, city of, sunk, 300.

God, justice of, 18, 21; wrath of, poured out, 19; works not in darkness, 68; lays down life, 68; invites all men to partake of goodness of, 69; commands that there be no priestcrafts, 68; commands all to have charity, 68; commands against all iniquities, 68; denies none that come to him, 69; all alike to, 69.

Gold, senine of, 161; seon of, 161; shum of, 161; limnah of, 161; antion of, 161; abundant among Nephites and Lamanites, 269.

Gospel, to be preached among Jews, 11; Gentiles to receive fullness of, 12; parts of, taken away, 16; to be with Nephites, 17; to be declared to seed of Nephi, 74; church to be built upon, 323; taught by Christ, 323; those who reject, called Ishmaelites, etc., 329; those who deny miracles know not, 341.

Grave, must deliver up its captive bodies, 48.

Great Spirit, Ammon called, 174, 178.

Great Spirit, Ammon teaches of, 176.

Great Spirit, Lamoni's father asks Aaron about the, 182.

Hagoth, launches ship near Bountiful and Desolation, 258; builds other ships, 258.

Healing of sick, 14.

Hearthom, son of Lib, 343; succeeds Lib as king, 357; kingdom taken from, 357.

Hebrew, language, altered by Nephites, 342.

Helam, baptized by Alma, 123; land of, 130; city of, 130; land of, taken by Lamanites, 130; guards set round about, 131; Alma and people depart from, 132; captivity of people in, 136.

Helaman, son of Alma, 198; commandment of Alma to, 207; Alma commits plates to, commanded to keep records, 208, 233; commanded to preserve directors, 209; to take care of sacred things, 211; account of Nephites in days of, 222; visited by Alma, 222; foretold by Alma of destruction of Nephites, 222; de-

clares word among people, 223; and brethren establish the church, 223; and brethren appoint priests and teachers over church, 223; and brethren opposed by Amalickiah, 223; and brethren high priests, 224; and high priests maintain order in church, 226, 231; preaches and baptizes, 229; persuades people of Ammon not to break oath, 239; chosen leader of sons of people of Ammon, 240; epistle of, to Moroni, 243; marches to city of Judea, 243; and army pursued by Lamanites, 244; and army defeat and capture Lamanites, 245, 246; and army return to Judea, 246; sends epistle to king of Lamanites, 246; takes city of Cumeni, 246; sends embassy to Governor at Zarahemla, 248; takes city of Manti, 249; Moroni reinforces, 255; returns to city of Zarahemla, 257; resumes preaching of word, 257; death of, 257.

Helaman, son of Benjamin, 98.

Helaman, son of Helaman, receives sacred things, 258; appointed chief judge, 261; servant of, kills Kishkumen, 261; filled judgment seat with judgment and equity, 263; Nephi and Lehi sons of, 263; death of, 264; words of, to sons, 265.

Helem, accompanies Ammon to land of Nephi, 107.

Hell, must deliver up dead, 48; chains of, 167; pains of, 167, 207; powers of, 229; gates of, not to prevail, 304.

Helorum, son of Benjamin, 98.

Hem, accompanies Ammon to land of Nephi, 107.

Hermounts, wilderness of, 145.

Heshlon, Shared flees to plains of, 362.

Heth, son of Com, 343, 355; embraces secret plans, 355; dethrones Com, 355; perishes by famine, 355.

Heth, son of Hearthom, 343; land of, 352; born in captivity, 357.

High priest, Alma, 130, 141; Alma retains office of, 148; Ammon, over people of Ammon, 195; could not condemn to death, 296.

High priests, of King Noah, 114; Abinadi examined by, 116; teach law of Moses, 116; flee into wilderness, 125; seize daughters of Lamanites, 125; seed of, of King Noah, 188; Helaman and brethren

king of, issues proclamation to his people, 226; Amalickiah given command of, 226; portion of, flee to Onidah, 226; Amalickiah seeks kingdom of, 226; king of, slain by servant of Amalickiah, 227; servants of king of, join people of Ammon, 227; queen of, summons Amalickiah, 228; Amalickiah made king of, 228; stirred up against Nephites, 228; approach city of Ammonihah, 229; astonished at preparation of Nephites, 230; attack Noah, 231; many slain among, 231; flee to wilderness, 231; driven out of east wilderness by Moroni, 232; Amalickiah prepares, for war against Nephites, 234; Amalickiah heads army of, 234; take cities, 235; met by Teancum, 235; retreat to Mulek, 236; Ammoron made king of, 236; armies of, march against Teancum, 237; chief captains of, flee from Lehi, 238; surrounded by Moroni and Lehi, 238; surrender to Moroni, 238; prisoners of, taken to Bountiful, 238; surrender to Moroni, 242; prisoners of, set to work to fortify Gid, 242; take Manti, Zeezrom, Cumeni, Antiparah, 243; overtaken by Antipus, 245; Helaman turned upon by, 245; captured by Helaman, 245, 246; prisoners of, sent to Zarahemla, 246; Helaman sends epistle to, 246; leave city of Antiparah, 246; lose city of Manti, 249; attack city of Nephihah, 250; capture Nephihah, 251; join people of Ammon, 256; flee from land of Moroni, 257; war on people of Moronihah, 258; wage war on Nephites, 260; surrounded and defeated by Moronihah and Lehi, 261; Nephites become, 262; go against Nephites in battle, 264; obtain possession of Zarahemla, 264; Nephi and Lehi preach to, 266; eight thousand of, baptized, 266; cast Nephi and Lehi into prison, 266; yield possession of land to Nephites, 268; become righteous people, 268; go to land northward, 268; grow in belief of God, 270; preach word of God, 270; destroy Gadiantons by preaching, 270; Samuel a prophet of, 280; join Gadianton robbers, 289; fight against Gadiantons, 289, 290;

unite with Nephites, 289, 290; curse taken from, 290; Christ appears to, 303; all converted to Christ, 327; a people called, 329; rejected gospel, 329; become exceedingly wicked, 329; war with Nephites, 330; beaten by Nephites, 330; war with Nephites, 331; drive Nephites out of Angola and land of David, 331; Aaron king of, 331; pursue Nephites to land of Jason, 332; come against Nephites again, 332; flee before Nephites, 332; Nephites make treaty with, 332; king of, sends epistle to Mormon, 333; Nephites beat, 333; drive Nephites out of Desolation, 334; come against Teancum, 334; repulsed by Nephites at Teancum, 334; come again to battle with Nephites, 334; regain Desolation, 334; offer women and children as sacrifices, 334; are driven from land by Nephites, 334; beat Nephites at Desolation, 335; come against Nephites at Jordan, are driven back, 335; beat Nephites again, 335; Moroni sends epistle to king of, 336; destroy Nephites at Cumorah, 337; at war among themselves, 338; put to death those who will not deny Christ, 365; take prisoners from tower of Sherizah and feed women on flesh of husbands, children upon flesh of fathers, 371; Moroni writes to, 372.

Lamb of God, Son of Eternal Father, 13; among men, 13; lifted upon cross, 14; multitudes fight against, 14; plainness in, 16; to be manifest to seed of Nephi, 17; book of, proceeded from Jew, 17; records to witness of, 17; all men must come to, 17; words of, 17; church of, 18; baptism of, 75; Holy Ghost descends upon, 75.

Lamoni, descendant of Ishmael, king of Lamanites, 173; Ammon becomes servant of, 173; traditions of, 175, 176; father of, king over all land, 175; taught by Ammon, 176; falls to earth, 176; arises, 178; teaches people, 178; and Ammon go to Middoni, 179; meets father of, 179; commanded to slay Ammon, 179; secures release of brethren of Ammon, 180, 181; returns to land of Ishmael, 182; builds synagogues, 182; and Anti-Nephi-

Lehi counsel with Ammon and brethren, 186.

Land northward, people depart into, 258; second migration into, 259; emigration to, from Zarahemla, 262; Nephi and Lehi and Lamanites go to, 268; whole face of, changed, 299; Lamanites give, to Nephites, 332.

Land of promise, 3, 5; plates carried to, 8; seed to be raised up in, 8; led to, 12, 14; mist of darkness upon, 14; visitations upon, 14; discovered, 15; to be led toward, 24; driven before wind toward, 27; Lehi and company arrive at, 28; beasts of every kind in, 28; ores found in, 28; Lehi speaks of, 35; decrees of God concerning, 344, 345; people who possess, will be free, 344; barges driven toward, 349, 350; people of Jared land upon, 350.

Land southward, Nephites give, to Lamanites, 332.

Language, of Lehi, 1; of Egyptians, 1; of people of Zarahemla corrupted, 95; people of Zarahemla taught, of Mosiah, 95; Benjamin teaches sons, of fathers, 98; of Egyptians, 98; of Nephites, 111; of Nephi taught among Lamanites, 131; confounded by the Lord, means of interpretation of, 138; no other people knew, of Moroni, 342; of Jaredites not confounded, 344; brother of Jared writes in confounded, 347; interpretation of, by Holy Spirit, 373.

Lasciviousness warned against, 82.

Law, preserved and executed, 143; of Moses, 7, 66; fulfilled in Christ, 66; words of Christ to be, 67; of Moses kept by Nephites, 82, 93, 99, 188, 195; of land exceedingly strict, 93; of Moses effective through atonement, 103; no, of God governing belief, 195; punishing men according to crimes, 195; Zoramites do not observe the, of Moses, 198; no, without punishment, 216, 217.

Laws, to be enacted by voice of people, 148; Pahoran refuses to alter, 234.

Lawyers skilled in their profession, 159, 160; Zeezrom, one of the, accuses Alma, 160; many, 168.

Leah of silver, 161.

Lebanon to become a fruitful field, 70.

Lehi, attacks army of Lamanites, 219; pursues Lamanites, 219; army of, east of Sidon, 220; appointed chief captain over city of Noah, 230; meets Lamanites at Bountiful, 238; and Moroni surrounded Lamanites, 238; given command of Mulek, 238; and Teancum given command of army, 255; forces sent to, 255; encamps around land of Moroni, 256; heads Coriantumr, 260.

Lehi, city of, 232; land of, source of contention, 233; people of, flee to Moroni, 233; established peace with Morianton, 234; taken by Amalickiah, 235; Moroni goes to land of, 256; Lamanites flee from, to land of Moroni, 256; land south called, 268.

Lehi, language of, 1; prays for his people, 4; vision of, 1; receives book, 2; prophesies, 2; mocked by Jews, 2; Jews angry at, 2; dream of, 2; commanded to depart into wilderness, 2; arrives at borders of Red Sea, 2; family of, 2, 3; builds an altar, 3; speaks to Laman and Lemuel, 3; dwells in tent, 3; sons of, flee from Laban, 4; comforts Sariah, 7; and Sariah offer sacrifices and burnt offerings, 7, 9; receives plates of brass, 7; plates contain genealogy of, 7, 8; descendant of Joseph, 7, 8, 39; prophesies, 7; record of, 8; sons of, to take wives, 8; gathers seeds, 9; dream of, 9; has vision of tree, 9; prophesies concerning coming of the Messiah, 11; speaks concerning Gentiles, 12; dwells in valley of Lemuel, 12; Gentiles to be numbered among seed of, 18; words of, hard to be understood, 19; sons of, dispute, 19; seed of, to come to knowledge of Redeemer, 20; commanded to take journey, 22; finds ball of brass, 22; inquires of the Lord, 22; chastened, 23; looks upon ball, 23; and family go into ship, 27; begets two sons in wilderness, 27; pleads for Nephi, 28; and company arrive at promised land, 28; tills the earth, 28; speaks to sons, 35; prophesies concerning his seed, 36; speaks to Zoram, 37; speaks to Jacob, 37; speaks to

among children of men, 18, 65; to be done, 70; shall proceed to do, 72.

Mary, mother of Christ, 102; Son of God to be born of, 153.

Mathoni, one of twelve, 313, 314.

Mathonihah, one of twelve, 313, 314.

Melchisedec, priesthood of, 166; king of Salem, 166.

Men, all commanded to write words of God, 73; Lord speaks to, according to their language, 75.

Messiah, coming of, 2, 11, 29; to be baptized, 11; to be slain, to rise, 12; to be manifest among Gentiles, 12; Gentiles to come to knowledge of, 12; Son of God, 12; Lamb of God, 15; to be manifest to children of men, 20; to be made manifest in latter days, 40; people wait for coming of, 45; Jews to be convinced of the true, 65; but one true, 66; name of, Jesus Christ, 66; signs of birth of, to be given, 67.

Metals, Nephi teaches people to work in, 43; Nephites become rich in, 93; mentioned in taxing, 113; used by Noah, 113, 114; gold and silver values of, 161; among Jaredites, 356, 357.

Micah, words of, 315, 316.

Middoni, Aaron, Muloki, and Ammah in prison at, 179; Antiomno, king of, 179; Lamoni and Ammon start to, 179; meet father of Lamoni, on journey to, 179; brethren of Ammon released from prison at, 180; Aaron, Muloki, and Ammah preach at, 181; they are cast into prison at, 181; Ammon and Lamoni return from, to land of Ishmael, 182; people converted in, 185.

Midian, land of, 186.

Minon, land of, 145.

Miracles, among disciples of Jesus, 328; ceased because of wickeness, 330.

Mocum, water replaces city of, 300.

Moriancumer, place called, 345.

Morianton, descendant of Riplakish, 343, 356; gains power over land and made king, 356; does justice, 356; builds cities and people prosper, 356; begets Kim, 356; death of, 356.

Morianton, land of, source of contention, 233; people of, take arms against people of Lehi, 233; people of, restored to land, 233; taken by Amalickiah, 235.

Morianton, leader of people of Morianton, 233; beats maidservant, 233; slain by Teancum, 233.

Moriantum, abominations of Nephites at, 371.

Mormon, about to deliver record to Moroni, 96; makes abridgment of plates, 96; finds small set of plates, 96; finishes record on plates of Nephi, 97; makes plates with own hands, 294; calling of, 294, 295; record of, 295; pure descendant of Lehi, 295; words of, 295, 328; writes things commanded, 322; makes record, 330; spoken to by Ammoron, 330; told to take plates of Nephi, 330; visited by Lord, 330; endeavors to preach, 330, 331; leader of Nephites, 331; withstands Aaron, 331; gets plates of Nephi, 332; flees to Shem, 332; teaches people, 333; gets epistle from king of Lamanites, 333; refuses command of Nephites, 333; writes to Gentiles and house of Israel, 333; gets all records hidden by Ammoron, 335; again takes command, 335; defends Jordan and other cities against Lamanites, 335; abridgment of record of, 335; speaks to house of Jacob, also to Gentiles, 335; finishes record, 336; writes epistle to king of Lamanites, 336; hides records in hill Cumorah, 337; wounded, 337; lamentation of, 337; speaks to remnant, 337, 338; slain in battle, 338; descendant of Nephi, 339; words of, 367; epistle of, to Moroni, 369; second epistle of, to Moroni, 371; has sacred records to deliver to Moroni, 372.

Mormon, Alma and followers flee to, 122; waters of, 122, 123, 124; place of, 122, 124; Jerusalem on the borders of, 181.

Moroni, chief captain of Nephites, 218; meets Lamanites in Jershon, 218; sends men to Alma, 219; takes part of army to near Manti, 219; takes part of army to hill Riplah, part to river Sidon, and Manti, 219; meets Lamanites near Sidon, 220; addresses Zerahemnah, 220; receives surrender of Zerahemnah, 221; addressed by Zerahemnah, 221; returns swords and weapons of Zerahemnah, 221; many Lamanites surrender to, 221; renews battle against Lamanites, 222; disarms and paroles Lamanites, 222; returns with army to land of Nephites, 222; writes on piece of garment, 224; prays for cause of Christians, 224; intercepts army of Amalickiah, 225; puts to death some of the Amalickiahites, 225; plants standard of liberty among Nephites, 226; fortifies land, 228; description of, 228; like Alma and Ammon, 229; appoints Lehi chief captain of city of Noah, 230; continues preparation for defense, 231; drives Lamanites from east wilderness, 232; maidservant tells, about people of Morianton, 233; sends army to head Morianton, 233; heads them at Desolation, 233; angry with king-men, 235; marches against king-men, 235; puts end to king-men, 235; sends orders to Teancum to fortify land Bountiful, 236; arrives at city of Bountiful, 237; holds counsel with Teancum and others, 237; takes possession of Mulek, 238; and Lehi surround Lamanites, 238; wounded, 238; Lamanites surrender to, 238; gives Lehi command of Mulek, 238; causes Lamanite prisoners to fortify Bountiful, 239; sends epistle to Ammoron, 240; Ammoron writes to, 241; appoints Laman to go to Gid, 241; arms prisoners, 242; Lamanites surrender to, 242; receives epistle from Helaman, 243; writes to Pahoran and receives answer, 251, 253; gives Lehi and Teancum command of part of army, 255; raises standard of liberty, 255; sends forces to Lehi and Teancum, 255; goes with Pahoran toward Nephihah, 255; makes night attack on Nephihah, 256; regains Nephihah, 256; goes to land of Lehi, 256; camps around land of Moroni, 256; returns to Zarahemla, 257; gives command of army to Moronihah, 257; death of, 257.

Moroni, city of, 232; Lamanites come into, 235; taken by Amalickiah, 235; sinks in sea, 299.

Moroni, son of Mormon, receives record from Mormon, 96, 337; leader of ten thousand Nephites,

337; finishes record of his father, 338; lone survivor of Nephites, 338; hides record, 339; instructs to search prophecy of Isaiah, 339; prophesies concerning coming forth of record, 339; teaches concerning resurrection, 341; writes of language, 342; gives account of ancient inhabitants, 343; commanded to seal up records of brother of Jared, 348; writes according to memory, 349; teaches concerning faith, 358; on faith and charity, 359, 360; bids farewell to Gentiles, 360; ends abridgment of record of people of Jared, 365; resumes writing, 365; writes words of Mormon, 367; epistle of Mormon to, 369; second epistle of Mormon to, 371; Mormon has sacred records to deliver to, 374; writes to Lamanites, 372; seals up records, 372, 373.

Moron, Coriantor son of, 343; son of Ethem, 343; reigns instead of Ethem, 358; wicked man battles with, and gets half of kingdom, 358; regains kingdom, 358; descendant of brother of Jared takes captive, 358; begets Coriantor, 358.

Moron, land of, where king dwelt, 351; near land of Desolation, 351; Noah takes Shule captive into land of, 351.

Moronihah, Moroni appoints, as commander of army, 257; Lamanites war against people of, 258; sends Lehi to head Coriantumr, 260; takes Zarahemla, 261; succeeds in obtaining many cities from Lamanites, 264, 265; preaches many things to people, 264; regains half of possessions, 264, 265.

Moronihah, city of, earth carried upon, 299, 300.

Moronihah, leader of ten thousand Nephites, 337.

Moses, plates of brass contain five books of, 7; Nephi reads words of, 30; to deliver people from Egypt, 40; to have power in rod, 40; spokesman for, 40; law of, kept by Nephites, 43, 66, 82, 93, 99; law of, taught, 93; law of, availeth nothing except through atonement, 103; law of, taught to people of Noah, 116; law of, not always to be taught, 118; law of, kept, 188, 195; Zoramites would not observe law of, 198; speaks of Son of God, 203; words of, 204; law of, Lamanites observe, 280, 285; contention concerning law of, 288; law of, fulfilled in Christ, 301, 308; law of, no longer observed, 327, 328; law of, given by faith, 359.

Mosiah, Amaleki speaks concerning, 95; warned to flee from land of Nephi, 95; language of, taught to people of Zarahemla, 95; unites with people of Zarahemla and is appointed king, 95; interprets engraving on stone, 95; death of, 95.

Mosiah, son of Benjamin, is given charge of sword of Laban, ball, or directors, plates of Nephi, 99; makes proclamation, 99; declared king, 101; consecrated king, 107; walks in way of Lord, 107; causes people to till the earth, 107; no contention under, 107; sends men to land of Lehi-Nephi, 107; receives records found by people of Limhi, 129, 138; receives people of Alma, 132; reads records of Zeniff and of Alma, 132; permits Alma to establish churches, 133; gives Alma authority over church, 134; sends proclamation, 135; sons of, unbelievers, 135; angel appears to sons of, 136; Ammon, Aaron, Omner, Himni, sons of, teach people of Zarahemla, 137; sons of, desire to preach to Lamanites, 137; sons of, refuse the kingdom, 138; translates records found by people of Limhi, 138; confers plates, record, interpreters on Alma, son of Alma, 138; asks will of people regarding king, 138; message of, to people concerning a king, 139; recommends judges, 139; loved by the people, 141; death of, 141; laws of, acknowledged by people of Nephi, 141, 160; sons of, met by Alma, 172; sons of, have spirit of, 172; sons of, preach to Lamanites fourteen years, 172; laws of, altered, 265.

Melek, land of, Alma teaches people of, 155; people of, baptized, 155; people of Ammon come into, 206.

Mulek, taken by Amalickiah, 235; Lamanites retreat to, 236; Teancum ordered to attack, 237; Jacob leader of Lamanites at, 237; taken by Moroni, 238; Moroni gives command of, to Lehi, 238; Nephi

and Lehi preach at, 266; land north called, 268.

Mulok, descendants of, 132.

Muloki, in prison, 179, 181; released, 180, 181; at Ani-anti, 181.

Murmur, brothers of Nephi, 4.

Murmuring of Laman and Lemuel, 3; of brothers of Nephi, 4; of Nephites, 127; against Nephites, 178; of the church, 135.

Nahom, Ishmael buried in, 23.

Narrow neck of land, Moroni orders Teancum to secure, 236.

Nations, all, to write words of Lord, 73; all, to be taught by men of own race, 194.

Nehor, land of, Corihor rebels and goes to, 351.

Nehor, teaches among people, 141, 142; slays Gideon, 142; pleads before Alma, 142; condemned to death, 142; executed on Manti, 142; profession of, 168, 170; Desolation of, 171; Amalickites and Amulonites after order of, 181, 187.

Nephi, birth of, 1; taught in learning of fathers, 1; afflictions of, 1; favored of the Lord, 1, 3; record of, 1, 2; account of, 2; plates of, 2; description of, 3; obedience of, 3; speaks to Sam, 3; to be ruler and teacher, 3; seed of, to be scourged, 3; and brethren to return to Jerusalem, 3; brothers of, murmur, 4; obedience of, 4; statement of, 4, 11, 12; genealogy of father of, 4; exhorts brethren, 4, 5, 8, 20, 22, 25, 27, 33, 42; and brethren return to land of inheritance, 4; offers to purchase records of Laban, 4; and brethren flee from Laban, 4; angel speaks to, 5; slays Laban, 6; obtains plates, 6; returns to father in wilderness, 6; record of, 8; descendant of Joseph, 8; returns to Jerusalem, 8; brethren rebel against, 8; bound with cords, 9; plates of, contain full account of people, 11; two sets of plates of, 11; reign and ministry of, 11; writes in book, 12; vision of, 12; angel appears to, 13; seed of, and of brethren, 14; angel speaks to, 18, 19; forbidden to write, 19; grieved by hardness of their hearts, 19; overcome, 19; sees fall of people, 20; takes daughter of Ishmael to wife, 22; breaks bow, 22; commanded to build ship, 24; makes tools, 24; stretches forth hand and brethren shaken by the Lord, 27; brethren offer to worship, 27; completes ship, 27; goes into ship, 27; bound with cords by brethren, 27; Lehi pleads for, 28; makes plates of ore, 28; makes records on plates, 29; reads words of Moses, 30; reads from plates of brass, 33; Joseph to hearken to, 41; speaks concerning Joseph of Egypt, 41; Laman and Lemuel and sons of Ishmael angry with, 42; ministered to by angels, 42; life sought by brethren, 43; and others depart in wilderness, 43; place and people named after, 43; teaches people in metals and wood, 43; builds temple, 43; refuses to be king, 44; consecrates Jacob and Joseph, 44; keeps records upon plates, 44; makes other plates, 44; Jacob speaks to people of, 44; writes words of Isaiah, 52; soul of, delights in plainness, 64; speaks concerning words of Isaiah, 64; declares Jerusalem had been destroyed, 65; prophesies destruction of his people, 67; promises to, to be remembered, 72; seed of, to be remembered, 72; prophesies concerning Jews and Gentiles, 73; mourns because of wickedness, 76; has charity, 77; commands Jacob to write on small plates, 78; anoints man to be king, 78; loved by people, 78; wields sword of Laban, 78; to be name of kings, 78; dies, 78; consecrated priests and teachers, 79; makes plates called plates of Jacob, 82; other plates of, 94; plates of, conferred on Mosiah, 99; language of, taught to Lamanites, 131; words of God to first, 146; Aminadi, descendant of, 159; son of Lehi, 159.

Nephi, people of, to fortify against Lamanites, 90; people of, till ground and raise animals, 92; Ammon and brethren go to land of, 107; Zeniff has knowledge of, 111; children of the daughters of Lamanites and priests take name of, 133; Alma speaks to people of, 133; land of, 136; Aaron goes to land of, 182; people of, converted, 185; armies of, set around Jershon,

193; account of people of, in days of Helaman, 222; people of, rejoice in peace, 222; Amalickiah goes to land of, 225; Amalickiah returns to land of, 227; Amalickiah possesses the city of, 227; Lamanites flee to land of, 231; peace among people of, because of diligence to word of God, 231; land of, in straight course from east to west sea, 232; Gadiantons gain many advantages over land of, 290; people of, prosper, 327; people of, proud in hearts, become exceedingly wicked, 329.

Nephihah, appointed chief judge, 148; dies, 233.

Nephihah, city or land of, 232; not taken by Lamanites, 235; people of, attacked by Lamanites, 250; city of, captured, 251; Moroni and Pahoran go to city of, 255; plains of, 255; Moroni enters, at night, 256; Moroni regains city of, 256.

Nephites, to write words of the Lord, 73; not Lamanites, 78; friendly toward Nephi, 79; grow hard in hearts, 79; desire many wives and concubines, 79; pride of, 80; excuse themselves in committing whoredoms, 80; to be scourged by Lamanites, 81; Lamanites more righteous than, 81; Jacob warns against sins of, 82; records of, to be preserved, 92; war with Lamanites, 93; culture of, 93; weapons of, 93; more wicked part of, destroyed, righteous spared, 94; drive out Lamanites, 95; people of, not so numerous as people of Zarahemla, 132; prepared to meet Amlicites, 144; war with Amlicites, 144; defeat Amlicites, 144; defeat Lamanites and Amlicites at Sidon, 145; Lamanite army attacks, 146; Zoram leads army of, against the Lamanites, 171; church established generally among people of, 171; nearly surrounded by Lamanites, 184; nearly surrounded by water, 184; Lamanites swear vengeance against, 188; great slaughter among, 193; separation of, from Zoramites, 198; war with Lamanites, 206, 217; give lands to people of Ammon, 218; obliged to contend with brethren, 218; Moroni, leader of, 218; meet Lamanites in Manti, 219; part of, attack Lamanites

broken people, a righteous kingdom, 355; begets Riplakish and dies, 355.

Shez, son of Shez, rebels against father, 355; smitten by robbers, 355.

Shiblom, leader of ten thousand Nephites, 337.

Shiblom, son of Com, 343, 357; brother rebels against, 357; brother of, puts prophets to death, 357; reigns, 357; famine and pestilence in days of, 357; slain, 357.

Shiblon of silver, 161.

Shiblon, son of Alma, 198; commandment of Alma to, 211; faithful among Zoramites, 211; declares word of God, 231; takes possession of sacred things, 257; death of, 258; confers sacred things upon Helaman, son of Helaman, 258.

Shiblum of silver, 161.

Shilom, Ammon and party at, 107, 108; city of, 108; land of, possessed by Zeniff, 111; walls of, repaired, 111; spies come to, 112; tower of Noah overlooks, 114; many buildings in, 114; tower on hill north of, 114; people of Limhi depart in wilderness of, 129; Amulon teacher over people in, 131; people converted in, 185.

Shim, Ammoron deposits sacred engravings in hill called, 330; Omer passed by hill, 353.

Shimnilom, people converted in city of, 185.

Ship, construction of, commanded, 24; completion of, 27; put forth in sea and driven before wind, 27; arrives at promised land, 28.

Shiz, brother of Lib, pursues Coriantumr, 363; three-day battle of, 363; repulsed three times, wounds Coriantumr 363; Coriantumr writes epistle to, 364; people of Coriantumr flee from, to waters of Ripliancum, 364; beaten by Coriantumr, 364; final battle of, with Coriantumr, 364; gets epistle from Coriantumr, 364; killed by Coriantumr, 365.

Shule, son of Kib, 343, 351; becomes mighty in judgment, 351; makes steel swords, 351; battles with Corihor, 351; restores kingdom to Kib, 351; made king by Kib, 351; gives Corihor power, 351; gives battle and taken captive by Noah, 351; replaced on throne by sons,

351; people of, prosperous, 351; given kingdom by Nimrod, 351; prophets come among people of, 351; is righteous, 351, 352; Omer son of, reigns, 352.

Shum of gold, 161.

Shurr, Coriantumr in valley of, 363.

Sidom, Alma and Amulek depart from Ammonihah to land of, 169; Zeezrom and those cast out from Ammonihah found at, 169; Alma establishes church at, 170.

Sidon River, Amlicites slain at, 144; Nephites defeat allies at, 145; dead cast into, 145; many baptized at, by Alma, 147; valley of Gideon east of river of, 152; Melek west of, 155; Lamanites march by head of, 218; army of Moroni secreted near, 219; Lamanites attacked at, 219; Lamanites surrounded at, 220; Lamanite dead cast into, 222; war by waters of, 330.

Sign sought by Sherem, 90.

Silver, senum, amnor, ezrom, onti, shiblon, shiblum, 161.

Siron, Corianton goes to, 212.

Solomon, Nephi builds temple after manner of temple of, 43; and David, 79; and David had many wives and concubines, which is an abomination, 80.

Son of righteousness shall heal, 67.

Souls, condition of, between death and resurrection, 214; of wicked, state of, 214.

Southward land, 184.

Spirit of body, restored, 49; speaks truth, 83.

Spirits of all men taken home to God, 214.

Spokesman, for Moses, 40; for choice seer, 40.

Star, new, appears, 288.

Stone, brought to Mosiah, 95; prepared for Gazelem, 209.

Stones, two given to brother of Jared, 347; sealed, 347.

Stones, used by Mosiah in translating, 138; smelted by brother of Jared, 346; description of, 346; touched by finger of Lord, 346, 349; put into vessels, give light, 349.

Storm, great, arises, 299.

Substance, people of church to impart of, 123, 143.

Sword of Laban, Nephi slays Laban with, 6; Nephi makes many swords after manner of, 43; Nephi wields,

78; Benjamin fights with, 97; Benjamin confers, on Mosiah, 99.

Teachers, Jacob and Joseph to be priests and, 44; to labor with own hands, 123, 135; consecrated by Alma, 147, 170; consecrated by Aaron, 185; appointed by Helaman and brother, 223; manner of ordaining, 366. (See Priests.)

Teancum, city of, Nephites flee to, 334; near Desolation, 334; Lamanites come against, 334; drive Nephites from, 334.

Teancum, leader of army which heads people of Morianton, 233; slays Morianton, 233; meets Lamanites, 235; defeats Lamanites, 236; kills Amalickiah, 236; ordered to secure narrow neck of land, 236; ordered to attack Mulek, 237; returns to city Bountiful, 237; holds council with Moroni and others, 237; Lamanites marched against, 237; and Lehi given command of part of army, 254, 255; forces sent to, 255; encamps around land of Moroni, 256; slain, 256.

Temple, built by Nephi, 43; Jacob teaches in, 79; people of Zarahemla gather to, 99; at land of Nephi, 114; Christ appears at, in Bountiful, 303.

Ten commandments quoted by Abinadi, 117, 118.

Teomner secrets himself in the wilderness, 249.

Three disciples, not to taste of death, 324; Moroni and father administered to by, 339.

Timber, land without, 262; shipped from land southward to land northward, 262.

Time measured only to men, 213.

Timothy, brother of Nephi, one of twelve, 313.

Tithes paid by Abraham, 166.

Tower, Noah builds, 114; Jared came from, 343.

Treasure hidden up, 331.

Tree, Lehi's vision of, 9; Nephi's vision of, 13; is love of God, 13; of life, 21, 216.

Tribes, Nephites divided into, 297; not to fight among themselves, 298; Christ to go to lost, 310; twelve, of Israel to be judged, 333.

Tubaloth, son of Ammoron, king of Lamanites, 260.

Twelve, follow Redeemer, 13; fought against, 14; all nations fight against, apostles, 14; ordained of God, 14; apostles to judge tribes of Israel, 14; twelve ministers to be judged by, 14; book goes forth from, apostles, 16; one of, apostles seen by Nephi, 19; chosen, 304; given power to baptize, 304; instructions to, 307, 308, 312, 313, 315; given power to give Holy Ghost, 313; names of, 313, 314; teach multitude, 314; baptized by Nephi, 314; Holy Ghost falls upon, 314; angels minister to, 314; pray, 314; told to write scriptures, 320; Christ shows himself often to, 322; commanded to judge, 324; Christ speaks to, 324; desires of, 324; promises to, 324; three of, not to taste of death, 324, 325; Christ touches all save three, 325; three of, caught up into heaven and changed, 325; all of, die except three, and others ordained in their stead, 328; cast into fire, 329; to judge people in this land, 333; in Jerusalem to judge twelve in this land, 333; words of Christ to, 365, 366; power given, to give Holy Ghost, 365, 366.

Vineyards, Noah plants, 114.

Virgin, Nephi sees, in vision, 13; mother of Son of God, 13; bears child in arms, 13.

Vision of Lehi, 1, 2; of Nephi, 12.

Voice, heard by all people, 300, 301; people hear, as out of heaven, 302.

Voice of the people, 128; Aaron chosen king by, 138; judges to be judged by, 140; is supreme, 144; against Amlici, 144; to enact laws by, 148, 160; obtain, concerning Anti-Nephi-Lehies, 192; contention concerning law settled by, 234; authorized Moroni to go against king men, 235; Pacumeni unites with, 259; condemns Paanchi to death, 259; laws and government established by, 265; laws given by, 297.

War, multitudes gather to, 14, 15; among all nations, 19; and contentions with Lamanites, 44; and rumors at Jerusalem, 65; and con-